Gangs

International Library of Criminology, Criminal Justice and Penology - Second Series

Series Editor:Gerald Mars and David Nelken

Gangs

Edited by

Jacqueline Schneider

Department of Criminology, University of Leicester, UK

and

Nick Tilley

Nottingham Trent University and Jill Dando Institute of Crime Science, University College London, UK

ASHGATE

Published by
Ashgate Publishing Limited
Gower House
Croft Road
Aldershot
Hants GU11 3HR
England

Ashgate Publishing Company
Suite 420
101 Cherry Street
Burlington, VT 05401-4405
USA

Ashgate website: http://www.ashgate.com

British Library Cataloguing in Publication Data
Gangs. – (International library of criminology, criminal
  justice and penology. Second series)
  1. Gangs
  I. Schneider, Jacqueline II. Tilley, Nick
  364.1'066

Library of Congress Cataloging-in-Publication Data
Gangs / edited by Jacqueline Schneider and Nick Tilley.
      p. cm. — (International library of criminology, criminal justice, and penology)
    ISBN 0-7546-2410-2 (alk. paper)
      1. Gangs—Cross-cultural studies. I. Schneider, Jacqueline. II. Tilley, Nick. III.
International library of criminology, criminal justice & penology.

HV6437.G34 2004
364.1'06'6—dc22

2004047717

ISBN 0 7546 2410 2

Printed in Great Britain by The Cromwell Press, Trowbridge, Wiltshire

Contents

Acknowledgements

The editors and publishers wish to thank the following for permission to use copyright material.

American Journal of Criminal Justice for the essay: Jacqueline L. Schneider (2001), 'Niche Crime: The Columbus Gangs Study', *American Journal of Criminal Justice*, **26**, pp. 93–105. Copyright © 2001 Southern Criminal Justice Association.

American Sociological Association for the essays: Robert K. Merton (1938), 'Social Structure and Anomie', *American Sociological Review*, **3**, pp. 672–82; Ruth Horowitz and Gary Schwartz (1974), 'Honor, Normative Ambiguity and Gang Violence', *American Sociological Review*, **39**, pp. 238–51.

Australian and New Zealand Journal of Criminology for the essay: Scott Poynting, Greg Noble and Paul Tabar (2001), 'Middle Eastern Appearances: "Ethnic Gangs", Moral Panic and Media Framing', *Australian and New Zealand Journal of Criminology*, **34**, pp. 67–90.

Blackwell Publishing Ltd for the essay: Walter B. Miller (1959), 'Lower Class Culture as a Generating Milieu of Gang Delinquency', *Journal of Social Issues*, **14**, pp. 5–19.

Canadian Criminal Justice Association for the essay: Robert M. Gordon (2000), 'Criminal Business Organizations, Street Gangs and "Wanna-be" Groups: A Vancouver Perspective', *Canadian Journal of Criminology*, January, pp. 39–60. Copyright © 2000 Canadian Criminal Justice Association.

Elsevier for the essay: Scott H. Decker and G. David Curry (2002), 'Gangs, Gang Homicides, and Gang Loyalty: Organized Crimes or Disorganized Criminals', *Journal of Criminal Justice*, **30**, pp. 343–52. Copyright © 2002 Elsevier Science Ltd.

Home Office for the essay: Karen Bullock and Nick Tilley (2002), 'Shootings, Gangs and Violent Incidents in Manchester: Developing a Crime Reduction Strategy', *Home Office Crime Reduction Research Series, Paper 13*, (Briefing Note), pp. 1–2.

Humanity and Society for the essay: Meda Chesney-Lind (1993), 'Girls, Gangs and Violence: Anatomy of a Backlash', *Humanity and Society*, **17**, pp. 321–44.

Journal of Australian Studies for the essay: Judith Bessant (1995), '"Hanging Around the Street": Australian Rockers, Sharpies and Skinheads of the 1960s and Early 1970s', *Journal of Australian Studies*, **45**, pp. 15–31.

Preface to the Second Series

The first series of the International Library of Criminology, Criminal Justice and Penology has established itself as a major research resource by bringing together the most significant journal essays in contemporary criminology, criminal justice and penology. The series made available to researchers, teachers and students an extensive range of essays which are indispensable for obtaining an overview of the latest theories and findings in this fast changing subject. Indeed the rapid growth of interesting scholarly work in the field has created a demand for a second series which like the first consists of volumes dealing with criminological schools and theories as well as with approaches to particular areas of crime criminal justice and penology. Each volume is edited by a recognised authority who has selected twenty or so of the best journal articles in the field of their special competence and provided an informative introduction giving a summary of the field and the relevance of the articles chosen. The original pagination is retained for ease of reference.

The difficulties of keeping on top of the steadily growing literature in criminology are complicated by the many disciplines from which its theories and findings are drawn (sociology, law, sociology of law, psychology, psychiatry, philosophy and economics are the most obvious). The development of new specialisms with their own journals (policing, victimology, mediation) as well as the debates between rival schools of thought (feminist criminology, left realism, critical criminology, abolitionism etc.) make necessary overviews that offer syntheses of the state of the art.

GERALD MARS
Visiting Professor, Brunel University, Middlesex, UK

DAVID NELKEN
Distinguished Professor of Sociology, University of Macerata, Italy;
Distinguished Research Professor of Law, University of Cardiff, Wales;
Honourary Visiting Professor of Law, LSE, London, UK

Introduction

This volume has been brought together by an American (Schneider) and an Englishman (Tilley). Both of us currently live in Nottingham, where official worries about gangs in Nottingham date back at least eight or nine hundred years. The legendary Robin Hood and his Merry Men were an archetypal, early Nottingham gang, operating in the Middle Ages. At the time of writing, we are both involved in a project that is looking at patterns of shooting in the city, in particular those associated with gangs, with a view to developing a preventive strategy. These circumstances shape the perspective we bring to gangs.

We wonder how much the situation for policing and criminological research has changed since Robin Hood's time. Although accounts of Robin Hood-type gangs have been widely documented through time and space, albeit often with some difficulty in separating myth from reality (see Hobsbawm, 1969), social science research investigating the nature and development of these groups really only began in the early 1900s. Volumes of analyses have been devoted to the study of gangs, their formation, structure, criminal activity, official responses to and the community's tolerance of them, with two pieces of work providing the impetus for present-day criminological and sociological gang research. In America, Fredrick Thrasher's (1927) seminal piece on gangs in Chicago provided the first systematic study on the nature and structure of criminal gangs. Since then, research, which largely tends to compile case-study analyses of particular groups or cities, has been built around the original ideas forwarded by Thrasher. In England, the number of studies devoted solely to gangs is relatively small in comparison to those generated in America. However, Stanley Cohen's (1972) work on the evolution or, more accurately, the social construction of the 1960s 'Mods' and 'Rockers' is crucial for the study of gangs and societal reaction to them. In England, modern-day accounts relate not only the Mods and Rockers, but have moved on to include the Teddy Boys of the 1950s, the Yardies, who are said to largely control the drug trade in several of England's larger cities, and other city-specific gangs that have persisted over significant periods (see, for example, Bullock and Tilley, Chapter 29, this volume).

Schneider (1995) identified three stages of gang research in the USA: the Exploratory Stage (pre-1950s); Theory Generation (1950s–1960s); and the Stage of Diversity (post-1960s). During the first stage, researchers documented as many characteristics and patterns of behavior amongst gangs and their members as possible. The works of Thrasher (1927), Merton (Chapter 1, this volume), Tannenbaum (1939), Shaw and McKay (1942) and Whyte (1943) provided the empirical observations necessary for the work of the next generation – the theoreticians. Cohen (1955), Bloch and Neiderhoffer (1958), Miller (Chapter 2, this volume), Cloward and Ohlin (1960) and Yablonsky (1962 and Chapter 3, this volume)[1] paid particular attention to hypothesis testing and theoretical development, which laid the foundation for researchers in the third stage. Research from the 1970s onwards lacks intellectual coherence. Contrary to the generations that preceded them, researchers delved into a number of different topical investigations. For example, some specialized in looking at the criminal nature of gangs; others looked at structural elements; and still others looked at demographic characteristics. The topics were diverse and did not tie in coherently with the body of works produced as a whole.

The essays in this volume are based loosely on themes running through the gang literature worldwide. Needless to say, selected essays represent only a small portion of the overall body of literature that exists. However, they do embody a comprehensive attempt to understand activity that appears to occur as a result of some group process. What is less clear from existing studies is the extent to which these suppositions feed moral panics or contribute to the misidentification or overspecification of a problem. In today's social science climate, the notion that gangs might well be nothing more than a group of likeminded people who engage in similar activities is tantamount to heresy.

Generally speaking, several underlying assumptions run throughout all gang research since the 1970s:

1. Gangs exist.
2. Gangs are purposeful.
3. Gangs commit crimes – frequently very serious types of crime.
4. Gangs survive beyond the lifetime of any given member.
5. Gangs direct the activities of their members.
6. Gangs require special social intervention to reduce their existence and criminality.
7. Gangs are social groups that often replace more traditional social institutions such as the family.
8. Gangs actively recruit and initiate new members.
9. Gangs have structure, albeit to varying degrees of formalization.
10. Gangs are instrumental groups that offer disenfranchised youths economic alternatives to those offered by mainstream society.

For obvious reasons, the above list is not exhaustive, but it does reflect the general themes coursing through the literature.

Theory and Concepts

Part I of this volume is organized around theory and concepts. In Chapter 1 Robert Merton situates anti-social behavior within the context of cultural values and class structure. His seminal essay, first published in 1938, has provided generations of structural sociologists and criminologists with the foundation for studying group phenomenon. Gang formation is caused by the lack of integration between means and ends for gang members. Continuing along these lines, Walter Miller (Chapter 2) examines patterns of behavior that result from lower-class groups having distinctly different cultural systems from those of the middle class. Delinquent gangs are merely a variant of what he terms 'adolescent street corner groups'. Building on Merton's earlier work, Miller believes that crime is a result of those attempting to achieve valued ends through means that are available uniquely to those in lower-class structures.

In Chapter 3 Lewis Yablonsky introduces the concept of a 'near-group' which, although originally postulated in 1959, seems to be growing in significance for today's researchers. Deviant groups and criminal gangs exist on a continuum of organizational characteristics, ranging from crowds through to highly organized criminal groups or firms. Perhaps the most enduring, but ignored, finding from Yablonsky is his observation that '[m]ost gang theorizing begins with an automatic assumption that gangs are defined sociological groups' (p. 32). He continues by stating that 'misconceived theories' pertaining to gangs and their developments are based on popular images reported in the press rather than on scientific observations.

Malcolm Klein and Lois Crawford (Chapter 4) call on Thrasher and Yablonsky's work to show a continuum of 'gangness' in terms of structure and activity. They compare gangs to other more benign social groups in order to identify distinguishing characteristics. Whilst they found similar characteristics for gangs and non-delinquent groups, delinquency appeared to be the main defining attribute of gangs. Klein and Crawford draw a distinction between the types of group in terms of internal and external cohesion. Internal sources of cohesion (goals, membership stability, group norms, and so on) appear to be less important to gangs than external mechanisms.

The final essay selected for Part I is based on work stemming from Canada. Robert Gordon (Chapter 5) uses his work to illustrate the need for Canadian-specific research to document gangs and their formation rather than relying on the work emanating from America or England. The work, however, builds on the notion set out by other authors in Part I – namely, that a continuum of gang behavior exists.

The History and Development of Gangs

Perhaps research has come full circle by needing to return to the historical roots of looking at gangs in terms of near-groups and cultural values. However, the question for new generations of gang researchers might well be this: to what extent do the activities within these groups resemble those of organized crime firms as opposed to those of groups of friends and associates who, from time to time, commit crimes when with one another?

Part II of this volume relates to the history and development of gangs, although none of the essays goes back as far as Robin Hood. Andrew Davies (Chapter 10) takes us back to the nineteenth-century 'scuttlers' in Manchester and Salford, showing how themes of masculinity, violence, territoriality and honor were to be found in these British working-class gangs. Anne Campbell, Steven Munce and John Galea (Chapter 6) compare groups in Britain and the United States in the period after the Second World War. For gangs to exist, they suggest, there must be face-to-face interaction, internal structure including leadership and role allocation, territoriality and stable membership. However, they argue that in Britain, unlike in the United States, there is little evidence of gangs with these attributes; British gangs can be better characterized as youth subcultures. In the different contexts of the United States and Britain, they highlight the relatively greater salience of class in Britain and race in the United States. In Chapter 7 R.G. Whitfield questions Campbell *et al.*'s conclusions, arguing that gangs have a long history in Britain and that class is of diminishing significance. He maintains that gangs comprise 'subcultures writ small'.

Judith Bessant (Chapter 8) looks at 'rockers', 'sharpies' and 'skinheads' in Australia in the 1960s and early 1970s. Like Campbell and her colleagues she refers to both the post-war growth in youth culture and the importance of class. She also notes the emergence of a collective identity amongst different groups as well as their rivalry, fights, mutual loyalty and territoriality. However, the groups she studied lacked exclusive membership, leadership or rules of behavior and, in this sense, they did not comprise 'gangs'. Scott Poynting, Grey Noble and Paul Tabar

(Chapter 12), also writing with an Australian focus, discuss the role of the media in creating a moral panic over ethnic gangs in Sydney at the end of the twentieth century. They draw on Leslie Wilkins's pioneering work on deviancy amplification (Wilkins, 1964), since adopted and developed by others, to interpret the response to Lebanese Australian young men and their adaptation to the treatment meted out to them. In relation to this theme, Cheryl Maxson, Kristi Woods and Malcolm Klein (Chapter 9) look at the role of migration as a mechanism for spreading gangs in the United States. However, they do not find it to play a major role. Christopher Adamson (Chapter 11) compares the developments of youth gangs amongst African-American and European-Americans in the United States since 1787. Whilst acknowledging some similarities – a basis in social disadvantage, mutual violence, defensive localism, a place to forge identity and potential source of social status – he highlights the very different experiences of these groups across time. In particular, he shows how variations in gang formation and activity need to be understood in terms of the differences in economic and structural conditions.

Defining Gangs

The essays relating to the history and development of gangs do, in some cases, explicitly raise questions of definition. Across all of them we see rather different formations, functions and activities across time, across country and across groups within a given country. It may be unhelpful to lump all these together as 'gangs'. Using an everyday scare term may occlude more than it reveals when attached to such diverse groups and social movements.

The task of researching gangs has been fraught with difficulties since the 1970s. Central to these difficulties are issues of definition and reliance on certain forms of data for analyses. These methodological issues have been acknowledged as limitations in most of the existing research, but they have not been explored as being potentially serious flaws contributing to the proliferation of myth, or as aggravating factors that exacerbate what is essentially a relatively uncomplicated social process. Although the term 'gang' is used universally by researchers, police, social workers, media and the general public, its meaning is not applied consistently. Hearing the word 'gang' conjures up a myriad images – from the acute, exclusive and manifest group loyalties and conflicts depicted tragically in *West Side Story* through the violent gangsters controlling the streets of Los Angeles to the group of youths skateboarding through the city centre. The degree of disparity between these, in terms of criminal activity, cohesion, purpose, and structure, reflects the disparities in the ways in which the term 'gang' itself is used.

Defining the term 'gang' is tricky, but perhaps essential. In order to conduct research or to implement plausible crime reduction initiatives, unambiguously and accurately capturing the target phenomenon is crucial. Winfree, Fuller, Vigil and Mays (1992, p. 29) describe the evolution of gang research as having an 'almost schizophrenic path', which they say is due to the lack of definitional consensus on the term. Horowitz (1990) not only excuses this imprecision, but also condones it. She says that because a number of special interest groups (that is, police, prison, media and schools) exist, they will need their own definitions and that these definitions will necessarily differ. According to Horowitz, problems may arise when policy-making comes into play; however, she offers no remedy for these problems except that the implications of having different definitions ought to be studied.

Nearly 15 years later criminal justice agencies still do not apply the term 'gang' in consistent or productive ways, if they apply it at all. Police organizations often take the lead in identifying local groups, gangs, their members and their specific criminal activities, although assumptions about what constitutes a gang, a gang activity or membership of a gang vary both between agencies and within them. Whatever view or views prevail, however, due to data protection issues and the sensitive nature of the information, these data are rarely shared with crime reduction partners. This opens the door for other agencies independently to adopt their own definitions, which help frame the varying perspectives found on the issue. The variations in definition are often not even recognized. The outcome is not only confused and incoherent local strategic and tactical decision-making, but also a situation that allows one agency to maintain an account of a problem even when data held by another agency may refute it. Crime and disorder partners could benefit from a more systematic approach in identifying the existence of gangs in the first instance, followed by ways of measuring their impact. In other words, crime and disorder partners should know:

1. what comprises a gang
2. if, given these parameters, gangs exist
3. what constitutes membership of a gang
4. whether the criminal activities of gang members reflect the wishes of the overall group.

The use of consistent definitional criteria may avoid the danger of overstating the existence of gangs and overestimating the problems they cause. It may also help prevent the over-sensationalization of the issue by the media.

Under current systems, ancillary issues arise relating to the ways in which police count numbers of gangs, numbers of members of gangs and the volume of crime attributable to gangs. The potential problem of circularity becomes important here. Anecdotal evidence often serves as the basis for classification, or intelligence information provides the justification for naming a particular gang and its membership. If it is then accepted, without independent corroboration, that gangs exist, information substantiating their existence can be constructed. This is not to say that officers, or even researchers, manufacture the evidence to support their presuppositions. Rather, if one assumes that a situation exists, a self-fulfilling prophecy begins: intelligence is sought and sources tasked in relation to the presumed problem, the intelligence is constructed and construed in terms of that presumed problem, and the original impression is reinforced.

What is also unclear from existing studies is the degree to which the aforementioned suppositions are supported simply because of the type of data used to study gangs. Police data serve as the basis for much, if not most, gang research. Either recorded crime data are used to analyze gang-related crime patterns or intelligence files are used to identify who belongs to specific gangs so that qualitative interviews can be conducted with 'known' gang members. The misidentification of someone as a gang member or as belonging to the wrong gang can severely affect research outcomes. To further complicate matters, knowing how to classify an incident as being 'gang-related' is important. Chicago and Los Angeles have taken the lead in trying to distinguish between 'gang-related' offences and all others. Their definitions as to what makes something 'gang-related' differ: Chicago's is more restrictive than that used in Los Angeles.[2] But what is not known is the extent to which these are reliable and valid measures of gang activities and their underlying motivations.

Future generations of gang researchers certainly have obstacles to overcome. Definitional issues and problems must be dealt with. It may be useful in future to differentiate more clearly between levels of gang organization and formalization. Some, for example, seem like ephemeral packs of predators, others like embryonic organized crime firms, others like chapters of national or international movements, and still others like territory-based friendship groups. It is unhelpful in criminological research to lump all these together. Detailed crime pattern analyses and network analyses should help work out the extent to which crime is committed in packs of loosely affiliated youths or in organized, purposeful criminal enterprises. It is important, too, to recognize that even when gang members do commit crime together, their behavior is not necessarily gang-motivated; it may more simply be a by-product of shared opportunities and interests. A key practical question is that of whether intervention and reduction strategies should change where crimes are committed by 'known gang' members. It may be more efficient and effective to concentrate on the acts themselves rather than the group membership of those engaged in them.

Parts III to VI of this volume represent that almost schizophrenic nature of gang research to which Winfree *et al.* (1992) refer. Parts III and IV are dedicated to activities that gangs routinely engage – violence and drugs. The role that girls play in criminal gangs is explored through a series of essays in Part V. Policy initiatives that are aimed at reducing or suppressing gang activities are included in the final chapters of the volume.

Gangs and Crime

Ruth Horowitz's and her colleagues' work with Chicano gangs provide a foundation that enriches our understanding about how these groups manage to exist amongst communities. Her work with Schwartz (Chapter 13) examines the normative process within a community that influences gang members' responses to various stresses and strains. Their findings showed that, within the Chicano gangs, adherence to a code of personal honor shapes the individual's reaction to insults. According to Short and Strodtbeck (1965), gangs provide an attractive alternative for gang members to find status given that they often lack appropriate socialization mechanisms that enable them to respond more appropriately to social strains. Using this hypothesis as the foundation for their work, Horowitz and Schwartz found that Chicano gangs operate under a different cultural experience. Social honor shapes the responses that these gang members make. Building on this, Horowitz demonstrated that, 13 years later, Chicano gangs are basically an accepted part of the community's social fabric (Chapter 14). Gang members will respond within a range of behaviors that are accepted amongst the general community. This enables the Chicano gang members to develop their own mechanisms of adaptation when pursuing culturally imposed expectations; however, the gang members must balance their pursuit with the tolerance of the community. If they operate outside the tolerance level, gangs are well aware that they jeopardize their perceived levels of legitimacy amongst the larger community.

The remaining essays in Part III look at gang activity from a structural viewpoint. Researchers use organizational elements in order to examine gang behavior and crime. For example, Jacqueline Schneider (Chapter 15) uses criminal histories of gang leaders in order to develop a profile of gang activity for each of the identified gangs in Columbus, Ohio, USA. Finding that some gangs specialize in certain types of criminal activity over other forms, she suggests that intervention and prevention activities might well benefit from using a more macro-approach rather than focusing on the activities of the individual gang member. In Chapter 16 Scott Decker and David Curry examine the social organization of gang homicides compared to non-gang-related killings. Finding that the majority of killings are intra-gang in contrast to the widely held belief that gangs kill rival gang members, Decker and Curry question the degree to which gangs are cohesive. Finally, in Chapter 17, Anthony Braga shows how patterns of youth homicide in Boston, USA, are clustered among the city's most prolific serious gun-crime offenders rather than amongst the more diffused street drug trade.

Drugs and Gangs

The essays in Part IV continue to take a structural perspective, but concentrate specifically on drugs-related crime. In Chapter 18 Jeffrey Fagan examines the social organization of drug-dealing in three American cities. His research identifies four types of gangs that had varying degrees of drug-dealing capabilities. Fagan concludes that gangs' varying degrees of organizational and social structures influence the degree to which the gangs are equipped to traffic drugs. Next, Malcolm Klein, Cheryl Maxson and Lea C. Cunningham (Chapter 19) examine the degree to which gangs play a part in the distribution of crack cocaine and the subsequent violence that is believed to accompany that distribution. Although they fail to demonstrate that gangs are the main impetus behind the drug's sale and associated violence, they do show that individual members do play a part. This important distinction between gangs' behaviors and the actions of their individual members is an important one to make. All too often, it is supposed that gangs act in unison for a greater purpose; however, research continues to struggle to find evidence to support this ideology. John Hagedorn (Chapter 20) continues along the lines that Klein and his colleagues set into motion. In large part, he finds that gangs are loosely organized groups of neighborhood-based groups that are not organizationally suited to large-scale drug-trafficking.

Girls and Gangs

Gang members are overwhelmingly male, and most of the literature is related to males as gang members. The essays collected in Part V, however, deal with girls and gangs. Anne Campbell (Chapter 21) reports on a full-time three-year study of three New York gangs and discusses the ways in which girls talk about their fights. She finds that the most discussed fights are one-on-one, and that most reported fights are domestic and are concerned with personal integrity rather than being gang-related. In Chapter 23 Karen Joe Laidler and Geoffrey Hunt report on a long-term study of ethnic gangs (African American, Latina and Asian American) in the San Francisco Bay area that began in 1991 and involved interviews with male and female gang members. They draw on 141 interviews with female respondents across three snowball samples taken at different times. They find that female, like male, gang members seek respect, but that the content of that respect differs. For males it has to do with power and control. For females, across ethnic groups, however, it is also associated with the pursuit of respectability, including 'being feminine'. Meda Chesney-Lind (Chapter 22) writes against an intense media interest at the time (1993) in girls' violence and highlights the almost exclusive treatment of males in gangs in the early literature. She notes the exaggerated accounts of growth in female gang criminality in particular violence, at the same time pointing out that, at earlier points, this has been understated. Chesney-Lind locates girl gang membership in the context of the severe social disadvantages experienced and interprets media responses as a means of demonizing the young women in gangs at the expense of addressing the racism and sexism to which they are responding.

Policy and Practice

Part VI concerns policy and practice. Anthony Braga, David Kennedy, Elin Waring and Anne Piehl (Chapter 28) discuss Boston's Operation Ceasefire, which achieved a rapid fall in the number of injuries and deaths caused by firearms. It did so by focusing not on gangs per se, but on a specific behavior in which they were engaged. The strategy, which involved the application of well-publicized leverage on gangs in relation to use of firearms, emerged from close cooperation between researchers at Harvard, including the authors, and practitioners from various agencies in Boston. In Chapter 29 Karen Bullock and Nick Tilley describe the findings of analyses undertaken in connection with an effort to mount a sister project in Manchester, England, using principles akin to those that had been applied in Boston.

Eric Fritsch, Tory Caeti and Robert Taylor (Chapter 26) report on a project in Dallas where three tactics were applied to reduce gang violence: 'aggressive curfew enforcement', 'aggressive truancy enforcement' and 'saturation patrol'. Their findings suggest that the aggressive curfew enforcement and aggressive truancy patrol were responsible for a statistically significant fall in violent gang-related offences, with minimal displacement. Other offences were not reduced. Irving Spergel and Susan Grossman (Chapter 25) describe the Little Village Gang Violence Reduction project in Chicago, which was directed by Spergel. The project comprised an inter-agency and community initiative focusing on violent youth gang problems, which were reduced over a four-year period. It involved a series of interrelated strategies including both social interventions and enforcement. Spergel and Grossman stress the close working practices and shared mission that developed between community youth workers – many of whom had once belonged to gangs – and police officers, probation workers, residents and representatives of local organizations, and the targeting of 'hard-core gang youths'. As with the Boston project the researchers also worked closely with those implementing the initiative.

In contrast, Karl Hill, James Howell, David Hawkins and Sara Battin-Pearson (Chapter 27) do not report an actual intervention. Instead they report a Seattle-based prospective study of risk factors at age 10 to 12 associated with gang membership at age 13 to 18, with a view to identifying potential points of preventive action. Gang membership was defined by an answer to the questions, 'Do you belong to a gang?' and 'What is the name of the gang?'. The strongest predictors at age 10–12 were the availability of marijuana in the neighborhood, living in a neighborhood where many youths are in trouble, living with one parent and another non-parent adult in the home, having initiated marijuana use, having engaged in violence, low academic achievement, and being identified as learning disabled at school. Exposure to multiple risk factors substantially heightened overall risk. The authors suggest measures that might impact on the identified risk factors.

John Hagedorn (Chapter 24) again does not report a specific program, but focuses instead on research-based policy recommendations. Drawing on three Milwaukee studies to show how deindustrialization has altered youth gangs, he shows how maturing out of gangs has been undermined by the loss of job opportunities in factories and their replacement with part-time work in the illegal drug economy. Older gang members then furnish models for new recruits. Hagedorn also looks at local neighborhood conditions, noting the lack of effective community institutions, and the presence of 'a checkerboard of struggling working class and poor families, coexisting, even on the same block, with drug houses, gangs, and routine violence' (p. 446). He stresses the ensuing tensions and absence of control. Hagedorn has four suggestions: that public spending and private investment be concentrated in the most impoverished areas; that programs be fully evaluated to see whether they are having an impact on gangs or those most in need; that family preservation programs be funded; and that large bureaucracies become more neighborhood-based and more open to input from clients and the neighborhoods they serve. These measures are directed at strengthening local institutions to complement major jobs programs.

Final Thoughts

We cannot, at this distance in time, be certain about Robin Hood and his Merry Men's significance or exploits, though the stories appear compelling and are echoed in various ways in many other parallel developments in places and times far from Sherwood Forest (Hobsbawm, 1969). Likewise with more modern forms of gangs, we have plenty of plausible myths and legends upon which to make suppositions about gangs and the kinds of things gangs do. It is, we think, hard to escape myth and legend even in present-day gang research. To us, local myths and legends appear to continue to play a part in shaping police work, as well as in the police data that are created and then processed by criminologists. This is not to say that we are locked into their reproduction or to their acceptance; rather, we need to be cautious and critical about the data that provide the foundation of our work and resulting ideology. Additionally, as researchers we need to work with agencies in order to help them avoid succumbing to assumptions that are all too easily confirmed and reproduced. We need to be in the business of demystification. We think that this volume makes a good start by bringing together a wide range of what we deem to be high-quality literature on the nature, composition, activities, social foundations for, and policy responses to, social phenomena labeled 'gangs'.

Notes

1   Due to the nature of this publication, the classic works of these authors are not included in this volume. We would be remiss if we did not suggest that the reader peruse these classics as they provide a rich source of background and theoretical rationale for the study of gangs.
2   For an incident in Los Angeles to be classified as 'gang-related' an identified member of the gang simply has to be taken to have committed the offence – regardless of whether the gang itself ordered the act. In Chicago, however, a more restrictive definition has been set. Here, for an offence to be recorded as 'gang-related' it must be ordered by the gang (for a detailed discussion see Maxson and Klein, 1990).

References

Bloch, Herbert and Neiderhoffer, Arthur (1958), *The Gang: A Study in Adolescent Behavior*, New York: Philosophical Press.

Cloward, Richard A. and Ohlin, Lloyd E. (1960), *Delinquency and Opportunity: A Theory of Delinquent Gangs*, New York: The Free Press.

Cohen, Albert K. (1955), *Delinquent Boys: The Culture of the Gang*, Glencoe, IL: The Free Press.

Cohen, Stanley (1972), *Folk Devils and Moral Panics: The Creation of the Mods and Rockers*, London: Paladin.

Hobsbawm, Eric (1969), *Bandits*, London: Weidenfeld and Nicolson.

Horowitz, Ruth (1990), 'Sociological Perspectives on Gangs: Conflicting Definitions and Concepts', in C. Ronald Huff (ed.), *Gangs in America*, Newbury Park, CA: Sage, pp. 37–54.

Maxson, Cheryl L. and Klein, Malcolm W. (1990), 'Street Gang Violence: Twice as Great, or Half as Great?', in C. Ronald Huff (ed.), *Gangs in America*, Newbury Park, CA: Sage, pp. 71–100.

Schneider, Jacqueline L. (1995), 'Organizational Perspectives and Patterns of Criminality Among Gang Leaders', unpublished doctoral dissertation, University of Cincinnati, USA.

Shaw, Clifford and McKay, Henry (1942), *Juvenile Delinquency and Urban Areas*, Chicago: University of Chicago Press.

Short, James and Strodtbeck, Fred (1965), *Group Process and Gang Delinquency*, Chicago: University of Chicago Press.

Tannenbaum, Frank (1939), *Crime and the Community*, New York: Columbia University Press.

Thrasher, Fredrick M. (1927), *The Gang: A Study of 1,313 Gangs in Chicago*, Chicago: University of Chicago Press.

Whyte, William Foote (1943), *Street Corner Society*, Chicago: University of Chicago Press.

Wilkins, Leslie T. (1964), *Social Deviance: Social Policy, Action and Research*, London: Tavistock Publications.

Winfree, L. Thomas jr, Fuller, Kathy, Vigil, Teresa and Mays, G. Larry (1992), 'The Definition and Measurement of "Gang Status": Policy Implications for Juvenile Justice', *Juvenile and Family Court Journal*, **43**, pp. 29–37.

Yablonsky, Lewis (1962), *The Violent Gang*, New York: Macmillan.

Part I
Theory and Concepts

[1]

SOCIAL STRUCTURE AND ANOMIE

ROBERT K. MERTON

Harvard University

THERE persists a notable tendency in sociological theory to attribute the malfunctioning of social structure primarily to those of man's imperious biological drives which are not adequately restrained by social control. In this view, the social order is solely a device for "impulse management" and the "social processing" of tensions. These impulses which break through social control, be it noted, are held to be biologically derived. Nonconformity is assumed to be rooted in original nature.[1] Conformity is by implication the result of an utilitarian calculus or unreasoned conditioning. This point of view, whatever its other deficiences, clearly begs one question. It provides no basis for determining the nonbiological conditions which induce deviations from prescribed patterns of conduct. In this paper, it will be suggested that certain phases of social structure generate the circumstances in which infringement of social codes constitutes a "normal" response.[2]

The conceptual scheme to be outlined is designed to provide a coherent, systematic approach to the study of socio-cultural sources of deviate behavior. Our primary aim lies in discovering how some social structures *exert a definite pressure* upon certain persons in the society to engage in nonconformist rather than conformist conduct. The many ramifications of the scheme cannot all be discussed; the problems mentioned outnumber those explicitly treated.

Among the elements of social and cultural structure, two are important for our purposes. These are analytically separable although they merge imperceptibly in concrete situations. The first consists of culturally defined goals, purposes, and interests. It comprises a frame of aspirational reference. These goals are more or less integrated and involve varying degrees of prestige and sentiment. They constitute a basic, but not the exclusive, component of what Linton aptly has called "designs for group living." Some of these cultural aspirations are related to the original drives of man, but they are not determined by them. The second phase of the social

---

[1] E.g., Ernest Jones, *Social Aspects of Psychoanalysis*, 28, London, 1924. If the Freudian notion is a variety of the "original sin" dogma, then the interpretation advanced in this paper may be called the doctrine of "socially derived sin."

[2] "Normal" in the sense of a culturally oriented, if not approved, response. This statement does not deny the relevance of biological and personality differences which may be significantly involved in the *incidence* of deviate conduct. Our focus of interest is the social and cultural matrix; hence we abstract from other factors. It is in this sense, I take it, that James S. Plant speaks of the "normal reaction of normal people to abnormal conditions." See his *Personality and the Cultural Pattern*, 248, New York, 1937.

SOCIAL STRUCTURE AND ANOMIE

structure defines, regulates, and controls the acceptable modes of achieving these goals. Every social group invariably couples its scale of desired ends with moral or institutional regulation of permissible and required procedures for attaining these ends. These regulatory norms and moral imperatives do not necessarily coincide with technical or efficiency norms. Many procedures which from the standpoint of *particular individuals* would be most efficient in securing desired values, e.g., illicit oil-stock schemes, theft, fraud, are ruled out of the institutional area of permitted conduct. The choice of expedients is limited by the institutional norms.

To say that these two elements, culture goals and institutional norms, operate jointly is not to say that the ranges of alternative behaviors and aims bear some constant relation to one another. The emphasis upon certain goals may vary independently of the degree of emphasis upon institutional means. There may develop a disproportionate, at times, a virtually exclusive, stress upon the value of specific goals, involving relatively slight concern with the institutionally appropriate modes of attaining these goals. The limiting case in this direction is reached when the range of alternative procedures is limited only by technical rather than institutional considerations. Any and all devices which promise attainment of the all important goal would be permitted in this hypothetical polar case.[3] This constitutes one type of cultural malintegration. A second polar type is found in groups where activities originally conceived as instrumental are transmuted into ends in themselves. The original purposes are forgotten and ritualistic adherence to institutionally prescribed conduct becomes virtually obsessive.[4] Stability is largely ensured while change is flouted. The range of alternative behaviors is severely limited. There develops a tradition-bound, sacred society characterized by neophobia. The occupational psychosis of the bureaucrat may be cited as a case in point. Finally, there are the intermediate types of groups where a balance between culture goals and institu-

---

[3] Contemporary American culture has been said to tend in this direction. See André Siegfried, *America Comes of Age*, 26–37, New York, 1927. The alleged extreme(?) emphasis on the goals of monetary success and material prosperity leads to dominant concern with technological and social instruments designed to produce the desired result, inasmuch as institutional controls become of secondary importance. In such a situation, innovation flourishes as the *range of means* employed is broadened. In a sense, then, there occurs the paradoxical emergence of "materialists" from an "idealistic" orientation. Cf. Durkheim's analysis of the cultural conditions which predispose toward crime and innovation, both of which are aimed toward efficiency, not moral norms. Durkheim was one of the first to see that "contrairement aux idées courantes le criminel n'apparait plus comme un être radicalement insociable, comme une sorte d'elément parasitaire, de corps étranger et inassimilable, introduit au sein de la société; c'est un agent régulier de la vie sociale." See *Les Règles de la Méthode Sociologique*, 86–89, Paris, 1927.

[4] Such ritualism may be associated with a mythology which rationalizes these actions so that they appear to retain their status as means, but the dominant pressure is in the direction of strict ritualistic conformity, irrespective of such rationalizations. In this sense, ritual has proceeded farthest when such rationalizations are not even called forth.

tional means is maintained. These are the significantly integrated and relatively stable, though changing, groups.

An effective equilibrium between the two phases of the social structure is maintained as long as satisfactions accrue to individuals who conform to both constraints, viz., satisfactions from the achievement of the goals and satisfactions emerging directly from the institutionally canalized modes of striving to attain these ends. Success, in such equilibrated cases, is twofold. Success is reckoned in terms of the product and in terms of the process, in terms of the outcome and in terms of activities. Continuing satisfactions must derive from sheer *participation* in a competitive order as well as from eclipsing one's competitors if the order itself is to be sustained. The occasional sacrifices involved in institutionalized conduct must be compensated by socialized rewards. The distribution of statuses and roles through competition must be so organized that positive incentives for conformity to roles and adherence to status obligations are provided *for every position* within the distributive order. Aberrant conduct, therefore, may be viewed as a symptom of dissociation between culturally defined aspirations and socially structured means.

Of the types of groups which result from the independent variation of the two phases of the social structure, we shall be primarily concerned with the first, namely, that involving a disproportionate accent on goals. This statement must be recast in a proper perspective. In no group is there an absence of regulatory codes governing conduct, yet groups do vary in the degree to which these folkways, mores, and institutional controls are effectively integrated with the more diffuse goals which are part of the culture matrix. Emotional convictions may cluster about the complex of socially acclaimed ends, meanwhile shifting their support from the culturally defined implementation of these ends. As we shall see, certain aspects of the social structure may generate countermores and antisocial behavior precisely because of differential emphases on goals and regulations. In the extreme case, the latter may be so vitiated by the goal-emphasis that the range of behavior is limited only by considerations of technical expediency. The sole significant question then becomes, which available means is most efficient in netting the socially approved value?[5] The technically most feasible procedure, whether legitimate or not, is preferred to the institutionally prescribed conduct. As this process continues, the integration of the society becomes tenuous and anomie ensues.

---

[5] In this connection, one may see the relevance of Elton Mayo's paraphrase of the title of Tawney's well known book. "Actually the problem *is not that of the sickness of an acquisitive society; it is that of the acquisitiveness of a sick society.*" *Human Problems of an Industrial Civilization,* 153, New York, 1933. Mayo deals with the process through which wealth comes to be a symbol of social achievement. He sees this as arising from a state of anomie. We are considering the unintegrated monetary-success goal as an element in producing anomie. A complete analysis would involve both phases of this system of interdependent variables.

SOCIAL STRUCTURE AND ANOMIE

Thus, in competitive athletics, when the aim of victory is shorn of its institutional trappings and success in contests becomes construed as "winning the game" rather than "winning through circumscribed modes of activity," a premium is implicitly set upon the use of illegitimate but technically efficient means. The star of the opposing football team is surreptitiously slugged; the wrestler furtively incapacitates his opponent through ingenious but illicit techniques; university alumni covertly subsidize "students" whose talents are largely confined to the athletic field. The emphasis on the goal has so attenuated the satisfactions deriving from sheer participation in the competitive activity that these satisfactions are virtually confined to a successful outcome. Through the same process, tension generated by the desire to win in a poker game is relieved by successfully dealing oneself four aces, or, when the cult of success has become completely dominant, by sagaciously shuffling the cards in a game of solitaire. The faint twinge of uneasiness in the last instance and the surreptitious nature of public delicts indicate clearly that the institutional rules of the game *are known* to those who evade them, but that the emotional supports of these rules are largely vitiated by cultural exaggeration of the success-goal.[6] They are microcosmic images of the social macrocosm.

Of course, this process is not restricted to the realm of sport. The process whereby exaltation of the end generates a *literal demoralization*, i.e., a deinstitutionalization, of the means is one which characterizes many[7] groups in which the two phases of the social structure are not highly integrated. The extreme emphasis upon the accumulation of wealth as a symbol of success[8] in our own society militates against the completely effective control of institutionally regulated modes of acquiring a fortune.[9] Fraud, corruption, vice, crime, in short, the entire catalogue of proscribed

---

[6] It is unlikely that interiorized norms are completely eliminated. Whatever residuum persists will induce personality tensions and conflict. The process involves a certain degree of ambivalence. A manifest rejection of the institutional norms is coupled with some latent retention of their emotional correlates. "Guilt feelings," "sense of sin," "pangs of conscience" are obvious manifestations of this unrelieved tension; symbolic adherence to the nominally repudiated values or rationalizations constitute a more subtle variety of tensional release.

[7] "Many," and not all, unintegrated groups, for the reason already mentioned. In groups where the primary emphasis shifts to institutional means, i.e., when the range of alternatives is very limited, the outcome is a type of ritualism rather than anomie.

[8] Money has several peculiarities which render it particularly apt to become a symbol of prestige divorced from institutional controls. As Simmel emphasized, money is highly abstract and impersonal. However acquired, through fraud or institutionally, it can be used to purchase the same goods and services. The anonymity of metropolitan culture, in conjunction with this peculiarity of money, permits wealth, the sources of which may be unknown to the community in which the plutocrat lives, to serve as a symbol of status.

[9] The emphasis upon wealth as a success-symbol is possibly reflected in the use of the term "fortune" to refer to a stock of accumulated wealth. This meaning becomes common in the late sixteenth century (Spenser and Shakespeare). A similar usage of the Latin *fortuna* comes into prominence during the first century B.C. Both these periods were marked by the rise to prestige and power of the "bourgeoisie."

behavior, becomes increasingly common when the emphasis on the *culturally induced* success-goal becomes divorced from a coordinated institutional emphasis. This observation is of crucial theoretical importance in examining the doctrine that antisocial behavior most frequently derives from biological drives breaking through the restraints imposed by society. The difference is one between a strictly utilitarian interpretation which conceives man's ends as random and an analysis which finds these ends deriving from the basic values of the culture.[10]

Our analysis can scarcely stop at this juncture. We must turn to other aspects of the social structure if we are to deal with the social genesis of the varying rates and types of deviate behavior characteristic of different societies. Thus far, we have sketched three ideal types of social orders constituted by distinctive patterns of relations between culture ends and means. Turning from these types of *culture patterning*, we find five logically possible, alternative modes of adjustment or adaptation *by individuals* within the culture-bearing society or group.[11] These are schematically presented in the following table, where (+) signifies "acceptance," (−) signifies "elimination" and (±) signifies "rejection and substitution of new goals and standards."

	Culture Goals	Institutionalized Means
I. Conformity	+	+
II. Innovation	+	−
III. Ritualism	−	+
IV. Retreatism	−	−
V. Rebellion[12]	±	±

Our discussion of the relation between these alternative responses and other phases of the social structure must be prefaced by the observation that persons may shift from one alternative to another as they engage in different social activities. These categories refer to role adjustments in specific situations, not to personality *in toto*. To treat the development of this process in various spheres of conduct would introduce a complexity unmanageable within the confines of this paper. For this reason, we shall be concerned primarily with economic activity in the broad sense, "the

[10] See Kingsley Davis, "Mental Hygiene and the Class Structure," *Psychiatry*, 1928, I, esp. 62–63; Talcott Parsons, *The Structure of Social Action*, 59–60, New York, 1937.

[11] This is a level intermediate between the two planes distinguished by Edward Sapir; namely, culture patterns and personal habit systems. See his "Contribution of Psychiatry to an Understanding of Behavior in Society," *Amer. J. Sociol.*, 1937, 42:862–70.

[12] This fifth alternative is on a plane clearly different from that of the others. It represents a *transitional* response which seeks to *institutionalize* new procedures oriented toward revamped cultural goals shared by the members of the society. It thus involves efforts to *change* the existing structure rather than to perform accommodative actions *within* this structure, and introduces additional problems with which we are not at the moment concerned.

SOCIAL STRUCTURE AND ANOMIE

production, exchange, distribution and consumption of goods and services" in our competitive society, wherein wealth has taken on a highly symbolic cast. Our task is to search out some of the factors which exert pressure upon individuals to engage in certain of these logically possible alternative responses. This choice, as we shall see, is far from random.

In every society, Adaptation I (conformity to both culture goals and means) is the most common and widely diffused. Were this not so, the stability and continuity of the society could not be maintained. The mesh of expectancies which constitutes every social order is sustained by the modal behavior of its members falling within the first category. Conventional role behavior oriented toward the basic values of the group is the rule rather than the exception. It is this fact alone which permits us to speak of a human aggregate as comprising a group or society.

Conversely, Adaptation IV (rejection of goals and means) is the least common. Persons who "adjust" (or maladjust) in this fashion are, strictly speaking, *in* the society but not *of* it. Sociologically, these constitute the true "aliens." Not sharing the common frame of orientation, they can be included within the societal population merely in a fictional sense. In this category are *some* of the activities of psychotics, psychoneurotics, chronic autists, pariahs, outcasts, vagrants, vagabonds, tramps, chronic drunkards and drug addicts.[13] These have relinquished, in certain spheres of activity, the culturally defined goals, involving complete aim-inhibition in the polar case, and their adjustments are not in accord with institutional norms. This is not to say that in some cases the source of their behavioral adjustments is not in part the very social structure which they have in effect repudiated nor that their very existence within a social area does not constitute a problem for the socialized population.

This mode of "adjustment" occurs, as far as structural sources are concerned, when both the culture goals and institutionalized procedures have been assimilated thoroughly by the individual and imbued with affect and high positive value, but where those institutionalized procedures which promise a measure of successful attainment of the goals are not available to the individual. In such instances, there results a twofold mental conflict insofar as the moral obligation for adopting institutional means conflicts with the pressure to resort to illegitimate means (which may attain the goal) and inasmuch as the individual is shut off from means which are both legitimate *and* effective. The competitive order is maintained, but the frustrated and handicapped individual who cannot cope with this order drops out.

---

[13] Obviously, this is an elliptical statement. These individuals may maintain some orientation to the values of their particular differentiated groupings within the larger society or, in part, of the conventional society itself. Insofar as they do so, their conduct cannot be classified in the "passive rejection" category (IV). Nels Anderson's description of the behavior and attitudes of the bum, for example, can readily be recast in terms of our analytical scheme. See *The Hobo*, 93–98, *et passim*, Chicago, 1923.

Defeatism, quietism and resignation are manifested in escape mechanisms which ultimately lead the individual to "escape" from the requirements of the society. It is an expedient which arises from continued failure to attain the goal by legitimate measures and from an inability to adopt the illegitimate route because of internalized prohibitions and institutionalized compulsives, *during which process the supreme value of the success-goal has as yet not been renounced.* The conflict is resolved by eliminating *both* precipitating elements, the goals and means. The escape is complete, the conflict is eliminated and the individual is a socialized.

Be it noted that where frustration derives from the inaccessibility of effective institutional means for attaining economic or any other type of highly valued "success," that Adaptations II, III and V (innovation, ritualism and rebellion) are also possible. The result will be determined by the particular personality, and thus, the *particular* cultural background, involved. Inadequate socialization will result in the innovation response whereby the conflict and frustration are eliminated by relinquishing the institutional means and retaining the success-aspiration; an extreme assimilation of institutional demands will lead to ritualism wherein the goal is dropped as beyond one's reach but conformity to the mores persists; and rebellion occurs when emancipation from the reigning standards, due to frustration or to marginalist perspectives, leads to the attempt to introduce a "new social order."

Our major concern is with the illegitimacy adjustment. This involves the use of conventionally proscribed but frequently effective means of attaining at least the simulacrum of culturally defined success,—wealth, power, and the like. As we have seen, this adjustment occurs when the individual has assimilated the cultural emphasis on success without equally internalizing the morally prescribed norms governing means for its attainment. The question arises, Which phases of our social structure predispose toward this mode of adjustment? We may examine a concrete instance, effectively analyzed by Lohman,[14] which provides a clue to the answer. Lohman has shown that specialized areas of vice in the near north side of Chicago constitute a "normal" response to a situation where the cultural emphasis upon pecuniary success has been absorbed, but where there is little access to conventional and legitimate means for attaining such success. The conventional occupational opportunities of persons in this area are almost completely limited to manual labor. Given our cultural stigmatization of manual labor, and its correlate, the prestige of white collar work, it is clear that the result is a strain toward innovational practices. The limitation of opportunity to unskilled labor and the resultant low income

---

[14] Joseph D. Lohman, "The Participant Observer in Community Studies," *Amer. Sociol. Rev.*, 1937, 2:890–98.

SOCIAL STRUCTURE AND ANOMIE   679

can not compete *in terms of conventional standards of achievement* with the high income from organized vice.

For our purposes, this situation involves two important features. First, such antisocial behavior is in a sense "called forth" by certain conventional values of the culture *and* by the class structure involving differential access to the approved opportunities for legitimate, prestige-bearing pursuit of the culture goals. The lack of high integration between the means-and-end elements of the cultural pattern and the particular class structure combine to favor a heightened frequency of antisocial conduct in such groups. The second consideration is of equal significance. Recourse to the first of the alternative responses, legitimate effort, is limited by the fact that actual advance toward desired success-symbols through conventional channels is, despite our persisting open-class ideology,[15] relatively rare and difficult for those handicapped by little formal education and few economic resources. The dominant pressure of group standards of success is, therefore, on the gradual attenuation of legitimate, but by and large ineffective, strivings and the increasing use of illegitimate, but more or less effective, expedients of vice and crime. The cultural demands made on persons in this situation are incompatible. On the one hand, they are asked to orient their conduct toward the prospect of accumulating wealth and on the other, they are largely denied effective opportunities to do so institutionally. The consequences of such structural inconsistency are psycho-pathological personality, and/or antisocial conduct, and/or revolutionary activities. The equilibrium between culturally designated means and ends becomes highly unstable with the progressive emphasis on attaining the prestige-laden ends by any means whatsoever. Within this context, Capone represents the triumph of amoral intelligence over morally prescribed "failure," when the channels of vertical mobility are closed or narrowed[16]

---

[15] The shifting historical role of this ideology is a profitable subject for exploration. The "office-boy-to-president" stereotype was once in approximate accord with the facts. Such vertical mobility was probably more common then than now, when the class structure is more rigid. (See the following note.) The ideology largely persists, however, possibly because it still performs a useful function for maintaining the *status quo*. For insofar as it is accepted by the "masses," it constitutes a useful sop for those who might rebel against the entire structure, were this consoling hope removed. This ideology now serves to lessen the probability of Adaptation V. In short, the role of this notion has changed from that of an approximately valid empirical theorem to that of an ideology, in Mannheim's sense.

[16] There is a growing body of evidence, though none of it is clearly conclusive, to the effect that our class structure is becoming rigidified and that vertical mobility is declining. Taussig and Joslyn found that American business leaders are being *increasingly* recruited from the upper ranks of our society. The Lynds have also found a "diminished chance to get ahead" for the working classes in Middletown. Manifestly, these objective changes are not alone significant; the individual's subjective evaluation of the situation is a major determinant of the response. The extent to which this change in opportunity for social mobility has been recognized by the least advantaged classes is still conjectural, although the Lynds present some suggestive materials. The writer suggests that a case in point is the increasing frequency of cartoons which observe in a tragi-comic vein that "my old man says everybody can't be Presi-

in a society which places a high premium on economic affluence and social ascent for all *its members*.[17]

This last qualification is of primary importance. It suggests that other phases of the social structure besides the extreme emphasis on pecuniary success, must be considered if we are to understand the social sources of antisocial behavior. A high frequency of deviate behavior is not generated simply by "lack of opportunity" or by this exaggerated pecuniary emphasis. A comparatively rigidified class structure, a feudalistic or caste order, may limit such opportunities far beyond the point which obtains in our society today. It is only when a system of cultural values extols, virtually above all else, certain *common* symbols of success *for the population at large* while its social structure rigorously restricts or completely eliminates access to approved modes of acquiring these symbols *for a considerable part of the same population*, that antisocial behavior ensues on a considerable scale. In other words, our egalitarian ideology denies by implication the existence of noncompeting groups and individuals in the pursuit of pecuniary success. The same body of success-symbols is held to be desirable for all. These goals are held to *transcend class lines*, not to be bounded by them, yet the actual social organization is such that there exist class differentials in the accessibility of these *common* success-symbols. Frustration and thwarted aspiration lead to the search for avenues of escape from a culturally induced intolerable situation; or unrelieved ambition may eventuate in illicit attempts to acquire the dominant values.[18] The American stress on pecuniary success and ambitiousness for all thus invites exaggerated anxieties, hostilities, neuroses and antisocial behavior.

This theoretical analysis may go far toward explaining the varying correlations between crime and poverty.[19] Poverty is not an isolated variable.

---

dent. He says if ya can get three days a week steady on W.P.A. work ya ain't doin' so bad either." See F. W. Taussig and C. S. Joslyn, *American Business Leaders*, New York, 1932; R. S. and H. M. Lynd, *Middletown in Transition*, 67 ff., chap. 12, New York, 1937.

[17] The role of the Negro in this respect is of considerable theoretical interest. Certain elements of the Negro population have assimilated the dominant caste's values of pecuniary success and social advancement, but they also recognize that social ascent is at present restricted to their own caste almost exclusively. The pressures upon the Negro which would otherwise derive from the structural inconsistencies we have noticed are hence not identical with those upon lower class whites. See Kingsley Davis, *op. cit.*, 63; John Dollard, *Caste and Class in a Southern Town*, 66 ff., New Haven, 1936; Donald Young, *American Minority Peoples*, 581, New York, 1932.

[18] The psychical coordinates of these processes have been partly established by the experimental evidence concerning *Anspruchsniveaus* and levels of performance. See Kurt Lewin, *Vorsatz, Wille und Bedurfnis*, Berlin, 1926; N. F. Hoppe, "Erfolg und Misserfolg," *Psychol. Forschung*, 1930, 14:1–63; Jerome D. Frank, "Individual Differences in Certain Aspects of the Level of Aspiration," *Amer. J. Psychol.*, 1935, 47:119–28.

[19] Standard criminology texts summarize the data in this field. Our scheme of analysis may serve to resolve some of the theoretical contradictions which P. A. Sorokin indicates. For example, "not everywhere nor always do the poor show a greater proportion of crime . . . many poorer countries have had less crime than the richer countries . . . The [economic] improve-

SOCIAL STRUCTURE AND ANOMIE 681

It is one in a complex of interdependent social and cultural variables. When viewed in such a context, it represents quite different states of affairs. Poverty as such, and consequent limitation of opportunity, are not sufficient to induce a conspicuously high rate of criminal behavior. Even the often mentioned "poverty in the midst of plenty" will not necessarily lead to this result. Only insofar as poverty and associated disadvantages in competition for the culture values approved for *all* members of the society is linked with the assimilation of a cultural emphasis on monetary accumulation as a symbol of success is antisocial conduct a "normal" outcome. Thus, poverty is less highly correlated with crime in southeastern Europe than in the United States. The possibilities of vertical mobility in these European areas would seem to be fewer than in this country, so that neither poverty *per se* nor its association with limited opportunity is sufficient to account for the varying correlations. It is only when the full configuration is considered, poverty, limited opportunity and a commonly shared system of success symbols, that we can explain the higher association between poverty and crime in our society than in others where rigidified class structure is coupled with *differential class symbols of achievement*.

In societies such as our own, then, the pressure of prestige-bearing success tends to eliminate the effective social constraint over means employed to this end. "The-end-justifies-the-means" doctrine becomes a guiding tenet for action when the cultural structure unduly exalts the end and the social organization unduly limits possible recourse to approved means. Otherwise put, this notion and associated behavior reflect a lack of cultural coordination. In international relations, the effects of this lack of integration are notoriously apparent. An emphasis upon national power is not readily coordinated with an inept organization of legitimate, i.e., internationally defined and accepted, means for attaining this goal. The result is a tendency toward the abrogation of international law, treaties become scraps of paper, "undeclared warefare" serves as a technical evasion, the bombing of civilian populations is rationalized,[20] just as the same societal situation induces the same sway of illegitimacy among individuals.

The social order we have described necessarily produces this "strain toward dissolution." The pressure of such an order is upon outdoing one's competitors. The choice of means within the ambit of institutional control will persist as long as the sentiments supporting a competitive system, i.e., deriving from the possibility of outranking competitors and hence en-

---

ment in the second half of the nineteenth century, and the beginning of the twentieth, has not been followed by a decrease of crime." See his *Contemporary Sociological Theories*, 560–61, New York, 1928. The crucial point is, however, that poverty has varying social significance in different social structures, as we shall see. Hence, one would not expect a linear correlation betweem crime and poverty.

[20] See M. W. Royse, *Aerial Bombardment and the International Regulation of War*, New York, 1928.

joying the favorable response of others, are distributed throughout the entire system of activities and are not confined merely to the final result. A stable social structure demands a balanced distribution of affect among its various segments. When there occurs a shift of emphasis from the satis-factions deriving from competition itself to almost exclusive concern with successful competition, the resultant stress leads to the breakdown of the regulatory structure.[21] With the resulting attenuation of the institutional imperatives, there occurs an approximation of the situation erroneously held by utilitarians to be typical of society generally wherein calculations of advantage and fear of punishment are the sole regulating agencies. In such situations, as Hobbes observed, force and fraud come to constitute the sole virtues in view of their relative efficiency in attaining goals,— which were for him, of course, not culturally derived.

It should be apparent that the foregoing discussion is not pitched on a moralistic plane. Whatever the sentiments of the writer or reader concern-ing the ethical desirability of coordinating the means-and-goals phases of the social structure, one must agree that lack of such coordination leads to anomie. Insofar as one of the most general functions of social organization is to provide a basis for calculability and regularity of behavior, it is in-creasingly limited in effectiveness as these elements of the structure become dissociated. At the extreme, predictability virtually disappears and what may be properly termed cultural chaos or anomie intervenes.

This statement, being brief, is also incomplete. It has not included an ex-haustive treatment of the various structural elements which predispose toward one rather than another of the alternative responses open to in-dividuals; it has neglected, but not denied the relevance of, the factors de-termining the specific incidence of these responses; it has not enumerated the various concrete responses which are constituted by combinations of specific values of the analytical variables; it has omitted, or included only by implication, any consideration of the social functions performed by illicit responses; it has not tested the full explanatory power of the analytical scheme by examining a large number of group variations in the frequency of deviate and conformist behavior; it has not adequately dealt with re-bellious conduct which seeks to refashion the social framework radically; it has not examined the relevance of cultural conflict for an analysis of cul-ture-goal and institutional-means malintegration. It is suggested that these and related problems may be profitably analyzed by this scheme.

---

[21] Since our primary concern is with the socio-cultural aspects of this problem, the psycho-logical correlates have been only implicitly considered. See Karen Horney, *The Neurotic Personality of Our Time*, New York, 1937, for a psychological discussion of this process.

[2]

Lower Class Culture as a Generating Milieu of Gang Delinquency

Walter B. Miller

The etiology of delinquency has long been a controversial issue, and is particularly so at present. As new frames of reference for explaining human behavior have been added to traditional theories, some authors have adopted the practice of citing the major postulates of each school of thought as they pertain to delinquency, and going on to state that causality must be conceived in terms of the dynamic interaction of a complex combination of variables on many levels. The major sets of etiological factors currently adduced to explain delinquency are, in simplified terms, the physiological (delinquency results from organic pathology), the psychodynamic (delinquency is a "behavioral disorder" resulting primarily from emotional disturbance generated by a defective mother-child relationship), and the environmental (delinquency is the product of disruptive forces, "disorganization," in the actor's physical or social environment).

This paper selects one particular kind of "delinquency" [1]—law-violating acts committed by members of adolescent street corner groups in lower class communities—and attempts to show that the dominant component of motivation underlying these acts consists in a directed attempt by the actor to adhere to forms of behavior, and to achieve standards of value as they are defined within that community. It takes as a premise that the motivation of behavior in this situation can be approached most productively by attempting to understand the nature of cultural forces impinging on the acting individual as they are perceived *by the actor himself*—although by no means only that segment of these forces of which the actor is consciously aware—rather than as they are perceived and evaluated from the reference position of another cultural system. In the case of "gang" delinquency, the cultural system which exerts the most direct influence on behavior is that of the lower class community itself—a long-established, distinctively patterned tradition with an integrity of its own—rather than a so-called "delinquent subculture" which has arisen

---

[1] The complex issues involved in deriving a definition of "delinquency" cannot be discussed here. The term "delinquent" is used in this paper to characterize behavior or acts committed by individuals within specified age limits which if known to official authorities could result in legal action. The concept of a "delinquent" individual has little or no utility in the approach used here; rather, specified types of *acts* which may be committed rarely or frequently by few or many individuals are characterized as "delinquent."

through conflict with middle class culture and is oriented to the deliberate violation of middle class norms.

The bulk of the substantive data on which the following material is based was collected in connection with a service-research project in the control of gang delinquency. During the service aspect of the project, which lasted for three years, seven trained social workers maintained contact with twenty-one corner group units in a "'slum" district of a large eastern city for periods of time ranging from ten to thirty months. Groups were Negro and white, male and female, and in early, middle, and late adolescence. Over eight thousand pages of direct observational data on behavior patterns of group members and other community residents were collected; almost daily contact was maintained for a total time period of about thirteen worker years. Data include workers' contact reports, participant observation reports by the writer—a cultural anthropologist—and direct tape recordings of group activities and discussions.[2]

Focal Concerns of Lower Class Culture

There is a substantial segment of present-day American society whose way of life, values, and characteristic patterns of behavior are the product of a distinctive cultural system which may be termed "lower class." Evidence indicates that this cultural system is becoming increasingly distinctive, and that the size of the group which shares this tradition is increasing.[3] The lower class way of life, in common with that of all distinctive cultural groups, is characterized by a set of focal concerns—areas or issues which command widespread and persistent attention and a high degree of emotional involvement. The specific concerns cited here, while by no means confined to the American lower classes, constitute a distinctive *patterning* of concerns which differs significantly, both in rank

---

[2] A three year research project is being financed under National Institutes of Health Grant M–1414, and administered through the Boston University School of Social Work. The primary research effort has subjected all collected material to a uniform data-coding process. All information bearing on some seventy areas of behavior (behavior in reference to school, police, theft, assault, sex, collective athletics, etc.) is extracted from the records, recorded on coded data cards, and filed under relevant categories. Analysis of these data aims to ascertain the actual nature of customary behavior in these areas, and the extent to which the social work effort was able to effect behavioral changes.

[3] Between 40 and 60 per cent of all Americans are directly influenced by lower class culture, with about 15 per cent, or twenty-five million, comprising the "hard core" lower class group—defined primarily by its use of the "female-based" household as the basic form of child-rearing unit and of the "serial monogamy" mating pattern as the primary form of marriage. The term "lower class culture" as used here refers most specifically to the way of life of the "hard core" group; systematic research in this area would probably reveal at least four to six major subtypes of lower class culture, for some of which the "concerns" presented here would be differently weighted, especially for those subtypes in which "law-abiding" behavior has a high overt valuation. It is impossible within the compass of this short paper to make the finer intracultural distinctions which a more accurate presentation would require.

order and weighting from that of American middle class culture. The following chart presents a highly schematic and simplified listing of six of the major concerns of lower class culture. Each is conceived as a "dimension" within which a fairly wide and varied range of alternative behavior patterns may be followed by different individuals under different situations. They are listed roughly in order of the degree of *explicit* attention accorded each, and, in this sense represent a weighted ranking of concerns. The "perceived alternatives" represent polar positions which define certain parameters within each dimension. As will be explained in more detail, it is necessary in relating the influence of these "concerns" to the motivation of delinquent behavior to specify *which* of its aspects is oriented to, whether orientation is *overt* or *covert, positive* (conforming to or seeking the aspect), or *negative* (rejecting or seeking to avoid the aspect).

The concept "focal concern" is used here in preference to the concept "value" for several interrelated reasons: (1) It is more readily derivable from direct field observation. (2) It is descriptively neutral—permitting independent consideration of positive and negative valences as varying under different conditions, whereas "value" carries a built-in positive valence. (3) It makes possible more refined analysis of subcultural differences, since it reflects actual behavior, whereas "value" tends to wash out intracultural differences since it is colored by notions of the "official" ideal.

CHART 1
FOCAL CONCERNS OF LOWER CLASS CULTURE

Area	Perceived Alternatives (state, quality, condition)	
1. *Trouble:*	law-abiding behavior	law-violating behavior
2. *Toughness:*	physical prowess, skill; "masculinity"; fearlessness, bravery, daring	weakness, ineptitude; effeminacy; timidity, cowardice, caution
3. *Smartness:*	ability to outsmart, dupe, "con"; gaining money by "wits"; shrewdness, adroitness in repartee	gullibility, "con-ability"; gaining money by hard work; slowness, dull-wittedness, verbal maladroitness
4. *Excitement:*	thrill; risk, danger; change, activity	boredom; "deadness," safeness; sameness, passivity
5. *Fate:*	favored by fortune, being "lucky"	ill-omened, being "unlucky"
6. *Autonomy:*	freedom from external constraint; freedom from superordinate authority; independence	presence of external constraint; presence of strong authority; dependency, being "cared for"

7

Trouble: Concern over "trouble" is a dominant feature of lower class culture. The concept has various shades of meaning; "trouble" in one of its aspects represents a situation or a kind of behavior which results in unwelcome or complicating involvement with official authorities or agencies of middle class society. "Getting into trouble" and "staying out of trouble" represent major issues for male and female, adults and children. For men, "trouble" frequently involves fighting or sexual adventures while drinking; for women, sexual involvement with disadvantageous consequences. Expressed desire to avoid behavior which violates moral or legal norms is often based less on an explicit commitment to "official" moral or legal standards than on a desire to avoid "getting into trouble," e.g., the complicating consequences of the action.

The dominant concern over "trouble" involves a distinction of critical importance for the lower class community—that between "law-abiding" and "non-law-abiding" behavior. There is a high degree of sensitivity as to where each person stands in relation to these two classes of activity. Whereas in the middle class community a major dimension for evaluating a person's status is "achievement" and its external symbols, in the lower class, personal status is very frequently gauged along the law-abiding-non-law-abiding dimension. A mother will evaluate the suitability of her daughter's boyfriend less on the basis of his achievement potential than on the basis of his innate "trouble" potential. This sensitive awareness of the opposition of "trouble-producing" and "non-trouble-producing" behavior represents both a major basis for deriving status distinctions, and an internalized conflict potential for the individual.

As in the case of other focal concerns, which of two perceived alternatives—"law-abiding" or "non-law-abiding"—is valued varies according to the individual and the circumstances; in many instances there is an overt commitment to the "law-abiding" alternative, but a covert commitment to the "non-law-abiding." In certain situations, "getting into trouble" is overtly recognized as prestige-conferring; for example, membership in certain adult and adolescent primary groupings ("gangs") is contingent on having demonstrated an explicit commitment to the law-violating alternative. It is most important to note that the choice between "law-abiding" and "non-law-abiding" behavior is still a choice *within* lower class culture; the distinction between the policeman and the criminal, the outlaw and the sheriff, involves primarily this one dimension; in other respects they have a high community of interests. Not infrequently brothers raised in an identical cultural milieu will become police and criminals respectively.

For a substantial segment of the lower class population "getting into trouble" is not in itself overtly defined as prestige-conferring, but is implicitly recognized as a means to other valued ends, e.g., the covertly valued desire to be "cared for" and subject to external constraint, or the overtly valued state of excitement or risk. Very frequently "getting into trouble" is multi-functional, and achieves several sets of valued ends.

8

Toughness: The concept of "toughness" in lower class culture represents a compound combination of qualities or states. Among its most important components are physical prowess, evidenced both by demonstrated possession of strength and endurance and athletic skill; "masculinity," symbolized by a distinctive complex of acts and avoidances (bodily tatooing; absence of sentimentality; non-concern with "art," "literature," conceptualization of women as conquest objects, etc.) ; and bravery in the face of physical threat. The model for the "tough guy"—hard, fearless, undemonstrative, skilled in physical combat—is represented by the movie gangster of the thirties, the "private eye," and the movie cowboy.

The genesis of the intense concern over "toughness" in lower class culture is probably related to the fact that a significant proportion of lower class males are reared in a predominantly female household, and lack a consistently present male figure with whom to identify and from whom to learn essential components of a "male" role. Since women serve as a primary object of identification during pre-adolescent years, the almost obsessive lower class concern with "masculinity" probably resembles a type of compulsive reaction-formation. A concern over homosexuality runs like a persistent thread through lower class culture. This is manifested by the institutionalized practice of baiting "queers," often accompanied by violent physical attacks, an expressed contempt for "softness" or frills, and the use of the local term for "homosexual" as a generalized pejorative epithet (e.g., higher class individuals or upwardly mobile peers are frequently characterized as "fags" or "queers"). The distinction between "overt" and "covert" orientation to aspects of an area of concern is especially important in regard to "toughness." A positive overt evaluation of behavior defined as "effeminate" would be out of the question for a lower class male; however, built into lower class culture is a range of devices which permit men to adopt behaviors and concerns which in other cultural milieux fall within the province of women, and at the same time to be defined as "tough" and manly. For example, lower class men can be professional short-order cooks in a diner and still be regarded as "tough." The highly intimate circumstances of the street corner gang involve the recurrent expression of strongly affectionate feelings towards other men. Such expressions, however, are disguised as their opposite, taking the form of ostensibly aggressive verbal and physical interaction (kidding, "ranking," roughhousing, etc.).

Smartness: "Smartness," as conceptualized in lower class culture, involves the capacity to outsmart, outfox, outwit, dupe, "take," "con" another or others, and the concomitant capacity to avoid being outwitted, "taken," or duped oneself. In its essence, smartness involves the capacity to achieve a valued entity—material goods, personal status—through a maximum use of mental agility and a minimum use of physical effort. This capacity has an extremely long tradition in lower class culture, and is highly valued. Lower class culture can be characterized as "non-intellectual" only if intellectualism is defined specifically in terms of control

9

over a particular body of formally learned knowledge involving "culture" (art, literature, "good" music, etc.), a generalized perspective on the past and present conditions of our own and other societies, and other areas of knowledge imparted by formal educational institutions. This particular type of mental attainment is, in general, overtly disvalued and frequently associated with effeminancy; "smartness" in the lower class sense, however, is highly valued.

The lower class child learns and practices the use of this skill in the street corner situation. Individuals continually practice duping and outwitting one another through recurrent card games and other forms of gambling, mutual exchanges of insults, and "testing" for mutual "conability." Those who demonstrate competence in this skill are accorded considerable prestige. Leadership roles in the corner group are frequently allocated according to demonstrated capacity in the two areas of "smartness" and "toughness"; the ideal leader combines both, but the "smart" leader is often accorded more prestige than the "tough" one—reflecting a general lower class respect for "brains" in the "smartness" sense.[4]

The model of the "smart" person is represented in popular media by the card shark, the professional gambler, the "con" artist, the promoter. A conceptual distinction is made between two kinds of people: "suckers," easy marks, "lushes," dupes, who work for their money and are legitimate targets of exploitation; and sharp operators, the "brainy" ones, who live by their wits and "getting" from the suckers by mental adroitness.

Involved in the syndrome of capacities related to "smartness" is a dominant emphasis in lower class culture on ingenious aggressive repartee. This skill, learned and practiced in the context of the corner group, ranges in form from the widely prevalent semi-ritualized teasing, kidding, razzing, "ranking," so characteristic of male peer group interaction, to the highly ritualized type of mutual insult interchange known as "the dirty dozens," "the dozens," "playing house," and other terms. This highly patterned cultural form is practiced on its most advanced level in adult male Negro society, but less polished variants are found throughout lower class culture—practiced, for example, by white children, male and female, as young as four or five. In essence, "doin' the dozens" involves two antagonists who vie with each other in the exchange of increasingly inflammatory insults, with incestuous and perverted sexual relations with the mother a dominant theme. In this form of insult interchange, as well as on other less ritualized occasions for joking, semi-serious, and serious mutual invective, a very high premium is placed on ingenuity, hair-trigger responsiveness, inventiveness, and the acute exercise of mental faculties.

Excitement: For many lower class individuals the rhythm of life fluctuates between periods of relatively routine or repetitive activity and

---

[4] The "brains-brawn" set of capacities are often paired in lower class folk lore or accounts of lower class life, e.g., "Brer Fox" and "Brer Bear" in the Uncle Remus stories, or George and Lennie in "Of Mice and Men."

sought situations of great emotional stimulation. Many of the most characteristic features of lower class life are related to the search for excitement or "thrill." Involved here are the highly prevalent use of alcohol by both sexes and the widespread use of gambling of all kinds—playing the numbers, betting on horse races, dice, cards. The quest for excitement finds what is perhaps its most vivid expression in the highly patterned practice of the recurrent "night on the town." This practice, designated by various terms in different areas ("honky-tonkin'"; "goin' out on the town"; "bar hoppin'"), involves a patterned set of activities in which alcohol, music, and sexual adventuring are major components. A group or individual sets out to "make the rounds" of various bars or night clubs. Drinking continues progressively throughout the evening. Men seek to "pick up" women, and women play the risky game of entertaining sexual advances. Fights between men involving women, gambling, and claims of physical prowess, in various combinations, are frequent consequences of a night of making the rounds. The explosive potential of this type of adventuring with sex and aggression, frequently leading to "trouble," is semi-explicitly sought by the individual. Since there is always a good likelihood that being out on the town will eventuate in fights, etc., the practice involves elements of sought risk and desired danger.

Counterbalancing the "flirting with danger" aspect of the "excitement" concern is the prevalence in lower class culture of other well established patterns of activity which involve long periods of relative inaction, or passivity. The term "hanging out" in lower class culture refers to extended periods of standing around, often with peer mates, doing what is defined as "nothing," "shooting the breeze," etc. A definite periodicity exists in the pattern of activity relating to the two aspects of the "excitement" dimension. For many lower class individuals the venture into the high risk world of alcohol, sex, and fighting occurs regularly once a week, with interim periods devoted to accommodating to possible consequences of these periods, along with recurrent resolves not to become so involved again.

Fate: Related to the quest for excitement is the concern with fate, fortune, or luck. Here also a distinction is made between two states— being "lucky" or "in luck," and being unlucky or jinxed. Many lower class individuals feel that their lives are subject to a set of forces over which they have relatively little control. These are not directly equated with the supernatural forces of formally organized religion, but relate more to a concept of "destiny," or man as a pawn of magical powers. Not infrequently this often implicit world view is associated with a conception of the ultimate futility of directed effort towards a goal: if the cards are right, or the dice good to you, or if your lucky number comes up, things will go your way; if luck is against you, it's not worth trying. The concept of performing semi-magical rituals so that one's "luck will change" is prevalent; one hopes that as a result he will move from the state of being "unlucky" to that of being "lucky." The element of fantasy

11

plays an important part in this area. Related to and complementing the notion that "only suckers work" (Smartness) is the idea that once things start going your way, relatively independent of your own effort, all good things will come to you. Achieving great material rewards (big cars, big houses, a roll of cash to flash in a fancy night club), valued in lower class as well as in other parts of American culture, is a recurrent theme in lower class fantasy and folk lore; the cocaine dreams of Willie the Weeper or Minnie the Moocher present the components of this fantasy in vivid detail.

The prevalence in the lower class community of many forms of gambling, mentioned in connection with the "excitement" dimension, is also relevant here. Through cards and pool which involve skill, and thus both "toughness" and "smartness"; or through race horse betting, involving "smartness"; or through playing the numbers, involving predominantly "luck," one may make a big killing with a minimum of directed and persistent effort within conventional occupational channels. Gambling in its many forms illustrates the fact that many of the persistent features of lower class culture are multi-functional—serving a range of desired ends at the same time. Describing some of the incentives behind gambling has involved mention of all of the focal concerns cited so far—Toughness, Smartness, and Excitement, in addition to Fate.

Autonomy: The extent and nature of control over the behavior of the individual—an important concern in most cultures—has a special significance and is distinctively patterned in lower class culture. The discrepancy between what is overtly valued and what is covertly sought is particularly striking in this area. On the overt level there is a strong and frequently expressed resentment of the idea of external controls, restrictions on behavior, and unjust or coercive authority. "No one's gonna push *me* around," or "I'm gonna tell him he can take the job and shove it. . . ." are commonly expressed sentiments. Similar explicit attitudes are maintained to systems of behavior-restricting rules, insofar as these are perceived as representing the injunctions, and bearing the sanctions of superordinate authority. In addition, in lower class culture a close conceptual connection is made between "authority" and "nurturance." To be restrictively or firmly controlled is to be cared for. Thus the overtly negative evaluation of superordinate authority frequently extends as well to nurturance, care, or protection. The desire for personal independence is often expressed in such terms as "I don't need *nobody* to take care of me. I can take care of myself!" Actual patterns of behavior, however, reveal a marked discrepancy between expressed sentiment and what is covertly valued. Many lower class people appear to seek out highly restrictive social environments wherein stringent external controls are maintained over their behavior. Such institutions as the armed forces, the mental hospital, the disciplinary school, the prison or correctional institution, provide environments which incorporate a strict and detailed set of rules defining and limiting behavior, and enforced by an authority system which controls and applies coercive sanctions for deviance from these rules. While under the jurisdiction of such systems, the lower class person generally expresses to his peers continual resentment of the coercive, unjust, and arbitrary exercise of authority. Having been released, or having escaped from these milieux, however, he will often act in such a way as to insure recommitment, or choose recommitment voluntarily after a temporary period of "freedom."

Lower class patients in mental hospitals will exercise considerable ingenuity to insure continued commitment while voicing the desire to get out; delinquent boys will frequently "run" from a correctional institution to activate efforts to return them; to be caught and returned means that one is cared for. Since "being controlled" is equated with "being cared for," attempts are frequently made to "test" the severity or strictness of superordinate authority to see if it remains firm. If intended or executed rebellion produces swift and firm punitive sanctions, the individual is reassured, at the same time that he is complaining bitterly at the injustice of being caught and punished. Some environmental milieux, having been tested in this fashion for the "firmness" of their coercive sanctions, are rejected, ostensibly for being too strict, actually for not being strict enough. This is frequently so in the case of "problematic" behavior by lower class youngsters in the public schools, which generally cannot command the coercive controls implicitly sought by the individual.

A similar discrepancy between what is overtly and covertly desired is found in the area of dependence-independence. The pose of tough rebellious independence often assumed by the lower class person frequently conceals powerful dependency cravings. These are manifested primarily by obliquely expressed resentment when "care" is not forthcoming rather than by expressed satisfaction when it is. The concern over autonomy-dependency is related both to "trouble" and "fate." Insofar as the lower class individual feels that his behavior is controlled by forces which often propel him into "trouble" in the face of an explicit determination to avoid it, there is an implied appeal to "save me from myself." A solution appears to lie in arranging things so that his behavior will be coercively restricted by an externally imposed set of controls strong enough to forcibly restrain his inexplicable inclination to get in trouble. The periodicity observed in connection with the "excitement" dimension is also relevant here; after involvement in trouble-producing behavior (assault, sexual adventure, a "drunk"), the individual will actively seek a locus of imposed control (his wife, prison, a restrictive job); after a given period of subjection to this control, resentment against it mounts, leading to a "break away" and a search for involvement in further "trouble."

Focal Concerns of the Lower Class Adolescent Street Corner Group

The one-sex peer group is a highly prevalent and significant structural form in the lower class community. There is a strong probability that the prevalence and stability of this type of unit is directly related to the prevalence of a stabilized type of lower class child-rearing unit—the "female-based" household. This is a nuclear kin unit in which a male parent is either absent from the household, present only sporadically, or, when present, only minimally or inconsistently involved in the support and rearing of children. This unit usually consists of one or more females of child-bearing age and their offspring. The females are frequently related to one another by blood or marriage ties, and the unit often includes two or more generations of women, e.g., the mother and/or aunt of the principal child-bearing female.

The nature of social groupings in the lower class community may be clarified if we make the assumption that it is the *one-sex peer unit* rather than the two-parent family unit which represents the most significant relational unit for both sexes in lower class communities. Lower class society may be pictured as comprising a set of age-graded one-sex groups which constitute the major psychic focus and reference group for those over twelve or thirteen. Men and women of mating age leave these groups periodically to form temporary marital alliances, but these lack stability, and after varying periods of "trying out" the two-sex family arrangement, gravitate back to the more "comfortable" one-sex grouping, whose members exert strong pressure on the individual *not* to disrupt the group by adopting a two-sex household pattern of life.[5] Membership in a stable and solidary peer unit is vital to the lower class individual precisely to the extent to which a range of essential functions—psychological, educational, and others, are not provided by the "family" unit.

The adolescent street corner group represents the adolescent variant of this lower class structural form. What has been called the "delinquent gang" is one subtype of this form, defined on the basis of frequency of participation in law-violating activity; this subtype should not be considered a legitimate unit of study per se, but rather as one particular variant of the adolescent street corner group. The "hanging" peer group is a unit of particular importance for the adolescent male. In many cases it is the most stable and solidary primary group he has ever belonged to; for boys reared in female-based households the corner group provides the first real opportunity to learn essential aspects of the male role in the context of peers facing similar problems of sex-role identification.

The form and functions of the adolescent corner group operate as a selective mechanism in recruiting members. The activity patterns of the group require a high level of intra-group solidarity; individual members must possess a good capacity for subordinating individual desires to general group interests as well as the capacity for intimate and persisting interaction. Thus highly "disturbed" individuals, or those who cannot tolerate consistently imposed sanctions on "deviant" behavior cannot

---

[5] Further data on the female-based household unit (estimated as comprising about 15 per cent of all American "families") and the role of one-sex groupings in lower class culture are contained in Walter B. Miller, Implications of Urban Lower Class Culture for Social Work. *Social Service Review*, 1959, *33*, No. 3.

remain accepted members; the group itself will extrude those whose behavior exceeds limits defined as "normal." This selective process produces
a type of group whose members possess to an unusually high degree both
the *capacity* and *motivation* to conform to perceived cultural norms, so
that the nature of the system of norms and values oriented to is a particularly influential component of motivation.

Focal concerns of the male adolescent corner group are those of the
general cultural milieu in which it functions. As would be expected, the
relative weighting and importance of these concerns pattern somewhat
differently for adolescents than for adults. The nature of this patterning
centers around two additional "concerns" of particular importance to this
group—concern with "belonging," and with "status." These may be conceptualized as being on a higher level of abstraction than concerns
previously cited, since "status" and "belonging" are achieved *via* cited
concern areas of Toughness, etc.

Belonging: Since the corner group fulfills essential functions for the
individual, being a member in good standing of the group is of vital
importance for its members. A continuing concern over who is "in" and
who is not involves the citation and detailed discussion of highly refined
criteria for "in-group" membership. The phrase "he hangs with us" means
"he is accepted as a member in good standing by current consensus";
conversely, "he don't hang with us" means he is not so accepted. One
achieves "belonging" primarily by demonstrating knowledge of and a
determination to adhere to the system of standards and valued qualities
defined by the group. One maintains membership by acting in conformity with valued aspects of Toughness, Smartness, Autonomy, etc. In
those instances where conforming to norms of this reference group at the
same time violates norms of other reference groups (e.g., middle class
adults, institutional "officials"), immediate reference group norms are
much more compelling since violation risks invoking the group's most
powerful sanction: exclusion.

Status: In common with most adolescents in American society, the
lower class corner group manifests a dominant concern with "status."
What differentiates this type of group from others, however, is the particular set of criteria and weighting thereof by which "status" is defined.
In general, status is achieved and maintained by demonstrated possession
of the valued qualities of lower class culture—Toughness, Smartness, expressed resistance to authority, daring, etc. It is important to stress once
more that the individual orients to these concerns *as they are defined
within lower class society;* e.g., the status-conferring potential of "smartness" in the sense of scholastic achievement generally ranges from negligible
to negative.

The concern with "status" is manifested in a variety of ways. Intra-
group status is a continued concern, and is derived and tested constantly
by means of a set of status-ranking activities; the intra-group "pecking
order" is constantly at issue. One gains status within the group by demon-

15

strated superiority in Toughness (physical prowess, bravery, skill in athletics and games such as pool and cards), Smartness (skill in repartee, capacity to "dupe" fellow group members), and the like. The term "ranking," used to refer to the pattern of intra-group aggressive repartee, indicates awareness of the fact that this is one device for establishing the intra-group status hierarchy.

The concern over status in the adolescent corner group involves in particular the component of "adultness," the intense desire to be seen as "grown up," and a corresponding aversion to "kid stuff." "Adult" status is defined less in terms of the assumption of "adult" responsibility than in terms of certain external symbols of adult status—a car, ready cash, and, in particular, a perceived "freedom" to drink, smoke, and gamble as one wishes and to come and go without external restrictions. The desire to be seen as "adult" is often a more significant component of much involvement in illegal drinking, gambling, and automobile driving than the explicit enjoyment of these acts as such.

The intensity of the corner group member's desire to be seen as "adult" is sufficiently great that he feels called upon to demonstrate qualities associated with adultness (Toughness, Smartness, Autonomy) to a much greater degree than a lower class adult. This means that he will seek out and utilize those avenues to these qualities which he perceives as available with greater intensity than an adult and less regard for their "legitimacy." In this sense the adolescent variant of lower class culture represents a maximization or an intensified manifestation of many of its most characteristic features.

Concern over status is also manifested in reference to other street corner groups. The term "rep" used in this regard is especially significant, and has broad connotations. In its most frequent and explicit connotation, "rep" refers to the "toughness" of the corner group as a whole relative to that of other groups; a "pecking order" also exists among the several corner groups in a given interactional area, and there is a common perception that the safety or security of the group and all its members depends on maintaining a solid "rep" for toughness vis-a-vis other groups. This motive is most frequently advanced as a reason for involvement in gang fights: "We *can't* chicken out on this fight; our rep would be shot!"; this implies that the group would be relegated to the bottom of the status ladder and become a helpless and recurrent target of external attack.

On the other hand, there is implicit in the concept of "rep" the recognition that "rep" has or may have a dual basis—corresponding to the two aspects of the "trouble" dimension. It is recognized that group as well as individual status can be based on both "law-abiding" and "law-violating" behavior. The situational resolution of the persisting conflict between the "law-abiding" and "law-violating" bases of status comprises a vital set of dynamics in determining whether a "delinquent" mode of behavior will be adopted by a group, under what circumstances, and how persistently. The determinants of this choice are evidently highly complex

16

and fluid, and rest on a range of factors including the presence and perceptual immediacy of different community reference-group loci (e.g.,
professional criminals, police, clergy, teachers, settlement house workers),
the personality structures and "needs" of group members, the presence in
the community of social work, recreation, or educational programs which
can facilitate utilization of the "law-abiding" basis of status, and so on.

What remains constant is the critical importance of "status" both for
the members of the group as individuals and for the group as a whole
insofar as members perceive their individual destinies as linked to the
destiny of the group, and the fact that action geared to attain status is
much more acutely oriented to the fact of status itself than to the legality
or illegality, morality or immorality of the means used to achieve it.

Lower Class Culture and the Motivation of Delinquent Behavior

The customary set of activities of the adolescent street corner group
includes activities which are in violation of laws and ordinances of the
legal code. Most of these center around assault and theft of various types
(the gang fight; auto theft; assault on an individual; petty pilfering and
shoplifting; "mugging"; pocketbook theft). Members of street corner
gangs are well aware of the law-violating nature of these acts; they are
not psychopaths, nor physically or mentally "defective"; in fact, since the
corner group supports and enforces a rigorous set of standards which
demand a high degree of fitness and personal competence, it tends to
recruit from the most "able" members of the community.

Why, then, is the commission of crimes a customary feature of gang
activity? The most general answer is that the commission of crimes by
members of adolescent street corner groups is motivated primarily by the
attempt to achieve ends, states, or conditions which are valued, and
to avoid those that are disvalued within their most meaningful cultural
milieu, through those culturally available avenues which appear as the
most feasible means of attaining those ends.

The operation of these influences is well illustrated by the gang
fight—a prevalent and characteristic type of corner group delinquency.
This type of activity comprises a highly stylized and culturally patterned
set of sequences. Although details vary under different circumstances, the
following events are generally included. A member or several members of
group A "trespass" on the claimed territory of group B. While there they
commit an act or acts which group B defines as a violation of its rightful
privileges, an affront to their honor, or a challenge to their "rep." Frequently this act involves advances to a girl associated with group B; it
may occur at a dance or party; sometimes the mere act of "trespass" is
seen as deliberate provocation. Members of group B then assault members
of group A, if they are caught while still in B's territory. Assaulted
members of group A return to their "home" territory and recount to
members of their group details of the incident, stressing the insufficient
nature of the provocation ("I just *looked* at her! Hardly even said any-

17

thing!"), and the unfair circumstances of the assault ("About *twenty* guys jumped just the *two* of us!"). The highly colored account is acutely inflammatory; group A, perceiving its honor violated and its "rep" threatened, feels obligated to retaliate in force. Sessions of detailed planning now occur; allies are recruited if the size of group A and its potential allies appears to necessitate larger numbers; strategy is plotted, and messengers dispatched. Since the prospect of a gang fight is frightening to even the "toughest" group members, a constant rehearsal of the provocative incident or incidents and the essentially evil nature of the opponents accompanies the planning process to bolster possibly weakening motivation to fight. The excursion into "enemy" territory sometimes results in a full scale fight; more often group B cannot be found, or the police appear and stop the fight, "tipped off" by an anonymous informant. When this occurs, group members express disgust and disappointment; secretly there is much relief; their honor has been avenged without incurring injury; often the anonymous tipster is a member of one of the involved groups.

The basic elements of this type of delinquency are sufficiently stabilized and recurrent as to constitute an essentially ritualized pattern, resembling both in structure and expressed motives for action classic forms such as the European "duel," the American Indian tribal war, and the Celtic clan feud. Although the arousing and "acting out" of individual aggressive emotions are inevitably involved in the gang fight, neither its form nor motivational dynamics can be adequately handled within a predominantly personality-focused frame of reference.

It would be possible to develop in considerable detail the processes by which the commission of a range of illegal acts is either explicitly supported by, implicitly demanded by, or not materially inhibited by factors relating to the focal concerns of lower class culture. In place of such a development, the following three statements condense in general terms the operation of these processes:

1. *Following cultural practices which comprise essential elements of the total life pattern of lower class culture automatically violates certain legal norms.*

2. *In instances where alternate avenues to similar objectives are available, the non-law-abiding avenue frequently provides a relatively greater and more immediate return for a relatively smaller investment of energy.*

3. *The "demanded" response to certain situations recurrently engendered within lower class culture involves the commission of illegal acts.*

The primary thesis of this paper is that the dominant component of the motivation of "delinquent" behavior engaged in by members of lower class corner groups involves a positive effort to achieve states, conditions, or qualities valued within the actor's most significant cultural milieu. If "conformity to immediate reference group values" is the major component of motivation of "delinquent" behavior by gang members, why is such behavior frequently referred to as negativistic, malicious, or rebellious? Albert Cohen, for example, in *Delinquent Boys* (Glencoe: Free Press, 1955) describes behavior which violates school rules as comprising elements of "active spite and malice, contempt and ridicule, challenge and defiance." He ascribes to the gang "keen delight in terrorizing 'good' children, and in general making themselves obnoxious to the virtuous." A recent national conference on social work with "hard-to-reach" groups characterized lower class corner groups as "youth groups in conflict with the culture of their *(sic)* communities." Such characterizations are obviously the result of taking the middle class community and its institutions as an implicit point of reference.

A large body of systematically interrelated attitudes, practices, behaviors, and values characteristic of lower class culture are designed to support and maintain the basic features of the lower class way of life. In areas where these differ from features of middle class culture, action oriented to the achievement and maintenance of the lower class system may violate norms of middle class culture and be perceived as deliberately non-conforming or malicious by an observer strongly cathected to middle class norms. This does not mean, however, that violation of the middle class norm is the dominant component of motivation; it is a by-product of action primarily oriented to the lower class system. The standards of lower class culture cannot be seen merely as a reverse function of middle class culture—as middle class standards "turned upside down"; lower class culture is a distinctive tradition many centuries old with an integrity of its own.

From the viewpoint of the acting individual, functioning within a field of well-structured cultural forces, the relative impact of "conforming" and "rejective" elements in the motivation of gang delinquency is weighted preponderantly on the conforming side. Rejective or rebellious elements are inevitably involved, but their influence during the actual commission of delinquent acts is relatively small compared to the influence of pressures to achieve what is valued by the actor's most immediate reference groups. Expressed awareness by the actor of the element of rebellion often represents only that aspect of motivation of which he is explicitly conscious; the deepest and most compelling components of motivation—adherence to highly meaningful group standards of Toughness, Smartness, Excitement, etc.—are often unconsciously patterned. No cultural pattern as well-established as the practice of illegal acts by members of lower class corner groups could persist if buttressed primarily by negative, hostile, or rejective motives; its principal motivational support, as in the case of any persisting cultural tradition, derives from a positive effort to achieve what is valued within that tradition, and to conform to its explicit and implicit norms.

[3]

THE DELINQUENT GANG AS A NEAR-GROUP*

LEWIS YABLONSKY

University of Massachusetts

This paper is based on four years of research and direct work with some thirty delinquent gangs in New York City. During this period I directed a crime prevention program on the upper West Side of Manhattan for Morningside Heights, Inc., a community social agency sponsored by fourteen major institutions including Columbia University, Barnard, Teacher's College, Union Theological Seminary, and Riverside Church.

Approaches used in data gathering included field study methods, participant observation, role-playing, group interaction analysis, and sociometry. The data were obtained through close daily interaction with gang boys over the four-year period during which I was the director of the project.

Although data were obtained on 30 gangs, the study focused on two, the Balkans and the Egyptian Kings. It was the latter which committed the brutal killing of a polio victim, Michael Farmer, in an upper west side park of New York City. The trial lasted over three months and received nation-wide attention. These two groups were intensively interviewed and contributed heavily to the formulation of a theory of near-groups. In addition to the analysis of the gang's structure, a number of delinquent gang war events produced vital case material.

There is a paucity of available theory based on empirical evidence about the structure of delinquent gangs. Two landmarks in the field are Thrasher's *The Gang* and Whyte's *Street Corner Society*. Some recent publications and

*This is a revised version of a paper delivered at The Eastern Sociological Meetings in New York City, April 11, 1959. The theory of near-groups and gang data presented in this paper is part of a forthcoming volume on gangs by the author.

controversy focus on the emergence of gangs and their function for gang members. Professor Cohen deals with gangs as sub-cultures organized by working-class boys as a reaction to middle-class values (1). In a recent publication Block and Nederhoffer discuss gangs as organizations designed to satisfy the adolescent's striving for the attainment of adult status (2).

Although partial group structuring has been extensively discussed in sociological literature on "groups," "crowds," and "mobs," my gang research revealed that these collectivity constructs did not seem to adequately describe and properly abstract the underlying structural characteristics of the delinquent gang. Consequently, I have attempted here to construct a formulation which would draw together various described social dimensions of the gang under one conceptual scheme. I call this formulation Near-Group Theory.

NEAR-GROUP THEORY

One way of viewing human collectivities is on a continuum of organization characteristics. At one extreme, we have a highly organized, cohesive, functioning collection of individuals as members of a sociological group. At the other extreme, we have a mob of individuals characterized by anonymity, disturbed leadership, motivated by emotion, and in some cases representing a destructive collectivity within the inclusive social system. When these structures are observed in extreme, their form is apparent to the observer. However, in viewing these social structures on a continuum, those formations which tend to be neither quite a cohesive integrated group nor a disturbed mal-functioning mob or crowd are often distorted by observers in one or the other direction.

A central thesis of this paper is that mid-way on the group-mob continuum are collectivities which are neither groups nor mobs. These are structures prevalent enough in a social system to command attention in their own right as constructs for sociological analysis. Near-groups are characterized by some of the following factors: (1) diffuse role definition, (2) limited cohesion, (3) impermanence, (4) minimal consensus of norms, (5) shifting membership, (6) disturbed leadership, and (7) limited definition of membership expectations. These factors characterize the near-group's "normal" structure.

True groups may manifest near-group structure under stress, in transition, or when temporarily disorganized; however, at these times they are moving toward or away from their normative, permanent structure. The near-group manifests its homeostasis in accord with the factors indicated. It never fully becomes a *group* or a *mob*.

THE GANG AS A NEAR-GROUP PATTERN

Some recent sociological theory and discourse on gangs suffers from distortions of gang structure to fit a group rather than a near-group conception. Most gang theorizing begins with an automatic assumption that gangs are defined sociological groups. Many of these misconceived theories about gangs in sociological treatises are derived from the popular and traditional image of gangs held by the general public as reported in the press, rather than as based upon empirical scientific investigation. The following case material reveals the disparities between popular reports of gang war behavior and their organization as revealed by more systematic study.

The official report of a gang fight, which made headlines in New York papers as the biggest in the city's history, detailed a gang war between six gangs over a territorial dispute.* The police, social workers, the press, and the public accepted a defined version of groups meeting in battle over territory. Research into this gang war incident, utilizing a near-group concept of gangs, indicates another picture of the situation.

N. Y. Daily News
NIP 200 — PUNK FIGHT NEAR COLUMBIA CAMPUS
by Grover Ryder and Jack Smee
A flying squad of 25 cops, alerted by a civilian's tip, broke up the makings of one of the biggest gang rumbles in the city's turbulent teen history last night at the edge of Columbia University campus on Morningside Heights.

N. Y. Herald Tribune
POLICE SEIZE 38, AVERT GANG BATTLE — RIVERSIDE PARK RULE WAS GOAL
Police broke up what they said might have been "a very serious" battle between two juvenile factions last night as they intercepted thirty-eight youths.

N. Y. Times
GANG WAR OVER PARK BROKEN BY POLICE
The West Side police broke up an impending gang fight near Columbia University last night as 200 teen-agers were massing for battle over exclusive rights to the use of Riverside Park.

N. Y. Journal-American
6-GANG BATTLE FOR PARK AVERTED NEAR GRANT'S TOMB COPS PATROL TROUBLE SPOT
Police reinforcements today patrolled Morningside Heights to prevent a teen-aged gang war for "control" of Riverside Park.

World-Telegram and Sun
HOODLUM WAR AVERTED AS COPS ACT FAST
38 to 200 Seized near Columbia
by Richard Graf
Fast police action averted what threatened to be one of the biggest street gang fights in the city's history as some 200 hoodlums massed last night on the upper West Side to battle over "exclusive rights" to Riverside Park.

*New York Newspaper Headlines — June 11, 1955:

Depth interviews with 40 gang boys, most of whom had been arrested at the scene of the gang fight, revealed a variety of reasons for attendance at the battle. There were also varied perceptions of the event and the gangs involved reported simply in the press as "gangs battling over territory." Some of the following recurring themes were revealed in the gang boys' responses.

Estimates of number of gang boys present varied from 80 to 5,000.

Gang boys interviewed explained their presence at the "battle" as follows:

> I didn't have anything to do that night and wanted to see what was going to happen.
>
> Those guys called me a Spic and I was going to get even. [He made this comment even though the "rival" gangs were mostly Puerto Ricans.]
>
> They always picked on us. [The "they" is usually a vague reference.]
>
> I always like a fight; it keeps up my rep.
>
> My father threw me out of the house; I wanted to get somebody and heard about the fight.

The youth who was responsible for "calling on" the gang war — the reputed Balkan Gang leader—presented this version of the event:

> That night I was out walkin' my dog about 7:30. Then I saw all these guys coming from different directions. I couldn't figure out what was happening. Then I saw some of the guys I know and I remembered we had called it on for that night.
>
> I never really figured the Politicians [a supposed "brother Gang" he had called] would show.

Another boy added another dimension to "gang war organization":

> How did we get our name? Well, when we were in the police station, the cops kept askin' us who we were. Jay was studying history in school — so he said how about The Balkans. Let's call ourselves Balkans. So we told the cops — we're the Balkans — and that was it.

Extensive data revealed this was not a case of two organized groups meeting in battle. The press, public, police, social workers, and others projected group conceptions onto a near-group activity. Most of the youths at the scene of the gang war were, in fact, participating in a kind of mob action. Most had no real concept of belonging to any gang or group; however, they were interested in a situation which might be exciting and possibly a channel for expressing some of their aggressions and hostilities. Although it was not necessarily a defined war, the possibilities of a stabbing or even a killing were high — with a few hundred disturbed and fearful youths milling around in the undefined situation. The gang war was not a social situation of two structured teen-aged armies meeting on a battlefield to act out a defined situation; it was a case of two near-groups in action.

Another boy's participation in this gang war further reveals its structure. The evening of the fight he had nothing to do, heard about this event and decided that he would wander up to see what was going to happen. On his way to the scene of the rumored gang fight he thought it might be a good idea to invite a few friends "just to be on the safe side." This swelled the final number of youths arriving at the scene of the gang fight, since other boys did the same. He denied (and I had no reason to disbelieve him) belonging to either of the gangs and the same applied to his friends. He was arrested at the scene of "battle" for disorderly conduct and weapon-carrying.

I asked him why he had carried a knife and a zip gun on his person when he went to the gang fight if he did not belong to either of the reputed gangs and intended to be merely a "peaceful observer." His response: "Man, I'm not going to a rumble without packin'." The boy took along weapons for self-defense in the event he was attacked. The possibilities of his being attacked in an hysterical situation involving hundreds of youths who had no clear idea of what they were doing at the scene of a gang fight was, of course, great. Therefore, he was correct (within his social framework) in taking along a weapon for self-protection.

These characteristic responses to the situation when multiplied by the numbers of others present characterizes the problem. What may be a confused situation involving many aggressive youths (belonging to near-groups) is often defined as a case of two highly mechanized and organized gang groups battling each other with definition to their activities.

In another "gang war case" which made headlines, a psychotic youth acted out his syndrome by stabbing another youth. When arrested and questioned about committing the offense, the youth stated that he was a member of a gang carrying out retaliation against another gang, which was out to get him. He attributed his assault to gang affiliation.

The psychotic youth used the malleable near-group, the gang, *as his psychotic* syndrome. Napoleon, God, Christ, and other psychotic syndromes, so popular over the years, may have been replaced on city streets by gang membership. Not only is it a convenient syndrome, but some disturbed youths find their behavior as rational, accepted, and even aggrandized by many representatives of society. Officials such as police officers and social workers, in their interpretation of the incident, often amplify this individual behavior by a youth into a group gang war condition because it is a seemingly more logical explanation of a senseless act.

In the case of the Balkans, the societal response of viewing them as a group rather than a near-group so-

lidified their structure. After the incident, as one leader stated it, "lots more kids wanted to join."

Another gang war event further reveals the near-group structure of the gang. On the night of July 30, 1957, a polio victim named Michael Farmer was beaten and stabbed to death by a gang varyingly known as the Egyptian Kings and the Dragons. The boys who participated in this homicide came from the upper West Side of Manhattan. I had contact with many of these boys prior to the event and was known to others through the community program I directed. Because of this prior relationship the boys cooperated and responded openly when I interviewed them in the institutions where they were being held in custody.*

Responses to my interviews indicated the near-group nature of the gang. Some of the pertinent responses which reveal this characteristic of the Egyptian King gang structure are somewhat demonstrated by the following comments made by five of the participants in the killing. (These are representative comments selected from over ten hours of recorded interviews.)

> I was walking uptown with a couple of friends and we ran into Magician [one of the Egyptian King gang leaders] and them there. They asked us if we wanted to go to a fight, and we said yes. When he asked me if I wanted to go to a fight, I couldn't say no. I mean, I could say no, but for old time's sake, I said yes.
>
> Everyone was pushin' and I pulled out my knife. I saw this face — I never seen it before, so I stabbed it.
>
> He was laying on the ground lookin'

*The research and interviewing at this time was combined with my role as consultant to the Columbia Broadcasting System. I assisted in the production of a gang war documentary narrated by Edward R. Murrow, entitled "Who Killed Michael Farmer?" The documentary tells the story of the killing through the actual voices of the boys who committed the act.

up at us. Everyone was kicking, punching, stabbing. I kicked him on the jaw or someplace; then I kicked him in the stomach. That was the least I could do was kick 'im.

They have guys watching you and if you don't stab or hit somebody, they get you later. I hit him over the head with a bat. [Gang youths are unable to articulate specific individuals of the vague "they" who watch over them.]

I don't know how many guys are in the gang. They tell me maybe a hundred or a thousand. I don't know them all. [Each boy interviewed had a different image of the gang.]

These comments and others revealed the gang youths' somewhat different perceptions and rationale of gang war activity. There is a limited consensus of participants as to the nature of gang war situations because the gang structure — the collectivity which defines gang war behavior — is amorphous, diffuse, and malleable.

Despite the fact of gang phenomena taking a diffuse form, theoreticians, social workers, the police, the press, and the public autistically distort gangs and gang behavior toward a gestalt of clarity. The rigid frame of perceiving gangs as groups should shift to the fact of gangs as near-groups. This basic redefinition is necessary if progress is to be made in sociological diagnosis as a foundation for delinquent gang prevention and correction.

THE DETACHED GANG WORKER

The detached-worker approach to dealing with gangs on the action level is increasingly employed in large cities and urban areas throughout the country. Simply stated, a professional, usually a social worker, contacts a gang in their milieu on the street corner and attempts to redirect their delinquent patterns into constructive behavior.

Because of the absence of an adequate perceptual framework, such as the near-group concept, detached gang workers deal with gang collectivities

as if they were organized like other groups and social organizations. The following principle stated in a New York City Youth Board manual on the detached gang worker approach reveals this point of view:

> Participation in a street gang or club, like participation in any natural group, is a part of the growing-up process of adolescence. Such primary group associations possess potentialities for positive growth and development. Through such a group, the individual can gain security and develop positive ways of living with other individuals. Within the structure of his group the individual can develop such characteristics as loyalty, leadership, and community responsibility (3, p. 107).

This basic misconception not only produces inaccurate reports and theories about gang structure but causes ineffectual work with gangs on the action level. This problem of projecting group structure onto gangs may be further illuminated by a cursory examination of detached gang-worker projects.

Approaching the gang as a group, when it is not, tends to project onto it a structure which formerly did not exist. The gang worker's usual set of notions about gangs as groups includes some of the following distortions: (1) the gang has a measurable number of members, (2) membership is defined, (3) the role of members is specified, (4) there is a consensus of understood gang norms among gang members, and (5) gang leadership is clear and entails a flow of authority and direction of action.

These expectations often result in a group-fulfilling prophecy. A group may form as a consequence of the gang worker's view. In one case a gang worker approached two reputed gang leaders and told them he would have a bus to take their gang on a trip to the country. This gang had limited organization; however, by travel-time there were 32 gang members ready to go on the trip. The near-group became more organized as a result of the gang worker's misconception.

This gang from a near-group point of view was in reality comprised of a few disturbed youths with rich delusional systems who had need to view themselves as leaders controlling hordes of other gang boys in their fantasy. Other youths reinforce this ill-defined collectivity for a variety of personal reasons and needs. The gang, in fact, had a shifting membership, no clarity as to what membership entailed, and individualized member images of gang size and function.

The detached worker, as an agent of the formal social system, may thus move in on a gang and give a formerly amorphous collectivity structure and purpose through the projection of group structure onto a near-group.

NEAR-GROUP STRUCTURE

Research into the structure of 30 groups revealed three characteristic levels of membership organization. In the center of the gang, on the first level, are the most psychologically disturbed members — the leaders. It is these youths who require and need the gang most of all. This core of disturbed youths provides the gang's most cohesive force. In a gang of some 30 boys there may be five or six who are central or core members because they desperately need the gang in order to deal with their personal problems of inadequacy. These are youths always working to keep the gang together and in action, always drafting, plotting, and talking gang warfare. They are the center of the near-group activity.

At a second level of near-group organization in the gang, we have youths who claim affiliation to the gang but only participate in it according to their emotional needs at given times. For example, one of the Egyptian Kings reported that if his father had not given him a "bad time" and kicked him out of the house the night of the homicide, he would not have gone to the corner and become involved in the Michael Farmer killing. This second-level gang member's participation in the gang killing was a function of his disturbance on that particular evening. This temporal gang need is a usual occurrence.

At a third level of gang participation, we have peripheral members who will join in with gang activity on occasion, although they seldom identify themselves as members of the gang at times. This type of gang member is illustrated by the youth who went along with the Egyptian Kings on the night of the Farmer killing, as he put it, "for old time's sake." He just happened to be around on that particular evening and went along due to a situational condition. He never really "belonged" to the gang nor was he defined by himself or others as a gang member.

The size of gangs is determined in great measure by the emotional needs of its members at any given point. It is not a measure of actual and live membership. Many of the members exist only on the thought level. In the gang, if the boys feel particularly hemmed in (for paranoid reasons), they will expand the number of their near-group. On the other hand, at other times when they feel secure, the gang's size is reduced to include only those youths known on a face-to-face basis. The research revealed that, unlike an actual group, no member of a near-group can accurately determine the number of its membership at a particular point in time.

For example, most any university department member will tell you the number of other individuals who comprise the faculty of their department. It is apparent that if there are eight members in a department of psychology, each member will know each other member, his role, and the total number of members of the department. In contrast, in examining the size of gangs or near-group participation, the size increases in almost direct relationship to the lack of membership clarity. That is, the second- and third-level members are modified numerically with greater ease than the central members. Third level members are distorted at times to an almost infinite number.

In one interview, a gang leader distorted the size and affiliations of the gang as his emotional state shifted. In an hour interview, the size of his gang varied from 100 members to 4,000, from five brother gangs or alliances to 60, from about ten square blocks of territorial control to include jurisdiction over the five boroughs of New York City, New Jersey, and part of Philadelphia.

Another characteristic of the gang is its lack of role definition. Gang boys exhibit considerable difficulty and contradiction in their roles in the gang. They may say that the gang is organized for protection and that one role of a gang is to fight. How, when, whom, and for what reason he is to fight are seldom clear. The right duties and obligations associated with the gang member's role in the gang varies from gang boy to gang boy.

One gang boy may define himself as a protector of the younger boys in the neighborhood. Another defines his role in the gang as "We are going to get all those guys who call us Spics." Still other gang boys define their participation in the gang as involuntarily forced upon them, through their being "drafted." Moreover, few gang members maintain a consistent function or role within the gang organization.

Definition of membership is vague and indefinite. A youth will say he belongs one day and will quit the next without necessarily telling any other gang member. I would ask one gang boy who came into my office daily

whether he was a Balkan. This was comparable to asking him, "How do you feel today?"

Because of limited social ability to assume rights, duties, and obligations in constructive solidified groups, the gang boy attaches himself to a structure which requires limited social ability and can itself be modified to fit his monetary needs. This malleability factor is characteristic of the near-group membership. As roles are building blocks of a group, diffuse role definitions fit in adequately to the near-group which itself has diverse and diffuse objectives and goals. The near-group, unlike a true group, has norms, roles, functions, cohesion, size, and goals which are shaped by the emotional needs of its members.

Gang Leadership Characteristics

Another aspect of near-groups is the factor of self-appointed leadership, usually of a dictatorial, authoritarian type. In interviewing hundreds of gang members one finds that many of them give themselves some role of leadership. For example, in the Egyptian Kings, approximately five boys defined themselves as "war counsellors." It is equally apparent that, except on specific occasions, no one will argue with this self-defined role. Consequently, leadership in the gang may be assumed by practically any member of the gang if he so determines and emotionally needs the power of being a leader at the time. It is not necessary to have his leadership role ratified by his constituents.

Another aspect of leadership in the gang is the procedure of "drafting" or enlisting new members. In many instances, this pattern of coercion to get another youth to join or belong to the gang becomes an end in itself, rather than a means to an end. In short, the process of inducing, coercing, and threatening violence upon another youth, under the guise of getting him to join, is an important gang leader activity. The gang boy is not truly concerned with acquiring another gang member, since the meaning of membership is vague at best; however, acting the power role of a leader forcing another youth to do something against his will becomes meaningful to the "drafter."

GANG FUNCTIONS

In most groups some function is performed or believed to be performed. The function which it performs may be a constructive one, as in an industrial organization, a P. T. A. group, or a political party. On the other hand, it may be a socially destructive group, such as a drug syndicate, a group of bookies, or a subversive political party. There is usually a consensus of objectives and goals shared by the membership, and their behavior tends to be essentially organized group action.

The structure of a near-group is such that its functions not only vary greatly and shift considerably from time to time, but its primary function is unclear. The gang may on one occasion be organized to protect the neighborhood; on another occasion, to take over a particular territory; and on still another, it may be organized in response to or for the purpose of racial discrimination.

The function of near-groups, moreover, is not one which is clearly understood, known, and communicated among all of its members. There is no consensus in this near-group of goals, objectives, or functions of the collectivity — much near-group behavior is individualistic and flows from emotional disturbance.

A prime function of the gang is to provide a channel to act out hostility and aggression to satisfy the continuing and momentary emotional needs of its members. The gang is a convenient and malleable structure quickly adaptable to the needs of emotionally disturbed youths, who are unable to fulfill the responsibility and demands required for participation in constructive groups. He belongs to the gang because he lacks the social ability to relate to others and to assume responsibility for the relationship, not because the gang gives him a "feeling of belonging."

Because of the gang youth's limited "social ability," he constructs a social organization which enables him to relate and to function at his limited level of performance. In this structure norms are adjusted so that the gang youth can function and achieve despite his limited ability to relate to others.

An example of this is the function of violence in the near-group of the gang. Violence in the gang is highly valued as a means for the achievement of reputation or "rep." This inversion of societal norms is a means for quick upward social mobility in the gang. He can acquire and maintain a position in the gang through establishing a violent reputation.

The following comments by members of the Egyptian Kings illustrate this point:

> If I would of got the knife, I would have stabbed him. That would have gave me more of a build-up. People would have respected me for what I've done and things like that. They would say, "There goes a cold killer."

> It makes you feel like a big shot. You know some guys think they're big shots and all that. They think, you know, they got the power to do everything they feel like doing.

> They say, like, "I wanna stab a guy," and the other guy says, "Oh, I wouldn't dare to do that." You know, he thinks I'm acting like a big shot. That's the way he feels. He probably thinks in his mind, "Oh, he probably won't do that." Then, when we go to a fight, you know, he finds out what I do.

> Momentarily, I started to thinking about it inside: den I have my mind made up I'm not going to be in no gang.

Then I go on inside. Something comes up den here come all my friends coming to me. Like I said before, I'm intelligent and so forth. They be coming to me — then they talk to me about what they gonna do. Like, "Man, we'll go out here and kill this guy." I say, "Yeah." They kept on talkin' and talkin'. I said, "Man, I just gotta go with you." Myself, I don't want to go, but when they start talkin' about what they gonna do, I say, "So, he isn't gonna take over my rep. I ain't gonna let him be known more than me." And I go ahead just for selfishness.

The near-group of the gang, with its diffuse and malleable structure, can function as a convenient vehicle for the acting out of varied individual needs and problems. For the gang leader it can be a super-powered organization through which (in his phantasy) he dominates and controls "divisions" of thousands of members. For gang members, unable to achieve in more demanding social organizations, swift and sudden violence is a means for quick upward social mobility and the achievement of a reputation. For less disturbed youths, the gang may function as a convenient temporary escape from the dull and rigid requirements of a difficult and demanding society. These are only some of the functions the near-group of the gang performs for its membership.

NEAR-GROUP THEORY AND SOCIAL PROBLEMS

The concept of the near-group may be of importance in the analysis of other collectivities which reflect and produce social problems. The analysis of other social structures may reveal similar distortions of their organization. To operate on an assumption that individuals in interaction with each other, around some function, with some shared mutual expectation, in a particular normative system as always being a group formation is to project a degree of distortion onto certain types of collectivities. Groups are

social structures at one end of a continuum; mobs are social structures at another end; and at the center are near-groups which have some of the characteristics of both, and yet are characterized by factors not found fully in either.

In summary, these factors may include the following:

(1) Individualized role definition to fit momentary needs.
(2) Diffuse and differential definitions of membership.
(3) Emotion-motivated behavior.
(4) A decrease of cohesiveness as one moves from the center of the collectivity to the periphery.
(5) Limited responsibility and sociability required for membership and belonging.
(6) Self-appointed and disturbed leadership.
(7) A limited consensus among participants of the collectivities' functions or goals.
(8) A shifting and personalized stratification system.
(9) Shifting membership.
(10) The inclusion in size of phantasy membership.
(11) Limited consensus of normative expectations.
(12) Norms in conflict with the inclusive social system's prescriptions.

Although the gang was the primary type of near-group appraised in this analysis, there are perhaps other collectivities whose structure is distorted by autistic observers. Their organization might become clearer if subjected to this conceptual scheme. Specifically, in the area of criminal beahvior, these might very well include adult gangs varyingly called the "Mafia," the "National Crime Syndicate," and so-called International Crime Cartels. There are indications that these social organizations are comparable in organization to the delinquent gang. They might fit the near-group category if closely analyzed in this context, rather than aggrandized and distorted by mass media and even Senate Committees.

Other more institutionalized collectivities might fit the near-group pattern. As a possible example, "the family in transition" may not be in transition at all. The family, as a social institution, may be suffering from near-groupism. Moreover, such standardized escape hatches of alcoholism, psychoses, and addictions may be too prosaic for the sophisticated intellectual to utilize in escape from himself.

For him, the creation and perpetuation of near-groups requiring limited responsibility and personal commitment may be a more attractive contemporary form for expressing social and personal pathology. The measure of organization or disorganization of an inclusive social system may possibly be assessed by the prevalence of near-group collectivities in its midst. The delinquent gang may be only one type of near-group in American society.

REFERENCES

1. Cohen, Albert K., *Delinquent Boys* (Glencoe: The Free Press, 1955).
2. Block, Herbert, and Arthur Nederhoffer, *The Gang* (New York: The Philosophical Library, 1958).
3. Furman, Slyvan S., *Reaching the Unreached* (New York: Youth Board, 1952).

[4]

Groups, Gangs, and Cohesiveness*

MALCOLM W. KLEIN

Senior Research Associate and Project Director, Youth Studies Center,
University of Southern California
Research Associate, John Tracy Clinic, Los Angeles, 1960-62
Ph.D. (Social Psychology), 1961, Boston University

LOIS Y. CRAWFORD

Research Associate, Delinquent Gang Project, Youth Studies Center,
University of Southern California
Assistant Social Research Analyst, NIMH Data Processing in Mental Retardation
Project, Pomona, California, 1962-65
B.A. (Psychology), 1951, Ohio State University

This paper is concerned with selected qualitative differences between juvenile gangs and other groups which have been the more traditional subject of empirical research. Two factors in particular are emphasized: gang cohesiveness and gang-related delinquent behavior. We take the position that the sources of gang cohesiveness are primarily external to the group, in contrast to the findings on most groups previously studied. Gang delinquency, in addition to being the partial consequence of gang interaction, serves as an additional reinforcer of gang cohesiveness. After a brief review of the literature, we draw the conclusions that available concepts and approaches to the measurement of group cohesiveness are somewhat insufficient for application to gang research. With the use of data drawn from a study of 576 male Negro gang members in Los Angeles we illustrate several alternate measurement procedures. We view these procedures as a first step toward a sorely needed investigation of the relationship between gang cohesiveness and gang delinquency.

IF A GROUP LACKS A TASK, purpose, or mission as a result of not being integrated into a demanding external system—as may in fact be the case for street-corner gangs—then it would fail to generate a major part of the rewards and sentiments which its members might expect to gain from it."[1]

This statement by Gordon, quoted by Short and Strodtbeck, derives from experience and data in the context of

* This paper will appear in *Gang Delinquency and Delinquent Subcultures*, James F. Short, Jr., ed. (New York: Harper and Row, 1967). An earlier version of this paper was presented at the annual meeting of the Pacific Sociological Association in Vancouver, B.C., April 1966. It reports one aspect of a larger project funded by the Ford Foundation and carried out in collaboration with the Los Angeles County Probation Department. The authors are grateful to LaMar Empey, Solomon Kobrin, Barbara Myerhoff, and George Newland for their constructive criticisms of an earlier draft.

1 Robert A. Gordon, "Social Level, Social Disability, and Gang Interaction," unpublished paper quoted in James F. Short, Jr. and Fred L. Strodtbeck, *Group Process and Gang Delinquency* (Chicago: University of Chicago Press, 1965), pp. 272-73.

the Chicago juvenile gang world. It also is the nub of the position we have taken on the basis of independently collected data and experience with Los Angeles gangs. This paper is concerned with selected *qualitative differences* between juvenile gangs and other groups which have been the more traditional subject of empirical research. Our emphasis will be upon group cohesiveness and the differential nature and function of this concept when the distinctions between gangs and other groups are taken into account.

The Sherifs[2] have adopted the position, in very strong terms, that separating gang phenomena from the generic peer group context does violence to one's perspective on gangs. We agree with the *intent* of the Sherifs' argument, believing that the understanding of gang dynamics must come in the conceptual context of general group concepts and findings. We hope to demonstrate, however, that the rather extreme position taken by the Sherifs commits one to the opposite error of emasculating the juvenile gang of just those characteristics which make it stand out as a social problem.

SOCIAL GROUPS

Laboratory g r o u p s, T-groups, fraternities, and the other group targets of most empirical research are frequently studied in terms of the interpersonal attraction of the members and derive their cohesiveness (whether natural or experimentally induced) from such factors as common goals, explicitness of goals, shared norms and values, and stability of membership. They further tend to

be characterized by behaviors and goals which are acceptable to society. Our understanding of group process and cohesiveness is colored by these facts.

It is a major thesis of this report that the existing literature on cohesiveness is less directly applicable to gangs because of qualitative factors which distinguish gangs from most other groups previously studied. As Lott and Lott observe in their review of empirical studies in the literature, while most researchers have subscribed to the position that group cohesiveness is the result of a number of independent forces, most investigations have focused on intermember attraction. Thus, they "assume that interpersonal attraction, liking, or positive attitudes among group members is central to the cohesiveness of small groups."[3]

JUVENILE GANGS

It is our contention that gang cohesiveness is based not only on these normal group processes but, to an even greater extent, on the interaction of these processes with negatively sanctioned behavior and attitudes. In the gang setting, cohesiveness and delinquent behavior are mutual interactors and reinforcers.[4] Indeed, the current literature on gangs bifurcates into these two major emphases or concerns with group variables.

One group of writers lays stress on

---

[2] Muzafer and Carolyn Sherif, *Reference Groups* (New York: Harper and Row, 1964), pp. 48-49.

[3] Albert J. and Bernice E. Lott, "Group Cohesiveness as Interpersonal Attraction: A review of relationships with antecedent and consequent variables," *Psychological Bulletin*, October 1965, pp. 259-309.

[4] This point—the interaction of normal group processes with delinquency involvement and the consequent impact on group structure—is overlooked by the Sherifs in their argument, although they quote Polsky on just this issue; see Sherif and Sherif, *op. cit. supra* note 2, p. 129.

group structure and cohesiveness per se. Thrasher,[5] for example, recognized great variation in the size and structure of the gangs under his purview. He distinguished between "diffuse" and "solidified" gangs. A group's position along the continuum between these two categories was determined by the amount of conflict with neighboring groups. In the same vein, Yablonsky has emphasized that gang cohesiveness varies as a function of conflict, or, more accurately, of shared sociopathic withdrawal from perceived environmental threat.[6]

The other major emphasis in the current literature has to do more specifically with the modal behavior patterns of gangs. As examples, one can cite Cloward and Ohlin's[7] conception of criminal, conflict, and retreatist groups; Spergel's[8] analysis of the relationship between neighborhood characteristics and conflict, racket, theft, and drug subcultures; and the Short and Strodtbeck[9] report of five behavior factors characterizing the activities of gang members.

Thus, variations in gang cohesiveness and in gang-related behavior

patterns are well established. It would appear, in addition, that group cohesiveness and group product are interdependent. The importance of this interdependence to the practitioner has been underscored by Bernstein.[10] It seems especially important at this point to investigate systematically the relationships between these two sets of variables. This paper presents preliminary analyses of the gang cohesiveness problem.

SOURCES OF COHESIVENESS

As noted above, most groups may be said to derive their cohesion primarily from "internal" sources—with respect to both origination and perpetuation of the group. In identifying these sources of cohesion as "internal" we recognize a certain semantic looseness, but our meaning may become clear when major sources of gang cohesiveness are examined.

It is our contention that internal sources operate with far less impact among gangs than among most groups and that, in contrast to other groups, gang cohesiveness derives from and is perpetuated by sources primarily external to the group. This contention is not new; most of the writers referred to above would be in sympathy with it. Cohen's[11] "reaction formation" analysis and Yinger's[12] discussion of "contraculture" are in the same tradition. We believe in addition, however, that elimination of external sources of cohesiveness of gangs, in most cases, would be followed by dissolution of a relatively

---

[5] Frederic M. Thrasher, *The Gang: A Study of 1,313 Gangs in Chicago*, abridged and with a new introduction by James F. Short, Jr. (Chicago: University of Chicago Press, 1963), particularly chs. 4 and 14.

[6] Lewis Yablonsky, *The Violent Gang* (New York: MacMillan, 1962), particularly ch. 13. Yablonsky's seemingly overstated interest in violence, paranoia, and sociopathic characteristics should not blind one to his legitimate contribution to the placement of gangs in the group-structure tradition.

[7] Richard A. Cloward and Lloyd E. Ohlin, *Delinquency and Opportunity: A Theory of Delinquent Gangs* (Glencoe: The Free Press, 1960).

[8] Irving Spergel, *Racketville, Slumtown, Haulburg: An Exploratory Study of Delinquent Subcultures* (Chicago: University of Chicago Press, 1964).

[9] Short and Strodtbeck, *op. cit. supra* note 1, ch. 4.

[10] Saul Bernstein, *Youth on the Streets: Work with Alienated Youth Groups* (New York: Association Press, 1964), pp. 98-100.

[11] Albert K. Cohen, *Delinquent Boys* (Glencoe: The Free Press, 1955).

[12] J. Milton Yinger, "Contraculture and Subculture," *American Sociological Review*, October 1960, pp. 625-35.

large proportion of gang membership. That is, only rarely does a gang develop a sufficient number of internally-oriented systems to perpetuate itself in the absence of external pressures. This position is the result of two concomitant observations: (a) that internal sources of gang cohesion are weak and (b) that strong external pressures are present. These two characteristics of delinquent groups provide an explanation for what Gerrard has described as "the intense but fragile quality of gang cohesion."[13]

To be more specific about the weak aspects of internal sources of cohesiveness, certain characteristics can be listed.

1. *Group qua group goals* are usually minimal. The most commonly expressed group goal is the protection of members against rival gangs. Clearly this falls under what we have termed an *external* source of cohesion. Gangs assigned a detached worker sometimes learn to verbalize goals such as self-betterment, improving their group image, and "holding their cool." However, such goals are far more easily verbalized than internalized and their general acceptance, when it does take place, is more often associated with gang dissolution than with solidification.

2. *Membership stability* in gangs is relatively low. We have observed large groups in which the combined subgroup memberships have totaled more than two hundred over a two- to three-year period, yet at any given point of time there may be only thirty or forty active members. In other words, turnover is high; many members affiliate with the group for brief periods of from a few days to a few

months, while others move out of the neighborhood or are incarcerated for periods sometimes exceeding a year. The bonds of member relationships are rendered even more transitory by the existence of intra-gang suspicions. Under these circumstances, it is hard to *conceive* of, much less observe, a continuing cohesive group. Even within gangs which have existed over several generations, the mobility factors mentioned above operate to reduce the stability of active membership, in spite of the fact that allegiance to a given group may persist for many years.

3. *Group norms* among gang members have received much attention in the literature, but few have been found which are distinguishable in kind from those of the social class from which gang members generally are drawn. Group *qua* group norms are relatively nonexistent in the gang world except as myths which are exploded upon test. For instance, it is often said that gang members are loyal, will not inform ("fink") on each other, and will come to each other's aid in time of threat, attack, or retaliation, yet most gang researchers report numerous occasions in which such behavior fails to materialize, or does so only among selected members. The one norm that does seem to be shared is that of acceptance of a wide variety of illegal acts. Again, however, this may be more class or subculture related than specifically gang related.

4. *Role differentiation* is difficult to observe in gangs. There are often official positions, such as president, vice-president, or war counselor, but the influence of the position incumbents is nebulous at best. Functional leadership related to different categories of activity is often present, but

[13] Nathan L. Gerrard, "The Core Member of the Gang," *British Journal of Criminology*, April 1964, pp. 361-71.

this leadership is unstable and tends to shift from one person to another during various phases of group development. A most illuminating experience in this regard is to question several members of a group about the respective roles which they expect others to assume during various anticipated future activities. Uniformity of expectation is *not* the standard finding of such an endeavor. The major agreement is on status, not role. In fact, the boys can seldom differentiate beyond the status dimension.

5. *Group names*—Gladiators, Vice Lords, Egyptian Kings—are assumed by many to indicate a common "we-feeling" among gang members. In fact, however, these names often change within a group and derive their greatest effect during conflict periods when cohesion is increased by external threat. Many gang names derive from street or neighborhood labels—Ochenta, Parks, White Fence —suggesting again an external rather than internal base for identification.

Thus, minimal group goals, membership instability, a paucity of unique group norms, little group role differentiation, and a lack of lasting identity with group names all militate against the formation of delinquent gangs based on internal sources of cohesion.

An exception is to be found among gangs with a long history, for gang tradition does seem to be a major internal source of cohesiveness. These traditions in Los Angeles extend over thirty or forty years. A boy growing up in the Clover, Hazard, or White Fence areas of East Los Angeles knows at an early age that gang membership is a highly salient opportunity. This perception is continually reinforced on the street, in school, and even in his home. In this sense, a boy living in such a neighborhood is initiated into the gang culture before he has an opportunity to make an independent decision.

In contrast to relatively weak internal sources, strong external sources of cohesion are everywhere apparent. Any informed layman can discourse on the perils of poverty, low educational performance, job skills, disrupted family relations, "social disability,"[14] and so on. It needs to be added only that these facts of urban life lead to withdrawal symptoms, as documented by Cohen and Hodges.[15] When a number of boys in a neighborhood withdraw from similar sets of environmental frustrations and interact with one another enough to recognize, and perhaps generate, common attitudes, the seeds of the group are sown. Added to threats of rival groups are the many ways in which society reinforces this tendency— police behavior, teacher reactions, lack of acceptance by adults on playgrounds and in local business establishments, etc. Adolescent behavior and adult and rival group reactions thus reinforce each other, and the range of alternatives open to these youngsters is decidedly restricted. The result is delinquent group cohesiveness, however tenuous.

THE DELINQUENT PRODUCT

Thus far little reference has been made to the deviant behavior associated with the gang. The *delinquent product* of gang interaction is the second factor which distinguishes the juvenile gang from groups that have provided the bulk of social science knowledge of group behavior.

---

[14] Short and Strodtbeck. *op. cit. supra* note 1, ch. 10.

[15] Albert K. Cohen and Harold M. Hodges, "Lower-Blue-Collar-Class Characteristics," *Social Problems*, Spring 1963, pp. 303-34.

Society does not disapprove of gangs because they are groups, or because their membership is adolescent, or because they are urban, or because of their normal, urban, adolescent group behavior. Gangs share all of these attributes with many non-delinquent youth groups. In addition, many other youth groups originate as expressions of opposition to adult expectations concerning their behavior. However, while all the activities of these spontaneous adolescent groups may not be condoned by society, such groups are not likely to engage in behavior which will result in social rejection. Society disapproves of juvenile gangs specifically because of that small portion of member behavior labeled as delinquent. It is this delinquent product of the group that causes the reaction. Society knows this, its agents know it, and so do the boys.[16]

We have tried to indicate that gangs are distinguishable from most groups on the basis of (a) a disproportionate measure of external sources of cohesion and (b) a socially disapproved group "product." Gangs are not the only such groups in existence. Consider for example other extremist groups—motorcycle clubs, beatniks, the Black Muslims, the KKK, and some inmate cultures. In most of these cases, however, there are specifiable common goals for which the groups are originated. This and sometimes other internal sources of cohesion distinguish them from the gang. The closest parallels to the juvenile gang may in fact be inmate cultures and San Francisco's now defunct North Beach beatnik colony.[17]

TRADITIONAL APPROACHES TO COHESIVENESS

In relating gang cohesiveness to gang-connected delinquency, one must choose among available conceptions and measures of cohesiveness or create new ones. A review of the literature strongly suggests that one should create new measures of cohesiveness to fit this particular problem.

Cohesiveness, like patient care in medical sociology or morale in industrial psychology, proves on examination to be a complex concept. It has been used as independent variable,[18] dependent variable,[19] intervening variable,[20] and hypothetical construct.[21]

---

[16] Parenthetically, it is often the failure to separate specific delinquent acts from the offender which makes for the inefficiency of many of our delinquency prevention programs. Perhaps due to stimulus generalization, it is the whole boy and the whole group which is condemned, rather than their delinquent product alone.

[17] Francis J. Rigney and L. Douglas Smith, *The Real Bohemia: A Sociological and Psychological Study of the "Beats"* (New York: Basic Books, 1961).

[18] J. Downing, "Cohesiveness, Perception, and Values," *Human Relations*, May 1958, pp. 157-66; A. Pepitone and G. Reichling, "Group Cohesiveness and the Expression of Hostility," *Human Relations*, August 1955, pp. 327-37; S. Schacter, N. Ellertson, Dorothy McBride, and Doris Gregory, "An Experimental Study of Cohesiveness and Productivity," *Human Relations*, August 1951, pp. 229-38.

[19] B. N. Phillips and L. A. D'Amico, "Effects of Cooperation and Competition on the Cohesiveness of Small Face-to-Face Groups," *Journal of Educational Psychology*, February 1956, pp. 65-70; H. P. Shelley, "Focused Leadership and Cohesiveness in Small Groups," *Sociometry*, June 1960, pp. 209-16; J. W. Thibaut, "An Experimental Study of the Cohesiveness of Underprivileged Groups," *Human Relations*, August 1950, pp. 251-78.

[20] R. S. Albert, "Comments on the Scientific Function of the Concept of Cohesiveness," *American Journal of Sociology*, November 1953, pp. 231-34.

[21] A. J. Lott and Bernice E. Lott, "Group Cohesiveness, Communication Level and Conformity," *Journal of Abnormal and Social Psychology*, March 1961, pp. 408-12.

It has been used as an experimental gimmick, induced so that relationships between other variables might be illuminated.[22]

Cohesiveness, nominally, has referred to mutual liking or acceptance,[23] attraction to group,[24] degree of shared norms or values,[25] and resistance to disruptive forces.[26] Operationally, it has been measured by coordination of efforts,[27] summated attractiveness scores,[28] reaction to threat,[29] choice of group over other alternatives,[30] ratio of in-group to out-group choices or contacts,[31] and so on.

So many dimensions of cohesiveness run through the literature that cohesiveness can hardly be considered a definitive concept. Resolution of this problem is perhaps best solved with reference to one's particular interests based on relevant theoretical concerns.

We have said that the delinquent product of the gang makes it a special case. Further, it is generally acknowledged that gang membership increases delinquency involvement. The question is, how much and why? The "why," we suggest, is in part a function of cohesiveness; the "how much" is ultimately an empirical question.

Why should high cohesiveness lead to high delinquency in the gang? It is not just the external sources of cohesiveness that bring this about; these have to do with gang formation before reinforcement. Most gangs theorists presently concur that, if offenses are affected by gang membership, it is because the antecedent deviant values, the requisite skills, and the opportunities for misbehavior are learned and reinforced through association with other members. Status forces are also operative. We would add only that these processes can occur and persist because the external sources of cohesion continually throw gang members together, forcing the kinds of interaction which are preliminary to increased gang-related offenses. These interactions become secondary sources of cohesion in conjunction with offense behavior, each reinforcing the other as the members mingle and verbalize the deviance which labels them as different.

[22] L. Berkowitz, "Group Standards, Cohesiveness, and Productivity," *Human Relations,* November 1954, pp. 509-19.

[23] B. N. Phillips and L. A. D'Amico, *op. cit. supra* note 19; Bernice Eisman, "Some Operational Measures of Cohesiveness and their Interrelations," *Human Relations,* May 1959, pp. 183-89; Warren O. Hagstrom and Hanan C. Selvin, "Two Dimensions of Cohesiveness in Small Groups," *Sociometry,* March 1965, p. 1, 30-43.

[24] Leon Festinger, "Group Attraction and Membership," *Group Dynamics, Research and Theory,* Dorwin Cartwright and Alvin Zander, eds. (Evanston, Ill.: Row, Peterson and Company, 1953), pp. 92-101; Annie Van Bergen and J. Koskebakker, "Group Cohesiveness in Laboratory Experiments," *Acta Psychological* (2), 1959, pp. 81-98; Hagstrom and Selvin, *op. cit. supra* note 23; Eisman, *op. cit. supra* note 23.

[25] Eisman, *op. cit. supra* note 23; Hagstrom and Selvin, *op. cit supra* note 23.

[26] Neal Gross and William E. Martin, "On Group Cohesiveness," *American Journal of Sociology,* May 1952, pp. 546-54.

[27] Cartwright and Zander, *op. cit. supra* note 24, p. 76.

[28] Lott and Lott, *op. cit. supra* note 21.

[29] A. Pepitone and R. Kleiner, "The Effects of Threat and Frustration on Group Cohesiveness," *Journal of Abnormal and Social Psychology,* March 1957, pp. 192-99.

[30] Sherif and Sherif, *op. cit. supra* note 2, p. 242.

[31] Gross and Martin, *op. cit. supra* note 26; Sherif and Sherif, *op. cit. supra* note 2; Leon Festinger, Stanley Schacter, and Kurt

Back, *Social Pressures in Informal Groups* (New York: Harper, 1950); P. R. Hofstaetter, "A Note on Group Cohesiveness," *American Journal of Sociology,* September 1952, pp. 198-200.

Some of the jargon, the "tough" talk, and the recounting of delinquent exploits engaged in by gang members probably serve the function of reinforcing the weak affiliative bonds within the group. Several writers have analyzed both individual and group offenses at critical points in gang development—points of low status and low cohesiveness—to indicate how these offenses revitalize failing group patterns.[32]

Thus a measure of cohesiveness which might relate most directly to gang delinquency must involve *member interaction*. It should not rely on members' verbal responses to an investigator, however, since those willing to respond are not likely to constitute a representative sample of the membership. Interviewing and questionnaire responses are of limited value for the task at hand.

Group *qua* group measures are also inappropriate for they reflect only *indirectly* a presumed summation of member interaction. This eliminates retaliations against rival groups as a measure, an infrequent occurrence in any case.

Index measures which are based on the attractiveness of gang participation as the numerator and alternatives as the denominator are suspect because the researcher cannot adequately assess these alternatives. We have attempted one such analysis, using average distance from member homes to evening meeting sites as representing a summation of barriers overcome to join in group activities. This measure yields findings which are highly gang-specific, rather than generalizable. In some groups it is related to attendance figures, in others it is not. The variance seems more a function of core than of fringe members in the analysis of between-gang differences, and variance is far greater between gang clusters than within subgroups of the same cluster.[33] All in all, we see little advantage in continuing to use this approach.

A SUGGESTED APPROACH

Another approach seems more promising. This method is not dependent upon member responses, presents fewer sampling problems, and is a direct measure of member interaction, our primary criterion. It requires the presence of an observer—in our case, a "detached worker."

For the past four years, the authors and their colleagues have been conducting studies of gang intervention practices employed by detached workers with Negro juvenile gangs in Los Angeles. As part of this project, we have received daily "Contact Reports" from the gang workers assigned to *four large Negro gang clusters* (involving sixteen separate gang groups). These Contact Reports give an account of all individuals seen by the workers in the course of each day. The report lists the names of the

[32] Short and Strodtbeck, *op. cit. supra* note 1, especially chs. 8 and 9; also see Leon Jansyn, *Solidarity and Delinquency in a Street Corner Group*, unpublished Master's thesis, University of Chicago, 1960.

[33] A gang "cluster" refers to a pattern of inter-gang affiliations commonly observed among traditional gangs in Los Angeles. Typically, a cluster consists of three or four age-graded male subgroups plus a girls' group. Each subgroup maintains its own self-identity, yet clearly affiliates with the overall cluster and its "generic" name. See Malcolm W. Klein, "Internal Structures and Age Distributions in Four Delinquent Negro Gangs," paper presented at the annual meetings of the California State Psychological Association, Los Angeles, 1964 (Youth Studies Center, University of Southern California, mimeo.) .

TABLE 1

	1	2	3	4	5	6	7	8	9	10	11	12	13	14	15	16	17	18	19	20	21	22	23	24	25	26	27	28	29	30	31	32	Total
1		2	0	12	1	5	0	0	4	0	0	17	0	18	1	2	0	5	0	4	17	5	1	9	0	0	5	0	0				108
2	2		0	3	0	2	0	0	2	0	0	2	4	2	0	2	0	2	0	6	4	2	0	2	0	2	0	0					39
3	0	0		0	0	0	0	0	0	0	0	0	0	0	1	0	0	0	0	2	0	0	0	0									1
4	12	3	0		1	9	3	0	11	1	0	0	18	0	11	1	7	0	4	0	2	16	6	0	1	7	1	0	0	0	0	0	114
5	1	0	0	1		0	1	0	0	0	0	3	0	1	5	0	0	0	1	14	21	1	1	0	5	10	1						66
6	5	2	0	9	0		0	0	6	2	0	7	0	7	0	4	0	4	0	2	11	6	0	5	0	4	0	0					74
7	0	0	0	3	1	0		0	0	0	0	0	0	0	3	0	0	0	0	0	0	0	3	0									10
8	0	0	0	0	0	0	0		1	0	0	0	2	0	2	0	0	0	0	1	0	1	0	0									7
9	4	2	0	11	0	6	0	1		1	0	0	18	0	14	0	3	0	6	0	2	15	5	0	9	0	5	0	0				102
10	0	0	0	1	0	2	0	0	1		0	0	2	0	0	1	0	1	0	0	0	0	0	0									8
11	0	0	0	0	0	0	0	0	0	0		1	0	1	0	0	0	1	0	1	0	0	0	0									3
12	2	0	0	0	0	0	0	0	0	0	0		3	2	1	0	0	0	2	1	2	0	0	0	0	0							11
13	17	4	0	18	3	7	0	18	2	1	3	2		37	1	5	0	5	0	6	40	6	0	1	11	1	0	5	0	4	3		202
14	0	2	0	0	0	0	0	0	0	0	0	1	3		2	0	0	0	2	2	0	0	0	0									10
15	18	2	0	11	1	7	0	2	14	0	1	0	37	0		1	3	0	5	0	4	34	5	0	12	1	0	4	0	0			162
16	1	0	0	1	5	0	0	0	0	1	0	1	0	0	1		0	1	0	0	2	1	0	0	0	3	6						23
17	2	2	0	7	4	3	0	3	1	0	5	0	3	0	3	0		2	10	2	0	3	0	2	0	5	5						57
18	0	0	0	0	0	0	0	0	0	0	0	0	0	3	1	0	1		0	0	0	0	0	0									1
19	5	2	0	4	0	4	0	6	1	0	0	5	0	5	3	0	2	6		4	0	5	0	4	0	0							57
20	0	1	0	0	0	0	0	0	0	0	0	0	0	1	0	0	0	0	0		0	0	0	0	0	0	1	0					3
21	4	6	0	2	0	2	0	2	0	0	2	6	2	4	0	2	0	2	0		4	2	0	0	2	0	0	2	0	0	0		44
22	17	4	0	16	1	11	0	15	0	1	2	40	2	34	1	10	0	6	0	4		6	0	1	11	1	0	5	0	0	0		189
23	5	2	0	6	6	0	0	5	0	0	6	0	5	0	2	0	4	0	2	0	5		0	5	0	4	0	0					58
24	0	0	0	14	0	0	0	0	0	0	0	0	0	0	0	0	0	0	0	0	0	2		0	0	0	0	0					16
25	1	0	0	1	21	0	0	0	0	0	0	1	0	2	0	0	0	0	1	0	2	1	0		2	1	0	0	0	3	0		33
26	9	2	0	7	1	5	0	0	9	0	0	0	11	0	12	1	3	0	5	0	2	11	5	0	1		0	0	4	0	0	0	88
27	0	0	0	1	1	0	0	0	0	0	0	1	0	1	0	0	0	0	1	0	0	0	1	0	0	13		0					19
28	0	0	0	0	0	0	0	0	0	0	0	0	0	0	0	0	0	0	0	0	0	0	0	0	1	0	0		0	0	0	0	1
29	5	2	0	0	5	4	0	1	5	0	0	5	0	4	2	0	4	0	2	5	4	0	4	0	0	4	0	0		0	0	0	52
30	0	0	0	0	0	0	0	0	0	0	0	0	0	0	0	0	0	0	0	0	0	0	0	0	0	0	0	0	1		0	0	1
31	0	0	0	0	10	0	3	0	0	0	0	4	0	3	5	0	1	0	0	0	3	0	0	3	0	0	13	0	0	1		2	45
32	0	0	0	0	1	0	0	0	0	0	0	3	0	0	6	0	0	0	0	0	0	0	0	0	0	0	0	0	0	0	2		12
Total																																	**1616**

Gangs

72 MALCOLM W. KLEIN, LOIS Y. CRAWFORD

Clique#1

Clique#2

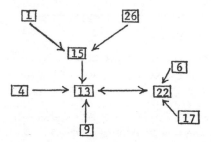 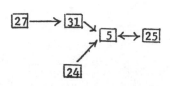

persons seen and indicates the site, duration, and mode of contact initiation in each case, as well as the content of the conversation between the worker and the person contacted. There is also an indication of the grouping of persons involved in each interaction situation. Thus, for any given gang member, it can be determined not only how often he has been seen by the worker during a specified time period, but also with which other members he is seen most frequently.

Approximately six hundred male and two hundred female gang members have been identified through these Contact Reports in combination with other data-collecting procedures. Most of these members have interacted with the detached workers numerous times.

Table 1 summarizes the intragroup companionship patterns for one gang over a six-month period and indicates how often each member contacted each of the other members in the presence of the worker. For example, member #1 was seen most often with members #13, 15, and 22, and he was never seen in the company of fifteen of the thirty-two members contacted by the worker during this time period.

Using data such as those presented in the model in Table 1, we explored the ability of various combinations of the data to differentiate one group from another. The indices explored are summarized below, using the data in Table 1 for illustrative purposes. The first five indices are measures of subgroup or clique cohesiveness.

1. *Number of Cliques.*—Any approach to analysis based on a factor analytic model can be used to reveal subgroupings among the members. For instance, if one applies the first steps of McQuitty's Elementary Linkage Analysis[34] to Table 1, two cliques emerge. The first involves members #1, 4, 6, 9, 13, 15, 17, 22, and 26 and the second involves members #5, 24, 25, 27, and 31. The relationships within each group are shown in Figure 1, following McQuitty's procedure.

In this illustration, we have *arbitrarily* limited potential clique members to those who have at least ten contacts with one other member. The arbitrariness introduced has no theoretical or statistical justification,

[34] Louis L. McQuitty, "Elementary Linkage Analysis for Isolating Orthogonal and Oblique Types and Typal Relevancies," *Educational and Psychological Measurement,* Summer 1957, pp. 207-29.

but this presents no problem so long as the index is used for *comparative* purposes, i.e., for comparing one group to another or comparing different time periods involving the same group.

One other cautionary note is required here. This analysis employs only those members contacted during the time period selected. In other situations, it might be preferable to include in the contact matrix all known gang members, whether contacted or not. This choice applies equally to the other indices cited below.

2. *Percentage of Members in Cliques.*—This index consists of the number of clique members divided by the total membership (however defined—see previous paragraph). In the case of Table 1, the index yields a figure of .44 (14 ÷ 32).

3. *Percentage of Clique Members with 50 per cent or More of Their Contacts within Their Own Cliques.* —The 50 per cent figure is obviously an arbitrary choice. This provides a measure of clique cohesiveness rather than of overall gang cohesiveness, although the two obviously will be positively related. In our illustration, all fourteen clique members fall above the 50 per cent figure, ranging from 58 per cent for number 31 to 100 per cent for number 24.

4. *Average Within-clique Over All-contacts Ratio.*—In this index, one determines, for each clique member, the ratio of his contacts within his clique to the sum of his contacts, then sums over all clique members and divides by the number of clique members. The index figure in our illustration is 77 per cent.

5. *Percentage of Clique Membership with Core Status.*—Most gang workers make a gross distinction be-

tween two classes of gang membership: core and fringe. Using the worker's designation as the operational definition of core and fringe status, this index states the ratio of core to fringe members within identifiable cliques.

The first five possible indices of gang cohesiveness all deal with clique membership. The potential importance of such indices is that the clique members clearly constitute friendship groups within a larger and somewhat amorphous collection of individuals. From a practical viewpoint, the practitioner concerned with decreasing the cohesive bonds of a juvenile gang must understand the nature and intensity of these bonds where they are the strongest, that is, within natural friendship groups. A suitable index of the relative extent and intensity of clique relationships is the first order of business.

The remaining indices refer to the entire matrix of contacts representing an attempt to measure total gang cohesiveness rather than the tightness of selected subgroups.

6. *Number of Contacts Per Cell.*—Referring again to Table 1, it can be seen that a total of 808 mutual contacts was made (1,616 contact notations in the two symmetric halves of the matrix). There are $\frac{32 \times 31}{2}$ or 496 possible combinations of individuals who might have made mutual contacts. This index divides the first figure by the second to arrive at an overall measure of the relative frequency of gang interaction (in the illustration, this figure is 1.63).

7. *Percentage of Empty Cells.*—It is one of the interesting facets of our obtained matrices that a number of gang members are never seen together, with the result that many of the matrix cells are empty. Much of this

lack of contact is due to age differentials among the members. Ages range from twelve to the early twenties and, as with all adolescents, friendship patterns are strongly related to the age dimension. Younger boys are seldom seen in the company of older boys within the gang. Another contributing factor is the inclusion of many fringe members, boys who have fewer contacts "across the board." This index provides a measure of these factors as they and others affect behavioral interactions. In the illustration, 68 per cent of the matrix cells are empty, indicating no observed contact between the individuals concerned.

8. *Percentage of Single-contact Cells out of All Contact Cells.*—Given the relatively high index figures resulting from index #7 (percentage of empty cells), we thought that we should obtain a similar measure among those boys who *were* in contact with each other. This index is derived by dividing the number of cells with only one entry by all cells containing one or more entries. In Table 1, the result is 78/322 or 24 per cent.

9. *Percentage of Empty and Single Cells.*—This is a combination of the numerators of the 7th and 8th indices, using the total number of cells as the denominator. For our example, the index percentage is 75 per cent.

Results

No doubt other combinations may occur to the reader, but the foregoing are sufficient to illustrate the general approach. We have been unashamedly exploratory in the absence of consistent theoretical guidelines in the literature on group cohesiveness. We had hoped that some of the above indices, along with meeting attendance and average residential "spread," as mentioned earlier, might be differentially related to the current status of the four gang clusters involved in our Los Angeles study. From many sources we know that gang Clusters A and B have continued the gang pattern far longer than have Clusters C and D. Further, we know from structural premises that cohesiveness declines with age beyond a certain point. In comparing the indices of cohesiveness taken from the workers' Contact Reports, we have found the following (see Table 2).

1. The number of identifiable sub cliques within a cluster seems unrelated to overall cluster patterns, but the proportion of boys identifiable as clique members *is* related. These proportions in Clusters A, B, C, and D are .42, .43, .16, and .15 respectively. Remember, throughout these items, that Clusters C and D are the ones with lower delinquency involvement.

2. The index based on the number of mutual contacts between members divided by the number of boys contacted, squared (actually n x n — 1), clearly differentiates between clusters. In the same order as above, the index figures are .81, .72, .20, and .32.

3. Similarly, the number of single mutual contact situations (two boys see each other just once during a standard period of time) over the number of all mutual contact situations yields indices of .54 for Cluster A., .35 for B, .73 for C, and .77 for D.

4. Among clique members, the proportion of in-clique contacts to all clique member contacts is related in a fashion similar to the above. For Clusters A, B, C, and D, the figures are .82, .73, .47, and .40.

5. The remaining indices failed to differentiate between the four groups.

TABLE 2
COHESIVENESS MEASURES IN FOUR GANG CLUSTERS

	Higher Delinquency Clusters		Lower Delinquency Clusters	
	A	B	C	D
a. Clique members/all members	.42	.43	.16	.15
b. Mutual contacts/n (n − 1)	.81	.72	.20	.32
c. Single contacts/all contacts	.54	.35	.73	.77
d. In-clique contacts/all clique contacts	.82	.73	.47	.40

That the indices listed refer to more than differences between clusters is revealed by a pilot analysis carried out on Cluster A. The older and younger members were compared on two indices over three consecutive six-month periods, with the results shown in Table 3.

TABLE 3
COHESIVENESS INDEX CHANGES AMONG OLDER AND YOUNGER MEMBERS OF CLUSTER A

Index	Age Group	July-Dec. '63	Jan.-June '64	July-Dec. '64
# Contacts	Older	.25	.25	.16
n(n − 1)	Younger	.21	.25	.29
# Non-single contacts	Older	.65	.54	.51
Total contacts	Younger	.60	.57	.70

Preliminary data indicate that the increase in cohesiveness among the younger boys and the decrease among the older boys parallels similar trends in recorded offense rates. In any case, it is clear from both tables that we are employing indices of some sensitivity. It remains to be shown just how directly they are related to gang offense patterns, but our hopes are high.

The development of these indices of cohesiveness is an effort to assess this group variable as it is found in delinquent gangs. Our concurrent d-e velopment of offense measures endeavors to ascertain the seriousness of the delinquent product.[35] The in-teraction patterns of these measures of gang cohesiveness and juvenile offenses, we believe, represent a sorely needed investigation in our understanding of group delinquency phenomena. If our investigation adds to the placement of these phenomena within the larger context of group process and outcome relationships, we shall be doubly rewarded.

[35] Richard I. Martin and Malcolm W. Klein, "A Comparative Analysis of Four Measures of Delinquency Seriousness," paper presented at the annual meeting of the Pacific Sociological Association, Salt Lake City, April 1965 (Youth Studies Center, University of Southern California, mimeo.).

[5]

Criminal business organizations, street gangs and 'wanna-be' groups: A Vancouver perspective[1]

Robert M. Gordon
School of Criminology,
Simon Fraser University,
Burnaby, B.C.

Le Greater Vancouver Gang Study (Étude des gangs du Vancouver mé-tropolitain) comporte une recherche détaillée sur 128 membres de gangs. Cette étude a pour objectif d'amasser des données (ex., âge et origine ethnique); de vérifier l'exactitude des classifications et des définitions des gangs et des groupes; de déterminer pourquoi des individus se joignent à des gangs. La recherche a concentré son attention sur trois groupes principaux: les associations criminelles d'affaires; les gangs de rue et les groupes de "wanna-be". Les raisons pourquoi il y a des vagues d'activités de gangs et de groupes demeurent difficiles à préciser, mais la recherche a pu identifier les principales raisons pourquoi des particuliers se mêlent aux associations criminelles, aux gangs et aux autres groupes. Ces raisons sont: la marginalité économique et ethnique, l'acquisition de biens, les appuis qu'on trouve auprès des membres d'un groupe, et la fuite devant les situations familiales violentes. Pour que des politiques et des programmes puissent être efficaces, ils doivent faire la différence entre les associations criminelles, les gangs de rue et les autres groupes marginaux et distinguer quels sont les facteurs qui sous-tendent l'adhésion initiale au groupe et la continuation de cette participation.

The Greater Vancouver Gang Study involved research on and with 128 known gang members. The goals included developing profile data (e.g., age and ethnicity); testing classifications and definitions of gangs and groups; and determining why individuals become involved with gangs. The research focussed upon three main groups: criminal business organizations; street gangs; and wanna-be groups. The causes of the waves of street gang and wanna-be group activity in Vancouver remain elusive, but the research identifies the main reasons why individuals become involved with organizations, gangs, and groups. These reasons include economic and ethnic marginality, material gain, the attraction of supportive peer groups, and flight from abusive family circumstances.

40   *Revue canadienne de criminologie*   *janvier 2000*

*To be effective, policy and programme responses must recognize the
differences between organizations, gangs, and groups, and the different
factors underpinning initial and continued membership.*

Introduction

Those interested in the "gang" phenomenon in Canada are
frequently surprised by the absence of a body of research that is
distinctively Canadian and publicly available. The first recorded
piece of work was a study of juveniles in street gangs in Toronto
in the 1940's undertaken by Rogers (Rogers 1945), and there is
an occasional reference to street gangs and youth gangs in other
publications (e.g., Ley 1975). Some research was also conducted
by Joe and Robinson on street gangs in the "Chinatown" area of
Vancouver in the late 1970's (Joe and Robinson 1980). Apart
from this, no organized and systematic research was undertaken,
and nothing was published, until quite recently.

The same appears to be true for the research and literature
on criminal organizations. Beare's (1996) recently published book
on organized crime (or criminal enterprises) in Canada is the
first major contribution to the field. A host of important
definitional, policy, and legislative issues are canvassed
(especially with respect to money laundering) and help pave the
way for new empirical research. Dubro's (1985; 1992) journalistic
accounts of the Mafia, and of Asian organized crime, in Canada
are illuminating, and the nature and form of Canadian organized
crime is usefully clarified in a recently released report of a pilot
survey of organized criminal activity conducted by the Canadian
Centre for Justice Statistics (1999). Wolf's (1991) ethnography
of biker gangs in Alberta still stands as the only insider's account
of what, for some analysts, is a criminal organization (e.g., Beare
1996; Canadian Centre for Justice Statistics 1999) but which,
in Wolf's view, is a subculture of rebels – a brotherhood of outlaws
– for whom crime is a casual rather than entrenched activity. It
is clear that the debate over the nature of biker gangs will
continue for some time and that an accurate picture is often
blurred by regional and other variations. As Wolf (1991: 268)
points out, there are tremendous differences between clubs and
between chapters, and those involved in the "full gamut of crime
remain a distinct minority". This is supported by one of the

findings in the report of the Centre for Justice Statistics (1999: 19) which acknowledges that "among all the motorcycle associations, only 1% fall into the underworld of organized crime".

Several pieces of Canadian gang research were coincidentally released in 1993. Three reports, each written for either the federal or the provincial levels of government (Fasiolo and Leckie 1993; Gordon 1993; Mathews 1993), and an unpublished M.A. thesis (Young 1993) examined different aspects of the gang phenomenon. In addition, Kennedy and Baron (1993) and Baron and Tindall (1993) published their studies of groups of street youth in part to understand better an apparent increase in youth violence. All of this work provided not only the answers to some pressing policy questions (e.g., to what extent are Canadian street gangs dominated by the members of visible ethnic minorities?) but also the building blocks for more comprehensive research such as the Greater Vancouver Gang Study.

Fasilio and Leckie's work (1993) on the coverage of gangs and gang activity by the Canadian media made an extremely valuable contribution to what was, at the time, a lively debate over news media amplification of the nation's street gang "problem." The authors undertook a content analysis of major national news magazines and the major daily newspapers published in urban centres such as Vancouver, Winnipeg, Toronto, and Montreal between July and October 1992. They found that the media characterized gangs and gang activity as widespread, a significant threat to society, and as a relatively new phenomenon. Gangs were depicted as a subject of "growing social concern" and the product of an ailing society; themes which, according to Young (1993), have been trumpeted by Canadian newspapers during every wave of urban street gang activity since at least 1945.

Fasilio and Leckie noted the absence of any historical reference or perspective in the stories and a focus that accentuated polarization along ethnic lines: "Asian gangs" were a particular menace. One consequence, the authors argued, was an unjustified increase in the fear of gangs and gang activity, and a similarly unwarranted concern over the extent to which immigrants who were members of visible ethnic minorities were responsible for gang related crimes. The reasons why gangs

42   *Canadian Journal of Criminology*   *January 2000*

emerged were largely ignored apart from some vague references to the consequences of immigration policies and practices. Generally, in the authors' view, the media were contributing to a moral panic.

Gordon's (1993) preliminary study of gang members in British Columbia correctional centres provided something of a counterfoil to the news media's pre-occupation with "Asian gangs" and "youth gangs." The files of 41 male inmates (adult and youth) who were identified as active gang members by the police and corrections personnel were examined and the inmates were asked to participate in interviews. Ten adults and 24 young offenders were interviewed, the goal being to obtain information about the activities and membership of gangs in the province (especially the Greater Vancouver area) and the reasons why young people, in particular, became involved with gangs. A secondary objective was to design and test some research definitions and instruments for use in a later study (i.e., the Greater Vancouver Gang Study).

The majority of incarcerated gang members were young adult males (the mean age was 19), rather than young offenders. This finding was of importance in combating the false perceptions created by the news media's use of the term "youth gangs." Also of importance was the finding that the largest single group of incarcerated gang members were individuals of European ethnic origin born in Canada (40 percent). The next largest group were individuals of Asian ethnic origin (34 per cent), the majority having been born in Canada. There were very few gang members of East Indian, aboriginal, and Hispanic origin, and only one black gang member in the sample. Overall, 32 per cent of incarcerated gang members were not born in Canada; a proportion higher than the proportion of immigrants in the provincial population and, therefore, the expected percentage (22 percent). This finding lent support to an hypothesized relationship between immigration and gang membership. As Gordon and Nelson (2000) have pointed out, however, the actual numbers of gang members in the study who were not born in Canada (14) is extremely small, especially when compared with the size of the immigrant population in the province as a whole (approximately 750,000 people).

The gang members who were interviewed indicated that they were not coerced or otherwise pressured into joining gangs and that the process of becoming involved was a gradual, rather than abrupt event. There was a slow drift towards involvement that was often initiated by a close relative or a friend who was already a member of a gang or who knew a gang member. A prospective member would spend time on the periphery of the group but might eventually be drawn in, undergo an initiation ceremony, and then become a full member. As Gordon (1993; 1995) points out, the process was neither strange nor surprising and was similar to the experiences of a young person joining a legitimate "gang" such as the boy scouts or a baseball team.

According to Gordon (1993), the availability of choices is a key to understanding a person's involvement in gangs. If an individual has no access to, or is not encouraged to join, a mainstream group, an "illegitimate" group may be chosen instead, an hypothesis reflecting the seminal work of Cloward and Ohlin (1960) that was supported, in part, by the research data. Nearly one half of the subjects had backgrounds filled with domestic problems including drug, alcohol, and physical abuse in the family coupled with school records of truancy, fighting, suspensions, and expulsions. The picture was one of troubled individuals from troubled backgrounds. When these problems were related to the reasons why the subjects became involved with gangs (as stated in interviews), it was clear that the choice of an illegitimate, rather than legitimate, group was a function of the absence of alternatives. The reasons why other subjects became involved with gangs were not so clear. Some became involved primarily to continue associations with friends, to make money, and for the relief of boredom, considerations that could not be satisfied by membership in a legitimate "gang".

Mathews' (1993) preliminary research in Toronto also involved interviews with youth gang members. The study was intended to allow young people a voice in the emerging debate on gangs and groups. Youth involved in gang activity were approached by experienced social services and police personnel and asked to participate in the study. Twelve young people aged from 14 to 21 years agreed and were interviewed. Interviews were also conducted with social workers, police officers, school officials, the parents of gang members, and some victims of gang activity.

Mathews recognized that the term "gang" can be misleading and that the term "gang/group" is a better way of describing the different kinds of gatherings of young people. Analysts and policy-makers should view the phenomenon along a continuum ranging from groups of friends who spend time together and who occasionally get into trouble, to more serious, organized criminal groups or gangs. Mathews also developed an exploratory "gang/group involvement cycle" and a multivariate causal model. The model accounts for the process of joining, remaining with, and leaving a gang by reference to several variables including individual vulnerability factors that can drive a young person into a gang/group (e.g., an abusive family environment), situational factors, the larger social context, and the nature of the responses to the youth's behaviour.

Young's (1993) study of the history of gangs in Vancouver filled a significant gap in Canadian gang research by providing the first socio-historical analysis of youth gang activity. Young scrutinized each daily edition of a major Vancouver newspaper for an 85-year period and, when articles reporting gang activity were found, these were cross checked against stories in other newspapers. Young argues that the first significant wave of street gang activity occurred between 1948 and 1959: the era of the "Hoodlum Gangs". These street gangs included the "Alma Dukes" and the "Vic Gang", and the characteristics and activities of these gangs were similar to those of street gangs in more recent times. The second wave of street gang activity occurred between 1970 and 1975 and consisted of two, seemingly unrelated clusters of gangs: the "Park Gangs" (e.g., the *Riley Park Gang* and the *Clark Park Gang*), and the "Chinatown Gangs" discussed by Joe and Robinson (1980). The Chinatown gangs of the early 1970's included some gangs that may have eventually evolved into criminal business organizations. The third, and most recent, wave of street gang activity began in 1985 and began to dissipate in the mid-1990's.

Young attempted to explain the wave like pattern during the post 1945 period by focusing on two independent variables: inward migration; and unemployment rates. A preliminary analysis of these variables indicated a slight positive relationship between inward migration rates and reported fluctuations in gang activity. Unemployment rates and fluctuations in gang activity were inversely related but Young cautions against the use of these results, beyond the development of hypotheses for future research.

The Greater Vancouver Gang Study

Method

The Greater Vancouver Gang Study was designed to build upon the existing but limited pool of knowledge about gangs and similar groups in Canada, and to inform policy and practice in British Columbia. The Study had four main goals: to develop profile data on known gang members (e.g., age, gender, and ethnicity); to test the validity of the classifications and definitions of gangs and groups proposed and discussed in preliminary studies; and to determine why individuals became involved with and left gangs. This third goal included identifying the processes of involvement and disengagement, with a particular emphasis on the psychological and sociological factors that propel individuals into gangs. The fourth goal was to examine the organization, composition, and activities of gangs, from the perspectives of those involved with, and those working with, gangs.

The research subjects were all adults and youth on the caseloads of corrections personnel in the Greater Vancouver area in January 1995, and those who were added to their caseloads during the following six months, who were identified by these personnel as being involved with "gangs". The group included individuals sentenced to terms of imprisonment and probation or those undertaking other forms of supervised community service. The main portion of the research took place during the first six months of 1995 and involved reviewing and extracting information from client files, interviewing clients who were willing to participate, and discussing individual cases with probation officers and police officers. The purpose was to obtain as many perspectives on a client as possible. A total of 128 subjects were included in the research and 33 agreed to be interviewed, in some cases with the assistance of a social worker or probation officer who spoke the subject's first language. The interviews were conducted in probation offices, "natural settings" in the community (e.g., coffee shops), and in correctional centres. In addition, there were 11 family visits and interviews each conducted by a qualified and experienced family therapist assisted by an experienced social worker who spoke the languages of the families.

Although the subjects were the entire population of "gang members" known to the provincial Corrections Branch at the time, they were not the entire population of gang members in the Vancouver area. The extent to which the subjects are representative of the larger gang population is impossible to determine (no "gang census" was available), and the proportion of the larger gang population represented by the research subjects is similarly impossible to ascertain. The estimated numbers of gangs and gang members varies considerably at any given moment, and from year to year, and even the best estimates offered by authoritative sources such as the police are only ever educated guesses. Communication breakdowns, rivalries, and territoriality affecting the police departments in the Greater Vancouver area also means that no single police unit has a comprehensive overview of the situation.

The status of the gang members involved in the research could not be determined with certainty. Police and probation officers offered their best opinions but it was not always clear whether a subject was a core member of a gang, an associate, or a peripheral (or wanna-be) member. In addition, the gang members involved in the research were those who had been caught, charged, and convicted, and this must be borne in mind when interpreting the results. Further challenges were posed by the perennial problem of defining gangs.

Defining "gangs"

One of the initial problems for the Study was finding an accurate and widely accepted definition of a "gang", and a "gang member". Similar difficulties are reported consistently in research reports and other literature on gangs, regardless of the location and objectives of the research, and the methods used by the researchers (e.g., Goldstein and Huff 1993; Mathews 1993; Klein, Maxson, and Miller 1995; Spergel 1995; Curry and Decker 1998). A valid and reliable answer to the question "what is a gang?" has been elusive and depends upon who is asked.

Different police departments and individual police officers have different conceptions and definitions (formal and informal), as do probation officers, corrections centre staff, researchers, policy-makers, and the members of "gangs" and criminal groups.

As the research proceeded, it became clear that small groups of offenders were being referred to as "gangs" when the members of these groups did not see themselves that way. Perhaps predictably, the primary offenders seemed to be the news media who used a range of inaccurate terms to describe groups (e.g., Asian gangs, and youth gangs), thereby generally distorting and amplifying the "gang" problem. In one case, a daily newspaper actually constructed a name for a small group of young offenders who, for several weeks, had been bullying high school students into parting with cash and possessions, and then began to refer to this group as a "gang". The name given by the newspaper – the "Back Alley Boys" – reflected both the chosen scene of crime (alleyways at the rear of houses) and the membership of the group (teen-age males), but it was an imposed name.

Another example of the problem of construction involved both the media and the police. The so-called "626 gang" was a group of eight youth and young adults who committed a series of armed robberies of banks, stores, and credit unions in the Greater Vancouver area, over a four month period in 1992. The group was named the "626 gang" by the police because they consistently used stolen Mazda 626 automobiles to drive to and escape from the scenes of their robberies. When members of the "gang" were interviewed it became clear that they had not chosen the "gang" name and did not see themselves as a "gang"; they were simply a group drawn together by friendship and a common interest in crime that decided to try its luck at armed robbery.[2]

Attaining a common and accurate understanding of a phenomenon (or phenomena) being studied, and about which policy and programming are being developed, is important. In the absence of common and widely accepted conceptions and definitions research, policy development, program development, and even police operations, both within and between jurisdictions, will be confused and confusing. The Greater Vancouver Gang Study took a grounded approach to the development of gang classifications and definitions. A typology was developed and tested prior to the main research and a great deal of time and effort was expended on this component. Six main types of groups that seemed to attract the label "gang" were identified: youth movements; youth groups; criminal groups; wanna-be groups; street gangs; and criminal business organizations.[3] The research concentrated on the last three types.

Criminal business organizations are organized groups that exhibit a formal structure and a high degree of sophistication. Organizations are comprised primarily of adults, including older adults. They engage in criminal activity primarily for economic reasons and almost invariably maintain a low profile, which is a characteristic that distinguishes them most clearly from street gangs. Organizations may have a name, examples being *Lotus*, *The Flying Dragons*, and *The Big Circle Boys (Dai Huen Jai)*. There were 24 members of criminal business organizations in the research, representing both the organizations named above and three other organizations.

Street gangs are groups of young people, mainly young adults, who band together to form a semi-structured organization the primary purpose of which is to engage in planned and profitable criminal behaviour or organized violence against rival street gangs. They can be distinguished from other groups (especially wanna-be groups) by a self-perception of the group as a gang; a name selected and used by gang members; and some kind of identifying marks such as clothing and colours. The members will openly acknowledge gang membership because they want to be seen as gang members by others. Street gangs will tend to be less visible but more structured, better organized, and more permanent than wanna-be groups. Examples include *Persian Pride*, *Midnight Rockers*, and the quintessential Vancouver street gang of the 1980's and 1990's: *Los Diablos*. There were 35 members of street gangs in the research, representing both the gangs named above and ten other gangs.

Wanna-be groups are clusters of young people who band together in a loosely structured group to engage in spontaneous social activity and exciting, impulsive, criminal activity including collective violence against other groups of youths. A wanna-be group will be highly visible and its members will openly acknowledge their "gang" involvement because they want to be seen by others as gang members. The group will have a local gathering area and a name, selected and used by its members, which may be a modified version of the name of either a local or an American street gang. The group may use clothing, colours, or some other kind of identifying marks. The group's name, meeting ground, and colours may fluctuate. Examples include a suburban wanna-be group known as *Los Cholos* that was active in Greater Vancouver during the early 1990's. There were 25 members of wanna-be groups in the research, representing *Los Cholos* and six other groups.

The categories and definitions are not perfect, partly because of inter-relationships between the groups that tend to blur boundaries. Some street gangs were allied to criminal business organizations, one example being the link between the street gang known as *Los Diablos* and the criminal business organization known as *Lotus* (Gordon 1998). During the late 1980's and early 1990's, *Los Diablos* acted as the drug retail and enforcement arm of *Lotus*, some key members of *Los Diablos* also being *Lotus* associates. Some criminal groups are affiliated with criminal business organizations, many of which have a cell-like (rather than pyramidal) organizational structure, each cell being potentially independent. Some wanna-be groups may have been created (in part) by former street gang members and may exhibit more gang-like characteristics than other wanna-be groups. Despite these overlaps and connections, the typology and its associated definitions reflected a reality that was recognized and endorsed by a variety of criminal justice practitioners and policy-makers.

Results: Why individuals become involved with organizations, gangs and groups

There is no single and simple answer to the frequently posed question, "why do individuals become involved with gangs?" This, in part, is because the question itself is not terribly useful. It makes more sense to ask why people become involved with criminal business organizations, or with street gangs, or with wanna-be groups. The answers differ.

In the case of criminal business organizations, answers begin to appear once the basic characteristics of their memberships are examined. Organization members included in the Study tended to be older males (mean age 27.8 years) who were better educated than the members of street gangs. They were less likely to be economically dis-advantaged, primarily because of the lucrative nature of their work with an organization. Criminal business organizations engage primarily in the supply of illegal goods and services (e.g., drugs), areas of commerce in which significant profits are made. Organization members were more likely to have migrated to Canada than, for example, street gang members (21 out of the 24), and more likely to be members of a visible ethnic minority (21 out of the 24). Sixteen of the 24 were of Vietnamese or Chinese ethnic origin.

Members of criminal business organizations and the corrections personnel responsible for their cases (e.g., probation officers) indicated that there was a social and cultural bond which attracted individuals to organizations and that addressed their sense of ethnic and cultural marginality in a predominantly Euro-Canadian environment. The importance of a shared language and a sense of belonging accounted for their continued involvement with organizations. Members consistently stated that, on arriving in Canada, there was a lack of resources and employment opportunities available to them. They had few marketable skills, and experienced significant difficulties in obtaining rewarding, legitimate employment because of significant language barriers. In order to overcome their economic marginality and achieve the economic status valued by the larger Canadian society, organization members were drawn into illegal activities. In short, and perhaps not surprisingly, membership of criminal business organizations (in Greater Vancouver) is ethnically shaped and meets the economic and social needs of both organization members and their families.

Particularly telling were the responses given to questions about leaving (as opposed to joining) criminal business organizations. Members were asked about the process of leaving, and any associated problems such as fear of retaliation. Two subjects stated that they had considered leaving but could not afford to do so, and the loss of significant income was a factor for most individuals. Organization members reported earning from $2,500 per week to up to $30,000 per month (tax-free) and members, police officers and probation officers all agreed that membership of a criminal business organization was a lucrative endeavour. The majority of subjects had minimal work skills and could not expect to earn a comparable income in a legitimate field. As one organization member put it, "what else could I do and make this kind of cash... I speak little English, and legal work means no money" (Gordon and Foley 1998: 34).

Understanding why individuals became involved with street gangs proved to be less straightforward. Thirty-five street gang members were included in the research (only one was female) and they tended to be much younger than the members of criminal business organizations (the mean age of street gang members was 18 years). Education levels were lower and they were more likely to be from economically disadvantaged backgrounds. More than 60 percent were born in Canada, although 85 percent were members of visible ethnic minorities – a significant over-representation.[4] These included individuals of Indo-Canadian (Fijian), Hispanic, Iranian, Chinese, and Vietnamese ethnic origin.

Discussions with street gang members and their probation officers indicated that individuals became involved with gangs for a variety of interconnected reasons. Although the prospect of material gain cannot be discounted as an explanation, the members of gangs were more likely to become involved as a result of peer group attraction. They wanted to belong to a friendly, supportive group that included their friends or close relatives and this included a desire to be with individuals from the same cultural and ethnic group; gang members felt ethnically marginalized.

Many street gang members wanted to escape from, and find rewarding alternatives to, exceedingly unpleasant family lives. Their recent domestic histories and current circumstances reflected common characteristics that transcended, in particular, ethnicity. Most had physically abusive parents resulting in a lack of bonding, fear, and frequent absences from home (to avoid abuse). Parents seemed unable to control or otherwise influence the behaviour of their children without recourse to ineffective and extreme physical discipline which, in some cases, had resulted in child protection interventions by the (then) Ministry for Social Services. Another common factor was poverty, resulting from a combination of single parenthood, an absent or unemployed father, additional dependant siblings, and an inability to obtain employment due to a combination of parental commitment to the dependants and a lack of English. In the case of some immigrant and ethnic minority families, these problems were compounded by isolation from the larger, surrounding community, and even from individuals and families within that community who shared the same ethnic background (Gordon and Foley, 1998: 52-53).

The relationships among variables such as ethnicity, family circumstances, and peer group attraction could not be measured precisely but, arguably, they are closely related.[5] A young person or young adult experiencing abuse or neglect in his family – and this seemed to be present in the case of most street gang members – will probably be strongly attracted to a welcoming, supportive, and accessible alternative which simultaneously improves his material well being. The choice of alternative is likely a product of availability and opportunity and, for some young males living in the inner urban areas of Vancouver in the late 1980's and early 1990's, a viable alternative existed in the form of street gangs. The peer group attraction that is evidently responsible for young males becoming involved with street gangs is probably no different than the attraction of other socially legitimate groups such as hockey teams and the boy scouts. There is a common tendency on the part of adolescents and young adults to group together and the main difference with respect to street gang members appeared to be their choice of "gang". This choice is, to some extent, a function of the opportunities available in communities.

Understanding why individuals became involved with wanna-be groups was clearer than in the case of street gang members. Twenty-five wanna-be group members were included in the research (only one was female) and they tended to be much younger than the members of criminal business organizations and street gangs (the mean age of wanna-be group members was 16.8 years). About 60 percent were born in Canada, and 68 percent were members of visible ethnic minorities. Although there was an over-representation of subjects from visible minorities,[4] the largest single ethnic group found amongst wanna-be group members was Canadian born individuals of European descent (28 percent).

Individuals involved with wanna-be groups tended to be involved in less serious and less organized forms of crime – shoplifting, thefts from vehicles, and minor assaults. The members of *Los Cholos*, for example, spent most of their time in the suburbs of Burnaby and Coquitlam bullying other adolescents. *Los Cholos* members wore purple clothing and their primary mission in life appeared to be persuading other teenagers to part with any items of purple clothing they happened to be wearing. The group did not have any particular objectives (or significant organization) and would occasionally attack adolescents and groups of adolescents for no apparent reason other than as a response to a comment, a glance, or an appearance.

Wanna-be group members tended to fit the profile of hard core young offenders. They came from economically disadvantaged circumstances and exhibited behavioral and scholastic problems at school due, primarily, to the distractions of their adverse family circumstances. A disproportionate number attended alternate schools and other learning centres. They became involved with wanna-be groups primarily because of their distressing family backgrounds, most of which were characterized by physical and sexual abuse, as well as neglect. The Case of "B" provides a good illustration.

> B was a 17 year old Canadian born subject of Aboriginal ethnic origin. He had a severe conduct disorder, severe anger management needs, and fetal alcohol syndrome. He was permanently removed from his home at age three. Prior to this he experienced physical and sexual abuse and was frequently neglected by his mother who had significant substance abuse problems (drugs and alcohol). B had been placed in more than 20 foster homes before the age of three. His adoptive parents divorced at which point he became unable to control the anger he felt and expressed. According to B's probation officer, his involvement in a wanna-be group seemed to meet his need to belong to a family.

54   *Canadian Journal of Criminology*   *January 2000*

In many cases, the wanna-be group was a replacement for the families that the members did not have, or that had rejected them. The group satisfied a variety of unmet emotional needs, especially the need for attachment – for a sense of belonging.

Discussion

The Greater Vancouver Gang Study was designed to expand the existing pool of knowledge of gangs and similar groups in Canada. The Study explored several possible explanations for "gangs" (inclusively defined), some of which were not supported by the data. The idea that the involvement of individuals in "gangs" was a function of their experiences with racism was not supported. Another hypothesis - that the involvement of individuals in "gangs" was a function of the messages and role models transmitted by the news and entertainment media – was also not supported. When the leaders and core members of criminal business organizations and street gangs were asked, in interviews, about the possibility that their behaviour had been shaped by the media (or words to that effect) most dismissed the idea as a joke.

There was some evidence to suggest that the *entertainment* media may shape the behaviour of individuals involved with wanna-be groups but only as an intervening, rather than an independent, variable. For example, police and probation officers reported that after the release of the popular movie "Colors" the behaviour and activities of young people who were already involved with gangs began to reflect the images portrayed in the film. Graffitti began to appear on walls and fences, wanna-be group members began to dress in "colours", and individuals and groups began to use the language – especially the idiom – of the actors in the film (e.g., the term "homes"). Other films may have had a similar impact, but "Colors" appears to have been the primary influence, for a while.

It is clear that membership of a visible ethnic minority is related to involvement in criminal business organizations, street gangs and, to a lesser extent, wanna-be groups. It is also evident that ethnicity is possibly more significant than whether or not a person was born in Canada (i.e., whether or not he is an immigrant). The problem lies in determining the role that ethnicity plays.

It is possible that the data used in the Greater Vancouver Gang Study were skewed or inaccurate in some way. In particular, it is possible that individuals from visible ethnic minorities are more easily caught and prosecuted, or are singled out for attention by a consciously or unconsciously biased criminal justice system. By definition, such individuals are more visible than individuals of Euro-Canadian ethnic origin, and their ethnicity may be (falsely) associated with "gang" involvement, primarily because of media-generated and other images. Alternatively, it is only individuals from visible ethnic minorities who are caught and prosecuted, while Euro-Canadian gang members remain undetected.

This is an important consideration and there is probably some negative labeling taking place on the part of some individuals working within the criminal justice system. However, police and probation officers in the Greater Vancouver area are generally sensitized to biases of this kind and labeling, alone, cannot account for the disproportionate representation of individuals from visible ethnic minorities who are identified as "gang" involved. In addition, there is concrete evidence in the form of police surveillance photographs and other hard data to confirm the involvement of such individuals in organizations and street gangs.

Another possibility is that the disproportionate number of individuals from visible ethnic minorities is a product of the lack of rewarding (materially and emotionally) economic opportunities for these individuals. This is an especially compelling explanation in the cases of those who were not born in Canada and who face significant language and skills barriers when they try to enter the legitimate job market. It may well be that experiencing the frustrations of attempting, but failing, to achieve material success in a highly materialistic society, results in a rejection of conventional ways of succeeding and an embracing of the unconventional ways. This may be especially prevalent amongst adolescents and young adults who are bombarded with achievement messages and who are raised on the idea of instant gratification for minimal effort (the so-called "MacDonald's Syndrome").

While the idea of "impatience" may be dismissed as unsubstantiated, there is ample evidence from the current research to underscore the importance of economic and, equally importantly, ethnic marginality as significant causal factors. Above all else, it is the economics of immigration and of ethnicity that seem to account best for a person's involvement in criminal business organizations and this should be explored in future research.

Conclusion

There are significant differences between criminal business organizations, street gangs, and wanna-be groups, with implications for policy and programme development. Dealing with a criminal business organization like *Lotus* requires a different strategy from one aimed at a street gang such as *Los Diablos*, or a wanna-be group such as *Los Cholos*. Unlike street gangs and wanna-be groups which tend to appear and disappear in waves (Young 1993), criminal business organizations are relatively constant (Dubro 1992). They are comprised of adult males of primarily Chinese or Vietnamese ethnic origin who migrated to Canada, and are involved in the provision of illegal goods and services. Clearly, organizations and their members are quite different from street gangs. And street gangs and organizations are quite different from wanna-be groups - a highly visible, noisy, and suburban phenomenon consisting of adolescent males from a variety of ethnic backgrounds who engage in random acts of collective violence and theft, some of which seemed quite pointless to all but the participants.

Although the development of specific recommendations for new policy and programming was not within the mandate of the Greater Vancouver Gang Study, the work did produce insights. It is clear that careful definition and classification of organizations, gangs and groups, and of their members, is critical to any effective policy and programming, but this may be hard to achieve. Policy and programming developments must address the needs of individuals from visible ethnic minorities who have recently migrated to Canada and who experience ethnic and economic marginality. The lack of language, and a lack of both money and the means to obtain money and material goods legitimately may result in individuals clustering in supportive groups where they are understood and can make money, albeit illegally. Whatever is being provided in the way of settlement services for immigrants is not reaching some individuals and families. This may be a function of the length of time during which services are provided for newly arrived immigrants, and especially those who are refugees.

Lastly, existing community-based anti-gang programming should be continued as an important preventative strategy, but must be expanded during the onset of a wave of street gang and wanna-be group activity. Anti-gang programming appears to be most effective when it is aimed at the supply of new gang and group members, rather than existing and well-established street gang members. Programs in high schools can reduce fear and intimidation, dry up the source of gang personnel, and help generate a broader, negative perspective of gang membership, especially amongst younger adolescents. A great deal is accomplished once gang membership is defined as "uncool" by the adolescent sub culture (Danesi 1994).

Further research into Greater Vancouver's street gangs started in May 1999. Phase 2 of the Greater Vancouver Gang Study is concentrating on the emergence, growth, activities, and eventually decline of three street gangs from the most recent period of gang activity: *Los Diablos;* the *East Vancouver Saints;* and *Gum Wah.* In each case, key issues of ethnicity and immigration will be considered (e.g., the impact of ethnic marginality) along with an examination of the relationships among the gangs, criminal business organizations, and wanna-be groups. A more detailed analysis of the factors responsible for the beginning of a wave of street gang (and wanna-be group) activity will also be undertaken.

Notes

1. The research associated with this article was funded by the British Columbia Ministry of the Attorney-General and the Department of Justice, Canada. The author gratefully acknowledges the support and encouragement of these government agencies and of the British Columbia Inter-Ministry Committee on Youth Violence and Crime. The principal researcher was Sheri Fabian, M.A. Major contributions were made by Jacquelyn Nelson, Ph.D., Lynda Fletcher-Gordon, M.S.W., Sergeant Jim Fisher of the Vancouver Police Department, and Mike White of the British Columbia Ministry for Children and Families.

2. Other examples of police constructed "gang" names surfaced during
    the research. These included the *"The Goof Troop"*, a name given by
    the police to a wanna-be group; *"The Ethnic Viets"*, a name given by the
    police to a conglomerate of criminal groups affiliated with a criminal
    business organization; and, *"The Pin-Heads"*, a name used by the police
    to identify the members of a criminal group led by one Mr. Pin.

3. Youth movements are extensive national, and often international, social
    movements characterized by a distinctive mode of dress or other bodily
    adornments, a leisure time preference, and other distinguishing
    features. The vagaries of adolescent fashion and other larger social
    and economic developments tend to determine the life spans of these
    movements. To the extent that birds of a feather will flock together,
    adolescents who subscribe to a movement often accumulate in groups
    and may be erroneously referred to, usually by the media, as a "gang".
    Examples include, the "zoot-suiters" (the 1940's and 1950's), the "mods
    and the rockers" (the 1960's); "skin-heads" (the 1970's and 1980's);
    and "punkers" (the 1980's and 1990's). Youth groups are sometimes
    referred to as "social gangs" insofar as they are comprised of small
    clusters of young people who "hang out" together in public places such
    as shopping malls, fast food outlets, and large convenience stores. They
    are often quite visible, noisy, and energetic and can seem intimidating.
    At one time, in the Vancouver area, these groups were referred to as
    "Mallies" because of their frequent appearance in large shopping malls.
    Criminal groups are small clusters of friends who band together, usually
    for a short period of time (no more than one year), to commit crime
    primarily for financial gain. They can be composed of young people
    and/or young (and not so young) adults and may be mistakenly, or
    carelessly, referred to as a gang.

4. More than three quarters of the research sample were members of visible
    ethnic minorities (78.0 percent). According to a 1994 projection for
    the Vancouver Metropolitan Area, approximately 59.0 percent of the
    general population of the Area were members of visible ethnic minorities
    (Gordon and Foley 1998; and Gordon and Nelson 1993).

5. The relationships among economic disadvantage and marginality,
    ethnicity and other variables will be examined more thoroughly during
    Phase 2 of the Greater Vancouver Gang Study, begun in the Spring of
    1999.

References

Baron, S. and D. Tindall
    1993   Network structure and delinquent attitudes within a juvenile
            gang. Social Networks 15: 255 - 273.

Beare, M.
    1996   Criminal Conspiracies: Organized Crime in Canada. Toronto:
            Nelson Canada.

Canadian Centre for Justice Statistics
  1999   Organized Crime Activity in Canada, 1998. Ottawa: Statistics
          Canada.

Cloward, R.A. and L.E. Ohlin
  1960   Delinquency and Opportunity: A Theory of Delinquent Gangs.
          Glencoe, Il: Free Press.

Curry, D. and S. Decker
  1998   Confronting Gangs: Crime and Community. Los Angeles:
          Roxbury.

Danesi, M.
  1994   Cool: The Signs and Meanings of Adolescence. Toronto:
          University of Toronto Press.

Dubro, J.
  1985   Mob Rule: Inside the Canadian Mafia. Toronto: MacMillan.

Dubro, J.
  1992   The Dragons of Crime: Inside the Asian Underworld. Markham:
          Octopus Publishing.

Fasilio, R. and S. Leckie
  1993   Canadian Media Coverage of Gangs: A Content Analysis. Users
          Report 1993-14. Ottawa: Ministry of the Solicitor General.

Goldstein, A. and C.R. Huff (eds.)
  1993   The Gang Intervention Handbook. Champaign: Research Press.

Gordon, R.M.
  1993   Incarcerated Gang Members in British Columbia: A Preliminary
          Study. Victoria: Ministry of Attorncy General.

Gordon, R.M.
  1995   Street gangs in Vancouver. In J. Creechan and R. Silverman
          (eds.), Canadian Delinquency. Toronto: Prentice Hall.

Gordon, R.M.
  1998   Street gangs and criminal business organizations: A Canadian
          perspective. In K. Hazlehurst and C. Hazlehurst (eds.), Gangs
          and Youth Subcultures: International Explorations. Transaction:
          New Brunswick.

Gordon, R.M. and S. Foley
  1998   Criminal Business Organizations, Street Gangs and Related
          Groups in Vancouver: The Report of the Greater Vancouver Gang
          Study. Victoria: Ministry of Attorney General.

Gordon, R.M. and J. Nelson
  1993   Census '93: The Report of the 1993 Census of Provincial
          Correctional Centres. Victoria: Ministry of Attorney General.

Gordon, R.M. and J. Nelson
  2000   Crime, ethnicity and immigration. In R. Silverman, James J.
          Teevan, and Vincent F. Sacco (eds.), Crime in Canadian Society
          (6th edition). Toronto: Harcourt Brace.

Joe, D. and N. Robinson
  1980   Chinatown's immigrant gangs. Criminology 18: 337 - 345.

Kennedy, L. and S. Baron
  1993   Routine activities and a subculture of violence: A study of violence
          on the street. Journal of Research in Crime and Delinquency
          30: 88 - 112.

Klein, M., C. Maxson, and J. Miller (eds.)
  1995   The Modern Gang Reader. Los Angeles: Roxbury Publishing.

Ley. D.
  1975   The street gang in its milieu. In G. Gappert and H. Rose (eds.),
          The Social Economy of Cities: Vol. 9 Urban Affairs Annual Review.
          Beverly Hills: Sage Publications.

Mathews, F.
  1993   Youth Gangs on Youth Gangs. Ottawa: Department of Justice.

Rogers, K.H.
  1945   Street Gangs in Toronto: A Study of the Forgotten Boy. Toronto:
          Ryerson Press.

Spergel, I.
  1995   The Youth Gang Problem: A Community Approach. New York:
          Oxford University Press.

Wolf, D.R.
  1991   The Rebels: A Brotherhood of Outlaw Bikers. Toronto: University
          of Toronto Press.

Young, M.
  1993   The History of Vancouver Youth Gangs: 1900 - 1985. Burnaby:
          Simon Fraser University, School of Criminology. Unpublished
          M.A. thesis.

Part II
The History and Development of Gangs

[6]

American Gangs and British Subcultures: A Comparison

Anne Campbell, Steven Munce and John Galea

THIS paper will attempt to examine the social, cultural and economic forces in Great Britain and the United States which gave rise to youth subcultures and gangs respectively. Although the two terms have sometimes been used interchangeably, in the context of this paper at least their denotation is quite distinct.

Short (1968) noted: "It is important to distinguish between gangs and subcultures, for most subcultures are not carried solely by a particular group. . .". Pfautz (1961) similarly stressed the absence of organized social and interpersonal structure which characterizes a subculture: ". . . social movements exhibit continuity beyond the concrete interacting situation because they develop a 'culture' in the sense of a set of ideas, theories, doctrines, values and strategic and tactical principles . . . they lack a fully developed and functionally effective social structure". In British sociology, youth subculture has come to denote a national social movement of teenagers and young people who share a common set of values, interests, and tacit ideology but not necessarily dependent on face-to-face interaction with other members or with any rigid criteria of entry, membership or obligation.

To offer a definition of a gang is no easy task. As a starting point, we can take the definition of Thrasher (1963) who described it thus: "The gang is an interstitial group originally formed spontaneously, and then integrated through conflict. It is characterized by the following types of behavior: meeting face to face, milling, movement through space as a unit, conflict and planning. The result of this collective behavior is the development of tradition, unreflective internal structure, esprit de corps, solidarity, morale, group awareness and attachment to a local territory." Such a view of gangs has not gone unchallenged. Yablonsky (1962) has queried the rigidity and stability of many of the definitional criteria. He argues that role definition and membership may be diffuse, that there is a lack of cohesiveness and limited consensus on gang objectives and norms. To the extent that this may be true, the gang becomes no more than a loose collectivity of individuals and becomes more akin to the friendship groupings which occur within English subcultures. However, in order to pursue the argument offered here, we will assume a rigorous definition of the gang which demands that it meet all the following conditions:

1. Presence of face-to-face interaction.
2. Internal structure, including leadership and role allocation.
3. Territoriality.
4. Stable membership.

These conditions set up a discriminative criteria since youth subcultures exhibit none of these attributes.

Great Britain has been the home of at least five major working-
class youth subcultures since the Second World War—Teddy Boys,
Mods, Rockers, Skinheads and Punks. Yet it has shown little evidence of structured gangs. Patrick (1973) claimed the existence of
gangs in Glasgow but close examination suggests that while there
were groupings of male youths known by territorial names, there
was little if any internal structure and stability of membership.
Cohen (1973) in his discussion of the Mods and Rockers disturbances of the 1960's, has noted that while some groupings of teenagers might be referred to as "The lot from Eltham" or the
"Walthamstow boys" these were simply for ease of reference and
did not imply any formal gang structure. The same may be true
of Patrick's Glasgow groups. What is more significant is the failure
of such writers as Mays (1954), Scott (1956) and Downes (1966) to
find any evidence of the structured gang in England. As David
Downes notes in his excellent work on British youth groups: "In
England, delinquent group structure is more fluid and less tangible
than in the States." (Downes 1966, p.122)

Reciprocally, the United States has produced a wealth of gangs.
In New York City alone in 1978, the Police Department knew of
at least 146 gangs with an estimated membership of 11,634. (Collins
1979). In a national survey, Miller (1975) estimated gang membership to range between 28,450 and 81,500 between 1973 and 1975.
Youth subcultures have been notable by their absence. Hippies did
achieve a substantial following but it was a middle-class movement
unlike the subcultures of Britain. Surfers and the attendant beach
boy lifestyle was again predominantly middle-class and membership
was constrained by geographical location. In this paper it will be
argued that the structure of gangs and subcultures respectively
spring directly from the dominant social, cultural and political
systems in which they are embedded.

The Rise of Youth

The post-war years saw the beginning of youth subcultures in
Great Britain with the appearance of the Teddy Boys (Fyvel 1963).
Although gangs at least in New York City have been traced back
tentatively to the mid-nineteenth century, youth gangs specifically
came to prominence also in the 1950's. This coincidence was most
likely the result of the "Baby Boom" immediately following the

Second World War. According to the United Nations Annual Yearbook (1949), the number of live births per 1,000 population rose between 1939 and 1948 by 41 per cent in the United States and 19 per cent in Great Britain. Thus by the end of the 1950's a sizeable proportion of the population was entering adolescence. They were doing so in a period of relative affluence. After the war and the rationing which attended and followed it, Britain entered a period of economic prosperity, which culminated in the 1960's. This affluence was particularly felt by the youth market who did not have the economic responsibilities of mortgages and families. A substantial part of their income was spent on leisure consumables— clothes, records, alcohol, cosmetics, movies and so on (see Fyvel 1963, Galbraith 1969). As a market they became important to the manufacturing and leisure industry. Teenage tastes in magazines, clothes and music were catered for. Being a "teenager" took on the connotation of a recognized chronological and social status whereas before, childhood and adulthood had merged with little fanfare. Youth was preoccupied with itself and the media increased this self-concious visibility by catering to it both in advertising and in broadcast content. Both in numerical size and in economic and cultural power, youth became a force to be reckoned with on both sides of the Atlantic.

At the same time there were important social and ideological differences between the two countries which profoundly affected the structuring of youth groups.

The Subcultures of Britain

Social class has always been a highly visible fact of British life reflected in the differences in language (Bernstein 1973, Rosen 1972), education (Ford 1969, Halsey 1956), job opportunity (Willis 1975), leisure (Willis 1976) and home life (Douglas 1964; Hoggart 1958). The long tradition of class division is manifest not only in day-to-day lifestyles but in national party politics. The Labour party in Britain represents the interests of the working class as an explicit and coherent platform. That the interests of the social classes are in direct conflict is clear from even a rudimentary understanding of current affairs. The working class in Britain recognize their cultural separation from the middle-class and take pride in it. The history of working class labor organization and unions have produced some of the most well-known political names of this century; MacDonald, Hardie, Shinwell, Jones, Feather. Culturally, writers such as Dickens, Lawrence, Sillitoe have written either from or about a working class lifestyle. Stories of life in the mines, the factories, the fishing boats are passed from generation to generation with pride. To be working class in Britain may be a source of economic dissatisfaction but not of cultural shame.

The reality of the class system in Britain is transmitted to the child, if not in the home then certainly at school. Until the late 1960's Britain operated an explicitly two-tier education system, where on the basis of a single examination at age eleven, children entered either grammar or secondary modern schools. The former were destined for clerical or professional jobs, the latter for semi-skilled or unskilled work. While this system was replaced by comprehensive schooling in the 1970's, there is evidence that a clear distinction still exists, in the eyes of the children at least, between those who will enter white-collar work and those who are bound for factories. (Hargreaves 1967; Willis 1975). Willis notes that by the second or third year of secondary (senior) school two distinct factions have developed; the "earholes" who continue to accept the schools evaluation of personal success in terms of academic achievement and the "boys" who establish their own culture which stresses the importance of personal style, opposition to authority and short-term hedonism. On a more formal level, Britain continues to adhere to a two-tier system in terms of secondary school graduation examinations; the General Certificate of Education (taken by "brighter" students and carrying considerably more prestige in terms of future employment potential) and the Certificate of Secondary Education—a definite second best. To compound this stratification process, Britain offers little in the way of continuing or remedial education to those who fail to achieve their secondary school examinations. To fail at age sixteen, almost inevitably means a future of limited and menial employment.

Much has been written on the problems of adjustment experienced by American youths who fail educationally and economically (Cohen 1955; Miller 1958; Cloward and Ohlin 1960). Downes (1966) in his study of the applicability of subcultural and strain theories to English youth noted:

". . . dissociation—not alienation is the normative response of working-class male adolescents to semi-skilled and unskilled work (and to no work at all). . . The English 'corner boy' successfully traverses the humiliations of school and job allocation by his re-affirmation of traditional working-class values." (Downes 1966, p.258).

A further reason for the solidarity of working class youth in Britain lies with the media. Great Britain is served by five or six major national papers. Thus the same news is available to all on a national level. Secondly, the newspapers assume quite distinct political positions with respect to their analysis of news material. Even the tabloid papers cater to right (*Daily Mail, Daily Express*) as well as left wing taste (*Daily Mirror*). Working-class teenagers have a means of receiving a consistent political analysis of events and this does much to foster their understanding of the position of the working class in Britain. Thirdly, the reporting of "youth" news does much to spread subcultures across the country. Stan Cohen (1973) has documented the way in which relatively minor disturbances in a South Coast resort town between Mods and Rockers received sensational publicity which grossly exaggerated the events, but which greatly popularized both movements among teenagers. More recently, the role of the media in distorting, amplifying and popularizing "Punks" has been documented. (Stevenson 1980).

Subcultural youth movements have been inextricably linked with the working class backgrounds from which they spring. The unifying factor in all of them from Teddy Boys to Punks has been an antipathy to the middle class and a pride in the youngsters' own class background. Their rejection of middle-class values has been evidenced in dress, music, alcohol and drug use and ideology—all of which have been in opposition not only to the adult world, but specifically to the *middle-class* adult world. All represent an attempt to discredit or ridicule the establishment rather than to emulate it and to re-affirm the cultural gap between the teenagers' own future of menial labor and the dedicated work-orientated life of the middle class. This does not represent a political or revolutionary threat—none of the subcultures have been sufficiently well struc- tured, let alone motivated, to do that—but rather a restatement of the intractability of the class system, the hopelessness of their position.

The challenge to the middle classes is expressed in the absence of structure as well as the ideology of youth groups (Downes 1966). Unlike American gangs, subcultures make no attempt to duplicate the institutions of "straight" society such as the family or the busi- ness corporation. They have no role allocation, no initiation rites, no specific requirements of membership. Similarly, status is not achieved within the subculture by the traditional means of wider society; money, job prospects, education and material possessions. Membership of a subculture bestows instant identity. It betokens the acceptance of the superordinate importance of leisure over work, of short term hedonism rather than dedication, of fun rather than money and in so doing, elevates these fundamentally working- class values into an implicit political ideology set against the middle class. They provide a readily accessible solution to failure in employment and academic fields by uniting such youths in a stance which not only lays the blame on the class system but which fiercely challenges any liberal or benevolent attempts to help them. They are working class and proud of it.

The Gangs of the United States
By contrast, the United States offers no such rationale for failure.

The American dream continues to stress the availability of power, income, and wealth to anyone prepared to commit himself whole-heartedly to its achievement. Economic success and affluence as goals are foisted indiscriminately on all sectors of the population and those who fail must take personal responsibility (see Cohen 1955). Social class is certainly more enigmatic and less incontrovert-ible than in Britain and consequently less available as a rationale for failure. Party politics in the States has done little to develop a sense of solidarity among the working class. Candidates for office rely heavily on endorsement and funding from specific pressure groups and lobbies. The result is piecemeal political platforms which fail to represent the overall position of the working class and do much to destroy its unity. Jews, blacks, women, inner city dwellers each feel a different candidate may help their position with little concern as to the cost of that help in terms of denying similar opportunities to others. The result has been to add to the fragmen-tation of the American working class.

The education system in the United States—in theory at least—offers equal opportunity to all class levels. Furthermore, for those who drop out or fail in high school, there is always the possibility of remedial action through the High School Equivalency Diploma. Ironically, though Britain offers government funding to candidates accepted to university, a smaller proportion of the population attain college education in Britain than in the States. Education is seen in the United States as an important entrance to upper income brackets and heightened social standing. Its doors remain open even to those who have failed at sixteen. The educational mach-inery operates in such a way as to publicly promote the impression of a classless and egalitarian society.

Cohen has suggested that the working class in America funda-mentally subscribe to the dominant value system of the middle class: "Though we refer to them as 'middle class' norms, they are really manifestations of the dominant American value systems and even working class children must come to terms with them" (Cohen 1955, p.87).

In contrast, Miller (1958) has suggested that there is a distinctive lower-class set of "focal concerns" and that delinquent gangs represent their extreme manifestation in action. However, a focal concern is, as Miller himself notes, a different thing than a value. Those events or attributes which occupy a substantial part of life do not necessarily carry with them the connotation of moral worth to the people who subscribe to them. To get drunken in search of "excitement" or to become involved in "trouble" may indeed, as Miller also notes, be seen as negative and counter-productive by those who engage in them. Working class values in Britain however carry positive moral overtones; a fair day's labor for a fair day's pay, belief in the defense of personal integrity and family loyalty, in the rejection of "loose" morality and financial debt to name but a few. (Hoggart 1958; Young and Wilmott 1957). To attribute a homogeneous set of focal concerns to the American lower class Miller himself notes may be an over-simplification: ". . . systematic research in this area would probably reveal at least four to six major subtypes of lower class culture. . ." (Miller 1958, supra note 3). It is our contention that ethnic differences are of critical importance in understanding working-class values. Certainly teenagers themselves perceive substantial differences between groups which often results in humor as well as prejudice. Blacks in New York, for example, poke fun at the fiestiness and machismo of Puerto Ricans. Regardless of the "objective" homogeneity or lack of it in working-class American culture, teenagers certainly note the differences in the value systems between ethnic groups.

The most visible and most publicised divisions in American society lie less in social class than in race, ethnicity, language, sex and urban versus rural location. Doubtless this is the result of the immigration into the country of diverse cultural groups and the formation of neighborhoods (and ghettos) in the cities. Italians, Chinese, Jews, Poles each settled in its own geographical and social locations perpetuating its own language, culture and political interests. (Glaser and Moynihan 1970; Lewis 1966). The cultural and linguistic divisions between neighborhoods created an in-group feeling among members of the same block or area. This division lay at the heart of the "turf" to which the gangs of the 1950's laid claim. The tradition of neighborhood bosses and vigilante groups long before had paved the way for them.

In terms of personal adjustment for youth who fail to "make it" educationally or economically, delinquency theorists of the 1950's and 1960's have argued that the burden of guilt falls on the self. To cope with this sense of personal failure, such youths group together with like minded others; their ties to conformity are broken (Hirschi 1969); they invert middle-class values in a process of reaction formation (Cohen 1955) or they withdraw legitimacy from the traditional means of attaining success (Cloward and Ohlin 1960). However in the period following the civil rights movements of the 1960's, the mode of adjustment appears to have altered. In New York City over the last fifteen months I have spoken with members of at least nine gangs on a regular basis. They show a clear awareness of racial issues and make reference to them frequently in accounting for their behavior. They point to the areas in which Puerto Ricans and blacks reside in the city, noting the disadvantages this gives in housing, health care, education and employment opportunity. Their dissatisfaction focuses predominantly on the plight of other members of their own local

American Gangs and British Subcultures: A Comparison   83

and racial group. It does not extend to the general position of the working class nationally. Furthermore they accept as unproblematic the prevailing ideology of capitalism. Their complaint is that American capitalism is insufficiently benign and operates on a discriminative basis. They do not invert middle-class values, most would be delighted to have a white-collar office job. Neither do they withdraw legitimacy from the Protestant ethic of hard work and job commitment. They certainly do not view the solution in revolutionary or even radical terms. The long-term solution as they see it lies in organised local pressure groups which will force the city to attend to the plight of ghetto people—to force decent education, better housing conditions and health care. As one gang member said:

Gino: If I'm eating a T-bone steak, I would like you to eat a T-bone steak. If I'm eating sirloin, I want him to have a sirloin. Because, goddamn, there is no reason why people have to go without in this goddamn society, as rich as this country is. People go with one meal a day, starving and then have to go on the streets and find means of getting food for their families. All we are asking for is to have the same that middle-class people are having. We are not asking for first-class action. The same thing that every middle-class person is having is what we want. We don't want to have what the goddamn President has because we know we ain't going to get it but damn, give us a break. Give us a shot at life—give us a break to be comfortable.
A.C.:   Do you want a revolution?
Gino: No. There's no revolution that goes without force or without violence. We are not talking about violence. We are just talking about getting ours whether its with words or something.

Most view prejudice as endemic to American life and their aim is to escape upward without regard to those who will take their place.

Connie: Well, now the blacks and Puerto Ricans don't have nothing to worry about—its the Cubans now. You know I saw a movie that said: "If there were no niggers we would have to invent them". The Cubans are taking over the oppressed group now. They're the oppressed group. Before that it was the Dominicans and the Haitians. There's always some group that somebody is going to pick on. But that's the way it is. Whenever you go into a new neighbourhood since you're the newcomer, you're always going to get all that hard stuff and everything until you finally fall into a category—whatever group. You either fit in or fit out. . . I think what it is, like I also noticed each individual has to have one person who they hate in life, like they got to have people they love. You've got to have someone you hate because these are all feelings that keep people going. So when it comes to society, society is just a group of people.

In the meantime, gangs exist as organised local groups committed to their own personal survival. They recruit predominantly from their own area, with an average ten block perimeter. Racially, they are predominantly black or Hispanic. The New York City Police Department estimate that of total gang membership in the city 54.7 per cent are Hispanic, 35.7 per cent black, 9.3 per cent white and 0.3 per cent other races (Collins 1979). The victims of their attacks are often other members of their own neighborhoods. In 1977, 84 per cent of New York City gang incidents were so directed. The fragmentation so evident in large scale American politics is painfully evident on the streets. Since the United States has no national daily newspapers, youth in one part of the country are relatively ignorant of others activities until it reaches the point of mass movement or violence. The net effect is that New York teenagers, already factioned within the city into their own areas, have virtually no knowledge of the situation of gang members in Chicago, Los Angeles or Philadelphia. The only group to be trusted is the gang itself. Everyone beyond that, including members of the same neighborhood or other gangs, are seen as "outsiders" and, therefore, potential victims.

While territorial street gangs may be seen as symptomatic of the overall fragmentation of American society, their acceptance of the prevailing ideology of the country is evidenced in the structuring of their groups. Gangs duplicate in organization the major institutions of American society; the family, the business corporation and the military. The family structure is particularly evident in mixed sex gangs where the male and female leaders are known respectively as "Pops" and "Moms" (Campbell 1980; Gale 1977). They are referred to on personal and romantic issues for guidance. Their right to discipline the members for irresponsible or selfish behavior is accepted unquestioningly. Moms and Pops take responsibility for ensuring members attendance in court or at the probation officer's office. They also take care of the family finances and are responsible for handing out "pocket money". In return, members are expected to contribute to household affairs by cleaning, cooking and shopping. "Mom" is treated with respect by all and male members make no sexual overtures to her. Other gangs operate on a corporate model with presidents, vice-presidents and spokesmen. Their turf or territory defines their area of business operation and here they may sell drugs, operate protection rackets, extort money, manage prostitution and traffic stolen goods. Their area is guarded against intrusion by other gangs who might attempt to profit from the same area. Other gangs have warlords and counselors of war who are responsible for parlays with other gangs, declarations of war and the acquisition of weapons. Unlike their English counterparts who express disdain for the middle-class and demonstrate their seperateness by denying its institutions and values, American gangs accept and duplicate the organization of the dominant society.

Implicit Ideologies

Both in Britain and the United States, youth groups have not remained unresponsive to the social and economic climate around them. While their respective structures have remained fundamentally intact, their orientation to society at large has altered.

In the mid-sixties in England, the affluence of youth was perhaps at its height. There was high employment and sufficient money for leisure to support a youth subculture that stressed more than any other the acquisition of consumer goods. The Mods laid great stress on personal grooming and appearance. Pants were worn tightly fitted on the hip, flared at the bottom over Italian shoes. Button-down collared shirts and either Parkahs or leather coats were worn. The vehicles of choice were motor scooters (as distinct from the motor bikes of the Rockers) and a status hierarchy existed between the various models and brands. The preferred music was The Who and The Small Faces. The intoxicants used were spirit alcohol (as opposed to beer) and amphetamines. Saturday nights were often costly in terms of suitable clothing, alcohol and music. More than any other subculture, it accepted the importance of consumables—of being "flash". It was no accident that this movement coincided with the prevalent ethos of working-class chic. The stars of the sixties were working-class youths who had made it in the straight world — Twiggy, David Bailey, Terence Stamp, The Beatles. The inverted snobbery reached the point where middle-class teenagers would affect Cockney accents. The Mods thrived on their stardom. Their class background was a source of pride. While accepting the bourgeois ethic of ownership, they rejected the "posers" who were not really of their background. Working class and proud of it had never been quite so easy to be.

The Skinheads who followed the Mods began in the south of England and were characterized by extremely close cropped hair. They wore heavy, steel-capped construction boots and pants which ended four inches above the ankle. They projected an image of toughness and aggression. Their appearance was the direct antithesis of the then prevalent Hippie. Hippies were a predominantly middle class movement and the Skinheads took pains to be as different as possible, to stress not only their separate class background but their contempt for love and peace. Many were football supporters and took pride in following their home team around the country on a Saturday terrorizing the opposing fans by mob attacks on them both in the football ground and outside. At that time also, the first generation of British-born West Indian and Pakistani youths were reaching adolescence. Both groups were considered fair game by the Skinheads who turned "Paki-bashing" into a recognized activity. With the recent advent of the National Front party in Britain, many found a political rhetoric to justify their aggression (see *The New York Times Magazine,* September 14, 1980).

By 1974 when the Punks made their appearance, Britain had entered a state of economic depression. Raised in the 1960's, with every expectation of a future of affluence and full employment, teenagers left school to find few jobs and a Labour government which seemed to be doing little to improve the situation. Britain could no longer boast a "Swinging London" and much of the music and entertainment was being imported from the United States. The mood of youth was disillusioned and angry. It found expression in the cynicism and anarchy of the Punk movement and its music. The songs expressed some of the dominant moods of Punk: "I'm so bored with the U.S.A.", "Anarchy in the U.K.", "God Save the Queen" and "White riot". Punks did their best to discredit the middle class and all of its values. Money was irrelevant, race issues were just a red herring, even romance and sexuality were decried as being a temporary opiate to keep people happy. Organised politics and personal salvation were both rejected. Life seemed hopeless and the only solution was to poke fun at those who took it seriously.

At the same time, in the United States the mood of the gangs was undergoing changes also. The 1950's street gangs were tightly organised units who attempted to salvage dignity in the symbolic defense of "turf" and demonstration of "heart". The focus of youth at that time set it apart as a chronological unit somehow separate from adulthood. As such, gangs directed their attention toward each other, rather than to society at large. Masculinity appeared to be at the heart of many of the activities. The Spanish and Italian need to demonstrate "machismo" and the displacement of the black male from the family unit (Rainwater 1966; Wallace 1978) lead to his appearance on the street and his defense in action of both personal integrity and gang loyalty. (Miller 1958; Cohen 1955). The territoriality at that time was related to the struggle between ethnic groups for social position, if not in the world at large at least in the ghettos.

The dramatic decrease in gang membership in the 1960's has not been fully accounted for. (Miller 1975; Collins 1979). Certainly heroin became widely available on the streets and an active market was created by pushers who would give the first couple of shots free. (Collins 1979; Gale 1977; Galea, forthcoming). Narcotics were antithetical to the all-for-one philosophy of the street gangs. Many of the potential members were drafted into the military. At the same time, the civil rights movement was enlisting support not just from middle-class university students but from the streets. The "Young Lords" was a movement for Puerto Rican liberation which drew much in name and dress from the street gang image. Radical groups like the Panthers and the Black Liberation Army became folk heros to teenagers on the street. However by the 1970's many of these heroes were dead or in jail. The impetus was drained away and after it all, the ghettos remained. As the 1970's wore on the economic situation grew worse. In some black areas of New York City unemployment was as high as 70 per cent. Gangs began to re-emerge. In New York, gang membership rose from an estimated 2,800 in 1971 to 18,226 in 1976 (Collins 1979). The mood however had changed. Being black or Hispanic was no longer a source of shame. Such youths now recognized and talked about the disadvantages they had to face in employment and education. The economic situation, the lack of jobs were reflected in the increase in property crimes. Miller (1975) in a study of six major United States cities reported that there was "greater stress on the use of violence as a means to the acquisition of money and saleable goods" (p.43). In New York, the percentage of crimes for profit (burglary, robbery, extortion) as a proportion of all gang crimes (the above plus homicide, dangerous weapon, narcotics, assault, rape, unlawful assembly) rose from 17 per cent in 1971 to 64 per cent in 1977 (Collins 1979; Marsh and Campbell 1978). While the gangs may have increased their awareness of the social disadvantages of minorities, they used the gang as a means of criminally exploiting those in a similar position to their own. The dog-eat-dog mentality engendered by the economic decline was visible in the behavior of street gangs. Unlike their British counterparts who in the 1970's re-affirmed their class position by challenging the status quo (albeit ineffectually), the American ghetto youth continued to subscribe to the predominant value of money and acquisition at almost any cost.

Conclusion

It has been argued that the differential structural response of youth in situations of economic disadvantage is a function of the historical and social differences in the predominant culture. We have also suggested that the activities and philosophy of youth movements are responsive to prevailing social and economic climates. In the coming years, Britain and the United States will be governed by political polities which favor decreases in spending in public areas which affect youth; education, housing, health care, and social security benefits. In both countries unemployment is steadily rising. Britain may now face the kinds of racial problems which the United States has already begun to deal with. Among British youth there is a new interest in "Two-tone" music—a blend of West Indian ska rhythm and rock. Perhaps this heralds an optimistic future for racial problems among youth. Much however depends on the ability of the Labour movement to unite itself and to welcome young people of all races into the development of an alternative political policy. In the United States, gangs in New York show signs of uniting across the barriers of race and turf. As the Republican party comes into office, perhaps it will serve to unite inner-city youth who stand to benefit least from such a government. The future promises an interesting comparison between the two countries in terms of the response of youth to the politics of conservatism.

REFERENCES

Bernstein, B. F. (1973) *Class, Codes and Control* (Volume 2), London: Routledge and Kegan Paul.

Brown, C. (1965) *Manchild in the Promised Land*, New York: Macmillan.

Campbell, A. (1980) *Gangs and Subcultures in New York and London*, Paper delivered to the American Society of Criminology Annual Meeting, San Francisco, California.

Cloward, R. A. & Ohlin, L. E. (1960) *Delinquency and Opportunity*, Glencoe: The Free Press.

Cohen, A. K. (1955) *Delinquent Boys: The Culture of the Gang*, Glencoe: The Free Press.

Cohen, S. (1973) Mods and Rockers: The Inventory of Manufactured News. In: *The Manufacture of News*, edited by S. Cohen and J. Young, Beverley Hills, California: Sage Pub.

Collins, C. (1979) *Street Gangs*, New York: New York City Police Department.

Douglas, J. B. (1964) *Home and School*, London: MacGibbon & Kee.

Downes, D. M. (1966) *The Delinquent Solution*, London: Routledge & Kegan Paul.

Ford, J. (1969) *Social Class and the Comprehensive School*, London: Routledge & Kegan Paul.

Fyvel, T. R. (1963) *The Insecure Offenders*, Harmondsworth: Penguin.

Galbraith, J. F. (1969) *The Affluent Society* (2nd ed.), Boston: Houghton Mifflin.

Gale, W. (1977) *The Compound*, New York: Ballantine.

Galea, J. (1979) *Youth Gangs in New York*, paper delivered to interdisciplinary Perspectives on Aggression (Conference), Oxford University, England.

Glazer, N. & Moynihan, D. P. (1970) *Beyond The Melting Pot*, Cambridge & London: M.I.T. Press.

Halsey, J. A. (1956) *Social Class and Educational Opportunity*, London: Heinemann.

Hargreaves, D. H. (1967) *Social Relations in Secondary School*, London: Routledge & Kegan Paul.

Hirschi, T. (1969) *Causes of Delinquency*, Berkeley: University of California Press.

Hoggart, R. (1958) *The Uses of Literacy*, Harmondsworth: Penguin.

Lewis, O. (1966) *La Vida*, New York: Random House.

Marsh, P. & Campbell, A. (1978) The Youth Gangs of New York and Chicago Go into Business, *New Society*, **46**, 67-69.

Mays, J. B. (1954) *Growing Up in the City*. Liverpool: University Press.

Miller, W. B. (1958) Lower Class Culture as a Generating Milieu of Gang Delinquency, *Journal of Social Issues*, **14**, 5-19.

Miller, W. B. (1975) *Violence by Youth Gangs as a Crime Problem in Major American Cities*, Washington: Government Printing Office.

New York Times Magazine (1980) (W. Borders) *The Fire this Time for the British*, September 14.

Patrick, J. (1973) *A Glasgow Gang Observed*, Bristol: Eyre Methuen.

Pfautz, H. W. (1961) Near-Group Theory and Collective Behavior: A Critical Reformulation, *Social Problems*, **9**, 167-174.

Rainwater, L. (1966) Crucible of Identity: The Negro Lower-class Family, *Daedalus*, **95**, 172-216.

Rosen, R. (1972) *Language and Class: A Critical Look at the Theories of Basil Bernstein*, Bristol: Falling Wall Press.

Scott, P. (1956) Gangs and Delinquent Groups in London. *British Journal of Delinquency*, **7**, 4-24.
5-19.167-174.1172-216.4-24.4-24.

Short, J. F. (Ed.) (1968) *Gang Delinquency and Delinquent Subcultures*, New York: Harper and Row.

Stevenson, R. (1978) *Sex Pistols File*, Suffolk: Panda Press.

Thrasher, F. M. (1963) *The Gang*. Chicago: University of Chicago Press. (Originally published 1927.)

Wallace, M. (1978) *Black Macho and the Myth of Superwoman*, New York: Dial Press.

Willis, P. (1975) *How Working Class Kids Get Working Class Jobs*, Birmingham: Centre for Contemporary Cultural Studies, Stencilled Occasional Paper.

Yablonsky, L. (1962) *The Violent Gang*, New York: Macmillan.

Young, M. & Willmott, P. (1957) *Family and Kinship in East London*, Harmondsworth: Penguin.

Anne Crawford Campbell, Ph.D.
Harkness Fellow, School of Criminal Justice,
Rutgets University, Newark, NJ07102, U.S.A.

[7]

American Gangs and British Subcultures: A Commentary

R. G. Whitfield

As this highly topical article comparing English and American gang structures and sub-cultures originates from the United States, we thought it appropriate to ask **Mr. Whitfield,** *a distinguished member of the Probation Service, to provide a commentary, which is printed below (The Editors).*

This is an ambitious paper in that it tries to account for apparent transatlantic differences in adolescent group behaviour by reference to a much broader social, economic and political canvas. With the under 21's accounting for something like half of those found guilty of indictable offences and with the bulk of juvenile offending taking place in small groups this must be an area of considerable interest. But how does it seem from this side of the Atlantic? Are the differences as marked as the authors claim and, if so, what are the implications?

From a British standpoint if it is true that gangs are not a part of the youth scene then this is surely a fairly recent phenomenon, for the literature of the 19th and 20th century contains plenty of reference to gang delinquency—groups like the Gonophs, Fagins Gang or the Swell Mob—and from the accounts given by men like Mayhew and Chesney they would seem to have met the requirements of the definition used in this paper. More recently, Hells Angels, who seem to have been superseded by the more peaceful Bikers, have certainly displayed a rigid structure, hierarchy and allocated roles as the hallmark of their operations.

If true gangs are no longer a part of the British scene, as the authors claim, have they, then, disappeared as part of a larger pattern of social change? This, it seems to me, is where the argument is weakest for I think any British reader would take issue with the rigid class structure portrayed by the authors. I do not think it has been true for twenty years and, in fact, observation of current subcultures produces some support for this. By basing themselves on a specific style of music, dress or ideas groups can and do surmount class boundaries much more effectively than those traditional gangs based on geographical territory.

One possible answer is that gangs are subcultures writ small; understandable, workable sub-divisions of a larger life-style which accepts a much greater degree of cross-class mobility than the authors of this paper allow. It may be that membership is not particularly stable or permanent; that affiliations may vary and loyalties

American Gangs and British Subcultures: A Commentary 91

change but the work of Patrick,[1] Welsh[2] and others suggests that we should not allow our preoccupation with the more obvious aspects of subcultures to decide that the gang is necessarily defunct.

On an ordinary Saturday in any large city in Britain a keen observer can still pick out groups of Skinheads, Rockabillies, Punks, Mods, Rude Boys, Bikers and Rockers, quite apart from the separate ethnic groups which exist in some areas. Apart from a desire to belong, to find security and identity in a group independent of the family, what does it all mean? When the first Mods and Rockers burst on an unsuspecting public with incidents of Bank Holiday violence, investigators into the phenomenon (and there were many) generally reached much the same conclusion; that the participants were not necessarily delinquent but they were bored with their lives aimless, so that casual violence of the kind they seemed to enjoy provided the necessary excitement and interest which were otherwise missing.

Life seems to have become much more complicated in the 17 years since that rash of trouble and so, too, has the variety of subcultures which abound. The authors of this paper are certainly right in identifying the way that most groups reject middle class values and conservative ideas in an increasingly cynical way. They are wrong, I think, to attribute this cynicism to disadvantaged, working class youth alone. Some of the most articulate and critical voices have come from other backgrounds, yet still been very much a part of the subculture from which they articulate their ideas. The result has seemed to some observers to have disturbing implications in a wider context than mere delinquency:

> *"All healthy societies can tolerate dissent, even vigorous dissent and the amount they can tolerate is often a good guide to the health of the society; but few can tolerate more than a minimal quantity of total rejection without becoming distinctly uneasy at what might happen if the rejection spread."*[3]

That rejection is all too apparent in the authors' survey—and in their foreboding about likely developments.

A whole range of sociologists—and particularly American ones, including Cohen, Matza, Ohlin, Miller and Cloward—have been fascinated by the phenomenon of group delinquency but it cannot be said that their findings conform to any neat pattern. Summar-

1. Patrick, J. (1973) *A Glasgow Gang Observed,* UK: Eyre Methuen.

2. Welsh, S. (1981) The Kid—The Manufacture of Excitement in Police-Juvenile Encounters, *British Journal of Criminology,* 21, 3.

3. Levin, B. (1972) *The Pendulum Years,* UK: Pan.

ising the evidence, Radzinowicz and King* noted:

> *"Boys drift in and out of gangs, in and out of crime and even the most troublesome spend most of their time surrounded by adults and conforming to their views. . ."*

The influence of the gang, they suggest, is much more limited (on both sides of the Atlantic) than sociologists or criminologists would have us believe. Only a small fraction of young people belong, at any stage, to what could be classed as a delinquent gang. Most of those experience it as a transient phase and certainly group offences become much less common as offenders grow older.

But Radzinowicz and King also quote Walter Miller's study of six American cities—referred to in this paper—which estimated a total of 2,700 gangs with 80,000 members and predicted continuing growth over the next few years. If we in Britain are to be similarly affected, the implications for crime rates and policing in large urban areas need to be looked at afresh. The authors of this study suggest that social, political and class differences have spared us the worst features of adolescent gangs in the past, but are unlikely to do so now that both economic problems and political responses in the U.K. and the U.S.A. are so similar. Whether one accepts their argument or not, we should do well to learn from the American experience and keep this important issue under review.

*Radzinowicz and King (1977) *The Growth of Crime*, UK: Hamish Hamilton.

(*R. G. Whitfield*)

[8]

'Hanging Around the Street': Australian Rockers, Sharpies and Skinheads of the 1960s and early 1970s.

Judith Bessant

The student movement, the New Left, 'cultural radicalism' and an insurgent 'youth culture' provide central points of reference for the ways in which popular memory and academic accounts understand and recall the 1960s and early 1970s.[1] These characteristic forms of social and political expressivity were no doubt important, even if historians differ about the significance of this period.[2] This article sets out to provide a counter-balance to the social history of 'youth' and the ways we have come to represent the 1960s and early 1970s in terms of distinctive forms of 'youth culture'. It focuses on the lives of young people whose experiences were either largely ignored at the time, or have since been mostly erased from the histories of that period.[3] It specifically challenges a dominant interpretation which has limited the representation of collective youth action of these two decades to the protesting students and to the anti-war and peace movements. It argues that we have a richer history in the 1960s and in the early 1970s of collective youth action and group formations than has been so far recognised by historians.

A more comprehensive picture of that period and an account of the history of 'youth' needs to be inclusive of the experiences of young people in the 1960s and early 1970s associated with groups of sharpies, the mods, rockers and skinheads.

Within our 'historical imagination' lies the desire to tell as much as possible about the whole story. Social revisionist historians of the 1960s took note of E.H. Carr's assertion that history was the story told by or about the winners, and their concern was to get into the historical records 'the views from below'.[4] That has generated an enormous 'new social history', which recognises the roles and experiences of marginalised groups like women, gays, blacks and others. However, for some groups of people the 'normal' assumptions and processes that inform history writing continue to restrict access to historical recognition.

The tendency not to remember the inconvenient or unpleasant collective memories of the past may be especially relevant for a generation of historians and writers, who reached maturity in the 1960s and 1970s, and who in many cases actively participated in the politics of that time, and who also now play a central role in the production of history and theory.[5] An understandable pride in the

1. See V. Burgmann, *Power and Protest: Movements for Change in Australian Society*, Allen & Unwin, Sydney, 1993; R. Gerster and J .Basset, *Seizures of the Sixties, The Sixties and Australia*, Hyland House, Melbourne, 1991; G. Langley, *A Decade of Dissent: Vietnam and the Conflict on the Australian Home Front*, Sydney 1992; I. Turner, 'The Vietnam Moratorium', *Meanjin*, vol. 29, no. 2, 1970, p.243; J. Cockington, *Mondo Weirdo; Australia in the Sixties*, Melbourne, 1992.
2. See G. Langley, *A Decade of Dissent*, Sydney, 1992, pp.x-xii.
3. D. Dunphy, *Cliques, Crowds and Gangs*, Melbourne, 1969 which offers (pp.108-143) a case study of Rockers.
4. E.H. Carr, *What is History?*, Harmondsworth, 1968, p. 34.
5. At the time much of the social theory of the collective forms of social and political action were produced by activists like Warren Osmond, Terry Irving, Dennis Altmann, Kelvin Rowley, John Playford, Humphrey McQueen, whilst New Left journals like *Australian Left Review* and *Arena* regularly reflected on the experiences and strategies of the social movements. See for example, R. Mortimer, 'Student Action-out of Nihilism', *ALR*, April-May 1970, pp. 173-8 and D. O'Neill, 'Student Movement Strategy', *ALR*, 1 April-May 1970, pp. 150-191, and W. Osmond, 'Student Revolutionary Left', *Arena*, no.19, 1969, pp. 22-7; D. Altmann, 'Students in the Electric Age', *Arena*, no.21, 1971 pp. 3-18; H. McQueen, 'Three Tactics for Student Power', *Arena*, no.18, 1969 pp. 16-22, 1969, pp. 16-22; R. Gordon (ed.), *The Australian New Left*, Melbourne, 1970.

achievements of the the 1960s, and as well as a possible vanity may well have played a part in the way the story of the 1960s and 1970s has been told, especially in terms of what may be seen as the history of Australian youth cultures.[6] Nevertheless, there were many experiences lived by young Australians through the 1960s and 1970s that have been given insufficient attention in Australian social and political history, which this article hopes to rectify.

Contemporary accounts produced in the 1960s and early 1970s generally saw the emergence of a youth movement as coincidental with a general 'counter-culture' and identical to a significant political movement of opposition.[7] Rozsack's account of the 'counter-culture' equated a wide range of cultural, musical, literary and religious impulses of oppositionality with the restlessness, idealism, spiritual searching and the commitment to change that was seen to have been immanent amongst all young people.[8] In Australia, contemporaries saw in the music of protest, new life-styles among the young, new clothing and hair styles, and a general ambience of protest and challenge, local signs of a 'global' counter-culturalism.[9] For some critics, especially those aligned with local conservative networks, the counter-culture was a sign of imported enthusiasms by spoilt brats, or worse of sinister manipulation by agents of International Communism intent on fomenting Fifth Columnist activities.[10]

The North American march into a ground and air war in Indo-China after 1963, and the introduction in 1966 of conscription for service in Vietnam, was a major catalyst in the revival of a durable anti-war/anti-conscription tradition in Australia which began to attract significant student support by 1968.[11] A political movement was by the last years of the 1960s grounded in the student population of universities in both Western societies and among certain of the Eastern bloc countries especially Cszechoslovakia, Yugoslavia and Poland.[12] In the West, the emergence of the 'New left' announced itself in opposition to capitalism, the authoritarian state and the substance of the foreign policy of the Western alliance and the general effects of a souless and mindless consumerist capitalism.[13] In his book, *One Dimensional Man* (1968), Marcuse argued that under the conditions of late-capitalism, most elements of the social order were too heavily implicated in the benefits of consumerism to be able to want to revolt; only the truly marginalised like the young – and especially students – could become a truly oppositional source of political and cultural challenge to the world of instrumental rationality and oppressive tolerance.[14] In Australia, local radicals praised the youthful 'need' to dissent. Ian Turner spoke of how

6.   Authors such as Verity Burgmann, Michael Hamel-Green, Barry York, Stuart MacIntyre, Dennis Altmann and others who have produced Australian texts on this period, or on general issues of social theory and social change, were also activists at the time.
7.   See for example, M. Charlesworth, 'The youth revolution', *Meanjin Quarterly*, vol 28, Spring, 1969, pp. 391-97; P. Allan, 'The Student Revolt in Australia', *Economic Review*, 1969, pp.29-32; S. Encel, 'Anatomy of the Student Revolution', *Blackacre*, 1970, pp. 34-6; P. Blizzard, 'Students as Agents of Social Change in Higher Education', *Australian Journal of Social Issues*, vol 6, no.1, 1971, pp. 36-53; J. Edwards, 'The Counter Culture: Melbourne: Where the Alternative Society Quietly Swings', *Australian Financial Review*, 17 March 1971.
8.   T. Roszack, *The Making of a Counter Culture*, London, 1969.
9.   P. Morgan, The State of Student Protest, *Current Affairs Bulletin*, vol. 46, no. 8, 1970; R. Ireland, *Roots of Student radicalism*, La Trobe University, 1971; B.A. Sheil, 'Student Politics- Current research', *Politics*, vol. 5, May 1970, pp.81-2; J. Bornstein, 'Student Unrest and the Universities', *Monash Reporter*, no.3, May 1971, pp.5-6, and J. Berry, 'The Vietnam Marchers', in H. Mayer (ed.), *Australian politics- A Second Reader*, Melbourne, 1969, pp.205-7.
10.   See e.g. G. Henderson, 'The Derived Nature of the Australian New Left', *Quadrant*, December 1969, pp. 66-70, and G. Henderson, 'Student Protest in the 1960s – an Australian view', *20th century*, vol. 24, Autumn, 1970, pp. 260-78; B.A. Santamaria, 'Morality and the new Wave', *Social Survey*, vol. 19. no.7. August 1969, pp.20-8. and G. Hawkins, 'The Youth Rebellion – is it Really so New?', *Australian*, 25 August 1970.
11.   See J. Spigelman, 'Student Activism in Australia – A History', *The Bridge*, vol. 5 nos. 3-4, 1970, pp. 35-8; K. Dalton, Secondary Student Dissent, *Victorian Liberal Leader*, June 1969, p. 3.
12.   See G. Statera, *Death of a Utopia: The Development and Decline of Student Movements in Europe*, Oxford, 1975.
13.   T. Roszack, *The Making of a Counter Culture*, London, 1968.
14.   H. Marcuse, *One Dimensional Man*, Boston, 1968.

a culture and sensibility are being transformed before our eyes. Politics takes on new dimensions; the young no longer see themselves as apprentices to old power structures; they demand policies and institutions which are responsive to their needs.[15]

Not everyone was convinced then or now that the 'youth movement' was that important, or that significant a threat culturally or politically. By the early 1970s writers such as Adelman argued that 'youth culture' was nothing more than pop music, clothes, marijuana and Che Guevara posters, and that, what was popularly represented in the media as a major threat to the Western political and moral order was both more superficial and less political because it was merely the expression of indulgent middle-class adolescents.[16] Others saw the proliferation of opposition and counter-culture as a quasi-natural and/or universal antagonism between the generations that was best explained in psycho-analytic terms.[17] Others maintained that the scale and significance of the New left and the counter-culture was not as great as popularly believed.[18] This view has been repeated in the more recent writing of Gerster and Bassett, and Alomes.[19]

Bolton also characterised the 1960s and early 1970s by the predominance of these forms of youthful expressivity, stressing their limited effect and their derivative character. Young Australians with alternative social visions were attracted to the 'counter-culture.[20] Similarly, Cockington typified the 1960s by reference to the drenching effects of a far reaching 'youth culture'.[21] Memoirs of the period also stress the effect of the politics of the international student movements.[22]

More recent and specialist historical analysis confirms the dominant view that 'youth cultures' or 'youth movements' defined the special quality of the 1960s – especially when associated with overt forms of political opposition to war, to conscription and to Government policy. York, too, stressed the 'marriage of a distinct youth culture' with the student protest movement.[23] These interpretations stressed the social movement character of the anti-war and student movements.[24] Oral histories like Langley's emphasised the moral and political purpose of the participants in the 1960s' anti-war and anti-conscription movements.[25] York also stressed the 'marriage' of a distinct youth culture with the student protest movement.[26]

If we are to tell more of the story of young people and forms of collective actions they engaged in we must not forget the lives and the expressivity of other youth groups, especially those who did not join the anti-war movement or go to university or join the 'counter-culture'. Recovering the experiences of young, predominantly 'working-class' sharpies, rockers, mods, and skinheads is part of the larger, mostly untold story of the experiences of adolescence that the category of 'youth culture' has tried to encompass.

This article is concerned with young people in the 1960s and 1970s other than the university-based life-world of protesting students. It deals with the life-worlds

15.   I. Turner, 'The Vietnam Moratorium', *Meanjin*, vol. 29, 1970, pp.233-4.
16.   C. Adelman, *Generations: A Collage on Youth Culture*, Harmondsworth, 1972.
17.   L. J. Feuer, *Conflict of Generations*, London, 1973.
18.   G. Little, *The University Experience*, Melbourne, 1970.
19.   See R. Gerster, J. Bassett, *Seizures of Youth: The 'Sixties and Australia'*, Melbourne, 1991, and S. Alomes, 'Cultural Radicalism in the Sixties', *Arena*, no.62, 1983, pp. 36-7.
20.   G. Bolton, *The Middle Way, 1942-1988, Oxford History of Australia* (vol.5), Melbourne, 1990, pp.165-8 and pp.189-202.
21.   J. Cockington, *Mondo Weirdo: Australia in the Sixties*, Melbourne, 1992, p.x.
22.   R. Erlich in H. Dow (ed.), *More Memories of Melbourne University*, Melbourne, 1985, p.169.
23.   B. York, *Student Revolt: La Trobe University 1967-1973*, Campbell, 1989, p. 21.
24.   J. McCalman, *Struggletown: Public and Private Life in Richmond, 1900-1965*, Melbourne 1985.
25.   A theoretical version of this can be found in G. Katsiaficas, *The Imagination of the New Left*, Boston, 1987, pp.17-28.
26.   B. York, *Student Revolt: La Trobe University 1967-1973*, Campbell, 1989, p. 21.

Judith Bessant

of the rockers, sharpies, mods and skinheads. It draws on a tradition and style of social history that relied on 'non-traditional sources and methods, including oral history.[27] There is no literary record of substance or an archive of official and authoritative documentation which can permit the construction of a minimal chronology. There are no great events. There is not even a large sample of the kind the modern social scientist presume to be the minimum for providing a solid basis for drawing 'credible' inductive generalisations about the 'sample'. What there is is a small number of people who are prepared to talk about their lives as 'youth' in the 1960s and early 1970s, many years after the event. What we have are the memories connected to larger autobiographical projects that we all constantly work on in the making of ourselves and the telling of stories that assures our identity.

Allowing for caveats about a 'history from below' which relies on oral sources and fragile memories, there is much that can be said about the lives of the 1960s and early 1970s rockers, mods, sharpies and skinheads.[28] For the purposes of this article the central focus is on the collective identities of these groups. This includes analysis of the meanings attributed by those young people to group membership as a basis of individual claims to status and identity.

The intention here is to recover a semblance of the social life and patterns of meanings that were internal to the life-worlds of young people who entered into the certain collective behaviour of their group. 'Culture' means here what Clendinnen identified as 'the characteristic ways of apprehending, evaluating, enjoying and managing the world in greeting, eating, fighting, producing and reproducing'.[29] In this way this article can be best understood as an attempt to reconstruct the culture of these various groups of young people.[30] The intention is to recover some of the sensibilities of young people's lives.

The article addresses a limited number of themes. Given the social scientific and popular obsessions with adolescent 'gangs', which in Australia goes back at least to the larrikin phenomena, the question is asked whether group members saw themselves as part of a 'gang'?[31] Or, did they see themselves as just young people 'hanging out' in loose and informal groups? Alternatively, given the more recent work of social movement theorists like Touraine and Melucci, did they understand themselves as part of a social movement? And if so, how did they see this?

Social Context.

From the late 1950s to the early 1970s we saw a series of 'youth cultures', mainly in 'working class' areas in Australia's cities. The earliest group were the bodgies and widgies who first appeared in the 1940s and remained through much of the 1950s. The focus of this article, however, is on the rockers, who were followed by sharpies, mods and skinheads. Their emergence was part of a larger process of economic, social and cultural change in the post-war years.

Fundamental transformations in Australian urban development involved the extension of suburbs offering cheap housing. The *White Paper on Full Employment*

27.   See P. Thompson, *The Voice of the Past: Oral History*, Oxford, 1978, and J. Murphy, 'The Voice of Memory: History, Autobiography and Oral Memory, *Historical Studies*, 1986, pp. 157-75.
28.   For the caveats see P. O'Farrell, 'Oral History: Facts and Fiction', *Quadrant*, November 1979, pp. 4-8.
29.   I. Clendinnen, *Aztecs: An Interpretation*, Cambridge, 1991, p.2.
30.   ibid.
31.   See J. Murray, *Larrikins: A Nineteenth Century Outrage*, Melbourne, 1975.

(1945) ushered in full (male) employment. Australia enjoyed progressive extension of what is now referred to as Fordist culture based on the interdependence of mass advertising, mass media, especially television after 1956, and the mass production of an array of new and affordable consumer goods, such as automobiles all of which provided a material frame in which to situate the elements of an emergent youth market.[32] This youth market was based on market differentiation of music, clothing, film and media production, fashion and popular entertainments for young people which determined to a large extent cultural differentiation. It engaged the availability of adolescent and young adult leisure time to maintain the various forms of 'youth culture'. This leisure time co-existed with an extension of mass secondary schooling for more and more Australian adolescents and on the consolidation of youth labour market, based jointly on the apprenticeship systems and on the ready availability of plentiful, low-status but steady full-time employment for 15-22 year olds. Australia through the 1950s and 1960s maintained a high level of male employment and a standard of per capita income enjoyed by only four or five other countries in the pattern and content of working and leisure lives which all provided an essential framework for the emergence of distinctive adolescent cultures. These cultures had a lot to do with the evolution of new forms of commodification involving clothing, music and 'fashion'.[33]

Were the emergence of 'youth cultures' during and after the 1950s just a reactive response by young people to advertising and production pressures and how much were they an autonomous and shaped response by young people?[34] Stratton's account of the bodgies emphasises the hegemony of production and consumption processes and the role of the media in constructing images of 'normal teenagers' and 'deviant and threatening teenagers' like the bodgies and widgies through the 1950s.[35]

In terms that have become very popular ways of thinking since Cohen's work on 'moral panics', and to the extent that the media of the 1960s noticed the existence of the mods, rockers and sharpies, it would be possible to replicate the kind of account which Stratton, Pearson and others have presented which focuses on the ways the media represented the threatening elements of youth cultures.[36] Such an account would tell how the media of the 1960s were content to slot the mods, rockers and sharpies into the true and tried formula of 'young mobsters and hooligans'. Fights in public places amongst groups of young people made for wonderful street theatre and even better opportunities for news coverage and commentary. By the mid-1960s the main 'youth cults', the mods and sharpies, had been involved in what the press referred to as mod/sharpie wars. 'Ugly stitched bottle gashes across the abdomen', broken noses and hospitalisation were the 'scars of war'. This was accompanied by heroic tales of regaining consciousness in the gutter with injuries to the head and 'a bunch of long hairs standing there laughing'.[37] Constant policepatrols were 'obviously' needed to keep 'mobs of

32.   S. Alomes, M. Dober, D. Hellier, 'The Social Context of Post-war Conservatism', in A. Curthoys, J. Merritt (eds), *Australia's First Cold War, 1945-1953*, Sydney, 1984, and P. Spearritt, *Sydney Since the Twenties*, Sydney, 1978.
33.   S. Ewen, *Captains of Consciousness*, New York, 1976.
34.   For a view which stresses the dominance of new modes of production and consumption, culturally mediated by the experience of the American presence after 1941 see J. Stratton, *The Young Ones Working Class Culture, Consumption and the Category of Youth*, pp.59-86; See J. Savage, *England's Dreaming: Sex pistols and Punk Rock*, London, 1991.
35.   J. Stratton, 'Bodgies and Widgies: Just Working Class Kids Doing Working Class Things', in R. White (ed.), *Youth Subcultures*, p. 88.
36.   See here, S. Cohen, *Moral Panics and Folk Devils*, Oxford, 1979, and G. Pearson, *Hooligan: A History of Respectable Fears*, London, 1987.
37.   *Pix/People*, 18 July 1974, p.8.

teenagers' on the move.[38] The press were interested when one hundred mods and
sharpies milled around the Southern Cross Hotel. Police broke up several
skirmishes before the mods and sharpies could organise their gangs. Law
enforcement agencies and the press reinforced the image of these groups as highly
dangerous, warranting extra caution and police powers to ensure public safety.[39]

While there are important issues that such an account raises, I suggest that the
experiences of young sharpies or skinheads had an authenticity that cannot be
deconstructed as a media-driven reflex. As has been argued elsewhere, too much of
the 'youth studies' tradition has been influenced by a certain style of sociology.[40]
This tradition has constructed the social actions of young people as an effect or
constrained consequence of structures such as class, gender, ethnicity. Following
the ethnographic tradition, this account focuses on the life-worlds and the
categories of the young people themselves. [41]

Who were they?

Each of the groups or 'sub-cultures' represented here had a high level of self-
consciousness. In terms of gender composition, rockers, sharpies, skinheads and
mods were predominantly male-dominated groups, with the male-female ratio
varying according to the particular time and group. The age of members ranged
from twelve years to those in their early twenties. The majority were in their mid
to late-teens. The ethnic background of group members was mainly Anglo-Saxon.
This was especially prominent in the case of skinhead groups whose identity was
derived in part from their vehement racism. Exclusionary practices on ethnic
grounds were common. Greeks, Italians and 'Asians' were generally not permitted
to join in, but instead often became the target of a violent 'bit of fun' or on
occasion, the objects of outright assault.

The people in this study lived either at home with their parents or
independently. There were also some whose living arrangements were restricted to
prison or youth detention centres. Family backgrounds did not vary. Most came
from self-described 'working-class' families. The education credentials of all
interviewees were 'limited' to mid-secondary school. Most left school at the
compulsory leaving age of 15 or 16 and most of the males then went out to work
as unskilled or semi-skilled labourers – in a factory, in the service sector or as an
apprentice. All of those interviewed worked full-time in their youth. Nearly all
spoke with considerable distaste about their years within the schooling system,
expressing hatred for most (but not all) teachers, a dislike for the way in which
authority and power was wielded in the schools, and what they saw as the futility
of their formal 'learning' experiences.

Rockers.

Rockers had been around for a long time by the 1960s. In most respects they
represent the continuation into the 1960s of the bodgie and widgie style. Dunphy
noted that, 'With their black jeans, striped sweaters and long greasy hair, the

38.   *Sun*, 15 August 1966; See also, Sun, 13 August 1966, Mods describe sharpies as 'trouble stirrers'.
39.   *Sun*, 22 August 1966.
40.   See A. Giddens, *Central Problems in Social Theory*, London, 1979, pp.50-1.
41.   A. Schutz, *Collected Papers*, 1964 p. 85.

rockers were typical bodgies'.[42] They were known for their enjoyment of both 'Latin American style' dancing and American rock and roll. As well as older siblings, many rockers of the 1960s also had fathers who provided 'rocker' role models and an introduction to rocker life. As young men those fathers saw themselves as 'the original' rockers and the first young Australians to be riding motor bikes and wearing leather jackets.[43] According to some accounts, rockers remained popular in some areas until the hippies started appearing in the late 1960s. Rivalry amongst some of the groups was strong which meant rockers spent quite some time fighting opposition groups such as the sharpies and in Sydney the surfies. In the early 1960s, as a Mod, 'Warren', saw what he believed to have been the tail end of the rockers epoch:

> In our generation there were still a few rockers around who would have been a few years older than us. They grew up on the end of the rocker era. Their big brothers were in the middle of the rocker era ... We thought, 'oh' fancy being a rocker. They had their own areas ... They had rocker dances ... We wouldn't go there for all the tea in China.[44]

Sharpies.
Sharpies emerged in the early to mid-1960s. They also were similar in many ways to their bodgie-widgie predecessors. Their home grounds, family and social backgrounds were the same as the bodgie-widgies of a generation earlier; their stylish expression in clothing was also similar.

The sharpies, called so because of their sharp, neat hair cuts, short on top and long at the back, and smart looking dress to almost respectable, 'now numbered about 200' in one area of Melbourne.[45] 'They used to wear cress neck T-shirts with white collars and tweed pants, not pegged (like the bodgie), but straight legged and sometimes baggy.'[46] Male and female sharpie dress was very similar except for the T-shirts and preference for corked platform shoes by the girls. The 'Sharps' or sharpies, like the bodgie-widges of the 1940s and 1950s lived mainly in inner city suburban areas; they wore short regularly trimmed hair. Sharpies were also like the earlier bodgies, and rockers and the later skins, in terms of their music, clothing styles, their 'disadvantaged working-class' background and the emphasis on toughness and masculinity.[47]

Sharpies like bodgies and widgies, had exaggerated outward conventions in terms of their physical appearance. Their clothes, hair and general styles were highly 'expressive'. They were fastidious to the point of obsession about 'the correctness' of their appearance; they wore clothes that were extremely expensive in proportion to their low incomes.

> As sharpies we took pride in what we wore. It used to cost a bit. I used to get about $70 a week pay. We got our pants tailor made. Through our clothing we let it be known we were sharpies.[48]

42.   D.Dunphy, *Cliques, Crowds and Gangs*, p.108.
43.   Interview, Stephen, January 1991.
44.   Interview, Warren, September 1993.
45.   *Sun*, 10 January 1966.
46.   Interview, Stephen Kelly, January 1991; See also, *Sun*, 13 August 1966.
47.   *Australian Womens Weekly*, 13 July 1966, p.60.
48.   Interview, David, August 1993.

Judith Bessant

The preoccupation with style and the gendered relations is epitomised in 'Alannah's' experience of sharpie life as 'a unisex thing'.

Cuffed pants, roman sandals were the shoes that were 'in' then – as well as platforms ... Cardigans with emblems on either side. 'Short hair ... scissor cut and flat over with one side parted – very Mia Farrow. We didn't go to the hairdressers, we went to the barbers to have our hair cut with the guys. We'd have our hair cut all the same – all on the same Saturday morning. We'd have our hair cut every two weeks because we couldn't let it grow too long.'[49]

Sharpie clothing was precise and immaculately tailored. Many did not wear jeans preferring tailored blue pin stripped and baggie trousers with 'Miller' western-styled shirts and a 'connie' cardigan with a coloured stripe across it. Platform shoes three to four inches high made sharpies look tall, although they were also said to be extremely difficult to walk in. 'Acropolis' platform shoes were top of the range for boys only, girls instead wore 'corkies' which went well with their tent dresses and under-sized T-shirts.[50] 'Treads' were another type of sharpie shoe, called so because the sole was made from the treat of the car tyre, and laced across the top of the foot. Those shoes were worn mainly by an off-shoot of the sharpies, 'the Droogs' who were a softer version of the sharpie – a cross between the sharpies and surfies.[51] Sharpies liked to be what they saw as 'smart looking' and perfect in their presentation almost to a point of parodying 'the proper, respectable' middle and upper classes. In the minds of some, they dressed too well.[52] They often imitated 'posh dress' to the point of burlesque mockery, whereby their own styles became a parody, a laughing impersonation, which could be read as expressive political statements.

Mods

Mods emerged in Australia in the mid-1960s heavily influenced by English fashion. Part of their style included bell-bottomed pants. They were seen as and saw themselves as 'smart' dressers. In the mind of one 14-year-old girl, the mods were 'really with it, but they still looked neat and tidy'. Their mod gear looks fab.'[53] The girls wore high R.M.William boots with pointy toes like the boys. They also wore blouses, skirts and jackets, and their shoulder-length hair was in a bobby style, curled up and under slightly. 'Sparkly' lipstick and make up lightly applied was also part of the image. The 'Cilla Black hair do, a 'bobbed short' style with a heavy fringe and 'side bangs'.[54] There was also a later Mod revival in the 1970s which ran across the sharpie era and paralleled the punks.

Skinheads

Of the four groups, the skinheads acquired early on a notoriety that has not waned. Skinheads appeared in Australia in the early 1970s.[55] Some sharpie groups based aspects of their style on the skinheads and vice versa. However, despite the

49. Interview, Alannah, (sharpie) 7 September 1993.
50. Interview, Debbie, January 1994.
51. ibid.
52. J. Tanner, New Directions For Subcultural Theory: An Analysis of British Working-class Youth Culture, in *Youth and Society*, vol. 9. June, 1978, pp.343-371.
53. *Australian Women's Weekly*, 18 May 1966, p.80.
54. *Australian Women's Weekly*, 1 June 1966, p.59; See also, The *Australian Women's Weekly*, 21 April 1965, p. 32; *The Australian Women's Weekly*, 12 May 1965, p.7.
55. Interview, Debbie, January 1994. For an account of the English experience see, M. Brake, The Skinheads: An English Working Class, *Youth and Society*, December 1974, pp.178-229.

similarities there was a general recognition amongst 'types' that skinheads were distinct and quite different from 'others'. There were subtle and clear markers of separateness. There were, for example, certain behaviour that non-skinheads did not engage in such as overt acts of racism. 'They [skinheads] hated anything that wasn't Australian.'[56] The clothing styles also symbolised a difference; they had visible markers: such as Doc Martin boots and shaven heads often with peroxide fronts or tails that went down their back. Skinheads wore canvas jeans, very rarely baggies like the sharpies and never 'treads'. 'Like the bikies it didn't matter how hot the weather was skinheads wore only long pants and heavy boots and often a jacket.'[57]

Being Part of the Group: Claims to space.

'Youth culture studies' have for a long time argued that for 'working-class' young people, claiming space, especially public or street space, has been an integral aspect of the politics of opposition. More strongly argued has been the popular preoccupation, shadowed by academic treatments of youth cultures, with the formation and activities of adolescent 'gangs'. While this has been a characteristic of American scholarship it is also a feature of British and Australian 'youth studies'.[58] It seems reasonable to conclude on the basis of this study that collective identity and collective action were important to the various groups of young people of the 1960s, although this does not support a notion of a virulent gang culture.

However, pointing to identity and claims over territory is not a distinguishing feature that can be used to divide off 'youth cultures' from 'the rest'. The language used to describe that space gives it special significance in the lives of those who live within it. The claims we make on particular places indicate that we draw on aspects of our human condition about which we feel very deeply and which give space significance, and which we proceed to fill-up with special and expressive activities and signs in which (amongst other things) our identity and our status are embodied and encoded. Because this is true for young people should not be a special surprise, although it has for a long time been a major source of annoyance and anxiety on the part of adults and owners of 'private property'.

Rival Brisbane sharpies and mod 'gangs' embodied their identity and separateness in their own respective places and 'gig spots'.[59] In Melbourne 'Warren' recalled

> ... lots of ... fights in the city. We used to go to discos like Sebastians. They were at the top end of town around Exhibition street. The sharpies were up around Southern Cross and Bourke street, Spring street. That was their side of town. We'd be walking up one way and the opposition would be walking the other way ... and then the fun would start and we'd run like hell.[60]

'Claiming' space was connected to identity. Certain locations were private, exclusive, almost sacred. For one sharpie group the Hampton beach on Port Phillip Bay was one such place. There was one special wall where most times of the day and night through the 1960s a particular group of young people, would meet regularly and sit around, drinking, smoking and catching up on the latest news. It

56.   Interview, Graham, August 1993.
57.   Interview, Debbie, January 1994.
58.   Australian studies like D. Dunphy, *Cliques, Crowds and Gangs*, pp.108-143 emphasised the gang character of Rockers. See also, P. Wilson (ed.) *Delinquency in Australia*, St. Lucia, 1977, pp.55-69; J. Walker, *Louts and Legends*, Sydney, 1988; and R. White, *No Space of their Own*, 1991.
59.   *Courier Mail*, 25 June 1967 (Interview with 17 year old).
60.   Interview, Warren, September 1993.

Judith Bessant

was a special congregating area for young people who enjoyed sitting along the wall, talking to each other.[61]

Where the groups came from and thus belonged geographically were important determining factors for their self-identity and for their social lives. Dunphy argued that for Manly rockers of the 1960s the places they hung out – and didn't hang out – were vital parts of the rockers' identity. For these young men, the wharf at Manly was the place to be and the nearby surf was the place to avoid.[62]

The importance of territory was evident in the 'need' felt by members to signal where they came from by wearing the name of their suburb printed boldly on the front of their T-shirts. Such messages not only stated a claim to certain space, but also declared to others their identity by reference to that territory. Signaling that information affirmed for group members a sense of belonging and solidarity.

> We were called Sharpies. We used to wear T-shirts with our suburbs and 'sharps' underneath to say where we came from.'[63]

Where the groups came from determined how group members saw and named themselves. There were for example the Borough Boys, the Melbourne Mods, the Bondi boys, the Heidelberg Boys, or the Richmond Sharpies.

Many rocker, sharpie, mod and skinhead groups emerged from previously formed friendship, family and local community-neighbourhood groups where group members grew up together, went to the same schools, clubs and football matches. Loyalty to their home turf and a strong sense of belonging to particular suburbs, specific streets or other locales such as shops, 'spots' on the beach were powerful influences in the constitution of collective identities and the building of group loyalty, solidarity and cohesiveness. For the Manly Rockers this even included a strong sense of affinity with the older men who worked on the wharves whose casual life and work cycles were as attractive as the sense of tribal loyalty from the old men to the young men, a loyalty which questions the traditional sociological view of youth cultures and generational politics as maintaining strict age-based boundaries.

> One night ... Ken was drunk and so was John and we had a bit of trouble with the surfies. The other wharfies ... and we all know each other. They're the same as us. The older wharfies are always fighting the surfies. If any of us smaller kids get into trouble with the surfies, the older boys grab 'em and there's a great brawl on.[64]

Territory provided an important marker of identity and putative status. Just as fundamental was appearance and style. Wearing the right clothes meant acceptance into the group. Without the correct garb no one would talk to you. Mods, however, contrasted dramatically with both the sharpie, rocker, skinhead and even punk groups. Part of the Mod 'attitude' was to look soft, non-masculine, 'respectable' and 'neat'; not tough or 'scruffy' like the sharpies and certainly not down and out like the later punks. Their approach was also not to reject mainstream fashion like the later punk of the 1980s, but rather to embarrass it with an over-the-top enthusiasm.

61.   Interview, Brad, September 1993.
62.   Dunphy, op.cit., p.113.
63.   Interview, Graham, August 1993.
64.   Dunphy, op.cit., p.114.

Being Mod was a huge fashion statement ... It was underground and I think that was important. You felt like you were the first there. It was a very tribal thing ... I worked, we weren't into thieving... That was the Mod philosophy, it wasn't like punks. Punks expected to be on the dole. You're not meant to have middle class punks are you? The mods were meant to look very middle class. You weren't meant to look like you were on the dole and a dirt bag. You had to look clean. You had to look respectable. You had to look different, but respectable.[65]

One's map of the universe was drafted according to where one stood as an individual member within one's group and where one's particular group/s stood in relation to others. As Warren explained: 'We thought we were above the sharpie. We used to wear designer jackets, the stuff they used to wear was pretty rotten ... As far as the Mods were concerned, Mods were at the top, sharpies underneath and the rockers down the bottom of the ladder.'[66]

Mods who had the capacity to anticipate, and to the limited extent that was possible, to set local fashion trends, offered a form of leadership to their peers. Their ability to 'set the trends' meant that they became models for others to follow and enjoyed the high status that came with such a role. It was important for a leading Mod to be 'cool', to be what they called a 'face' which implied acute awareness of the subtleties in Mod fashion.

We tried to be a face ... A face is a person that other people looked up to, not so much a cult leader but some-one who knows what's going on, how to dress well, knows what is going to be fashionable ... That's what mods called 'a face' ... They were the best at dressing ... [67]

Groups and Inclusion-Exclusion.

Group identity was sharply delineated within the dynamics of intergroup rivalry. Justification for membership was couched mostly in terms of self-protection and mutual support and justified by repetitive provocations where conflict could be generated and thus vindicate the *raison d'être*.

Inner city and suburban young people 'hung out' together 'to survive'; an important attraction of gang or group life was said to have been the protection that numbers provided. Groups varied in their size from twenty to fifty young people who would walk around the streets together, and on special occasions like dances there were often many more gathered together. As well as safety, there was a sense of power gained from belonging to a big group.

When you've got that many people together, it's an army, you can do anything you like, no-one is going to touch you.[68]
There would be mutual respect. If you came from St Kilda that was it. Prahran, St Kilda and Collingwood they were the strong ones ... they were the toughest, the craziest.[69]

Solidarity, a sense of belonging and the protection that membership to particular groups attracted young people like 'Brad' who became a member of a sharpie 'gang' in the 1960s. To 'Brad' the local sharpies were a 'terrific and tough gang'.

65.   Interview, Ian, June 1992.
66.   Interview, Warren, September 1993.
67.   Interview, Terry, August 1993.
68.   Interview Brad, (sharpie) 4 September 1993.
69.   ibid.

Judith Bessant

> A sense of belonging to an organisation...[was] always very strong ... Everyone
> wants to belong to something ... It's in our nature – belonging, especially for
> kids... and to belong to something was very special. And especially if no-one else
> could belong too ... You *had* to be a sharpie, it was as simple as that.[70]

Protection was a vital factor for a 'quality life' within their immediate socio-
economic and cultural contexts. For 'Rick' being in a gang provided both security
and freedom of movement that was otherwise not possible within his antecedent
social setting.

> You had a lot of resentment on the streets towards people who were into punk
> rock. That's why we'd hang around in groups our own kind. You could travel
> places then [within the groups] and you didn't have to do it surreptitiously.[71]

The group gave protection not only from hostile 'youth groups' but also from
the police. When needed they also gave support, security and reassurance in times
of domestic, family and economic strife. Group members were fiercely loyal to each
other both collectively as well as individually – 'to mates'. 'You always stood by your
mates! Right or wrong, you'd always support them no matter what'. [72] Loyalty was
vital for maintaining the cohesiveness of the group – and individual identity.

Rick's identity as a gang member relied considerably on acknowledgment by
others that he belonged to a particular group. Being publicly viewed and associated
with 'his group', being recognised as part of it made him '... feel pretty cool
walking down the street ... I liked the reactions. People would avoid you. It was
always better to get any reaction. I did not want to blend in'.[73] The responses of
others re-affirmed in Rick's mind who he was. It made him feel proud and strong
to be identified as part of a 'gang' with such a tough reputation.

Stephen's experience was similiar. Living in Eltham, a semi-rural Melbourne
suburb in the 1960s, most of his mates came from 'in town'. Reflecting on 'the
qualities' of 'the city guys', he described them as 'real survivors'. Most of those he
mixed with came from the inner city Housing Commission flats and they had to be
tough to survive in 'that world'.

> ...[the sharps] came from places like Collingwood. And they all had maroon cars,
> really light maroon cars and they had umbrellas and the points were really sharp
> and they used to stab you in the leg, not enough to damage you, but enough to
> really hurt. They came twice and it was pretty even [the fights], and there was the
> third time I wasn't there. I was going up the country with a mate and I slept at his
> place in Heidelberg and went up to get the paper that morning and right across
> the front page was 'Eltham – wild brawl'.[74]

Gangs or Social Movements?

Since the 1970s a counter-response in social theory associated with the work of
Melucci and Touraine has seen contemporary transformations as more than simply
that to do with labour-economic domains. Touraine and Melucci see such
collective energies as directed towards the creation of innovative cultural forms,

70.   ibid.
71.   Interview, Rick, September 1993.
72.   Interview, Tony, July 1993.
73.   Interview, Rick, September 1993.
74.   Interview with Stephen, January 1991.

ways of living and struggles over control in shaping public life and cultural patterns of meaning.[75] This approach has seen the dissolution of older narratives about society in which most of youth studies has been constituted. This shift towards a theory of social action also has important consequences for rewriting the history of 'youth' and in particular youth politics as a field of social action.

Social movements contest to establish identities that have a capacity for action in opposition to the dominant forms of identities – shaping forces.[76] Basic to our contemporary ways of living is social conflict or contest centred around the ability to shape and create cultural models. In this sense the notion of social movement provides a more insightful understanding of the life-worlds of rockers sharpies, mods and skinheads, than do the more popular and limited concepts of 'youth culture' that rely on the notion of structurally determined responses either to 'society', 'capitalism', 'patriarchy' etc.

The flexibility of group membership, to a large extent, determined whether groups saw themselves as a 'gang' or not. Not having a closed or at least a restricted membership meant for some that they were not a gang. The relative ease with which members joined and left meant that they were not a gang, but rather a loose group or collective of young people who liked each other's company and some of the same things. Terry's group was '... called 'the Melbourne Mods'. We didn't think of ourselves as a gang, you had people who were floating in and out all the time.'[77]

The loose sense of association is well represented:

> [We were] ... all pretty much affiliated. It was all one scene, but we used to hang out in our own areas with our friends. You could say there was a division between you and another punk group, but you were all associated ... My area was north and central Perth. There were about 50 to 60 in the group in my area. They used to have every year this thing called a punk picnic. We'd all get together, every single one of us ... That was a pretty bizarre event for a groups of anarchists. We'd also see each other at social activities, at parties, pubs and other places.[78]

Although the term 'gang' was frequently used in the interviews, when questioned the dominant view was that gangs were more structured than 'just groups' and had restricted membership, leaders and clear although often informal rules of behaviour.

'Terry' saw his Mod group not as a gang; a 'gang' to his mind was closed and formal. The Melbourne Mods 'were more of a movement ... I followed that movement and they called it an alternative movement.'[79]

> We used to knock around with the Chelt guys a bit ... If I was in a group I would have been in Moorabbin even though I lived in Hampton. It changed around. I'd go with different groups around the joint. It depended on where you were and what you did. Then I had other mates who were not sharps.[80] There wasn't a set amount of people. It was just who you were with. You had your friends, your

75. A. Touraine, *The Voice and the Eye: An Analysis of Social Movements*, Cambridge, 1981; See also, A Touraine, *The Post-Industrial Society: Tomorrow's Social History: Classes, Conflict and Culture in the Programmed Society*, London, 1974; J.Keane, P. Mier, (eds) *Alberto Melnni, Nomads of the Present: Social Movements and Individual Needs in Contemporary Society*, London, 1989.
76. J. Gusfield (ed.) *Protest, Reform and Revolt: A Reader in Social Movements*, New York, 1970; H. Toch, *The Social Psychology of Social Movements*, London, 1966.
77. Interview, Terry, August 1993.
78. Interview, Rick, September 1993.
79. Interview, Terry, August 1993.
80. Interview, Brad, (sharp), 4 September 1993.

Judith Bessant

mates and then there were acquaintances and sometimes one wouldn't be there and some-one else would. There were groups throughout the whole area – there might be 30 of you, there might not be all of you at once. There might be a group in town and you might be in a group of ten in another pub some where.[81]

The 1960s groups boundaries were not rigid, but porous and easily penetrated. The terms of association allowed for the frequent and unchallenged comings and goings of members. The fluidity of some groups also meant that someone could belong to one or a number of compatible groups, often at the one time. For inner city sharpie groups like Brad's membership 'changed around considerably'. 'Attributes' such as the group's status, toughness, style and strength formed the basis for relations between the groups: 'I'd be with different groups around the joint. It depended on where you were and what you did. Then I [also] had mates who weren't sharps.'[82]

Crossing over from one group to another, or even multiple memberships was common; and movement between certain types of groups was also considered to be quite acceptable within certain limits. As Graham explained: 'There were a couple of skinheads who wanted to be sharpies because their groups and area went a bit silly. We [sharps] influenced them in the end and a lot came over to us.'[83]

Music was a powerful force that crossed many group boundaries. Hair styles and the fun involved in experimenting with looks also brought some young people together. Although the 'bobby cut' was popular amongst some girl Mods, female Mods also played with 'harder sharp and skin looks':

> [We] experimented with the 'rude look'. A lot of girls were a cross over between skinheads [and mods]. You had the 'rude girls and the rude boys ... They had skinhead bloke style hair cuts but with a fringe. It was like an out grown crop... they'd leave their fringe down with sharpie tails. It was also similar to a sharpie style cut.[84]

Violence and Identity

Part of the image for groups like rockers, sharpies and skinheads included displays of hostility and violence directed especially at those they 'looked down on'.[85] Rockers were frequently observed 'hanging out' in a 'threatening manner' on the week-ends around the local picture theatres, milk bars, town halls and street corners. There were also activities for amusement that tested strength and toughness; one of these was taking turns in strapping each other to the telegraph pole on the corner at the local milk bar, then setting light to a fire underneath the captive and timing to see how long they could stand the pain. Within the group such 'tests' established whether or not the individual had 'real guts'. They also gauged manliness, tested their 'the captives' trust of other group members and their credentials for continued membership as well as clarifying the ranking or hierarchy within the group.[86]

81.   ibid.
82.   Interview, Brad, September 1993.
83.   Interview, Graham, August 1993; see also Interview, Brad, September 1993.
84.   Interview, Terry, August 1993.
85.   'Teenage Weekly' (supplement), in *Australian Women's Weekly*, 19 February, 1964, pp. 14-15.
86.   Interview, Carolyn, July 1993.

Most of the identity making conflict arose when 'different' groups hostile to each other such as the skinheads and the mods crossed paths. It was also made clear that certain groups could under no circumstances put foot on 'enemy' turf without such trespassing signifying major trouble. 'Others' did not usually deliberately venture into 'hostile' space unless it was intended as an act of provocation. Despite the fact that each group had their own space that was clearly tagged, and therefore known to belong to a particular group where 'outsiders' were not permitted, there were many occasions when conflicting groups came together and dances were one such place. Going to a dance did not necessarily mean dancing together or socialising, on the contrary dances meant a self-enforced segregation between the groups. 'Sharpie girls wouldn't dance with Mods, although they might with skinheads. Mods wouldn't dance with sharpies. We were segregated. Mods were on one side. We'd have our corner somewhere and sharpies would have their corner on the other side.'[87]

Violence, in the form of fights or assaults like 'beating up' others was one way that group members produced meanings about their worlds and their place in it. It was a way also of establishing new rules, or reaffirming and enforcing old rules and reputations within groups. Fights helped work out how groups should behave towards each other; who were the toughest, the biggest dare-devils and the most outrageous. One 1960s rocker remembered the way in which stories of bravery and reputations travelled through the network:

> ... guys from Collingwood that knew guys from Richmond that knew guys from Spotswood that knew other top guys from each of these gangs ...They knew of each other and had this respect for each other. Guys from other gangs knew who they were and respect them ... All the real tough guys I've ever met never had to talk about how tough they were.[88]

The lives of many young people, particularly the males were regularly organised around group fights and public displays of bravado. This is not to say that physical fights were exclusively male activities. Girls also 'went in boots and all when they needed to'; it is however accurate to say that overt physical violence was predominantly a male activity.[89] Individual and collective moralities are important factors in understanding the violence of these groups. Moral issues often motivated group members to action particularly if it was over issues such as assaults on one's personal integrity or the 'need' to protect space or kind (mates). Many rockers, sharpies and skinheads became involved in violence because they often saw themselves as moral ambassadors. For the skinheads 'the long hairs – the Mods', and their 'whimpy', soft and effeminate appearance was a major affront. 'Bashing the shit out of those fag long hairs', helped reassert the normative status of what it meant to be 'Australian' and 'masculine'. Such violence also demonstrated the virility of the perpetrators, their strength and the toughness of 'real men'. These young men were morally obliged to 'fight the good fight' for Australia's national identity and racial hygiene, for the defence of heterosexuality (against the 'poofy mods') sometimes simply to counter an affront to their integrity because someone had moved in on 'their sheila'.

87.   Interview, Warren, September 1993.
88.   Interview, Stephen, January 1991.
89.   Interview, Jane, August 1993.

Judith Bessant

The formation of groups such as the sharpies, rockers, mods and skinheads provide insights into understanding what drove rival gangs to fight so often and so savagely over claims to space. One would expect to hear explanations of the same sort coming from warriors justifying defence of their ancestral home lands or as the result of an affront to some arcane code of honour. Graham remembered how 'we were all very toey about other people. We more or less knew everybody.' [90] Graham's stake in what he saw as the need to protect his home were primary reasons for 'giving others a good hiding'. 'We belonged to that suburb. We were born and breed in that suburb ... Fights were with other groups who came into our area that we didn't know – there would always be a fight on. We didn't care if they were sheilas or blokes, we'd just get stuck into them, we didn't care.' [91]

Considerable time was spent as members of sharpies groups enjoyed each other's company over a few drinks while 'guarding' points of entry into 'their area'.

> We lived ... near the railway station. People used to get around then by train and we could always tell if a heap of skinheads or sharpies got off the train. We used to always sit out the front of the station and listen to music and drink and watch the trains stop and go past. ... We just didn't like what they were doing. It was our area and wanted them to back off... We didn't care if they were girls or boys, we'd kick them out ... If they wanted to look like that and hang around out part of Richmond, we'd think up some excuse to bash them. [92]

Rick described what his group was about:

> we were just on about fucking up the establishment, everything. Parents hated it ... It wasn't just the clothes and hanging out in groups, there was a bit more to it. It was about creating chaos. We did some bizarre and very strange things. [93] Bucking the system was fun, it meant not wanting what every one else wanted. In the fifties they did it, in the seventies we did it.' [94]

Even less violent Mods did not mind causing bother for a bit of fun. Terry 'and his mates' took delight in gate crashing parties. They once visited a home in the affluent area of Prahran, in inner city of Melbourne 'for a stir'.

> I don't know who's house it was, but it was one of those wild over-the-top parties. It became a near riot. One of the neighbours came out and abused people. I think he may have hit some-body and gone back into the [his] house. A whole lot of people [Mods] grabbed the trolley in the street and started bashing his door down. In the end the guy jumped out and pulled a gun on us. It was a revolver he said: freeze or I'll shoot you, you motherfucker... He was waving the gun around. There were about 40 of us. Someone in the group said, 'It's a bloody fake', and he slammed the door shut. [95]

A Sydney boy elaborated on how group conflict took place over claims to space:

> We had a snack bar which was our territory, and they [the long hairs] tried to 'muscle in'. We turned up. There were bike chains and studded belts, bits of paling fence and even a few shivs. It was all over in five minutes and there was blood everywhere. I reckon we won. They didn't come back. [96]

90.   Interview, Graham, August 1993.
91.   ibid.
92.   ibid.
93.   Interview, Rick, August 1993.
94.   Interview, Alannah, (sharpie), 7 September 1993.
95.   Interview, Terry, August 1993.
96.   *Sun-Herald*, 26 February 1967.

Young sharpie groups ... got a few hidings from a few of the bikie groups in Richmond. They told us to get a decent hair cut or they won't let us in that part of Richmond again. So if we went down that part we disguised ourselves. They were blokes but we were only kids.[97]

Paradoxically there was also often a degree of solidarity between groups of 'the same kind' who occupied shared areas. In other words, two or more like groups could cohabit the same space with little or no hostility. This meant that sharpie groups from one part of town quite happily mixed with those from another areas. Graham who belonged to the Burnley-Richmond Sharps, (named after the inner city suburbs of Melbourne that was their home) '...ventured into other areas, but we knew a lot of different gangs, different sharpies in those areas. When we ventured into those areas we were pretty safe'.[98]

Group members also shifted from one group to another if there were attractive offerings such as more opportunities to get into 'good fights'. The fact that Mods were on the recipients of much violence was for one ex-skinhead an excellent reason for swapping camps.

He [a skinhead] came into the Mods scene ... He said ... no-one picks on skinheads, you look too threatening. I could get into more fights when I was a mod and that's why he was in it [the Mod scene] he liked the fights. He said that when he was a mod people would start on him. He said blokes half his size would come up and start on me. They'd say: who are you, you pooftah, you weirdo pooftah? He said that when I was a skinhead no-one would touch me because people associated skinheads with Nazi bastards ... so he became a mod and we thought it was funny. He'd dress like a gympy poof to have people start on him.[99]

★ ★ ★

Anthony Giddens suggested that understanding our social world requires a three-fold exercise of the imagination which involves an historical, anthropological and critical sensitivity.[100] To date most of the literature and our popular memory of the 1960s and early 1970s is dominated by the imprint of 'the student movement and middle-class radicalism'. What is needed and what is attempted here is a challenge to the dominant aspects of how we have come to understand our social history. Doing so attempts to imaginatively reconstruct elements of the social lives that have been to a large extent forgotten and ignored. The ethnographic approach here provides material that hopefully challenges the idea that 'working class youth cultures' were in some way invisible' or not important enough to warrant being written into our history of that period. A fuller development of the subject is not possible here. However what is possible is an opening up of one aspect of our social history that others may feel warrants further attention and deeper explorations.

Australian Catholic University

97.   Interview, Graham, August 1993.
98.   ibid.
99   Interview, Terry, September 1993.
100.   A. Giddens, *Sociology: A Brief but Critical Introduction*, London, 1982, p.13.

[9]

Street Gang Migration: How Big a Threat?

by Cheryl L. Maxson, Kristi J. Woods, and Malcolm W. Klein

Deeply imbedded within the twin contexts of gang proliferation and drug market expansion is public concern about gang migration—the movement of gang members from one city to another. That concern is reflected in the reports of State legislative task force investigations; government-sponsored conferences; and law enforcement accounts at the local, State, and Federal levels.[1] In these documents the evidence cited is most often anecdotal, rarely the result of a systematic assessment of the prevalence, nature, and consequences of gang migration.

With a single exception, the findings of research on this topic contrast sharply with the perspective presented in the government and law enforcement reports as well as in the media. These research studies show that the impact of gang migration is far less than has been believed.[2]

Resolving the disparate views

The disparity between the empirically based studies and the law enforcement and media reports can be resolved through analysis of the *patterns* of gang migration. The study whose findings are summarized here examines these patterns by drawing on a nationwide sample of cities and reporting information from law enforcement, community informants, and gang members.

The study revealed that although overall the pattern of migration and the characteristics of migrants point to a less dramatic effect than has been believed, variations in the dominant patterns may explain that belief. Because this study is the first to investigate gang migration systematically and on a national scope, it should be viewed as exploratory.[3] (See "How the Information Was Gathered.")

National scope of gang migration

Gang migration, broadly defined, is widespread. Of the 190 larger cities (those with a population of more than 100,000), 155 (80 percent) cited at least some migration, as did another 555 smaller cities. These cities are located throughout the country: 44 percent in the West, fewer in the Midwest and South (26 and 25 percent, respectively), and only about 5 percent in the Northeast.

Gang migration is a recent phenomenon; relatively few cities (13 percent) report their first gang migration as occurring before 1986. In most cities the emergence of local, indigenous gangs either preceded the onset of migration (54 percent)

How the Information Was Gathered

The study was conducted in four phases. In the first phase, cities that had experienced gang migration were identified through a questionnaire sent to law enforcement agencies in 1,105 cities. The number included all 190 U.S. cities with populations over 100,000 and a number of smaller cities and towns. "Candidate" cities also were obtained from law enforcement contacts, researchers, and survey respondents. Ninety-two percent of the police departments contacted responded to the survey.

The 480 cities in which at least 10 migrants arrived the past year became the basis for the law enforcement interview part of the study (phase 2). Interviews were conducted in 226 of these cities[4] and produced the detailed descriptions of gang migrant characteristics, crime patterns, and law enforcement responses. The telephone interviews with community respondents in a sample of 42 of these cities constituted the third phase.

The case studies of three cities, selected as exemplars of three patterns of gang migration, comprised the fourth and final phase of the study. The cities were Lawndale and Napa, California, and Milwaukee.

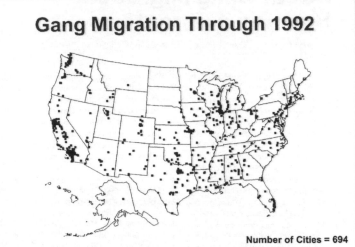

Gang Migration Through 1992

Number of Cities = 694

Gang members have migrated to cities large and small throughout the United States.

or occurred the same year (41 percent); in just 5 percent, the onset of migration preceded the emergence of local gang problems.

Numbers. Estimates of the total number of migrants vary widely, from as low as a dozen and under (30 percent of the 600 cities that could provide figures) up to the thousands (16 cities, or just 3 percent). A more reliable but still quite variable estimate is the number of migrants who arrived the previous year. Less than half (47 percent) of the cities reported the arrival of 10 or fewer migrants in that period, while only 34 (5 percent) estimated as many as 100 or more recent arrivals.

Thus, although in recent years hundreds of cities have seen the arrival of gang members, their numbers have been relatively low. As a result, their potential for increasing local gang activity and crime rates would appear to be limited.

Characteristics of gang migrants and migration

More detailed information was drawn from interviews with law enforcement gang experts in the cities that reported at least 10 migrants in the previous year.

Age, gender, ethnicity. For each of these cities, the migrants' age ranged from 13 to 30, with the typical age about 18 years. Female gang migrants were uncommon, as were Asians and whites. Compared with the ethnic distribution of gang members nationally, migrants were somewhat more likely to be black. About half the cities reported that at least 60 percent of their migrants were black; in 28 percent they were predominantly Hispanic. These characteristics are roughly similar to those of gangs in general.

Place of origin. Where do gang migrants come from? Cities within the Los Angeles area were cited by 63 percent of the respondents. One-third mentioned Chicago area cities, with far fewer reporting the New York or Detroit areas. About one-fourth cited the *city* of Los Angeles

(rather than the larger Los Angeles area) as their *primary* source of migrants; Chicago was noted by 14 percent.

The primary source of migration was typically within 100 miles of the destination city; only 12 percent cited primary source cities more than 1,000 miles away. A regional migration pattern, or a clustering of three or more source cities within 30 miles of each other, was evident in about one-fourth of all cities.

Motives/length of stay. The average length of stay was typically 3 months or longer; only about one-fourth of the cities reported typical visits shorter than a month. This pattern is consistent with the motivations for migration. When police officers were asked to select which of several reasons explained why *most* of the gang members who moved to their city did so, they cited family moves (39 percent) along with stays with relatives and friends. Combined into a category of "social" primary motivations, these reasons accounted for 57 percent of the cities.

The second most frequently cited primary motivation was drug market expansion (20 percent of the cities). This the researchers combined with other criminal opportunity motivations to create a category of "extra-legal attractions" that accounted for 32 percent of the total in the destination cities.

Influence on local gangs and crime

The ways in which migrants participated in gangs in the destination cities exhibited no dominant pattern. In about one-third there was a prevailing pattern in which migrants recruited for former gangs or to establish branch operations. In about 20 percent, migrants largely joined pre-existing local gangs, and about the same percentage reported that migrants retained their affiliation with their former gang only. Few respondents felt that migrants discontinued gang activity altogether; however, this is difficult to determine, since individuals who ceased gang activity might be less likely to come to the attention of the police.

Effect on crime. Most officers interviewed (86 percent) reported that migrants have had an impact on local crime rates or patterns, primarily through increases in thefts (50 percent of the cities), robberies (35 percent), other violent crimes (59 percent), and gun use or sophistication of firearms used (36 percent). Migrants were somewhat or heavily involved in drug sales in about three-fourths of the cities, according to the law enforcement respondents. This pattern extended to both black and Hispanic gang migrants, with rock or crack cocaine most commonly distributed by blacks, and marijuana by Hispanics. But despite the reportedly widespread involvement of gangs in drug sales, gang migrants were generally not perceived as having a substantial impact on the local drug market, probably because of their relatively low numbers.

Variations in the dominant pattern

These general characteristics might obscure more specific patterns that would have different implications for criminal justice response. The researchers examined motivations to migrate, involvement of migrants with drugs, and number of migrants and found that only on the first factor did differences emerge. The larger cities and cities in the South were more likely than other sites to attract migrants drawn by the

prospect of extra-legal activities. Migrants to these cities also traveled longer distances, stayed less time, were more likely to be older, and tended to be black. In cities where social reasons for migration predominated, migrants were more likely to be Hispanic.

Local responses to gang migration

Law enforcement officers were asked about the use of specific strategies and their effectiveness in reducing the volume of gang migrants or their impact. Most departments have not developed specific strategies to deal with gang migrants (e.g., targeting of entry points). Many responded to questions about strategy by citing their gang intelligence and operational activities. Analysis revealed informational and operational coordination to be weak.

Although the officers cited several strategies for dealing with gang migrants, including routine field contacts, arrests, and use of informants, few viewed them as effective. Selective enforcement of violations (e.g., use of narcotics laws) and gang sweeps and other suppression strategies were less common but were perceived to be effective by a majority of officers. Although prevention was rarely mentioned (by 15 percent), it was considered effective by more than half the departments using it.

The reasons for gang migration are far more complex than has been believed.

Joint efforts with other agencies. Collaboration of the police with community agencies and institutions was reported in nearly two-thirds of the cities, most often taking the form of information exchange or gang awareness education. However, this rarely involved service referrals or direct participation in service provision. Although officers in more than half the cities viewed community collaboration as an effective response to migration, less than one-fourth could provide the name of someone outside law enforcement who was informed about gang migration.

Lack of innovation. Not only were the strategies not viewed as particularly effective, but they did not meet the study's definition of "innovative and promising" responses to gang migration. The officers reported that they saw the adverse impacts of gang migration as substantial, yet their views were not reflected in departmental policy or systematic enforcement approaches. Only 18 percent of the officers said their department sees gang migration as a severe problem, while fully one-third said their department sees it as a minor problem or not a problem. This departmental assessment may help explain the absence of innovation, and that absence also likely reflects the recent occurrence of migration and its relatively minor role in the overall gang problem in many cities.

Community response

The interviews with community respondents revealed several locales that have recently recognized the problem and were just beginning to work with police. Of the 42 respondents, only four reported that *no* steps had been taken. But of those in which steps had been taken, only three mentioned migrants specifically. All three included the involvement of law enforcement and school or housing authority collaboration to identify migrants or to share information about newcomers.

In the remaining responses, an array of prevention or intervention activities related to gangs or to crime generally—not to migrants—were noted. Over half specified distinct roles for law enforcement, a confirmation of the high levels of police/community collaboration reported in the interviews with police. Little attention was given to the development of coordinated responses to gang migration.

Case studies

Indepth studies of three cities that experienced a high volume of migration revealed that the reasons for migration are far more complex than has been believed. They also revealed a range of relationships between newcomers and established gangs, and great variety in the

level and nature of connections with gangs in the departure sites.

In general, migrants reported getting in less trouble with the law in their destination city. For policymakers the issue then becomes weighing such reduced gang activity against concern with the spread of gang culture from city to city.

In all three cities, remedies were directed at gangs in general rather than gang migrants. One city adopted a social service approach geared to individuals. In another, there seemed to be little in the way of services directed to at-risk youth.

Policy implications

Although the attempts to identify promising law enforcement and community strategies that address gang migration were not successful, the study findings suggest several directions that local and Federal policy might take. The findings indicate that the core policy issues are as follows:

1. Migration is not the cause of local gang problems.

Most cities had local gangs before the onset of migration, and many respondents felt their city would have a gang problem regardless of migration. In view of the generally small number of migrants, it may be appropriate that there is little

Communities must continue to invest in targeted prevention and intervention.

specificity in programs to deal with gangs and in law enforcement strategies.

Communities are grappling with the root causes of gang activity, and they must continue to invest in targeted prevention and intervention. The variety of such programs described by community respondents, coupled with high levels of police-community collaboration, suggest that such efforts are under way in many cities. More active recruitment of gang migrants into these programs could yield benefits for them as well as for the larger community.

2. The adverse effects of migrants are substantial, according to law enforcement officers, yet few departments have policies or coherent strategies to address them.

Special intervention strategies might be warranted if gang migrants present unique threats. However, the evidence to substantiate concern about this threat is mixed. Because the demographics of gang migrants are roughly similar to those of the country's gang population in general, there is little support for the contention that only the "worst" gang members migrate.

This is not to say that the law enforcement accounts of substantial adverse effects on local gang dynamics and crime patterns should be dismissed. The data are necessarily perceptual, but the views of the

officers interviewed were quite consistent—gang migrants commit a lot of crime and exacerbate local gang problems. In view of the officers' *perceptions*, the lack of departmental policies and strategies was surprising.

3. Different types of migration require different responses.

The finding that drug market expansion and other illegal pursuits are the primary motivation in one-third of the cities indicates that judicious exercise of interdiction and suppression may be beneficial. However, a proactive social service policy might fare well even in these cities.

Since social reasons were far more common as a migration motive, gang prevention and early intervention programs that provide alternative activities and opportunities may be more promising in these cities than aggressive law enforcement.

4. The need for developing a national file of gang members is not supported by the study.

In the past few years, some Federal law enforcement agencies have joined with local police officials to promote establishment of a national file on gang members. In light of the findings of this study, the costs and benefits of such an undertaking should be weighed carefully. The majority of gang migrants were found not to travel great distances, so a national gang data base would not yield substantial benefits.

On the other hand, because a substantial minority report clusters of "source cities" within 30 miles of one another, regional gang data bases may be useful.

Future research

Future research should include systematically organized ethnographies of several carefully selected migration cities. Study of selected sites could much more effectively investigate migrants' influence on local gang cultures, the transition of gang members to their new environments, and the critical junctures in shifting gang identities. A nationwide survey of law enforcement should be repeated in order to update the findings reported here.

Close attention should be paid to migration patterns. As the current study revealed, the primary reasons for relocation are associated with the characteristics of the migrants and the destination cities.

Systematic assessment of response strategies, now in their infancy, is very much needed before more effective policies can be developed. As suggested here, some gang migrants may be responsive to social programming. Communities could be encouraged to provide such programs on an experimental basis and assess their effectiveness with gang migrants as well as with local gang clients and at-risk youths.

Systematic assessment of response strategies, now in their infancy, is very much needed before more effective policies can be developed.

The issues of foreign gang immigration and emigration, the diffusion of gang culture through the media, and criminal profiles of gang migrants also require further assessment. Migrants' individual histories of criminal activity should be investigated to identify the circumstances in which relocation to a different city might prove an effective crime *reduction* technique. Judges and family members employed this tactic years before gang migration studies were conducted. It is time that we identify the conditions in which such moves should be encouraged.

Notes

1. Bonfante, Jordan, "Entrepreneurs of Crack," *Time*, February 27, 1995; Hayeslip, D.W., Jr., "Local-Level Drug Enforcement: New Strategies," *NIJ Reports*, 213 (March–April 1989):2–6; California Council on Criminal Justice, *State Task Force on Gangs and Drugs: Final Report*, Sacramento, California: CCCJ, 1989; Genelin, M., and B. Copelin, *Los Angeles Street Gangs: Report and Recommendations of the Countywide Criminal Justice Coordination Committee Interagency Gang Task Force*, Los Angeles, California: Interagency Gang Task Force, 1989; McKinney, K.C., *Juvenile Gangs: Crime and Drug Trafficking*, Juvenile Justice Bulletin, Washington, D.C.: U.S. Department of Justice, Office of Juvenile Justice and Delinquency Prevention, September 1988; and National Drug Intelligence Center, *Bloods and Crips Gang Survey Report*, Johnstown, Pennsylvania: NDIC, 1994.

2. Rosenbaum, D.P., and J.A. Grant, *Gangs and Youth Problems in Evanston*, Evanston, Illinois: Northwestern University Center for Urban Affairs and Policy Research, 1983; Hagedorn, John, *People and Folks: Gangs, Crime, and the Underclass in a Rustbelt City*, Chicago: Lakeview Press, 1988; Huff, C. Ronald, "Youth Gangs and Public Policy," *Crime and Delinquency*, 35 (1989): 524–537; Zevitz, R.G., and S.R. Takata, "Metropolitan Gang Influence and the Emergence of Group Delinquency in a Regional Community," *Journal of Criminal Justice*, 20 (1992):93–106; and Waldorf, Dan, "When the Crips Invaded San Francisco: Gang Migration," *The Gang Journal*, 1(4) (1993). The exception is the study by Skolnick, J.H., et al., "The Social Structure of Street Drug Dealing," *American Journal of Police*, 9(1) (1990):1–41; and Skolnick, *Gang Organization and Migration*, Sacramento, California: Office of the Attorney General of the State of California, 1990.

3. A related study is Maxson, Cheryl L., *Street Gangs and Drug Sales in Two Suburban Cities*, Research in Brief, Washington, D.C.: U.S. Department of Justice, National Institute of Justice, September 1995 (NCJ 155185).

4. Information gathered from cities with drug gang migrants only is not included in this report but may be found in the final, unpublished report submitted to NIJ.

Cheryl L. Maxson, Ph.D., is director of the Center for the Study of Crime and Social Control at the Social Science Research Institute, University of Southern California (USC). Kristi J. Woods is a doctoral candidate at USC. Malcolm W. Klein, Ph.D., is director of the USC Social Science Research Institute.

The research for this study was supported by NIJ grant 91–IJ–CX–K004. The full, final report will be available from the National Criminal Justice Reference Service.

The authors gratefully acknowledge the research assistance of Lea Cunningham and Karen Sternheimer and the field staff of Napa, Milwaukee, and Lawndale. Staff in the police departments and community agencies generously shared their knowledge, as did many gang members. Members of NIJ's Gangs Working Group contributed expertise in selecting case study sites.

[10]

YOUTH GANGS, MASCULINITY AND VIOLENCE IN LATE VICTORIAN MANCHESTER AND SALFORD

By Andrew Davies   University of Liverpool

> It is surprising how few people, outside of the police and those residing in the imme-
> diate neighbourhoods where the outrages occur, really know what "scuttling" is. In
> the first place, the "scuttler" is not a thief, nor does he aspire to be a highwayman;
> he does not "scuttle" for any actually dishonest purpose.
>
> ### WHAT IS A SCUTTLER?
>
> A "scuttler" is a lad, usually between the ages of 14 and 18, or even 19, and
> "scuttling" consists of the fighting of two opposed bands of youths, who are armed
> with various weapons.
> Alexander Devine, *Scuttlers and Scuttling: Their Prevention and Cure* (Manchester,
> 1890), p. 2.

Historians are well aware that Britain's cities have a history of conflict between rival youth gangs. In their influential studies of "hooliganism", Stephen
Humphries and Geoffrey Pearson have both pointed to the existence of violent
gangs such as the "scuttlers" of Manchester and Salford during the late nineteenth and early twentieth centuries.[1] However, in the absence in Britain of a
tradition of research in empirical sociology to parallel the classic Chicago studies
of the gang during the 1920s and 1930s, our knowledge of youth-gang formation
in British cities prior to the Second World War remains patchy.[2]

The most detailed historical exploration of the culture of the British youth
gang is to be found in the work of Stephen Humphries. In *Hooligans or Rebels?*
(1981), Humphries adopted a class-centred approach through which he was concerned to show that violent gangs emerged in inner-city areas characterised by
deprivation and high levels of unemployment. Street-gang culture, Humphries
asserted, "offered working-class youth the opportunity to conquer its feelings of
hunger, failure and insignificance and to assert a proud and rebellious identity
through which its members could feel masters of their own destiny."[3] According
to Humphries, weapons were possessed by "a small minority" of gangs, but were
"carried largely as symbols of defiance and resistance" and were rarely used.[4] In
Humphries' account, "serious violence" was most likely to escalate when established street gangs turned against newly arrived immigrant groups, especially in
periods of economic decline. The severity of assaults upon young Jewish immigrants in East and South London during the 1890s, for example, reflected acute
anxieties over competition in local labour and housing markets.[5]

Humphries thus situated his analysis of street gangs within a broader discussion
of class and ethnicity. By contrast, he showed little concern with gender, noting
only in passing that "the assertion of masculinity" was one of the focal concerns
of the working-class street gang.[6] My aim in the present paper is to develop a
more nuanced analysis of confrontations between rival gangs in relation to masculine notions of honour and reputation. Moreover, by exploring the broader

350 journal of social history winter 1998

relationship between masculinity and violence in the working-class districts of late Victorian Manchester and Salford, I propose to show that gang conflicts were rooted in a much wider association between "hardness" and masculine status which permeated working-class culture.[7] "Hardness", or toughness, was considered a quintessential masculine virtue. Considerable kudos was derived from displays of fighting prowess and the ability to withstand pain, and boys and youths continually tested each other's mettle in order to prove themselves, and thus their masculinity, in the eyes of their peers.[8] In addition to courting peer respect, displays of male bravado were intended to impress young women, and youths assumed a chivalrous obligation to avenge perceived insults to their female associates. Working-class youths commonly regarded their "sweethearts" as their property, and the attentions of rival suitors constituted clear infringements of male honour.[9]

Gang conflicts provided a systematic means for young men to prove themselves against their peers, and affrays were invested with great significance by the participants. Borrowing from the anthropologist Gary Armstrong, it is possible to see late Victorian youth gangs as contriving "theatres of hostility."[10] Gangs of youths entered rival districts or city centre music-halls seeking confrontations in which honour and reputation might be acquired or maintained by defeating, and thus shaming, rival gangs. Equally, gang members were obliged to resist such incursions upon their own territory in order to defend their honour. Considerable prestige was derived from displays of prowess in "scuttling" affrays, although it is important to point out that the reputations of prominent gang members carried most weight among their peers and rivals. Even within the neighbourhoods which gangs claimed as their territory, adults' views of the gangs and their activities were, to say the least, highly ambiguous.[11]

Humphries drew his examples of hooliganism from a range of British cities. He did not attempt to undertake a systematic study of youth-gang violence in a specific urban context. I would suggest that if we are to develop a more rigorous and nuanced understanding of the nature of gang conflicts, it is necessary to adopt a narrower focus. The analysis which follows is based upon a sample of 250 cases of gang-related crimes of violence reported in the Manchester and Salford press between 1870 and 1900. A total of 717 young people were charged in these cases, with offences ranging from disorderly conduct to wilful murder. Significantly, 93.7 percent of those charged were male. Gang violence does therefore appear to have been an overwhelmingly masculine concern, and the discussion which follows focuses exclusively upon masculinity and violence. Nonetheless, it is important to acknowledge that young women formed a small but active minority of those involved in gang conflicts, and I have examined a series of cases involving "female scuttlers" in some depth elsewhere.[12]

An overview of the cases in my own sample suggests that a number of Humphries' central claims in his analysis of youth gangs are flawed. Contrary to Humphries' assertions, gang violence was by no means confined to the poorest and most notorious "slum" neighbourhoods. Moreover, scuttling affrays were characterised by the widespread use of weapons. Perhaps most importantly, my research suggests that gang conflicts in Manchester and Salford do not appear to have been structured to any significant extent by either short-term economic trends or ethnic tensions. Gang violence, rooted in local codes of toughness and manliness, appears to have been a recurring feature of local working-class life during the last three decades of the nineteenth century.

Of course, historians of crime need to be extremely cautious in using press reports as a source, not least in studies of street violence.[13] The local press reported only a small percentage of the cases heard in the Manchester and Salford police courts, and press reports may have exaggerated the extent to which scuttling was a new phenomenon in the early 1870s. Moreover, although the proceedings of cases which were heard at the higher courts of quarter sessions or assize were often reported in some depth, the majority of scuttling cases were dealt with at the police courts and were only briefly covered if at all by the local press. Significantly, for cases heard at the police courts, journalists appear to have frequently given accounts which were closely based upon police testimony in court. This version of events tended to be reproduced as a factual report.[14] The competing narratives of those accused of gang violence were only rarely reported, even in fragments. However, I would strongly endorse Humphries' assertion that violent youth gangs were not an invention of the late Victorian press.[15] Accounts of scuttling gleaned from local newspapers are examined below alongside depositions (the sworn statements of witnesses) from cases heard at quarter sessions and assize courts during the 1890s, working-class memoirs published during the 1930s and 1940s, and oral history interviews conducted in Salford in the 1970s.

This paper is divided into four empirical sections. The first provides a brief overview of the pattern of gang conflicts in late Victorian Manchester and Salford. Secondly, I propose to examine the diverse role models available to boys growing up in working-class districts across the conurbation, and the broader relationship between masculinity and violence which formed the backdrop to young men's involvement in gangs. Thirdly, I aim to explore the nature of scuttling confrontations and the meanings attached to gang violence by the participants. The nature of gang conflicts as male contests over honour and reputation is then explored in more depth in a case-study of John Joseph Hillyar, a prominent Salford scuttler during the 1890s.

I

Scuttling gangs were neighbourhood-based youth gangs which were formed in working-class districts across the Manchester conurbation, from the independent county borough of Salford to the west of the city to the townships of Bradford, Gorton and Openshaw to the east.[16] Contrary to Humphries' assertion that gang violence was underpinned by deprivation, the gangs were formed in a wide range of neighbourhoods, from the central "slums" to the more prosperous working-class neighbourhoods in manufacturing districts such as Gorton and Openshaw. In addition to fierce local rivalries between gangs from adjacent neighbourhoods, there were wider antagonisms between gangs from Manchester and those from the borough of Salford.[17] Press reports suggest that gang conflicts erupted in Manchester in the early 1870s and flared periodically for three decades, before declining in both frequency and severity by the late 1890s. It is difficult to trace a causal relationship between levels of violence and downturns in the trade cycle. The years 1878–1879, 1884–1886 and 1892–1895 saw high levels of cyclical unemployment in Manchester, yet the most intense escalation of gang conflicts appears to have occurred in 1889–1890. Indeed, 1889 was a year of "exceptionally good trade."[18]

Territory, rather than ethnic identity or religious affiliation, formed the basis of allegiance to the gangs.[19] Manchester and Salford had substantial Irish Catholic populations, clustered, during the late nineteenth century, in the poorer working-class districts close to Manchester city centre. However, even in those districts with the highest concentration of Irish Catholic households, Catholic and Protestant families occupied the same streets and their children shared the fierce loyalty to street and immediate neighbourhood found throughout the working-class districts across the Manchester conurbation.[20] An intense local pride was reflected in the names adopted by scuttling gangs. The "Bengal Tigers" (from Bengal Street in Manchester's Ancoats district) and the more prosaically-named "Hope Street, Salford" were identified by their territorial rather than ethnic allegiances, although both gangs were drawn from districts where a substantial minority of local families were of Irish Catholic origin.

As Alexander Devine (police court missionary and pioneer of the local Lads' Club movement) pointed out, scuttlers were drawn overwhelmingly from the fourteen to nineteen age group. In occupational terms, they were employed in a wide range of semi-skilled and unskilled manual occupations. The ranks of the most prominent gangs included many factory workers as well as general labourers and carters, and it would be highly misleading to characterise scuttling gangs as drawn from the lumpenproletariat or a distinct "criminal class."[21] It is rare, however, to find cases involving apprentices. This is perhaps unsurprising as apprentices clearly had more to lose if they were imprisoned for crimes of street violence. Nonetheless, the absence of apprentices is of some importance. As Keith McClelland has recently remarked, the learning of a trade was in itself a vital source of identity for a young working-class male, not least because his gender identity was enhanced as he absorbed "the mysteries of the craft in learning his skills."[22] For those in semi-skilled or unskilled occupations, gang membership offered an alternative form of masculine identity, which embodied very different notions of status. Significantly, although gang conflicts do not appear to have been structured by sectarian allegiances, many prominent scuttlers had Irish Catholic backgrounds. Again, however, this is unsurprising. Irish Catholics faced widespread discrimination in local labour markets and were over-represented in the ranks of unskilled manual workers.[23]

I have only been able to trace five fatalities inflicted by gang members during the period from 1870 to 1900.[24] Nonetheless, scuttlers appear to have carried weapons as a matter of course, and by the late 1880s, knives were increasingly used in affrays to inflict wounds (usually to the body) which required hospital treatment.[25] However, scuttlers' customary weapons were thick leather belts with heavy brass buckles. The straps of the belts, which were ornately decorated, were wrapped tightly around the wrist so that the buckle, which could fracture a skull, might be used to strike at opponents.[26] In the early 1890s, staff at the Manchester Royal Infirmary informed the police that "scarcely a day passed" without the admission of someone who had been injured in a scuttling affray.[27] Clashes between rival gangs attracted many lurid headlines in the local press, but the police court news columns also contained frequent reports of attacks by gangs upon individuals. In some of the most brutal instances, isolated scuttlers were confronted by members of a rival gang, but assaults were also made upon people who had no connection with gangs themselves. These included both local people who complained about a gang's activities, and occasionally, passersby who strayed into territory to which a scuttling gang laid claim.

Scuttlers were intensely style-conscious. Fashion was by no means a feminine preserve among young people in working-class districts, but it is significant that male gang members appear to have been much more concerned with their appearances than other young men in similar occupations.[28] Style was used by scuttlers to signify "hardness". Gang members distinguished themselves from other young men in working-class neighbourhoods by wearing a uniform of pointed clogs, "bells" (bell-bottomed trousers, cut "like a sailor's" and measuring fourteen inches round the knee and twenty-one inches round the foot) and "flashy" silk scarves. Their hair was cut short at the back and sides, but they grew long fringes which were worn in a parting and plastered down on the forehead over the left eye. "Pigeon-board" peaked caps were also worn tilted to the left, and angled to display the fringe.[29] This style of dress carried both status and risk, however, as any young man who adopted such fashions became a target for gangs from rival districts.

II

In order to develop an analysis of the relationship between masculinity and violence, it is useful to consider the role models for boys growing up in working-class neighbourhoods in Manchester and Salford before 1900. Contemporary anxieties were frequently centred on popular fiction, especially the "penny dreadfuls," which were seen as glorifying crime and criminals and prompting imitation on the part of a youthful working-class readership. As Alexander Devine put it, "there is no doubt that they engender a morbid love of horrors and atrocities that may account to some extent for the many acts of violence committed by lads of this class."[30] Scuttlers certainly borrowed from popular culture, occasionally when naming gangs, for example.[31] However, the assertion that popular fiction was one of the causes of gang violence is, of course, impossible to substantiate and my concern here is with the more tangible role models available to boys growing up in working-class districts.

In the working-class neighbourhoods of late Victorian Manchester and Salford, there co-existed a range of very different conceptions of what "being a man" entailed. As the principal wage-earners in most families, men claimed the status of breadwinner, stressing their capacity to provide for their wives and children, and thus deriving their standing as men in part from their role within the household. However, another pervasive conception of manliness centred upon a very different set of virtues, including toughness—expressed both in a man's physical labour and in his everyday public conduct—and the capacity to drink heavily, which earned a man peer recognition, as a "hard" man, or "*man's*" man. Of course, the categories of breadwinner and "hard" man were not mutually exclusive. Many men managed to subscribe to elements of both notions of what it meant to be a man, adopting different personas in different contexts. Others, however, were more clearly distinguished either as "family" men or as heavy-drinking, "hard" men, and boys growing up in such districts were therefore faced

354   journal of social history   winter 1998

with quite diverse role models.[32] For young men in their mid- to late-teens, the status of breadwinner was usually unattainable. Within the family, most were restricted to the role of supplementary wage-earner and were subject to the authority of their fathers. The role of the "hard" man, which was available to them, thus appears to have been especially attractive.

Boys growing up in working-class neighbourhoods witnessed countless demonstrations of male violence.[33] Frequently, they were victims of such violence themselves. As Robert Roberts pointed out, corporal punishment was widespread and frequently very severe in working-class families, even for trivial offences. Fathers inflicted beatings with belts and canes, and Roberts recalled the case of a woman who boasted in his parents' shop how "My master [husband] allus flogs 'em till the blood runs down their back!"[34] Retrospective accounts also suggest that many (although by no means all) households were characterised by high levels of marital violence, largely perpetrated by men upon their wives.[35] In such families, boys learned quickly that violence was a customary means by which men vented their anger. Even those children who grew up in entirely peaceable households frequently witnessed violence on the streets. Domestic confrontations spilled out on to pavements and quarrels between neighbouring families could erupt into mass brawls involving both men and women.[36]

Fights between adult men were often bound up with drunkenness, and frequently occurred either inside public houses or in the streets outside. Displays of fighting prowess earned considerable local reputations, occasionally glimpsed in the courtroom boasts of men such as Samuel McGowan, who admitted to the sobriquet of "the Salford fighting man" following an altercation outside the Bridge Inn in Ordsall, Salford, in May 1885.[37] Similarly, John Crawley, a labourer from the Hanky Park district in Salford, bragged in court in 1887 that "there was not many others could lick him about Ellor Street at fighting."[38] "Fair fights", in which two men fought willingly with their fists, were an accepted means of settling an argument and rarely led to criminal charges unless police officers intervened at the scene. Breaches of this fighting code, in which a man was forced to fight against his will, or in which injuries were inflicted by kicking or the use of weapons, could prompt working men to initiate prosecutions for assault or wounding.[39] Fights outside public houses at closing-time at weekends assumed the status of a spectator sport in working-class districts. Children were enthusiastic observers, as William Bowen recalled in his account of his childhood in Greengate in Salford during the 1880s:

> I can remember as a boy one Sunday afternoon, after closing time, a glorious summer afternoon, a crowd came out of a public house with two men stripped to their naked waists who began to fight and they fought until their naked bodies were streaming with blood. I thought, when I am a man I would like to be able to fight like that.[40]

As Bowen's account graphically suggests, fighting was an intensely public spectacle in which men proudly demonstrated their sheer physical power through their capacity to withstand pain. Watching these displays, boys were left in little doubt that toughness was one of the quintessential masculine virtues.

As Michael Childs has recently noted, boys from all strata of the working class were taught by their fathers to "stand up for themselves" from an early age, and to fight back if provoked by other boys.[41] Laying down codes of appropriate behaviour to their sons appears to have been a common way for men to validate their own masculinity. Billy Doyle, for example, who was born in Greengate in 1882, told how his father tried to prevent him from helping his mother with the housework. "A lad hadn't to do anything. We had flag floors and we mustn't clean the floor and 'They're not going to make a girl of my lad.' That was his idea." His father even punished him for losing in a fight, and Doyle recalled how "if I got a good hiding outside [my father]'d give me another one for getting a good hiding."[42] The emphasis on the need to be prepared to fight was further consolidated by peer group pressure among boys. Joe Toole, who was born in 1887, grew up in Ordsall and became the first Labour M.P. for South Salford in 1923. In his autobiography, *Fighting through Life*, Toole reflected on the emergence of a succession of famous local boxers:

> No wonder we turned out fighters for you! You had to fight to survive in my early days in Salford. If you were not fighting for a living, you had to periodically defend your skin, which included your honour; if you declined a challenge to fight, you took a back seat at all games; and if you didn't swear vigorously, nobody believed what you said.[43]

Thus boys learned by example that violence was both a necessary and legitimate means of self-assertion.

Upon entering the world of full-time work, youths were again expected to demonstrate a willingness to stand up for themselves. Challenges to fight had to be accepted in order to gain peer-group acceptance in the workplace, and retrospective accounts suggest that youths continually tested each other's mettle. In a semi-autobiographical account of his Manchester childhood, Bart Kennedy told how fights between youths employed in a machine shop in Ancoats were prompted by the most trivial disputes. Fights were almost nightly events, and custom dictated that new arrivals were forced to accept the first challenges they faced. If they refused, they would be bullied relentlessly. Fights between youths, as between men, were highly public affairs. Generally taking place at the end of the working day, or on weekend evenings, they drew large crowds of onlookers who heaped praise on those who acquitted themselves well. Fights were held in the streets or on patches of open ground within working-class districts, and in Kennedy's account, youths were expected to fight "fair up," using only their fists.[44]

Reports in the local press lend support both to Kennedy's claim that youths fought with their workmates in order to prove themselves and to his depiction of a fighting code governed by the principle of fairness. In May 1889, for example, sixteen-year-old John Rowlands challenged "any lad of his own size" in Derbyshire's glassworks in Ordsall to fight him. Arthur Jones took up the challenge, and they went to a plot of vacant land opposite the works where they took off their coats, watched by a crowd of their workmates. They started to fight and Rowlands struck Jones several blows to the head and body, knocking him to the ground. Jones "appeared to have some sort of fit" and died shortly afterwards. When apprehended, Rowlands told the police "I will give myself up; but it was a fair fight. We shook hands before we fought." Convicted of manslaughter at the Liverpool assizes, he was sentenced to one day's imprisonment. The judge accepted witnesses' accounts of Jones' death as an "unfortunate accident."[45]

In a milieu in which youths tended to regard their "sweethearts" as their property, fights also frequently stemmed from quarrels over the affections of young women. The police court news columns of the local press are littered with tales of assaults and woundings committed by jealous suitors upon their rivals. In such cases, those who felt that their honour had been affronted frequently abandoned any notion of the "fair fight" and sought revenge with knives.[46] Similarly, young men were doubly keen to avenge insults suffered in the company of the young women with whom they were "walking out." Such insults were deeply felt, as young men were obliged to defend their honour not only among their peers but also in the eyes of their "sweethearts". In July 1890, for example, twenty-year-old George Smith of Pendleton, Salford, was sentenced to two months' imprisonment with hard labour for unlawfully wounding Patrick Cooney. Smith had been standing with his "sweetheart" when Cooney walked by, making a remark to them as he passed. Smith rushed after Cooney and stabbed him in the back with a knife. In court, Smith justified his action by claiming that Cooney had used "very dirty language" to them.[47]

Mirroring the behaviour of older men, youths were at times equally violent in their treatment of women. Young women who spurned a would-be suitor's advances could face violent retribution. In May 1897, for example, Thomas Buckley of Greengate was fined twenty shillings following a vicious assault upon Mary Madely. She told how Buckley had accosted her at 9:30 p.m. one evening, pulling her shawl from her head and asking her to accompany him for a drink. When she refused, he struck her in the face with his fist, then butted her twice.[48] Other Salford youths, upholding a tradition of male violence within the home, were charged with assaults upon their mothers and other female relatives. In February 1890, Joseph Hargreaves, aged nineteen, was gaoled for a month after assaulting his mother and smashing her furniture. In court, she told how "she was frightened of her son, who came home blind drunk every night."[49] Violence therefore appears to have been a common feature in the everyday lives of young men in working-class districts. Some aped the behaviour of older men in their violence towards women, whilst many fought with rival youths, whether to avenge insults or simply to prove themselves against their peers. This broader culture of male violence formed the backdrop to young men's involvement in violent gangs.

III

Gang conflicts constituted arenas in which young men could prove themselves both individually and collectively by more systematic means. Gangs both issued and resisted challenges in order to enhance their reputations and to maintain their honour. Public displays of aggression and acts of violence in affrays between rival gangs allowed those on the brink of adulthood to derive considerable status, and to imagine themselves as "hard" men. As Humphries has remarked, gang membership provided young men in working-class districts with a source of identity and excitement, and offered an opportunity to assert a form of power. In Humphries' terms, for young men who possessed little or no formal economic or political power, gang membership offered at least a partial and temporary "solution" to the experience of inequality and subordination in other spheres of life.[50] We might usefully add, however, that gang membership provided a means for youths to attempt to consolidate their gender identities, and that the collective assertions of power in which gangs engaged offered frequent opportunities for male bravado. The imagined identity of the "hard" man was given dramatic expression by the members of scuttling gangs. James Rook, for example, a twenty-one-year old labourer, was convicted of assault after a gang rampaged through Chapel Street, Salford's main thoroughfare, at pub closing-time on a Saturday night in January 1889. As he struck out at passers-by, Rook was reported as shouting that he "could beat any man in Salford."[51]

Confrontations between rival scuttling gangs could take one of three forms, and it is worth examining these in turn in order to demonstrate the limited extent to which gang members were bound by the code of the "fair fight." Firstly, any gang which was aggrieved by the actions of a rival formation could issue the challenge "Will your best lad fight our best lad?" If the challenge was accepted, it was understood that only fists were to be used.[52] Press reports occasionally enable us to document such encounters. In May 1892, for example, Thomas Callaghan, a "king" among the scuttlers according to the Manchester police, was convicted of fighting and creating a disturbance in Hulme. According to the arresting officer, Callaghan was fighting with another man in the centre of a ring formed by scuttlers armed with belts and knives. In court, Callaghan admitted the offence, but alleged that the other man hit him first.[53] On these occasions, clashes between rival scuttlers appear to have been governed by the wider convention in which men were expected to fight "fair up."[54]

The vast majority of affrays reported by the local press, however, took the form of full "scuttles". These were characterised by Charles Russell, another leading figure in the local Lads' Club movement, as "set combats" between gangs which were "twenty or thirty strong."[55] In these collective encounters, it was understood that weapons would be used by both sides.[56] Typically, full-scale scuttles were prompted by territorial infringements. Scuttling gangs staked control over territory through the occupation of strategic street corners and public houses. Incursions by one gang into the territory of another were treated as deliberate acts of provocation, and it possible to trace vendettas between gangs across the Manchester conurbation. In June 1890, for example, the Salford police told how the Hope Street and Ordsall Lane gangs had clashed once or twice a week over a period of eighteen months in which they had "carried on a dangerous sort of guerilla warfare," armed with sticks, belts and knives.[57] The feud resulted in a series of police court cases and two trials. Hostility between the two gangs was perpetuated as both attempted to salvage their honour by avenging woundings inflicted by their adversaries.[58] Similarly, in October 1890, eleven youths aged between seventeen and nineteen were convicted of riot and sentenced to nine months' imprisonment with hard labour following an affray in Gorton in East Manchester. A gang from the neighbouring district of Bradford had made a

journal of social history winter 1998

series of raids upon Gorton, leading to fights with bricks, stones and heavily-buckled belts, culminating in a "pitched battle" on Sunday 20 October.[59] In such collective encounters, the principle of fighting "fair up" was clearly abandoned. Although scuttlers appear to have sought to wound rather than murder their opponents, feuds between rival gangs generated intense hostility and the use of weapons such as belts and knives was customary in the pursuit of status and reprisal.

In the third form of confrontation, assaults were made by a number of scuttlers belonging to one gang upon an isolated member of a rival formation. Such incidents were not uncommon and, as Alexander Devine noted, were "done for the purpose of terrorising and showing the superiority of one set over another."[60] Gangs were quick to interrogate individual scuttlers from rival districts who ventured into their territory, and appear to have regarded such territorial infringements as challenges to their honour irrespective of whether the hostile party numbered one or thirty. As the *Manchester Guardian* noted in 1898, the scuttler's uniform was like "a red rag to a bull" in rival districts. A Manchester youth, asked by the *Guardian* to describe how he would go about provoking a fight, stated simply "Suppose you want someone to fly at you ... you just soap your hair down over your left eye and put on a pigeon-board cap. Then you go into Salford. Then-you-go-into-Salford."[61] Again, the notion of the "fair fight" was abandoned when gangs made collective assaults upon lone rivals. Particularly brutal assaults were made as acts of reprisal, and it is significant that on the rare occasions when scuttling conflicts did lead to fatalities, the victims tended to be isolated and outnumbered in attacks of this sort.[62]

Territorial encroachments were not the only perceived insults which precipitated gang violence. Gang members also kept collective watch over their female associates. In effect, this amounted to an extension of their territorial claims. Charles Russell claimed that:

> The gravest troubles generally arose from attentions paid to the sweetheart of a member of one gang, by a member of another—a *casus belli* of first importance, and most dangerous consequences.[63]

Local journalists, following police officers and, on occasion, gang members themselves, were quick to blame young women for inciting gang conflicts. As the *Manchester Guardian* put it, "Everyone likes to feel herself a Helen of Troy."[64] However, gang members required little encouragement to interpret the actions of youths from rival districts as challenges. In February 1897, for example, James Tynan and Peter Fleming, two Manchester youths, were savagely assaulted after they walked Kathleen Whitham and Catherine Chambinzetti home to Greengate in Salford following an evening at a Manchester music-hall. Tynan was "keeping company with" Whitham, but upon arriving in Greengate, he and Fleming were immediately accosted by a gang of around a dozen local youths, one of whom shouted "This lot is out of Manchester." Tynan and Fleming were surrounded and struck with belts. According to Fleming, William Hopwood shouted "If you come this way, we will rip your bleeding hearts out," before stabbing Tynan. The knife punctured Tynan's lung, almost killing him.[65] In the eyes of the Greengate youths, Tynan and Fleming had committed two offences. Firstly, it was deemed an affront for Manchester youths to come into Salford.

Moreover, it transpired that sixteen-year-old Hopwood was "keeping company with" Chambinzetti, and was sufficiently aggrieved by the sight of his "sweetheart" with Tynan and Fleming to inflict a near fatal knife wound.

If the notion of the "fair fight" was widely disregarded in gang violence, scuttlers nonetheless claimed to adhere to a code of honour by asserting that they did not assault those who were not themselves gang members.[66] This is, however, unconvincing. As Alexander Devine complained in 1890:

> It often happens that a lad simply going to and from his work, and quite innocent of anything in the way of "scuttling," will be attacked, and possibly left on the ground bleeding. A lad with whom I am acquainted was a short time ago going on an errand to Miles Platting, and was there set upon and stabbed in the calf of the leg by a number of lads.[67]

Most of the victims of such assaults appear to have been young males. However, the local press occasionally reported the severe beatings suffered by adults who attempted to intervene on behalf of youths who were being assaulted by scuttlers, and there is evidence that witnesses called to testify against gang members in court were subjected to widespread harassment.[68] Assaults upon adults passing through streets which gangs claimed as their territory appear to have been less common, but occasional instances, sometimes motivated by racism and anti-semitism, were reported by the local press, and even young children in the company of their parents were vulnerable in such instances.[69] Moreover, gang members, in common with young men in working-class districts more generally, were also periodically convicted for assaults upon women, including their "sweethearts," mothers, aunts and sisters-in-law.[70] However, the perpetrators of such assaults may well have insisted that acts of violence against women should not be classed as "scuttling", since, in their own terms, they only "scuttled" rival gang members.

It is important to stress that participation in scuttling affrays was not universal among young working-class males, even in those areas where the gangs were strongest. Some young men, like Joe Toole, were willing to risk ostracism by their erstwhile peers. Telling how he was increasingly drawn to the local libraries in his youth, Toole recalled how:

> The lads at the street corner began to miss me. They now referred to me as a snob, who was learning more than was good for him. At this juncture, the Ordsall lads had a feud with the "She Battery" mob in Regent Road, Salford ... and they needed help to save the "honour" of the gang. They received no assistance from me. A new world had opened up for me which was quite unknown for them.[71]

Those who resisted such requests from scuttling gangs were sometimes dealt with more severely, and the local press reported cases where young men were beaten up for refusing to assist local gangs in an affray, or for a refusal to contribute to collections to pay the fines of those convicted for scuttling.[72] As noted earlier, however, the "hard" man was only one of the role models available to boys within working-class neighbourhoods. Other more respectable models of mature masculinity, provided by local autodidacts and political or trade union activists, were mirrored in the lifestyles of youths who eschewed the street corner for more respectable, "improving" pursuits.

IV

In order to develop a more detailed analysis of scuttling affrays in relation to masculine notions of honour and reputation, I now propose to examine a series of cases involving John Joseph Hillyar, a leading Salford scuttler during the 1890s. Hillyar's "career" as a gang member neatly illustrates the existence of a status hierarchy among scuttlers, and confirms the importance attached to the cultivation of both individual and collective reputations for fighting prowess. Before examining some of the affrays in which Hillyar took part, it might be useful by way of context to sketch his background and outline his history of court appearances. Hillyar was born in Fermoy, a market town in County Cork, in 1873, but moved to Salford during his childhood. At the time of the 1891 census, he was recorded as living in the Salford district of Ordsall with his mother and step-father, a furnace man.[73] Hillyar himself was working as a labourer in a copper works. He was involved in a series of court cases (I have so far traced eleven) between 1889 and 1899 arising out of incidents reported as cases of scuttling. These ranged from clashes between rival gangs to assaults either by or upon individual rivals. In eight of the eleven cases, Hillyar faced charges himself, ranging from disorderly conduct to unlawful wounding and attempted murder. In the remaining three cases, Hillyar appeared twice as prosecutor and once as a witness. His court appearances were made at the police courts and quarter sessions in both Salford and Manchester, and on one occasion, at the Manchester assizes. Significantly, from November 1893, Hillyar adopted the alias John Joseph Elliott, perhaps in an attempt to shed his string of previous convictions.[74] This was unsuccessful, however. He was too well-known to the local police forces.

Ten of the eleven cases occurred between 1889 and 1894, when Hillyar was aged between fifteen and twenty-one. He received six custodial sentences during this period, including three terms of two months' imprisonment and one of six months', and he was reported as living at a series of addresses in Salford and in neighbouring districts in Manchester between 1891 and 1895, which suggests that he was living in lodgings by the time that he was in his late teens. Hillyar received his longest sentence, of five years' penal servitude, following a conviction for attempted murder in 1895. He carried the scuttler's customary weapon of a brass-buckled belt as well as a knife, and he fought with rivals who were similarly armed. On at least three occasions, his own injuries were sufficiently serious to require hospital treatment.

A review of some of the cases involving Hillyar serves to illustrate a number of wider points about the nature of scuttling conflicts. His first conviction, on the relatively innocuous charge of throwing stones in Quay Street, Salford, was in June 1889, when he was aged fifteen.[75] Five months later, he was convicted of riot and sentenced to fourteen days' imprisonment with hard labour, following an incident in the Adelphi district of Salford. Hillyar was apprehended by the police whilst in possession of a butcher's knife. He had been struck on the head with belts, and was bleeding when he was taken into custody.[76] By the time he was aged seventeen, Hillyar was well-known to the members of rival gangs, and a third case shows how youths with prominent reputations were singled out by the members of opposing gangs during affrays. In May 1891, Hillyar was one of two youths who were severely injured by the members of a Manchester gang in an affray outside the "Cass," a popular music-hall in Manchester city centre. Thomas Callaghan, the "king" of the London Road scuttlers, was reported to have threatened Hillyar inside the music-hall. In the subsequent affray, which occurred in the streets outside, Callaghan allegedly struck Hillyar on the head with an iron bar. Hillyar fell to the ground, and was surrounded and kicked by the rival gang. He spent nearly two weeks in hospital recovering from his injuries.[77] The "Cass" was a common site of confrontations between rival gangs. In August 1891, Hillyar was himself sentenced to two months' imprisonment for stabbing a Bradford scuttler during an affray in the gallery.[78]

A further case confirms that although rival gangs fought to establish the collective supremacy of one gang over another, individual reputations for scuttling prowess were also fiercely contested. In November 1893, Hillyar (by now using the alias Elliott) was charged with unlawfully wounding Peter McLaughlin in New Bridge-street, Salford. According to police evidence in court, when apprehended Hillyar admitted that he had committed the offence, declaring that "McLaughlin thinks he is the champion scuttler in Salford, and he has got to see there is some one who can — take him down."[79] Hillyar was subsequently indicted at the Salford quarter sessions in January 1894. It was alleged that he had accosted McLaughlin (who presumably was wearing the scuttler's customary bell-bottomed trousers) with the words "Hallo, sailor! What do you say if I cut you in pieces?" before stabbing him in the back with a dagger. Hillyar was sentenced to six months' imprisonment with hard labour.[80] Shortly after his release, Hillyar and his companions were set upon by a gang of around fifty youths in Salford, and Hillyar in turn was stabbed in the chest. In view of the timing of the assault, it is at least possible that it was intended in part as a reprisal for Hillyar's stabbing of Peter McLaughlin.[81]

At the Manchester assizes in February 1895, Hillyar was indicted for the attempted murder of William Willcock, a Salford collier. Willcock alleged that Hillyar had struck him with a belt and stabbed him several times in the back in an incident which took place in Manchester city centre on a Sunday night in December 1894. The police officer who apprehended Hillyar stated that he had admitted to the offence. However, at the trial Hillyar claimed "He had a knife, and I did it in self-defence. They keep following me from all nations. I could only go in one part of Manchester, and then certain people were not satisfied until they had got me in prison again."[82] Hillyar, displaying a strong sense of his own importance, thus claimed that he was a marked man, singled out by rivals from across Manchester and Salford. Nonetheless, on this occasion, he was sentenced to five years' penal servitude.[83]

Each time that he appeared in court, Hillyar protested his innocence, usually pleading that he had acted only in self-defence.[84] However, he also played at times to the public gallery, conscious that his peers were assembled there. Reports of court proceedings in scuttling cases frequently testify to the presence of gang members as on-lookers, and to the "considerable uproar at the back of the court" which greeted the announcement of sentences.[85] At the Salford quarter sessions in 1894, for example, when sentenced to six months' imprisonment for unlawfully wounding Peter McLaughlin, Hillyar shouted "I will swing for it when I come out," as the Recorder of Salford announced the sentence.[86] Whilst signalling his defiance to the Recorder and to the police (as well as to the watching journalists), Hillyar's display of bravado may well have been intended for his peers, as much to impress his own associates as to intimidate McLaughlin.

A series of points emerge from these accounts. Firstly, this brief profile suggests that a clear status hierarchy among scuttlers, and the reputations of prominent gang members like Hillyar and Thomas Callaghan, spanned the working-class districts across the Manchester conurbation. Salford scuttlers clashed with rival gangs drawn both from Manchester and from the townships to the east of the city, such as Bradford and Openshaw. On Friday and Saturday nights, the city centre formed a contested terrain, as gangs drawn from as far apart as Salford and Bradford confronted each other in music-halls, nearby beerhouses and the surrounding streets. In these conflicts, the reputations of the leading figures were constantly adjusted, whether enhanced or undermined. Moreover, scuttlers who were worsted in an affray frequently appear to have launched revenge attacks in attempts to salvage their reputation and honour.[87] It seems likely that leading scuttlers such as Hillyar were the most famous working-class youths in late Victorian Manchester and Salford. They attracted more press coverage at this time than any local sporting figures, for example. However, whilst the leaders of scuttling gangs enjoyed considerable prestige among their peers and rivals, they also faced the constant danger of surprise assault. Just as Hillyar stabbed Peter McLaughlin, he in turn was subject to assaults by individual rivals who sought to enhance their own reputations at his expense.[88]

Hillyar's reputation was such that he was recalled, by his alias of Elliott, in an oral history interview conducted as part of Paul Thompson's project on "Family Life and Work Experience before 1918." In an interview which took place in February 1970, Arthur Collier, who was born in the Hanky Park district in 1885, described the scuttlers when he was asked about "rough" districts in Salford. Collier declared "Oh, they were terrible. They always wore belts you know, scuttler's belts with brass buckles on."[89] Asked whether he knew any scuttlers personally, he replied:

> Oh yes, I knew a lot of them. There was Red Elliott ... he was one of the leaders ... He wore a jersey which said "Red Elliott" on it and "King of Scuttlers" ... He stabbed a fellow on Hope Street bridge ... where the Prince of Wales [public house] is.[90]

According to Arthur Collier, the stabbing occurred as "Red Elliott" fought against the Hanky Park scuttlers in a "row over girls". This incident took place in July 1899, and was widely reported in the local press. John Joseph Hillyar (who was still using the alias Elliott) was alleged to have wielded a belt and a knife during the affray. Now aged twenty-five, and currently on a ticket-of-leave from his sentence of five years' penal servitude, Hillyar was considerably older than the vast majority of those convicted of scuttling. In some ways, he must have seemed an anomalous figure in court, not least when it is considered that one of the young women present at the scene appears to have been only fifteen years old. Nonetheless, Hillyar was described in court by his old title as a "King of Scuttlers."[91] Significantly, this title was first used by the Salford press to describe Hillyar in 1893, which raises the intriguing possibility that a label originally devised by a journalist was adopted by Hillyar, for whom the title must have formed an ironic yet welcome mark of his status.[92]

It is important to note that scuttlers were themselves willing to use the criminal justice system. Although gang members generally attempted to avoid police interference at the scene of affrays, even those like Hillyar with strings of previous convictions of their own would sometimes initiate prosecutions against their rivals.[93] This raises the possibility that such prosecutions followed deals struck between gang members and the police, in which scuttlers agreed to prosecute their rivals in return for escaping criminal charges themselves. Alternatively, however, it is conceivable that gang members felt justified in complaining to the police in cases where they had been set upon without warning, or by superior numbers. Moreover, it is equally plausible that prosecutions were viewed as an alternative means of revenge for scuttlers who had been worsted in affrays. For those whose honour had been undermined by defeat, the courts may have constituted an alternative arena of conflict, and it appears that gang members may have attempted to manipulate the criminal justice system against specific rivals. Hillyar's plea, when charged with attempted murder in February 1895, that his enemies were determined to pursue him and to bring prosecutions against him, suggests that his rivals were as keen to see him in prison as the police.

V

In conclusion, it is tempting to reverse Humphries' characterisation of gang members as "rebels". When their activities are examined from a gendered perspective, we might view Hillyar and his rivals as striving to embody the working-class ideal of the "hard" man, and thus as reproducing established patterns of male behaviour. Seeking to prove themselves through displays of aggression and fighting prowess, scuttlers both dramatised and endorsed the customary association between "hardness" and masculine status which permeated life in working-class districts. In cultural terms, therefore, scuttlers were archly conservative. Moreover, Humphries' emphasis upon gang members' alienation from respectable society must be qualified, as scuttlers were not, in any literal sense, outlaws.[94] Gang members did sometimes fight with police officers in their efforts to evade arrest, and displays of bravado in the dock frequently signalled their defiance of those sitting in judgement upon them. However, under certain circumstances, gang members were willing to use the law themselves and to co-operate with the police in bringing prosecutions against their adversaries. Perhaps the much smaller number of young women who took an active part in gang violence were more rebellious than their male counterparts, as female scuttlers clearly transgressed the codes of womanly conduct embedded in dominant Victorian ideals of femininity.[95]

Considerable peer-group prestige was at stake in scuttling affrays, and feuds between rival gangs generated a momentum of their own as gang members sought to avenge defeats and thus to salvage their honour. Youths tended to be more likely than older men to take part in street violence, reflecting in part the more precarious masculine identities of those aged in their mid- to late teens. For youths who had not yet reached the peak of their physical strength, and had still to qualify for the most physically-demanding (and high-status) forms of manual work, gang conflicts provided an alternative arena for displays of masculine prowess. Yet even Hillyar and his closest rivals were not regarded

364   journal of social history   winter 1998

as the "hardest" men in Salford. Scuttlers sought out confrontations with rival youths, but do not appear to have pitted themselves against older "hard" men, such as local prize fighters. Indeed, for all the efforts of gang members to prove themselves, scuttling with knives and belts may well have been viewed almost as a boyish practice by men aged in their twenties and thirties, very few of whom ever chose to involve themselves in gang conflicts.

It must be stressed that within working-class neighbourhoods, there were sharply differentiated conceptions of what being a man entailed. Scuttlers generally drew upon notions of "hardness" rather than the alternative models of virtuous manhood provided by the breadwinner or the respectable artisan. Even in districts with powerful local gangs, such as Ordsall in Salford, gang membership was not universal among youths in semi- or unskilled occupations. Unfortunately, in the absence of autobiographical accounts by former gang members, it is not possible to examine why certain youths joined gangs whilst others, from comparable backgrounds, did not.[96] The absence of scuttlers' memoirs also makes it difficult to chart the behaviour of gang members over the course of the life cycle. There is fragmentary evidence that some scuttlers subsequently made domineering and violent husbands, and many gang members no doubt maintained reputations as neighbourhood "hard" men in later life.[97] Others, however, may well have become increasingly respectable once they took on "men's" work and the adult responsibilities of breadwinner and householder. Scuttling therefore appears to have been a pre-eminently youthful activity, in which young men on the brink of adulthood acquired both individual and collective status in the eyes of their peers.

School of History
Liverpool L69 3BX United Kingdom

ENDNOTES

This paper is drawn from a project on "Youth Gangs and Urban Violence: Manchester, Salford and Glasgow, 1860–1939" funded by the Economic and Social Research Council as part of a Research Programme on *Crime and Social Order*, award number L210252006. For permission to consult the Registers of Prisoners' Offences (hereafter P.O. Registers) held at the Salford Magistrates' Court, I am grateful to John Davies, Clerk to the Court. I also wish to thank Claire Langhamer for her meticulous work in entering a sample of offences from 1889–1890 into a database.

Earlier versions of this paper were presented at conferences held at the Roehampton Institute, London, in May 1995, and the Martin-Luther-Universität Halle-Wittenberg in September 1996. I am grateful to Laura Craig-Gray and Jon Lawrence for a series of discussions of the themes raise here. For further constructive criticism, I wish to thank John Archer, Penny Fraser, Jill Greenfield, Karen Hunt, Martha Kanya-Forstner, Sean O'Connell, Geoff Pearson, Ian Taylor, John Tosh and Pamela Walker.

1.   Stephen Humphries, *Hooligans or Rebels? An Oral History of Working-Class Childhood and Youth 1889–1939* (Oxford, 1981); Geoffrey Pearson, *Hooligan: A History of Respectable Fears* (London, 1983).

2.   There are no British studies which compare with Frederic M. Thrasher, *The Gang: A Study of 1,313 Gangs in Chicago* (Chicago, 1927) or William F. Whyte, *Street Corner Society: The Social Structure of an Italian Slum* (Chicago, 1943). For a critical overview of the historical development of the contrasting North American and British literatures on

youth and crime, see Geoffrey Pearson, "Youth, Crime and Society," in Mike Maguire, Rod Morgan and Robert Reiner (eds), *The Oxford Handbook of Criminology* (Oxford, 1994).

3. Humphries, *Hooligans or Rebels?* p. 179.

4. Humphries, *Hooligans or Rebels?* pp. 190–93.

5. Humphries, *Hooligans or Rebels?* pp. 193–8. Few historians would now endorse Humphries' claim that ethnic violence was a "misdirected expression" of class consciousness among white working-class youths.

6. Humphries, *Hooligans or Rebels?* pp. 179–80. Humphries turned his attention more directly to the issue of masculinity in a subsequent account of sexual behaviour among gang members. See his *A Secret World of Sex. Forbidden Fruit: The British Experience 1900–1950* (London, 1988), ch. 6. In the case of the late Victorian youth gang, sexual behaviour is extremely difficult to assess given the paucity of the available sources.

7. For a recent assessment of notions of "hardness", see Paul Willis, *Common Culture: Symbolic Work at Play in the Everyday Cultures of the Young* (Milton Keynes, 1990), p. 103–9.

8. For an insightful discussion of peer recognition as a component of the transition to manhood, see John Tosh, "What Should Historians do with Masculinity? Reflections on Nineteenth-century Britain," *History Workshop Journal* 38 (1994): 184.

9. For Humphries' treatment of these themes, see *Secret World of Sex*, pp. 147–8.

10. Gary Armstrong, "False Leeds: The Construction of Hooligan Confrontations," in John Williams and Richard Giulianotti (eds), *Games Without Frontiers: Football, Identity and Modernity* (Aldershot, 1994), p. 301. My analysis of gang conflicts as contests over honour has been strongly influenced by this pioneering work on football hooliganism.

11. I have discussed the issue of broader working-class attitudes towards scuttling gangs in a separate paper, as yet unpublished, entitled "A Carnival of Knives and Belts: Youth Gangs and Street Violence in Late Victorian Salford."

12. Andrew Davies, " 'These Viragoes are No Less Cruel than the Lads': Young Women, Gangs and Violence in late Victorian Manchester and Salford," *British Journal of Criminology* (forthcoming).

13. Rob Sindall, *Street Violence in the Nineteenth Century: Media Panic or Real Danger?* (Leicester, 1990).

14. The one-dimensional nature of police court news reporting was highlighted by Andrew Barrett, "Newspapers as a Source for the History of Crime," paper presented to the Historians of Crime, Policing and Punishment in the North West group, November 1994.

15. Humphries, *Hooligans or Rebels?* p. 176.

16. Manchester's municipal boundaries were significantly extended during the late nineteenth century. Bradford was incorporated in 1885, and Openshaw and West Gorton in 1890. See Alan Kidd, *Manchester* (Keele, 1993), p. 154.

17. *Manchester Guardian*, 5 February 1898.

18. Alan J. Kidd, " 'Outcast Manchester': Voluntary Charity, Poor Relief and the Casual

Poor 1860–1905," in Alan J. Kidd and K.W. Roberts (eds), *City, Class and Culture: Studies of Social Policy and Cultural Production in Victorian Manchester* (Manchester, 1985), pp. 51, 68.

19. See the comments of the Mayor of Manchester to the Home Secretary, *Manchester Guardian*, 13 December 1890. Neither of the principal commentators on scuttling featured ethnicity or sectarianism in their accounts of the conflicts. See Devine, *Scuttlers and Scuttling* and Charles E. B. Russell, *Manchester Boys: Sketches of Manchester Lads at Work and Play* (Manchester, 1905). Only in the first reports of scuttling in the Manchester press, following disturbances in the Rochdale Road district of Manchester during the autumn of 1871, were the conflicts characterised in terms of sectarian violence. See the *Manchester Courier*, 25 October 1871. Sectarianism appears to have been rapidly superseded by territorial rivalries as gang conflicts spread across the conurbation by the mid-1870s.

20. Steven Fielding, "A Separate Culture? Irish Catholics in Working-class Manchester and Salford, c. 1890–1939," in Andrew Davies and Steven Fielding (eds), *Workers' Worlds: Cultures and Communities in Manchester and Salford, 1880–1939* (Manchester, 1992), pp. 26–8, 36–7.

21. See the insistent comments of local stipendiary magistrates to the Home Secretary, *Manchester Guardian*, 13 December 1890. I have profiled the occupational and family backgrounds of the members of Salford's Hope Street gang in "A Carnival of Knives and Belts" (forthcoming).

22. Keith McClelland, "Masculinity and the 'Representative Artisan' in Britain, 1850–80," in Michael Roper and John Tosh (eds), *Manful Assertions: Masculinities in Britain since 1800* (London, 1991), p. 81.

23. Fielding, "A Separate Culture?", pp. 28–9, 37.

24. The most heavily-publicised fatality occurred in the Ancoats district of Manchester in May 1892. See the *Manchester Guardian*, 12 May 1892.

25. See the account of a series of cases involving the Salford scuttler John Joseph Hillyar, below.

26. Devine, *Scuttlers and Scuttling*, pp. 2–3. For an account of an affray in which a Salford youth suffered a fractured skull, see the *Salford Chronicle*, 10 February 1894.

27. James Bent, *Criminal Life: Reminiscences of Forty-Two Years as a Police Officer* (Manchester, 1891), p. 225.

28. On the youthful dedication to fashion in Manchester's working-class districts, see the colourful descriptions in local magazines such as *The Shadow*, 20 March 1869 and *The City Lantern*, 6 August 1875.

29. *Manchester Guardian*, 5 February 1898, Russell, *Manchester Boys*, p. 51. I am grateful to David Taylor of Manchester Central Reference Library for the first of these references.

30. Devine, *Scuttlers and Scuttling*, p. 5.

31. Four Salford scuttlers, members of "Buffalo Bill's Gang", were convicted following an affray in January 1890, *Salford Chronicle*, 25 January, 1 February 1890.

32. The notion of multiple masculinities is beginning to be developed across a range of social science disciplines. For a wide-ranging critical survey, see R. W. Connell, *Masculinities* (Cambridge, 1995). For a discussion of the contrasting lifestyles of "family" men and

"hard" men in working-class districts in the early twentieth century, see Andrew Davies, *Leisure, Gender and Poverty: Working-Class Culture in Salford and Manchester, 1900–1939* (Buckingham, 1992).

33. Paul Thompson highlighted the range of violence both suffered and witnessed by the children of two poor Salford families at the close of the nineteenth century in his "Voices from Within," in H. J. Dyos and Michael Wolff (eds), *The Victorian City: Images and Realities*, vol. I (London, 1976), pp. 73–9. See also Michael J. Childs, *Labour's Apprentices: Working-Class Lads in Late Victorian and Edwardian England* (London, 1992), pp. 106–9.

34. Roberts, *Classic Slum*, pp. 28–9.

35. Ellen Ross, "Fierce Questions and Taunts: Married Life in Working-Class London, 1870–1914," *Feminist Studies* 8, 2 (1982).

36. Robert Roberts, *A Ragged Schooling: Growing up in the Classic Slum* (Manchester, 1976), p. 118.

37. *Salford Weekly Chronicle*, 30 May 1885.

38. *Salford Weekly Chronicle*, 3 September 1887.

39. See the case of Michael Green and John McGratton, *Salford Weekly News*, 12 June 1875.

40. Henry Hill, *The Story of Adelphi: Sixty Years' History of the Adelphi Lads' Club* (Salford, 1949), p. 121.

41. Childs, *Labour's Apprentices*, p. 107.

42. Thompson, "Voices from Within," pp. 74–6. I have retained the pseudonym 'Doyle' used by Thompson. The term "flag floors" is used here to denote bare stone floors.

43. Joe Toole, *Fighting through Life* (London, 1935), pp. 5–6.

44. Bart Kennedy, *Slavery: Pictures from the Depths* (London, 1905), pp. 138–46. For an account of the frequent and public fights between youths in Greengate in Salford, see the *Sphinx*, 19 June 1869.

45. *County Telephone*, 25 May 1889; *Manchester Guardian*, 30 May 1889.

46. See, for example, the case of William Choularton, *Salford Reporter*, 13 January 1894.

47. P.O. Register, 8 July 1890, case no. 18; *Salford Chronicle*, 12 July 1890.

48. *Salford Chronicle*, 22 May 1897.

49. *Salford Reporter*, 8 February 1890.

50. Humphries, *Hooligans or Rebels*, p. 208. See also Barbara Weinberger, "L'Anatomie de l'Antagonisme Racial et de la Violence Urbaine: Les Bandes à Birmingham dans les Années 1870," *Déviance et Société* 15, 4 (1991): 417.

51. P.O. Register, 21 January 1889, case no. 11; *Salford Weekly Chronicle*, 26 January 1889.

52. *Manchester Guardian*, 5 February 1898.

53. *Manchester Guardian*, 24 June 1892.

54. *Manchester Guardian*, 5 February 1898.

55. Russell, *Manchester Boys*, pp. 52–3.

56. *Manchester Guardian*, 13 December 1890, 5 February 1898.

57. *Manchester Courier*, 7 June 1890.

58. The feud between the two gangs is explored in depth in Davies, "Carnival of Knives and Belts."

59. *Manchester Courier*, 22 October 1889; *Manchester Guardian*, 23 October 1889.

60. Devine, *Scuttlers and Scuttling* p. 3.

61. *Manchester Guardian*, 5 February 1898.

62. *Manchester Guardian*, 12 May 1892.

63. Russell, *Manchester Boys*, p. 52.

64. *Manchester Guardian*, 5 February 1898; *Salford Reporter*, 3 June 1899.

65. *Salford Chronicle*, 30 January, 13, 27 February 1897; *Salford Reporter*, 30 January 1897.

66. Charles E. B. Russell and Lilian M. Rigby, *Working Lads' Clubs* (London, 1908), p. 12; *Manchester Guardian*, 5 February 1898.

67. Devine, *Scuttlers and Scuttling*, p. 3.

68. *Salford Weekly News*, 1 April 1882; *Salford Chronicle*, 10 June 1893.

69. *Salford Weekly News*, 26 May 1877; *Salford Chronicle*, 20 June 1891.

70. See, for example, the case of John Devaney, *Manchester Guardian*, 31 October 1890.

71. Toole, *Fighting through Life*, p. 48. Providence Street, Salford was labelled the "She Battery" by locals, on account of the prostitutes who worked from the street, drawing the majority of their clients from a nearby barracks.

72. For two from a series of such cases, see the *Salford Weekly News*, 15 March 1879 and 21 August 1880.

73. The 1891 census recorded the family as living at 29 Woden Street. I have taken the spelling of Hillyar from the census entry. The local press generally used the alternative of Hillier.

74. *Salford Chronicle*, 18 November 1893.

75. P.O. Register, 4 June 1889, case no. 11.

76. P.O. Register, 7 November 1889, case no. 3; *County Telephone*, 9 November 1889; *Salford Chronicle*, 9 November 1889.

77. *Manchester Guardian*, 5, 13, 20 May, 13 June 1891; *Salford Reporter*, 9 May 1891.

78. *Manchester Guardian*, 28 August, 1 September 1891. The "Cass" was the popular name for the Casino music-hall, previously known as the People's Concert Hall. One of Manchester's most popular music-halls, the audiences were notoriously "rough". See Toole, *Fighting through Life*, p. 2.

79. *Salford Chronicle*, 18 November 1893.

80. *Salford Reporter*, 13 January 1894.

81. *Salford Reporter*, 21, 28 July 1894; *Salford Chronicle*, 1 September 1894.

82. *Salford Reporter*, 2 March 1895.

83. *Salford Reporter*, 2 March 1895.

84. For examples of Hillyar's pleas of self-defence, see the reports of his court appearances in the *Manchester Guardian*, 28 August, 1 September 1891; *Salford Reporter*, 13 January 1894; *Salford Reporter*, 2 March 1895.

85. *Salford Reporter*, 2 March 1895.

86. *Salford Reporter*, 13 January 1894.

87. *Manchester Guardian*, 13 June 1891.

88. For example, in a case reported in the *Manchester Evening News*, 9 May 1892, Hillyar alleged that he had been stabbed as he was leaving a ragged school in Deansgate, by a youth named William Wood, who was sentenced to a month's imprisonment.

89. "Family Life and Work Experience" interviews, Qualidata Archive, University of Essex, tape no. 90. I am grateful to Professor Thompson for his permission to consult this tape. The pseudonym "Collier" was used by Paul Thompson in "Voices from Within," pp. 77–9.

90. Ibid. I have re-transcribed this extract, which was originally cited in Thompson, "Voices from Within," p. 78. I am grateful to Dave Moore for alerting me to this reference.

91. *Salford Chronicle*, 29 July, 5 August 1899; *Salford Reporter*, 29 July, 5 August 1899.

92. *Salford Reporter*, 13 January 1894. Further thanks are due to Dave Moore for this reference.

93. For reports of cases in which John Joseph Hillyar brought prosecutions against rival scuttlers, see the *Manchester Evening News*, 9 May 1892; *Salford Reporter*, 21, 28 July 1894; *Salford Chronicle*, 1 September 1894.

94. Humphries, *Hooligans or Rebels?* p. 208.

95. Davies, "Young Women, Gangs and Violence."

96. The same question has vexed anthropologists studying football hooligan gangs in modern Britain. See Armstrong, "False Leeds", p. 321, and his "Like that Desmond Morris?" in Dick Hobbs and Tim May (eds), *Interpreting the Field: Accounts of Ethnography* (Oxford, 1993), p. 37.

97. See the portrayal of "Mr Carey", the father of a childhood friend, by Robert Roberts, *Ragged Schooling*, pp. 75, 79, 102, 119.

[11]

Defensive localism in white and black: a comparative history of European-American and African-American youth gangs

Christopher Adamson

Abstract

The activities of European-American and African-American youth gangs have been closely linked to the operation of changing racial and class structures. In this article, I compare European-American and African-American youth gangs in four historical periods: the seaboard city, 1787–1861; the immigrant city, 1880–1940; the racially changing city, 1940–1970; and the hypersegregated city, 1970–1999. I show that the differences between European-American and African-American gangs can be traced to the race-specific effects of labour, housing and consumer markets, government policies (especially crime control policies), local politics and organized crime on European-American and African-American communities. I conclude that European-American youth gangs facilitated cultural assimilation because of their close ties with formal and informal political authorities and organizations which commanded substantial social and economic power, whereas African-American youth gangs reinforced cultural separation because of their embeddedness in racially segregated, economically marginalized and politically powerless communities.

Keywords: Youth gangs; United States; ethnicity; race; assimilation; segregation.

In a country like the United States in which race and class have been the central structuring principles of urban life, we would expect significant differences in the patterns of historical development of European-American and African-American youth or street gangs. Indeed, the effects of racial and class structures on the behaviour of American youth gangs have been so profound that scholars who have sought to develop race-invariant theories of gangs and delinquency have been stymied.[1] Over the last fifty years, those criminologists and sociologists who have been sensitive to the differential effects of joblessness, residential segregation and the availability of public services on white and black communities have acknowledged the absurdity of attempts to construct a single, race-invariant model of youth-gang behaviour.[2]

This is not to say that there are not similarities between white and black gangs.[3] It is true, for example, that both white and black youth gangs have been affected by economic disadvantage, family disruption and social disorganization. Gangs of both races have been predators upon, and protectors of, the communities in which they are embedded. For black and white teenagers, the gang has been a place in which to forge an identity and achieve social status. And just as white youth gangs have attacked vulnerable blacks, black youth gangs have attacked vulnerable whites. For both races, the gang has performed important community functions which can be subsumed under the rubric of defensive localism. These functions include the defence of territory, the policing of neighbourhoods, the upholding of group honour, and the provision of economic, social, employment, welfare and recreational services.

Despite these similarities, white and black youth gangs are profoundly different historical creations. They originated at different times, and their respective relationships to labour, housing and consumer markets, governmental institutions, formal and informal political authority, organized crime and agencies of crime control have been different. In the historical analysis which ensues, I compare the effects of these structural relationships on white and black youth gangs.

White youth gangs in the seaboard city, 1787–1861

Black youth gangs did not exist as a recognized social problem until the great migration of the 1910s when large numbers of African-Americans came to the northern cities. Indeed, it was only with the massive second great migration of the mid-twentieth century, when a far more intractable urban ghetto was created, that politicians, prosecutors, police officials and social workers began to view African-American youth gangs as a threat to social order. In the nineteenth century, the assumptions of caste militated against the formation of territorial gangs of free black youth. No doubt groups of three or more young blacks got together on many occasions, and certain newspapers, such as the *North American and United States News Gazette* in 1853, did point to the existence of black youth gangs in Philadelphia (Davis 1982, p. 190). It is significant, however, that these black gangs were neither named nor territorial. At a time when African-American gatherings and parades were regarded with suspicion, the appearance of boisterous gangs of black teenagers on street corners, even in areas inhabited by many blacks, would have been dangerously provocative (Litwack 1961, p. 102).

White youth gangs, in contrast, existed at the very inception of the republic. In the late 1780s, for example, prison reformers commented on

274   *Christopher Adamson*

the baneful presence of gangs of young people hanging out on Philadelphia's street corners (Meranze 1996, p. 94). The activities of white gangs, which became an increasingly visible presence in the ante-bellum city, were geared to the defence of local neighbourhoods. Gang youth, who were generally subservient to prominent adults in the community, upheld the local racial order.

By the 1820s white boys in their teens and early twenties were gathering on street corners in New York's Bowery and Five Points districts, Boston's North End and Fort Hill, and the outlying Southwark and Moyamensing sections of Philadelphia. These gangs of boys fought youths from other neighbourhoods for control of street corners and open lots. For example, New York's Smith Vly Boys, a gang which took its name 'from the marsh, or lowlands (Dutch *Vly*) in the lower, eastern part of the city', fought several Broadway gangs for control of the high ground on present-day Grand Street, then called Bunker Hill (Gilje 1987, p. 261). The Roach Guards, named in honour of a Five Points liquor seller, took on the Chichesters, the Plug Uglies and the Dead Rabbits. The Roach Guards' battle uniform was 'a blue stripe on the pantaloons, while the Dead Rabbits adopted a red stripe, and at the head of their sluggers carried a dead rabbit impaled on a pike' (Asbury 1928, p. 23). The impoverished suburbs of Philadelphia were home to a large number of turf-defending white gangs whose 'verminous designations', as *New York Tribune* reporter George Foster (1848, p. 35) put it, 'were written in chalk or charcoal on every dead-wall, fence, and stable door'.

It is important to recognize that white gangs were often multi-ethnic, especially in neighbourhoods that were not rigidly segregated by ethnicity. Dutch, English, Welsh, Scots-Irish, Irish Catholics, Germans and persons of mixed ancestry could be found in the same territorially defined youth gang. Territory was often more important than ethnicity in shaping the formation of white youth gangs. New York's Bowery gangs, such as the O'Connell Guards, the Atlantic Guards, the American Guards and the True Blue Americans – some of which were nativist and Protestant, others Irish Catholic – put aside their ethnic differences in order to defend their territory against Five Points gangs[4] (Asbury 1928, p. 28; Sante 1991, p. 200).

It is central to this article's argument to recognize that white youth gangs enjoyed a measure of support from the adult population. To be sure, gang boys annoyed adults by swearing and carrying on loudly in the streets; and their drinking, fighting, disrespect for property and theft disrupted the fabric of social life. But white gangs were sponsored by politically powerful adults, who rewarded them for defending the local neighbourhood. In some instances, youth gangs served an informal policing function. Gang boys in New York, for example, 'served as informal neighborhood constabularies'. They 'stood about on street corners with a studied watchful glower, making sure, as one New Yorker recalled, that anyone who was 'exotic or unfamiliar' would not cause trouble or linger too long' (Wilentz 1984, p. 262). Gang boys also considered it their duty to protect young women in the neighbourhood. In the Bowery young toughs chased after prowling outsiders and voyeuristic 'aristos' seeking sexual liaison with Bowery girls (Stansell 1987, p. 95).

It was thus a hallmark of white defensive localism that street gangs were subservient to powerful adults in the community. Gangs allied themselves with social and political clubs and often took direction from political bosses, who depended on them to mobilize the vote and protect polling places on election days. Membership in a youth gang could lead to a career in local politics. Thus William McMullen, Philadelphia's influential saloon keeper, alderman, prison inspector and political boss, started his career as a member of the Killers, one of the city's violent Irish-Catholic fighting gangs.

White youth gangs patrolled streets and secured neighbourhood boundaries. The Killers, for example, won the support of the people of Moyamensing by protecting them from nativist invaders and by occasionally distributing food to the poor (Silcox 1989, p. 46). However, white youth gangs like the Killers also participated in collective attacks on free blacks. Given the caste assumption of black ontological inferiority, white gang boys looked upon black Americans as a people to whom the rules of honour-based conflict did not apply, and viciously assaulted inoffensive black women and elderly black men during riots.

In the 1830s young Irish and native-born workingmen expressed their contempt for New York's African Americans by savagely attacking black patrons of white drinking and eating houses, and by destroying the property of successful black tavern keepers (Kaplan 1995, pp. 606–9). In Philadelphia, in 1834, a 'party of half grown boys' precipitated a three-night riot by attacking a tavern with an interracial clientele. A mob then invaded the streets and alleys of Moyamensing, assaulting free blacks, looting their homes, destroying their furniture and bedding, and forcing many of them to flee into the city or across the Delaware. Many of the rioters described their activities as 'hunting the nigs' (Runcie 1972, p. 190). In 1849 Philadelphia's Killers burnt down the California House Tavern, an establishment owned by a mulatto who had married a white woman. As in 1834, a mob then proceeded to hunt down pedestrians on the streets of the African-American section of Moyamensing, killing three blacks and injuring at least two dozen others (Feldberg 1980, p. 59; Laurie 1980, p. 156).

The Irish antipathy towards African Americans was partly fuelled by competition for jobs on the docks, shipyards and building construction sites, and partly rooted in a *herrenvolk* republicanism which sought to deprive free blacks of any of the rights enjoyed by white citizens and members of the producing classes (Roediger 1991, p. 147). This antipathy found its ugliest expression in New York City's draft riot of 1863 and in

276   *Christopher Adamson*

Philadelphia's voting day riot of 1871 (Lane 1986, p. 10; Bernstein 1990, p. 66). The impulse of Irish-Catholic youth gangs to victimize African Americans became an undeniable element in the century-long cultural transformation of the United States from a haven of Protestant purity to a white republic that included Catholics. Poor Irish immigrants strove to assimilate or, as Noel Ignatiev (1995, pp. 163–76) has put it, to 'become white' by victimizing African Americans. As early as the ante-bellum period, then, belonging to a white gang facilitated the cultural assimilation of European immigrants.

White youth gangs in the immigrant city, 1880–1940

A significant number of the 13.5 million people who came to the United States from South, Central, and Eastern Europe between 1880 and 1924 settled in the cities of the Northeast and Midwest. The economic hardship and cultural dislocation experienced by many immigrant parents made it difficult for them to adequately discipline their children, let alone supervise their school work or guide them into rewarding employment. Immigrant children, who found themselves caught between the old-world communal practices of their parents and the norms of an often hostile host society, frequently got together in corner groups and gangs.

White youth gangs in the immigrant city were often multi-ethnic, generally subservient to ward politicians, resolutely territorial, delinquent in varying degrees and virulently racist. In 1927 the country's foremost gang expert, Frederic Thrasher, highlighted the involvement of immigrants in the youth gangs of Chicago. He noted that 70.4 per cent of Chicago's 10–24-year-old males were boys of foreign extraction, while a *'whopping'* 87.4 per cent of the city's gangs were gangs of foreign boys. In contrast, 25.7 per cent of Chicago's 10–24-year-old males were American (that is, native white parentage) boys, while a *'miniscule'* 5.3 per cent of the city's gangs were gangs of American boys (Thrasher 1936, p. 193, Table 5).

Progressive-era white youth gangs, like their ante-bellum predecessors, were often multi-ethnic. Thrasher's data include myriad examples of ethnically mixed white gangs. For example, the Tent Gang, which stole tinned goods from railroad cars, was made up of Italian and Polish boys. The Elstons, who fought 'innumerable battles of fists and bricks' against the Polish Belmonts, were Irish and Swedish. The O'Brien Juniors, known for their tradition of initiating new members by 'kicking them around', included Irish, Scottish, and Swedish boys. The Twelfth Street Boundary Gang was composed of Polish, Bohemian and Greek lads. Italian boys were invited to join a Jewish gang in the Maxwell Street area 'because of their compatibility and their residence in the area' (Thrasher 1936, pp. 136, 180, 258, 282, 310).

Thrasher determined the race and ethnicity of 880 out of the 1,313 gangs known to exist in Chicago at the time. If we exclude the sixty-three Negro gangs, the twenty-five mixed Negro-white gangs, and the five miscellaneous gangs, as shown in Table 1, then 787 of these 880 gangs were European-American gangs. Of this number, 351 gangs (or 44.6 per cent) were of mixed European-American ethnicity. Such a large percentage of ethnic mixing within gangs reflected the fact that immigrant Chicago was ethnically heterogeneous. As Thomas Philpott (1978, pp. 139–42) has revealed, the average number of nationalities in Chicago's immigrant neighbourhoods was twenty-two. None of the immigrant groups represented more than 50 per cent of the population in their neighbourhoods, except for the Poles, who constituted 54 per cent of their neighbourhood.

As in the ante-bellum period, white youth gangs often attached more importance to the defence of territory than to the promotion of the honour of a specific ethnic identity. Feuds between rival white gangs were typically about turf, and so persisted even when the ethnic composition of the feuding gangs changed. Moreover, many white gang boys interviewed by Thrasher expressed an existential disinterest in the question of ethnicity. 'Aw, we never ask what nationality dey are', said a Polish boy. 'If dey are good guys, dey get in our gang. Dat's all we want.' To be sure, ethnicity and territory sometimes converged. For example, Jewish boys in Chicago were at risk when they travelled unprotected through

Table I *Race and nationalities (ethnicities) of gangs in Chicago*

Race or ethnicity	Number of gangs	Percentage of total gangs
Mixed ethnicities	351	39.89
Polish	148	16.82
Italian	99	11.25
Irish	75	8.52
Negro	63	7.16
American – white	45	5.11
Mixed negro-white	25	2.84
Jewish	20	2.27
Slavic	16	1.82
Bohemian	12	1.36
German	8	.91
Swedish	7	.79
Lithuanian	6	.69
Miscellaneous	5	.57
Total	880	100.00

Source: Thrasher (1936, p. 191). The term ethnicity has been substituted for nationality.

solidly Polish territory (Thrasher 1936, pp. 215, 197). In ethnically poly-
glot white areas, however, the impetus for gang conflict was usually territorial rather than ethnic.

Politically powerful adults did not approve of many of the things that
white gangs did, such as breaking windows, reporting false fire alarms,
cutting cable lines, defacing street signs, disturbing the peace at night,
insulting people on the sidewalk, pilfering from stores, breaking into
private dwellings, and looting factory yards and construction sites
(Philpott 1978, p. 73). Nevertheless, those adults sponsored white street
gangs, and rewarded them for playing a key role in neighbourhood
defence, especially since urban governments and police forces were
weak, ineffective and often corrupt. While adults frowned on activities
which undermined the quality of community life, they approved of the
youth gang's role in keeping strangers, especially blacks, off their streets
and beaches, and out of their parks, baseball diamonds, swimming pools,
saloons and dance halls (Spear 1967, p. 206; Kusmer 1976, p. 185).

Ward politicians and street gang leaders often reached a mutually beneficial understanding. The former would pay the rent of an apartment
that could serve as a gang clubhouse, while the latter would distribute
campaign leaflets, put up posters, hustle up votes, and chase opponents
from polling booths on election days. Ward bosses could mitigate the
police harassment of gangs, and gangs could turn over a share of the proceeds of their illegal activities.

Local politicians legitimized street gangs by sponsoring neighbourhood athletic clubs. Cook County's Democratic Commissioner, Frank
Ragen, set up the Ragen Athletic Club on Chicago's Halsted Street. This
club was home to Ragen's Colts, a fighting gang of Irish youth ranging in
age from seventeen to thirty. This gang, whose motto was 'Hit me and
you hit a thousand', provided a *de facto* policing service for the community. Ragen Colt territory was the Back of the Yards district west of
Wentworth Avenue extending south from 43rd to 63rd Street. Any black
who made the mistake of crossing Wentworth Avenue risked being seriously injured. In 1918 the poet, Langston Hughes, then a high school
student, made this mistake and was badly beaten up. Yet, every working
day, thousands of black labourers had to cross Wentworth Avenue and
make their way through hostile Irish and Polish streets in order to get to
the stockyards (Tuttle 1970, pp. 103, 199).

Youth gangs served as nuclei for the white mob during the race riots
in East St. Louis in 1917, Philadelphia in 1918 and Chicago in 1919
(Rudwick 1964, pp. 41–57; Tuttle 1970, pp. 32–66; Franklin 1975, p. 340).
The Chicago Commission on Race Relations, which investigated the
causes of the city's five-day riot, concluded that 'the riot would not have
gone beyond the first clash' were it not for the involvement of local gangs
and athletic clubs (1922, pp. 11–17). Members of Ragen's Colts, for
example, drove into the Black Belt at night, setting fire to wooden

porches and shacks, and firing their guns at the windows and roofs of tenement buildings.

Approximately two-fifths of the violent confrontations between whites and blacks during the Chicago riot occurred in Bridgeport. Young people in this cohesive Irish-Catholic neighbourhood belonged to the Hamburg Social and Athletic Club. The youth gang known as the Hamburgs or Hamburgers were active participants in the street fighting. As the journalist Mike Royko (1971, p. 37) has noted, it is likely that one of the Hamburgs, the seventeen-year-old boy, Richard J. Daley, future mayor of the city, was caught up in the violence.

Another gang active in the riot, the Dirty Dozen, armed themselves with 'revolvers, blackjacks, and knives, and started out to get the "niggers"'. An ex-gang member recounted that about twenty gang members stopped a 'street car filled with colored people' at 35th and State Streets, which was about 'five miles or more from their own territory'. In the ensuing fracas, a 'colored woman' slashed a boy by the name of Shaggy Martin across the heart with a razor. Infuriated by this, the white gang extracted vengeance by killing two blacks and seriously injuring five others (Thrasher 1936, p. 47). This kind of racial violence was an offshoot of the politics of white defensive localism in the cities of the Progressive era.

Black youth gangs in the immigrant city, 1880–1940

The immigrant city was the birthplace of the African-American youth gang. Most of our knowledge of the black youth gangs of this period comes from Thrasher's research. Whereas African-American boys accounted for approximately 3.8 per cent of Chicago's total boy population, African-American gangs made up 7.4 per cent of the total number of city gangs (Thrasher 1936, p. 193). The finding that the involvement of African-American boys in gangs was greater than their representation in the overall population of young people makes sense in the light of the fact that they were barred from unionized factory jobs, clerical positions and even unskilled, part-time positions.

Thrasher also found some racial mixing in the gangs of Progressive-era Chicago. As Table 1 reveals, twenty-five of the 880 gangs of known race and ethnicity were mixed 'Negro-white' gangs. Although only 2.8 per cent of the total, this percentage is relatively high when considered in the light of the small number of racially mixed gangs reported in the far more racially segregated cities of the second half of the twentieth century.

To be sure, white ethnic mixing in gangs was far more extensive than racial mixing. As Table 1 shows, 28 per cent (25 of 88) of Chicago's African-American gangs were racially mixed, while 44.6 per cent (351 of 787) of the city's European-American gangs were of mixed white ethnicity. The existence of racially mixed youth gangs was because African

280   *Christopher Adamson*

Americans often lived interspersed among whites. The arrival of southern blacks in Chicago's Jewish neighbourhoods created friction, but 'the Negro boys brought in by this migration', one of Thrasher's informants stated (1936, p. 216), 'are being received in a friendly way by Jewish boys, and Jewish gangs are now fraternizing with the negroes'.

Whereas the white youth gangs of this period derived support from local political authorities and were aggressive in the defence of turf, black youth gangs existed in communities that were not yet large enough or ecologically distinct enough to sanction the vigorous defence of turf.[5] In Washington and Philadelphia, African Americans, many of whom worked as domestic servants, lived in unmapped alleys and streets behind the elegant houses of their white employers (Borchert 1980, p. 135; Lane 1986, p. 21). In New York, prior to the black settlement of Harlem in the 1910s, African Americans lived on many different blocks between 20th and 63rd Streets (Osofsky 1966, p. 12). On Chicago's South Side, less than a dozen blocks were 'entirely Negro' in 1910 (Spear 1967, p. 20). 'We have no LITTLE AFRICA in Cleveland,' an African-American clerk boasted in 1915. 'There is not yet a single street in this city that is inhabited by nothing but Negroes' (Kusmer 1976, p. 42). As late as 1930, following two decades of migration from the South, blacks were widely dispersed throughout Pittsburgh (Gottlieb 1987, pp. 66–67). In the same year, most of Milwaukee's blacks lived in white residential areas (Trotter 1985, p. 67). In none of these cities was the black population large enough for the formation of territorially aggressive black youth gangs. In the 1919 Chicago riot, according to the Commission investigating its causes, African-American gangs played an insignificant and largely defensive role (1922, pp. 11–17).

The exclusion of African Americans from urban political structures, their subordinate role in organized crime and the hostility of predominantly white police forces also inhibited the rise of turf-defending black street gangs. The white business élite, real estate developers, city politicians, police forces and dominant figures in organized crime conspired to locate the vice industry in areas of the city that were inhabited by large numbers of black people.[6] Yet, the illegal economy associated with prostitution, gambling and the provision of bootleg alcohol was largely controlled by whites. In Chicago's 'Levee', Detroit's 'Paradise Valley', or Cleveland's 'Roaring Third', white crime syndicates hired young black males to work as bouncers in speakeasies, as lookouts in brothels, and as numbers runners. Black entrepreneurs who attempted to establish their own rackets were ruthlessly suppressed. In Harlem, for example, Dutch Schultz relied on the police to wrest control of the policy racket away from Stephanie St. Clair (Schatzberg and Kelly 1996, p. 90). The racial order upheld by corrupt politicians, police forces, and white criminal syndicates permitted neither collective forms of illegality by black adults nor the aggressive defence of turf by black youth.

White youth gangs in the racially changing city, 1940–1970

White youth gangs at mid-century continued to defend turf and uphold the racial order, and derive support for doing so from political leaders and organized crime figures. Ethnically heterogeneous areas continued to produce ethnically mixed gangs. Irish, Italian, Polish, Serbian and Mexican boys who lived on the same block or street in South Chicago joined the same gang and fought similarly mixed gangs from other blocks (Kornblum 1974, p. 74). In New York's Spanish Harlem, one particular Italian gang included 'maybe twenty guys who were Puerto Rican' (Wakefield 1957, p. 126). In Boston's Roxbury, the Senior Bandits and the Outlaws were predominantly Irish Catholic, but also included a few Protestants of British ancestry, French Canadians, and Italians (Miller 1969, pp. 16–20).

Elsewhere in Boston, the intermarriage of Irish and Italian families affected gang fighting. For many years, Charlestown's Irish-American gangs had been at feud with Italian-American youth from the North End. The bridge across the river was the site of battles which dragged on for hours and involved hundreds of adolescents armed with bottles, two-by-fours (timber planks), and slingshots. With the intermarriage of Irish and Italian families, however, Italian families began to settle in Charlestown. Thereafter Charlestown's residents began to view 'the Champas, Saccos, and Castranovas as "our Italians" or "white Italians" to distinguish them from "the goddamned Italians" across the bridge' (Lukas 1985, p. 155).

The traditional role which white youth gangs played in neighbourhood defence became more important during the 1950s when the influx of southern blacks created a tidal wave of urban racial transition.[7] Adults seeking to keep their neighbourhoods white formed neighbourhood improvement and homeowners' associations which mobilized youth gangs to do much of their dirty work. In the housing riots which occurred in the Chicago neighbourhoods of Fernwood and Englewood in 1947 and 1949, roving youth gangs terrorized the South Side, hauling blacks off streetcars and attacking University of Chicago students assumed to be sympathetic to racial desegregation (Hirsch 1983, p. 54). White youth gangs targeted black teenagers in neighbourhoods like Oakland, Kenwood, Hyde Park, Woodlawn, Park Manor and Englewood that were undergoing partial or complete racial transition. In the early 1960s, a large white gang attacked participants in the so-called 'wade-ins' – protests against the segregation of Chicago's beaches. This kind of activity was supported by adults. Gang boys who chased black pedestrians out of their neighbourhoods were, James Short and Fred Strodtbeck (1965, pp. 193, 114) noted, 'spurred on to greater efforts by adults of the area who offered advice and encouragement'.

In Detroit, white homeowners' associations relied on youth support in their militant response to racial change. When a black family purchased

282   *Christopher Adamson*

a home in a white neighbourhood, youth gangs could be counted on to throw stones and bottles at the newcomer's house, pile garbage on his lawn, block his driveway or slash his tires (Sugrue 1996, pp. 247–58). During the late 1950s, in what was then still the Italian section of Manhattan on the Upper East Side, much of the gang fighting was, according to a local settlement house worker, 'a reflection of the insecurity of the adults, who felt very hostile toward the Puerto Ricans and Negroes' who were moving in (Spergel 1964, p. 64). In mid–1960s Brooklyn, white adults moving out of Crown Heights, East Flatbush, Brownsville, Bushwick and Red Hook sanctioned youth gang violence directed at minority newcomers. Italian youth gangs in East New York vandalized a black realty office and grocery store, and armed themselves with lug wrenches to keep blacks off their streets and out of their parks (Connolly 1977, p. 134).

White street gangs were active at Chrysler Corporation's Dodge Main Plant in Detroit's Hamtramck municipality during the 1950s. The local chapter of the United Automobile Workers, in its efforts to uphold male white supremacy, 'drew support from neighborhood street gang members who had taken work in the plant' (Boyle 1997, p. 507). However, the usual way for white street gangs to uphold white supremacy was by terrorizing black newcomers in neighbourhoods threatened with racial change. In this regard, multi-ethnic white gangs signified that social solidarity among whites at mid-century was increasingly founded on a common identification with territory rather than on a particularistic identification with a specific European ethnic or cultural heritage (Kornblum and Beshers 1988, p. 219).

African-American youth gangs in the racially changing city, 1940–1970

The rapidly growing urban black population led to an increase in the number of African-American youth gangs.[8] With the creation of large areas of concentrated black poverty, black youth gangs began to defend themselves and enter adjoining white territory. However, extreme ghettoization ultimately cut black youth off from white areas of the city so that black youth gangs began to prey on each other. While black gang boys received moral support from adults for defending turf, they received little concrete political or economic support because of the relative powerlessness of adults in disadvantaged black communities. The exclusion of black youth from legal jobs as well as from opportunities in white-controlled criminal syndicates resulted in an increase in violent gang feuding among black youth.

Initially, the geographic expansion of the black ghettos led to an increase in fighting between black and white youth gangs. As early as the 1940s, teenagers in Detroit's densely populated ghetto, Paradise Valley, hung out on street corners and got into fights with white gangs in parks and playgrounds (Thomas 1992, p. 119). During the 1943 riot, black youth gangs adopted the same tactics that white gangs had traditionally used against black people. They assaulted white students and factory workers returning home on streetcars, and they hurled bricks at unsuspecting white motorists (Lee and Humphrey 1943, p. 28). In Chicago, black youth were no longer the passive victims of white violence. In 1957, when a white gang killed a black youth at 59th Street and Kedzie, black gangs retaliated and seriously assaulted twelve whites (Hirsch 1983, p. 291). Black gangs increasingly challenged whites over the use of streets, bridges, beaches, parks, school playgrounds, restaurants, ballrooms and roller rinks. Black teenagers on Chicago's South Side took on the Diablos, a white gang which tried to keep them out of the Capitol Theater. Reminiscing about the night his gang fought their way into the theatre, a former gang member, interviewed for the film *The Promised Land* (1995), remarked ironically, 'that was my first experience of integration'.

However, one effect of the doubling of black spatial isolation in northern cities between 1930 and 1970 was that turf-oriented black youth gangs became increasingly likely to prey on each other (Massey and Denton 1993, p. 46).[9] Turf rivalries on Chicago's West Side enmeshed the Imperial Chaplins and the Clovers, forerunners of the Vice Lords and the Egyptian Cobras (Perkins 1987, p. 28). Black-on-black gang warfare was endemic to the massive public housing estates constructed in the middle of slum neighbourhoods. One of wartime Chicago's largest youth gangs, the Deacons, was born in the Ida B. Wells housing project just a few years after its completion in 1941. The Deacons took on the Destroyers, who lived to the north of the projects, and the 13 Cats, who occupied the area south of Oakwood Boulevard (idem). From the Governor Henry Horner Homes, a project which opened on the Near West Side in 1957, the Vice Lords and Black Souls, a faction of the Devil's Disciples, fought with white gangs located in the neighbourhood to the north. When the whites moved away, the Vice Lords and Black Souls fought each other (Kotlowitz 1991, p. 18). In the early 1960s, Devil's Disciples, Blackstone Rangers, and Vice Lords began to carve up sections of the two-mile-long, quarter-of-a-mile-wide strip of twenty-eight identical sixteen-storey buildings along State Street that comprised the Robert Taylor Homes (Lemann 1991, p. 226).

As the population of vast areas of Philadelphia's north side became exclusively black in the 1960s, gang fighting became increasingly intraracial. In 1973, for example, two North Philadelphia gangs, the Valley gang and the Norris Street gang, fought over an abandoned area known as the 'graveyard' which consisted of '3 or 4 acres of smashed brick and twisted tailpipe' (Lieber 1975, p. 42). In Los Angeles, conflict-oriented black gangs began to form in the housing projects in Watts during the 1950s. A

284   *Christopher Adamson*

little farther north in the Florence/Firestone district, which was under-going racial transition, the Slausons emerged partly in response to attacks by whites on defenseless blacks. However, white flight led to turf- and honour-based rivalries between the Slausons and various Watts gangs. A few years after the formation of the first Crip gang in 1969, marauding Crips, belonging to different sets, such as the West Side Crips, Main Street Crips and Grape Street Watts Crips, began to victimize youth living on Piru Street in Compton, who then banded together for protection. The Pirus, Brims, Bishops, Blood Fives, Swans, and other gangs formed the nucleus of the Blood Nation. By the early 1980s not only were Crips fighting Bloods, but different Crip sets were also locked in deadly turf- and honour-based feuds (Valentine 1995, pp. 45–50; Quicker and Batani-Khalfani 1998, pp. 18–20).

Extreme racial segregation in Chicago, Milwaukee, St. Louis and Cleveland has virtually eliminated confrontations between black and white youth gangs (Dawley 1973; Hagedorn 1988; Decker and Van Winkle 1996; Huff 1996). In New York, however, black-white gang violence has persisted in places where black housing projects were built near white working-class neighbourhoods. In South Brooklyn, for example, the proximity of the predominantly black Red Hook Houses to Carroll Gardens, an Italian neighbourhood of brownstones, has been the source of more than thirty years of interracial youth violence (Barron 1997; Martin 1997).

The increased violence associated with gang fighting in impoverished African-American neighbourhoods can be traced to growing joblessness among youth, especially in cities like Philadelphia, Cleveland, Detroit and St. Louis. Another reason why a destructive conflict subculture began to emerge among African-American youth was that opportunities for illegal work as bouncers or numbers runners declined. By 1940 Italian gangsters had seized control of numbers gambling in Boston, New York, Philadelphia, Cleveland and Detroit, and, in 1952, Sam 'Mooney' Giancana took over Chicago's lucrative black-operated policy racket (Pinderhughes 1987, p. 147; Schatzberg and Kelly 1996, pp. 78, 102). The failure of black street gangs during the 1950s and 1960s to develop into criminal organizations, or even to provide major services to white criminal organizations, reflected their inability to influence the operation of crime or to launder money because of the political and economic marginality of urban black communities (Ianni 1974).

Richard Cloward and Lloyd Ohlin were among the first sociologists to recognize, in their influential book, *Delinquency and Opportunity* (1960), that social disorganization and community breakdown brought about by political and economic marginality tend to decrease the involvement of youth in income-producing illegality and increase their participation in gang-fighting. A weakened community fabric, they argued, increases the degree to which gang youth resort to violence to win social status. Their argument was empirically extended by Irving Spergel (1963, p. 250), who discovered that sophisticated, income-producing forms of youth crime, such as burglary, larceny and narcotics selling, were more frequent on Chicago's South Side, whereas crimes of violence, such as murder, manslaughter, assault and robbery, occurred more frequently among youthful offenders on the West Side. Gangs on the South Side, a much older, established ghetto community, engaged in criminally oriented behaviour, whereas the trend on the newly settled and rapidly growing West Side pointed towards a future in which growing numbers of black youth, unable to find legal work and excluded from illegitimate economic opportunities, would participate in turf- and honour-based gang violence.

The social scientists who undertook detailed studies of gang delinquency during the 1950s and early 1960s recognized that the greater social disorganization of black neighbourhoods made it more difficult for adults to control the violence of young people. Spergel (1964, pp. 40–43) compared patterns of delinquency in Slumtown, a structurally isolated, mixed Puerto Rican and African-American ghetto in Manhattan north of 100th Street and east of Fifth Avenue, with those in Racketville, an Italian section of Manhattan north of 86th Street between Second Avenue and the East River. He found that 'bopping' or gang fighting was four times more frequent in Slumtown. Not only were parents in Slumtown unable to help their children find either legal or illegal jobs, they were also unable to supervise their children's activities at school and in the street.

Whereas the youth of Slumtown resorted to fighting as a means of achieving 'rep', the Italian youth of closely knit Racketville rarely fought among themselves. As a local street-club worker reported, these kids

> may decide every few months to go out and get a "spick", but there isn't a constant tension or pressure to participate in a gang fight as in other neighborhoods. Fighting isn't the usual subject of conversation among the Italian kids (Spergel 1964, p. 41).

Racketville's white youth gangs were discouraged from fighting each other by politically powerful adults. Moreover, those adults, some of whom were affiliated with locally tolerated organized crime families, rewarded youth gangs and street-corner groups for upholding the racial order by chasing Puerto Ricans and blacks out of Racketville. A similar situation existed in Chicago's white neighbourhoods (Short and Strodtbeck 1965, pp. 107–14).

The behaviour of white and African-American youth gangs during the 1960s reflected the profound differences in the social organization of white and black neighbourhoods. The journalist Walter Bernstein (1968), in a 1957 article in *The New Yorker*, described how local community

286   *Christopher Adamson*

resources, such as the availability of the American Legion Hall for
dances, were effectively used to discourage Italian-American gangs from
fighting in the Park Slope neighbourhood of Brooklyn. Adults in socially
organized, resource-rich white communities were able to control the
violent excesses of their young people, whereas the growing joblessness,
political powerlessness and social disorganization of inner-city black
neighbourhoods made it far more difficult for adults in those neighbourhoods to prevent young people from fighting over turf and honour.

White youth gangs in the hypersegregated city, 1970–1999

Continued suburbanization during the 1970s and 1980s decreased the
number of white youth gang members relative to minority youth gang
members.[10] Nevertheless, just as in previous eras, white youth gangs and
corner groups were positively sanctioned by politically powerful adults
for their role in upholding the racial order. During the late 1970s in South
Philadelphia, members of a white youth gang called the Counts, according to a local informant, 'had the blessing and support of their parents'
when they attacked blacks who ventured into their turf (Skogan 1990,
p. 25). The people of Canarsie, an Italian-Jewish enclave in South Brooklyn, who, in 1972, objected to the busing of African-American children
from Brownsville, approved of youth groups who armed themselves with
iron pipes and heavy sticks and attacked 'blacks they took to be suspi-
ciously out of place' (Reider 1985, p. 179).

Similar incidents occurred in Boston during that city's busing crisis of
the mid–1970s. Charlestown's notorious Green Store Gang won
approval from adults in the community for intimidating black families
living in the Bunker Hill projects and adjacent Charles Newton development (Lukas 1985, pp. 157–8). In Dorchester, four street-corner gangs –
the Roseland Street gang, the Shawmut Station gang, the Mather Street
gang and the Wainright Park gang – tried to force a black family, the
Debnams, out of the neighbourhood. The boys in these gangs did what
the adults in the neighbourhood wished they could do but felt self-
conscious about doing. They drove by the Debnam's house at all hours
honking and shouting racial slurs, threw rocks and bottles through their
windows, exploded firebombs in their driveway, and removed planks of
wood from their fence. The boys recalled that the community had failed
to defend itself 'when their parents lived west of Washington Street', and
vowed that this time they would not 'let the colored push us out' (Lukas
1985, p. 525).

In the Bensonhurst section of Brooklyn, an 80 per cent white neighbourhood which experienced significant job loss and a decline in its
Italian population during the 1980s, white youth gangs upheld the racial
order (Alba 1995, p. 12). In the 1990s, Bensonhurst's Avenue T Boys
specialized in the practice of going on 'missions'.[11] 'That's when,' as one

boy described it, 'you go look for people who don't belong in the neighborhood and you beat 'em up. Sometimes we go out lookin' for blacks
to jump. Sometimes we look for anybody who ain't supposed to be there'.
Another boy revealed that by 'taking care of people who don't belong in
the neighborhood, you get respect. Especially if it is some of the blacks
from the Marlboro projects' (Pinderhughes 1997, pp. 132, 134).

The adult population within communities like Bensonhurst and
Charlestown, besides sanctioning youth gangs for upholding the racial
order, strove to curb gang behaviour, such as petty theft, vandalism, disorderly conduct and drug dealing, which detracted from the quality of
life in the neighbourhood. Their ability to do so was facilitated by their
political influence, their close ties with local police forces, and, most
important, their economic power. White parents used their contacts with
neighbours and local employers to get their children jobs and keep them
out of trouble. The father of one of the Avenue T Boys, for example,
owned a construction business and hired his son and other gang members
(Pinderhughes 1997, p. 57). Even in economically declining blue-collar
neighbourhoods, then, white adults were rarely so cut off from the labour
market that they were unable to find entry-level jobs for their children.
Boys with jobs were more likely to leave the gang in their early twenties,
and the youth gang itself was less likely to be a troublesome presence.

Black youth gangs in the hypersegregated city, 1970–1999

Since 1970 one effect of declining manufacturing and service employment on black ghettos is that black youth gangs have become far more
troublesome. Between 1970 and 1982, the number of black men aged
between 18 and 29 in the country's central cities who were either unemployed or marginally attached to the labour force increased from 24 per
cent to 54 per cent (Lichter 1988, p. 782). The growing concentration of
joblessness in increasingly segregated African-American ghettos has
meant that black parents have been less effective than white parents in
finding jobs for their children (Sullivan 1989, p. 74; Kasinitz and Rosenberg 1996, p. 187). Moreover, the kinds of job available to young inner-
city black males are typically poorly paid, part-time positions in the
secondary labour market which fail to insulate them from the influence
of gangs (Crutchfield 1995, p. 205).

Black male joblessness, which more than doubled levels of ghetto
poverty during the 1970s, has also disrupted family and community life
(Lynn and McGeary 1990). The withdrawal or breakdown of government
services in jobless ghettos has aggravated the difficulties which impoverished African-American parents face in caring for, supervising and edu-
cating their children (Sampson 1987; Anderson 1990).[12] The fact that
policing policies in places like North Philadelphia have been lax, on the
one hand, or irrationally severe, on the other, has created an atmosphere

288   *Christopher Adamson*

of danger on the streets, giving rise to a code of violence and legitimiz-
ing the tendency of young men to join a corner group of running buddies
or a street gang for physical protection and psychological peace of mind
(Anderson 1998, p. 81).[13]

The vast majority (84 per cent) of the gang members in St. Louis interviewed by Decker and Van Winkle (1996, p. 65) said they joined a gang
because they found it impossible to live without some form of protection
against the violence of rival gangs in nearby neighbourhoods. Young
males growing up in underpoliced housing estates are most likely to live
in fear of assault. A boy who joined Chicago's Black Disciples at the age
of fifteen explained:

> Around here, if you're not in a gang, they still think you're in a gang.
> You can't walk to school. You can't go where you want, when you
> want, so you might as well be in a gang. Then at least when trouble
> starts, you ain't by yourself. You got some aid and assistance (Terry
> 1994, p. A26).

Police have also contributed to the inner-city gang problem by the
harshness and irrationality of certain of their responses (Tonry 1995,
pp. 105–16; Miller 1996, pp. 80–86). William Chambliss (1994) has
described policing and sentencing policies in Washington, DC whereby
deproletarianized black males were repeatedly arrested and given long
prison sentences for minor drug offences. Blacks have been five times
more likely than whites to be arrested for drug-related offences, and thus
account for much of the nearly fourfold increase in the proportion of
drug offenders in US prisons – from 5.7 per cent in 1979 to 21.5 per cent
in 1991 (Sampson and Lauritsen 1997, pp. 327, 354). The incarceration of
adults has hurt black teenagers by depriving them of parental guidance
at home, and the incarceration of teenagers has led directly to their
future joblessness by isolating them from job networks and exposing
them to the gangs operating behind bars. The mutually reinforcing
effects of joblessness, incarceration and gang involvement have made it
increasingly difficult for gang members to 'age out' of black street gangs
(Hagedorn 1988; 1994a; 1998).

Adult authority has been particularly powerless in curbing gang violence in African-American housing projects. Certainly the fact that
women and children comprise over 90 per cent of the population of many
housing estates has made it easy for young male gang members to intimidate tenants. But the real reason why tenants have found it difficult to
stand up to gangs is that they cannot rely on the social services of city
and county governments. Whereas parents in white communities have
relied on social workers, school teachers, truant officers and the police to
deal with troublesome youth, African-American parents living in isolated housing projects have discovered that social workers, school

teachers and truant officers are often reluctant to visit, and city and housing police are often incompetent. In the early 1990s tenants at Chicago's Robert Taylor Homes felt that gangs did a better job of protecting them than did the housing police.

> At least the gangs is giving us something, so lot of us prefers to help them 'cause we can *always* go to them and tell them to stop the shooting. Police don't do anything for us and they can't stop no shooting anyway (quoted in Venkatesh 1997, p. 95).

Parents in many of Chicago's housing projects have been unable to insulate their children from gang sniper fire, or prevent gangs from commandeering apartments as places to store weapons and stash drugs (Venkatesh 1996, p. 250; Belluck 1997, p. A1). Because of the breakdown of public services, some gangs have taken on a *de facto* community service role. As early as the 1960s, the Blackstone Rangers helped to pay the rents of the destitute elderly and obtained medical service for prostitutes (Sale 1971, p. 76). Since then, gangs have tried to provide a range of welfare, maintenance and recreational services. They have repaired apartments, sponsored picnics, barbecues and basketball tournaments, paid bail bonds for people in trouble with the law, and purchased groceries, clothing and sneakers for needy children (Kotlowitz 1988; Venkatesh 1997, p. 101).

African-American street gangs have progressed further in the direction of organized crime in Chicago than in the larger, less rigidly segregated, and more ethnically diverse cities of New York and Los Angeles. Over the years, the FBI and local agencies of law enforcement have targeted Jimmie Lee's Conservative Vice Lords, Larry Hoover's Black Gangster Disciples, and Jeff Fort's Black P. Stone Nation, a branch of which evolved into the criminal mob known as El Rukns, for their involvement in prostitution, drug-selling, gambling, theft, intimidation and extortion (Spergel 1995, p. 45; Schatzberg and Kelly 1996, pp. 200–4). Although unable to corrupt a white-controlled police force, Chicago street gangs have increasingly left their imprint on local politics. As Kotlowitz (1991, p. 39) noted, politicians aligned with one gang have not been safe on the turf of a rival gang.

One of Chicago's most powerful gang leaders, who derived much of his income from illegal activities occurring at rundown housing projects, made his home in a solidly middle-class black neighbourhood (Pattillo 1998). In this respect, he resembles Italian mafia leaders who have purchased homes in quiet residential districts. Despite this similarity, it would stretch the meaning of the term to suggest that black street gangs in Chicago or other American cities have become a mafia. At best, they are a proto-mafia. While the spread of the illegal drug economy has blurred the boundaries between organized drug gangs and turf-defending street gangs, the consensus among criminologists is that most

290   *Christopher Adamson*

African-American street gangs lack the organizational structure, leadership and discipline needed to operate highly sophisticated illegal drug manufacturing and selling businesses.[14]

The name of one of Chicago's street gangs, the Vice Lords, conveys the nature of much African-American organized crime. Vice or vice-related illegality is contingent on a form of lordship – the military capacity to use violence or the threat of violence to control territory. In the 1990s, for example, Larry Hoover required heroin- and crack-dealing individuals and crews operating in Gangster Disciple turf to 'devote one day a week to selling drugs strictly for him' (Terry 1997, p. 12). The Italian and Jewish syndicates of the 1920s were unable to completely prevent bloodshed related to factional disputes over the extraction of tributary surplus from illegal operations. Black street gangs have been even less successful in preventing bloodshed, especially since 1985. In Milwaukee, a surge in gang-related violence during the 1990s resulted from battles to control the cocaine market (Hagedorn 1998, p. 95). In Chicago, two 'brother gangs' that were not traditionally in dispute – the Black Gangster Disciples and the Black Disciples – quarrelled over drug markets, resulting in forty-five feud-related homicides between 1987 and 1994 (Block *et al.* 1996, pp. 11–12).[15]

The relative organizational weakness of contemporary African-American street gangs, their orientation towards extracting tribute from small-scale, local illegal operators and the intensity of their fights over turf are indicative of the fact that African-American neighbourhoods remain ghettoized and excluded from both legitimate and illegitimate opportunity structures.

Conclusion

Over the last two hundred years, white youth gangs have facilitated the cultural assimilation of non-Hispanic European immigrants into American society. Irish Catholic, German, Swedish, Polish, Bohemian, Slovak, Lithuanian, Jewish, Italian, Serbian and Greek boys internalized from the culture of the ethnically mixed gang a sense of whiteness and Americanness. For white immigrants, the youth gang facilitated cultural assimilation because of its close ties with formal and informal political authorities and organizations which commanded substantial political and economic power. For African Americans, in contrast, the youth gang has reinforced cultural separation because of its embeddedness in racially segregated, economically marginalized and politically powerless communities.

Black youth gangs only appeared with the shift from caste- to class-specific forms of segregation which did not really get underway until the second quarter of the twentieth century. Racially mixed gangs were rare in Thrasher's day, and, with increasing racial segregation since then, have become even more rare. Since 1950 continuous economic restructuring resulting from deindustrialization and commercial disinvestment has progressively weakened institutions of social control in the poorest urban black neighbourhoods. Lacking access to the organizational resources available to white parents, African-American parents and community leaders have found it difficult to curb youth gang violence. This was the case during the crack-related epidemic of violence which spread throughout the inner cities in the late 1980s.

The evidence of this article shows, first, that the causes of this epidemic were structural, not cultural; and, second, that a cultural predisposition towards violence has been far more characteristic of white than black youth gangs. African-American youth gangs have certainly resorted to violence in coping with social and cultural structures of racism and class oppression, but these same structures have been continuously reinforced by white youth gangs which, in performing their role in neighbourhood defence, have engaged in much socially harmful, violent and vicious conduct.

Acknowledgements

I am grateful to an anonymous *ERS* reviewer for a helpful critique, and thank Arnold Hirsch, Irving Spergel, Walter Miller, John Quicker, Joan Moore, and Frederick Wright for responding to my requests for information. Tom Finlay, librarian at the Centre of Criminology, University of Toronto, kindly obtained research material through Interlibrary loan.

Notes

1. I use the terms youth gang and street gang interchangeably. A great deal of youth or street gang activity is non-delinquent. Some scholars (for example, Klein 1995, p. 75) insist that a predisposition towards law-violating behaviour be a defining element of the youth or street gang. Others (for example, Short, Jr. 1997, pp. 81–2) do not. Walter B. Miller (1982) introduced the term 'law-violating youth group' to cover the countless cliques, crews, crowds, bands, rings and groups of three or more associates or running buddies which are not recognized as youth or street gangs by urban police forces.

2. See, for example, discussions by Miller (1969), Suttles (1969; 1972), Spergel (1984; 1986), Bursik and Grasmik (1993, p. 134).

3. The word 'white' in this article refers only to persons of *non-Hispanic* European background. On the links between the country's various Latino ethnicities and cultures and youth gangs, see Moore (1978; 1991); Horowitz (1983); Vigil (1988); Sullivan (1989); Sanchez-Jankowski (1991) and Padilla (1992). On the impacts of residential segregation, economic restructuring and government neglect on Latino communities and their youth gangs, see Moore and Pinderhughes (1993); Moore and Vigil (1993); Chincilla, Hamilton, and Loucky (1993); and Sullivan (1993).

14. In pointing out that some ante-bellum youth gangs were multi-ethnic, I am not denying the existence of violent conflict between nativist and Irish Catholic gangs. One of Philadelphia's powerful nativist gangs, the Shifflers, named itself after George Shiffler, a

292   *Christopher Adamson*

nativist political leader who was killed during the Kensington riots of 1844. This disturbance also radicalized the Schuylkill Rangers, one of the city's violent Irish Catholic gangs (Clark 1973, p. 11; Laurie 1980, p. 151).

5.   In 1920 African Americans accounted for 7.4 per cent, 4.3 per cent, 4.1 per cent, 4 per cent, and 2.7 per cent of the populations of Philadelphia, Cleveland, Detroit, Chicago and New York respectively (Osofsky 1966, p. 128; Spear 1967, p. 16; Kusmer 1976, p. 10; Lane 1986, p. 7; Thomas 1992, p. 26).

6.   On the zoning of vice in black areas of New York, Chicago, Detroit, Cleveland, Pittsburgh, Milwaukee and Philadelphia, see, respectively, Osofsky (1966, p. 14); Spear (1967, p. 25); Katzman (1973, p. 171); Kusmer (1976, p. 48); Bodnar, Simon and Weber (1982, p. 227); Trotter (1985, p. 24); Lane (1986, p. 122).

7.   From 1950 to 1960, the percentage of African Americans in northern cities increased dramatically, from 18 to 29 per cent in Philadelphia, from 16 to 29 per cent in both Cleveland and Detroit, and from 14 to 23 per cent in Chicago (Massey and Denton 1993, p. 45).

8.   By 1970 African Americans accounted for 21 per cent of the population of New York City, around 33 per cent of the population of both Philadelphia and Chicago, 38 per cent, 41 per cent, and 44 per cent of Cleveland's, St. Louis' and Detroit's populations, respectively, 54 per cent of Newark's population, and 71 per cent of the population of Washington, DC (US Bureau of Census 1975, p. 23).

9.   For an analysis of how the public housing, urban renewal, and highway building initiatives taken by governments and the private sector ghettoized African Americans during the 1950s and 1960s, see Bowly (1978), Hirsch (1983), Goldstein and Yancey (1986), Bauman (1987), Massey and Kanaiaupuni (1993), Mohl (1993), Kusmer (1995), Sugrue (1996). For an analysis of how suburbanization and suburban shopping mall construction siphoned off tax revenue and eroded the fabric of the central cities, leading to housing deterioration and abandonment, see Taub, Taylor and Dunham (1984, pp. 6–7); Jackson (1985, p. 284); Darden *et al.* (1987, p. 24); Miller and Wheeler (1990, p. 159); Lazare (1991 p. 270); Wilson (1996, pp. 34–50).

10.   Curry (1995, n.p. Table 10) reviewed surveys of recent law enforcement data on the race and ethnicity of gang members in the United States, and concluded that between 1975 and 1992 white gang membership declined from 8.8 to 4.4 per cent of total gang membership, while African-American gang membership remained constant at about 48 per cent. Interpretation of these data is problematic, since the surveys defined gangs differently and were not based on random samples.

11.   This name is fictitious. The gang's real name did, however, derive from the turf it defended. Although loosely organized and lacking a leadership hierarchy, specialized roles, and initiation rites, this gang was well-known throughout the metropolitan area. It was 'a community institution, having existed for years, with its membership being continually regenerated by the newer, younger members of the community' (Pinderhughes 1997, p. 54).

12.   On housing abandonment, unsafe buildings, inadequate trash collection, the withdrawal of fire and ambulance services, underfunded schools and the closing of libraries, parks and recreational facilities, see Wallace (1990a; 1990b); Skogan (1990, p. 36); Weir (1994, p. 337); Kelley (1997, pp. 49–53).

13.   At Chicago's Robert Taylor Homes during the late 1970s, city police officers rarely got out of their cars after dark (Lemann 1991, pp. 295–7). At Chicago's Henry Horner Homes during the 1980s, the city police frequently ignored reports of gang shootings (Kotlowitz 1991, p. 18). In North St. Louis during the early 1990s, officers in the 5th Police District freely admitted that they did not always respond to calls from residents, and often failed to file reports or follow up on assaults and vandalism (Ward 1997, p. 183).

14.   See Fagan (1989); Klein, Maxson and Cunningham (1991); Hagedorn (1994b); Maxson (1995). Decker and Van Winkle (1996, p. 153) reported that gang involvement in drug selling in St. Louis during the early 1990s was 'generally poorly organized, episodic, non-monopolistic, carried out by individuals and cliques on their own' and never the gang's

raison d'être. Hagedorn (1998, p. 391) concluded that Milwaukee's black street gangs, despite their increasing involvement in drug dealing between 1988 and 1993, were not likely to mutate into organized criminal syndicates. For a description of Detroit's specialized drug gangs, see Mieczkowski (1986); Taylor (1990); Adler (1995).

15. African-American gangs have also feuded with Hispanic-American gangs in areas where the two groups live in relatively close proximity. In Los Angeles, for example, fighting between the African-American Venice Shoreline Crips and the Hispanic-American Culver City Boys resulted in eleven deaths during the summer of 1997 (*New York Times*, 20 June 1999, "Courts in Los Angeles Help Fight Gang Crime").

References

ADLER, WILLIAM M. 1985 *Land of Opportunity*, New York: Atlantic Monthly Press

ALBA, RICHARD D. 1995 'Assimilation's quiet tide', *The Public Interest*, no. 119, pp. 3–18

ANDERSON, ELIJAH 1990 *Streetwise: Race, Class, and Change in an Urban Community*, Chicago, IL: University of Chicago Press

—— 1998 'The social ecology of youth violence', in Michael Tonry and Mark H. Moore (eds), *Youth Violence. Crime and Justice: A Review of Research*, Chicago, IL: University of Chicago Press. vol. 24, pp. 65–104

ASBURY, HERBERT 1928 *The Gangs of New York*, New York: Knopf

BARRON, JAMES 1997 'Beating shatters a fragile Brooklyn truce', *The New York Times*, 23 September, p. C27

BAUMAN, JOHN F. 1987 *Public Housing, Race, and Renewal: Urban Planning in Philadelphia, 1920–1974*, Philadelphia, PA: Temple University Press

BELLUCK, PAM 1997 'Chicago school in gang crossfire tries to duck but not run', *The New York Times*, 17 November, p. A1

BERNSTEIN, IVER 1990 *The New York City Draft Riots*, New York: Oxford University Press

BERNSTEIN WALTER 1968 'The cherubs are rumbling', (first published in *The New Yorker*, 1957), in James F. Short, Jr. (ed.), *Gang Delinquency and Delinquent Subcultures*, New York: Harper & Row, pp. 22–55

BLOCK, CAROLYN, CHRISTAKOS, ANTIGONE, JACOB, AYAD and PRZYBYL-SKI, ROGER 1996 'Street gangs and crime: patterns and trends in Chicago', Chicago, IL: Illinois Criminal Justice Information Authority

BODNAR, JOHN, SIMON, ROGER and WEBER, MICHAEL P. 1982 *Lives of Their Own: Blacks, Italians, and Poles in Pittsburgh, 1900–1960*, Urbana, IL: University of Illinois Press

BORCHERT, JAMES 1980 *Alley Life in Washington: Family, Community, Religion, and Folklife in the City, 1850–1970*, Urbana, IL: University of Illinois Press

BOWLY, JR., DEVEREUX 1978 *The Poorhouse: Subsidized Housing in Chicago, 1895–1976*, Carbondale, IL: Southern Illinois University Press

BOYLE, KEVIN 1997 'The kiss: racial and gender conflict in a 1950s automobile factory', *Journal of American History*, vol. 84, no. 2, pp. 496–523

BURSIK, JR., ROBERT J. and GRASMIK, HAROLD G. 1993 *Neighborhoods and Crime*, New York: Lexington

CHAMBLISS, WILLIAM J. 1994 'Policing the ghetto underclass: the politics of law and law enforcement', *Social Problems*, vol. 41, no. 2, pp. 177–94

CHICAGO COMMISSION ON RACE RELATIONS 1922 *The Negro in Chicago*, Chicago, IL: University of Chicago Press

CHINCHILLA, NORMA, HAMILTON, NORA and LOUCKY, JAMES 1993 'Central Americans in Los Angeles: an immigrant community in transition', in Joan W. Moore and Raquel Pinderhughes, (eds), *In the Barrios: Latinos and the Underclass Debate*, New York: Russell Sage, pp. 51–78

294 *Christopher Adamson*

CLARK, DENNIS J. 1973 *The Irish in Philadelphia*, Philadelphia, PA: Temple University Press

CLOWARD, RICHARD A. and OHLIN, LLOYD E. 1960 *Delinquency and Opportunity*, New York: Free Press

CONNOLLY, HAROLD X. 1977 *A Ghetto Grows in Brooklyn*, New York: New York University Press

CRUTCHFIELD, ROBERT D. 1995 'Ethnicity, labor markets and crime', in Darnell F. Hawkins, (ed.), *Ethnicity, Race, and Crime*, Albany, NY: SUNY Press, pp. 194–211

CURRY, G. D. 1995 'National youth gang surveys: a review of methods and findings', *Report Prepared for the National Youth Gang Center*, December, Tallahassee, Florida

DARDEN, JOE T., HILL, RICHARD C., THOMAS, JUNE and THOMAS, RICHARD 1987 *Detroit: Race and Uneven Development*, Philadelphia, PA: Temple University Press

DAVIS, SUSAN G. 1982 ' "Making night hideous": Christmas revelry and public order in nineteenth-century Philadelphia', *American Quarterly*, vol. 34, no. 2, pp. 185–99

DAWLEY, DAVID 1973 *A Nation of Lords: The Autobiography of the Vice Lords*, Garden City, NY: Anchor

DECKER, SCOTT H. and VAN WINKLE, BARRIK 1996 *Life in the Gang*, New York: Cambridge University Press

FAGAN, JEFFREY 1989 'The social organization of drug use and drug dealing among urban gangs', *Criminology*, vol. 27, no. 4, pp. 633–69

FELDBERG, MICHAEL 1980 *The Turbulent Era: Riots and Disorder in Jacksonian America*, New York: Oxford University Press

FOSTER, GEORGE G. 1969 'Philadelphia in slices', (1st edn 1848), *The Pennsylvania Magazine of History and Biography*, vol. 93, no. 1, pp. 23–72

FRANKLIN, VINCENT P. 1975 'The Philadelphia race riot of 1918', *The Pennsylvania Magazine of History and Biography*, vol. 99, no. 3, pp. 336–50

GILJE, PAUL A. 1987 *The Road to Mobocracy: Popular Disorder in New York City, 1763–1834*, Chapel Hill, NC: University of North Carolina Press

GOLDSTEIN, IRA and YANCEY, WILLIAM L. 1986 'Public housing projects, blacks, and public policy: the historical ecology of public housing in Philadelphia', in John M. Goering, (ed.), *Housing Desegregation and Federal Policy*, Chapel Hill, NC: University of North Carolina Press, pp. 262–89

GOTTLIEB, PETER 1987 *Making Their Own Way: Southern Blacks' Migration to Pittsburgh, 1916–1930*, Urbana, IL: University of Illinois Press

HAGEDORN, JOHN M. 1988 *People and Folks: Gangs, Crime and the Underclass in a Rustbelt City*, Chicago, IL: Lake View Press

—— 1994a 'Homeboys, dope fiends, legits, and new jacks', *Criminology*, vol. 32, no. 2, pp. 197–219

—— 1994b 'Neighborhoods, markets, and gang drug organization', *Journal of Research in Crime and Delinquency*, vol. 31, no. 3, pp. 264–94

—— 1998 'Gang violence in the postindustrial era', in Michael Tonry and Mark H. Moore (eds), *Youth Violence, Crime and Justice: A Review of Research*, Chicago, IL: University of Chicago Press, vol. 24, pp. 365–419

HIRSCH, ARNOLD R. 1983 *Making the Second Ghetto: Race and Housing in Chicago, 1940–1960*, New York: Cambridge University Press

HOROWITZ, RUTH 1983 *Honor and the American Dream*, New Brunswick, NJ: Rutgers University Press

HUFF, C. RONALD 1996 'The criminal behavior of gang members and nongang at-risk youth', in C. Ronald Huff (ed.), *Gangs in America*, 2nd edn, Newbury Park, CA: Sage, pp. 75–102

IANNI, FRANCIS A. J. 1974 'New mafia, black, Hispanic and Italian styles', *Society*, vol. 11, no. 3, pp. 26–39

IGNATIEV, NOEL 1995 *How the Irish Became White*, New York: Routledge

JACKSON, KENNETH T. 1985 *Crabgrass Frontier: The Suburbanization of the United States,* New York: Oxford University Press

KAPLAN, MICHAEL 1995 'New York city tavern violence and the creation of a working-class male identity', *Journal of the Early Republic,* vol. 15, no. 4, pp. 590–617

KASINITZ, PHILIP and ROSENBERG, JAN 1996 'Missing the connection: social isolation and employment on the Brooklyn waterfront', *Social Problems,* vol. 43, no. 2, pp. 180–96

KATZMAN, DAVID M. 1973 *Before the Ghetto: Black Detroit in the Nineteenth Century,* Urbana, IL: University of Illinois Press

KELLEY, ROBIN D. G. 1997 *Yo' Mama's DisFUNKtional: Fighting the Culture Wars in Urban America,* Boston, MA: Beacon Press

KLEIN, MALCOLM W., MAXSON, CHERYL L. and CUNNINGHAM, LEA C. 1991 '"Crack", Street Gangs, and Violence', *Criminology,* vol. 29, no. 4, pp. 623–50

KLEIN, MALCOLM W. 1995 *The American Street Gang: Its Nature, Prevalence and Control,* New York: Oxford University Press

KORNBLUM, WILLIAM 1974 *Blue Collar Community,* Chicago, IL: University of Chicago Press

KORNBLUM, WILLIAM and BESHERS, JAMES 1988 'White ethnicity: ecological dimensions', in John H. Mollenkopf (ed.), *Power, Culture and Place: Essays on New York City,* New York: Sage, pp. 201–221

KOTLOWITZ, ALEX 1988 'Chicago street gangs treat public housing as private fortresses', *The Wall Street Journal,* 30 September

—— 1991 *There Are No Children Here,* New York: Anchor

KUSMER, KENNETH 1976 *A Ghetto Takes Shape: Black Cleveland, 1870–1930,* Urbana, IL: University of Illinois Press

—— 1995 'African Americans in the city since World War II: from the industrial to the post-industrial era', *Journal of Urban History,* vol. 21, no. 4, pp. 458–504

LANE, ROGER 1986 *Roots of Violence in Black Philadelphia 1860–1900,* Cambridge, MA: Harvard University Press

LAURIE, BRUCE 1980 *Working People of Philadelphia, 1800–1850,* Philadelphia, PA: Temple University Press

LAZARE, DANIEL 1991 'Collapse of a city: growth and decay of Camden, New Jersey', *Dissent,* vol. 38, Spring, pp. 267–75

LEE, ALFRED M. and HUMPHREY, NORMAN D. 1943 *Race Riot,* New York: Dryden Press

LEMANN, NICHOLAS 1991 *The Promised Land,* New York: Vintage

LICHTER, DANIEL T. 1988 'Racial differences in underemployment in American cities', *American Journal of Sociology,* vol. 93, no. 4, pp. 771–92

LIEBER, J. B. 1975 'Philadelphia's brotherly death', *The Nation,* no. 220, pp. 42–7

LITWACK, LEON 1961 *North of Slavery: The Negro in the Free States, 1750–1860,* Chicago, IL: University of Chicago Press

LUKAS, J. ANTHONY 1985 *Common Ground,* New York: Knopf

LYNN, JR. LAURENCE E. and McGEARY, MICHAEL G. H. (eds) 1990 *Inner-City Poverty in the United States,* Washington, DC: National Academy Press

MARTIN, DOUGLAS 1997 'At the scene of a beating, a line divides 2 worlds', *The New York Times,* 28 September, p. A19

MASSEY, DOUGLAS S. and DENTON, NANCY A. 1993 *American Apartheid: Segregation and the Making of the Underclass,* Cambridge, MA: Harvard University Press

MASSEY, DOUGLAS S. and KANAIAUPUNI, SHAWN M. 1993 'Public housing and the concentration of poverty', *Social Science Quarterly,* vol. 74, no. 1, pp. 109–22

MAXSON, CHERYL L. 1995 'Street gangs and drug sales in two suburban cities', *Research in Brief,* September, Washington, DC: National Institute of Justice

MERANZE, MICHAEL 1996 *Laboratories of Virtue: Punishment, Revolution, and Authority in Philadelphia, 1760–1835,* Chapel Hill, NC: University of North Carolina Press

296   *Christopher Adamson*

MIECZKOWSKI, THOMAS 1986 'Geeking up and throwing down: heroin street life in Detroit', *Criminology*, vol. 24, no. 4, pp. 645–66

MILLER, CAROL POH and WHEELER, ROBERT 1990 *Cleveland: A Concise History, 1796–1990*, Bloomington, IN: Indiana University Press

MILLER, JEROME G. 1996 *Search and Destroy: African-American Males in the Criminal Justice System*, New York: Cambridge University Press

MILLER, WALTER B. 1969 'White gangs', *Transaction*, vol. 6, no. 10, pp. 11–26

—— 1982 'Gangs, groups, and serious youth crime', in Rose Giallombardo (ed.), *Juvenile Delinquency*, 4th edn, New York: Wiley and Sons, pp. 311–28

MOHL, RAYMOND A. 1993 'Race and space in the modern city: interstate–95 and the black community in Miami', in Arnold R. Hirsch and Raymond A. Mohl (eds), *Urban Policy in Twentieth-Century America*, New Brunswick, NJ: Rutgers University Press, pp. 100–58

MOORE, JOAN W. 1978 *Homeboys: Gangs, Drugs and Prisons in the Barrios of Los Angeles*, Philadelphia, PA: Temple University Press

—— 1991 *Going Down to the Barrio: Homeboys and Homegirls in Change*, Philadelphia, PA: Temple University Press

MOORE, JOAN W. and PINDERHUGHES, RAQUEL 1993 'Introduction', in Joan W. Moore and Raquel Pinderhughes (eds), *In the Barrios: Latinos and the Underclass Debate*, New York: Russell Sage, pp. xi–xxxix

MOORE, JOAN W. and VIGIL, JAMES DIEGO 1993 'Barrios in Transition', in Joan W. Moore and Raquel Pinderhughes (eds), *In the Barrios: Latinos and the Underclass Debate*, New York: Russell Sage, pp. 27–49

OSOFSKY, GILBERT 1966 *Harlem, The Making of a Ghetto: Negro New York, 1890–1930*, New York: Harper and Row

PADILLA, FELIX M. 1992 *The Gang as an American Enterprise*, New Brunswick, NJ: Rutgers University Press

PATTILLO, MARY E. 1998 'Sweet mothers and gangbangers: managing crime in a black middle-class neighborhood', *Social Forces*, vol. 76, no. 3, pp. 747–74

PERKINS, USENI EUGENE 1987 *Explosion of Chicago's Black Street Gangs: 1900 to Present*, Chicago, IL: Third World Press

PHILPOTT, THOMAS L. 1978 *The Slum and the Ghetto: Neighborhood Deterioration and Middle-Class Reform, Chicago, 1880–1930*, New York: Oxford University Press

PINDERHUGHES, DIANNE M. 1987 *Race and Ethnicity in Chicago Politics: A Reexamination of Pluralist Theory*, Urbana, IL: University of Illinois Press

PINDERHUGHES, HOWARD 1997 *Race in the Hood: Conflict and Violence among Urban Youth*, Minneapolis, MN: University of Minnesota Press

[THE] *PROMISED LAND*, 1995 Film Narrated by Morgan Freeman, The BBC

QUICKER, JOHN C. and BATANI-KHALFANI, AKIL 1998 'From boozies to bloods: early gangs in Los Angeles', *Journal of Gang Research*, vol. 5, no. 4, pp. 15–21

REIDER, JONATHAN 1985 *Canarsie: The Jews and Italians of Brooklyn Against Liberalism*, Cambridge, MA: Harvard University Press

ROEDIGER, DAVID R. 1991 *The Wages of Whiteness*, New York: Verso

ROYKO, MIKE 1971 *Boss: Richard J. Daley of Chicago*, New York: Signet

RUDWICK, ELLIOTT M. 1964 *Race Riot at East St. Louis, July 2, 1917*, Carbondale, IL: Southern Illinois University Press

RUNCIE, JOHN 1972 '"Hunting the nigs" in Philadelphia: the race riot of August 1834', *Pennsylvania History*, vol. 39, no. 2, pp. 187–218

SALE, R. T. 1971 *The Blackstone Rangers*, New York: Random House

SAMPSON, ROBERT J. 1987 'Urban black violence: the effect of male joblessness and family disruption', *American Journal of Sociology*, vol. 93, no. 2, pp. 348–82

SAMPSON, ROBERT J. and LAURITSEN, JANET L. 1997 'Racial and ethnic disparities in crime and criminal justice in the United States', in Michael Tonry (ed.), *Crime and Justice*, vol. 21, Chicago, IL: University of Chicago Press. pp. 311–74

SANCHEZ-JANKOWSKI, MARTIN 1991 *Islands in the Street: Gangs and American Urban Society*, Berkeley, CA: University of California Press

SANTE, LUC 1991 *Low Life*, New York: Farrar, Strauss, Giroux

SCHATZBERG, RUFUS and KELLY, ROBERT J. 1996 *African-American Organized Crime, A Social History*, New York: Garland

SHORT, JR. JAMES F. 1997 *Poverty, Ethnicity and Violent Crime*, Boulder, CO: Westview Press

SHORT, JR. JAMES F. and STRODTBECK, FRED L. 1965 *Group Process and Gang Delinquency*, Chicago, IL: University of Chicago Press

SILCOX, HARRY C. 1989 *Philadelphia Politics from the Bottom Up: The Life of Irishman William McMullen, 1824–1901*, Philadelphia, PA: The Balch Institute Press

SKOGAN, WESLEY G. 1990 *Disorder and Decline: Crime and the Spiral of Decay in American Neighborhoods*, New York: Free Press

SPEAR, ALLAN H. 1967 *Black Chicago: The Making of a Negro Ghetto, 1890–1920*, Chicago, IL: University of Chicago Press

SPERGEL, IRVING A. 1963 'Male young adult criminality, deviant values, and differential opportunity in two lower-class neighborhoods', *Social Problems*, vol. 10, no. 3, pp. 237–50

—— 1964 *Racketville, Slumtown, Haulburg*, Chicago, IL: University of Chicago Press

—— 1984 'Violent gangs in Chicago: in search of social policy', *Social Service Review*, vol. 58, no. 2, pp. 199–226

—— 1986 'The local gang in Chicago: a local community approach', *Social Service Review*, vol. 60, no. 1, pp. 94–131

—— 1995 *The Youth Gang Problem: A Community Approach*, New York: Oxford University Press

STANSELL, CHRISTINE 1987 *City of Women: Sex and Class in New York, 1789–1860*, Urbana, IL: University of Illinois Press

SUGRUE, THOMAS J. 1996 *The Origins of the Urban Crisis: Race and Inequality in Postwar Detroit*, Princeton, NJ: Princeton University Press

SULLIVAN, MERCER 1989 *'Getting Paid': Youth, Crime and Work in the Inner City*, Ithaca, NY: Cornell University Press

—— 1993 'Puerto Ricans in Sunset Park, Brooklyn: poverty amidst ethnic and economic diversity', in Joan W. Moore and Raquel Pinderhughes (eds), *In the Barrios: Latinos and the Underclass Debate*, New York: Russell Sage, pp. 1–25

SUTTLES, GERALD 1969 'Anatomy of a Chicago slum', *Transaction*, vol. 6, no. 4, pp. 16–25

—— 1972 *The Social Construction of Communities*, Chicago, IL: University of Chicago Press

TAUB, RICHARD P., TAYLOR, D. GARTH and DUNHAM, JAN D. 1984 *Paths of Neighborhood Change: Race and Crime in Urban America*, Chicago, IL: University of Chicago Press

TAYLOR, CARL S. 1990 *Dangerous Society*, East Lansing, MI: Michigan State University Press

TERRY, DON 1994 'Gangs: Machiavelli's descendants', *The New York Times*, 18 September, p. A26

—— 1997 'Chicago trial could end long reach of man said to run gang from jail', *The New York Times*, 23 March, p. A2

THOMAS, RICHARD W. 1992 *Life for Us Is What We Make It: Building a Black Community in Detroit, 1915–1945*, Bloomington, IN: Indiana University Press

THRASHER, FREDERIC 1936 *The Gang: A Study of 1,313 Gangs in Chicago*, (1st edn 1927), 2nd edn, Chicago, IL: University of Chicago Press

TONRY, MICHAEL H. 1995 *Malign Neglect: Race, Crime and Punishment in America*, New York: Oxford University Press

TROTTER, JR., JOE W. 1985 *Black Milwaukee: The Making of an Industrial Proletariat, 1915–1945*, Urbana, IL: University of Illinois Press

298   *Christopher Adamson*

TUTTLE, JR. WILLIAM M. 1970 *Race Riot: Chicago in the Red Summer of 1919,* New York: Atheneum

VALENTINE, BILL 1995 *Gang Intelligence Manual: Identifying and Understanding Modern-Day Gangs in the United States,* Boulder, CO: Paladin Press

VENKATESH, SUDHIR A. 1996 'The gang in the community', in C. Ronald Huff (ed.), *Gangs in America,* 2nd edn, Newbury Park, CA: Sage, pp. 241–55

—— 1997 'The social organization of street gang violence in an urban ghetto', *American Journal of Sociology,* vol. 103, no. 1, pp. 82–111

VIGIL, JAMES DIEGO 1988 *Barrio Gangs: Street Life and Identity in Southern California,* Austin, TX: University of Texas Press

WAKEFIELD, DAN 1957 *Island in the City: The World of Spanish Harlem,* Boston, MA: Houghton Mifflin

WALLACE, RODRICK 1990a 'Urban desertification, public health and public order: "planned shrinkage", violent death, substance abuse and AIDS in the Bronx', *Social Science and Medicine,* vol. 31, no. 7, pp. 801–13

WALLACE, DEBORAH 1990b 'Roots of increased health care inequality in New York', *Social Science and Medicine,* vol. 31, no. 11, pp. 1219–27

WARD, CAROLYN M. 1996–97 'Policing in the Hyde Park neighborhood of St. Louis: racial bias, political pressure, and community policing', *Crime, Law and Social Change,* vol. 26, no. 2, pp. 161–86

WEIR, MARGARET 1994 'Urban diversity and defensive localism', *Dissent,* vol. 41, Summer, pp. 337–42

WILENTZ, SEAN 1984 *Chants Democratic: New York City and the Rise of the American Working Class, 1788–1850,* New York: Oxford University Press

WILSON, WILLIAM J. 1996 *When Work Disappears: The World of the New Urban Poor,* New York: Knopf

CHRISTOPHER ADAMSON is a sociologist who has taught at Hofstra University, Hempstead, Long Island, New York.
ADDRESS: 23 Admiral Road, Toronto, Ontario M5R 2L4, Canada.

[12]

Middle Eastern Appearances: "Ethnic Gangs", Moral Panic and Media Framing

Scott Poynting
University of Western Sydney

Greg Noble
University of Western Sydney

Paul Tabar
Notre Dame University, Beirut

This article details a moral panic in 1998–2000 about "ethnic gangs" in Sydney's south-western suburbs and analyses its ideological construction of the links between ethnicity, youth and crime. It documents the racisms of labelling and targeting of immigrant young people which misread, oversimplify and misrepresent complex and class-related social realities as racial, and the common-sense[1] sharing of these understandings, representations and practices by "mainstream" media, police and vocal representatives in state, local and "ethnic" politics. The data used in this analysis are largely comprised of English-language media extracts, press, radio, television — both commercial and government-funded; and national, state and local in circulation, supplemented by interview material, from an ethnographic pilot study, with Lebanese-Australian youth, Lebanese immigrant parents, ethnic community workers, community leaders and police.

This article details a recent moral panic about "ethnic gangs" in Sydney's south-western suburbs, following the stabbing to death of Korean-Australian schoolboy Edward Lee in Punchbowl in October 1998 and the shots fired at Lakemba Police Station in November 1998.

The paper traces a triangle of inter-relations between a police service which has not yet overcome a culture of racism (Chan, 1997), the ethnocentric mainstream media, the populism of state politicians in the context of an election campaign and a climate of anti-immigrant scapegoating, and the incorporation of "ethnic leaders" beholden by a political patronage style of multiculturalism. It demonstrates how

Address for correspondence: Scott Poynting, Senior Lecturer, School of Cultural Inquiry, University of Western Sydney, Locked Bag 1797, Penrith South DC NSW 1797, Australia. E-mail: s.poynting@uws.edu.au

SCOTT POYNTING, GREG NOBLE AND PAUL TABAR

these interests inter-reacted to foment a "moral panic" over "ethnic youth gangs", in which virtually an entire ethnic community in south-western Sydney — and especially its young men — were criminalised, and the problems of youth crime were racialised, legitimising a law-and-order crackdown which arguably garnered votes for the government but severely damaged police-community relations.

Data and Method

The data used in this analysis are largely comprised of English-language media extracts: press, radio, television — including both commercial and government-funded media; and those with national, state and local audiences — over the period October 1998 to March 2000. The authors examined over this period all articles in national, state, or local newspapers in Australia which had identifiable references to "youth and gangs", "youth and crime", "ethnicity and gangs", or "ethnicity and crime"; supplemented by a sampling of electronic media — including talk-back radio — over the period October 1998 to March 1999, and selected for analysis for this article the reportage of events in western Sydney in late 1998 and their after-math. These were collated to identify established patterns in ideological themes, especially those related to racialisation, and to trace the "amplification spiral" in the developing moral panic. This analysis is made alongside the interpretation of some preliminary material from a pilot study using ethnographic methods, involving open-ended, semi-structured one-to-one interviews at home and in the workplace with young Arabic-speaking background people, Lebanese immigrant parents, police and Police Service workers, and community workers and leaders, about — among other things — their experiences of these media representations. The interviews were conducted in English by two of the authors, tape-recorded and transcribed for analysis by the research team. (All interviewees' names given are pseudonyms).

The Making of a Moral Panic

The moral panic was precipitated by the stabbing to death on 17 October 1998 of a fourteen year-old schoolboy, Edward Lee, in a suburban street, outside the birthday party of a teenage friend. The press described the victim as "the only child of Korean parents who live in Canterbury" (Clennell & Kennedy, 1998, p. 3), and reported the incident as follows:

> The Year 9 student at Canterbury Boys' High School was stabbed on Saturday night after he and four friends went to the party in Telopea Street, Punchbowl, and became involved in a footpath brawl with about 20 men police described as of Middle Eastern appearance (Murphy & Power, 1998, p. 2).

From the beginning, the crime was causally linked by police and media to ethnicity, the perpetrators were described in racial terms, and the spectre of "ethnic" gangs was raised by police and media, feeding off each other. Commercial television news reports (eg Channel Nine) the night after the killing were linking it to a "gang" and faithfully circulating the police description of racial phenotypes clearly referring to Lebanese immigrants.

MIDDLE EASTERN APPEARANCES: "ETHNIC GANGS", MORAL PANIC AND MEDIA FRAMING

> Police refused yesterday to comment on whether the killing was racially motivated but said they were investigating other recent shootings in the area, including two "kneecappings" last week, the first of which involved men of Middle Eastern appearance and the second involving Asian men (Clennell & Kennedy, 19/10/98, p. 3).

Here, police and media symbiotically act as "amplifiers", while "structuring", defining or focusing on the crime — in this instance "ethnic gang" crime — in ways which highlight and thus find more of it (Hall, Critcher, Jefferson, Clarke & Roberts, 1978, p. 38).

Two weeks after the Punchbowl stabbing, following a fortnight of heavily publicised "zero tolerance" policing and a campaign of "stop and search" by police directed at — mainly Lebanese-background — young men in the neighbourhood, gunshots were fired into nearby Lakemba police station. While no-one was injured, there ensued a spiralling of press briefings from police spokespeople, comment on talkback radio, statements by parliamentarians and other public figures, letters to the editor, press editorials.

Presented here is an outline of the fomentation of a "moral panic", as defined by Stanley Cohen (1987, p. 9):

> A condition, episode, person or group of persons emerges to become defined as a threat to societal values and interests; its nature is presented in a stylized and stereotypical fashion by the mass media; the moral barricades are manned by editors, bishops, politicians and other right-thinking people; socially accredited experts pronounce their diagnoses and solutions; ways of coping are evolved or (more often) resorted to; the condition then disappears, submerges, or deteriorates and becomes more visible.

We sketch here the accelerating phase of this cycle of moral panic, which can be viewed as a "deviancy amplification spiral" (Hall, Critcher, Jefferson, Clarke & Roberts, 1978, p. 38).

We can follow the logic of the argument drawn from Leslie Wilkins (1964) without accepting the terms of 1960s deviancy theory in which it originated. For example, the cultural practices of immigrant young men, in gathering in public spaces, are forbidden by local government regulations and defined as illegal: "Less tolerance leads to ... more acts being defined as crimes" (Wilkins, 1964, p. 90). Police are called upon to take action to disperse the groups and prevent their gathering: "more action against [those defined as] criminals" (Wilkins, 1964, p. 90). Yet if an original purpose for the grouping in the first place was felt to be defensive and reassertive of dignity in the face of racist humiliation (Poynting, Noble & Tabar, 1999), and if the police action is perceived as discriminatory and demeaning, then this will clearly increase the motives to gather in this way. If, moreover, part of the reason for the grouping is to engage in a form of masculine cultural resistance (Poynting, Noble and Tabar, 1998), then the responses of the police give meaning to and a rationale for that resistance (Tomsen,1996, p. 193). Loader (1996, p. 101) refers to the counterproductivity of "the paradox of face" in an overly negative police response to youthful "acting up" in public space. Goode and Ben-Yehuda (1994, p. 24, citing Cohen, 967, pp. 280–1) point to the connection, drawn in Staney Cohen's seminal work, between the "diffusion" of sensitivity towards a particular "folk devil", and the "escalation" of the moral panic about it: "on more

SCOTT POYNTING, GREG NOBLE AND PAUL TABAR

than one occasion, the over-zealousness of police resulted in an escalation of the conflict, where, for instance, by insisting that the crowd "move along", some of "the more labile members" of a crowd were provoked to resist, "blows were exchanged, which led to their arrest".

Finally, if this oppositional and confronting collective practice by minority young people leads to moral outrage expressed in the media and articulated by politicians, leading, in turn, to further attention to the offences and demands for police intervention, then the whole process spirals in ever-increasing cycles until countervailing forces produce a winding down. The focus of the present article is on the part played by the media in the first phase — the amplification — of this cycle, and its inter-relationship with the operation of the police and with interventions of political representatives.

It should be noted that the events in question began in the months leading up to the New South Wales state election in March 1999, in which each of the two major parliamentary parties tried to outbid each other in "law and order" promises. In early November 1998, the NSW Director of Public Prosecutions, Mr Nick Cowdery, QC, publicly criticised what the Herald termed "the State Government's law and order push, describing many of its policies as 'ill-conceived' and potentially dangerous". He also condemned the Coalition Opposition proposals for tougher sentencing, and cautioned against the developing "law and order auction" between the major political parties, being abetted by sections of the media. Mr Cowdery argued against Government claims that its law and order push just responded to concern in the electorate, saying that "to a very large extent they are the ones who are creating that community concern" (Garcia, 1998, p. 8). The Premier ignored this counsel in favour of the populist "tough on crime" stance which had been a platform of his successful 1995 election campaign; with this discourse now rearticulated in the context of some virulent anti-immigrant ideology linking immigration with (among other evils) crime, an ideology which had been a factor in Australian politics since the 1996 election to the Federal Parliament of the Independent (and former Liberal Party) candidate for Oxley, Pauline Hanson. The tactic was reflected in favourable editorials and arguably in opinion polls; on the eve of the election, the *Sun-Herald* reported a 9% rise in approval rating over the previous five weeks for Mr Carr, while "Opposition Leader Kerry Chikarovski, battling grim opinion polls, ... pledged tough new law and order measures" in an apparent attempt to regain popularity (Walker & Chulov, 1999, p. 1).

The "law and order" strategy had already worked for Bob Carr in the previous (1995) New South Wales election, in which his slogan had been "tough on crime and tough on the causes of crime". Already in 1994, the *Sun-Herald* was referring to "Labor's anti-gang strategy", reporting that, "initiating what was to prove a bipartisan policy on law and order, Carr has promised that if elected next year, he will crack down on gangs". In this earlier context, he had made derogatory remarks about "roaming gangs of youth (with) their baseball caps turned back to front" (Wynhausen, 1994, p. 29). Since then, the electoral success in the 1996 federal election and later in the state of Queensland of the anti-immigration populism of the One Nation party, with its scapegoating of ethnic minorities for everything from unemployment, disease, decline of national identity, environmental degrada-

MIDDLE EASTERN APPEARANCES: "ETHNIC GANGS", MORAL PANIC AND MEDIA FRAMING

tion — and crime — had primed the media, and politicians looking to play them in the election campaign, for another "ethnic youth gangs" moral panic.

The earlier "gangs" moral panic with all the attributes set out by Cohen (1987, p. 9) had developed over 1993–4, following the 1993 murder, alleged to be associated with "Asian gangs", of anti-drug campaigner MP, John Newman, in outer-western Cabramatta (Collins, 1994); and an anti-police "riot" by Lebanese youth at an Arabic Day Carnival in the inner-western suburb of Tempe (Ethnic Affairs Commission of New South Wales, 1994). In this conjuncture, Cunneen's (1995, see also Cunneen and Spiers, 1995) timely probing of the stereotyping of "ethnic gangs" focused mainly on the targeting of South-East Asian young people, though he concludes that Pacific Islanders and Lebanese are also particularly subjected to discrimination and harassment (Cunneen, 1995, p. 120). A report from Pulse Consultants commissioned by the New South Wales (NSW) Police Service drew attention in 1994 to the unwitting conferral of status on "gangs" by heavy-handed policing, and cautioned against "unnecessary aggression" (cited in Legislative Council Standing Committee on Social Issues, 1995, p. 289). The NSW Parliament's Legislative Council Standing Committee on Social Issues concluded that "media beat-ups about youth gangs contribute to [the status] problem" and recommended that "media organisations should be informed that stories on gangs are creating the problem they purport to reveal. Politicians should be equally mindful of their responsibilities" (Legislative Council Standing Committee on Social Issues, 1995, p. 289). The present article provides considerable empirical evidence of the extent to which that advice has gone unheeded: the links traced here of a "deviancy amplification spiral" between political demands, media representations, and police informing of these and responses to these, go some way towards explaining this.

We develop in this paper our ideology critique along lines suggested by Pearson's (1983), definitive "history of respectable fears" in his book, Hooligan, and informed by recent research on the criminalisation of young people from ethnic minorities and the racialisation of crime in Australia (White, 1996, 1999; Cunneen, 1995; Pe-Pua, 1996, 1999). The ideological elements here examined include: the supposed foreignness of the phenomena of street crime, the supposed newness of the problem, the myth of youth out of control — especially of their families, calls for harsh discipline, moral outrage at a "wall of silence", appeals to the "community".

Pearson (1983, p. 212) makes use of the concept of "myth", arguing that law-and-order doomsayers are engaging in mythology: "Law-and-order myths restrict attention to the facts of the immediate present, while turning a blind eye towards the over-flowing evidence of the past" (1983, p. 212). In this article, we draw on a theory of ideology using the term in the "negative" sense (Larrain, 1979, 1983, 1994) sometimes portrayed as mythologising or blinding. All ideology in this sense can be seen as the manifestation of real social relations at the (immediate) level of appearances, in ways which preempt and distract (or "blind", if you will) from a deeper understanding of these relations. Racism is here taken to be one form of ideology, in which cultural, historically contingent factors are presented as natural, and determinants of class relations are often taken to be effects of "race".

In understanding racism thus as ideology, we are deploying the concept of racialisation proposed by Bob Miles (1989), whose development of the notion was

SCOTT POYNTING, GREG NOBLE AND PAUL TABAR

premised on the recognition that "race" was not a scientific category but an ideological construct. Miles argued that social relations are "racialised", refracted through the prism of "race" as a key form of social perception. The concept of racialisation has largely gone out of favour for various reasons (see Solomos & Back, 1996), but one of the major problems was that Miles saw it purely as an "ideological effect". Yet racialisation is not simply an issue of representation, but of social practices through which political, economic and social relations are structured (see Hage, 1998 for a parallel argument about racism as practice, not ideology). Connected to this, the concept was used primarily to suggest processes of marginalisation and containment, without recognising the extent to which 'racialised' subjects contest and transform the processes of racialisation (Gilroy, 1987), fashioning "new ethnicities" in the spaces available (Hall, 1988).

Racialisation here, in contrast, is being deployed to capture the complex social dynamic which takes place between structural dimensions of social, economic and political marginalisation and the cultural representation of social relations — the "ways of seeing" which the frame the experience of social relations but which are negotiated through processes of self-identification. Especially important here, as we will explore, are the ways in which "social problems" such as "ethnic youth gangs" are constructed by the racialised perceptual schemas employed to address such "problems".

Racialisation is also a complex social process in that it involves an array of social actors and institutions — the media, politicians, community leaders, the police, ordinary members of the relevant communities, and of course in this case the young people themselves. And it is dynamic in that there are competing processes of structuration and resistive agency: attempts to label, contain and regulate are met with attempts to resist and transform these processes. We should perhaps note that in some ways "ethnicisation" is a more appropriate term in the Australian context, given that ethnicity has a key role in public and private discourse, but racialisation captures better the stronger sense of racism — institutionalised and attitudinal — activated by these processes.

Central to the processes of racialisation is the creation of a racialised Other: a "them" against whose "difference" a dominant national, ethnic "us" is defined. This entails the production of knowledge about this Other — a set of characteristics or behaviours, even a pathology — deployed to explain social and cultural difference, and to rationalise social exclusions (Said, 1979; Goldberg, 1993, 150–151). This also involves the projection of anxieties about social problems onto the Other, which becomes seen as the cause of those problems, the source of conflict and disorder. In this case, we trace the intersection of an interlocking set of processes within racialised discourse: the racialisation of youth groups, the criminalisation of this racialised youth as part of a larger history of the construction of youth as a social problem (see Clarke, J. et al., 1976), and the ensuing racialisation of crime itself.

Youth Crime as Foreign, "Ethnic" Youth as Criminal

As White, Perrone, Guerra and Lampugnani (1999, p. 11) point out, the predominant impression conveyed by most media coverage is that groups of ethnic minority young people being sociable together in public spaces are "gangs" and that these

MIDDLE EASTERN APPEARANCES: "ETHNIC GANGS", MORAL PANIC AND MEDIA FRAMING

"gangs" are "entirely negative, dangerous and threatening". Moreover, such groups are invariably reported in terms of race: "Middle-Eastern appearances" and the like. In the context of the periodic moral panics about "ethnic youth gangs", there is an increasing tendency for the media (and those whom they influence) to equate, say, "young Lebanese" or "young Vietnamese" with being a (criminal) "gang member". "The result is an inordinate level of public and police suspicion and hostility being directed towards people from certain ethnic minority backgrounds" (White, et al.,1999, p. 11).

We found just such a process of racialisation at work in the media moral panic traced here. From the first reports, imparted by police via the media, that a "gang" was involved in the stabbing of Edward Lee and that those seen fleeing from the scene of the crime were of "Middle Eastern appearance", "ethnic gangs" became defined as a threat. "Police sources" were quoted in the tabloid press as being aware of a constant "turf war over drugs in Bankstown" entailing fights between "Lebanese and Vietnamese gangs" (Temple & Trute, 20/10/98, p. 5).

Sercombe (1999, p. 11) underlines the importance of well-established links between newspaper journalists and police, such that youth subcultures are most often represented in the media via police sources in the context of criminal activity. Schlesinger and Tumber (1994, pp. 1–2) have noted the closeness of the interconnections and the effects of the exchanges between the world of police and criminal justice professionals and that of specialist crime-reporting journalists. Grabosky and Wilson (1989, pp. 26–42) have also noted the "symbiotic" relationship between police and journalism, while insisting that the power lies more with the police. We show here how such "source" relations tied the reportage of the crimes at issue to a demonising of young men of Arabic-speaking background in public space. Certainly, our interviews with police officers serving in the area overwhelmingly demonstrated their conflation of the categories of "gangs" as organised criminals, with the concept of "gangs" used to denote friendship groups of Lebanese-Australian teenagers, and the treatment of the latter as criminals was thus part of their common sense. This was a fully shared and daily lived part of policing discourse, although each interviewee contradictorily also distinguished between professional criminals and kids who were experienced as a nuisance (Poynting, Collins, Noble & Tabar, 1999).

Numerous "right-thinking people" were thus led to prescribe a law and order crackdown on "ethnic" youth in the Canterbury-Bankstown area. For example, a former New South Wales police officer, who spoke on air with right-wing radio talkback presenter, Alan Jones, counselled that a "show of force" was the most effective approach to dealing with Lebanese young men on the streets. He said that police in Australia were seen as soft on gangs compared with those in the United States, where gangs fear the police because they "do not take a backward step" (2UE, 4/11/98). This expression was later closely echoed by several of the police in the area whom we interviewed: the most successful approach, they found, was "Don't take a backward step". Others advocated "zero tolerance" and being "proactive" towards Arabic-speaking background youth.

The "get tough" prescription was duly fulfilled. Channel Two television news on 2 November 1998 reported the Police Commissioner as claiming "a tough public

SCOTT POYNTING, GREG NOBLE AND PAUL TABAR

crackdown on ethnic gangs." National Nine News said that, the previous Friday, "130 police made a clean sweep of the area, arresting 24 people on more than 70 charges".

Young people from the targeted groups, of course, saw things differently:

> We said we're waiting for a lift with his Dad. They [police] said, "We don't care. We don't want to see you in any of Bankstown: McDonald's on Rickard Road, Timeout , Bankstown Square, kebab shop, anywhere". "Then where are we supposed to wait?" They said, "We don't care; we'll lock youse up"' (Male teenager interviewed on 7:30 Report ABC TV 2/11/98).

A male seventeen-year old Sunni Muslim youth whom we interviewed said that police "like picking on Lebanese people ... everywhere you go you can't move, you see police behind us, stopping us, taking our details ... they are just racists" (Ahmad, 24/9/99).

A mature-aged, female ethnic community worker whom we interviewed, said that the police:

> were targeting young people indiscriminately. ... Every time there are a group of three or four, they are told to break up or they will be arrested ... They [police] were putting up barricades and searching cars. ... They [young people] couldn't hang around Bankstown Station. ... The bottom line is people were being harassed for the sheer fact that they were young people of Lebanese background. They were being harassed by the police when they had no reason to harass them (Raja, 20/5/99).

Police publicised, in connection with the stabbing, supposedly drastic recent increases in robbery rates, and took the opportunity afforded by the public outcry (which they stimulated) to deploy a special "Strike Force" "to reduce street crime including drug dealing, car theft and armed robberies" (Kennedy, 1998a). Arguably in retaliation for the concentrated campaign of police harassment such as that reported above, some youths calling themselves "the Bankstown Boys"[2], three days after the stabbing, interrupted police radio transmissions with abusive threats to the police. Judging from their voices, later broadcast on television news, their manner was youthful, taunting, bold; the tone was more that of a schoolyard insult than the threat of a dangerous gangster[3]. The defiance was conveyed with deliberately offensive masculinity, but it would strain credulity to take literally the threat that the "Bankstown Boys" were coming to "root" the policemen's "mums" (Bearup, 2/11/98, p. 4). Police and press, however, at the time appeared to be treating the threats seriously[4], with proclaimed precautions of "Armed escorts for officers after radio threats" (Kennedy, 1998a). As early as October 28, the *Daily Telegraph* reported that police in the area were acquiring bullet-proof vests (*Daily Telegraph*, 2/11/98, p. 5). Police Commissioner Ryan intoned, "I'm not having my officers threatened by anyone; *I don't care where they come from*" (22/10/98, Radio 2BL News).

Where they (or their parents) were believed to come from was an issue, of course. The radio threats were "made in both English and a Middle Eastern language", the *Herald* noted (Kennedy, 1998a). Police Minister Paul Whelan characterised this menace as "cowardly" and "un-Australian" (*Sunday Telegraph*, 25/10/98, p. 19), setting a theme that would be referred to ad nauseam over the

MIDDLE EASTERN APPEARANCES: "ETHNIC GANGS", MORAL PANIC AND MEDIA FRAMING

coming weeks, rising to a crescendo with the shots fired into the police station the following weekend.

There was widespread consensus that the November 1 shooting-up of Lakemba police station was, like the radio threats, a response to the police crackdown of the previous weeks. National Nine News reported the following day that the Police Commissioner, Mr Ryan "is in no doubt this is payback". Commissioner Ryan said, "We're reducing crime figures; we're catching robbers, we're locking people up and I think this is a retaliation for that." The dog squad and mounted police were involved (Jamieson, 1998, p. 4), in the "clean sweep of the area" (Usher, 1998) suggesting a degree of intimidation of young people on the streets: horses are not very useful these days for catching robbers, but are very handy for "moving on". One male Lebanese-background community worker whom we interviewed spoke of having a meeting between a sympathetic journalist and the group of school students who had been named as the "Punchbowl Boys" and portrayed as a criminal gang on the front page of the Daily Telegraph (Casey & Ogg 1998, p. 1). "A few minutes later the police were there with their dogs. ... The kids dispersed; they shit themselves. I felt for them as well; I felt personally threatened. ... It wasn't written in the newspaper; I wonder why."

"The dog squad, mounted police, and uniformed and non-uniformed officers – 130 men and women in total" conducted a well-publicised "swoop" on the Bankstown CBD, with the purpose of "re-establishing, however fleetingly, their control over the streets ...", reported the Bulletin (Martin, 1998, p. 27) cooperating in both the publicity and the myth that the streets had been beyond control. The target of this campaign by 130 officers with guns, horses and dogs, was "stolen property, outstanding warrants, truancies from schools, anti-social and offensive behaviour" (Rowlands & Ogg, 1998:9). The Courier Mail quoted the head of the Lakemba Islamic Welfare Centre, Sheikh Khalil Chami, as saying,

> "There had to be some revenge from this gang" after police targeted the Arab community in their crime crackdowns. "This is just about all people are talking about on Arabic radio — that police were unjustifiably stopping and searching anyone of Middle-Eastern appearance" (Ogg & Casey, 1998b).

The local press reported "46 cautions, 199 separate marches and 247 move-alongs" from the blitz (The Torch 1998, p. 7). The Weekend Australian of 7–8 November reported kids in Lakemba the previous Tuesday just hanging around, being sociable, being moved on by police (Wynhausen & Safe, 1998:13). Sydney talkback radio echoed approval across many stations of the 24-hour "crackdown" by 130 police in the small suburban shopping stretch; Gareth McCray on commercial radio station 2KY, for instance, reporting that 200 people had been searched and 6 knives seized (30/10/98)[5]. Graham Richardson, of Radio 2GB said, "It's about time the police got stuck into these people" (30/10/98). Commissioner Ryan, interviewed after the shooting, on Phillip Clark's radio talkback on the Australian Broadcasting Corporation's (ABC) station 2BL, said that police were targetting ethnically based gangs in their crackdown and that therefore such a gang could be responsible for the shooting (2/11/98).

One tabloid editorial compared the shooting to Northern Ireland, Israel and Kashmir (Daily Telegraph, 2/11/98, p. 10), next to a Warren cartoon drawing

SCOTT POYNTING, GREG NOBLE AND PAUL TABAR

comparisons with New York. Comparisons to Northern Ireland were made by the Police Commissioner and the Leader of the Opposition, Mr Collins (*Sydney Morning Herald*, 2/11/98, p. 5; Murphy, 3/11/98, p. 6). More pointedly, the *Courier-Mail* sensed "a grim echo of Beirut" (Charlton, 1998). Mr Collins, apparently without irony and not referring to the police, also compared the events to a "South American dictatorship" (ABCTV News, 2/11/98). Canterbury Council councillor Barbara Coorey drew parallels with "some third world country where police are placed in danger" (Ogg & Casey, 1998, p. 5). An unnamed police officer said, "we are dealing with ethnic-based gangs who have come from harsh environments where life is cheap" (Bearup, 1998, p. 4)[6].

The act was denounced as "un-Australian" by, among others: Lakemba Police Commander Morris West (Ogg & Casey, 1998, p. 5), Muslim leader Taj Al Hilali, Mufti of Australia (Humphries & Marsh, 1998, p. 1), *The Inner Western Suburbs Courier* (1998b, p. 4). New South Wales Premier, Bob Carr, said the culprits were "trying to destroy the Australian way of life" (Casey and Ogg, 3/11/98, p. 1).

This epithet, "un-Australian", was also used widely in the media when Cabramatta MP John Newman was shot and killed in 1994 (*Sydney Morning Herald*, 1994, p. 1), and when two men were beaten with baseball bats outside a Korean restaurant in Kings Cross in 1996 (*Sydney Morning Herald*, 1997, p. 14).

Mukherjee (1998, 1999) points out that it was noted by the Committee to Investigate Conduct of Migrants, in the 1950s at the beginning of the Australian postwar immigration wave, that

> If an Australian commits a misdemeanour, responsibility for it is attributed to him individually. If a migrant commits a similar misdemeanour it is usually reported in such a way that the fact that he is a migrant, rather than the crime itself, is featured and responsibility for the offence is thus shared by the whole migrant population (Commonwealth Immigration Advisory Council, 1952, p. 14, cited in Mukherjee, 1999, p. 3).

Journalist Tony Stephens perceptively predicted the onset of what he called the "Lazlo Toth syndrome", named after an Australian citizen who vandalised the Michelangelo sculpture in the Vatican in the 1970s, and was repeatedly referred to in the Australian press as a "Hungarian carrying an Australian passport" (1998, p. 5). The ideological linking of aliens with criminality is thus not new in Australia; the resurgence over the past two years of labelling of Asian immigrants with drugs (as well as illicit gambling, disease, immorality and taking White Australians' jobs) is but the latest manifestation of a racist theme over a century old in Australia.

Recourse to guns and knives was portrayed in the context of the current moral panic, by Kevin Moss, Labor MP for Canterbury, as evincing an altogether foreign style of masculinity. Moss claimed, without a shred of evidence, that the attackers of the police station were Lebanese, and continued:

> This area is full of little mug lair hoods who have been spoiled rotten by their fathers since they could walk, have never been in a fight down the back lane with their fists and the only way they know how to get their way is by pulling knives and guns on people (cited by Humphries & Marsh, 1998, p. 1).

MIDDLE EASTERN APPEARANCES: "ETHNIC GANGS", MORAL PANIC AND MEDIA FRAMING

This is reminiscent: Pearson cites the Hytner Report on the British Moss Side "riots" of 1981 as bewailing the "un-Britishness" of using a knife in a fight, despite the historical record that a century earlier infamous English gang fights had been typified by just that (1983, p. 209). At that time, too, the weapon was portrayed as "un-English" and "foreign": Italian or French (Pearson, 1983, p. 131).

The characterisation of crime, especially youth street crime, as culturally alien, imported from abroad, is firmly implanted in the English language. The *Macquarie Dictionary* (1981, p. 1707) still lists the term, "street Arab" for street kids inclined to larceny; Partridge (1972, p. 29) dates the usage from England in the mid-nineteenth century. Pearson (1983, p. 159) records that they were also referred to as "English kaffirs" and "Hottentots". The word, "thug", of course, was imported from India to denote "a brutal, vicious or murderous ruffian, robber or gangster", from the Hindi name of "a former body of professional robbers and murderers in India who strangled their victims" (*Macquarie Dictionary*, 1981, p. 1803)[9]. The word, "assassin", borrowed from Arabic during the Crusades, originally denoted hashish-crazed Muslim fanatics banding together to attack and kill Crusaders (*Macquarie Dictionary*, 1981, p. 141).

A New Problem?

As well as being represented in the media as alien, the problem of youth gangs there constructed was also presented in this case, as previously, as if it were a new one, or reaching unprecedented crisis. Cohen's (1987, p. 46) seminal analysis of the mods and rockers panic makes the point that these subcultures "didn't become news because they were new; they were presented as new to justify their creation as news". Pearson (1983) points out that over three centuries of moral panics about young people and street violence invariably involve the reactionary appeal to some golden age of the past when such things were unheard of. His history is cleverly written backwards, in search of this mythical age of tranquillity "twenty years" ago or "before the war", and reaches back to the beginning of the century — the seventeenth — with outrage about long-haired, streetfighting, offensively behaving apprentices (1983, p. 193). In some ways this ideology is timeless: a function of aging, as nostalgia rehabilitates the folk devils of the past, and the physical vulnerabilities of the aged cast youthful boisterousness in more threatening light. Yet it is overwhelmingly the youth of the *working class* who are represented as the threat (ever since this class came into being), and the moral panics tend to arise in conjunctures of more generalised social crisis or disruption.

In a region with the demographics of contemporary Canterbury-Bankstown, these age and class relations are complicated by, and sometimes ideologically represented as, relations of ethnicity. The influx of migrants to these suburbs over the last two decades, and their age profile, means that many elderly Anglos, when confronted by youth, experience this as confrontation by *ethnic* youth.

Generational frictions within ethnic communities, moreover, are often compounded by the different experiences of migration, and different relations to the "home" culture, of middle-aged and young immigrants, and of first and second generation immigrants. Thus the "timeless" discourse of moral decline with regard to the young is read, particularly by conservative elders, as "losing" their culture

SCOTT POYNTING, GREG NOBLE AND PAUL TABAR

and their values. The age-old complaint of lack of respect for elders is thus refracted through the prism of loss of respect for the old ways of the homeland. Pronouncements of some "ethnic community leaders" thus readily lend themselves to the reactionary discourse of falling moral standards, diagnoses of laxity and indulgence, and prescriptions of stern discipline.

Commissioner Ryan pronounced after the 1 November shooting that "Sydney had entered "a whole new ball park" of violence' (Bearup, 1998b, p. 33). NSW Premier Bob Carr described the attack as "something we haven't witnessed before" (Ogg and Casey, 1998, p. 5). Opposition Leader Peter Collins dubbed the event a "turning point in Australia's criminal history", stating, "I am unaware that any police station has been shot up in Australia like this before" (Murphy, 1998, p. 6). The *Courier-Mail* announced "a new dimension to Australian crime" (Charlton, 1998). The *Herald* hyperbolised, "The nature of policing in this state had been changed forever" (Bearup, 1998b, p. 33). ABC news journalist Michael Brissenden observed that "This attack has already been painted as a loss of innocence. Suddenly, Australia is no longer immune from acts of urban terror" (ABCTV, 2/11/98). *The Australian* echoed Peter Ryan by announcing "'A new era of crime", growing in a way where 'violence is becoming the norm'". (Crawford, 1998, p. 1). A Lakemba resident, Ali, is quoted by the same newspaper, the following day, as saying, "It used to be very good here. I don't feel safe any more. The country is much changed" (Jackson, 1998, p. 5). "Gone are the days we could safely walk the streets day or night and leave our house doors and windows open", lamented the editorial of a local paper (*Inner Western Suburbs Courier*, 1998a, p. 4). The *Telegraph* editorialised, "Until this morning, acts of terrorism were largely confined to the foreign news sections of this newspaper" (1998b, p. 10).

If we follow Pearson's lead, we can test the novelty of this outbreak of violent crime by looking back a generation, for the good old days when the streets held no fear and property was safe. In 1986 we find, however, something rather less tranquil: newspaper headlines, "War in the west", "Bankstown battleground" and "Race hate grips Bankstown" (Marsh, 1998:43). Looking much further back, as one letter to the *Herald* (6/11/98, p. 22) waggishly pointed out, Ned Kelly and his "ethnic" gang were shooting at police in Australia 120 years ago — with the associated moral panic about lawlessness and banditry being symptoms of social malaise (Clark, 1987, pp. 161–2).

The working-class Teddy Boy subculture of the 1950s, nowadays domesticated as nostalgia, in its day was represented in a moral panic as a dangerous American import: "It is deplorable. It is tribal. And it is from America. ... We sometimes wonder whether this is the negro's revenge", grieved the *Daily Mail* in 1956 over the advent of rock 'n roll (cited in Pearson, 1983, p. 24). A similar theme of the national working class drawing perilously on American popular culture could be found in Australia at the same time, in moral panic over the "Bodgies" (Stratton, 1993; Braithwaite & Barker, 1978), who were also mythologised as the reincarnation of the "larrikin" (Irving, Maunders and Sherington, 1995, pp. 103–5). In that same year of 1956, a pamphlet published by New South Wales Teachers Federation activists complained:

MIDDLE EASTERN APPEARANCES: "ETHNIC GANGS", MORAL PANIC AND MEDIA FRAMING

Already at the Conference of the N.S.W. Teachers' Federation evidence had been given that at Newtown some individuals had been influenced by the "cult of violence" (one boy having been found carrying a knife, and saying, "I'm going to carve up a teacher in this place one of these days"). After the film "Blackboard Jungle" had been released and seen by thousands of teen-agers, pupils were noticed "draped around the playground chanting the film's theme song, 'Rock around the Clock'".

Teachers had for long been contending with anti-social attitudes on the part of certain boys – instances of "bodgie" behaviour and dress, the carrying of dagger-like and stiletto-type knives, vandalism, undermining of school regulations on uniform, contempt for teacher authority (Woodcock, 1957, p. 1).

Compare the picture of working-class youth painted by the *Telegraph* in November, 42 years later: "Punchbowl Homeboys ... ape the black homeboy gangs in the United States — they wear the same baggy jeans, sportswear such as FILA and adidas, and listen to rap music" (Casey & Ogg, 1998, p. 4). The protagonists offered to be photographed with their guns, but the journalists proudly record that they ethically declined. The tabloid front page photo shows pretty clearly that the young men are having fun ridiculing the reporters (Casey & Ogg, 1998, pp. 1–4), and our interview of one of those present (a schoolmate of the others who declined the *Telegraph's* invitation to be photographed) corroborates this[10]. Or another example: "Their clothes proclaim their identity — shiny sportsgear with trademarks writ large like badges of honour. Their music is the gangsta rap of 2Pac Shakur; their language is a hybrid of American trash talk, English and Arabic" (Stevenson, 1998, p. 32).

The myth of newness allows the "respectable fears" projected ideologically onto these youth subcultures to be experienced as having come about "since the war", permitting their representation as products of postwar immigration or foreign imports.

Youth Out of Control

Under the banner, "Ethnic gangs have the upper hand", an outraged reader wrote (from distant Tweed Heads) to the *Telegraph* (3/11/98, p. 12), expostulating, "The elders of the Arabic communities should be ashamed to show their faces in Sydney and for letting their offspring do as they please. I'm more than sure it would not be tolerated in their homeland." Judicial lenience was to blame and deportation was the remedy, he claimed. Surprisingly congruent was the opinion of the leading Muslim cleric, Taj al Hilali, who said that the laxity of Australian law was part of the problem and that the perpetrators "did not "deserve to be Australian citizens'" (Humphries, 1998, p. 5). Interviewed by Alan Jones on Radio 2UE (10/11/98), Richard Miter, a spokesperson for the Lebanese Muslim Association said that Lebanese parents worry that their children are losing the best of their tradition. Jones responded that parents feel that they are not allowed to discipline their children as they see fit. Sheik Chami, of the Lebanese Welfare Centre in Lakemba complained to the *Australian* that "the Government doesn't allow parents to discipline" kids (Jackson, 1998, p. 5). The Mufti of Australia, Taj Al Hilali, quoted in

SCOTT POYNTING, GREG NOBLE AND PAUL TABAR

the *Australian*, urged legislators to "go back 25 years". "The law doesn't give the power for families to control their kids", he said (Humphries, 1998, p. 5). He recommended giving curfews the force of law (English, 1998, p. 2). Parents in the community were "struggling to supervised their young children", he remarked (Jamal, 1998, p. 6). He complained on ABCTV news about a lack of respect by young people in the Lebanese community. The reporter explained, "The weekend attack has shocked local Lebanese as much as anyone else. Some say they've lost control of their young people and they're causing a growing divide within their local community (2/11/98). The *Telegraph* took up the refrain: "The constant complaint among Lebanese adults is that they are unable to control their children". It quotes a Bankstown interpreter as saying, "At the age of 14 or 16, they cannot stop their children from doing what they want to do" (Stevenson, 1998, p. 33). "Lebanese community leader and councillor for Canterbury Council, Michael Hawatt was also reported as saying 'his community had lost control of its young'" (Humphries & Marsh, 1998, p. 1).

Councillor Coorey asserted, "there's a lack of discipline within the family unit"; Sheik Khalil concurred (Casey, 1998, p. 4). Superintendent West also blamed "dysfunctional families" (Cornford, 1998, p. 4).

Many of the parents and community leaders we interviewed indeed conveyed some sense of loss of control over their young folk, and many blamed "Western" laxity and prescribed stern discipline from the State. Yet virtually all found the police "zero tolerance" campaign against gatherings of Lebanese-background young people in public spaces to be discriminatory and uncalled for. Not surprisingly, none saw their own family as "dysfunctional" or lacking in discipline.

The *Herald* divulged that the Premier's strategy in calling together religious and community leaders to address the problem "amused some police", and quoted one policeman as saying, "If it had happened in the Eastern suburbs or on the North Shore, and they were Anglo kids, would he have called in all the local priests and vicars?" "His point was that the youths whom police are seeking are not turning up at Lakemba Mosque each day for prayer sessions. They are outside the influence of the sheiks, and their parents", explained the *Herald* (Bearup, 1998b, p. 43).

This misses several points. Religion may, in complex and not necessarily devout or orthodox ways, serve as a focal point for precisely the disaffection which local youth are directing at police. For example, a car full of defiant youths drove past Lakemba police station the day after the shooting, with one raising a fist and shouting, "Tell them Mohammed says, 'sucked in'" (Cornford, 1998, p. 4). The *Daily Telegraph* quotes "the brother of the Imam of Lakemba Mosque" as witnessing worshippers wearing firearms and carrying knives (Casey & Ogg, 1998, p. 4). Of course, they may have been carrying these for defence. Lakemba Mosque was placed under private security guard (Jamal, 1998, p. 6) and then protective police guard after threats against it were made in a racist backlash against the Lebanese community (Safe, 1998, p. 13), concomitant with the moral panic traced here. Several cases of assault and injury of Lebanese Australians were reported (*Daily Telegraph*, 1998c, p. 2).

Nor were the meetings aimed at coopting the killer(s) of Edward Lee or the attackers of Lakemba Police Station; rather, as we discuss below, police and politi-

MIDDLE EASTERN APPEARANCES: "ETHNIC GANGS", MORAL PANIC AND MEDIA FRAMING

cians were appealing to "the Lebanese community" to inform on the perpetrators. Moreover, the Lebanese communities, outraged at what they saw as slanders and slurs directed against them, had to be placated (Tabar, Poynting & Noble, 1998; Collins, Noble, Poynting &Tabar, 2000). Threats by community leaders for legal action against the Premier for racial vilification needed to be quickly allayed by the State Government in an election campaign where the "ethnic vote" is a strong consideration. Populist "law and order" policies in the leadup to the state election may garner votes, but crucial constituencies in culturally diverse electorates require reassurance when they feel their people are being targeted . Finally, the State sought to enlist community cooperation in the social control of youth deemed to be out of control.

The complaints about Lebanese youths' lack of respect for the elders of their community and their culture, both those complaints emanating from adult members of Lebanese communities and the repetitions of these from politicians and public commentators, are also misplaced. Those who take the trouble to listen to the young people themselves will hear a different account. Indeed, the authors' ethnographic work in the Lakemba-Bankstown area in 1996 found that their respect for what they saw as their communities' culture, including their religions, was experienced by Lebanese teenagers in friendship groups labelled as "gangs", as constitutive of their identity and restorative of dignity in the face of everyday racist humiliation (Poynting, Noble & Tabar, 1998).

> But here [Lakemba], because of our religion, and close to a mosque, and heaps of Muslim friends. ... There is always something that they will respect. For example, religion; they respect their parents. Like respect for what you are. Like for what you do, not what you are. You know what I mean? (Mohammed, male, 16 years old secondary school student).

The kids framed by the *Telegraph* told a similar story — not that presented in the photograph and the headlines: "... their Lebanese blood [sic] unites them, driven together by persecution and insults suffered by their families."

> ... the fact is wherever we go the cops just hassle hassle hassle us because we're Lebanese.

> If you insult one of us, then you insult our brother, and if you insult our brother, you insult our father, our mother, and put shame on our whole family.

> Respect us, and we'll respect you (Casey & Ogg, 1998, p. 4).

"Wall of Silence"

From the first public statements following the Edward Lee murder, police spokesmen and political leaders appealed to residents of the neighbourhood, and specifically to members of "the Lebanese community", to come forward with information. The process of racialisation constructs a monolithic "community" out of the diversity of religions, politics, settlement histories, ages, class backgrounds, labour market positions and much more, as if they were homogeneous and were uniformly responsible for crimes committed in their neighbourhoods (Collins et al., 2000).

SCOTT POYNTING, GREG NOBLE AND PAUL TABAR

This racialisation, and the experience of being blamed, in fact militate *against* the willingness of immigrant communities to cooperate with the police. Moreover, when people find themselves, their families, their neighbours and friends targetted in an aggressive police "crackdown" on groups of their young people gathering together sociably in public spaces, this tends to make them even less inclined to cooperate with police and state leaders in their search for culprits (Poynting, 1999). Denied their citizen rights — including the right of assembly, freedom of movement, assumption of innocence until proven guilty — they are nevertheless hectored in the media about their civic responsibilities. "We already know our citizenship duty", retorted Maan Abdallah of the Lebanese Community Council (*Australian*, 1998, p. 1), who deemed it "unhelpful to give any crime an ethnic dimension" (English & Walsh, 1998, p. 4).

The Mufti of Australia, Taj al Hilali, was reported as saying that "many young people distrusted the police, whom they saw as being quick to point the finger at the Lebanese community" (Jamal, 1998, p. 6). Tony Stewart, Labor MP for Lakemba, who arranged to meet with local youth along with the Mufti, concurred: "They're very apprehensive. They don't trust the police …" (Humphries, 1998, p. 5). Premier Carr, after denouncing "Lebanese gangs" in the media, "urged Lebanese community leaders to 'work harder' in encouraging people with information on the crime to pass it on to police" (English and Walsh, 1998, p. 4).

The Monday after the weekend of the stabbing of Edward Lee, police were complaining of the reticence of locals to provide information; more people must have witnessed the events of the suburban street at 7:15 pm on the Saturday. The local area commander of the police cautioned that "Concealing a murder was a serious offence" (Clennell & Kennedy, 1998, p. 3). The following day, the police superintendent cited cultural reasons for "the reluctance of ethnic groups to talk to police" (Temple & Trute, 1998, p. 5). The next day he pointed to "barriers of language and cultural differences"[11], and stated that "people with vital information were not coming forward". "We know there are people in the street who witnessed this event," he said (Trute, 1998, p. 21). A fortnight later, after the police station shooting, the headlines were strident: "Street where no-one talks", accused the *Telegraph*, next to an aerial photograph of the suburban street and above another of the sign bearing its name (Trute & Stevenson, 1998, p. 7). "They all know Edward's killer, but won't talk", alleged the *Herald*'s front page in unison, indicting the unnamed "they" for precisely the "serious offence" warned of by the area commander (Kennedy, 1998b, p. 1). "They" knew who they were. As state MP for Lakemba, Tony Stewart, said, "The word is out on the Lakemba grapevine that these mongrels have to be found so the discrediting of the Arabic-speaking community is put to an end" (Harris, Sutherland & Woodley, 1998). "Police hit gang wall of silence", headlined the *Herald*'s cover story, doing its part in applying the pressure (Bearup, 1998c, p. 1).

Superintendent Madden knew the phenomenon: "We have had other stabbings in other streets — it's not uncommon for us to find a wall of silence in the community" (Trute & Stevenson, 1998, p. 7). While he may have been referring to the Lebanese community — and certainly they were held responsible by the Premier, the local MP, several police spokesmen, the three major daily newspapers, repeated letters to the editor, numerous talkback demagogues and their interlocutors — for the "wall of silence", it is indeed a longstanding and widespread occurrence. Yet when walls of silence are complained of by police and media in other instances, such as the Leigh Leigh rape and murder in Newcastle in 1989 (Lyons, Lewis & Watkin, 1989, p. 1; Lewis, 1989, p. 3), they are never represented as *Anglo-Celtic* intransigence. The taboo against "dobbing", "lagging", "grassing" to officialdom and especially the coercive arm of the state is recognisable from these very words as a part of *working-class* culture. Loader (1996, pp. 96–101), for instance, gives ample evidence of such working-class sanctions against informing police in contemporary Edinburgh.

Nor is it a particularly new phenomenon, any more than it is an "ethnic" one. George Morgan records that the "larrikin" moral panic in 1890s Sydney peaked with the daylight murder of a sailor in the Rocks, which was linked with a gang known as the Millers Point Push. *The Bulletin* bewailed that "through an elaborate system of terrorism it is often impossible to obtain evidence, and the witness who testifies against the "push" thereafter carries his life in his hands'(8/7/1893, cited in Morgan, 1997). Pearson (1983, p. 86) records similar occurrences in the late nineteenth-century English moral panic about the original "hooligans", who are shown, in attacks on police, to have been "acting in concert with their neighbours, reflecting the fact that in many working-class neighbourhoods hostility towards the police was a remarkably cohesive force"[12] which was often triggered by unfairness or arbitrary use of power by police. He argues that such cases manifested "complex structures of loyalty and tradition" which run counter to the ideology handed down from above about law-abiding and civil responsibility (1983, pp. 86–88).

We contend that the recent moral panic in south-western Sydney, one hundred years later, is also a matter of (though not reducible to) class relations. It is the ideology of racism, offering superficial diagnoses and remedies at the level of appearances — Middle-Eastern appearances — which makes these appear as relations of ethnicity, while class interests disappear from the account in the construction of an overwhelming "community" consensus about what the real problem and its causes are.

Conclusion

By the end of 1999, the current moral panic was beginning to calm down. Goode and Ben-Yehuda (1994, p. 38) point out that, "… by their very nature, moral panics are *volatile*; they erupt fairly suddenly (although they may lie dormant or latent for long periods of time, and may reappear from time to time) and, nearly as suddenly, subside." The "law and order auction" had helped to deliver the Labor Government election success in March 1999, and "ethnic crime" was out of the headlines. Then, on 17 September 1999, following a day of police raids and arrests in south-western Sydney, eight men and a teenage boy were charged with a range of offences, including three who were charged in relation to the shooting of Lakemba Police Station. Four were already in prison on remand on other charges. The press made a point of the fact that one grasped the Koran in court. With media image taking precedence over the convention of innocence until guilt is proven, the

SCOTT POYNTING, GREG NOBLE AND PAUL TABAR

Police Commissioner pronounced that, following these arrests, the streets of Sydney were "significantly safer" (Kennedy, Bearup and Connelly, 1999, p. 6).

As at April 2000, there had still not been any arrests for the murder of Edward Lee. The police harassment of Lebanese-Australian young men in Sydney continues. In relation to one of the other charges of those already in prison on September 17, magistrate Pat O'Shane, found on 29 November 1999 that the two young men charged had no case to answer. She remarked, moreover, that the police had no lawful reason to stop these men when they did, and that Sydney police had a history of chasing and harassing young people (Gibbs, 1999a, pp. 1,4; 1999b, p. 9). There was an outcry from press, police spokesmen and politicians, but it was directed at the magistrate rather than the police. "The DPP [Director of Public Prosecutions] overruled the decision a fortnight later by issuing an ex officio indictment", reported the *Telegraph* (Peterson, 1999), announcing the eventual gaoling of one of the young men.

NSW Police Commissioner, in February 2000, "stirred up a hornets' nest", blaming "Lebanese gangs for some of the recent violence in Sydney's south-west,", according to the tabloid *Sun-Herald* (2000), which applauded his plain speaking: "Some, he maintains, are protected by 'crooked lawyers' who coach them in courtroom tactics. Others are shielded by their own communities ...". The commercial television program, *A Current Affair*, showed on 27 March 2000, a high-profile "stop and search" manoeuvre by numerous police, along Telopea Street, Punchbowl, accompanied by two teams of dogs and the tabloid TV crew. They did find a small packet of marijuana seeds behind the seat of one car, but the media lamented their inability to prosecute anyone. Two police area commanders were interviewed on the program, and stressed that they did not have "no go" areas in their commands.

Media harassment of the ethnic communities also abated somewhat after the end of 1998, then flared up again. There was repeated blame for the "wall of silence". In March 1999, *Daily Telegraph* columnist Ray Chesterton (1999) had ranted:

> There has to be co-operation and a genuine attempt by ethnic leaders to rid NSW of the cowardly vermin waging a war that is murdering innocent people. The police appeal for help to convict a primarily Lebanese gang ... Police privately believe the gang is mainly Lebanese. But in accordance with the sickening political correctness that blights this nation, they can only talk of nationalities [sic] that are of Mediterranean/Middle Eastern. ... If help in convicting these leaders is not forthcoming from the ethnic community, multiculturalism could be as dead as [murdered "gang leader"] Danny Karam.

On the day of the September 1999 arrests, the *Herald* (Bearup, 1999, p. 6) headlined "Another day in Telopea Street: 'We see nothing'", the broken English referring to the lack of informants over the murder of Edward Lee the previous October. "It was a death witnessed by 20 people. Yet, when the police came asking, no-one saw a thing, and no-one has yet been charged with his murder". On that day in the ignominious street, the tipped-off reporter described how the car of one of the local young men was towed away for testing.

MIDDLE EASTERN APPEARANCES: "ETHNIC GANGS", MORAL PANIC AND MEDIA FRAMING

> Some of the boys were unhappy and began hassling both the police and tow-truck operator. One of the men approached a *Herald* photographer: "You take any more photos, I'll break your camera and I'll break your face. I don't give a f—- if the coppers charge me".

> A policeman stood nearby — they'd been copping the same all day (Bearup, 1999, p. 6).

It's easy to see where the reporter's sympathies lie and why; he relies on the police for stories. But the young Lebanese-Australian men of the area had been copping much the same from the police, the papers, and politicians not just for a day, but nearly for a year.

This article has provided evidence of the recent and ongoing criminalisation of Lebanese-background youth in Western Sydney in conjunction with the racialisation of crime in the region. The mechanisms of this racialisation have been investigated through analysing in the media, in the case of the moral panic here presented, the timeless ideological elements of racialisation of street crime, the seeming newness of the ("ethnic") "gang" problem, the assumption that ("ethnic") youth are out of control and in need of strong discipline, and appeals to the ("ethnic") "community" to break the "wall of silence". White (1996, p. 305) has argued that whether the issue is perceived as one of "ethnic youth gangs", or as problems experienced by young people from ethnic minorities, depends largely upon a social "frame of reference" — one too often constructed by the media. The NSW Parliament's Legislative Council Standing Committee on Social Issues (1995, p. 303) recommended that "both the media and politicians should be responsible in their reporting of so-called youth "gangs"" We have demonstrated here that the mainstream media, in a symbiosis with the police and political leaders, have rather continued their framing of young people with "middle Eastern appearance".

Acknowledgments

The authors wish to acknowledge a foundation grant from the University of Western Sydney, Macarthur, which has assisted the research for this paper, an earlier version of which was presented at the Annual Conference of the Australian Sociological Association, Queensland University of Technology, Brisbane, 3rd December 1998. We thank all our interviewees who gave of their time and their trust — both those actually quoted here pseudonymously and the greater number who inform the background.

Endnotes

1   We are here using the term "common sense" in the way deployed by Antonio Gramsci (1971).
2   Interestingly, the appellation, "Bankstown Boys", was used in 1931 by a group of young men involved in the anti-eviction movement, upon whose picket the police had fired shots on 17 June, and "captured 16 bleeding and battered prisoners", according to Nadia Wheatley &

SCOTT POYNTING, GREG NOBLE AND PAUL TABAR

Drew Cottle (1999, p. 9) and who evinced — perhaps not surprisingly — "a working-class dislike of police" (Wheatley & Cottle, 1999, p. 7).

3   We interviewed a 17 year old unemployed Sunni Muslim man who said he was friends with the "Bankstown Boys". He said that they were all Lebanese, and listed members' ages as "about 16, 18, 17, 13, 14, 20". He said "they like going out; they go night clubbing, they go there, they do this but they are not into crimes, no nothing. It's just like going out like family, you know, like family, like to go out, you know what I mean?" He admitted to streetfighting, and professed to have "bashed" a policeman who had hit his friend with a baton.

4   Also taken very seriously by police and media was the firecracker tossed from a car at Bankstown Police Station on 4 November 1998, reported on radio news as a possible "pipe bomb" (John Laws, Radio 2UE, 4/11/98); the rattling of windows becoming "Blast Rocks Police Station" on tabloid front pages (Crosweiler, 1998, p. 1).

5   The "knives" pictured in the *Telegraph* under the headline, "Sydney's night of knives", as a result of four months' "blitz" (another one) by police under new legislation, included school type paper scissors, hairdresser's scissors, a screwdriver and a corkscrew (Milohanic, 1998:5).

6   Compare the comments by police and public officials quoted by Mike Davis, made during a police "get tough" campaign, ostensibly against crack cocaine dealing in Los Angeles: "This is Vietnam here" (1988, p. 38), a comparison with the "murderous militias of Beirut" (1988, p. 38), and with "Haiti under the Tontons Macoutes" (1988, p. 46).

7   Nor was the more recent (September 1998) *Sydney Morning Herald* report, "Offduty police bashed with iron bar" couched in terms of ethnicity.

8   The *Melbourne Herald* of 4 April 1870, used the word rather less indulgently, for instance, when it reported that, "Three larikins … had behaved in a very disorderly manner in Little Latrobe Street" (cited in *The Penguin Dictionary of Historical Slang*, 1972, p. 524). The *Bulletin* of 8 January 1881 observed that, "The Larrikins who demonstratively display their evil propensities and outrageous proclivities in full public view do not as a rule belong to the well-to-do classes. They are the idle, the uncared for, the wilful, and the depraved" (cited in Gorman, 1990:viii) — but they were not *foreign*.

9   See Pearson (1983, p. 131) for a contemporaneous comparison with Indian *thuggee* during the English "garotting" panic of 1862. The garotte, of course, is French; the stiletto, Italian.

10 The photograph was "the subject of a complaint to the press council". "We sort of made everything up", says Easy E, "but we were only kids having fun, know what I mean?" "They've made everyone hate us even more than they hate us", says Gaz" (Wynhausen & Safe, 1998, p. 13). It was revealed on ABC Triple J radio that in the staging of the photo, one of the group of friends, a Tongan immigrant, was excluded by reporters because he did not look "Middle Eastern".

11 See Dixon (1998) for a well argued and evidenced refutation of these "explanations".

12 As, indeed, it was for the "Bankstown Boys" of 1931 (see Note 2).

References

Australian (1998, 3 November). Police search for shooting witness. *Australian*, p. 1.

Bearup, G. (1998a, 2 November). Fight to restore confidence. *Sydney Morning Herald*, p. 4.

Bearup, G. (1998b, 2 November). Under Fire .*Sydney Morning Herald*, pp. 33,43.

Bearup, G. (1998c, 4 November). Police hit gang wall of silence. *Sydney Morning Herald*, p. 1.

Bearup, G. (1999, 18 September). Another day in Telopea Street: "We see nothing". *Sydney Morning Herald*, p. 6.

Braithwaite, J. & Barker, M. (1978). Bodgies and widgies: Folk devils of the fifties. In P.R. Wilson & J. Braithwaite (Eds.), *Two faces of deviance: Crimes of the powerless and the powerful* (pp. 26–45). St Lucia: Queensland University Press.

MIDDLE EASTERN APPEARANCES: "ETHNIC GANGS", MORAL PANIC AND MEDIA FRAMING

Casey, M. (1998, 2 November). Community in crisis as tension turns to gunfire. *Daily Telegraph*, p. 4.

Casey, M. & Ogg, M. (1998, 3 November). Dial-a-Gun: Gang says it's easier than buying a pizza. *Daily Telegraph*, pp. 1,4.

Chan, J. (1997). *Changing police culture: Policing in a multicultural society*. Cambridge: Cambridge University Press.

Charlton, P. (1998, 3 November). A grim echo of Beirut. *The Courier-Mail*.

Clark, M. (1987). *A short history of Australia* (3rd ed.). New York: Mentor Books.

Clarke, J. et al., (1976). Subcultures, culture and class: A theoretical overview. In S. Hall & T. Jefferson (Eds.), *Resistance Through Rituals*. London: Unwin Hyman.

Clennell, A. & Kennedy, L. (1998, 19 October). Kneecappings may be linked to boy's murder. *Sydney Morning Herald*, p. 3.

Cohen, S. (1987). *Folk devils and moral panics: The creation of the Mods and Rockers* (3rd ed.). Basil Blackwell: Oxford.

Collins, J. (1994). John Newman and John Chinaman: Challenging Asians stereotyping *Australian Quarterly* 66(4), 27–48.

Collins, J., Noble, G., Poynting, S. & Tabar, P. (2000). *Kebabs, kids, cops and crime*. Sydney: Pluto Press Australia.

Commonwealth Immigration Advisory Council (1952). [First] Report of Committee Established to Investigate Conduct of Migrants (Typed report), cited in Mukherjee, S. (1999, p. 3.)

Connell, R.W. & Irving, T. (1980). *Class structure in Australian history*. Melbourne: Longman Cheshire.

Cornford, P. (1998, 2 November). Lakemba was vulnerable and easy to get away from. *Sydney Morning Herald*, p. 4.

Crawford, B. (1998, 2 November). Terror Australis: police in the firing line. *The Australian*, p.1.

Crosweiler, A. (1998, 4 November). Blast rocks police station: Arrests after new attack. *Daily Telegraph*, p.1.

Cunneen, C. (1995). Ethnic minority youth and juvenile justice: Beyond the stereotype of ethnic gangs. In C. Guerra & R. White, *Ethnic minority youth in Australia* (pp. 111–120). Hobart: National Clearinghouse for Youth Studies.

Cunneen, C & Spiers, M (1995). Police and justice. In Z. Antonios (Ed.), *State of the Nation: A report on people of non-English speaking background*. Canberra: Australian Government Publishing Service.

Daily Telegraph (1998a, 2 November), Two weeks of tension, threats and violence, *Daily Telegraph*, p. 5

Daily Telegraph, (1998b, 2 November) Anarchy pulls the trigger. *Daily Telegraph*, p. 10.

Daily Telegraph, (1998c, 4 November) Man stabbed as tensions increase. *Daily Telegraph*, p. 2.

Davis, M. (1988). Los Angeles: Civil liberties between the hammer and the rock. *New Left Review* 170, 37–60.

Dixon, D. (1998). Walls of silence. Paper presented to the Future of Australian Multiculturalism Conference, Research Institute for Humanities and Social Sciences, University of Sydney, 7–9 December.

English, B. (1998, 4 November). Parents told to control children. *Daily Telegraph*, p. 2.

Ethnic Affairs Commission of New South Wales (1994). *Police and ethnic communities*. Sydney: Ethnic Affairs Commission of New South Wales.

Finch, L. (1998). On the streets — Working class youth culture in the nineteenth century. In K. Healey, (Ed.), (1998) *Youth and the law*. Balmain: The Spinney Press. (reprinted from R. White (Ed.), (1993) *Youth subcultures — Theory, history and the Australian experience*. Hobart: National Clearinghouse for Youth Studies.)

Garcia, L.M. (1998, 13 November). Prosecutor lashes new law and order push. *Sydney Morning Herald*, p. 8.

SCOTT POYNTING, GREG NOBLE AND PAUL TABAR

Gibbs, S. (1999a, 27 November) Accused shooter harassed: magistrate. *Sydney Morning Herald*, p. 9.

Gibbs, S. (1999b, 30 November). O'Shane frees gunman and lashes police. *Sydney Morning Herald*, pp. 1,4.

Gilroy, P. (1987). *There ain't no black in the Union Jack*. London: Unwin Hyman.

Goldberg, D. (1993). *Racist culture*. Oxford: Blackwell.

Goode, E. & Ben-Yehuda, N. (1994). *Moral panics: The social construction of deviance*. Oxford: Blackwell.

Gorman, C., (Ed.). (1990). *The larrikin streak: Australian writers look at the legend*. Sydney: Pan Macmillan.

Grabosky, P. & Wilson, P. (1989). *Journalism and justice: How crime is reported*. Sydney: Pluto Press.

Gramsci, A. (1971). *Selections from the prison notebooks of Antonio Gramsci*. New York: International Publishers, (ed. and trans. Q. Hoare and G. Nowell-Smith).

Hall, S. (1988). New ethnicities. In K. Mercer (Ed.), *Black Film/British Cinema*. London: ICA.

Hall, S., Critcher, C., Jefferson, T., Clarke, J. & Roberts, B. (1978). *Policing the crisis: Mugging, the state, and law and order*. London: Macmillan. \

Harris, T., Sutherland, T & Woodley, B. (1998, 4 November). No let-up in attack on gangs, says, Carr. *The Australian*.

Humphries, D. (1998, 4 November). Lebanese youths and police to meet. *The Australian*, p. 5.

Humphries, D. & Marsh, J. (1998, 3 November). Lakemba backs police: attack was un-Australian. *Sydney Morning Herald*, p. 1.

Inner Western Suburbs Courier (1998a, 2 November). Victims of crime, p. 4.

Inner Western Suburbs Courier (1998b, 9 November). It is not Australian, p. 4.

Irving, T., Maunders, D. & Sherington, G. (1995). *Youth in Australia: Policy administration and politics*. Melbourne: Macmillan.

Jackson, S. (1998, 3 November). Families cower under lock, key. *The Australian*, p. 5.

Jackson, S., Harris, T. & Nason, D. (1998, 3 November). Call to community on shooting. *The Australian*, p. 5.

Jamal, N. (1998, 3 November). Islamic chief warns on rush to judgment. *Sydney Morning Herald*, p. 6.

Jamieson, T. (1998, 2 November). Take control of streets, Carr told. *Sydney Morning Herald*, p. 4.

Kennedy, L. (1998a, 22 October). Armed escorts for officers after radio threats. *Sydney Morning Herald*.

Kennedy, L. (1998b, 5 November). The all know Edward's killer, but won't talk. *Sydney Morning Herald*, p. 1.

Kennedy, L., Bearup, G. & Connolly, E. (1999, 18 September). Ryan claims "safe streets" as raids net 9. *Sydney Morning Herald*, p. 6.

Larrain, J. (1979). *The concept of ideology*. London: Hutchinson.

Larrain, J. (1983). *Marxism and ideology*. London: Macmillan.

Larrain, J. (1994). *Ideology and cultural identity*. Cambridge: Polity Press.

Lewis, J. (1989, 11 November). Tragic community suffers trial by rumour and suspicion. *Sydney Morning Herald*, p. 3.

Loader, I. (1996). *Youth, policing and democracy*. London: Macmillan.

Lucas, T. (1998). Youth gangs and moral panics in Santa Cruz, California. In T. Skelton & G. Valentine (Eds.), *Cool Place.s* London: Routledge.

Lyons, J., Lewis, J. & Watkin, A. (1989, 7 November). A night of savagery: Leigh's last hours. *Sydney Morning Herald*, p. 1.

Mackenzie, J. (1998, 6 November). "Lebanese" problem is Australia's. *Sydney Morning Herald*, p. 22.

Marsh, J. (1998, 7 November). A question of context. *Sydney Morning Herald*, p. 43.

MIDDLE EASTERN APPEARANCES: "ETHNIC GANGS", MORAL PANIC AND MEDIA FRAMING

Martin, B. (1998, 10 November). Urban warfare .*The Bulletin*, pp. 26–27.

Miles, R. (1989). *Racism*. London: Routledge.

Milohanic, S, (1998, 15 November). Sydney's night of knives: Police seize 1100 weapons in four-month blitz. *Daily Telegraph*, p. 5.

Morgan, G. (1997). The *Bulletin* and the larrikin moral panic in nineteenth century Sydney. *Media International Australia 85*, 17–24.

Mukherjee, S. (1998). Crime in our society, paper presented to the "Ethnicity and Crime Under the Microscope: Dispelling the Myths' Forum of the Ethnic Communities' Council of NSW, Sydney, 2 November.

Mukherjee, S. (1999). Ethnicity and crime. Paper presented at the 3rd National Outlook Symposium on Crime in Australia, convened by the Australian Institute of Criminology, Canberra, 22–23 March.

Murphy, D. (1998, 3 November). Collins calls for tough laws, safety equipment. *Sydney Morning Herald*.

Murphy, D. & Power, B. (1998, 20 October). Agony over murdered son. *Sydney Morning Herald*, p. 2.

New South Wales Parliament Legislative Council Standing Committee on Social Issues (1995). *A Report into Youth Violence in New South Wales*. Sydney: New South Wales Parliament.

Ogg, M. & Casey, M. (1998a, 2 November). An act of war: Gang fires 18 shots at police station. *Daily Telegraph*, pp. 1,4–5.

Ogg, M. & Casey, M. (1998b, 2 November). Police dig in against gang attack. *Courier-Mail*.

Partridge, E. (1972). *The Penguin dictionary of historical slang* (abridged by J. Simpson). Harmondsworth: Penguin.

Pearson, G. (1983). *Hooligan: A history of respectable fears*. London: Macmillan.

Pe-Pua, R. (1999). Youth and ethnicity: Images and constructions. In R. White (Ed.), *Australian youth subcultures: On the margins and in the mainstream* (pp. 120–126). Hobart: National Clearinghouse for Youth Studies.

Pe-Pua, R. (1996). *"We're just like other kids": Street-frequenting youth of non-English speaking background*. Canberra: Australian Government Publishing Service.

Peterson, A. (1999, 22 December). White city gunman sent to jail. *Daily Telegraph*.

Poynting, S. (1999) When "zero tolerance" looks like racial intolerance: "Lebanese youth gangs", discrimination and resistance. *Current Issues in Criminal Justice 11*(1).

Poynting, S., Noble, G. & Tabar, P (1998). "If anyone called me a wog, they wouldn't be speaking to me alone": Protest masculinity and Lebanese youth in Western Sydney. *Journal of Interdisciplinary Gender Studies 3*(2), 6–94.

Poynting, S., Noble, G. & Tabar, P. (1999). "Intersections" of masculinity and ethnicity: A study of male Lebanese immigrant youth in Western Sydney. *Race, Ethnicity and Education 2*(1), 59–77.

Poynting, S., Collins, J., Noble, G. & Tabar, P. (1999). "Bankstown Boys" and "Boys in Blue": Ethnic youth, police and the conflict of masculinities. Paper presented to the Annual Conference of the Australian Sociological Association, Monash University, 8 December.

Rowlands, L. & Ogg, M. (1998, 30 October). 24 arrests as police swoop to reclaim "their patch". *Daily Telegraph*, p. 9.

Safe, G. (1998, 7–8 November). Police at odds over gun links. *The Weekend Australian*, p. 13.

Said, E. (1979). *Orientalism*. New York: Vintage.

Schlesinger, P. & Tumber, H. (1994). *Reporting crime: The media politics of criminal justice*. Oxford: Clarendon Press.

Sercombe, H. (1999). Boots, gangs and addictions: Youth subcultures and the media. In White, R. (Ed.), *Australian youth subcultures: On the margins and in the mainstream* (pp. 5–15). Hobart: Australian Clearinghouse for Youth Studies.

SCOTT POYNTING, GREG NOBLE AND PAUL TABAR

Solomos, J. & Back, L. (1996). *Racism and society*. Basingstoke: Macmillan.

Stephens, T. (1998, 2 November). Hard questions for a horrified city: Now, hard questions for a city in terror. *Sydney Morning Herald*, pp. 1,5.

Stevenson, A. (1998, 7 November). Cultural crossfire. *Daily Telegraph*, pp. 32–3.

Stratton, J. (1993). Bodgies and widgies: Just working-class kids doing working-class things. In R. White (Ed.), *Youth subcultures: Theory, history and the Australian experience* (pp. 87–91). Hobart: National Clearinghouse for Youth Studies.

Sunday Telegraph, Ethnic leaders' help on stabbing. *Sunday Telegraph* 25 October, p. 19.

Sun-Herald (2000, 27 February). When ethnic seems to be the hardest word. *Sun-Herald* Editorial.

Sydney Morning Herald (1994) State MP shot dead in drive-by attack. *Sydney Morning Herald* 6 September, p. 1.

Sydney Morning Herald (1997, 5 February) "Ethnic" crime. *Sydney Morning Herald*, p. 14.

Sydney Morning Herald (1998b) Scene is from Northern Ireland, says shocked Ryan. *Sydney Morning Herald*, 2 November, p. 5.

Tabar, P., Poynting, S. & Noble, G. (1998). "They don't deserve to be Australian": The politics of representation among a migrant community. Paper presented to the Annual Conference of the Australian Sociological Association, Queensland University of Technology, Brisbane, 1–4 December, 1998.

Temple, W. & Trute, P. (1998, 20 October). Across the divide. *Daily Telegraph*, p. 5.

The Torch (1998, 4 November). Police operation targets criminals. *The Torch*, p. 7.

Tomsen, S. (1996). Ruling men? Some comments on masculinity and juvenile justice. *The Australian and New Zealand Journal of Criminology* 29, 191–4.

Trute, P. (1998, 21 October). Mother's tears for her "precious thing". *Daily Telegraph*, p. 21.

Trute, P. & Stevenson, A. (1998, 5 November). Street where no one talks: Appeal for witnesses to show courage. *Daily Telegraph*, p. 7.

Usher, M. (1998, 2 November). Station shootup, *National Nine News*.

Walker, F. & Chulov, M. (1999, 21 March). We'll shame young crims: Fading Coalition plays crime card. *The Sun-Herald*, p. 1.

Wheatley, N. & Cottle, D. (1999). Sydney's Anti-Eviction Movement: Community or conspiracy? *Labour History* (forthcoming).

White, R. (1996). Racism, policing and ethnic youth gangs. *Current Issues in Criminal Justice* 7(3), 302–313.

White, R. (1996). Youth gangs. In R. White (Ed.), *Australian youth subcultures: On the margins and in the mainstream* (pp. 36–45). Hobart: National Clearinghouse for Youth Studies.

White, R., Perrone, S., Guerra, C. & Lampugnani, R. (1999). *Ethnic youth gangs in Australia: Do they exist? Report No. 2: Turkish Young People*. Melbourne: Australian Multicultural Foundation.

Wilkins, L.T. (1964). *Social deviance: Social policy, action and research*. London: Tavistock Publications.

Woodcock, L. G.(1956). *The Lewis case and you*. Sydney: Liberty Press.

Wynhausen, E. (1994, 10 July). The politics of gang warfare. *The Sun-Herald*, p. 29.

Wynhausen, E. & Safe, G. (1998, 7–8 November). Gunshots that broke our peace. *The Weekend Australian*, p. 13.

Part III
Gangs and Crime

[13]

HONOR, NORMATIVE AMBIGUITY AND GANG VIOLENCE*

RUTH HOROWITZ

University of Chicago and Institute
for Juvenile Research

GARY SCHWARTZ

Institute for Juvenile Research

American Sociological Review 1974, Vol. 39 (April): 238–51

This paper examines the social context in which gang violence occurs in a Mexican American community. We argue that gang violence arises in situations where one party impugns the honor of his adversary. This sort of conduct violates the norms of interpersonal etiquette and constitutes, in Goffman's terminology, a violation of "personal space." Gang members fluctuate uneasily between conventional and honor bound responses to these kinds of insults. The paper outlines a theory of normative ambiguity that deals with this movement between two antithetical codes for conduct.

I. INTRODUCTION

This paper examines the social context in which gang violence occurs in an inner city, Chicano community. We will look at the ways a gang member's adherence to a code of personal honor shape his response to what he perceives as an insult. Our approach to what Albert Cohen (1965:9) calls the "microsociology of the deviant act" focuses on the normative "processes whereby acts and complex structures of action are built, elaborated and transformed."

Our data consist of approximately fifty episodes of inter-gang violence. These incidents involved one or more members of a gang of male teenagers with whom we had regular contact for over a year.[1] Our information comes from two sources: our own rather limited firsthand observations of violent incidents and more abundant reports of the participants in them.[2]

As we define it, a clash between peers must satisfy three conditions to be classified as an instance of gang violence. First, at least one party to a face-to-face encounter must feel that the presence of the other party in this setting or his behavior on this occasion endangers his safety and impugns his dignity. In light of the actor's definition of the situation as threatening and provocative, he must make

members) were generally ambivalent. They were willing to let the fieldworker spend as much time as she wished in the park with them. She went to their parties with them, accompanied them to court, etc. But, past a certain point, intimacy with the field worker became problematic for most gang members. It was only after she stopped hanging around with the group that some members began to reveal things about themselves that were never mentioned when she was with the group. In this paper we refer to "gangs" in accordance with the literature on conflict-oriented street groups, but they are called "clubs" by their members and most people in the community.

[2] Participant accounts of violence are edited to suit the audience to whom they are addressed. Nevertheless, comparing our own observations of violent incidents with those of our informants, we believe they are substantially correct. While it is easy to embellish one's role in a fight or omit significant details about what transpired, it is impossible to fabricate the entire incident because gang fights are public events. Inasmuch as others participate in them and everybody talks about them, an individual could not invent tales of his valor on the battlefield without corroboration by his opponents or allies. Gang members were quick to dismiss persons whose claims exceeded their deeds.

*The research for this paper was supported by an Illinois Law Enforcement Grant, no. 2-09-25-0410-03, Joseph Puntil, Project Director. We would like to thank Dr. Merton S. Krause for his detailed criticisms of an earlier draft of this paper. Don Merten also gave us valuable comments on this draft as did the entire ILEC research seminar at the Institute for Juvenile Research.

[1] Contact with the gang was made by "hanging around" the park where they congregated until someone noticed that there was a new person on the scene. Shortly after the field worker arrived on the scene, the "main man" of the Lions asked her what she was doing in the community. She told him that she was writing a book about the community, and she subsequently acquired many nicknames (e.g., Lois Lane, after the girl reporter in Superman comics).

As a well-educated person (who also speaks Spanish fluently) the field worker received a certain amount of deference, but as a woman she was definitely an inferior being in the eyes of the gang. Hence relations with the gang (but not with some

a decision on the spot. If he does not assume the role of an aggressor, he may play the part of a victim. Second, the actor must respond to this emotionally charged situation in a way that visibly reveals his resolve (i.e., he feels his words, gestures or actions express a definite intention) to inflict physical injury on his antagonist or by actually doing so. Third, the actor must account for his conduct on this occasion in terms of his status as a member of a gang.[3]

In brief, we are concerned with incidents that are part of a longstanding rivalry between gangs or that give rise to these kinds of animosities. Any provocative or threatening incident can become the basis for a collectively held grievance. But, until it does, we feel that physical conflict between peers should not be classified as gang violence.

Street gangs in this community are jealous of their "name."[4] They wear sweaters with special insignia and stake out street corners or a section of a local park as their hang-out. But they do not claim or defend entire city-block areas of the community as their exclusive "turf."

Gang ideology is simple. The members of these groups believe that they must respond to insults in kind. In theory, derogation of one of their members affects their collective honor. In practice, gang members pursue offenses committed by the members of other gangs less vigorously when a peripheral rather than a core member of the group reports that he was attacked or insulted.

The gang's organization is rudimentary. A

few officers collect dues regularly, although there are no formal guidelines for allocating funds. These all male groups are internally stratified according to age linked distinctions (e.g., midgets, juniors, seniors). Ethnicity, friendship and a common stake in the outcome of contests with other groups constitute the basis of gang solidarity.[5]

Judging from self-report studies, official statistics reflect only part of the actual incidence of delinquency (Erickson and Empey, 1963). Miller's (1966) thorough documentation of the activities of gangs over a two year period in a multi-ethnic, bi-racial, inner-city area of Boston provides us with reliable information about the relative frequency of different types of gang violence. Miller points out that there is much more verbal than physical violence among gangs and that assaults were less common than theft. Most crimes against persons were simple assaults. Fights that pitted entire gangs against each other were much less frequent than inconclusive skirmishes between a few members. There was little evidence of the widespread use of deadly weapons and *no* guns were used. Miller concludes that "the practice of violent crimes was an essentially transient phenomenon of male adolescence" (1966:111).

Miller may be correct about the comparatively low level of gang violence in the inner city. But his conclusion about its severity is no longer true. The reason for the change in the character of gang violence is obvious. Gangs now rely on guns to defend themselves against the predations of other groups and as a potent weapon against formidable opponents. A number of the members of the group we studied had been shot, and there has been a small but steady number of deaths from gang violence in the area.[6]

---

[3] We use account in the technical sense of the word (Scott and Lyman 1970). That is, if called on to explain his violent conduct, the gang's member's rationale should state or imply that he was involved in the incident "because he was a Lion."

[4] In this respect, the Mexican-American community differs markedly from the Italian area studied by Suttles (1968) and Kobrin, et al. (1967). In a study of the criteria of status among street groups in this community, Kobrin, et al., (1967) found that ascriptive criteria such as ethnicity and family connections to the local political-criminal power structure were as important as fighting prowess in the overall-all reputation of a particular gang in the area. In the Chicano community, gangs are not integrated into the adult sector of community life. Nor do adults control semi-legitimate or legitimate opportunity structures that distinguished street gangs with "connections" from those without them. Consequently, fighting ability establishes a group's reputation in the Chicano community.

[5] Many young men join specific gangs because a friend or relative is a member, but there are several cases where brothers are members of different and sometimes antagonistic gangs. Age-grade groups who share the same name sometimes form separate gangs and "hang" in different locations. They may or may not be allies.

[6] In June 1973 the initiator of a partly successful area-wide peace movement was shot while standing in the corner in the park on the western section of the community, talking about peace to a group who was having problems with another gang. At a memorial ceremony, it was estimated that fifty gang members had been killed in gang conflicts over the past five years. This did not stop the shooting even

II. THEORIES OF INTERPERSONAL VIOLENCE.

Following recent discussions of interpersonal aggression (Toch 1969; Lofland 1969; Short and Strodtbeck 1965), we assume that gang violence is a response to perceived threats to an actor's self-esteem. In this context, threat ultimately refers to acts that imperil an individual's physical safety. However, except in the case of a direct attack, threat arises out of an actor's interpretation of the intentions of others.

Lofland (1969) argues that an actor's perception of the desire of others to cast him in a depreciated role or derogatory light creates an embittering, foreboding sense of danger and provocation. In Lofland's words, an individual senses imminent "social defacement and disgrace" when he believes that others want to belittle, demean or embarrass him. A sudden or drastic reduction in his self-esteem becomes particularly ominous when he thinks others are treating him as an inherently weak or unworthy human being.[7]

A person doubts his own efficacy or suspects that he has been exposed as a lesser person when he believes he has been publicly humiliated. Toch (1969:122) describes the resultant spiraling anger and distrust:

> Each person comes to see the other as representing what he views as hateful or threatening or humiliating or fear-inspiring. As a result, he reacts negatively and the other person reciprocates, which reinforces the original preconception. The confrontation that finally takes place is between two symbols rather than between two real people.

The symbols to which Toch alludes are permeated with moral meanings. How a person responds to depreciation by another reveals what kind of person he is. His status as a moral agent, as a person who has the will and the fortitude to right flagrant wrongs, has been questioned. He feels that whatever he does (even if he does nothing) will elicit the approval or disapproval of others. His conception of himself as an admirable or contemptible person hangs in the balance.

By treating violence as a response to threat to an actor's self-esteem, we do not imply that it is necessarily a defensive reaction. Toch (1969) points out that "self-image promoters" habitually precipitate violent situations in which they can demonstrate their power, courage and importance. Conversely, "self-image defenders" are extraordinarily sensitive to any action that appears to discredit their image of themselves as persons with whom others do not trifle. We shall see that a heightened concern with personal honor makes a person both a self-image defender and promoter, i.e., one demands deference from others and is sensitive to any act that suggests that one is not worthy of respect.

Gang members subscribe to a code of personal honor that stresses the inviolability of one's manhood and defines breaches of interpersonal etiquette in an adversarial idiom. Any act or statement that challenges a gang member's "right" to deferential treatment in face-to-face relations is interpreted as an insult and hence as a potential threat to his manhood. For these youth, honor revolves around a person's capacity to command deferential treatment (i.e., "respect") from others who are, in other respects, like themselves.

Pitt-Rivers (1966) observes that honor is an issue that arises between social equals. Those who are clearly superordinates and subordinates do not engage in contests over honor. Honor is a double-edged value. Refusal to grant another's claim to precedence amounts to an insult. On the other hand, willing acceptance of his claim to social superiority is tantamount to humiliation. Honor, then, introduces an undercurrent of tension in interpersonal relations. Those sensitive to imputations that they lack honor are ever watchful for slights that betray contempt.

People who live in an honor-based culture or subculture are often portrayed as vain, hyper-sensitive and contentious, always

---

though all the gangs in the area, except the gang that shot him, were present for the service.

[7] This state of affairs becomes especially critical when a person whose dignity or worth is assailed in face-to-face relations cannot draw on a past record of conventional social accomplishments to protect his self esteem. A person whose biography is based on valued social roles is in a better position to neutralize or negate the destructive intent of a direct insult than a person whose biography is deficient or ambiguous in this respect. People who feel that their position in the world is secure can respond to penetrating derogations of their character with a retort that, in effect, says, "who are *you* to say that to me?" In addition, people who are immersed in an honor-based subculture, where the desire to back away from a face-to-face confrontation is thought of as cowardly and unmanly, are particularly vulnerable to this sort of provocation.

HONOR, NORMATIVE AMBIGUITY AND GANG VIOLENCE

searching for insults that lurk behind seemingly innocent statements or actions. Honorbound cultures or subcultures do not always have elaborate classifications of various kinds of insults, although they usually designate certain situations or occasions as the most appropriate places to raise and settle questions of honor. However, in all honor based cultures or subcultures people are likely to interpret any act that disturbs the delicate equilibrium between social equals as a possible sign of a deeper, more pervasive disrespect for the other person's character. Here one does not need to go out of one's way to insult another person. The possibility of insult inheres in any transaction between persons who are not exempted by kinship or close friendship from the constant effort to determine whether another person shows sufficient respect for one's person and position in the community (cf. Campbell 1964).

In some cases, the members of street gangs raise the issue of honor explicitly by casting aspersions on the character of potential opponents. However, honor is more often a tacit issue in disputes over informal but nonetheless jealously guarded rights associated with interpersonal etiquette. These young men are alert to any sign that indicates others are ready to withhold the respect to which they feel rightfully entitled. The standard maneuver that signals this state of affairs involves what Goffman (1971:44) aptly describes as incursions on the "personal territories of the self": "If territory-like preserves are the central claim in the study of co-mingling, then the central offense is an incursion, intrusion, encroachment, presumption, defilement, besmearing, contamination – in short a violation."

From a polite, middle-class perspective, these moves look like exaggerated forms of bad taste: a calculated violation of the standards of ordinary decency and good manners. For gang members, these maneuvers constitute intrusions, by either word or deed, on the personal space they see as the foundation of their self-respect and social dignity.

Whatever the specific issue, Pitt-Rivers (1966) notes that honor touches the person directly. It does so in two ways. In the first place, honor is an individual attribute. One cannot transmit or confer one's honor to others, although the members of groups share honor insofar as they must remove any stain

on their reputation. Moreover, as Pitt-Rivers observes, honor never depends on how an individual performs the duties of an office or a role. Honor adheres to those actions which reflect personal decisions and judgements. What a person does or says in this context is construed as a manifestation of his character, as something he intended to do or say. Since he is held personally responsible for his conduct, disputes over honor are settled by recourse to personal rather than legal forms of justice.

In the second place, honor inevitably devolves on the integrity of one's physical being (cf. Pitt-Rivers, 1966:22,27). Dishonor is experienced as a loss of one's manhood – the physical capability of backing claims to a dominant position in interpersonal relations and of resisting similar claims by others.

To say that gang violence emerges in situations where honor is at issue does not take us very far. Honor sensitizes actors to violations of their person which are interpreted as derogations of fundamental properties of the self. There are, of course, other ways of responding to insult besides violence. Violence is triggered by the normative framework within which people attempt to resolve interpersonal difficulties as well as by the values to which they give their allegiance. We shall argue that for these young men there is an inherent ambiguity in the rules that *should* govern the selection of the appropriate means for resolving perceived violations of interpersonal etiquette.[8]

By normative ambiguity we do not mean that the norms of proper interpersonal behavior are themselves imprecise, ill-formulated, or confused. These young men share with the

---

[8]We assume that in our society people expect to find normative guidelines for resolving interpersonal dilemmas that affect the maintenance of the public order. This is especially the case when the issues dividing the contending parties bear on the legitimacy of conventional moral norms. Seen this way, the word "should" does not refer to the disjunction between what a person "ought" to do and the existential demands of the situation in which he finds himself. Instead, it refers to a lack of normative specification in the rules that govern interpersonal etiquette in our culture [for a comparison between "tight" normative systems such as ours and those that maintain "loose" connections between general norms and situational conduct, see Ryan and Strauss (1954).] And this absence of normative specification occurs in a very special domain of our culture: situations that involve personal honor.

rest of our society a coherent, if uncodified, body of understandings about what constitutes good manners, behavior that shows consideration for the sensibilities of others and respect for their person. In this context, normative ambiguity refers to the absence of higher-order rules for reconciling contradictions between conflicting codes for conduct in situations where one or both parties feel that ill-mannered behavior of others is a sign of calculated disrespect.

In its most primitive form, normative ambiguity refers to the following situation. If someone insults me, I have two courses of action besides ignoring the entire matter. I can return the insult and escalate the probability of a violent encounter. Or I can treat his conduct as a boorish mistake that reflects poorly on his lack of judgment and tact, not on my character. In this way I defuse a potentially explosive situation. What is ambiguous here is that there are few rules for determining on what occasions and for what offenses I should respond in one or the other manner.

What appears to outsiders as a slight disruption of the flow of ordinary social discourse often becomes highly charged for gang members. Such presumably "minor" questions of interpersonal etiquette as who will sit or stand where at a party or who has the right to possess a sweater with group emblems can become intensely problematic. This is not because these young men lack the social skill to resolve these matters in a conventional manner. In contrast to the severe social disability that characterizes black gangs studied by Short, Strodtbeck (1965b), and Gordon (1967) Chicano gang members are quite adept at the nuanced behavior required by conventional society. These young men know how to do the "right" thing on these occasions, and they quite often follow the spirit as well as the letter of the laws of proper decorum.[9]

Perhaps the best way to convey the consid-

erable facility these young men display in switching from street to conventional modes of behavior is to describe their conduct at cotillions. A cotillion is a party given for a girl by her parents and relatives on her fifteenth birthday. It involves a religious ceremony and a dinner and dance for two or three hundred guests. The girl, her escort and fourteen other couples attend the affair in formal dress, and the entire event is marked by the sort of protocol one sees at expensive weddings.

Gang members not only attend these affairs regularly but are often part of the ceremonial party. At one cotillion, the gang we studied attended in their best clothes. When they were not dancing, the gang stood quietly and conversed in a polite, subdued manner. Unlike their conduct on the street, gang members avoided the loud profanity and rough joking that would reflect poorly on their ability to blend into the scene. There was an open bar. Gang members did not rush to finish all the liquor, but drank in a way that was befitting the relaxed, goodnatured sociability such an event is supposed to stimulate. Characteristically, one of the gang members noticed that the field worker was tired from helping serve the food and repeatedly offered her his chair. Since this was the first time they had ever seen her in "fancy" clothes, a number of them went out of their way to compliment her on her appearance.

When a gang member believes that a violation of his personal space was meant as an insult, he enters, to speak metaphorically, a state of normative ambiguity. He must choose between conventional and honor bound responses to this situational impropriety. And these codes for conduct point to quite different courses of remedial action.

The conventional response falls into the broad category of interpersonal strategies Goffman calls impression management. With respect to situational improprieties, impression management implies that the actor maintains enough distance from the on-going course of action to deflect any imputations of unworthiness away from himself and back on the "objective" properties of the situation. For example, if a person at a gathering bumps into another person he can say "excuse me" in a way that puts the onus for the violation of the other's personal space on the setting that brings them together. He thereby extricates himself from a difficult situation by

---

[9]Gideon, age twenty, and president of the Lions, took the fieldworker to lunch at a restaurant outside the community. In a confident manner, he got the waiter to give him a good table away from the door, ordered expertly from a large menu for himself and the fieldworker, paid the bill and left a reasonable tip. Compare this to Short's (1965a) discussion of a Black gang leader's anxieties over his own and his girl friend's table manners at a YMCA dinner.

HONOR, NORMATIVE AMBIGUITY AND GANG VIOLENCE   243

providing the other with adequate grounds for treating the offense as accidental. Impression management demands a "cool" orientation to potentially conflictful situations.

To continue with the bumping incident, if the person who commits the offense says, in effect, I take no cognizance of your feelings in this matter, then honor becomes an issue. In contrast to impression management, honor demands total involvement in the immediate consequences of actions that violate one's personal space. One not only takes insults seriously but refuses to postpone or otherwise delay a satisfactory resolution of the issue. In order to succeed at impression management one often must disassociate one's feelings about the moral validity of the other's conduct from one's estimate of the costs and benefits of alternative approaches to him. One contrives to appear spontaneous while self-consciously following a particular line of action. This allays any doubts the other may have about the congruence between one's public performance and private motives.

Honor, on the other hand, impels one to take an unequivocal stand, to choose decisively and openly between divergent courses of action, and to enforce one's claim to deference as a non-negotiable right. One may even have to defend an inadvertent slip as a deliberate expression of one's character. The effort here is to be what one wants others to think one truly is.

Honor, then, entails the consummation of an expressive value. Direct action takes priority over rational assessment of rights and wrongs and over the long-run consequences of an intransigent posture toward insults. This does not posit a Newtonian law of interpersonal relations: to every insult there is a direct and equal reaction. However, there is clearly a tendency toward "momentum" in situations of normative ambiguity.

One can legitimately respond to a certain amount of provocation by impression management. But over time violations of one's personal space are resolved decisively only by actions that return the insult in kind, preferably with interest added for accrued damages. This means that provocation builds in a dramatic fashion for gang members. Not every incident merits instant retaliation. But at some point one must respond in a way that visibly reinforces one's reputation. The repeated failure to do so is tantamount to an admission of weakness. To use the idiom of the street gang, one's pride ultimately tips the precarious balance between honor and impression management in favor of violence. Thus, relatively minor incidents have a notable tendency to snowball, and it is this movement toward a violent resolution of perceived violations of personal space that we call momentum.

The idea that gang members gravitate uneasily between conventional and honor bound responses to provocation is analogous, in some respects, to Matza's (1964) conception of delinquent "drift." Matza argues that subcultural delinquency does not depend on criminal norms that prescribe various modes of illegal conduct. Instead, a delinquent "exists in a limbo between convention and crime, responding in turn to the demands of each, flirting now with one, now the other, but postponing commitment, evading decision" (Matza 1964:28).

So too, the gang member's refusal to commit himself wholeheartedly to either street or conventional values puts him in a position to invoke either the norms of the gang or of the legitimate world to justify his conduct. He can freely admit that killing is morally wrong and that fighting is foolhardy, and, at the same time, contend that one must defend one's honor even if this leads to homicide. We believe that as long as a young man remains in the gang he rarely becomes acutely conscious of this dilemma. It is only after a variety of circumstances push him toward a conventional or street career that he may see that the capacity to operate smoothly in two contrasting social settings involves what the larger society regards as allegiance to two antithetical codes for conduct.

Unlike the idea of drift, the concept of normative ambiguity links the fluctuation between conventional and violent behavior among street groups to the normative structure of interpersonal relations, not to the latent impact of the law (as Matza claims) on those who are brought before it. Normative ambiguity, however, is not a social-psychological anomaly of lower class life. Nor is it a condition everyone in our society faces but, under the harsh conditions of inner city life, becomes a major dilemma for those who claim special status in this world. We believe that normative ambiguity links the "situation of company" to use Matza's terminology, to the structural position of the Chicano community in the wider society.

In this community, young people who are not in gangs also experience the tension between the excitement of street life and conventional aspirations and goals. But, for reasons that go beyond the scope of this study, gang members do not seem to see this as a matter of deliberate choice until relatively late in their adolescence. Instead, gang violence serves as a symbolic vehicle through which the contradictions between the desire to "make it" in American society and the real probability of actually succeeding is repeatedly enacted but never resolved. In other words, gang fights reflect the tension between street and conventional values that is built into the structural position of this community in the larger society. We suspect that gang members experience this contradiction (although they are not the only persons given to violent defenses of personal honor) with great intensity because they are not able at this point in their lives to confront openly the disparity between the course of their lives and their desire to have a conventional adult career.

III. THE COMMUNITY

Almost all of the residents of this area refer to it as 32nd street. Many of the small businesses that cater to a Mexican-American clientele are located along 32nd street. This community is bounded on the north and east by railroad tracks, on the south by a canal, and on the west by a major thoroughfare. Factories ring the southern fringe of the area.

The ethnic composition of this community of 44,500 persons has undergone a marked transformation in the last decade. Before 1960, the area had a predominantly middle European character. Since that date, the percentage of Mexican-Americans has risen dramatically from 30% to about 55% of the total population in the area.[10]

The ecological setting of this community does not distinguish it from other inner-city ethnic enclaves that are called "slums." But, as Suttles (1968) has recently shown, this word masks a great deal of social diversity. Similarly, composite indices of the socio-economic rank of urban communities based on standard ecological and demographic variables sometimes are misleading. In a recent, well-publicized study of how eighty-five communities in this city ranked on these indicators, the 32nd street area ranked 84th from the top.[11] Yet a closer look at the statistics on employment reveal that this community is relatively free of the un- and under-employment associated with deprived inner-city areas.[12] A glance at the well-kept houses and small apartment buildings in the community belies any vision of such areas as uniform islands of deteriorated housing.

Lenski's (1954) concept of status inconsistency characterizes the marginal situation of this community in the socio-economic system of the city. If income, education and ethnicity are three important criteria of a group's status in the larger society, this community ranks relatively high on one criterion, relatively low on another and is difficult to rank on the third. The majority of the Chicano families in this community have fairly substantial incomes.[13] Their educational level, however, is low by middle class standards.[14]

Looking at the picture based on income and education, one might say that this is a stable working class population with a somewhat low level of education. The status inconsistency in this case lies in the contradiction between their limited success and their desire for a better future and the fact that

[10] The 1960 census did not include a category on the Spanish speaking; but there were 11,650 (24%) Latins born in Mexico, or at least one of their parents was born there. This does not include those of Mexican descent whose parents were born in the United States. According to the 1970 census there were 24,463 residents of Latin descent (55%). The percent is considerably lower than that estimated by a local survey of the neighborhood. See, "Action Research in a Chicano Community," S. Schensul,

paper presented at the annual meetings of the American Anthropological Assn., Toronto, 1972, which asserts that the percentage of Spanish speaking residents is closer to seventy.

[11] This ranking was done by a prominent urbanologist using 1970 census data and was published in a major metropolitan newspaper.

[12] Only 4.45% of the male labor force is categorized by the census as unemployed.

[13] The 1970 census data indicate that the median family income was $8,560, and the percentage of families below the poverty level was 17.7.

[14] Only 21% of the population have finished high school, and many do not even start but drop out in the seventh or eighth grade. The percentage of those graduating from high school has not increased significantly; but of those graduating, many more are going to college.

these people, by virtue of where they live, are seen as "poor, inner-city residents." As far as their social identity in the larger society is concerned, the generalized stigma attached to residence in inner-city, ethnic neighborhoods is not congruent with their "hidden affluence" or the older generation's acceptance of the "work ethic."

The members of this community do not identify with the embattled residents of urban ghettos except on those occasions when minority groups confront the establishment over common grievances. Many do not feel that they are subjected to quite the same sort of racial derogation as blacks and Puerto Ricans, although they too have to force the larger society to recognize their cultural heritage as valid. Chicanos by and large feel that they differ socially and culturally from their less fortunate neighbors in the inner-city. At the same time, they are well aware of the fact that Mexican-Americans are not accepted as social equals by the dominant Anglo society. While ethnicity does not scale as neatly as income or education, we think that it is a highly ambiguous component of the Chicano status in the wider society. They fit somewhere in the "middle" of a vague status hierarchy based on ethnicity.

Mexican-Americans are outsiders in the urban community. Few people in positions of power and influence mention this community in announcements of decisions that affect the welfare of inner city residents. The community has no representatives on the city council or in the state legislature. The majority of local precinct workers who constitute the infrastructure of the regular democratic organization in the city are still drawn from the older ethnic groups that have traditionally dominated city politics. These few Mexican-Americans who are precinct captains do not align themselves with local groups, and their loyalty to City Hall is understood by everyone in the community.

Similarly, only a tiny percentage of policemen (178 out of approximately 13,000) have Latin backgrounds, and recently residents of this community publicly demonstrated against the failure of the local transit agency to recruit and hire Latin bus drivers. The local public schools are the source of widespread discontent. The high school which serves both black and Latin areas as well as a shrinking white population gives some credence to

Hollywood versions of the "blackboard jungle." Armed guards patrol the halls, girls are afraid to use the washrooms out of a justified (judging from personal accounts) fear of being raped, and racially-tinged fights are a common occurrence. In the senior class of 1973, two hundred of that class of four hundred graduated. None of those students who go to college are accepted on the basis of standard admission criteria. According to the school newspaper, only two out of approximately two thousand students had an A average in the spring quarter of 1973. Some of the more affluent or ambitious families (28%) send their children to Catholic schools.

The community has not accepted the low educational standards of the schools passively. During the summer of 1972, the community successfully removed an elementary school principal who had been a sore point for parents and students alike. In the spring of 1973, community groups publicly picketed the school board for a new high school.[15] Bypassing local agencies, some of the residents of the community obtained federal funding for drug, mental health, remedial education, and college preparatory programs operated by local persons.

On the whole, the members of this community meet the basic requirements for inclusion in what mainstream America views as the socially respectable and politically significant segments of the working class. Mexican-Americans hold steady jobs and make a decent living. Very few intact families are on welfare. They clearly want their children to get ahead in the world and believe that education is the stepping-stone to upward mobility. The majority of young people in this community speak English fluently and command the verbal skills necessary to negotiate their way through urban institutions.

As an ethnic enclave in the inner city, this community receives little in the way of vital social resources. The schools in the community offer little hope for young people who want something more than a low level white-collar or blue-collar job.[16] Highly motivated,

---

[15] The protests were both violent and peaceful. During the takeover of the school no officials would negotiate with them about their demands. Consequently, several police cars were wrecked and a few policemen sustained minor injuries.

[16] A recent study which commanded headlines in daily newspapers compared reading scores in this

achievement oriented young people have to forgo many of the pleasures of a normal adolescence in order to maintain the arduous struggle to pull themselves up by their academic bootstraps. This means that they avoid the excitement and the risks of street life — a police record might jeopardize their movement into professional or semi-professional occupations.

On the other hand, gang members have not opted out of the American dream. Rather, they are hedging their bets. They measure themselves against a code of personal honor that has local currency. But they have not closed the door completely to the possibility that they will find the right track to success. The phenomenon of normative ambiguity exposes the marginal position of Mexican-Americans in American society. Many young men cannot afford to relinquish their allegiance to a code of personal honor until the ideology of success through educational achievement yields tangible results for persons who are not unusually gifted, motivated and willing to forgo the company of a male peer group. Whatever prestige or status they will acquire now comes from their peers, although they know that their reputation on the streets is not a marketable commodity elsewhere.

IV. GANG FIGHTS

Not every young person who comes into contact with street life becomes a gang member. Yet once he attaches himself to a group this bond is not easily dissolved. He is expected to support his fellow gang members in fights with the members of other gangs, and those who violate this norm sometimes are severely chastised. Not all the street groups in the area, however, are equally attracted to fighting.[17] The Lions — the group with whom

we had the closest, most continuous contact — are known throughout the area as one of the toughest gangs. Out of the present membership of sixty our material concerns thirty-one of the more active members of the "Little" and "Junior" segments of the Lions. Their ages range from sixteen to twenty.

All of the Lions participate in violent episodes, although some obviously relish these occasions more than others. Yet for the thirty-one "Little" and "Junior" Lions, there seem to be two divergent paths along which some of the members are moving. Eight seem to have organized their lives in order to facilitate a conventional adult career.[18] Eight appear deeply immersed in street life. And the other fifteen members do not seem to have decided whether they will spend part of their youth in correctional institutions or will get a job or the schooling that eventually takes them out of the orbit of street life.

Apart from these differences, perhaps the single most important indicator of a gang member's commitment to conventional adult career is his attitude toward going to jail. Those who gravitate toward a more global street existence (i.e., for whom gang activities are more than a way to spend "free" time) seem to take the police and courts more casually than their more "achievement oriented" counterparts. This is not to say that the street-oriented gang members are more prone to violence.[19] But when they are

---

city's schools against a national norm. The national average was the fiftieth percentile, but the scores in the high school that serves this community for the ninth and eleventh grade were as follows: in 1971 and 1972, ninth grade, fifteenth percentile, the eleventh grade was thirteenth percentile. These scores were not much different from other inner city schools; but, for the purposes of comparison, the ninth graders in a white, middle class high school, scored 70 in 1971 and 1972; the eleventh grade scored 69 and 64 in 1971 and 1972.

[17] The Red Shirts (aged 18-22) are not basically a fighting gang, although previously most were members of fighting gangs. Their dues are used for parties, not for buying weapons. But they do ally themselves with other gangs "when necessary."

Martin, twenty-two, is a student at a local city junior college, a draftsman, and a Vietnam veteran. He decided not to die in the streets:

> You should grow up and out of violence, then if you don't bother anyone, they won't bother you. I can't go back to what I did before Nam. It's stupid to die without a war. It's better to fight the rich people. Politicians are corrupt. The change has got to be political 'cause guerrilla warfare isn't worth it . . . .We need leaders. Martin Luther King was brilliant and made sense but if you get involved, people step on your face and will think you're corrupt . . . .What I need to make me happy is money to travel . . . .

[18] Predictions about the careers of gang members can be made with increasing accuracy as the members get older. With increasing age, violence becomes more problematic. Until he has to decide whether he will stay on the streets or seek a conventional job, it is very difficult to predict in which direction a particular gang member will go.

[19] Ronnie, who has instigated many fights, is probably headed for a fairly conventional career. He was the first of three Lions to graduate from high

HONOR, NORMATIVE AMBIGUITY AND GANG VIOLENCE 247

charged with crimes that may lead to long-term incarceration, they tend to see the entire arrest and trial process as a lottery in which one takes one's chances, especially since many feel that they can buy their way out of jail or go to Texas until things quiet down. The gang members who have a greater stake in a conventional career tend to see such matters as a crisis – although they too have usually spent some time in jail.

Whatever the balance between a particular gang member's commitment to conventional as opposed to street values, he experiences the tension between them. We shall illustrate this proposition with capsule biographies of three gang members: one who is making it in terms of the criteria for success in the larger society; one who could go in either direction; and one who seems destined to remain in the street world for the forseeable future.

Dennis is a long-standing member and central figure in the Lions. He is nineteen, married and has one child. Dennis fights "when necessary."

> You got your pride, don't you. You can't let anyone step on you. We know when we do wrong, we really do, but sometimes you have to do things. Like five guys come toward you and do something to you – we fight back, man, we really fight 'em. You know even if we're outnumbered and you know you're going to get killed. But you do anyways. You have to protect yourself, you know we got pride and there's some things we *have* to do. I know other people will say "excuse me" or "it must be a mistake" and walk off. We can't do that. It's not in us. I know the consequences when I do something wrong.

Dennis often carries a gun and has been involved in several shootings. In November of 1971 he was stopped by two plainclothes detectives, frisked and charged with unlawfully carrying a gun. At the time, there had been several altercations with the Junior Greeks, and the Lions were prepared for trouble. Dennis found that this arrest upset his life more than he anticipated. He had no prior criminal convictions. Three months be-

fore this incident he got a white-collar job in a downtown bank and had a perfect attendance record. He enjoyed his work and was proud of his progress on the job. Dennis was fired unceremoniously from his job after his employers discovered that he was on trial for a felony.

After this, Dennis enrolled in a GED program (a high school diploma equivalent). He had previously completed the eleventh grade but he said that things were too "hot" to return to school for his senior year. Since his marriage, he spends less of his time at the park where the Lions and Greeks hang out which is a staging ground for gang fights. Recently, he has been a marshall at community political demonstrations and marches.

Gideon is twenty, married and has two children. He is the leader of the Lions and a seventh grade drop-out. He wanted to follow his older brother into the army but was turned down because of an extensive police record. When interviewed by another young man from the community on a local radio show, he confided to the field worker that he was worried that he was not articulate enough. His attitude toward school is representative of "fence-sitters":

> I really liked being in school. It was more fun goofing around in school 'cause my friends were there. Out on the streets it wasn't so much fun. I would have rather stayed in school but they kicked me out . . . But I felt much better out in the streets than at home.

At nineteen Gideon enrolled in and finished an automobile repair course and worked regularly for six months. At the present time he is pending trial on three or four charges such as assault and battery and carrying an unregistered gun. He recently has been hired by a local community action group as a street worker, and he takes the job seriously.

Yet he has not given up his dedication to a code of personal honor. Quite recently, he was at a dance when his friend requested a gun he had lent Gideon. Gideon was apparently offended by the manner in which the gun was requested. His friend sensed Gideon's anger and a fight ensued. Gideon then proceeded to beat him up in front of everyone.

By his own estimate, Harold has had serious contact with the legal system twenty-

---

school at the age of seventeen. He is the only one of six brothers to graduate. His mother wanted him to finish so badly that she sent him to parochial school. Six months after his graduation he was involved in an accidental murder, and he decided to get out quickly and joined the army.

six or twenty-seven times. He is a seventh grade drop-out and most of the people in the community think he is a "loser." He has been convicted of burglary, aggravated assault and attempted murder. He is presently trying to avoid trial on an accumulated assortment of charges and has been keeping company with a group that engages in burglary and robbery.

However, Harold does not admit that his life does not fit into conventional patterns. One night the Lions were joking about girls, and the field worker asked Harold how many mistresses he was going to have after he got married. He was genuinely hurt by the suggestion that he was not capable of settling down; and furthermore, he replied that he would not marry a girl unless he really loved her. Harold has applied for several jobs and is always turned down.

Along with the Blue Dolphins, a girl's gang, the Senior Greeks occupy the park with the Lions during the spring and summer. The Senior Greeks and Lions (who are about six or seven years younger than the Senior Greeks) had been at war from the summer of 1969 until a "peace conference" was held in June of 1970. During that time, five persons were killed and many more were wounded. The hostilities began over what is now called a misunderstanding – the Lions were fighting another gang and beat up a Greek in the melee. The Greeks returned the insult, and then the Lions killed a Greek.

To illustrate the role that insults play in precipitating gang violence, we will use a typical incident involving the Senior Greeks and the Angels. A girl was giving a party for the Angels though most of the girls present were girlfriends of the Greeks. One of the girls tells what transpired:

> They (the Greeks) had just come in and said, "hey, you can't hide anything from us." So they went out and were hanging on the front steps drinking. I told my boyfriend that I was going to a confirmation (that night) and he wasn't too mad (at finding his girl at a party with the Angels). The police came and told them (the Greeks) to take their party inside. Rock (a Greek) demanded that his favorite song be played. The Greeks tried to cool him down but then they started slugging and fighting all over the place. The girls were screaming to stop but more guys were getting in it. Henry Bain was having a good fight, punching a guy up, and one of the Angels

pulled a gun. The Greeks weren't packed so they split to Dagwood's for the heats. While they split through the back the police came through the front.
> The Greeks came back and wounded a couple of the Angels. They also blamed two girls for betraying them to the police and said they would beat their asses. They are my friends and I don't want to see their asses kicked but I can't help because they'll kick mine too. The Greeks hang around my place and I really like having them over but sometimes they get out of hand. My boyfriend doesn't mind if I go to other parties as long as I don't hang with a club they're at war with. And I don't rat on the guys – if I do I'm in bad shape.

The following is an abbreviated chronicle of the clashes between the Lions and the Aces over a period of fifteen months. Twenty-five conflict-laden incidents were recorded by the field worker over this period but not all eventuated in fights or shootings. We have selected incidents to highlight the cummulative nature of gang violence. Since momentum is a subjective state of apprehension and anticipation, it is difficult to document the way isolated incidents coalesce in the actor's mind to form a state of undeclared warfare.

Late one August evening in 1971, three Aces walked up to Alfred (a "Little" Lion) and his girl, Kimberly. They were sitting on a bench in part of the park that "belongs" to neither the Greeks or Lions. The Aces took out a gun and were threatening to kill Alfred when his quick thinking girlfriend explained that he was a brazer (a recent immigrant from Mexico) and could not speak English. The Aces claimed that Alfred was a Lion and that since Kimberly's sister was going with an Ace she should not hang around with a Lion. She assured them that Alfred was not a Lion and that she was loyal to the Aces. The next night the Lions assembled in the park but the Aces did not return.

A few nights later the Senior Greeks, the Nobles and the Lions were waiting for the Aces. Someone had seen a carload of them earlier. The Greeks were "packed" (i.e., armed). The field worker counted five guns and about thirty-five Lions were present. They continually asked each other, "do you think they'll come?" They did not show up that night.

Late in January of that year there was a battle between the Lions and the Junior

Greeks and Aces. According to the Lions, they were taunted by the Junior Greeks when they were walking along minding their own business. Ronnie (a Lion) struck one of the Greeks and the fight began. Some Aces spotted them from a car and joined the battle on the side of the Junior Greeks. Ronnie was struck forcefully on the head with a crowbar but continued fighting. Harold stabbed one of the Aces who had to be taken to the Hospital. Later that afternoon the Lions argued about whether the Ace had been stabbed two or three times. They left again to find the Greeks. Amos threatened to knife Pierre because he did not participate in the fight but excused Nen because he had been shot twice recently. Around eight that evening all the Lions returned to the park. The Greeks had fired several shot gun blasts at them but missed. The Lions retreated since they were not armed at the time. Some Greeks were arrested by the police. The following Saturday night Ronnie was alone and was stabbed in the back by the Ace who previously hit him with a crowbar. The Senior Greeks disowned the Junior Greeks and let the Lions know that they would not take the Junior's side in future fights between the Juniors and the Lions.

Similar incidents continued, fed by rumors often carried by girls who report who was carrying guns and where they were last seen. The tension between these groups is intensified by the fact that they attend the same dances and move freely, often in cars, in the same part of the city. Provocation is a standard ploy in sustaining conflict. Those who take the initiative in insulting the other group have, in effect, demonstrated their superiority for the moment.

Moreover, the members of these groups seek one another out for the purpose of laying down the gauntlet. For instance, an Ace threw a brick through Amos' (a Lion) mother's window in early February of 1972. Amos and two other Lions ran into this Ace late in April. Amos beat the Ace unconscious with the butt of his gun, but he regained consciousness a few days later and identified Amos as his assailant. Amos said he should have killed him but did not have ammunition for the gun at that time.

While such activities strike an outsider as highly dangerous, both personally and legally, gang members talk about their experience with the courts in ways that support Matza's (1964) description of the vagaries of the legal system. The experience of Alaster, a Lion, is a case in point. He and another Lion and their two girlfriends were on their way to church in order to confess before they stood up at a wedding. Quite by accident, they met some Greeks who demanded to know whether they were Lions. According to Alaster:

> I said, of course, and one of the Greeks pulled a gun. I was packed too. I managed to get my heat out and shoot him. I went to my sister's house and ordered a pizza and then I was going to go to Texas (just about everyone on 32nd has relatives in Texas) but the police caught me and I spent nine months in and out of court. I got me a good lawyer—he told me to plead not guilty but I pleaded guilty and the judge liked me and let me off. He told me not to go back to 32nd street again (the courts charged Alaster with murder in self-defense and ordered him to live with his sister in the suburbs). I never had anything against that guy — personally I never saw him before.

The issues, as we said before, that precipitate gang violence seem obscure because they strike persons who lack a heightened sensitivity to violations of one's personal space as intrinsically trivial. Perhaps the single most pointed insult one group can level at another group is to appropriate their sweaters.

Doodles started a fight with the Rockheads. He said that he had heard that one of them had a Lion's sweater but could not trace the source of the rumor. The source and reliability of the information is, to these young men, of less importance than allowing an insult to go unchallenged. According to Doodles:

> You know I heard it somewhere about the sweater. They insulted us, so I jumped on them and started the fight.

Not only do apparently minor slights lead to serious fights but the fights themselves seem to snowball. Ofttimes many people become involved for such obscure reasons that "peace conferences" have to be held. For example, the Lions thought that they saw a Wildcat wearing a sweater they had previously lost in a battle with the Aces. Bumpkin started a fight with one of the Wildcats and the rest of the Lions joined him.

Since the Wildcats were outnumbered, they retreated to a nearby house that happened to belong to one of the Nobles. The Lions began throwing rocks at the windows and the Nobles entered the fray. Though nobody knows how the Angels got involved in the fight, they were there too. By the end of the day, two young men had been shot.

We could add many more such incidents, but the pattern is essentially the same. Gang violence occurs when honor becomes a pressing issue in interpersonal relations and when the participants feel that they cannot gracefully talk their way out of a situation that impugns their dignity and self respect. The same young men show considerable poise and tact in the etiquette that surrounds interpersonal relations. They made certain that the field worker had a comfortable seat at a party or did not have to walk on the side of the street nearest the curb. This display of elegant manners is not a disguise for hidden aggression. Rather, the capacity to manage situations with great respect for the symbolic nuances of "good manners" co-exists with a desire to avenge any sign of disrespect.

V. CONCLUSION

Of all the studies of gang delinquency to date Short and Strodtbeck (1965b) focus most specifically on the factors that produce gang violence. Short and Strodtbeck argue that these young men are attracted to an alternative "status universe" in part because they lack the verbal and interpersonal skills that constitute social competence in our society. They prove their worth in terms of the standards of the conflict-oriented gang.

They have conventional personal goals. But they are socialized in a manner that deprives them of the ability to achieve even a modicum of success in the larger society:

The family does not equip the child with role-playing facility adequate to the demands of such instititutions as the school, and the unsatisfactory experiences in the school further narrow the range of role-playing opportunities which later facilitate job success – "getting along" with employers and fellow workers, and more than this, "getting along" in new and strange situations generally. The ability to move easily from one role to another and to adjust rapidly to new situations is a much

cultivated art in modern society, particularly among upwardly mobile persons. This ability is inculcated in their children by middle class parents at an early age, and this may prove to be one of the major differentiating areas of early family experience between gang and non-gang boys within the lower class (Short and Strodtbeck, 1965:236).

On the whole, the members of Chicano gangs were not distinguished by the sort of social ineptness Short and Strodtbeck refer to as a poorly developed capacity to assume roles congruent with the demands of diverse social situations in an urban society. Most of the members of the street gang we studied were quite adept in role taking – though we prefer to call this talent impression management. As they grow older, these young men can deal quite effectively with employers, the courts and school administrators.[20] Even those young men who dropped out of school very early were by and large able to hold jobs for relatively long periods of time. Almost all the older participants in the street gang milieu (e.g., the Senior Greeks) combined their activities in this sphere with steady working-class jobs, although they tended to spend more of their leisure time in bars than on the streets. Finally, it was not unusual for the field worker to encounter a gang member whom she had assumed was a "loser" who had enrolled in a special college program.

One of the important differences between the black ghetto Short and Strodtbeck studied and the Chicano community is that the former has a more "closed" and the latter a more "open" relationship to the street world. Chicano groups, as a rule, do not mark out entire city block areas of their neighborhoods as their sovereign domain (cf. Keiser, 1969). Nor do they usually force unaffiliated young men in the neighborhood to join their gang

---

[20] Several gang members who are also street workers are involved in a court advocacy program. A Senior Greek describes his job in the following terms:

First you have to go to see who the judge is and what kind of mood he is in. You have to get the feel of the situation, then you know how to present the dude's case for a lower bond. Of course, if he's got a record you've got to be careful and it's tough . . . .

HONOR, NORMATIVE AMBIGUITY AND GANG VIOLENCE   251

against their wishes. The "openness" of the street world in this community reveals that alternatives to the gang exist for young people even if these routes to conventional careers look tenuous from a middle class perspective.

In sum, we suggest that Chicano young men experience their position in the social structure differently than their counterparts in black ghettos. In the Chicano community, most adults obtain at least some of the things associated with success in our society. But this sort of success, by itself, does not resolve the problems inherent in their marginal status in the larger society. We believe that gang members in the Chicano community experience the contradiction between their relatively favorable economic prospects (judging from the ability of others to get moderately well-paying jobs) and the restrictions imposed by the larger society on their aspirations in terms of what we have called normative ambiguity. In other words, these young men fluctuate between commitment to conventional and street values. This tension is never formally resolved but rather is lived through until one is old enough to decide whether one is going to move away from the risks of street life.

This means that involvement in conflict-oriented street gangs depends, as Short and Strodtbeck point out, on social marginality in the larger society. But in this community a code of personal honor rather than social disability per se sustains the traditions of conflict-oriented gangs. Nor do we find that violence in this community is closely related to threats to a young man's status within the gang. The notion of an alternative "status universe" captures a vital ingredient of street life. It refers to more than a young man's concern about his position vis-à-vis his peers. Decreased self-esteem, as Short and Strodtbeck argue, is a critical variable in the precipitation of violent incidents. But in the Chicano community self-esteem is embedded in a code of personal honor that includes all breaches in interpersonal etiquette, not only those that threaten one's standing among one's peers.

REFERENCES

Cohen, Albert
  1965 "The sociology of the deviant act." American Sociological Review 30 (February): 5-14.

Campbell, J. K.
  1964 Honour, Family and Patronage: A Study of Moral Values in a Greek Mountain Community. London: Oxford University Press.

Erickson, Maynard and Lamar Empey
  1963 "Court records, undetected delinquency and decision making." Journal of Criminal Law, Criminology and Police Science 54: 456-69.

Goffman, Irving
  1971 Relations in Public. New York: Harper and Row.

Gordon, Robert A.
  1967 "Social level, disability, and gang interaction." American Journal of Sociology 73 (July): 42-62.

Kobrin, Solomon, Joseph Puntil, and Emil Peluso
  1967 "Criteria of status among street groups." Journal of Research in Crime and Delinquency (January): 98-118.

Lenski, Gerhard
  1954 "Status crystallization: a non-vertical dimension of social status." American Sociological Review 19 (August):405-13.

Lofland, John
  1969 Deviance and Identity. New York: Prentice-Hall.

Matza, David
  1964 Delinquency and Drift. New York: Wiley.

Miller, Walter
  1966 "Violent crimes in city gangs." Annals of the American Academy of Political and Social Science 364:96-112.

Pitt-Rivers, Julian
  1966 "Honour and social status." In Honor and Shame. Edited by J. Peristiany. Chicago: University of Chicago.

Ryan, Bryce and Murray Strauss
  1954 "The integration of Singhalese society." Research Studies of the State College of Washington 22:179-227.

Scott, Marvin and Stanford Lyman
  1970 "Accounts." In Social Psychology through Symbolic Interaction. Xerox College Publishers.

Short, James F. Jr.
  1965a "Social structure and group processes in explanations of gang delinquency." Pp. 155-88 in M. and C. Sherif (eds.), Problems of Youth. Chicago: Aldine.

Short, James F. Jr. and Fred Strodtbeck
  1965b Group Process and Gang Delinquency. Chicago: University of Chicago Press.

Suttles, Gerald
  1963 The Social Order of the Slum. Chicago: University of Chicago Press.

Toch, Hans
  1969 Violent Men. Chicago: Aldine.

[14]

Community Tolerance Of Gang Violence*

RUTH HOROWITZ, *University of Delaware*

This paper explores the maintenance of tolerance in relationships between community residents and violent gang members. How can parents and other non-gang residents experience their neighborhood as orderly and remain tolerant of violence when approximately five gang members are killed in their community each year? In the Chicano community I studied, gang members are not outsiders but are members of family networks in which they behave appropriately. I show that tolerance varies in degree and may be fragile, but that it is generally maintained through active negotiation between community residents and gang members. Locally, the meaning of gang violence is articulated within the cultural framework of honor which allows residents to understand, if not approve of gang violence. However, I also examine how this precarious negotiated order collapses and intolerance results when violent confrontations disrupt community affairs, such as dances or weddings, or when families become implicated in their sons' violent activities.

All social groups are occasionally confronted by troublesome behavior, and the reactive strategies they employ to define, punish, or treat such behavior as "deviant" have been a fertile ground for research. However, much less attention has been devoted to the phenomenon of tolerance of threatening or disturbing behavior. How and why people tolerate actions they do not support are complex questions. Tolerance of non-approved conduct may vary in degree. For instance, Lofland (1983:5) distinguishes between *negative* and *positive* toleration. Negative toleration is the ability "to put up with" another's differences or potentially problematic conduct simply because of lack of awareness or limited contact between self and other. On the other hand, positive toleration involves the ability to maintain a relationship with another in open awareness and "with at least a mild appreciation" of their personal or behavioral differences (Lofland, 1983:5).

This paper presents a case study of these and other tolerant responses to the violent behavior of gangs in a Chicago Chicano community. I focus on the processes through which violent acts and their meaning are interactionally negotiated and mutually understood among gang members, non-gang youths, and adult members of the community. By analyzing how these groups collaborate to maintain a sense of predictability and safety in their families and neighborhood (Wallace, 1980)—and by examining occasions where this tenuous sense of order collapses—I attempt to show why community members are generally able to tolerate conduct that outsiders condemn as senseless acts of violence.

Tolerance and Negotiated Order

Few studies of violent gangs have considered the question of community tolerance. Some research on other forms of troublesome behavior indicates that the smaller the social distance between the actor and the audience, the greater the reluctance of the audience to categorize the actor as deviant (Pfuhl, 1978; Rubington and Weinberg, 1978; Yarrow et al., 1955). Such

* An Earlier version of this paper was presented at a conference on "Juvenile Violence—Juvenile Justice," Milwaukee, Wisconsin, 1985. The author thanks Jeff Davidson, Carl Klockers, Lyn Lofland, James Short, and the anonymous *Social Problems* reviewers for their comments. Correspondence to: Department of Sociology, University of Delaware, Newark, DE 19716.

findings highlight a need to examine how tolerant or intolerant reactions to gang violence are contingent on the relationships between gang members and various community audiences.

More specifically, the ability of community members to maintain a tolerant stance toward the potentially disturbing or life-threatening behavior of gangs may depend fundamentally on the different "awareness contexts" that characterize their relationships to gang members. As Glaser and Strauss (1964:670) describe it, an awareness context is "the total combination of what each interactant in a situation knows about the identity of the other and his own identity in the eyes of the other." Even in close relationships, such as between family members, all parties may not be fully or equally aware of each others' identities outside of the relationship. Levels of tolerance may be affected not only by the degree of awareness (i.e., aware, suspicious, unaware) in a relationship, but also by the extent to which interactants acknowledge their awareness of others' identities (i.e., pretense or no pretense). For example, parents may openly acknowledge an awareness that their son is a "good boy" at home while being unaware or covertly suspicious of his identity on the street as a gang member. However, awareness contexts are always subject to revision or dramatic change in the face of new evidence about alternative identities—e.g., if parents discover their son was involved in a street fight.

In stressing the importance of awareness contexts, I do not mean to imply that tolerance simply amounts to a passive state of ignorance about gang members' behavior and identities. All parties to such relationships actively participate in the construction and maintenance of negative as well as positive toleration (Lofland, 1983). In this respect, my approach is similar to Becker and Horowitz's (1972) study of civility in San Francisco, where they found that toleration of a wide range of conduct and groups was based on mutual accommodations worked out between actors and audiences through a process of negotiation.

Furthermore, I will focus on the negotiated character of moral judgments about the violent acts of gangs in relation to community standards of conduct. Here, my analysis contrasts with Lemert's (1951:54) early conception of community tolerance, which treated the relationship between acts and cultural standards as basically unproblematic: "societal reaction tends to be a pure function of the interaction of deviation and the norms of the groups which are transgressed" (also see Scott, 1972). A view of community reaction as a direct function of rule-violations fails to account for the active manipulation of standards or situational maneuvers involved in the interactional construction of tolerance. For instance, analysts of urban life point out that tolerance may be maintained by avoiding contact with groups whose conduct is problematic (Karp et al., 1977; Lofland, 1973; Suttles, 1972)—in a sense, avoidance ("spacial myopia") mediates between standards and conduct. However, as Stokes and Hewitt (1976:844) point out, even when contacts between groups or with potentially disruptive behavior are unavoidable, audiences and actors often collaborate in "aligning actions" that "sustain a relationship (but not necessarily an exact correspondence) between ongoing conduct and culture in the face of recognized failure of conduct to live up to cultural definitions and requirements." Accordingly, I deal with tolerance and other community reactions to gang violence as a process of negotiation "among people interacting with one another and not simply [as] a question of applying rules or principles to conduct" (Stokes and Hewitt, 1976:844).

The people I studied—Chicano gang members, non-gang youths, and adults on 32nd Street—routinely collaborated to maintain a sense of order and mutual tolerance in their community. I will examine how most community members were generally able to avoid awareness of the violent acts of their sons and neighbors or to align such acts with cultural standards of honor. However, as I will also show, the presumption of order was precarious and subject to collapse on those occasions where accommodations between gangs and their neighbors failed, and violence intruded into the affairs of the rest of the community. People become baffled, upset, and shocked when the routine flow of events is disrupted (cf. Scott, 1972)—and they may focus their fear and outrage toward the source of this disorder. Just as tolerance is embedded in a cultural and social order that is continually negotiated, a break-down of this negotiated order can lead to intolerance of gang violence.

Setting and Methods

On 32nd Street, violent gangs were prevalent: they had guns; they shot at or stabbed each other and, occasionally, non-gang youths; and they sometimes killed people. The major-ity of community residents were poor and poorly educated. According to census data, there were 44,000 residents in the approximately 150 square block area, but some local estimates ranged as high as 70,000.[1] Some people chose to stay in the neighborhood; others were un-able to move because of their ethnic status or lack of income. However, most residents did not retreat behind heavily barricaded doors; in fact, people spent a good deal of time outdoors and walked around the community at all hours of the day and night.

Some local residents estimated that close to 70 percent of the male population, at least for a short period (a few months), joined one of the eight major gangs. Most of the gangs were divided into age-graded groups such as the Tinys, Midgets, Littles, Juniors, and Seniors. Acts of expressive violence by one or more gang members were relatively common, and the chances that other community residents would witness such violent events were quite high. Most conflicts did not end in a death; however, the number of gang-related deaths averaged about five per year during the period of my research.[2]

My research was conducted over a three-year period using participant-observation tech-niques. I spent long periods daily with the gang members in the streets, on their park bench, at dances, at parties, and in their homes while I was living in the community. I developed very close ties with some gang members and was often invited to their basement clubhouse while some members of their gang were excluded. Many of them would talk to me individu-ally about their lives, but others never spoke to me privately. If there were questions about an event, someone would say, "Ask Ruth, she's writing it all down." I also spent considerable time with many unaffiliated male youth and with a variety of female groups (see Horowitz, 1983, 1986 for further details).

Most of the gang data reported here concerns the Lions, which had approximately 30 core members. When I started the research, the Lions were 15 to 18 years old and made up the "Littles" segment of the gang. They split up a year later into the "Littles" and "Juniors"; however, they remained closely affiliated and continued to spend time on the same bench. When I returned to do a restudy seven years after the first meeting with the group, most of the original group were Seniors, who were married, were working, and had children. They still spent many of their evenings on the same bench. When I showed up at the park, the first thing anyone said was, "Ruth, where have you been?" It immediately seemed as though I had never left.

In the following analysis, I first explore the meaning of gang violence to gang members

1. Arguments have been made that the Spanish-speaking population is greatly undercounted in the U.S. census. In part this may be explained by language barriers and fear of immigration officials.

2. According to Chicago police department statistics, the Hispanic neighborhoods had the highest rates and num-bers of gang-related homicides. The rates have remained fairly stable over the years. During the period of 1971-1975, I could account for four or five gang-related deaths each year. There were 16 homicides in the 1978-1981 period on 32nd Street, and 20 additional murders during the same period in a contiguous neighborhood (Spergel, 1984). Many of these may have involved residents from 32nd Street or relatives as there is much interaction between the two communities. The five Hispanic areas comprise 12.4 percent of the city population and 51.9 percent of all gang homicides (Spergel, 1984). Local leaders often place the estimated number of gang-related murders higher than police estimates, due in part to different definitions of "gang-related." However, this number sometimes may be inflated for political purposes such as demands for additional resources. More people are directly affected than just the families of victims, as there is often more than one perpetrator of the murder. This is important for the individuals and families not only if caught, but as potential victims of revenge attacks.

and other community members and the processes by which groups (non-gang males and family) in varying relationships to gang members contsruct and maintain their presumption of order. Second, I examine the conditions under which gang violence becomes the solvent that destroys the apparent safety and order of the neighborhood. Third, I focus on how the distinct meanings attributed to gang violence by outsiders create a situation in which violence is not understood or tolerated. Finally, I consider some of the reasons why gang violence continues to be tolerated by parents.

Honor, Violence, and Etiquette

The cultural framework of *honor* and its extensive pattern of moral meanings permeates many of the social relationships on 32nd Street. A strong emphasis on the value and symbols of personal honor is generally found in Mediterranean and Latin societies (Peristiany, 1966). On 32nd Street the man of honor supports his family, accumulates no long-standing debts, protects the chastity of his women,[3] and guards against any aspersions on his masculinity. He is independent and dominant. These criteria are generally understood by community residents as a basis for evaluating actions. Should a man's honor be questioned publicly, violence is an expected response. On such occasions residents know the meaning of others' actions, where violence fits into the scheme of things, and what options are available and sensible.

Honor revolves around a man's ability to command deference in interpersonal relations. An individual suspects he is viewed as weak when he believes he has been publicly humiliated—that is, his right to deferential treatment in public has been challenged. In order not to test another man's claims to precedence inadvertently, men follow strict rules of etiquette in daily life: hands are shaken in greeting, bumping into others is assiduously avoided, and staring is eschewed. Polite and proper interactions indicate respect for others and allow unproblematic interaction to occur. Any violation might be regarded as an intended slight. A situation defined as a test of honor or a character contest is a fateful situation, a situation consequential to the participants with a problematic outcome (Goffman, 1967:216).

If contests of honor are to be avoided, adherence to the rules of courtesy and etiquette is essential. Following the rules of etiquette allows for safe management of face-to-face interaction and is expected during all social occasions. There is often at least one large, formal social occasion in the community every week. Weddings and *quinceañeras* (a 15-year-old girl's birthday party) tend to be elaborate affairs planned months in advance; frequently more than two hundred guests attend, and those who stand up as part of the bridal party or escort the 15-year-old wear formal, matching attire. The families serve dinner and typically have an open bar. Gang members attend such affairs regularly, often as escorts in rented tuxedos, and behave appropriately. Politeness demonstrates respect.

Moreover, the social skills learned and used in the family are employed on the job and in school. Many of the gang members work, and they are well aware of the different cultural interpretations of interaction in different settings. They carefully separate their behavior and identities on the job from their activities in the streets so that employers remain ignorant of their gang membership. A striking example of this involved a member of the Lions who worked at a large downtown bank as a computer operator. For several months he had not missed a single day of work, was on time, and always wore a tie. The bank management regarded him as one of their best trainees until they discovered that he was charged with a felony for carrying a gun on 32nd Street. He could not understand why they fired him because, as he explained it, it was unnecessary to take a gun into the bank. On 32nd Street on a Saturday when the Lions were expecting "trouble," it was.

---

3. A woman's shame (a premarital loss of virginity or an extra-marital affair) reflects on the male family members, as it indicates a man's inability to control the lives of his women and a failure to maintain his dominant position.

This ability to understand varying audience definitions of gang violence allows gang members to adjust their conduct towards the audience found in a particular setting. In return, by defining gang violence within a framework of honor, community members are able to understand such violence and to construct a partial basis for its toleration. However, this negative toleration does not amount to approval because gangs have changed the traditional notion of honor. Therefore, audiences must construct their own appraisals and evaluations of situations in which they encounter gang violence. Different audiences employ different strategies to maintain their presumption of order and achieve varying degrees of tolerance.

Gang Violence as an Extension of Honor: Acceptance and Tolerance

Gang-Gang Interaction: Acceptance

In the process of developing a distinctive social identity, gang members have distorted the traditional notion of honor. In general, the man of honor on 32nd Street is sensitive to challenges; however, gang members view the means of maintaining honor—displays of toughness— as an essential criterion of status and as a prime reason for involving one's self in such situations.[4] That is, gang members seek out and initiate challenges to another's honor as one way of publicly asserting their claim to precedence and enhancing their reputation by demonstrating their toughness. Other gang members almost routinely accept that definition of the situation and respond violently.

While it may be the intent of the initiator of a challenge to demean the other (requiring an immediate response of violence), the normative ambiguity of such encounters allows for alternative responses. The challenge may be defined as an intended insult and a character contest ensues. However, it is also possible that the individual who is insulted may view the actions of the initiator as the result of poor manners and as unintentional, allowing him to place the onus on the properties of the situation and to ignore or excuse the actions of the initiator. Here the situation is defined as routine, inconsequential, and unproblematic. The initiator then may leave the scene, if excused, or make further provocative actions if he wants the other to see his actions as demeaning. This negotiation process may terminate rapidly or continue until a fight is finally provoked. For example, on one occasion after a dance, someone knocked into Gilberto, President of the Lions; but Gilberto said, "Excuse me," and walked away. The young man looked as though he would pursue the encounter, but he turned away and melted into the crowd. I asked Gilberto about the incident, and he explained that there would have been no contest. The young man was no one important, no one worth fighting.

When the gang members define an act as intentional and demeaning, they respond with violence. These encounters may occur in the streets, parks, or club houses. Most terminate with a few bruises, but they occasionally end in death. After one encounter in which two of the Lions were jumped and beaten up in an alley, the other members gathered to discuss how they could regain the reputation they had lost when their two members were beaten. Several weeks later, there was a fight after a dance and the Lions declared themselves on top again. The potential combatants know what options are available and know the possible consequences of each move. The presumption of orderliness, therefore, remains intact. While gang members generally agree on the kind of incidents that can be defined as demeaning, the exact meaning of each incident must be negotiated by the immediate participants. This process is crucial, for the ordering of social relationships may hinge on the outcome of each new encounter (Anderson, 1978). While gang members may not approve of any one member's con-

---

4. Erlanger (1979) argues that violence is not the only means of maintaining machismo and that it is a result of estrangement. My data also support the notion that a gang member may gain status in a variety of ways; however, I have discussed this topic elsewhere (Horowitz, 1983; Horowitz and Schwartz, 1974).

struction of a particular encounter, in general, violence as a response is approved and demonstration of toughness is one means of achieving status.

Non-Gang Youth: Positive Toleration

Gang membership does not define the boundaries of friendship, although it generally delimits the boundary of complete approval of gang violence. There are youths who spend time in the same settings as gang members and interact with them freely and fairly frequently; however, they generally do not actively seek situations in which they can challenge the reputation of others in order to enhance their own status. While they may defend their honor when provoked, developing a reputation as "tough" is generally not a central concern.

During my field work, many non-gang youths spent time at one of the parks where two of the reportedly toughest gangs (Lions and Senior Greeks) were located. Several of these young men talked constantly with the gang members and attended the same classes and parties. War stories of previous fights were shared and thoroughly discussed. However, unaffiliated young men did not fully approve of gang members' activities and sometimes referred to them as "crazy" (fighting too much over small incidents) or explained that they would never instigate fights like gang members did. Yet, they understood gang violence; it is intelligible, sensible, and, in its context, proper. They concluded that they rarely would be challenged to fight and could remain safely watching an incident evolve, leave the area or, on certain occasions, voluntarily become involved.

Generally, non-gang youths relate to members in an atmosphere of positive toleration. Some even swear allegiance to come to the aid of a threatened gang. At one private party, the members of the Lions gang expected the arrival of one of the gangs with whom they were "at war." Several unaffiliated young men volunteered to help out, and all waited at the party until long past midnight when everyone finally staggered home. Yet, on another occasion, they left the park when the Lions were expecting to fight some Junior Greeks.

These young men understand that they generally can remain as an uninvolved audience because gang members symbolically segregate themselves from non-gang youth. Gang members evaluate themselves as having the highest status and no one of high status gains much by challenging someone of lesser status. As members of a gang, they cannot issue a challenge in the name of the gang to a non-gang individual. With no one to back up the person challenged, the fight would be too unequal and little would be gained by the gang member. One peripheral member of the Lions challenged a non-gang member and lost. When he asked for assistance from the group, they laughed at him and he stopped hanging around. Moreover, even if a non-gang youth interprets the actions of a gang member as casting aspersions upon his honor, the situation evolves in a sensible and fitting manner; they fight to maintain their honor. For example, a gang member may question the non-gang youth's toughness. On the one hand, the non-gang member may choose not to interpret the behavior of the other as offensive and walk away. On the other hand, he may interpret the action of the other as demeaning and react violently. On one occasion, Jamie, an unaffiliated youth, and a Junior Greek fought after the Junior Greek publicly called Jamie a name. Jamie felt that his heroic effort in the fight was sufficient to maintain his honor. There also were fights between gang and non-gang youths over questions of chastity: "I'll get him if he ever says that about my sister in my presence." The meaning of such actions, from the perspective of the non-gang member, is one of upholding his honor, not of gaining a reputation as a tough man.

While unaffiliated young men do fight, most define those situations as defending their honor, not as asserting their toughness and developing their reputation. Although they regard gang members' efforts to develop a reputation with admiration or, at least, sympathy, these young men remain symbolically separate from gang members and generally refrain from openly challenging others.

The Family: Negative Toleration

Considerable work is often required on the part of both parents and gang members to insure the parents' presumption of order and their continued toleration of gang violence. While most parents do not approve of fighting to better one's reputation, they understand the use of violence to uphold one's honor. While few parents would acknowledge that they think it important or good for their son to be a gang member or want him to be constantly fighting,[5] most would see violence—and, occasionally, deadly violence—as a proper and justifiable response to offenses against famiy honor. In one instance a gang member shot and killed his father after finding him a number of times with several different young girls. Not only did the father publicly flaunt his infidelities, but he was often out of work and did not support his family well. There was considerable support for the son's actions within the community and his mother fought for his release. Fighting to maintain one's honor is understood and generally approved under certain conditions, particularly if a man or his family is demeaned publicly.

The use of violence by gang members to enhance reputation has a different quality than violence to defend honor. When violent acts are employed as a means to demonstrate toughness, most parents do not approve of such activities. One father referred to all gang members as hoodlums. To maintain their presumption of order, parents may steadfastly avoid acknowledging that their sons are in gangs and that young men are hurt or even killed within a few blocks of their homes. They actively strive to maintain their negative toleration; they will put up with gang violence as long as it does not enter their social world. However, the gang members must cooperate for the parents' unawareness to continue.

Parents often can maintain the fiction of their son's conventional conduct outside the home if he behaves properly when at home. An honorable son respects his parents and elders by deferring to them and behaving according to the rules of etiquette. What he does in the street need not be consistent with his behavior at home. The possibility of segmenting actions by social setting is supported by the expectation that men be independent. Parents encourage their male children from an early age to play away from the house, partly to encourage independence and to compensate for lack of space. Consequently, what boys do outside the home may not interfere or be consistent with their home life. A boy who is a "good son"—who respects his parents and behaves appropriately at home—can also be a tough gang member. Most gang members agree that street behavior should not be brought into the home. One of the Lions explained that he deserved to be beaten by his mother for coming home drunk and rowdy. Inebriation was appropriate, but he thought that he should not have gone home while drunk.

While some parents appear to remain largely ignorant of what occurs in the streets, other parents, if pressed, acknowledge suspicions about their son's involvement in gang violence. However, to make his behavior more consistent with their standards, they may argue that he never starts any fights and that his particular gang is really a group of nice young men. For instance, the mother and aunt of a member who had a reputation as one of the toughest members of a wild gang told me that his gang was just a few young men who had grown up together. Parents are never told stories of fights and participants rarely receive severe wounds that cannot be explained away. Gang members' accounts for injuries were sometimes outrageous, but parents rarely questioned their sons. One son explained that the large gash over his

---

5. Many of the parents of these young people grew up outside of Chicago and were not in gangs. However, there was at least one father of one of the Lions who was very young, had been a gang member in a nearby neighborhood, and came to the park on a number of occasions to gossip with the young men. He occasionally applauded their efforts. This appeared atypical in this relatively newly formed neighborhood with a short history of gangs. In Los Angeles, where gangs have long histories and where sons may follow fathers into a gang, such behavior might be more common (Moore, 1978).

eye was a result of falling against a locker, and another explained that the ugly wound on his shin was a result of falling. In fact, he had been hit with a bat.

The generally held expectation that sons grow out of gang membership helps parents remain tolerant. Parents can refer to examples of gang members who have grown up and obtained a good job or attended college. When confronted by a son's gang membership, parents often argue that "Boys will be boys" or "He'll grow out of it."

While parents and gang members have developed techniques that facilitate the routine flow of activities, both adults and young gang members must work especially hard to maintain the parents' presumption of order at some social occasions. For example, parents sometimes talk about minimizing the number of gang members invited to weddings and *quinceañeras*. Exclusion, however, is generally impossible. When anyone is asked to be part of the bridal or *quinceañera* party, the entire family is invited. Additionally, many of the gang members are sought as escorts and people often attend uninvited.

Gang members also work to see that such events progress as planned. Respect for and knowledge of the rules of etiquette allow the gang members to work towards this smooth construction of an event. Gang members generally behave appropriately, find chairs for ladies, drink enough to get drunk but not enough to become too rowdy, and wear their best clothes. During the many public dances I attended over a two-year period, male gang members never fought inside a dance—only girls did. Although guns were passed in to the people at the dances and there were many rumors of impending fights, the fights usually occurred outside the dance or party and away from any crowds. Rumors of potential fights also circulated during many of the weddings and *quinceañeras*, but few of the rumored conflicts materialized. Two gangs who were "at war" attended a wedding. Each claimed that they were going to "get the others"; but they managed to stay on either side of the room, explained that they had to get more of their men, and claimed they did not have enough guns to fight. In all these situations, the events evolved as planned, and the presumption of order was maintained. The gang members and other guests collaborate so that everyone experiences the situation as orderly and routine.

Additionally, spatial segregation allows gang fights to occur without disrupting others' presumptions. Fights rarely last very long; the majority of time is spent talking about a fight, making preparations, and waiting for it to occur. Fights are confined generally to public places (streets, alleys, and parks) that allow others to leave the setting. When several gangs held a peace conference at the park, no one was sure what was going to occur. All girls and unaffiliated males disappeared from the park that Sunday afternoon about 15 minutes before most of the gang members arrived. Whenever the Lions were expecting "trouble," the girls would leave. Sometimes parents admonish smaller children not to hang around locations where gang members have their fights. Moreover, there is typically some warning before a fight. If a large number of young men wearing their colors walk intently down the street, and if people do not want to see a fight, they need not follow them. Only people whose homes border the area where the fight occurs may be forced to observe it.

Another form of gang violence involves the use of a car—riding by some enemy group and shooting at them. This is done quickly and is observed only by the people who happen to be in the immediate vicinity. Other chance encounters may occur in back alleys, but these are typically observed by few. Segregation of violent conduct and parents' work at explaining the conduct of their children help to permit the adults to maintain their presumption of order. They do not want to know about violence or see it; however, this is not always possible. The presumption of order is fragile and sometimes evolves into disorder.

Segregation Failures: Intolerance

Gang violence does not always develop in a manner that others can understand or think of as proper. Life is disrupted when violence occurs where people think it ought not to impinge. It can be terrifying and change the lives of family, friends, and the gang members themselves.

The Family: Awareness

Gang members generally work hard to avoid fights on social occasions so that others can maintain their presumption of order. However, gang members find that this is not always possible. At times they must fight; it is sensible and appropriate from their perspective.

The setting of the fight is critical. When a fight occurs at a party, there is no way for the audience to escape. During the period of observation, most weddings and *quinceañeras* proceeded smoothly. In other instances, however, major battles took place. During a *quinceañera* a small girl was shot accidentally when two gangs clashed. At one wedding the groom was arrested for assault. When several members of the wedding party were arrested along with the groom, some of the girls in the party became hysterical along with the bride and the couple's family. The only people who remained calm were some older gang members who were uninvolved in the fight. When fights occur indoors, they disrupt the flow of regularly occurring talk and activity. While gang members feel they have made a valid choice, others are angry at the disturbance and fear that they or their families might be hurt. Their co-presence makes escape impossible and such an abrupt intrusion of violence into community affairs is neither expected nor evaluated as fitting by others. The presumption of order cannot be maintained and the audience becomes terrified.

A fight is also viewed as insulting to the family giving the party. People who spend the money, time, and effort to make a nice affair deserve respect from their guests and violence demonstrates lack of respect. Talk after a fight focuses on the incident, not on the social occasion. People sometimes place the blame on the family. One young girl cried several days after a fight at her *quinceañera*. She was convinced that her family would lose respect after failing to control the guests.

Moreover, when relatives are involved in a serious fight, families can no longer remain unaware or maintain the pretense that a family member is not a gang member. Parents become baffled, upset, confused, and angry at the sudden failure of the social arrangements that allow them to tolerate conduct they do not fully approve.

However, the evolution from order to disorder may also proceed more slowly. Occasions do occur when families must begin to deal with the knowledge that a young man may not be a "nice boy" as distinct from "one of those gang members." Families are sometimes struck by the disjuncture between street life and the conventional world when a son is arrested or hurt badly or when a family member is threatened. The conflict is explicit and has to be faced or explained away. Many families continue to attempt to view their son as a "good son," unwittingly and unwillingly pulled into trouble by bad youth. This makes the conduct comprehensible. Sometimes the problem is managed by sending him to relatives in another state or Mexico. The work to maintain the presumption of order may continue for an extensive period. One mother, who had her 18-year-old son released from detention over 20 times, finally refused to bail him out on his 27th (by his own count) arrest. This is an extreme case, but it is interesting that his mother bailed him out almost every time before the last when he moved permanently to another state. To account for her long history of tolerance for her son's arrests, she explained that he was a "good boy."

Occasionally, a family member is threatened by a gang and the conflict is brought into the home. In one such instance, an enemy of the Lions threw a brick through the window of the home of a Lion's mother. She was very upset and could not understand why someone would want to hurt her family. Threats are sometimes made toward family members who are supposed to relay them to their brothers. The family cannot help but experience disruption in their lives and come to feel that gangs are dangerous and that their activities should be stopped. The father of a 16-year-old girl's child was involved in a conflict with an enemy gang. When the gang came looking for him at her house, her family, very upset by their involvement, sent the young woman to live with relatives and carefully watched the streets for several weeks. The discovery that a "nice boy" is involved in violent activities peels away the carefully constructed barriers that most relatives employ to maintain a presumption of orderliness. When someone else's son is hurt, he might have been "no good"; but kin are viewed generally as "good boys." However, except for sending sons away, parents make few efforts to control them.

Non-Gang Youth: Perhaps You Are Tough

Many of the non-gang youth are good fighters, and some are viewed as "tough warriors" by gang members. Consequently, such non-gang members are always at risk of being challenged by individual gang members who could improve their status by winning a fight. One young man transferred to a private school after being challenged more than five times in one semester. It was a great sacrifice for his family, and he started to work after school and on weekends to pay the tuition.

The symbolic segregation of gang and non-gang youth is tenuous. There is always a possibility that gang members may choose to redefine the identity of the non-gang male as a potential gang member, making the presumption of order difficult for the non-gang individual. For example, one young man who socialized frequently with the Lions was challenged by some of the Lions to fight. They told him that he had to become a member because he knew too many of their secrets. Several gang members beat him up. To avoid further confrontations, he enlisted in the military. When a gang redefines the symbolic boundaries between gang members and others, the situation, from the perspective of non-gang youth, no longer evolves as expected or in a proper and fitting manner; they cannot tolerate such behavior.

Gangs: What Makes an Honorable Man?

Fighting in schools disallows the presumption of order for some gang members. Much work by some gang members goes into avoiding such confrontations. Gang members, in order to avoid being so identified, may transfer to public schools outside the community or to parochial schools. Some even quit school to avoid fights. For example, Carlos, a gang member, dropped out his junior year claiming:

> Shit, I nearly was blown away in school yesterday. This dude pulls out a .45 and sticks it in my stomach. You know you can't trust them chicks. They pack the heats for the dudes. That chick [who handed the gang member the gun] was supposed to be going out with a friend of ours.

For gang members like Carlos, becoming a participant can have serious consequences—being expelled or arrested—that might disrupt their futures. They want their lives to evolve as planned and seek to avoid settings where a fight might jeopardize future plans.

Even the young men who remain gang members as they mature begin to feel that gang violence is less acceptable. They are no longer sure that they should remain symbolically segregated from other adults. They begin to tolerate rather than approve of violence. While the majority of youth drop out of the gangs by 18 or 20, some maintain their affiliation as Seniors along with marriage, fatherhood, and steady employment (Horowitz, 1982). Several of the gangs on 32nd Street had Senior groups. The Lions gang continued to fight as the members entered their twenties even though they individually began to think that they were too old to use toughness and their identities as warriors as indicators of status. When one member of the Lions who had been institutionalized for two years returned to the street, he failed to notice that the others had changed. He wanted to start fights and the others kept putting him off. Such "trouble" held increasing risks and older members rarely instigated fights.

Over their years together, gang members had developed very close ties and depended upon each other, a potentially dishonorable situation. In an honor-based subculture, suspicions of dependency may be evaluated as weakness and, to gang members, these suspicions can only be mitigated by demonstrated toughness. They were, in fact, dependent upon each other; therefore, to remain together as men with claims to being tough, they publicly had to declare a willingness to fight. The tension between maintaining identity in the street world of juvenile gangs and developing an image as a responsible adult began to make the presumption of orderliness more difficult to maintain. Adulthood and demonstrations of toughness began to appear increasingly incongruous.

Yet, the older gang members' sense of self-worth remained partly dependent on interaction with peers who remained in the streets, and they continued to act to maintain the respect of street peers (Horowitz, 1982). They did not feel free to discuss the ambivalence they were experiencing about toughness: now they were tough only so that they could remain together rather than hanging together because they are tough. Although each privately began to experience a lack of order in his own life, the basis upon which gang members evaluated social relationships remained almost the same. They felt that they had to fight even if they were no longer entirely sure it was fitting.

Outsiders' Views of Gang Violence: Intolerance

While most of the community residents I have discussed are situationally intolerant of gang violence, some groups are intolerant of gang activities in any context. The framework of honor does not inform their interpretation of gang violence. For teachers and other outside "helping" personnel, the meaning of the youth's violence is obscure. Young people are feared and violence is not understood and never develops as expected; there is no presumption of order.

Law enforcement officials and the public often regard gangs as a symbol of disorder. The police in many cities have "gang intelligence units," and the government has funded many gang prevention and intervention programs—e.g., the Chicago Area Project (Kobrin, 1959) and the Mid-City Project (Miller, 1962). Juvenile justice workers and police surveyed in many major cities still see gang violence as a major problem (Miller, 1975).

Such outsiders view the world of the young people on 32nd Street as dangerous and unappealing. One of the youth centers run by social workers from outside the community did not permit teens to use its facilities, because "They are all just troublemakers." Many teachers avoided "unnecessary contact" with students by retreating from the community as quickly as possible at the end of each working day. During my field work, few teachers attended events in the neighborhood. High school dances were held in the afternoons because school authorities were afraid of what might happen at night.

Some teachers have so little understanding of honor and violence that they fail to see how their own behavior is interpreted by students. A counselor expelled Jesús from high school on his sixteenth birthday for extended absences. Jesús called his mother and told her about his situation. The counselor, overhearing the conversation, laughed at him and Jesús punched him. Jesús could have ignored the laugh, defining the counselor as ignorant, but it told him that the counselor had no respect for him. Jesús felt that the only way he could regain his dignity was to punch him.

Teachers fail to distinguish gang members from non-gang individuals and to acknowledge any differences. One teacher said, "They should all be frisked every day." Most of the members neither wear their insignia, advertise their affiliations, nor act differently than others in school, and most school personnel rarely venture into the community. Gang members are generally pushed and pulled out of school by their lack of interest and the possibility of excitement in the streets. For example, most of the eighth-grade teachers were unaware that the boy chosen as the best dressed by his class was an active member of the Lions. He was outside drinking when his prize was announced at the graduation dinner-dance. He left school the following year for lack of interest—not misbehavior. For many teachers, their lack of understanding of gangs and other young people in the community leads to a fundamental intolerance of youth. The community is defined as a dangerous place, one to be avoided whenever possible.

Conclusion

In the Chicano community I studied, gang members are not cut off from the adult world, nor do they reject adult authority. On the other hand, their behavior is neither completely acceptable to adults, nor are they completely integrated into the social world of adults. While parents do not approve of gang violence, it is understood as a distortion of their notion of honor. As individuals, gang members are part of community and family life and accept the more conventional world of adults. Chicano youth act independently from their parents yet participate in many of the same social events and accept the authority of their parents in the home. However, in other communities the relationship between these social worlds appears to be simpler. Short and Strodtbeck (1965) found that black gangs were acceptable to community adults and integrated into the adult world, whereas white gangs were cut off from their parents and rejected adult authority. My analysis suggests that the cultural link between the street world and the conventional world—particularly the framework of honor—at least partially accounts for the Chicano gang's complex relationship to parents and other community members.

While the presumption of order is precariously maintained for most community members, it is unclear whether families' tolerant responses to violence are embedded in a context of freedom of choice or are indications of powerlessness. Can parents exercise sufficient control over their sons' behavior and their own actions that they need not openly condemn gang violence? Or, is toleration one of the few options available to parents who are unable to control the behavior of youth but unwilling to hand them over to the authorities?

Part of the difficulty in answering these questions is that the gang members are neither perceived as dangerous strangers (Merry, 1981) nor are they protecting the local area from strangers (Suttles, 1968, 1972), which might give them some legitimacy. The issue exists because gang members are not strangers; they are relatives and friends. Family and neighborhood networks are too extensive to pretend that gang members do not belong. Their activities are dangerous but they are not regarded as dangerous people.

Controlling the gang members' activities appears almost impossible and moving away from gang territories is usually too costly, both financially and socially. Close supervision of sons' activities runs against parents' own cultural understandings of honor. An honorable man is supposed to be independent and the honor of the family is embedded in the conduct of all its members. Thus, parents are caught in a cultural dilemma. On the one hand, a young man must be taught to be independent. He should, therefore, be on his own outside the home and ought to stand up to others' claims of precedence. On the other hand, to jeopardize the honor of the family by continuously fighting and getting into trouble with the law is not right. While they do not approve of their sons' gang activities, parents often feel that to try to control those activities is to fail to turn their sons into men. However, to call in outside agents (police) to control gang violence is not a viable solution because to question publicly a son's moral character is to question the honor of the family. While parents often punish daughters by keeping them indoors for untoward behavior, they rarely do that to sons. Occasionally, if things get very bad, they send a son out of the state or country to relatives. Beyond this, parents feel that there is little they can do—the pull of the streets is too strong.

When there is little they feel that they can do to deter violence and the perpetrators are people whom they love, parents have little choice but to cooperate with the gang members in negotiating a sense of order. As long as violence is ecologically segregated from "parental space," parents can do their part to maintain a pretense of unawareness of the gang identity of their children. Even when parents become aware of conduct that fails to measure up to their standards, they work to align such actions with the cultural framework of honor and their familial conception of a "good son." This cannot be achieved without the cooperation of the gang members who respect the need to segregate their violent actions by time and place and who offer reasonable accounts for their conduct that can be accepted by their parents.

In contrast to studies that have ignored the relationship of gangs to other community residents, this analysis has shown how non-gang community residents, but not outsiders, manage to co-exist successfully with violent gangs. If community audiences were to react to gang members as deviant, they would be faced with several dilemmas. Above all, they would have to reject beloved family members. To control gang violence, they would have to call in the authorities, thus publicly questioning family honor. The cultural and existential solution is to work with gang members to maintain a relationship of mutual toleration and to engage in negotiations which allow community life to proceed in an orderly, if tenuous, fashion.

References

Anderson, Elijah
    1978   A place on the Corner. Chicago: University of Chicago Press.
Becker, Howard and Irving L. Horowitz
    1972   Culture and Civility in San Francisco. New Brunswick, NJ: Transaction Books.
Erlanger, Howard
    1979   "Estrangement, machismo and gang violence." Social Science Quarterly 60:235–48.
Glaser, Barney and Anslem Strauss
    1964   "Awareness contexts and social interaction." American Sociological Review 29:669–79.
Goffman, Erving
    1967   Interaction Ritual. New York: Doubleday.
Horowitz, Ruth
    1982   "Masked intimacy and marginality: adult delinquent gangs in a Chicano community."
            Urban Life 11:3–26.
    1983   Honor and the American Dream. New Brunswick, NJ: Rutgers University Press.
    1986   "Remaining an outsider: membership as a threat to research rapport." Urban Life
            14:409–30.
Horowitz, Ruth and Gary Schwartz
    1974   "Honor, normative ambiguity and gang violence." American Sociological Review
            39:238–51.
Karp, David H., Gregory P. Stone and William C. Yoels
    1977   Being Urban: A Social Psychological View of City Life. Lexington, MA: D. C. Heath and
            Company.
Kobrin, Solomon
    1959   "The Chicago Area Project: a twenty-five year assessment." The Annals of the American
            Academy of Political and Social Science 322:1–29.

450   HOROWITZ

Lemert, Edwin
    1951   Social Pathology. New York: McGraw Hill.
Lofland, Lyn
    1973   A World of Strangers. New York: Basic Books.
    1983   "Urban relationships and urban people: creating cosmopolitans." Paper presented at the annual meetings of the Society for the Study of Symbolic Interaction, Detroit.
Merry, Sally
    1981   Urban Danger. Philadelphia, PA: Temple University Press.
Miller, Walter B.
    1962   "The impact of a 'total-community' delinquency control project." Social Problems 10:168–91.
    1975   "Violence by youth gangs and youth groups as a crime problem in American cities." U.S. Department of Justice: U.S. Government Printing Office.
Moore, Joan
    1978   Homeboys. Philadelphia, PA: Temple University Press.
Peristiany, G. J.
    1966   Honor and Shame. Chicago: University of Chicago Press.
Pfuhl, Edwin
    1978   "The unwed father: a 'non-deviant' rule breaker." Sociological Quarterly 19:113–28.
Rubington, Earl and Martin Weinberg
    1978   Deviance, The Interactionist Perspective, Third edition. New York: Macmillan.
Scott, Robert A.
    1972   "A proposed framework for analyzing deviance as a property of social order." Pp. 9–36 in Robert A. Scott and Jack Douglas (eds.), Theoretical Perspectives on Deviance. New York: Basic Books.
Short, James and Fred Strodtbeck
    1965   Group Process and Gang Delinquency. Chicago: University of Chicago Press.
Spergel, Irving
    1984   "Violent gangs in Chicago: in search of social policy." Social Service Review 58:199–226.
Stokes, Randall and John Hewitt
    1976   "Aligning actions." American Sociological Review 41:838–49.
Suttles, Gerald
    1968   Social Order of the Slum. Chicago: University of Chicago Press.
    1972   The Social Construction of Community. Chicago: University of Chicago Press.
Wallace, Samuel E.
    1980   The Urban Environment. Homewood, IL: Dorsey Press.
Yarrow, Marion, Charlotte Schwartz, Harriet Murphy, and Leila Deasy
    1955   "Psychological meaning of mental illness in the family." Journal of Social Issues 4:12–24.

[15]

NICHE CRIME:
The Columbus Gangs Study†

JACQUELINE L. SCHNEIDER††
University of Portsmouth

ABSTRACT: *Even though researchers have studied gangs for many years now, very little is known about the criminal activity of gang leaders. The purpose of this study is to examine the types of criminal activities in which gang leaders participate. Analysis of the criminal histories of 83 gang leaders from Columbus, Ohio, suggests that gangs there specialize in certain types of crime. These data imply that gang suppression policies might be more effective if they target specific niches of the crime market.*

INTRODUCTION

Criminal youth gangs, in existence as early as 1760 in this country (Bonn, 1984), have become permanent fixtures in many American cities. The ability to survive changing social and economic conditions has made the criminal gang an enduring and dangerous institution. As Monti (1994, p. 143) points out:

> [w]hen places as different as inner-city slums and suburban townships have gangs, one must submit that either persons in both places share the same values and moral vision or that their unique views about what is right or wrong cannot tell us much about where gangs will develop.

Despite volumes of research, there is very little information about the structure of gangs and even less about gang leaders. What is known is that leaders direct criminal activity (Monti, 1994) and that members gain status within the gang through criminal activity (Strodtbeck & Short, 1983). Given this orientation, the purpose of this paper is to examine the types and frequencies of criminal activities for which identified gang leaders were arrested between 1986 and 1994 in Columbus,

† *The Office of Criminal Justice Services of the State of Ohio funded this research under Grant No. 91-JJ-C010682. The author wishes to thank Dr. Michael R. Sutton of Nottingham Trent University for his contributions to this article.*

†† *Direct all correspondence to: Jacqueline L. Schneider, Shrewsbury Police Station, Clive Road, Monkmoor, Shrewsbury SY2 5RW, Shropshire, England. E-mail: drjschneider@hotmail.com.*

Ohio. The aim here is to determine whether leaders and their gangs specialize in certain types of offenses. Before delving into the current project, a brief discussion of leadership and gang organization is provided.

GENERAL LEADERSHIP ISSUES

One problem that confronts researchers is the multitude of definitions surrounding leadership. As Stogdill (1974, p. 259) wryly notes, there are "almost as many definitions of leadership as there are persons who have attempted to define the concept." Leadership has been defined from many perspectives. Some observers focus upon the personal traits of individual leaders. Others look at actions, interactions, role relationships, the perceptions of followers, the influence the leader has on tasks, and the overall influence the leader exerts on the organization (Barnard, 1938; Bennis, 1959; Davis, 1977; Katz & Kahn, 1978; Tannebaum & Massarik, 1957). Essentially, leaders "are people whom others want to follow and who command the trust and loyalty of others" (Hellriegel, Slocum, & Woodman, 1983, p. 393).

One can classify leaders according to the functions they perform. These focal points may include planning, organizing, and persuading (Coffin, 1944). Another aspect might include control (Davis, 1951). Other considerations would be goal definition, clarifying and administering goals, assigning and coordinating tasks, motivating members, creating an atmosphere of loyalty, representing the overall group, and sparking the membership into action (Gross, 1961). To perform such functions successfully, leaders need to have influence over other members in the organization. Quite often, this influence extends beyond the realm of "official" authority to less structured networks. According to Kast and Rosenzweig (1970, p. 196), the "greatest sources of authority involve the manner in which [the leader] builds alliances in [the] environment–with peers . . . associates, superiors, subordinates, and other interested parties."

Leadership is the process by which group members and activities are influenced so that organizational goals are achieved (Hellriegel et al., 1983). Few organizations could survive without the existence of some leadership component (Curry & Decker, 1998). Leadership is a vital element within any organization because leaders are in an excellent position to recruit new members and plan activities (Schneider, 1998). Given that leaders can sway members, one might assume that the activities of the group represent the desires and motivations of its leaders. It seems likely, therefore, that the criminal activities gang leaders commit will reflect the type of gang they run, as well as the kind of actions its individual members undertake.

THE INFLUENCE OF GANG LEADERS

Although researchers have been interested in gang studies since the 1920s, the topic of gang leaders has not been the focal point of systematic study. Oddly enough, the concept of leadership within gangs is a neglected area. The few studies that have mentioned leaders have done so briefly and have limited the materials to a short description of "what constitutes a leader."

Marsh and Campbell (1978) point out that Hispanic gang leaders in New York City tend to gravitate toward the position of a "spokesperson" rather than becoming a director of activities. In contrast, Thrasher (1927, p. 311) describes the gang leader as being "the chap of the readiest wit, [around whom] the gang crystallizes; and what he is, the gang also becomes." The leader is also portrayed as an expert in an area of criminality and the source of envy by other members.

Thrasher (1927) studied hundreds of different gangs and described several types of leaders. A good leader had a great deal of physical prowess, which would enable him to defend himself and other members. He would be regarded as the best fighter. The primary trait of the "natural leader" was "gameness," which encompasses the notions of fearlessness and bravery. Demonstrating "gameness" is necessary to lead the gang and, in some instances, this trait can become exaggerated to exhibit "the dare-devil" type of personality. Leaders also must be quick and firm decision makers. A leader, put simply, is a man of action. The leader has the ability to justify a decision—right or wrong—to the whole group. In essence, Thrasher (1927) concluded that boys with the strongest physical capabilities and the most powerful imaginations proved to be the best leaders of Chicago gangs.

Whyte (1943) also looked at leaders in his study of an Italian-American neighborhood. Leaders formed the focal point of the group. Without them, the other members had no ability to coordinate common activities. The leader is more resourceful and independent than his followers. He is also confident, fair minded, respected, and skillful in particular areas.

Several decades later, Krisberg (1975) visited gang leadership in Philadelphia. The Urban Leadership Training Program was designed to redirect the activities of known gang leaders to more positive community roles. Not surprisingly, Krisberg (1975) found that leaders exerted the most influence on other gang members. They taught techniques of gang warfare and controlled group activities. Leaders also promoted gang ideology by preserving the gang's historical background and confirming its purpose. Without leaders providing this continuity and mentoring to the younger members, the gang could not continue to thrive.

GANG STRUCTURE AND ORGANIZATION

Research concentrating on the effects that gang leaders have upon their organizations is rare. Much of the work since Thrasher's (1927) exploratory study has either aspired to construct general theories of delinquency or has focused upon various consequences of the gang phenomenon.

There is a general debate in the literature concerning the extent to which gangs are structurally organized for the purpose of committing specific crimes. Writers in this area believe that gangs are simply a collectivity of youths without any unification of purpose and with no firm leadership structure (Hagedorn, 1988; Klein, 1971, 1995, 1998). Felson (1988) provides a particularly succinct overview that supports this conclusion by noting that the police tend to "overdo their coding of gang involvement." He refers to the "juvenile gang fallacy" as a "myth-busting device" to show that most gangs are loosely structured and unorganized groups of individuals.

One stream of debate contends that gangs are "loosely organized" with leaders having little or no formal control mechanisms over other gang members' activities (See Klein, 1995; Strodtbeck & Short, 1983). However, Bloch (1968) serves as a reminder that gang structure and the organization of individual gangs vary over time. Therefore, it should come as no surprise that another line of research shows that gangs are highly organized, with a clear delineation of leadership roles and organizational structure (Bloch & Neiderhoffer, 1958; Hagedorn, 1988; Huff, 1994, 1995; Keiser, 1979; Knox 1991; Krisberg 1975; Sanchez-Jankowski, 1991; Whyte, 1943). Although Hagedorn's (1988) research supported the notion that gangs exhibited little formal organization, he also found that the gangs in Milwaukee "prize strong leadership, and have no hostility to a hierarchical organization" (p. 15).

Picking up on Felson's (1988) observation, Monti (1994) examined the arguments about the importance of gang influence upon crime. He noted that while some crimes committed by gang members may not require or have official sanctions from the gang,

> some acts do require the collaboration of many, if not most, members of the gang. Furthermore, much is done with the tactic approval of the larger group, and other actions would not be initiated without it (Monti, 1994, p. 146).

Sanchez-Jankowski (1991) reported that gangs establish particular codes in order to maintain the leader's authority, legitimacy, and control. These rules enable the gang to cope with any leadership changes. National research on gangs has found that leaders and leadership roles vary significantly over time (Huff, 1995). What remains constant, however, is the fact that gangs do have, as part of their structure, a leadership dimension that remains steadfast in the organization.

Interestingly, very little research is devoted to examining the influence of a gang leader's offending on the crimes other gang members commit. One would think that the behavior of gang members would mirror that of their leaders. Shaw (1969, p. 87) explained that:

> [t]he criminal group has its heroes, its big shots, its prominent persons who have gained prestige and power in the delinquent world. Such persons are well known in the delinquency areas of the city and are often emulated by the younger members of different groups.

Some writers have suggested that gangs evolve into sophisticated profit-seeking entities. Knox (1991) found that some gangs perceive themselves to be types of organizations rather than gangs, as such. Some gangs are said to grow into highly organized groups with specific criminal agendas, such as Taylor's (1990) corporate gangs. Following along those same lines, Monti's (1994) research revealed that gang members sold drugs cooperatively and that some gangs specializing in drug dealing systematically recruited new members to support that function. Further, these highly organized gangs put a percentage of their profits away for a bail fund and to buy weapons.

Monti (1994, p. 115) argued "gangs may not cause crime in the sense that they brought lawlessness to an otherwise law-abiding community." Rather, what gangs do is to make more efficient and extensive those activities that are an accepted part of the area's unconventional or hidden economy. In this sense, gangs do make crime a more serious or pronounced part of the community's routine and its residents' habits, thereby implicating everyone in its activities. While not all gang members engage in organized criminal activities, enough of them do to cause considerable problems.

Clearly, only some, not all, gang members are involved in organized criminal activity. While the majority of Klein's (1971, 1995, 1998) extensive research depicts gangs as participating in a wide range of activity, his work with Maxson (1996) identified a type of gang structure, the specialty gang, as having a much more focused and purposive existence. These gangs are much less versatile in their offending behavior than other more traditionally structured gangs. It seems fair to say that discussions about the extent of gang involvement in crime and the degree of criminal organization simply reflect the extent to which these elements exist within gangs, rather than whether they exist at all.

GANGS IN COLUMBUS, OHIO

The city of Columbus began to experience increasing levels of violence and drug trafficking, clearly associated with youth gangs, during the mid-1980s. Although officials initially were extremely cautious to use the word "groups" rather than "gangs," they eventually switched and began referring to them as "gangs." Four main reasons accounted for this change. They include the more routine involvement in illegal activities, the more deliberate involvement in illegal activities, the greater tendency to claim "turf" (which initially meant localities but later included "markets"), and the identification of leaders. The recognition of a growing youth "group" problem led to the formation of a police juvenile task force in 1986. The task force eventually became a permanent gang unit within the Columbus Police Department (CPD).

The increase in gang activity in Columbus was traced back to the arrival of a gang member from the Los Angeles Crips. Interviews with older gang members revealed that this person helped introduce the gang mentality and operational skills into an economically deprived neighborhood within the city. Once it was known that the Crips were operating in Columbus, other smaller gangs began surfacing. At one point, rival gangs actually merged so they could combat the Crips more effectively in both violent and economic terms.

THE COLUMBUS GANG LEADERS STUDY

Preliminary interviews with members of the CPD Gang Unit suggested that each gang tended to specialize in its own areas of criminal behavior. Therefore, the decision was made to analyze the official arrest histories of Columbus gang leaders and hard-core members to determine whether such offense specialization existed. Other sources of data, such as school or court records, were not accessed for comparative analyses. It was felt that if these types of agencies were approached, the anonymity of the research subject might be jeopardized. Additionally, the risk of identifying these individuals as being gang-affiliated in situations where that information might not have been known far outweighed any potential benefit from the data collected.

For the purposes of this study, a "leader" is a person who plays a prominent role and is instrumental in planning the agenda of the gang. "Hard-core" members are those individuals who are actively and exclusively committed to the gang and its activities. Since Huff (1995) had discovered that the positions of leaders and hard-core members seemed fluid and shifted continuously, it was agreed that hard-core members should be included along with leaders in the study group. As a result, the study included the "kingpins" (chief of operations) of the individual gangs and other members who were likely, at one time or another, to have participated in key leadership roles.

SAMPLING PROCEDURE

Sampling involved a two-step process. The first effort required having two former members of the CPD Gang Unit compile a list of all persons known to be involved in local gang activity. While the exact number of individuals active in gangs is not known, it was estimated that the number was well above 900 participants. This procedure resulted in the identification of 176 gang members.

The second step called for the submission of this list to a panel of three police officers who had considerable expertise regarding gangs in the Columbus area. The task for these experts was to identify gang members who exhibited leadership responsibilities and anyone else who had made leadership contributions.

Each officer reviewed the list of 176 names and identified whom they thought were gang leaders. In addition, each expert was asked to assess how "exclusively committed" or "hard-core" each nonleader was in 1986. Panel members distinguished known leaders from hard-core members and associates. An associate was defined as someone who was marginal to the operational functions of the gang. In this assessment, a score of "A" was assigned to "very hard-core" gang members and a "B" to subjects who were "less hard-core."

After each expert independently completed this assessment, the subjects' names were placed on a leader list. Names which received a score of "B" from all three experts ($n = 45$) were eliminated from the pool of prospective research participants, leaving a new total of 131 names for continued review. Of the 131 remaining names, 67 were agreed to be leaders of gangs. Seven received "AAA" ratings; 16 captured "AA" ratings; and 30 were given a rating of "A." Eleven individuals were rated as inactive.

Following this exercise, the panel members met to review the 30 names that had captured a single "A" rating. The ensuing discussion revealed that seven of the 30 had sufficient involvement in gang activities during 1986 to merit inclusion in the final pool. The remaining names were added to the "inactive group."

In sum, the assessment identified 67 persons identified as leaders. Seven subjects were classified as "AAA," 16 as "AA," 7 as "A," and 34 were rated as inactive. All those considered to be inactive in gangs during 1986 were then eliminated from this list. The final roster identified 97 young men, purported to have leadership or hard-core member standing, who played instrumental roles in the formation and continuation of gang activities from 1986 to 1992.

THE DATA

Only 83 of the 97 subjects had formal adult arrest records and criminal histories were obtained for each of them. The remaining 14 had juvenile arrests, but this information was restricted and could not be secured for the present study. The CPD generated these offense histories by accessing local crime records, as well as computerized records maintained by the State of Ohio and the Federal Bureau of Investigation.

Given the access to these inclusive systems, the completeness of reported criminal arrests is virtually assured. However, it is appropriate at this point to highlight some limitations with the sample used for this study. First, it was chosen by law enforcement officials. Consequently, there may be some unknown elements of bias within the sampling procedure. Second, others who have had dealings with gangs were not asked for their input as to who they thought were instrumental in the planning and organizing of gang activities. Finally, the information generated from this work may be limited in its usefulness to just the Midwest region. Without similar studies in other geographical areas, it would be imprudent to extend the results to other areas.

It is important to note that official arrest data are based only on those offenses known to law enforcement officials and that these figures may represent, to some degree, particular enforcement practices in Columbus. In addition, incidents the authorities did not know about or any incidents that officials disposed of informally are not tabulated. Although official "rap sheets" may not lend an accurate representation of crime in a given area (Geerken, 1994), they can provide a useful indication of patterns and trends of criminal careers (DeLisi, 2001).

The vast majority of gangs in the Columbus area in 1986 were comprised of black members. As such, the sample represented not only the membership of the gangs, but also those persons in command at that time. All the members of the sample were black males.

Records were collected from the time of first arrest up to and including January 26, 1994. The mean age of the 83 leaders at the time of the study was 27, with a range from 22 to 33. The mean age at the time of first arrest was 21.3 years. The youngest recorded age at first arrest was 18 and the oldest was 30.

FINDINGS

Gang leaders committed 78 different types of crimes during this time period for a total of 834 offenses. As Table 1 shows, the largest arrest category is crimes of violence (307 with a mean of 3.70 per person), which accounted for 36.8% of all the arrests. Most of these arrests are for assault ($n = 100$). Property offenses are the second largest category with gang leaders being arrested 239 times (28.7% of the total) for an average of 2.88 arrests. Drug offenses (154 total arrests) rank third out of the five categories. Overall, the majority of arrests (73.3%) are for non-index crimes.

TABLE 1
Arrest Histories of Columbus Gang Leaders, 1980-1994

Offense Type	f	%	Mean
Violent	307	36.8	3.70
Property	239	28.7	2.88
Drugs	154	18.5	1.85
Weapons	54	6.5	0.65
Other	80	9.6	0.96
Total	834	100.1	10.05

Table 2 presents the affiliation of gang leaders and their arrest distributions. One can view this information as a criminal profile for each major gang as represented by leaders' arrests. The Crips appear to be responsible for more crimes of violence than other Columbus gangs. One-third of all violent arrests involved Crips leaders. The Enforcers at 26% are a close second. Turning to property crime, the Freeze Crew and Crip leaders are the most frequently arrested. The Freeze Crew accounts for 58 (or 37.7%) of the 154 drug arrests. Their average of 2.90 drug arrests per leader is double the mean for the entire sample (1.85). Together, leaders of the Freeze Crew and the Crips account for over 60% of all weapons arrests.

TABLE 2
Gang Leader Affiliations by Arrest Histories, 1980-1994

Gang Affiliation	Number of Leaders	Arrests	Percentage Distribution of Arrests				
			Violent	Property	Drugs	Weapons	Other
Crips	27	235	32%	29%	21%	32%	21%
Dozen Cousins	10	107	11	7	20	19	21
East Columbus Assassins	7	65	9	8	4	6	13
Enforcers	14	154	26	13	12	15	20
Freeze Crew	20	237	20	37	38	28	18
Other	5	36	3	5	6	2	6
Total	83	834	101%	99%	101%	102%	99%
n			307	239	154	54	80

$\chi^2 = 71.916$, $df = 20$, $p < .001$

In essence, these data show that some gangs specialize in certain types of offending. Insofar as arrest data serve as a "proxy" for criminal behavior, the differences between the gangs are statistically significant ($\chi^2 = 71.916$, $df = 20$, $p < .001$). Therefore, it appears that further examination of gang organizational specialization or "niche crime" is warranted.

DISCUSSION

As with legitimate organizations, positions of leadership are essential for the continued operation and survival of illegitimate enterprises. The arrest patterns of gang leaders in Columbus, Ohio, demonstrate a tendency to commit particular forms of criminal activity. It appears that these gangs are, to some degree, operating within their own crime niches. If this observation is correct, then one potential way to attack the business operations of these gangs is to disrupt the various markets for their offending. For example, if a gang specializes in the distribution of drugs, efforts must target the influx and sales of drugs in that region. Better still, officials might consider implementing market reduction programs to reduce offending opportunities (Sutton, 1998; Sutton & Schneider, 1999; Sutton, Schneider & Hetherington, 2001). The market reduction approach is an innovative strategy that refocuses policing efforts on the markets that drive criminal opportunities. Rather than targeting offenders, this approach identifies the underlying conditions (i.e., types of drugs in demand or property most often stolen) that motivate offenders to commit crime. In gang-suppression or reduction projects, it might be beneficial for practitioners to examine what criminal activities the gang is involved in and then design appropriate intervention measures for these offense-specific conditions.

It was something of a surprise to find that drug offenses ranked third at 18.5% of the arrests. Past research has emphasized the importance of the gang-drug connection (Curry & Decker, 1998; Hagedorn, 1988; Huff, 1995; Sanchez-Jankowski 1991). Therefore, one might have anticipated a higher percentage of drug-related arrests. However, the findings from the Columbus Gangs Study are in line with results from other recent studies. For example, Klein (1995, p. 126) argues that gang structures and organizations are unsuitable "for effective drug distribution." They simply lack the ability to relocate elsewhere for the purpose of selling drugs.

Weapons arrests seem disproportionately low in Columbus, especially given the number of gang members on the street and the apparent "gang requirement" that members carry firearms (Schneider, 1998). Given the surge in gang-related homicides, drive-by shootings, and other violence in the 1990s (Curry & Decker, 1998), it is somewhat of a surprise that there are not more arrests for weapons-related crimes. Overall, there are only 54 charges (6% of all arrests) filed for weapons-related crimes (0.65 per leader). One possibility is that hard-core members and leaders may appreciate the seriousness of violence and restrain themselves accordingly (Monti, 1994). Another potential explanation is that leaders have the luxury of ordering such activities and members in the lower rungs of the gangs carry out these actions.

The findings from this research suggest that gangs no longer fit the mass media's stereotype of semi-organized groups of young men. If further evidence is found to support this conclusion, new anti-gang policies will need to emerge. Rather than developing approaches designed to impede individuals from joining or maintaining their allegiance to the gang, efforts will need to be redirected at stopping the specialized organizational growth of these criminal enterprises. In addition, further research is needed to look into the particular activities which sustain the organizational life of a gang and how gangs provide impetus or support for criminal careers. More fully integrated strategies need to be developed to make gangs less attractive to young people, with an overall aim to reduce crime and criminality.

CONCLUSION

It appears that gangs are specializing in particular areas of criminal behavior and adapting to local demands for stolen property, drugs, or violence. One possible explanation for these arrest patterns is that the gangs have developed a certain degree of organization, indicating their ability to create or adapt to "market" niches. If such is the case, then there is a need to examine existing anti-gang policies. Policies that are directed at organizational practices, rather than individual members, may be more effective. At the very least, policies directed at both organizations and individuals may be warranted.

REFERENCES

Barnard, C. (1938). *The function of the executive*. Cambridge, MA: Harvard University Press.

Bennis, W. G. (1959). Leadership theory and administrative behavior. *Administrative Science Quarterly, 4*, 259-301.

Bloch, H., & Niederhoffer, A. (1958). *The gang: A study in adolescent behavior*. New York: Philosophical Press.

Bloch, H., & Niederhoffer, A. (1968). Leadership and the power situation. In J. F. Short (Ed.), *Gang delinquency and delinquent subcultures*. New York: Harper & Row.

Bonn, R. L. (1984). *Criminology*. New York: McGraw-Hill.

Coffin, T. E. (1944). A three-component theory of leadership. *Journal of Abnormal Social Psychology, 39*, 63-83.

Curry, G. D., & Decker, S. H. (1998). *Confronting gangs: Crime and community*. Los Angeles, CA: Roxbury Publishing Co.

Davis, K. (1951). Learning to live with informal groups. *Advanced Management, 16*, 17-19.

Davis, K. (1977). *Human behavior at work* (5th ed.). New York: McGraw-Hill.

DeLisi, M. (2001). Extreme career criminals. *American Journal of Criminal Justice, 25*, 239-252.

Felson, M. (1998). *Crime and everyday life* (2nd ed.). City, CA: Pine Forge Press.

Geerken, M. R. (1994). Rap sheets in criminological research: Considerations and caveats. *Journal of Quantitative Criminology, 10*, 3-21.

Gross, E. (1961). Dimensions of leadership. *Personnel and Guidance Journal, 40*, 213-218.

Hagedorn, J. M. (1988). *People and folks*. Chicago, IL: Lake View Press.

Hellriegel, D., Slocum, J. W., Jr., & Woodman, R. W. (1983). *Organizational behavior* (3rd ed.). St Paul, MN: West.

Huff, C. R. (1994). *Youth gangs and drugs*. Columbus, OH: Ohio Office of Criminal Justice Services.

Huff, C. R. (1995). *Criminal behavior of youth gangs*. Washington, DC: National Institute of Justice.

Kast, F. E., & Rosenzweig, J. E. (1970). *Organization and management: A systems approach*. New York: McGraw-Hill.

Katz, D., & Kahn, R. (1978). *The social psychology of organizations* (2nd ed.). New York: John Wiley and Sons.

Keiser, R. L. (1979). *The vicelords: Warriors of the streets*. New York: Holt, Rinehart, & Winston.

Klein, M. W. (1971). *Street gangs and street workers*. Englewood Cliffs, NJ: Prentice-Hall.

Klein, M. W. (1995). *The American street gang: Its nature, prevalence, and control*. New York: Oxford University Press.

Klein, M. W. (1998). Street gangs. In M. Tonry (Ed.), *The handbook of crime and punishment*, (pp. 111-131). New York: Oxford University Press.

Klein, M. W., & Maxson, C. L. (1996). *Gang structures, crime patterns, and police responses.* Los Angeles, CA: University of Southern California, Social Science Institute.

Knox, G. W. (1991). *An introduction to gangs.* Berrin Springs, MI: Vande Vere Publishing.

Krisberg, B. (1975). *The gang and the community.* Berkeley: University of California.

Marsh, P. E., & Campbell, A. (1978, October 19). The sex boys on their own turf. *New Society, 46*(837), pp. 133-135.

Monti, D. J. (1994). *Wannabie gangs in suburbs and schools.* Cambridge, MA: Blackwell.

Sanchez-Jankowski, M. (1991). *Islands in the street: Gangs and American urban society.* Berkeley: University of California Press.

Schneider, J. L. (1998). Following the leaders: Patterns of arrests among gang leaders. *The Police Chief, 65*(4), 40-50.

Shaw, C. (1969). Juvenile delinquency: A group tradition. In J. F. Short (Ed.), *Gang delinquency and delinquent subcultures.* New York. Harper & Row.

Spergel, I. A. (1995). *The youth gang problem: A community approach.* New York: Oxford University Press.

Stodgill, R. M. (1974). *Handbook of leadership: A survey of the literature.* New York: Free Press.

Strodtbeck, F. L., & Short, J. F., Jr. (1983). The response of gang leaders to status threats: An observation on group process and delinquent behavior. *American Journal of Sociology, 68,* 571-578.

Sutton, M. (1998). *Handling stolen goods and theft: A market reduction approach.* Home Office Research Study 178. London: Home Office.

Sutton, M., & Schneider. J. L. (1999). Theft, stolen goods, and the market reduction approach: Operation radium and operation heat. In S. Brito & T. Allen (Eds.), *Problem-oriented-policing: Crime-specific problems critical issues and making POP work* (pp. 27-61). Washington, DC: Police Executive Research Forum.

Sutton, M., Schneider, J., & Hetherington, S. (2001). Tackling theft with the market reduction approach. *Crime reduction research series paper 8.* London: Research and Statistics Directorate, Policing and Reducing Crime Unit, Home Office.

Tannenbaum, R. & Massarik, F. (1957). Leadership: A frame of reference. *Management Science,* 4, 1-19.

Taylor, C. S. (1990). *Dangerous society.* East Langsing, MI: Michigan State University Press.

Thrasher, F. M. (1927). *The gang: A study of 1,313 gangs in Chicago.* Chicago: University of Chicago Press.

Whyte, W. F. (1943). *Street corner society.* Chicago: University of Chicago Press.

[16]

Gangs, gang homicides, and gang loyalty: Organized crimes or disorganized criminals

Scott H. Decker*, G. David Curry

527 Lucas Hall, Department of Criminology and Criminal Justice, University of Missouri-St. Louis, 8001 Natural Bridge Road, St. Louis, MO 63121-4499, USA

Abstract

Gang members contribute disproportionately to homicide. This article examines gang homicide during its peak in the mid-1990s in St. Louis, a city with high homicide rates and large gang problems. The article addresses two related questions, the differences between gang and non-gang homicides, and the social organization of gang homicide. Marked differences between gang and non-gang homicides were found. These differences centered primarily on guns and the similarity of victim and offender characteristics. Gang homicides most often occurred within gang factions rather than between factions. Gangs were unable to organize homicides in an effective manner, which reflected the disorganized character of gangs and the neighborhoods in which they reside. The findings of this article raised important questions about the cohesiveness of gangs. © 2002 Elsevier Science Ltd. All rights reserved.

Introduction

> ... my boy Victor got shot a while, well not even a while back. It hurt me so bad because this is by another Crip. They, they had, they was beefin' about something that happen between them. So Loc Man shot Victor so Victor's set went shootin' at Loc Man. I mean, and it was Crip against Crip and that hurt me so bad. I was like, "It ain't even supposed to be like this." Columbus (OH) gang member

Gang members account for a disproportionate amount of violence. That fact is well known, but the way that gang violence is organized is not well understood. As the quote above illustrates, some gang violence occurs within gangs, rather than between

* Corresponding author. Tel.: +1-314-516-5038; fax: +1-314-516-5048.
E-mail address: c1911@umsl.edu (S.H. Decker).

rival gangs. This is inconsistent with the dominant popular and law enforcement image of gangs as oppositional groups whose organizational structure leads them to violence with rivals. In addition, the dominant law enforcement view of gangs as well-organized groups suggests that most gang violence occurs between rivals rather than among members of the same gang grouping (Conly, 1993; Jackson & McBride, 1985).

Despite considerable attention to the study of gang crime, the analysis of gang homicide in particular and gang violence in general has not paid attention to the role of gang rivalries in homicide. That is, the extant research literature has largely ignored the issue of whether gang violence occurs within or between gangs. The implications of such a study are important, as they have a direct bearing on the role of the organizational structure of gangs. This study used the results of an analysis of gang homicides to provide insight into the role of one aspect of gang organization—gang cohesion and solidarity—on gang homicides.

344   S.H. Decker, G.D. Curry / Journal of Criminal Justice 30 (2002) 343–352

The involvement of gang members in violence has been a topic of concern since Thrasher (1927). Contemporary research has emphasized the role of firearms (Bjerregaard & Lizotte, 1995; Kennedy, Braga, & Peihl, 1997), threat and contagion (Decker, 1996), the spatial concentration of gang violence (Block, 1991, 1996; Cohen & Tita, 1999; Kennedy et al., 1997; Rosenfeld, Bray, & Egley, 1999), and the role of drugs (Block, 1996; Kennedy et al., 1997; Klein & Maxson, 1994) in gang violence.

One of the elements central to the discussion of gang violence is defining what counts as a gang homicide. This significance of definitional issues is demonstrated by a comparison of Chicago and Los Angeles Police Department definitions of gang crimes. In Chicago, a crime must be motivated by gang concerns to be counted as a gang crime. This definition is more strict than that used in Los Angeles, resulting in far fewer "gang" crimes. For Los Angeles, a gang crime includes a wider range of behavior. This more permissive definition includes all crimes that are "gang related"; that is, any crime is counted as a gang crime if it involves a gang member or a gang motive. The differences were made clear by the Maxson and Klein (1990) analysis, which applied the two definitions to Los Angeles homicides. They found that the Los Angeles definition yielded twice as many gang crimes as did the Chicago definition, underscoring the salience of definitions for understanding the problem of gang homicide.

One goal of research was to ask increasingly specific questions made possible by more sophisticated measurement, better data, improved analysis tools, or some combination of the three. This research expanded the understanding of gang violence specifically, and gang homicide more broadly, by conducting a microanalysis of gang homicides that included the gang affiliation—if any—of victims and perpetrators in St. Louis homicides for the years 1994–1996.[1] By knowing the gang affiliation of perpetrators and victims of homicide, one could speculate about the ability of the gang as an organization to control and target the behavior of its members.

St. Louis was labeled as an "emerging" gang city by Spergel and Curry (1993, p. 262) in the 1988 OJJDP National Youth Gang Survey. The term "emerging" was applied to cities that had developed gang problems since 1980. In contrast, the survey staff identified a set of cities with more long-term gang problems as "chronic." In addition to having identified gang problems prior to 1980, chronic cities had at least some gangs that were organized and engaged in serious criminal activities. As noted below, most research on gang homicide had been conducted in the cities that Spergel and Curry identified as chronic, particularly Los Angeles and Chicago. By examining gang homicides in a city where gang problems emerged in the late 1980s and became more lethal in the 1990s, patterns of gang homicide that might have been similar to or different from those observed in chronic gang cities could be identified.

The goal of this article is to examine the nature of gang homicides in an emerging gang city to determine how well violence is organized within gangs. The hypothesis that guides this analysis is that well-organized gangs (e.g., groups that function in corporate-like fashion) will engage in relatively few acts of homicide against their own members, preserving group solidarity and cohesion. For such groups, cohesion, solidarity, and leadership mitigate against internecine violence. Correspondingly, gangs with low levels of internal organization are expected to experience higher levels of intragang homicide. It is likely that the inability of these groups to control the behavior of their members may reflect a lower level of organization and control. The results of this analysis have important implications for the understanding of the nature of gang organization particularly for understanding the nature of gang crime.

Gang violence and homicide

The significance of gang homicide

It is important to understand gang homicide for a number of reasons. First, the precipitous increase in homicides in urban America in the early 1990s occurred at about the same time as the increase in the number of gangs, gang members, and gang-related crimes (Klein, 1995; Miller, 2001). Separating the contribution of gangs to the overall increase in homicide was an important contribution to our understanding of the rise in homicides. In this context, gang homicides were important because they might spark corresponding increases in violence, particularly retaliatory violence. Second, and closely related, was the apparent contribution of the drug–gun-diffusion process (Blumstein, 1995; Blumstein & Wallman, 2000) to the growth in homicide, and the obvious links to gangs. Blumstein and Wallman specified a temporal model in which relatively disorganized street drug sales—primarily crack cocaine—generated the need for protection in the form of guns. As more guns were drawn to urban drug markets, they eventually became diffused throughout the youthful population and contributed to the sudden spike in youth homicide recorded between 1990 and 1994. Despite debate about the extent to which gangs control drug markets, the extensive participation of gang members in drug sales has been well documented by a number of observers (Decker & Van Winkle, 1996; Fagan, 1989;

S.H. Decker, G.D. Curry / Journal of Criminal Justice 30 (2002) 343–352   345

Hagedorn, 1994; Maxson & Klein, 1985; Padilla, 1992; Vigil, 1988). Thus, gangs might play an important role in facilitating drug sales and the concomitant need for protection. A final reason to examine gang homicide as a separate category of fatalities was the proportion of fatal events that such offenses represented. In Chicago (Block, 1996), gang-motivated homicides represented approximately one-quarter of all homicides between 1993 and 1995, and gang-motivated homicides accounted for 45 percent of all homicides in Los Angeles County between 1994 and 1995 (Maxson, 1999). Clearly, gang homicides had contributed disproportionately to the dramatic increases in homicide recorded during the early 1990s. Yet, it was often difficult to disentangle gang homicides from the modal category of all homicides, those in which young, minority males were killed by firearms. In addition, the nature of gang affiliation might provide important insights about the extent to which gang homicides involved rivals or non-gang members.

Characteristics of gang homicide

It is important to understand why gang homicide should be studied as a special subcategory of homicides. Gang homicides can be distinguished from other homicides by virtue of a number of characteristics. These characteristics include: (1) spatial concentration; (2) weapon use; (3) race of victim and perpetrator; (4) location; (5) drug involvement; (6) age; (7) sex; and (8) victim–offender relationship.

Unlike Los Angeles and Chicago, Boston was not a chronic gang city. The findings regarding gang homicides in Boston (Kennedy et al., 1997), however, were consistent with those reported by Block for Chicago and Maxson (1999) for Los Angeles. Kennedy et al. (1997) reported an especially strong spatial concentration among gang homicides. These events disproportionately involved gun assaults, weapons, and drugs. This finding was similar to that reported by Rosenfeld et al. (1999) for St. Louis, as well as by Cohen, Cork, Engberg, and Tita (1998) and Cohen and Tita (1999). The correspondence across chronic and emerging gang cities suggested that a similar underlying process was at work in these cities, regardless of gang status. While these studies did not represent the nation, their consistency was rather striking. The role of firearms in gang-related homicides had been documented for a number of other cities (Bjerregaard & Lizotte, 1995; Decker, Pennell, & Caldwell, 1996) and remained one of the strongest correlates of gang homicide.

Maxson, Gordon, and Klein (1985) examined over 700 homicides from the Los Angeles Sheriff and Police departments between 1978 and 1982. They found that gang homicides were more likely

to occur between members of the same ethnic group and involve younger offenders and victims than non-gang homicides. In addition, gang homicides were more likely to have multiple participants, occur on the street, and involved the use of automobiles. Perhaps the most prominent feature of gang homicides, however, was the use of firearms. Gang homicides were significantly more likely to involve the use of firearms than other homicides, perhaps the most important finding from their research.

Chicago, another "chronic" gang city with serious levels of gang violence, had also been the site of research on gang homicides. Carolyn Block had tracked the pattern of homicides in Chicago over the last thirty years, documenting and examining the correlates of such events. Her examination of gang homicides (1991) revealed a pattern not dissimilar from that reported by Maxson et al. in Los Angeles. Specifically, Block (1991, 1996) found that gang homicides had a strong spatial concentration, and that the risk of being a victim or perpetrator peaked between the ages of fifteen and nineteen. The Chicago homicide data supported the conclusion that most gang-related homicides involved the use of firearms. Finally, Block reported that intragang violence was more common than might be expected. This finding was noteworthy, as most gang research (Maxson, 1999) reported a strong intergang character to gang violence. This contrast provided the central focus for the current analysis.

Theories of gang homicide

Despite the level of gang homicide, there have been few attempts to develop theoretical explanations for this behavior. The dominant explanations have followed two distinct approaches: (1) community explanations and (2) explanations that emphasize the role of collective behavior. Explanations based on community characteristics pointed to the role of community structure and other social correlates, including correlates of community social control, in the generation of patterns and trends in homicide. Those explanations that emphasize collective behavior pointed to the role of social processes such as retaliation. The former approach emphasized the spatial distribution of individual and neighborhood characteristics, while the latter highlighted dynamic social processes.

Curry and Spergel (1988) provided a community explanation for gang homicide. They examined both homicide and gang delinquency among Latinos and African Americans in Chicago. They concluded that gang homicides had a significantly different ecological pattern than did non-gang homicides. In addition, Curry and Spergel (1988) concluded that gang

346 *S.H. Decker, G.D. Curry / Journal of Criminal Justice 30 (2002) 343–352*

homicides conformed to classic models of social disorganization and poverty. They argued that viewing gang groups as a function of mobility patterns was a productive conceptual means of understanding gang homicides. The strong spatial concentration of gang homicides in neighborhoods characterized by poverty and social change was a consistent theme throughout the literature (Block, 1991; Kennedy et al., 1997; Wilson, 1987).

Decker (1996) emphasized the role of collective behavior in explaining gang violence, especially the spikes in violence that were observed over time. Decker argued that "threat" played a central role in the explanation of gang homicides, especially the retaliatory character of many gang homicides. This perspective grew from the work of Short (1989), who identified a process by which gang violence could be seen as a group phenomenon rather than acts of individuals. From this perspective, gang violence could escalate rapidly, as one event precipitated another. Such an approach emphasized the dynamic social processes that resembled collective behavior among informal groups and led to retaliatory violence between gangs and gang members.

Klein and Maxson (1987, p. 219) and Maxson (1999) provided support for the "escalation hypothesis." From this perspective, gang violence could best be understood as a series of reciprocal actions between rival gangs. This reciprocity was largely a function of the rivalries that existed between gangs. Such rivalries were the consequence of a number of factors (drug turf, neighborhood dominance, symbolic ascendance, etc.) that over time were sublimated to the more immediate need to dominate turf, a rival, or both. Klein and Maxson also reported that gangs had weak internal structures and generate little cohesion among members. As such, they were generally ineffective mechanisms for generating compliance among members. It should be noted that these findings were drawn from a chronic gang city, Los Angeles.

Taken together, these studies suggested that gangs were not well organized and had weak control over their members, and that rivalries could lead to violence within and between gangs. In addition, these studies pointed to the transitory nature of gang membership, reinforcing the notion that gangs might not be organizations capable of controlling the behavior of their members. This leds to the conclusion that gangs were not effective organizations for carrying out the mission of a group of individuals.

The conceptual argument

Typically, examinations of gang homicide in chronic cities have examined differences between gang and non-gang events. Such analyses highlighted the gang status of victims and perpetrators. In this analysis, a dimension in the social organization of gang homicide was considered, which had not been examined in prior research, the choice of victims by gang perpetrators and the gang status of offenders and victims.

Prior research on St. Louis gangs suggested a pattern of gang activity that was not organized (Decker, 1996; Decker & Van Winkle, 1996). As less organized groups, gangs in St. Louis were characterized as lacking effective leadership, with little internal discipline and few well-defined roles, and failed to invest profits from gang-related crime into the gang. This behavior was characterized as collective behavior, subject to the dynamics of contagion with considerable variation over time. It is not well understood at present whether gang homicides in an emerging gang city with loosely organized gangs are committed primarily against rival gang members, against gang members more generally (including members of one's own gang), or against a variety of individuals, both gang and non-gang members.

Two specific questions formed the basis of this analysis. First, the extent to which gang homicides shared characteristics with other "youth homicides" was examined. Here, the correlates of gang homicides were compared with other youth homicides. This was important as a premise to the argument that gang homicides were indeed different from other forms of homicide, particularly youth homicide. Next, the social organization of gang homicide was analyzed. Four categories of gang homicide framed this part of the analysis: (1) homicides committed by members of one gang against members of rival gangs; (2) homicides committed by members of one gang against members of their own or allied gangs; (3) homicides committed by gang members against non-gang members; and (4) homicides committed by non-gang members against gang members.

The implications of such an analysis were important to understanding the variation in urban street gangs specifically, and patterns of youth violence more generally. A strong pattern of gang homicides between rival groups indicated that the divisions between gangs were quite distinct and provided a potent mechanism for governing the behavior of gang members. Such a pattern would strengthen the argument that the organizational structure of the gang was effective in generating loyalty and creating discipline among its members. When members of the same gang kill each other or their allies, such a pattern indicated far different things about the nature of gang organization, loyalties, and discipline within the gang. If the perpetrators of gang homicides committed their offenses against a broader range of individuals, including members of their own gang, it was

S.H. Decker, G.D. Curry / Journal of Criminal Justice 30 (2002) 343–352 347

more difficult to conclude that the gang effectively controlled the behavior of its members. A pattern in which non-gang members were chosen as victims, or in which gang members were killed by non-gang members, suggested that gang homicide, as a special category of offenses, did not have as much theoretical or operational validity in cities where gangs and gang membership were not especially stable for any length of time.

The conceptualization of gangs as groups occupying particular locations in a socially evolving environment found support in the approach of environmental ecology (Vila, 1994). Gang problems in St. Louis emerged in the late 1980s. In that period, gangs often emerged and developed in response to neighborhood rivals, typically based on a collective awareness of other developing gangs. This led field researchers (Decker & Van Winkle, 1996) to identify perceived "threat" from other gangs as the key element in gang emergence and expansion in St. Louis. Members were drawn to gangs by their individual-level perceptions of threat from other gangs, just as gangs as organizations used conflict and the potential for intergang violence as principles around which to organize and recruit. This emergence was compatible with the view of gangs as loosely organized groups with shifting leadership, loyalty, and membership. Gangs formed and grew in response to collective threats of violence from other gangs. It was little wonder that researchers had found that violence, in thought and deed, pervaded almost every aspect of gang activity (Decker, 1996).

It was important to understand organizations such as gangs in the context of their environments, particularly in the amount and nature of resources that could be collectively mobilized by such organizations. Levels of organization within communities themselves played a special part (Bursik & Grasmick, 1993) in the emergence and nature of gangs and gang violence. The presence of gangs in neighborhoods was associated with weak network ties, either among individual residents or between residents and institutions. Especially noteworthy among youths who became involved in gangs were deficits in social capital (Coleman, 1988; Decker & Van Winkle, 1996; Short, 1990). This lack of social capital was linked to the well-documented marginality of gang members (Hagedorn, 1998; Vigil, 1988) and their inability to access the resources and relationships available to them. Gangs represented collective responses to perceived threats and were organizationally infused with the capacity to engage in violence, where there was already a deficit of personal and collective resources to develop social structure and resolve conflicts in a nonlethal manner. These deficits reflected the environment in which most urban gang members found themselves, poor underclass neighborhoods. The objective character-

istics of such neighborhoods accounted for the loose, fluid organization of gangs reported by most researchers (Hagedorn, 1998; Klein, 1995; Spergel, 1995). A community foundation of weak social structure should correspond to comparably weak correlations between stated organizational goals and outcomes among groups in such communities, particularly groups with little social capital. In the context of the gang and gang violence, such actions might not reflect stated group goals—such as the protection of and loyalty to the group—and would often occur within the gang and external to the gang, as well as between rival gang groups. Such a perspective was consistent with the dynamic and conflict-ridden nature of urban life for many of the individuals who join gangs and might be involved in a broad pattern of offending. In short, it was expected that disorganized communities would produce disorganized behavior among the members of those communities, particularly the adolescents of those communities.

In this research, the homicide event was used as the unit of analysis. Following the advice of James F. Short (1998), a measure of the gang as a group was used: the gang affiliation of victims or perpetrators in gang homicides. This theoretical and methodological commitment was particularly relevant in St. Louis, where the universal cultural currency of gangs as collective activity was the conflict between Crips and Bloods. An enmity borrowed from California gangs, either through migration or media, the Crips-versus-Bloods distinction provided a special vitality to accounts offered by St. Louis gang members describing their commitments, rivalries, and behavior (Decker & Van Winkle, 1996). Though the declaration of hostility to the opposing faction was ubiquitous among gang members of both Crip and Blood gangs, if gang structures were weak and ineffective mechanisms for insuring the compliance of their members, the outcomes of gang violence might be quite different. Characterized by low social capital and organizations with weak ties to social institutions, gangs appeared to be ineffective mechanisms for controlling the most fundamental behavior of their members—violence.

Data and methods

St. Louis was an appropriate site for the current analysis. It was a city that experienced high rates of violent crime, consistently ranking among the U.S. cities with the five highest rates of homicide and robbery. For example, in 1993, the city of St. Louis recorded a total of 261 homicides resulting in a homicide rate just under seventy per 100,000 citizens, compared to the U.S. rate of just over nine per

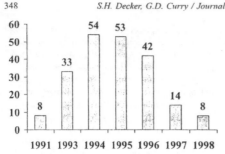

Fig. 1. Gang-related homicides in St. Louis for selected years.

100,000. Since St. Louis is a quite compact city, comprising only sixty-one square miles, it therefore intensified the spatial concentration of the violent crime problem. The city had experienced many of the conditions common to Midwest industrial cities, a fleeing middle class, eroding tax base, declining employment in the industrial sector, and substantial population loss. Law enforcement surveys indicated that there were approximately 33 gangs and 1,300 gang members in 1991 (Curry, Ball, & Fox, 1994) and 70 gangs and 4,000 gang members in 1997 (National Youth Gang Center, 1999).

The data for this study were drawn from the case files of the St. Louis Metropolitan Police Department Homicide Division and verified with the Gang Intelligence Unit that originated in 1989. Units within law enforcement agencies are always subject to variations in crime problems and resources dedicated in response to the assessments of such problems, as well as the transfer or retirement of key personnel. Details on victim–offender relationships and demographics were available in the Homicide Division's case records. The University of Missouri-St. Louis Homicide Project had converted the Homicide Division's records from 1970 to present into a computerized data set. One variable in that data set was whether or not the homicide was "gang related." The Homicide Division did not record the specific gang affiliation of offenders or victims. That was available from the Gang Intelligence Unit.

The analysis proceeded in several steps. First, the basic trend in gang homicides in the 1990s in St. Louis was reviewed. Following that, gang and non-gang homicides for the years 1994–1996 were examined in greater detail using the data from the Homicide Division. These years were selected for two reasons. First, these were the peak years of gang-related homicide in St. Louis, and second, these were the years for which both Homicide Division and Gang Intelligence Unit data on homicides were available.[2] Three primary demographic factors dominated the distinction between gang and non-gang

homicides. These were the race, age, and sex of victims and offenders. Next, comparisons between gang-related and non-gang homicides were made, controlling for age, sex, and race of offenders. This analysis allowed the identification of those factors that in addition to age, sex, and race of offenders distinguished gang from non-gang homicides. Specifically, age was examined within this diminished age range and the circumstances of gang and non-gang homicides including the method of inflicting death, location of homicide, whether or not it was drug related, and victim–offender relationship. Finally, using the offender–victim gang affiliation data from the Gang Intelligence Unit, this analysis examined the extent to which gang homicides involved rival gang members as perpetrators and victims, occurred between members of the same or allied gangs, or represented conflicts between gang members and non-gang members.

Findings

Gang homicide has become a significant problem in St. Louis. Following the pattern of many Midwest cities with an emerging gang problem, the early and mid-1990s was the period of most intense gang violence. This pattern is reflected in Fig. 1, which presents the number of gang-related homicides by year, and the fraction of city homicides accounted for by gang homicides for the years 1991 through 1998. As Figs. 1 and 2 depict, there was a rather dramatic growth in the number and fraction of gang-related homicides from 1991 to the peak year, 1994. In 1994, gang homicides achieved a brief stability, representing approximately one-quarter of all the homicides in the city. In 1997 and 1998, gang homicide declined somewhat more rapidly than the general decline in homicides.[3]

Table 1 compares gang and non-gang homicides as identified by the UMSL Homicide Project's data

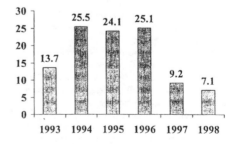

Fig. 2. Gang-related homicides as % of all homicides in St. Louis for selected years.

S.H. Decker, G.D. Curry / Journal of Criminal Justice 30 (2002) 343–352   349

Table 1
Gang versus non-gang homicides

| | Homicide type | | | | | |
| | Non-gang | | Gang | | | |
	n	%	n	%	Significance	Total n
Suspect: African American	394	90.8	77	100	.01	511
Victim: female	84	15.6	9	11.3	n.s.	617
Victim: White	82	15.3	1	1.3	.001	617
	Mean	n	Mean	n	Significance	Total n
Mean age of victim	31.9	534	22.7	80	0.001	614
Mean age of suspect	26.7	431	20.1	79	0.001	511
Mean number of suspects	1.4	432	1.5	79	n.s.	511

coded from the case files of the St. Louis Metropolitan Police Department Homicide Division. At first, a number of distinct differences appeared to exist. In gang homicides, the suspect and the victim were significantly more likely to be African Americans. Similarly, the offender and the victim were on the average younger than offenders and victims in non-gang homicides. All of the gang homicide suspects were males.

Since offenders in gang homicides were more likely to be African American, male, and younger, for the comparison group, gang and non-gang homicides in which the suspects were African American males under age twenty-five were chosen. The comparison of gang and non-gang homicides for this subset of all homicides are shown in Table 1.

Differences between the two types of homicides narrowed once this subset of homicides was examined, but statistically significant differences still remained. Non-gang homicide victims were significantly older. Though the difference narrowed considerably, gang homicide offenders were still younger than non-gang homicide offenders. There was a perfect correlation between the use of a gun and the classification of a homicide as gang related by the Gang Intelligence Unit. Gang homicide offenders and victims were slightly more likely to know one another. These characteristics underscored both the distinctive nature of gang homicide, as well as the fact that gang homicides shared many correlates with typical homicides in St. Louis: Both categories were dominated by young, African American males who killed their victims with guns. These data were consistent with the findings reported by Block in Chicago, Maxson and Klein in Los Angeles, and Kennedy et al. in Boston (Table 2).

The next issue examined in the analysis was a key for this research: the extent to which gang homicides occurred between rival gangs, within gangs or gang alliances, or involved non-gang members. In this analysis, the data on gang-related homicides provided by the St. Louis Police Department Gang Intelligence Unit were used to assess homicides. Gang affiliation of offender and victim were recorded for only seventy-two homicides in comparison to the seventy-seven gang-related homicides recorded from the Homicide Division data used in Table 1. In St. Louis in the mid-1990s, there were two main gang divisions, Bloods and Crips (Decker & Van Winkle, 1996), and Crip gang members outnumbered Blood members by at least a two-to-one margin. Here, data that reflected the extent to which gang homicides

Table 2
Homicide African American male suspects 25 and under

| | Non-gang | | Gang | | |
	Mean	n	Mean	n	Significance
Mean victim age	28.1	238	22.7	72	.001
Mean suspect age	20.3	239	19.2	72	.001
Mean number of suspects	1.6	239	1.5	72	n.s.
	n	%	n	%	Significance
Victim: female	30	12.0	8.0	11.7	n.s.
Location					
Inside	45	18.8	7	9.7	n.s.
Outside	134	56.1	38	52.8	
Automobile	51	21.3	20	27.8	
Other	9	3.80	7	9.72	
Weapon					
% Gun	208	89.3	70	100.0	.01
Victim–offender relationship					
% Stranger	52	26.8	13	22.4	.05
% Acquaintance	26	18.3	3	5.2	
% Intimate	110	56.7	34	58.6	
% Unknown	6	3.1	8	13.8	
Drug related	125	52.3	33	43.1	n.s.

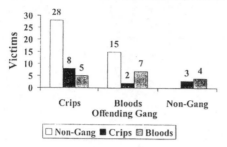

Fig. 3. Gang-related homicides by status of offender and victim 1994-1996 ($n = 72$).

occurred within Crip and Blood factions, between the two factions, or involved non-gang members were presented. The data to support this analysis are presented in Fig. 3.

Fig. 3 clearly reveals a picture of gang homicide at odds with the view that gangs control the pattern of violence that their members engage in. More Blood gang members (sixteen) were killed than Crips, and the largest portion of them (nine; 43.8 percent) were killed by non-gang members. Crips were more likely to be killed by other Crips than by members of their main rivals, the Bloods. This did not present a picture of gang homicide in which loyalty to fellow gang members controlled the choice of targets and victims for violence. Similar findings emerged for homicides involving Blood gang members. The majority of Crip gang victims (eight) or 61.5 percent of all Crip

victims, were killed by other Crips. Non-gang victims were more likely to be killed by Crips (65.1 percent) than by Bloods.

The picture offered by these data did not support a vision of gang homicide in which gangs deliberately targeted rival gang members, and offended in a highly patterned manner. Indeed, quite the opposite view was suggested by the data. The overwhelming majority of gang members were killed by non-gang members, and when gang members were killed by another gang member, it was most likely to be by someone from their own gang faction. These conclusions had implications for the way gang homicide was viewed, particularly in cities that had high rates of lethal violence. It might be that in such cities, gang status failed to add significantly to the risk for violence. Alternatively, gang membership might involve members in activities that placed them at risk for violent victimization as a consequence of activities related to gang membership, such as drug sales or other offenses, which were likely to draw the attention of active offenders in the neighborhood. The differences between gang and non-gang homicides are examined below.

The final part of the analysis looked only at gang-related homicides in order to compare the gang affiliations of offenders and victims. Table 3 shows the differences to be few across the four types of homicides considered. Non-gang members who killed gang members were significantly older than gang members who were offenders in gang-related homicides identified by the Gang Intelligence Unit.

Table 3
Gang homicide characteristics by gang affiliation

	Intrafaction	Interfaction	Attack on nonaffiliate	Attacked by nonaffiliate	Total	Significance
n	15	7	43	7	72	
Age of suspects	18.9	20.0	19.7	24.7	20.0	.05
Age of victims	20.6	23.8	23.8	19.9	22.7	n.s.
Number of suspects	1.60	1.29	1.56	1.00	1.49	n.s.
% Female (victims)	6.3	25.0	11.6	12.5	12.0	n.s.
Location						
% Inside	6.3	25.0	9.3	25.0	12.0	n.s.
% Outside	68.8	62.5	51.2	25.0	53.3	
% Automobile	18.8	12.5	30.2	37.5	26.7	
% Other location	6.3	0.0	9.3	12.5	8.0	
Weapon						
% Gun	100.0	100.0	97.6	87.5	97.3	n.s.
Victim-offender relationship						
% Stranger	0.0	20.0	34.3	0.0	22.4	n.s.
% Acquaintance	7.7	0.0	5.7	0.0	5.2	
% Intimate	61.5	40.0	54.3	100.0	58.6	
% Unknown	30.8	40.0	5.7	0.0	13.8	
Drug-related incident	18.8	37.5	58.1	62.5	48.0	.05

S.H. Decker, G.D. Curry / Journal of Criminal Justice 30 (2002) 343–352   351

Intrafaction gang killings were more likely to involve male offenders while females were more likely to be killed in interfactional incidents. Neither of the two types of homicides that involved gang members as offenders and victims were as likely to be classified as drug related by the Homicide Unit of the St. Louis Police Department as the homicides that involved violence between gang members and nonmembers. This could be interpreted to indicate that there was not as much overlap between gang conflicts and drug conflicts as some researchers have suggested. At least, this was the case in St. Louis.

Discussion

Cloward and Ohlin (1960) argued that gangs lack the structure and corporate capability to coordinate activities effectively. This observation had not been effectively challenged by empirical research in the forty years since it was made. The research presented here supports that conclusion, despite claims about more organized gangs. Gangs have been characterized in the research literature (Klein, 1995) as loosely organized confederations that coalesce irregularly over issues that emerge and vanish from the streets. That patterns of gang violence reflect the structural characteristics of gang membership is only logical.

Hagedorn (1998) concluded that the escalation of gun ownership in gang neighborhoods had implications that extended far beyond drug sales. As such, it was reasonable to expect that the presence of firearms led to lethal violence in circumstances that might otherwise have been settled with less-than-lethal means (Cook, 1991). As Rosenfeld et al. (1999) pointed out, gang members were involved in a variety of crimes that were not motivated by membership, but rather reflected the concerns and activities of young, urban offenders. The recent review of gang homicide research by Maxson (1999) found that the correlates of gang and non-gang homicides had narrowed over time. Taken together, this research provided support for the conclusions regarding the corporate structure and control of gang violence. To put a fine point on these findings, individuals at risk for violence were likely to engage in violence. When such individuals were gang members, that risk was elevated.

The fact that St. Louis gang members committed homicides within their own gang affiliation lends credibility to the view that gangs lack the characteristics of effective social organizations. Gang members were more likely than others to have access to the means of inflicting lethal violence, motives for doing so, and the opportunities to commit homicides. The fact that members of their own gang were most often the victims of their violence reflects the lack of

corporate control, restrictions of geography and age, and proximal nature of most youthful conflict.

Notes

1. While many studies have examined patterns in gang homicide, few have examined the micro-characteristics of homicides.

2. The Gang Unit participated in the U.S. DOJ Anti-Gang Initiative in 1994–1997.

3. The numbers of gang-related homicides for years 1991, 1993, 1997, and 1998 used to construct Figs. 1 and 2 were taken from St. Louis Police Department responses to national gang surveys of law enforcement agencies (Curry, Ball, & Decker, 1996; Curry et al., 1994; National Youth Gang Center, 1999).

Acknowledgments

We gratefully acknowledge the cooperation of the St. Louis Metropolitan Police Department for providing the data for this study. Sergeants Terry Sloan, Gary Hill, and Robert Ogilve are to be commended for their work in this regard, as is the Director of Planning, Larry Pattison. We also acknowledge our colleague, Jody Miller, for her insightful contributions to this article. Her contributions have meant more to us than she knows. This project was supported in part by funding by the Office of Community Oriented Policing Anti-Gang Initiative. The opinions expressed here are those of the authors and are not necessarily those of the funding or cooperating agencies.

References

Bjerregaard, B., & Lizotte, A. J. (1995). Gun ownership and gang membership. *Journal of Criminal Law and Criminology, 86,* 37–57.

Block, C. R. (1991). Gang homicide in Chicago: patterns over time, area of city, and type of victim. Presented to the Midwestern Criminal Justice Association. Chicago, Illinois.

Block, C. R. (1996). *Street gangs and crime. Research bulletin.* Chicago, IL: Illinois Criminal Justice Information Authority.

Blumstein, A. (1995). Youth violence, guns, and the illicit-drug industry. *Journal of Criminal Law and Criminology, 86,* 10–36.

Blumstein, A., & Wallman, J. (2000). The recent rise and fall of American violence. In A. Blumstein & Wallman J. (Eds.), *The crime drop in America* (pp. 1–12). New York: Cambridge.

Cohen, J., Cork, D., Engberg, J., & Tita, G. E. (1998). The role of drug markets and gangs in local homicide rates. *Journal of Homicide Studies, 2*, 241–262.

Cohen, J., & Tita, G. E. (1999). Spatial diffusion in homicide: an exploratory analysis. *Journal of Quantitative Criminology, 15*, 451–493.

Conly, C. (1993). *Street gangs: current knowledge and strategies*. Washington, DC: National Institute of Justice.

Cook, P. J. (1991). The technology of personal violence. In M. Tonry (Ed.), *Crime and Justice vol. 14* (pp. 1–7). Chicago: University of Chicago Press.

Curry, G. D., Ball, R. A., & Fox, R. J. (1994). *Gang crime and law enforcement record keeping. Research in brief*. Washington, DC: National Institute of Justice.

Curry, G. D., & Spergel, I. A. (1988). Gang homicide, delinquency, and community. *Criminology, 26*, 381–405.

Decker, S. H. (1996). Collective and normative features of gang violence. *Justice Quarterly, 13*, 243–264.

Decker, S. H., Pennell, S., & Caldwell, A. (1996). *Arrestees and guns: monitoring the illegal firearms market*. (Final report). Washington, DC: National Institute of Justice.

Decker, S. H., & Van Winkle, B. (1996). *Life in the gang: family, friends and violence*. New York: Cambridge.

Fagan, J. E. (1989). The social organization of drug use and drug dealing among urban gangs. *Criminology, 27*, 633–669.

Hagedorn, J. M. (1994). Neighborhoods, markets and gang drug organization. *Journal of Research in Crime and Delinquency, 32*, 264–294.

Hagedorn, J. M. (1998). *People and folks: gangs, crime and the underclass in a Rustbelt City*. Chicago: Lakeview Press.

Jackson, R. K., & McBride, W. D. (1985). *Understanding street gangs*. Sacramento, CA: Custom Publishing.

Kennedy, D. M., Braga, A. A., & Piehl, A. M. (1997). The unknown universe: mapping gangs and gang violence in Boston. In D. Weisburd, & J. T. McEwenx (Eds.), *Crime mapping and crime prevention* (pp. 219–262). New York: Criminal Justice Press.

Klein, M. W. (1995). *The American street gang*. New York: Oxford.

Klein, M. W., & Maxson, C. L. (1987). Street gang violence.

In M. E. Wolfgang, & N. Weiner (Eds.), *Violent crime, violent criminals* (pp. 198–234). Beverly Hills, CA: Sage.

Klein, M. W., & Maxson, C. L. (1994). Gangs and crack cocaine trafficking. In D. L. MacKenzie & C. D. Uchida (Eds.), *Drugs and crime* (pp. 42–58). Thousans Oaks, CA: Sage.

Maxson, C. L. (1999). Gang homicide. In D. Smith & M. Zahn (Eds.), *Homicide studies: a sourcebook of social research* (pp. 239–254). Newbury Park, CA: Sage.

Maxson, C. L., Gordon, M. A., & Klein, M. W. (1985). Differences between gang and nongang homicides. *Criminology, 23*, 209–222.

Maxson, C. L., & Klein, M. W. (1990). Street gang violence: twice as great, or half as great? In C. R. Huff (Ed.), *Gangs in America, vol. 1*. Newbury Park, CA: Sage.

Miller, W. B. (2001). *The growth of youth gang problems in the United States: 1970–1998*. Washington, DC: OJJDP.

Padilla, F. M. (1992). *The gang as an American enterprise*. New Brunswick: Rutgers.

Rosenfeld, R.B., Bray, T., & Egley, H. A., Jr. (1999). Facilitating violence: a comparison of gang-motivated, gang-affiliated, and non-gang youth homicides. *Journal of Quantitative Criminology, 15*, 495–516.

Short, J. F. (1998). The level of explanation problem revisited: the American Society of Criminology 1997 Presidential address. *Criminology, 36*, 3–36.

Short, J. F., Jr. (1989). Exploring integration of theoretical levels of explanation: notes on gang delinquency. In S. F. Krohn, M. D. Krohn, & A. E. Liska (Eds.), *Theoretical integration in the study of deviance and crime: problems and prospects* (pp. 243–260). Albany, NY: State University of New York Press.

Short, J. F., Jr. (1990). Gangs, neighborhoods, and youth crime. *Criminal Justice Research Bulletin, 5*, 1–11.

Thrasher, F. (1927). *The gang*. Chicago: University of Chicago Press.

Vigil, D. (1988). *Barrio gangs*. Austin, TX: University of Texas Press.

Vila, B. (1994). A general paradigm for understanding criminal behavior: extending evolutionary ecological theory. *Criminology, 32*, 311–360.

[17]

Serious Youth Gun Offenders and the Epidemic of Youth Violence in Boston

Anthony A. Braga[1]

Boston, like many other major cities, experienced a sudden increase in youth homicides during the late 1980s and early 1990s. Research evidence suggests that the recent epidemic of urban youth violence was intensely concentrated among criminally active young black males residing in disadvantaged urban neighborhoods rather than all young black males residing in disadvantaged black neighborhoods. Other researchers, however, suggest that there was a diffusion of guns and gun violence from youth involved in street crack markets to youth outside the drug trade who armed themselves primarily for self-protection against the armed criminally active youth. In this paper, criminal history data are analyzed to determine whether the criminal profile of Boston arrested youth gun offenders changed over time and micro-level data on youth gun assault incidents in Boston are examined to unravel whether there were noteworthy changes in the nature of these violent events over time. The results of these analyses suggest that the youth violence epidemic in Boston was highly concentrated among serious youth gun offenders rather than a diffusion of guns away from the street drug trade, gangs, and criminally active youth.

KEY WORDS: youth violence; epidemic; guns; gangs; diffusion.

1. INTRODUCTION

Although overall homicide rates in the United States declined between the 1980s and 1990s, youth homicide rates, particularly incidents involving firearms, increased dramatically. Between 1984 and 1994, juvenile (younger than 18) homicide victimizations committed with handguns increased by 418%, and juvenile homicide victimizations committed with other guns increased 125% (Fox, 1996). During this time period, adolescents (ages 14–17) as a group had the largest proportional increase in homicide commission and victimization, but young adults (ages 18–24) had the largest absolute

[1]Program in Criminal Justice Policy and Management, John F. Kennedy School of Government, Harvard University, 79 John F. Kennedy Street, Cambridge, MA 02138. Voice: (617) 495-5188 E-mail: Anthony_Braga@harvard.edu

increase in numbers, and there was a good deal of crossfire between the two age groups (Cook and Laub, 1998). All of the increase in youth homicide was in gun homicides (Cook and Laub, 1998). For many cities, the bulk of this dramatic increase in youth homicide occurred in the late 1980s and early 1990s. In Boston, youth homicide (ages 24 and under) increased more than threefold—from 22 victims in 1987 to 73 victims in 1990 (see Fig. 1). Youth homicide remained high even after the peak of the epidemic. Boston averaged about 44 youth homicides per year between 1991 and 1995.

Like many other major cities, Boston experienced a sudden downturn in youth homicides during the latter part of the 1990s. The number of Boston youth homicides decreased to 26 in 1996, and further dropped to 15 youth homicides in 1997. The low level of youth homicides continued through 1998 (18 victims), 1999 (15 victims), and 2000 (18 victims). An interagency problem-oriented policing intervention, which tightly focused criminal justice attention on a small number of chronically offending gang-involved youth, was associated with the significant reduction in youth homicide and non-fatal gun violence (Braga *et al.*, 2001). The implementation and impact of this intervention has been extensively documented elsewhere (see, e.g., Kennedy *et al.*, 1996; Kennedy *et al.*, 2001). This paper does not examine the downturn in youth homicide in Boston. Rather, it examines the importance of serious youth offenders in the sudden upswing of youth violence in Boston between 1984 and 1995.

To some observers, the recent epidemic of youth violence resembled a "flood in a canyon" as it was intensely concentrated in a particular demo-

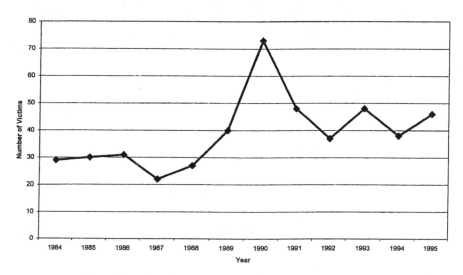

Fig. 1. Youth homicide in Boston ages 24 and under, 1984–1995.

graphic group—black males under age 25 residing in disadvantaged urban neighborhoods (Cook, 1998; Cook and Laub, 2002). The involvement of armed youth in street crack-cocaine markets and street gangs has been nominated as important dimensions of the epidemic (see, e.g., Reiss and Roth, 1993). This suggests that the epidemic was narrowly channeled among criminally active youth rather than all youth residing in disadvantaged black neighborhoods. Blumstein (1995), however, suggests that there was an indirect diffusion of guns from youth involved in street crack markets to youth outside the drug trade who armed themselves primarily for self-protection against the armed criminally active youth. In turn, the presence of firearms in the hands of these other young people transformed the settling of ordinary disputes from the use of physical force to shootings. The diffusion hypothesis presents a very different image of the trajectory of the youth violence epidemic relative to the intensification, or "flood in the canyon," perspective.

This paper assesses the extent to which youth violence was concentrated among criminally active offenders by examining the criminal profile of youth arrested for gun crimes over the course of Boston's youth violence epidemic. Section 2 briefly summarizes the existing literature on the youth violence epidemic and describes the relevant dimensions of Boston's youth violence epidemic. Sections 3 and 4 describe the data collection methodology, detail the statistical models used to analyze the data, and present the results of the quantitative analyses. The conclusions drawn from the research findings are discussed in Section 5.

2. THE EPIDEMIC OF YOUTH VIOLENCE

2.1. Key Elements of the Youth Violence Epidemic

Although the direct causes of the youth violence epidemic remain somewhat elusive, a concrete story emerged that seems to fit with experience and research evidence. Moore and Tonry's (1998) synthesis of key events provides a useful framework and is quickly summarized here. In the late seventies and early eighties, changes in structural factors produced conditions in inner-city minority communities that were ripe for an epidemic. The social and economic structure of many urban neighborhoods collapsed under a variety of social and economic pressures. Employment opportunities disappeared and small businesses moved away from the inner city. Under these economic pressures, families broke apart and children grew up under increasingly adverse conditions. In response to these conditions, some youth joined gangs in search of affiliation and security. Gangs produced fear and rivalries and caused other gangs to form and more youth to join gangs.

An epidemic of crack cocaine hit these troubled communities during the mid to late eighties. Some existing youth gangs and other youth not involved in gangs participated in street-level drug markets and armed themselves with guns to protect themselves and resolve business disputes. The arming of youth participating in street drug sales produced both dangerous conditions on the street and a cultural style that encouraged other youth to acquire guns in response. A large supply of available guns made it possible for other youth to acquire guns out of self-protection, style, and status concerns. The widespread arming of youth in these disadvantaged neighborhoods made conflicts much more lethal.

This story of the unfolding of the youth violence epidemic is often referred to as the "Blumstein hypothesis" as he was among the first to summarize the existing literature and present hard data supporting key elements of the story. In the period 1985–92, Blumstein (1995) documents three major changes: homicide rates by youth 18 and under doubled, while there was no growth in homicide rates by adults 24 and older; the number of homicides juveniles commit with guns more than doubled, while there was no change in non-gun homicides; and the arrest rate of non-white juveniles on drug charges more than doubled while there was no growth in the drug arrest rate for white juveniles.[2] Blumstein (1995) suggests that drug sellers in the expanding street-level crack markets actively recruited juveniles in disadvantaged inner-city neighborhoods. Juveniles provided a willing and cheap supply of labor, and were also less vulnerable to harsh punishments imposed by the adult criminal justice system. These armed juveniles were fairly tightly networked with other young people in the neighborhoods and guns "diffused" to other youth who went to the same schools and walked the same streets. Guns, rather than fists or other weapons, were used to settle disputes among youths with deadly results.

Cork (1999) closely examined the linkage between crack market activity and youth gun homicide suggested by Blumstein (1995). In a sample of 53 cities, he finds a sudden increase in youth gun homicide within 3 years of a similar, sharp increase in crack arrests among youth. Across the cities, there was temporal variation in the initiation of crack markets in the cities. However, the common temporal lag across the cities in the sudden appearance of crack markets followed by an upsurge in youth homicide provides compelling evidence on the plausibility of the Blumstein hypothesis (Cork, 1999). City-level studies in Pittsburgh (Cohen and Tita, 1999) and St. Louis (Rosenfeld *et al.*, 1999), using micro-level data on the circumstances of youth homicides, suggest that youth gangs were the dominant factor in

---

[2]While Blumstein (1995) notes that there was no growth in homicide rates by adults 24 and older, homicide victimization rates for 25–34 year olds did increase (Cook and Laub, 2002).

the growth of youth homicides. These studies found that crack markets did precede the epidemic of youth homicide and gang members were involved in the street-level drug trade. However, the increase in youth homicide in both Pittsburgh and St. Louis was linked to the emergence of intergang conflicts that spread from gang youth to nongang youth. Other research has suggested that, although crack markets may have sparked the youth violence epidemic, crack was no longer the main driver of youth violence. Rather, the youth violence epidemic had become "decoupled" from crack trafficking as violence was became more importantly tied to a complex mix of fear, gangs, guns, and subcultural norms guiding appropriate responses to resolving interpersonal disputes (Kennedy et al., 1996).

While these studies may not agree on the specifics of the trajectory of gangs, crack markets, and increases in youth violence, there seems to be a general consensus that guns diffused from youth who were involved in gangs and/or drug sales to other youth. It remains unclear, however, whether these other armed youth were active offenders, generally non-offending young people, or both. Research suggests that youth who acquire guns for "protection" are significantly more likely to commit guns crimes and street crimes such as robbery when compared with youth who own guns for sport and youth who don't own guns (Bjerregaard and Lizotte, 1995). Gang members are also much more likely to own guns for "protection" than for sporting purposes (Bjerregaard and Lizotte, 1995). To some observers, the important predisposing condition for the youth violence epidemic was the existence of young people either disposed, or sufficiently susceptible, to the use of violence as a means to acquire wealth, status, or resolve disputes (Howell and Hawkins, 1998). For inner-city youths involved in street social networks and street crime, social identity and position in social status hierarchies were tied closely to possessing guns and using guns to defend against status threats (Wilkinson and Fagan, 1996; Fagan and Wilkinson, 1998).

While survey research of both high school students residing in high-violence areas and incarcerated youth has demonstrated that guns have become a central feature of adolescent life for inner-city males (Sheley and Wright, 1995), the available evidence suggests it is likely that the youth violence epidemic was largely concentrated among active offenders rather than non-offending youth. Criminological research has long noted that a relatively high proportion of homicide victims and homicide offenders have a prior criminal record (see, e.g., Wolfgang, 1958). In particular, homicide offenders are likely to commit their murders in the course of long criminal careers consisting primarily of nonviolent crimes but including larger than normal proportions of violent crimes (Swersey and Enloe, 1975; Dawson and Boland, 1993). Homicide victims and offenders are likely to share social networks and have similar social milieus (Singer, 1981; Reiss and Roth, 1993). This is also true for nonfatal serious violence (Garofalo, 1987; Lauritsen *et al.*, 1991). Recent city-level studies of urban youth homicide problems have documented the same concentration of chronic offenders among youth homicide victims and youth homicide offenders (for a summary, see Braga *et al.*, 2002).

2.2. Characteristics of the Youth Violence Epidemic in Boston

As described earlier, Boston experienced a sudden upswing in youth homicide, measured as victims ages 24 and under, between 1988 and 1989 that peaked in 1990. Relative to the 1990 peak, the yearly number of youth homicides decreased in 1991 but stabilized and remained notably higher through 1995 when compared with the pre-epidemic years of 1984 through 1987 (Fig. 1). As Fig. 2 reveals, Boston gun assault incidents show a slightly different trajectory when compared with youth homicides. Gun assault incidents increased steadily from 796 in 1985 to a peak of 1241 in 1990. Unlike youth homicides, gun assault incidents decreased steadily after the 1990 peak to 802 in 1995. Arrests for youth gun assault offenders and youth gun possession offenders also show a large increase over the course of the 1980s (Fig. 3). However, arrests for youth gun offenders peaked one year later in 1991 and then decreased steadily through 1995. Survey research suggests that Boston high school students were slightly less likely to report

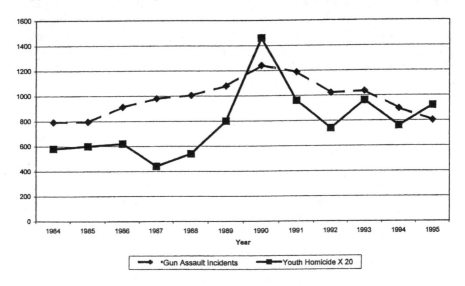

Fig. 2. Boston youth homicide and Boston gun assault incidents, 1984–1995.

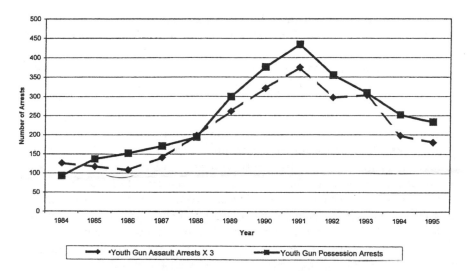

Fig. 3. Boston gun assault and gun possession arrests ages 24 and under, 1984–1995.

carrying a gun between 1993 (10.0%) and 1995 (8.5%) (Kann *et al.*, 1995; 1996). Like most other large cities in the United States, crack appeared in Boston before the significant increases in youth violence. Independent sources suggest crack first appeared in Boston in 1986, about two years before the sudden upswing in youth homicide between 1988 and 1989.[3]

A close examination of youth gun and knife homicide incidents between 1991 and 1994 revealed that these incidents primarily involved young black males and were largely concentrated within Boston's poorer neighborhoods of Roxbury, Dorchester, and Mattapan (Kennedy *et al.*, 1996). The problem of youth homicide was also concentrated among a small number of chronically offending gang-involved youth. Only about 1,300 gang members—less that 1% of their age group city-wide—in 61 gangs were responsible for at least 60% of all the youth homicide in the city. Chronic disputes, or "beefs," among gangs appeared to be the most significant driver of gang violence (Braga *et al.*, 1999). A majority of the youth homicide

[3]The National Institute on Drug Abuse's Community Epidemiology Working Group, which was established to provide ongoing community-level surveillance of drug abuse through the collection and analysis of epidemiological and ethnographic data, suggests that data on crack use and sales in Boston were first reported in 1986 (Kozel, 1997). A close examination of Drug Abuse Warning Network data by Grogger and Willis (2000) also suggests that crack use also appeared in Boston in 1986. In his rigorous statistical analysis of the upswing of youth gun homicides in American cities, Daniel Cork (1999) reports 1988 as the significant change point in the trajectory of juvenile gun homicides in Boston.

victims and youth homicide offenders had prior, and often extensive, criminal histories and involvement with the criminal justice system (Kennedy *et al.*, 1996).

These detailed analyses only examined youth violence after the peak in 1990 and provide little insight on changes in the nature of youth violence over the course of the epidemic. Moreover, the analyses focus on the most extreme form of youth violence—homicide— and offer little direct information on youth carrying guns or engaging in non-fatal gun violence. This paper seeks to unravel whether the criminal profile of youth gun offenders changed over the course of the youth violence epidemic in Boston by analyzing data on the criminal background of youth arrested for gun possession and gun assault offenses. If non-offending youth increasingly participated in gun crimes as the epidemic progressed, arrested gun offenders would be less likely to have extensive criminal histories. If serious youth offenders increasingly participated in gun crimes as the epidemic progressed, arrested gun offenders would be more likely to have extensive criminal histories. No change in the criminal profile of arrested gun offenders would be expected if the same types of offenders committed gun crimes or if serious youth offenders and non-offending youth participated in similar numbers equally over the course of the epidemic.

3. DATA

To assess whether the criminal profiles of youth involved in gun crime in Boston changed over time, criminal history information was collected on gun assault and gun possession offenders, ages 24 and under, arrested between 1984 and 1995. A random sample, stratified by year, of 30 youth gun assault offenders and 30 youth gun possession offenders per year was selected; the final sample had 720 individuals for the 12 year period.[4] It is important to recognize that these were not panel data. Rather, the data were organized as a set of 12 unique cross-sectional samples of randomly selected youth gun arrestees.

Although police decision-making practices introduce bias to arrest data as a measure of offending activity (Black, 1970), criminologists commonly use arrest data as a proxy for offenders. The demographic characteristics of offenders are usually unknown whereas the demographics of arrestees are

---

[4]The yearly sampling of youth gun assault arrestees and youth gun possession arrestees was based on the number of unique people arrested per year, not on the total number of arrests for those offenses per year. This was done to ensure that each arrested offender in a given year had the same probability of being included in the sample. Across the 12 years, only 13 individuals appeared twice (3.6%, 26 of 720 cases). Leaving these individuals out of the analyses made no substantive differences in the results described here.

easy to establish (Blumstein, 1995). Studies that have compared victim reports of the demographics of offenders with those of arrestees, for personal crimes such as robbery and aggravated assault, find the two tend to be closely related (Hindelang, 1978). Arrest data were also the only available yearly data that includes the minimum amount of information (name and date of birth) to obtain adult and juvenile criminal history data from the Criminal Offender Record Information (CORI) system maintained by the Massachusetts Criminal History Systems Board. CORI data include information on all arraignments in Massachusetts State and local courts. Thus, any non-Massachusetts offenses or locally committed crimes prosecuted in Federal court would not be captured. Adult and juvenile arraignment histories were generated by running the names and dates of birth of the sampled youth gun offenders through the CORI system. The number of arraignments an individual had before being arrested for the gun crime that led to his/her inclusion in the sample were coded and entered into a computerized database. In other words, if an individual was arrested for a gun assault in September of 1991, only those arraignments on his/her record prior to this date were included in the analysis. The CORI system includes all adult and juvenile arraignments of any individual arraigned in Massachusetts State and local courts since 1981. If an individual was arraigned in 1981, their entire history of adult and juvenile arraignments up to that point in time was entered into the computerized CORI system. As such, these data include all prior arraignments for an individual, not simply arraignments post 1981.[5]

Table I presents the summary statistics of the sample of Boston youth gun offenders. The age of the arrested gun offenders in this sample ranged from 12 to 24, with a mean age of 19.1. Slightly more than 80% of the arrested gun offenders were African-American. Nearly 16% of the arrested gun offenders were White, almost 1% of the arrested gun offenders were Asian, and other races comprised slightly more than 2% of the arrested gun offenders. Nearly 71% of the individuals in the sample had been arraigned at least once before being arrested for a gun possession or assault offense. The mean number of total prior arraignments was 6.4, with one individual having 54 prior arraignments. For the entire sample, the "average" arrested youth gun offender in Boston had nearly two prior violent crime arraignments, nearly two property crime arraignments, and nearly one prior drug offense arraignment.

[5]These insights on the quality of the criminal history data were provided by Professor Jack McDevitt of Northeastern University, who is a member of the Massachusetts Criminal History System Board's research review committee (Personal interview, December 10, 1999).

Table I. Summary Statistics of Sampled Boston Youth Gun Offenders, 1984–1995 ($N = 720$)

Quantitative Variables	Mean	Std. Dev.	Min–Max
Age of arrested gun offender	19.1	2.6	12–24
Total prior criminal arraignments	6.4	8.3	0–54
Total prior drug crime arraignments	0.9	1.9	0–14
Total prior violent crime arraignments	1.8	3.1	0–25
Total prior property crime arraignments	1.7	2.9	0–24
Qualitative Variables	N	%	
African-American	582	80.8	
White	115	15.9	
Asian	6	0.8	
Other	17	2.4	
Male	690	95.8	
Female	30	4.2	
Arrested for gun assault offense	360	50.0	
Arrested for gun possession offense	360	50.0	
At least one prior arraignment	509	70.7	

4. ANALYSIS

4.1. Simple Trends in the Criminal Profile of Boston Arrested Youth Gun Offenders

Between 1984 and 1995, the percentage of arrested Boston youth gun offenders with a criminal record and the average number of prior arraignments per arrested youth gun offender increased. Figure 4 presents the yearly percentage of Boston arrested youth gun offenders that had at least one prior juvenile and/or adult arraignment. In 1984, only 53.3% of arrested youth gun offenders had a prior criminal record. This percentage increased steadily through 1995, when 83.3% of arrested youth gun offenders had a prior criminal record. Figure 4 also reveals a similar linear increase in the yearly percentage of Boston arrested youth gun offenders that had at least one prior juvenile and/or adult drug arraignment. In contrast to the assertion of the "Blumstein hypothesis" that youth gun violence diffused away from drug markets, the percentage of Boston arrested youth gun offenders involved in drug crimes increased over the course of the gun violence epidemic. Figure 5 presents the yearly mean number of prior adult and juvenile arraignments for Boston arrested youth gun offenders. The mean number of prior arraignments increased linearly from 3.75 arraignments in 1984 to 9.28 arraignments in 1995.

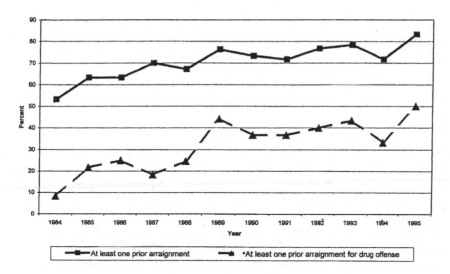

Fig. 4. Percent of arrested youth gun offenders with at least one prior arraignment.

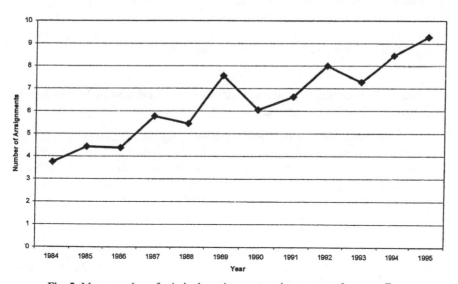

Fig. 5. Mean number of criminal arraignments prior to arrest for gun offense.

4.2. The Negative Binomial Regression Model

Prior adult and juvenile arraignments are distributed in the form of rare event counts. There are well-documented problems associated with treating event count variables, which are discrete, as continuous realizations of a normal data generating process (see King, 1989, p. 126). As such, methods such as standard mean difference tests and ordinary least squares regression that assume population normality of the dependent variable should not be used to analyze count data (see Gardner *et al.*, 1995, pp. 393–394). Rather, Poisson regression is generally used to estimate models of the event counts (Long, 1997). The Poisson regression model has the defining characteristic that the conditional mean of the outcome is equal to the conditional variance. However, in practice, the conditional variance often exceeds the conditional mean (Long, 1997). When a sample count distribution exhibits ·this "overdispersion," it is unlikely that a Poisson process generated it. Assuming a Poisson process, when the true process generates overdispersed data, results in the same coefficient estimates but underestimates coefficient variances. This results in spuriously large test statistics on the hypothesis that the true coefficient is equal to zero in the population (Gardner *et al.*, 1995, p. 399). As will be demonstrated in the formal analysis, the distributions of counts of prior arraignments of arrested Boston youth gun offenders were overdispersed. When count data are overdispersed, it is appropriate to use the negative binomial generalization of the Poisson regression model. As Long (1997) describes, the negative binomial regression model is an extension of the Poisson regression model that allows the conditional variance of the dependent variable to exceed the conditional mean through the estimation of a dispersion parameter.

4.3. Negative Binomial Regression Analysis of the Criminal Record of Boston Arrested Youth Gun Offenders

Changes in the criminal profile of Boston youth offenders arrested for gun crimes were examined by estimating four negative binomial regression models with the following dependent variables: the total number of prior arraignments, the number of prior arraignments for property crimes, the number of prior arraignments for drug crimes, and the number of prior arraignments for violent crimes. The independent variables were age of the offender, sex of the offender, race of the offender, type of gun arrest offense, and year of arrest. The demographic variables were included in the regression models to safeguard against any changes in criminal profile in a particular year that may have been an artifact of sampling error rather than a substantive change (e.g., by chance, sampling may have selected a higher number of females in a given year). Excluding the demographic variables from the models do not substantively change the results. Any small discrepancies between the two model specifications are noted below in the discussion of the results of the fully-specified model.

Age was entered into the equation as a continuous variable. Sex, race, gun arrest offense, and year of arrest were coded as dummy variables.

Following the conventions of constructing dummy variables, the most frequent category for each variable was selected as the reference category. As such, the sex variable was coded '1' for females; the race variable was coded '1' for Whites, Asians, and other races; the gun arrest offense variable was coded as '1' for offenders arrested for gun assault. Gun offenders arrested in 1995 were coded as '1' in the Year 1995 variable and coded as '0' on all other year variables. Gun offenders arrested in 1984 and 1985 served as the reference category for the other year dummy variables. These years serve as good pre-epidemic reference points as the numbers of youth homicide incidents in Boston were stable in 1984 and 1985 (Fig. 1). For convenience, the years 1989 and 1990 will be referred to as the "epidemic years" and the years 1991 through 1995 will be referred to as the "post-epidemic years."

Inserting the total number of prior arraignments as the dependent variable, the basic model was as follows:

> Count of total prior arraignments = Alpha + Age + Race + Sex + Gun Arrest
> Offense + Year 1986 + Year 1987 + Year 1988 + Year 1989 + Year 1990 +
> Year 1991 + Year 1992 + Year 1993 + Year 1994 + Year 1995. + Error

The parameters for the independent variables were expressed as incidence rate ratios (i.e., exponentiated coefficients). Incidence rate ratios are interpreted as the rate at which things occur; for example, an incidence rate ratio of 0.40 on the sex dummy variable would suggest that, controlling for other independent variables, women were associated with 60% fewer prior arraignments relative to men. To ensure that the coefficient variances were robust to violations of the homoskedastic errors assumption of linear regression models, Huber/White/sandwich robust variance estimators were used. Following social science convention, the two-tailed 0.05 level of significance was selected as the benchmark to reject the null hypothesis of "no difference."

Table II presents the results of the negative binomial regression models. For the four models, the alpha coefficient is statistically significant. This confirms that the data were significantly overdispersed and, as such, were distributed as a negative binomial process rather than a Poisson process.[6]

---

[6]Table II reports the z-scores for the test that alpha = 0. Another method to determine whether the data are distributed negative binomial is to calculate a likelihood ratio test of whether adding alpha to the count data model significantly improves the fit of the Poisson model to the data. Stata 7.0 calculates this likelihood ratio test when a negative binomial model is run with standard variance estimators (StataCorp, 2001, p. 387). Since the reported models were run with robust estimators that assume the errors may have unknown correlation, this likelihood ratio test, which assumes independence, could not be run. However, when the models were run with standard variance estimators, the likelihood ratio tests that alpha = 0 were statistically significant. The chi-square results were: 3759.77 for total arraignments, 492.33 for drug crime arraignments, 1094.53 for property crime arraignments, and 1081.81 for violent crime arraignments. These results assert that the probability that these data would be observed conditional on the process being Poisson is zero.

Table II. Results of Negative Binomial Regression Models ($N = 720$)

Variable	Total crime	Property crime	Drug crime	Violent crime
Age	1.14 (6.96)*	1.11 (4.27)*	1.18 (5.57)*	1.10 (3.91)*
Race	1.13 (0.91)	1.52 (2.46)*	0.47 (−3.07)*	0.77 (−1.33)
Sex	0.50 (−2.56)*	0.85 (−0.51)	0.21 (−2.78)*	0.52 (−2.00)*
Gun arrest offense	1.28 (2.74)*	1.16 (1.21)	1.44 (2.49)*	1.64 (3.94)*
Year 1986	1.23 (0.88)	1.14 (0.42)	1.88 (1.69)	0.78 (−0.76)
Year 1987	1.71 (2.59)*	1.63 (1.71)	2.16 (1.93)	1.62 (1.69)
Year 1988	1.48 (1.64)	1.28 (0.73)	3.15 (2.72)*	1.48 (1.36)
Year 1989	2.15 (4.11)*	1.91 (2.72)*	6.00 (5.32)*	1.57 (1.77)
Year 1990	1.82 (2.97)*	1.39 (1.34)	6.35 (5.18)*	1.84 (1.98)*
Year 1991	2.04 (3.55)*	1.06 (0.23)	5.71 (4.84)*	1.82 (2.26)*
Year 1992	2.25 (4.21)*	1.53 (1.68)	6.01 (5.16)*	1.97 (2.45)*
Year 1993	2.22 (4.19)*	1.18 (0.64)	9.44 (6.66)*	1.88 (2.32)*
Year 1994	2.49 (4.55)*	1.48 (1.61)	4.89 (4.44)*	2.81 (3.53)*
Year 1995	2.74 (5.22)*	1.51 (1.79)	9.75 (6.80)*	2.55 (2.95)*
Ln alpha	0.562 (8.41)*	0.891 (10.45)*	0.934 (8.42)*	0.821 (9.31)*
Alpha	1.754 (14.98)*	2.437 (11.73)*	2.543 (9.02)*	2.272 (11.35)*
Log likelihood	−2012.95	−1194.37	−804.29	−1205.49
Pseudo R^2	0.0169	0.0120	0.0635	0.0232
Wald chi-square	91.71*	39.60*	117.57*	57.94*

*$P < 0.05$.
Note: Binominal regression model coefficients were expressed as Incidence Rate Ratios with respective Z-scores in parentheses. Gun offenders arrested in 1984 and 1985 were included in the reference category. For all four models, the Wald chi-square statistic was distributed with 14 degrees of freedom.

For all models, controlling for other independent variables, as the age of the arrested youth gun offender increased, the count of prior arraignments significantly increased. While there were no significant differences in the total number of prior arraignments and prior violent crime arraignments, holding other variables constant, African-American youth gun offenders had significantly higher counts of prior drug offense arraignments and significantly lower counts of prior property crime arraignments relative to youth gun offenders who were White, Asian, and belonged to other racial groups. Controlling for other variables, female youth gun offenders had significantly lower counts of total prior arraignments, prior drug crime arraignments, and prior violent crime arraignments relative male youth gun offenders. Individuals arrested for gun assault offenses had significantly higher counts of total prior arraignments, prior drug crime arraignments, and violent crime arraignments relative to individuals arrested for gun possession offenses, holding other variables constant.

The negative binomial regression models revealed significant changes in the criminal profile of gun offenders arrested in Boston between 1984 and

1995. Youth gun offenders arrested during the epidemic and post-epidemic years had larger numbers of prior arraignments when compared with youth gun offenders arrested in the pre-epidemic years. Relative to youth gun offenders arrested in 1984 and 1985, holding other variables constant, the total number of prior arraignments significantly increased in 1987, were not significantly different in 1988, significantly increased in 1989, and remained significantly higher through 1995. The total count of prior arraignments for arrested gun offenders had increased by 82% in 1990 and by 174% in 1995, relative to the total count of prior arraignments for gun offenders arrested in 1984 and 1985. The period of sustained higher counts of prior arraignments for youth gun offenders arrested during the epidemic and post-peak epidemic years was also significantly different from the counts of prior arraignments for youth gun offenders arrested in prior years. A likelihood ratio test revealed that the coefficients for the year 1989 through year 1995 dummy variables were jointly significantly different from zero (chi-square = 34.51, 7 degrees of freedom, $P < 0.05$).

These results were primarily driven by increases in prior arraignments for drug and violent offenses. With the exception of a significant increase in 1989, controlling for other variables, the counts of prior property crimes of arrested youth gun offenders were not significantly different in later years relative to 1984 and 1985.[7] It is important to note that the lack of significant changes in the counts of prior property offenses over time provides some additional confidence that the observed changes in drug and violent prior offenses was not an artifact of some change in the overall quality of the criminal history data over time. Relative to youth gun offenders arrested in 1984 and 1985, holding other variables constant, the total number of prior arraignments for drug offenses significantly increased in 1988 and remained significantly higher through 1995. The count of prior drug arraignments for arrested gun offenders had increased by a factor of 6 in 1990 and by nearly ten-fold in 1995, relative to the count of prior drug arraignments for gun offenders arrested in 1984 and 1985. A likelihood ratio test revealed that the coefficients for the year 1988 through year 1995 dummy variables were jointly significantly different from zero (chi-square = 58.07, 8 degrees of freedom, $P < 0.05$). The significant change in the count of prior violent offenses for youth gun offenders arrested in Boston started two years later. Relative to youth gun offenders arrested in 1984 and 1985, holding other variables constant, the count of prior arraignments for violent offenses significantly increased in 1990, the height of the youth homicide epidemic,

---

[7]The count of prior property crimes of arrested gun offenders in 1989 was not significantly different from 1984 and 1985 in the binomial regression model without the demographic control variables.

and remained significantly higher through the post-peak epidemic years.[8] The count of prior violent arraignments for arrested gun offenders had increased by 84% in 1990 and more than doubled by 1995, relative to the count of prior arraignments for gun offenders arrested in 1984 and 1985. A likelihood ratio test revealed that the coefficients for the year 1990 through year 1995 dummy variables were jointly significantly different from zero (chi-square = 14.51, 6 degrees of freedom, $P < 0.05$).

4.4. Changes in the Nature of Youth Gun Assault Incidents

The simple trend analyses and the more rigorous negative binomial regression models suggest that youth gun offending in Boston was concentrated among more serious youth gun offenders over the course of the youth violence epidemic. However, these results provide little insight on whether the nature of youth gun assaults in Boston changed over the course of the epidemic. To unravel whether there were noteworthy changes in the nature of these violent events, data on youth gun assault incidents, for youth ages 24 and under, were closely examined for three years that represented distinct periods in Boston's youth homicide epidemic—1987, 1990, and 1995. The analyses were limited to one high-risk police district due to limitations of the Boston Police Department (BPD) incident data. The computerized BPD gun assault incident data do not capture the age of the victim. Information on the age of the gun assault victim was only available from hard copies of gun assault incident reports. Since the collection and coding of this information was a time consuming task, these data were collected for District B-2, which covers most of Boston's Roxbury neighborhood, has a very dense concentration of gangs, and experienced a third of Boston's youth homicide incidents between 1991 and 1995 (Kennedy *et al.*, 1996).

Table III presents the results of an analysis of B-2 youth gun assault incidents. Handguns were used in about 90% of B-2 youth gun assault incidents in 1987 and 1990, and increased slightly to 96% of B-2 youth gun assault incidents in 1995. Youth gun assaults in B-2 were more likely to occur in a public fashion after 1987. In 1987, slightly more than 70% of B-2 youth gun assault incidents occurred outside; during 1990 and 1995, youth gun assault incidents occurring outside increased to 85%. Similarly, B-2 youth gun assaults were more likely to result in a wound after 1987. Only

---

[8]In the binomial regression model without the demographic control variables, the count of prior violent crimes for arrested gun offenders significantly increased, relative to 1984 and 1985, beginning one year later in 1991. The alternative specification revealed the count of prior violent arraignments for arrested gun offenders had increased by 72% in 1990 relative to 1984 and 1985, but was not statistically significant at the 0.05 level ($P = 0.082$).

Table III. District B-2 Gun Assault Incidents, Victims Ages 24 and Under

	1987	1990	1995
	(N = 153)	(N = 244)	(N = 155)
Type of Firearm			
Handgun	91%	90%	96%
Shotgun	3%	6%	1%
Rifle	1%	3%	0%
Unknown	5%	1%	3%
Location			
Inside	18%	12%	10%
Outside	71%	85%	85%
Not clear	11%	3%	5%
Wound Inflicted	40%	56%	56%
Number of Wounds	(N = 61)	(N = 138)	(N = 92)
One	72%	72%	62%
Two or more	28%	28%	38%

CASE FATALITY RATE = [Number of B-2 youth gun homicides/Number of B-2 youth gun assault incidents] * 100

Number of B-2 youth gun homicides	5	14	16
Number of B-2 youth gun assaults	153	244	155
Case fatality rate	3.3	5.7	10.3

40% of B-2 youth gun assaults resulted in a wound in 1987; in 1990 and 1995, 56% of B-2 youth gun assaults resulted in wounds. In those instances where a youth was wounded, the number of multiple gunshot wounds increased from 28% in 1987 and 1990 to 38% in 1995. Finally, case fatality rates were calculated to estimate the percentage of B-2 youth gun assaults that were fatal in each of the three years. These data suggest an increase in the intent to kill over time (Table III). In 1987, 3.3% (5 of 153) of youth gun assaults resulted in a fatality; in 1990, 5.7% (14 of 244) of youth gun assaults resulted in a fatality; by 1995, 10.3% (16 of 155) of youth gun assaults resulted in a fatality. Although the absolute number of B-2 youth gun assaults in 1995 was essentially the same as 1987, the likelihood of a youth gun assault resulting in a fatality in B-2 tripled.[9]

These analyses suggest intensification in B-2 youth gun violence between 1987 and 1995. Post 1990, B-2 youth gun assault incidents were increasingly committed in a public fashion, more likely to result in a wound, more likely to result in multiple wounds, and more likely to result in death.

[9]A similar analysis of the rapid increase in homicide in Harlem between 1968 and 1974 found that the increase in killing was the result of an increase in the case-fatality rate of gun assaults rather than an increase in the number of gun assaults (Swersey and Enloe, 1975).

These results could be influenced by changes in the technology of the handguns used by youth in B-2. Unfortunately, the micro-level data to examine these changes were not available. However, as Fig. 6 reveals, there was a gradual shift from six-shot revolvers to higher capacity semiautomatic pistols among all crime handguns recovered by the BPD between 1981 and 1995.[10] Table IV reveals that the caliber of these recovered handguns also changed during this time period. Two themes were evident: the yearly percentage of .22 and .38 caliber handguns decreased over this time period while the yearly percentage of .380 and 9 mm caliber handguns increased, particularly in 1995. Between 1991 and 1995, previous research revealed that firearms associated with youth, especially with gang youth, tended to be newer semiautomatic pistols (Kennedy *et al.*, 1996). Unfortunately, without micro-level data on the guns used in the B-2 incidents, the possible effects of these technological changes on the observed results of our youth gun assault incident analysis remain unclear. Since few gun assault incidents involve large numbers of shots fired, the larger capacity of semiautomatic pistols relative to revolvers may not be relevant (Kleck, 1997). The decrease in low-powered .22 caliber handguns may suggest an increase in the overall lethality of crime guns recovered in Boston. However, possible changes in lethality associated with shifts among medium-powered .38, .380, and 9 mm handguns are less significant.[11]

5. CONCLUSION

Boston's youth violence epidemic, as measured as a homicide problem, started in 1988, was preceded by the arrival of crack in 1986, and was contained mostly within Boston's young black male population residing in a few disadvantaged neighborhoods. Gangs and criminally active youth were at the core of the Boston's violence problem. The negative binomial regression models reveal that the criminal profile of youth gun offenders significantly changed as the youth violence epidemic progressed. Beginning in 1988, arrested youth gun offenders were significantly more likely to have higher counts of prior drug arraignments and, beginning in 1990, were significantly more likely to have higher counts of prior violent offenses. These results suggest that the youth violence epidemic was concentrated

---

[10]These data on handguns recovered in crime by the BPD were generated through an analysis of the comprehensive records kept by the BPD's Ballistics Unit. While these data provide consistent information on the basic features of recovered handguns, the data do not consistently capture the location of the recovery or the demographics of the offender associated with the recovery.

[11]For an informed discussion of the lethality of different firearm calibers, see Karlson and Hargarten (1997).

Table IV. Yearly Percentages of Top Calibers of Handguns Recovered in Boston, 1981–1995

Year	Total handguns recovered	.22	.25	.32	.357	.38	.380	9 mm
1981	650	20.6%	12.8%	12.2%	5.4%	33.2%	3.4%	4.2%
1982	697	21.3%	10.2%	12.2%	6.3%	33.7%	5.6%	3.4%
1983	568	23.2%	11.1%	13.9%	6.9%	32.9%	2.8%	2.5%
1984	597	20.1%	14.9%	11.6%	7.0%	31.8%	4.5%	2.5%
1985	565	18.8%	13.8%	12.9%	6.5%	32.9%	5.1%	3.7%
1986	631	19.0%	16.0%	15.1%	6.3%	28.8%	3.8%	3.0%
1987	459	23.9%	16.6%	10.5%	6.1%	27.6%	3.7%	6.3%
1988	556	17.2%	17.2%	9.5%	7.4%	30.0%	5.8%	6.1%
1989	595	16.8%	14.1%	12.7%	6.9%	27.8%	5.5%	11.4%
1990	805	16.0%	14.2%	10.1%	7.5%	22.8%	9.6%	12.9%
1991	829	14.5%	17.5%	11.0%	6.9%	17.0%	11.8%	14.5%
1992	766	14.2%	16.1%	10.6%	7.6%	18.8%	10.8%	14.9%
1993	613	15.6%	16.0%	10.1%	5.4%	19.2%	13.2%	14.3%
1994	622	12.2%	14.6%	7.9%	6.1%	18.2%	13.8%	19.6%
1995	583	9.1%	13.7%	7.9%	5.8%	11.7%	17.0%	25.6%

among more serious youth gun offenders rather than non-offending youth. The higher counts of prior drug convictions underscore the continuing importance of involvement in the street level drug trade as a risk factor for youth gun offending.

The results of the simple trend analyses and negative binomial regression models could, of course, be influenced by enforcement bias introduced by a deliberate focus by Boston police on street drug markets and perceived gang areas. It is possible, in theory, that there was a volume of youth carrying guns in Boston that did not come to the attention of the police, for instance guns carried by otherwise non-offending youth that armed themselves out of fear. If such youth actually used their guns to settle interpersonal disputes, however, they stood at least some likelihood of coming to police attention as gun assaulters. If non-offending youth contributed meaningfully to the gunplay in the youth violence epidemic, their likelihood of coming to police attention as gun carriers would have increased over time as the police adjusted their enforcement response beyond street drug markets and gang turf areas. While guns may have been possessed and carried by non-criminal Boston youth, these analyses suggest they did not contribute much to the epidemic of youth violence. The preponderance of youth homicide victims and youth homicide offenders in Boston involved gang-involved chronic offenders (Kennedy *et al.*, 1996) and the non-lethal gun crime that comes to the attention of the Boston police was similarly concentrated among serious youth offenders.

The further analyses of gun assault data in District B-2 suggest that the nature of violent gun events also changed over the course of the youth violence epidemic. Boston gun assault incidents and arrests for youth gun crimes declined notably after their respective 1990 and 1991 peaks. Youth homicides, however, declined from the 1990 peak to 1991 and remained relatively high through 1995. In District B-2, there is evidence that gun violence intensified during the 1990 through 1995 time period as youth gun assault incidents were increasingly public in fashion and lethal. Coupled with the results from the regression models, these findings paint a picture of Boston youth gun violence that was highly concentrated among serious youth offenders who carried high capacity semiautomatic pistols and used their guns in an increasingly deadly way. In Boston, the youth violence epidemic was an intense "flood in a canyon" rather than a diffusion of guns away from the street drug trade, gangs, and criminally active youth.

ACKNOWLEDGMENTS

The research described herein was supported under award #95-6-12 from the Alfred P. Sloan Foundation. Points of view in this document are those of the author and do not represent the official position of the Sloan Foundation. The author would like to thank Stephen Brimley, Christiana Briggs, Ellsa Gold, and Linda Braga for their valuable research assistance and David Kennedy for his helpful comments.

REFERENCES

Bjerregaard, B., and Lizotte, A. J. (1995). Gun ownership and gang membership. *J. Crim. Law Criminol.* 86: 37–58.

Black, D. (1970). The production of crime rates. *Am. Soc. Rev.* 35: 733–748.

Blumstein, A. (1995). Youth violence, guns, and the illicit-drug industry. *J. Crim. Law Criminol.* 86: 10–36.

Braga, A. A., Kennedy, D. M., and Tita, G. (2002). New approaches to the strategic prevention of gang and group-involved violence. In Huff, C. R. (ed.), *Gangs in America*, Third edition, Sage Publications, Thousand Oaks, CA.

Braga, A. A., Kennedy, D. M., Waring, E. W., and Piehl, A. M. (2001). Problem-oriented policing, deterrence, and youth violence: An evaluation of Boston's Operation Ceasefire. *J. Res. Crime Delinq.* 38: 195–225.

Braga, A. A., Piehl, A. M., and Kennedy, D. M. (1999). Youth homicide in Boston: An assessment of supplementary homicide reports. *Homicide Stud.* 3: 277–299.

Cook, P. (1998). The epidemic of youth gun violence. In *Perspectives on Crime and Justice: 1997–1998 Lecture Series*, National Institute of Justice, U.S. Department of Justice, Washington, DC.

Cook, P., and Laub, J. (1998). The unprecedented epidemic in youth violence. In Tonry, M., and Moore, M. (eds.), *Youth Violence, Vol. 24. Crime and Justice: A Review of Research*, University of Chicago Press, Chicago.

Missing Data Problems in Criminological Research   53

Cook, P., and Laub, J. (2002). After the epidemic: Recent trends in youth violence in the United States. In Tonry, M. (ed.), *Crime and Justice: A Review of Research, Vol. 29*, University of Chicago Press, Chicago.

Cohen, J., and Tita, G. (1999). Diffusion in homicide: Exploring a general method for detecting spatial diffusion processes. *J. Quant. Criminol.*15: 451–494.

Cork, D. (1999). Examining space-time interaction in city-level homicide data: Crack markets and the diffusion of guns among youth. *J. Quant. Criminol.* 15: 379–406.

Dawson, J., and Boland, B. (1993). Murder in large urban counties, 1988, *Bureau of Justice Statistics Special Report*, U.S. Department of Justice, Washington, DC.

Fagan, J., and Wilkinson, D. (1998). Guns, youth violence, and social identity in inner cities. In Tonry, M., and Moore, M. (eds.), *Youth Violence, Vol. 24. Crime and Justice: A Review of Research*, University of Chicago Press, Chicago.

Fox, J. A. (1996). *Trends in Juvenile Violence: A Report to the United States Attorney General on Current and Future Rates of Juvenile Offending*, Bureau of Justice Statistics, U.S. Department of Justice, Washington, DC.

Gardner, W., Mulvey, E. P., and Shaw, E. C. (1995). Regression analyses of counts and rates: Poisson, overdispersed Poisson, and negative binomial models. *Psychol. Bull.* 118: 392–404.

Garofalo, J. (1987). Reassessing the lifestyle model of criminal victimization. In Gottfredson, M., and Hirschi, T. (eds.), *Positive Criminology*, Sage Publications, Newbury Park, CA.

Grogger, J., and Willis, M. (2000). The emergence of crack cocaine and the rise in urban crime rates. *Rev. Econ. Stat.* 82: 519–529.

Hindelang, M. J. (1978). Race and involvement in common law personal crimes. *Am. Soc. Rev.* 43: 93–109.

Howell, J., and Hawkins, J. (1998). Prevention of youth violence. In Tonry, M., and Moore, M. (eds.), *Youth Violence, Vol. 24. Crime and Justice: A Review of Research*, University of Chicago Press, Chicago.

Kann, L., Warren, C., Harris, W., Collins, J., Douglas, K., Collins, M. *et al.* (1995). Youth risk behavior surveillance—United States, 1993. *MMWR Morb. Mortal. Wkly. Rep.* 44: 1–57.

Kann, L., Warren, C., Harris, W., Collins, J., Douglas, K., Collins, M., *et al.* (1996). Youth risk behavior surveillance—United States, 1995. *MMWR Morb. Mortal. Wkly. Rep.* 45: 1–85.

Karlson, T., and Hargarten, S. (1997). *Reducing Firearm Injury and Death: A Public Health Sourcebook on Guns*, Rutgers University Press, New Brunswick, NJ.

Kennedy, D. M., Braga, A. A., and Piehl, A. M. (2001). Developing and implementing Operation Ceasefire. In *Reducing Gun Violence: The Boston Gun Project's Operation Ceasefire*, National Institute of Justice, U.S. Department of Justice, Washington, DC.

Kennedy, D. M., Piehl, A. M., and Braga, A. A. (1996). Youth violence in Boston: Gun markets, serious youth offenders, and a use-reduction strategy. *Law Contemp. Probl.* 59: 147–196.

King, G. (1989). Event count models for international relations: Generalizations and applications. *Int. Stud. Q.* 33: 123–147.

Kleck, G. (1997). *Targeting Guns: Firearms and Their Control*, Aldine de Gruyter, NY.

Kozel, N. (1997). *Identifying and Monitoring Emerging Drug Abuse Problems*, National Institute on Drug Abuse, National Institutes of Health, Washington, DC.

Lauritsen, J., Sampson, R., and Laub, J. (1991). The link between offending and victimization among adolescents. *Criminology* 29: 265–292.

Long, J. S. (1997). *Regression Models for Categorical and Limited Dependent Variables*, Advanced Quantitative Techniques in the Social Sciences, Volume 7, Sage Publications, Thousand Oaks, CA.

Moore, M., and Tonry, M. (1998). Youth violence in America. In Tonry, M., and Moore, M. (eds.), *Youth Violence, Vol. 24. Crime and Justice: A Review of Research*, University of Chicago Press, Chicago.

Reiss, A. J., and Roth, J. (eds.). (1993). *Understanding and Preventing Violence*, National Academy Press, Washington, DC.

Rosenfeld, R., Bray, T. M., and Egley, A. (1999). Facilitating violence: A comparison of gang-motivated, gang-affiliated, and nongang youth homicides. *J. Quant. Criminol.* 15: 495–516.

Sheley, J., and Wright, J. (1995). *In the Line of Fire: Youth, Guns, and Violence in Urban America*, Aldine de Gruyter, New York.

Singer, S. (1981). Homogeneous victim-offender populations: A review and some research implications. *J. Crim. Law Criminol.* 72: 779–788.

StataCorp (2001). *Stata Statistical Software: Release 7.0. Reference H-P.* Stata Corporation, College Station, Texas.

Swersey, A., and Enloe, E. (1975). *Homicide in Harlem*, Rand Corporation, New York.

Wilkinson, D., and Fagan, J. (1996). The role of firearms in violence "scripts": The dynamics of gun events among adolescent males. *Law Contemp. Probl.* 59: 55–90.

Wolfgang, M. (1958). *Patterns in Criminal Homicide*, University of Pennsylvania Press, Philadelphia.

Part IV
Drugs and Gangs

[18]

THE SOCIAL ORGANIZATION OF DRUG USE AND DRUG DEALING AMONG URBAN GANGS*

JEFFREY FAGAN
Rutgers University

Youth gangs are a major part of the urban landscape. Gang members always have been involved in collective and individual violence and, in recent years, in drug use and drug dealing. Involvement in drug dealing recently has been associated with increased violence among gangs. However, variation in organizational and social processes within gangs suggests that there also will be variation in drug-crime relationships among gang members. Analyses of the drug-crime relationships were conducted from interviews with 151 gang members in three cities. Four types of gangs were identified, and similar gang types were observed in the three cities. All gang types had high involvement in drug use, but drug dealing varied. The severity of collective gang crime was associated with the prevalence of drug use within a gang. Drug dealing occurred among gangs with both high and low involvement in violence and other crimes. Involvement in cocaine, opiates, and PCP occurred among both violent and nonviolent gangs, as well as among gangs with different involvement in drug dealing. The results suggest that the drug-crime relationship is skewed and spurious for gang members, similar to relationships among nongang inner-city adolescents. Members of violent gangs more often reported the existence of several features of social organization and cohesion in their gangs, independent of gang involvement in drug use and dealing. Similar to other urban adolescents, for gang members violence is not an inevitable consequence of involvement in drug use or dealing.

INTRODUCTION

Youth gangs have been part of the American urban landscape for nearly two centuries (Spergel, 1989). In the modern era, Thrasher's (1927) classic study found more than 1,300 gangs in Chicago alone in the 1920s and noted the consistency of gang formation and social processes in a spectrum of predominantly European immigrant groups. Chicano and Mexican gangs

---

* This research was supported by Grant 87-JN-CX-0012 from the U.S. Department of Justice; the paper reflects the views of the author and not the opinions or policies of the Department of Justice. James Deslonde (1942-1987) was co-principal investigator for this research. Joseph Weis and an anonymous reviewer provided valuable comments on earlier versions of the paper.

634   FAGAN

have persisted in most Latino communities in California since the large waves
of immigration began after the Mexican revolution (Moore, 1978). Gang formations have continued to be cultural institutions in Latino communities in
the United States, from the Pachucos of the World War II era, who were
involved in the infamous "Zoot Suit" riots, to the Vato Locos, who inhabit
the street corners of East Los Angeles and several other southwestern cities.
Gangs have also long established their presence in African-American communities in many large eastern and midwestern cities (Suttles, 1968).

The terms "gang" and "violence" often appear together in both the popular and social scientific literature. Gang research has emphasized violence by
gang members, despite empirical evidence that violence is prevalent but infrequent among gang members and has different origins and subjective meanings
across social and situational contexts (Hagedorn, 1988; Horowitz, 1983;
Klein and Maxson, 1989; Vigil, 1988). Yablonsky (1963) found violence to
be the driving organizational force and normative behavioral fabric for street
gangs. Miller (1975), however, found that although violence did occur
among gangs, it was perhaps the least prevalent of all major gang-specific
behaviors; gang members actually tried to avoid violence and engaged in ritualistic forms of violent interactions that minimized injury. Keiser's (1969)
ethnographic research on the Vice Lords of Chicago reports that "gangbangs" or street fights between gangs were the most infrequent occurrence of
Vice Lord gang life. More recently, Moore (1978) in East Los Angeles and
Horowitz (1987) in Chicago found that violence among Latino gangs served a
variety of specific functions, ranging from organizational maintenance to
social control.

In this decade, adolescent violence has been associated with drug use and
drug selling (Elliott and Huizinga, 1984; Wish and Johnson, 1986). Although
the relationship among drug use, drug selling, and serious youth crime is consistently strong, gangs are diverse, complex, and shifting organizations whose
members participate variably in crime, drug use, and drug dealing
(Hagedorn, 1988; Klein and Maxson, 1989; Spergel, 1989). Accordingly, this
study examines the extent and nature of the interaction of drug use, dealing,
and violence among gang members in urban areas characterized by the social
disorganization cited in early gang research (e.g., Shaw and McKay, 1943)
and in more recent studies of violence by adolescents (Laub, 1983; Shannon,
1984) and gang members (Curry and Spergel, 1988).

DRUG INVOLVEMENT OF GANG MEMBERS

There is great diversity among gangs and gang members in the nature of
their affiliation, social organization, and involvement in delinquency and violence (Bookin-Weiner and Horowitz, 1983; Dolan and Finney, 1984; Klein
and Maxson, 1989; Spergel, 1984). Drug use is also a diverse phenomenon in
gangs, as is the relation of drug use to gang violence (Stumphauzer et al.,

DRUG USE AND DRUG DEALING AMONG GANGS 635

1981). Although much gang violence is unrelated to drug involvement, there is evidence that the rates and severity of substance use and involvement in drug trafficking may be higher in gangs than among other urban youths.

DRUG SELLING

Whether to finance personal drug use, as an avenue to gang affiliation or social status, or as a means of income, the lure of drug sales for inner-city youths is apparent. Dolan and Finney (1984), Moore (1978), and Spergel (1984), among others, suggest that gang members may be involved more often in drug trafficking than other adolescents (cf., Klein et al., 1988). Until this decade, most gang studies suggested that gang involvement in drug trafficking was minor and confined generally to "soft" drugs, such as marijuana. Notable exceptions were Spergel (1966) and Moore (1978), who found close connections between gang membership and both drug use and selling.

Recent evidence suggests that gang members may have greater involvement in drug distribution, particularly of "hard" drugs, than other youths. Analyses of gang involvement in rock cocaine trafficking (Klein et al., 1988) suggest that gangs in Los Angeles frequently are involved in drug selling. They also report, however, that gang members may be less involved in cocaine trafficking and its growth than nongang members in Los Angeles during 1983–1985, the period when rock cocaine emerged in that city.

Mieczkowski (1986) reports the use of violence among organizations of adolescent heroin sellers in Detroit, and Cooper (1987) describes Detroit youth gangs organized around crack cocaine distribution. In several Chicago neighborhoods, gangs control drug sales to juveniles (Recktenwald and Sheppard, 1984; Spergel, 1984). Dolan and Finney (1984) show the economic lure of drug sales for gang members, relative to other economic opportunities. Klein (1985) suggests that the sudden emergence of rock or crack cocaine provided unique economic opportunities, of which Los Angeles gangs quickly took advantage.

Drug selling offers several roles for gang members. Moore (1978) shows how minor roles in drug selling were entry-level jobs for adolescents at the early stages of gang affiliation. Older gang members have more "important" roles in directing drug trafficking activities. For others, drug involvement may be both a job and a form of social "glue" that binds them to the gang in the pursuit of drugs and the money to finance drug use. Drug distribution may also provide economic support for other gang activities and income for individual gang members.

DRUG USE AMONG GANG MEMBERS

Until recently, little distinction has been made regarding patterns of drug use among gangs and the relationship among drug use, gang cohesion, and

636   FAGAN

gang activities. Stumphauzer et al. (1981) note that patterns of drug use varied within and among Los Angeles gangs. Dolan and Finney (1984) and Campbell (1984) illustrate the commonplace role of drug use in gang life among both male and female youths. Vigil (1988) describes a variety of meanings and functions of drug use among Chicano gang members in East Los Angeles, from social "lubricant" during times of collective relaxation to facilitator of ritual behaviors, such as *locura* (exaggerated and spontaneous) acts of aggression or violence. In these contexts, drug use provides a means to social status and acceptance, as well as mutual reinforcement, and it is a natural social process of gang life.[1]

Feldman et al., (1985) observed three distinct styles of drug involvement and its relationship to violence among Latino gangs in San Francisco. The styles were determined in part by the role and meaning of drug use in gang social processes. The *fighting* gangs consisted of young men who were antagonistic toward other gangs. They aggressively responded to any perceived move into their turf by other gangs or any outsider. Drug use and selling were evident among these gangs, but they were only situationally related to their violence through territoriality. Violence occurred in many contexts unrelated to drug use or selling, and it was an important part of the social process of gang affiliation. The *entrepreneurial* gangs consisted of youths who were concerned with attaining social status by means of money and the things money can buy. They very often were active in small-scale illegal sales of marijuana, oral amphetamines, and PCP. Fighting and violence were part of this style, but again they were situationally motivated by concerns over money and/or drugs. The last style was evident in gangs whose activities were *social* and recreational and gave little or no evidence of fighting or violence.

Drug use is not allowed in some youth gangs regardless of the gang's involvement in drug selling. Chin (1986) found that drug use was rejected entirely by nearly all Chinese gangs in New York City, despite their active involvement in heroin distribution. They used violence to protect their business territories from encroachment by other gangs and to coerce their victims to participate in the gang's ventures. These gangs were hierarchically organized, had strict codes, and meted out violent consequences for rule violations by members. Cooper (1987) described organizations of adolescent crack sellers in Detroit that prohibited drug use among their members. Leaders in these groups were wary of both threats to efficiency and security if street-level sellers were high and the potential for cooptation of their business goals if one

---

1. Vigil (1988) notes that these patterns are confined to substances that enhance gang social processes—alcohol, marijuana, and phencyclidine (PCP). Among Chicano gangs, heroin involvement is seen as a betrayal of the gang and the barrio: one cannot be loyal to his or her addiction and the addict ("tecato") culture and maintain loyalty to the gang.

DRUG USE AND DRUG DEALING AMONG GANGS 637

of their members became a consumer of their goods. The gangs were organized around income, and they saw drug use as detracting from the selling skills and productivity of the members. Expulsion from the gang resulted from breaking this rule, but other violent reprisals also were possible.

Mieczkowski (1986) studied street-level adolescent drug runners in heroin-dealing organizations, also in Detroit, and found a rejection of heroin use by members of the runner organizations. These groups, however, accepted recreational use of other drugs by members, primarily marijuana and cocaine in social situations not involved with dealing. They particularly found danger in being high on any drug while on the job, and superiors in these organizations enforced the prohibition against heroin use while working by denying runners their consignment and thereby shutting off their source of income. Violence was occasionally used by superiors (crew bosses) to enforce discipline. Sellers looked down on their heroin-using customers, despite having tried it themselves at some point in their lives. Their own experience with heroin in part explains their general disapproval of heroin use.

ROLE OF SOCIAL ORGANIZATION

The discovery of diverse patterns of criminality and drug involvement among gang members and gangs suggests that there are factors in the social organization of gangs and processes of affiliation or cohesion that either encourage or discourage these patterns. Such diversity also exists among general adolescent populations (Fagan et al., in press; Schwendinger and Schwendinger, 1985; White et al., 1987), which suggests that gangs reflect patterns of affiliation and collective behavior that are similar to those of other adolescent subcultures. Accordingly, violence, which historically has been taken as a defining feature of gangs, and drug involvement may more accurately be conceptualized as contingent behaviors among adolescents. Such contingencies rarely have received theoretical or empirical attention in prior research.

Little research has examined whether diverse patterns of drug involvement among gangs are influenced by the social organization of gangs, their processes of affiliation, and their strategies for maintaining behavioral norms. That gangs have specific social structures that vary by gang and locale has been well validated (see Klein and Maxson, 1989, for a review of this literature). This diversity extends also to the coexistence of conventional and deviant values (Keiser, 1969). The ethnographic literature on gang involvement strongly suggests that gangs have a natural social structure, are well stratified, and appear to undergo developmental sequences not unlike other social groups or organizations (Hagedorn, 1988; Horowitz, 1983; Moore, 1978; Vigil, 1988). Moreover, the reasons for gang affiliation are quite varied, ranging from social status, to protection from other gangs, to economic opportunity (Anderson and Rodriguez, 1984; Erlanger, 1979). These motivations, in

638 FAGAN

turn, may lead to quite different levels of involvement in drug use or sales and other criminal activities.

METHODOLOGICAL ISSUES

The study of drug use and selling among gangs is complicated by several methodological concerns. First, research on gangs reflects a lack of consensus on the basic definitions and characteristics of gangs. Definitions of gangs in the 1950s and 1960s reflected etiological interests as well as the attributes of the social areas where gangs were most visible. Klein (1971) found gang membership to be a transitory phenomenon that atrophied as gang members approached adulthood, though the upper end of the age range may have increased in recent years (Klein and Maxson, 1989). Moore's (1978) study of Mexican-American communities in East Los Angeles found that gang membership and identity often extend well into adulthood. In her study, gang activities continued in prisons and through illicit drug trade long after members fade from view as street corner youths. But the length of affiliation with gangs is likely to reflect the motivation for the initial affiliation, the cohesiveness of the particular gang, and specific social or personal circumstances that may influence an individual's life-style decisions during the transition to adulthood. Klein and Maxson (1989) suggest that the definition of gangs has evolved in concert with changes in social policy on how to control gangs, specifically their violent behaviors and, more recently, drug involvement.

Second, the definition of "gang crime" also varies across jurisdictions, depending on the interests of the definer. The determination of a "gang-related offense" is a subjective process and likely to vary by city, agency, and researcher (Klein and Maxson, 1989). The distinctions between youth groups and gangs have varied over the years, as have the distinctions between gang crimes and nongang delinquent acts. Law enforcement agencies disagree, for example, on whether any crime committed by a known gang member should be labeled as a gang crime regardless of the specific context or meaning of the event. Spergel (1989) cites extraordinary variability in gang-related homicides in Chicago and Los Angeles, which he suggests, is attributable to the differences in criteria for labeling an event as "gang-related." Obviously, such definitional issues will bear on methodological decisions in gang research, empirical knowledge of gangs, and theory development.

Third, the concentration of large numbers of gangs in urban areas such as Los Angeles and Chicago presents sampling problems that raise questions of external validity. The traditional gang, with its unstable membership, shifting leadership, and fluid norms, also presents sampling difficulties. Short and Strodtbeck (1965) concluded that it is difficult if not impossible to develop probability samples of gangs and gang members due to the constant changes in gang membership and identity.

DRUG USE AND DRUG DEALING AMONG GANGS 639

Gang research generally has relied on either ethnographic studies of gangs or analyses of official records from law enforcement and other social agencies on gangs, gang activity, and gang members. Few efforts have been made to study gang members systematically using survey methods with random or theoretical samples. Researchers confront a number of problems. Gang members span a broad age range. Initiates and "juniors" often are early adolescents. "Veteranos" and "OGs" (old guys) continue their gang involvement until 30 to 40 years of age, although their gang participation may be infrequent and marginal. Uncovering features of gang life also poses difficulties. Members tend to conceal their own activities or not be aware of the activities of others. To overcome suspicion about researchers and problems of gaining access to the concealed aspects of gang life, ethnographic research has been the dominant mode of gang research.

The measurement and theoretical advances of the past decade in delinquency research (Elliott et al., 1985; Hindelang et al., 1981) have not been applied to gang research. Klein and Maxson (1989), among others, noted the paradigm shift in the past decade from etiological research on gang formation and behaviors to crime control and suppression, and blamed it for the limited advances in theory and knowledge about gangs since the work of the late 1970s. Major consequences have been the inability to answer important and basic questions on gang formation and to compare gang and nongang youths, gangs of different behavioral orientations, and the variation in gang processes and behaviors in different social contexts.

PURPOSE OF STUDY

This study examines patterns of individual and collective crime, drug use, and drug dealing among gangs and gang members in three cities. First, variations among gangs in their patterns of drug involvement and other criminal activity are determined empirically from samples of gang members in specific neighborhoods in each city. Second, whether social organizational features and subcultural processes within gangs mediate these patterns is analyzed from gang members' self reports on gang structures and processes.

The relationship between drug use and youth crime is well established in research on adolescents (Elliott et al., 1985; Fagan et al., in press; White et al., 1987) and young adults (Chaiken and Chaiken, 1989; Gandossy et al., 1980). Goldstein (1985) has described the different ways that drug involvement contributes to violence. Among gang members, there is a positive correlation between group crimes and violence (Klein and Maxson, 1989; Piper, 1985; Tracy and Piper, 1984). There also appear to be discrete patterns within gangs on these behaviors (Dolan and Finney, 1984; Feldman et al., 1985). In addition, Fagan et al. (in press) show that drug use occurs among both violent delinquents and nondelinquent youths, and that violence occurs with and without drug involvement. Accordingly, it seems that while drug

640   FAGAN

involvement contributes to patterns of violence, the relationship is contingent on unique factors in what appear to be parallel but independent subcultures.

The diversity of gang structures and criminal activities observed in earlier studies suggests that drug involvement will vary in its contribution to other criminal activity, particularly violence. Whether organizational features of gangs influence their drug involvement has not been studied. The extent to which violence and drug use among gang members and gangs are spuriously related or reflect variation in gang structures or their subcultures, has also been neglected in theory and empirical research. Gang research, however, has illustrated the relationship between gang violence and social organizational factors, such as cohesion and hierarchy. This suggests that distinct subcultural processes or differences in the social organization of youth networks may mediate the occurrence and severity of these behaviors within discrete social networks of youths (Schwendinger and Schwendinger, 1985).

The interactions among drug involvement, violence, other gang and nongang crimes, and the social organization of gangs are examined in this study. If drug use is spuriously associated with violence among inner-city adolescents, then variation also may be expected in drug-crime relationships among gang members.[2] That is, crime and violence among gangs should occur independently of substance use.[3] Drug selling and violence, however, are positively associated among adolescents, as are serious drug use (of cocaine, heroin, and PCP) and violence. Since violence among gangs is associated with gang structure and cohesive social processes, then serious drug involvement among gangs should occur for those gangs with more formal structures and social processes.

METHODS

SAMPLES

Surveys were conducted in 1984 and 1985 in three inner-city, "high crime" neighborhoods in A- and B-level SMSAs: South Central Los Angeles, the University Heights section of San Diego, and the neighborhoods on the west side of Chicago.[4] By limiting the study to inner-city areas, gang behaviors and processes could be examined in areas with high concentrations of the

---

2. Although drug use and violence share common etiological processes, they are equally likely to appear independently or together.

3. Temporal order must be considered in these relationships. Drug selling, particularly of rock cocaine or crack, is a relatively recent event for African-American gangs in Los Angeles. Gang violence preceded their involvement in rock trafficking. However, the Detroit findings (e.g., Cooper, 1987) suggest that violence in drug-selling organizations developed simultaneously with their formation, though it existed in other Detroit gangs long before crack was available in the city.

4. A-level metropolitan areas have populations greater than 1,000,000; B-level areas, populations of 250,000 to 1,000,000. Analyses determined the homogeneity of the study

DRUG USE AND DRUG DEALING AMONG GANGS 641

ecological correlates of violence and other crimes (Sampson, 1986). Gang problems in all three cities have been extensively documented (Maxson and Klein, 1983; Pennell and Curtis, 1982; Spergel, 1984).

Respondents ranged in age from 13 to 20 years, were predominantly from minority groups, and were male. The final sample included 151 gang members, spread evenly among the three sites. The sampling procedure employed purposive "snowball" samples of gang members (Biernacki and Waldorf, 1981). This is an optimal choice, given the difficulty of identifying a gang universe from which to sample randomly (Short and Strodtbeck, 1965). This strategy was chosen instead of sampling from law enforcement rosters of known gang members because of the potential variability across cities in the definition of gang member and gang crime (Klein and Maxson, 1989; Spergel, 1989). The snowball strategy provided flexibility in targeting, locating, and recruiting members of all known or emerging gangs. Moreover, because the snowball process involves respondents nominating other respondents and identifying other possible chains of respondents, the likelihood of excluding specific gangs is minimized.

Gang members were recruited through intermediaries chosen from neighborhood-based organizations and agencies in each study neighborhood. Intermediaries included gang intervention programs, social service organizations, and neighborhood advocacy groups. The organizations were chosen because of their detailed knowledge of local gang scenes, their neutrality with respect to intra-gang conflicts or conflicts with law enforcement, and their access to a variety of gang members with different types of gang affiliation and activity. Their knowledge of local gang networks also minimized omission of unknown networks of gangs in their areas.

The management of chains was a critical task to ensure that all known gang networks were included, that no specific gang was overrepresented, and

---

neighborhoods with respect to their ecological characteristics. This procedure was necessary to determine whether samples from different cities could be aggregated. The census tract for each respondent's neighborhood was recorded, and 10 variables were extracted from 1980 census data. These variables represented the domains identified by Laub and Hindelang (1981) as sources of social area effects that explain differences in serious juvenile crime: demographic, labor force, poverty, and housing characteristics. Two validation checks were made. First, analysis-of-variance comparisons were made to determine whether the social area characteristics for the samples were comparable; 6 of 10 census variables were comparable. Second, two comparability checks were conducted to determine the homogeneity of samples across sites. Chi-square analyses of demographic and socioeconomic variables were used to compare sample characteristics; the results were not statistically significant. Also, means for selected explanatory and demographic variables were compared for each site versus the pooled sample from the remaining sites to determine if the exclusion of any site affected the pooled distribution of the inner-city sample.

that unknown networks were not excluded from the samples, and to incorporate any new (unanticipated) gangs that were discovered during the nomination part of the interview. Decisions on management of the chains were made by research staff in consultation with staff from the intermediary organizations. The sample of gangs represented by respondents was reviewed periodically with staff from the intermediary organizations to determine whether members of all gangs active in the neighborhood were included in the sample. One limitation of the data was the reliance on only one source to validate the representativeness of the sample of neighborhood gangs. Moreover, though representative of the study neighborhoods, the gang samples may not be representative of gangs active throughout each city.

Two recruitment processes were used. First, gang members were asked by intermediaries to refer others within their gang or gangs they knew but with whom they were not actively in conflict. A short screening interview, administered by volunteers from the intermediary organizations, determined their eligibility. Second, referrals were solicited from social agencies that routinely deal with gang members. The intermediary agencies and the neighborhood volunteers were known to and involved with gang members in several ways: mediators of gang disputes, counselors for school or family problems, organizers of neighborhood recreational activities, or monitors at school events. Volunteers worked in these organizations only if they had no personal ties to or experiences with (e.g., victimization) gangs or gang members.

The use of the gang chains also permitted stratification by age, an important factor given the correlation of age with specific roles within gangs (Klein and Maxson, 1989). Because of the hierarchical structure of the gangs in these areas, a variation of the typical chain referral procedure was used.[5] Gang members were solicited as groups. Accordingly, in approaching gang members, they were asked to suggest members of different ages and with different roles in the gang (e.g., "juniors" or "wannabes," "people who make or enforce the rules," and older gang members).

Gangs and gang members met the definition used by Klein (1971:13):

> we shall use the term [street gang] to refer to any denotable . . . group [of adolescents or young adults] who (a) are generally perceived as a distinct aggregation by others in the neighborhood, (b) recognize themselves as a denotable group (almost invariably with a group name), and (c) have been involved in a sufficient number of [illegal] incidents to call forth a consistent negative response from neighborhood residents and/or enforcement agencies.

This definition restricted the eligible gangs and members to those involved in illegal activities. Although most gang members and even members of street-

---

5. In such procedures, subjects are often asked to nominate "someone just like you."

DRUG USE AND DRUG DEALING AMONG GANGS 643

corner groups or youth groups are involved in at least some minor delinquency (including drug use), this definition excludes the unknown percentage of youth groups or gangs who do not commit illegal acts. Accordingly, the Guardian Angels, an anticrime gang, would not meet this definition, nor would a Chinese secret society (Chin, 1986).

SURVEY PROCEDURES

The surveys were conducted in groups of 10 in the facilities of the intermediary organizations; several sessions were scheduled to accommodate working youths and those with other commitments. To avoid repeats, volunteer proctors from the intermediary agencies who were familiar with neighborhood youths monitored attendance and selected out repeaters. Together with the researchers, they kept anonymous records of the number of participants from each gang in the sample. Care was taken to avoid inadvertent contact between rival gangs, mainly through scheduling and using a facility on "neutral" turf for all contacts.

In each case, the surveys were described as voluntary and anonymous. Neither names nor identifiers were requested anywhere on the survey forms. Participants received a stipend for their participation (e.g., coupons from local record stores, T-shirts, or caps), which were handed out at the completion of the session.

Survey items were read aloud by research staff while respondents followed along on the survey form. The proctors also held up large displays of the response sets for sequences of items (e.g., delinquency or drug use items). In addition, two or three volunteers from local neighborhood organizations were stationed in the rear of the rooms to answer respondents' questions and provide other assistance as needed. Care was taken these volunteers neither knew nor recognized the gang members. The volunteers were selected to be older than the gang members (usually, about 25 years of age) and were residents of the neighborhood.[6] Both male and female volunteers were used.

MEASURES AND CONSTRUCTS

The survey included demographic items, self-reported delinquency and drug use/sales measures, and items on respondents' perceptions of whether members of their gang participated in various types of gang activities (both legal and illegal), involvement in school or work, family life, and family approval of, or participation in the gangs. Other items asked about gang structures and roles, gang activities and organization (e.g., recruitment, enforcement of gang discipline), other gangs in the area (e.g., colors, turf,

---

6. The intermediary agencies asked prospective volunteers if they had contact with gang members in their neighborhoods; they declined offers of assistance from those who either had been victims of gang violence or who personally knew active gang members.

conflicts, activities), and items on gang relations with law enforcement and other social agencies.

Self-reported delinquency (SRD) and gang delinquency items included questions on specific acts that reflected "high consensus" deviance (Thio, 1983), primarily acts that harm, injure, or do damage. A 27-item index included behaviors that, with the exception of homicide and sexual assault, included all Uniform Crime Report (UCR) Part I offenses and many Part II offenses. The categorical response set for self-reports ranged from "never" to "several times a year" for the past year. Similar to other studies (e.g., Elliott et al., 1985), the recall period was 12 months, from "Christmas a year ago to this past Christmas." Such anchoring techniques enable respondents to reconstruct behaviors. For reports of gang activities, responses asked only for how many members of the gang were involved (from "none" to "all or nearly all"). Indices were constructed from aggregations of homogeneous behaviors to be consistent with UCR categories, using a procedure similar to that used by Elliott and Huizinga (1984). Indices were derived by summing the reported incidence or prevalence scores for nonoverlapping items within scales. The items and index construction are shown in the appendix.

The questions for alcohol and drug use followed the same format and response sets as the SRD items. Drug sales was included as a SRD item. Questions about personal use of substances were included in separate items. Two alcohol items (beer or wine; whiskey, gin, vodka, or other liquor) and seven illicit drug (marijuana, cocaine, heroin or opiates, hallucinogens, amphetamines or "speed," barbiturates or "downers," and inhalants or "glue sniffing") items were included. Individual substances were used to capture what ethnographic data suggest are distinct drug use patterns by youth network and locale (Feldman et al., 1979).

Gang structure and process measures covered recruitment and initiation processes, enforcement of gang hierarchy and leadership forms, and the range of legitimate and illegitimate activities by gang types. "Natural social controls" within gangs also were covered, including various forms of leadership, assessments of their strength (from the unanimity of gang members' responses), and the diversity versus concentration of leadership.

Overall, the SRD measures have strong explanatory power in both cross-sectional and longitudinal studies of serious delinquency and under a variety of sampling conditions, including samples of institutionalized male delinquents and general populations of male adolescents from six inner-city neighborhoods (Fagan et al., 1986). Fagan et al. (1987) validated the SRD items with both male and female adolescents in the same inner-city neighborhoods using both demographic and theoretical variables. Reliability analyses included calculation of consistency measures (Cronbach's alpha) for each SRD index, and again for site-specific calculations. In general, reliabilities

DRUG USE AND DRUG DEALING AMONG GANGS 645

were at least adequate (alpha = .70) or excellent (alpha = .90) for the gang samples, both within and across cities.

RESULTS

INCIDENCE AND PREVALENCE OF DELINQUENCY AND DRUG USE BY GANG MEMBERS

Table 1 summarizes the self-reports by gang members of their involvement in each type of behavior in the prior year and their reports of the behaviors of others members of their gang. The table shows the percentage of gangs involved in each behavior during the prior year, based on reports by individual gang members about their gangs. Two measures of individual acts by gang members are reported: the percentage of gang members reporting at least one act in the prior year (prevalence) and the frequency of those behaviors among individual gang members reporting at least one act. For gang members reporting at least 1 act, the percentages of those reporting 3 or more such acts and 12 or more such acts (at least 1 act per month) are shown. Because gang members were carefully sampled to avoid overrepresentation by members of any individual gang, redundancy was minimized.[7]

PREVALENCE

Collective and individual involvement in drug use and nondrug crimes was high. There is general concordance in respondents' reports of the prevalence of gang involvement in each crime type and their own involvement. Both violent and nonviolent crimes are common behaviors within gangs and among their members in these cities, similar to patterns found by Tracy and Piper (1984) among male gang members in Philadelphia. Felony theft (theft of property or goods worth more than $100) was the most prevalent crime type for collective behaviors, more prevalent than minor theft.[8] Extortion was the most prevalent individual act. Drug selling also was prevalent as a collective behavior of the gangs, but it was not as prevalent among their

---

7. The number of gang members involved in specific behaviors was not asked. This decision was intended to protect respondents against reprisals from other gangs and to minimize their disclosure of information that might attract the attention of law enforcement agencies and thus discourage truthful reporting.

8. Also, felony assault was more prevalent than minor assault as both a collective and individual act. In general adolescent samples (e.g., Elliott and Huizinga, 1984), minor assault and minor theft are more prevalent and frequent, respectively, than felony assault and felony theft. In inner-city adolescent samples (e.g., Fagan et al., 1986), similar trends were found among institutionalized male delinquents and school dropouts. The differences for this sample may reflect actual differences between gang members and other adolescents, sampling artifacts (the inclusion of only males in the sample), design artifacts (item and index construction that emphasized more serious criminal acts), and enhancements by gang members in reports of their behaviors.

646   FAGAN

Table 1.   Prevalence and Frequency of Collective and
           Individual Behaviors of Gang Members in Prior
           Year (N = 151)

Self-reported Offense-specific Behaviors	Gang Acts, Prevalence*	Individual Acts		
		At Least Once	Regular: Three or More Times	Frequent: Twelve or More Times
Felony Assault	55.6%	53.0%	27.8%	14.8%
Minor Assault	45.7	45.5	16.9	8.9
Robbery	59.6	57.8	35.8	22.0
Felony Theft	67.5	64.2	37.6	22.0
Minor Theft	58.3	56.4	35.4	23.6
Vandalism	55.0	59.8	34.0	19.7
Illegal Services	53.0	48.3	27.6	15.5
Weapons	53.6	58.6	34.4	18.9
Extortion	57.6	67.5	36.0	21.1
Drug Sales	62.9	51.3	23.8	14.1
Alcohol	72.8	79.2	50.4	40.8
Marijuana	67.5	73.6	44.8	33.6
PCP, Psychedelics	53.6	51.4	32.7	22.4
Speed, Barbiturates	51.0	48.1	26.9	17.3
Cocaine	53.6	48.2	35.0	13.4
Heroin, Other Opiates	41.7	40.8	16.5	12.6

* Percentage of respondents reporting that "a few" or more gang members were
involved in that behavior in the prior year.

members. Alcohol and marijuana were the most prevalent drugs used, both
collectively and individually. The prevalence estimates for other drugs also
are quite high. Heroin use, generally infrequent among adolescents (Johnson
et al., 1985), was used in over 40% of the gangs and by a similar percentage
of gang members.

The individual prevalence rates for both drug use and delinquency were
higher for gang youths than for general adolescent populations in inner cities.
Fagan et al. (1986) analyzed self-reports from a general adolescent sample
from six inner-city neighborhoods. They reported that 23.6% of the male
adolescents were involved in felony theft, and 13.9% were involved in robbery in the prior year.[9] The prevalence of felony robbery, felony theft, marijuana use, and drug sales among individual gang members in this study
generally are closer to prevalence rates for institutionalized juvenile offenders

---

9.   In those samples, 13% identified themselves as gang members.

DRUG USE AND DRUG DEALING AMONG GANGS 647

than for other inner-city male adolescents (Cernkovich et al., 1986; Fagan et al., 1986). Among the institutionalized delinquents in the Fagan et al. (1986) sample, for example, 82% were involved in felony theft and 58% in robbery.

FREQUENCY

For individual gang acts, the percentage reporting "regular" (three or more acts in the prior year) and "frequent" (12 or more acts) involvement was calculated from the percentage of those reporting at least one act. Fewer gang members reported regular and frequent individual acts than reported any involvement. A small percentage of gang members were involved frequently for most criminal acts, a widely observed epidemiological pattern in delinquency research (e.g., Elliott and Huizinga, 1984; Wolfgang et al., 1972). For most drug use and nondrug crime categories, regular involvement was reported by many of those reporting any involvement, and frequent involvement was reported by many of those reporting regular involvement. However, for alcohol and marijuana use, there were only small differences in the number of respondents reporting regular and frequent involvement.

Among violent offenses, fewer gang members reported frequent felony and minor assault than any other (nondrug) delinquent behaviors. Robbery was one of the most frequent acts; 22% reported 12 or more robberies in the prior year. Robbery, felony theft, minor theft, and extortion were the most frequent self-reported individual acts. Also, the fewest respondents reported both regular and frequent minor assaults and drug sales, although they appear to be both more frequent and more prevalent among gang members than other adolescent groups (Elliott and Huizinga, 1984; Fagan et al., in press). For drug use, the percentages of respondents reporting frequent marijuana and alcohol use were highest. Among all behaviors, the disparity between regular and frequent use was least for these two categories. Cocaine and heroin use were reported by the smallest number of gang members in all frequency categories, though the percentages in each category still exceed those in most general adolescent population estimates (see Elliott and Huizinga, 1984; Fagan et al., in press).

Overall, violent acts (other than robbery) and drug sales were the individual behaviors least often reported as frequent by gang members. The involvement of a relatively small percentage of gang members in frequent violence, together with their more frequent participation in nonviolent crime, suggests that gang violence still is a relatively infrequent behavior for gang members compared with nonviolent behaviors. The prevalence of frequent violence among gang members in the sample, however, is still higher than among other adolescents.

Finally, Table 1 affords a comparison of frequent crime participation between gang members and nongang youths. There are nearly twice as many

648   FAGAN

"frequent" violent offenders among the gang members in this study compared
with males in other adolescent samples (e.g., Wolfgang et al., 1972). Tracy
(1979) found similar differences between gang and nongang members among
males in Philadelphia. The percentage involved in frequent serious violent or
property delinquent acts in this study is higher than in both the National
Youth Survey (Elliott and Huizinga, 1984) and general inner-city adolescent
samples (Fagan et al., 1987). Using similar item and index construction,
those studies found that less than 9% reported three or more serious or violent behaviors in the prior year. For virtually all crime types and drug categories, frequent participation by gang members in this study exceeds self-
reports of involvement in similar behaviors among nongang youths. The
number of gang members reporting frequent participation was higher than for
institutionalized male delinquents in virtually all drug and nondrug behavior
categories (Cernkovich et al., 1986; Fagan et al., 1986).

TYPOLOGIES OF DRUG INVOLVEMENT AMONG GANGS

Typologies were developed to classify gangs on their patterns of drug use,
selling, and other criminal behaviors. Groups were constructed from gang
members' reports on whether members of their gang were involved in each of
the drug use and delinquency behaviors in the indices in Table 1. The groups
reflect differences between gangs in the joint distributions of drug use, drug
selling, and nondrug crimes, but they should be interpreted only as illustrative of the patterns and not reified as existing types of gangs. Also, the procedure of obtaining reports by gang members about others in their gang raises
validity concerns. Gang violence, for example, often occurs as group offenses,
which leads to exaggerations of the extent of collective gang involvement (see
Reiss, 1986, on group offending). Also, gang members may not be well
informed about the behaviors of others in the gang (Klein and Maxson,
1989).

There are two choices for identifying dimensions for typology development: either accept the original behavioral measures or use transformed
scores. The latter promises to reconcile anomalies within the raw data and
root out sampling artifacts. But transformations, such as log linear models or
factor analytic procedures, have their own implicit biases and assumptions,
which may introduce new meaning into the distributions.[10] Thus, the raw
scores were used here to avoid biases inherent in the transformation procedures. This selection seemed appropriate given the categorical response sets
and the unique sample construction procedures.

Typology development was based on the 11 offense-specific indices and the

---

10.   In other words, the loss of critical information from truncating positively skewed
distributions may alter the actual meaning and interpretation of this unique feature of
delinquency data (see Elliott and Huizinga, 1983).

DRUG USE AND DRUG DEALING AMONG GANGS 649

10 drug-use items in the appendix. An iterative partitioning method was used to identify patterns of drug use, drug sales, and criminality of the gangs as reported by their gang members. Squared Euclidean distance (Ward's centroid method) was used as the similarity measure (Aldenfelder and Blashfield, 1984). A k-means pass was used as the method to assign cases to clusters. The result was a nonhierarchical cluster analytic solution that optimizes the minimum variance within clusters. This approach to grouping subjects uses their relative proximity in a specified dimensional space. The nonhierarchical centroid method is less useful than the hierarchical models as a heuristic tool because it displays neither agglomerative nor diversive linkages (e.g., dendograms). This weakness was addressed by running sequential solutions that specify cluster sizes of from three to seven. Comparisons of each successive iteration approximated a divisive hierarchical analysis.

The four-cluster solution was selected based on the shifts in cluster membership in successive iterations and on the conceptual integrity (i.e., face validity) of the solution. The validation procedures relied on interpretation plus the face validity and internal consistency of the aggregate behavioral characteristics of each group and the overall sample classification. This is a purely classificatory procedure, with no questions of statistical significance in the derivation procedure. The clusters are a heuristic tool that is instructive for partitioning the gangs into groups for descriptive purposes, but they should be regarded cautiously as distinct types of gangs.

Table 2 shows cluster membership and the mean prevalence score for each of the cluster dimensions. Each offense-specific index includes several items, so that index scores varied by the number of behaviors that members reported for their gang.[11] Analysis-of-variance tests for all index scores were significant ($p = .001$). Table 3 summarizes the results and shows the relative degrees of gang involvement for each dimension of gang behavior. The descriptions below include the percentage of gangs in each type (based on individual gang members' reports about collective acts of their gang).

- Type 1 (28 percent) is involved in few delinquent activities and little drug use other than alcohol and marijuana use. These gangs also have low involvement in drug sales (most likely to finance their own drug use). This is basically a social group whose patterns of use reflect general adolescent experimentation in drug use and delinquency. This type of gang appears to be a "social gang."
- Type 2 (7 percent) gangs have few members involved in nondrug criminal behaviors, but relatively high prevalence of several types of drug use, drug sales, and one type of delinquency—vandalism. Their drug sales, in the absence of other forms of crime, are likely to be supportive of their own drug use. Their extensive involvement in

---

11. See Fagan et al. (1986) for an item-scale mapping.

Table 2. Gang Drug and Crime Behaviors, by Type of Gang

Gang Behaviors	Gang Type			
	1	2	3	4
(N)	(43)	(10)	(56)	(42)
Felony Assault	.09	.00	1.36	1.48
Minor Assault	.00	.00	.63	.81
Robbery	.05	.00	2.02	2.38
Felony Theft	.09	.00	4.00	4.40
Minor Theft	.00	.00	1.73	2.31
Vandalism	.00	1.50	1.18	1.48
Illegal Services	.07	.00	.75	.88
Weapons	.02	.00	1.93	2.52
Extortion	.02	.00	.77	.86
Drug Sales	.16	1.50	1.07	1.67
Alcohol	.44	1.50	1.55	1.67
Marijuana	.23	.80	.84	.88
Cocaine	.02	.70	.66	.86
Heroin	.00	1.50	.34	1.36
PCP, Psychedelics	.09	2.10	.64	2.45
Speed, Barbiturates	.09	2.60	.57	2.60

NOTE: Scale scores are mean prevalence scores for ordinal measures of gang members' participation in each behavior in the prior year. ANOVA tests for gang-type differences were significant ($P < .000$) for all scales.

drug use suggests that their affiliation may be based on mutually supportive patterns of drug use and dealing to support group and individual drug use. This type seems to be a "party gang" that otherwise manifests several of the subcultural and organizational features of gangs.

- Type 3 (37 percent) gangs appear to include serious delinquents who have extensive involvement in several types of delinquent acts, both serious and nonserious, and both violent and property offenses. This type of gang's involvement in drug sales, however, is far lower than for the "party gangs," as is their use of serious substances (cocaine, heroin, amphetamines, and PCP). The absence of extensive involvement in serious drug use and drug sales suggests that drugs play a secondary role in their criminal activities and that drug use is most likely recreational or social in nature (Fields, 1985). This group resembles serious delinquents identified in other studies of inner-city

DRUG USE AND DRUG DEALING AMONG GANGS 651

adolescents, and the members can be appropriately called "serious delinquents."

- Type 4 (28 percent) gangs differ from the third group only in their extensive involvement in serious drug use and higher rates of drug sales. We might speculate that their criminality and drug sales are linked and that rather than social drug use, their drug use and selling reflect a systemic relationship with other criminal acts. As shown below, this is a highly cohesive and organized type, and it is probably at the highest risk for becoming a more formal criminal organization. At this stage, they appear to be more of an incipient, or nascent "organization."

Table 3. Drug and Alcohol Use, Drug Dealing, and Other Behaviors, by Type of Gang (Summary)

Behaviors	Gang Type			
	1	2	3	4
(N)	(43)	(10)	(56)	(42)
Violent Crime	Low	Low	High	High
Felony Property Crime	Low	Low	High	High
Other Property Crime	Low	High	High	High
Weapons	Low	Low	High	High
Drug Sales	Low	High	Medium	High
Alcohol	Low	High	High	High
Marijuana	Low	High	High	High
Cocaine, Heroin, PCP	Low	High	Medium	High

The typology suggests that the complex relationship between substance use and dealing and delinquency observed among inner-city adolescents (Fagan et al., in press) also applies to gang members. Use of cocaine, PCP, and other serious drugs appears to be a routine feature of gang life only for gangs who otherwise are involved marginally in nondrug crimes. Drug selling is evident among both violent and nonviolent gangs, but it is not evident among one gang type that reports frequent violence. However, involvement in serious drug use occurs together with higher rates of drug selling in another gang type.

The high prevalence of drug use among "social" gangs and of drug use and selling among "party" gangs suggests that drug involvement is not inextricably linked to violence. Table 3 shows a high prevalence of violence among gangs with both high and moderate involvement in drug selling and also with low-to-moderate involvement in serious substances. One must look to factors other than drug involvement to explain violence among gang members. On the other hand, Table 2 implies that a strong relationship exists among violence, serious crime, frequent intoxication, and drug dealing among gang members, just as there is among other inner-city adolescents. The relationship among gang violence, nonviolent crimes, drug selling, and drug use is complex. Violence occurs in gangs with distinct drug use patterns, but rarely among gangs that also are not involved with drug use and drug selling.

Variation in gang violence by city is well established (Spergel, 1989). Whether this represents variation in ecological and community stability factors, historical processes of gang formation, police responses, ethnic differences and acculturation processes, or other factors is unknown. It is possible that the gang types simply represent city differences or ethnic variation within the sample. Accordingly, gang types were compared by city to determine if patterns reflected specific patterns within cities or valid representations of natural variation among gangs in different ecological settings.

Differences were evident, though not statistically significant ($p = .078$), by city (Table 4). In Los Angeles, there was a higher percentage of "social" gangs and a lower percentage of "organizations" than in the other two cities. Recent evidence on gang violence in Los Angeles suggests that Los Angeles gang members in this study underreported gang involvement in violence (Baker, 1988; Klein et al., 1988). Their responses may reflect the complex role of the intermediary group with gangs, the local schools, and the police, or simply denial by gang members of their violence. Nevertheless, the consistency between Chicago and San Diego, together with the minor differences in Los Angeles for all but type 1, supports the generalizability of the gang types across disparate urban settings. Also, ethnic differences seem to be unrelated to gang type. Respondents in Los Angeles and Chicago primarily were African-American gang members, while respondents in San Diego included both Chicano and Asian gangs. The similarity in distributions among cities suggests that there may exist differences within ethnic groups in gang types. Conclusive evidence of such variations requires more systematic study across ethnic groups.

CORE AND MARGINAL INVOLVEMENT IN GANG DELINQUENCY AND DRUG USE

Members of gangs vary by role, reason for affiliation, and extent of participation in delinquent activities. Gang membership and roles also shift over time, as members move in and out of various roles. Membership tenure varies, as does the length of time for members to move up from less important to more visible roles. Dropping back from leadership also is not uncommon (Moore, 1978; Vigil, 1988). Roles within gangs also may vary according to the nature of the activity—leaders for drug selling may differ from leaders or

DRUG USE AND DRUG DEALING AMONG GANGS 653

Table 4.   Distribution of Gang Types, by City

City	Gang Type			
	1	2	3	4
Chicago	22.0%	4.0%	36.0%	38.0%
Los Angeles	38.0	12.0	36.0	14.0
San Diego	25.5	3.9	39.2	31.4
N	43	10	56	42
Percent	28.5	6.6	37.1	27.8

Chi-square = 11.38   p = .078

soldiers in "gangbanging." Spergel (1989) refers to gang members with different leadership roles as "floaters." Despite the diversity and fluidity of gang affiliation and roles, there is consensus that core members are involved in a wider range of delinquent acts than fringe or situational members. Research on gangs has not examined the complicating role of involvement in drug use or sales, however.

Table 5 shows the percentage of respondents within gang types who reported "regular" substance use or delinquency in the past year—that is, those who reported more than "a few" (three or more) occasions in that time.[12] The behavior categories are the same ones used to construct the gang typology. Comparisons across gang types for all variables were significant. The results show that regular participation by individuals increased with the seriousness of collective gang acts. That is, a higher percentage of members in seriously delinquent gangs (types 3 and 4) reported regular or frequent participation (more than three times in the prior year) than in the other gang types. There are exceptions, though. The percentage of "party" gang members reporting regular assault and robbery was similar to reports from members of "serious delinquents" or the "organizations." Also, fewer members of "party gangs" reported regular involvement in drug use than in the "social gangs." The small number describing their gang as "party gangs" (10 gang members) leaves this group more vulnerable to sampling error than the others. Whether this is an artifact of the gang members selected or an anomaly of the design is not clear.

Nevertheless, there is variation in the extent and nature of individual participation in delinquency and drug use—that is, marginal or infrequent involvement in serious delinquent acts exists within gangs together with core

---

12. This is the threshold used by Dunford and Elliott (1984), Elliott and Huizinga (1984), and Fagan et al. (1987, in press) to classify "multiple index" offenders from others in typological schemes using self-reported annual frequencies.

Table 5. "Regular" Self-reported Substance Use and Other Delinquency, by Type of Gang

Self-reported Behaviors	Gang Type				Significance, p (Chi-square)
	1	2	3	4	
Felony Assault	12.0	33.3	28.9	35.9	.04
Minor Assault	4.4	33.3	15.6	27.5	.001
Robbery	4.3	50.0	40.9	47.2	.001
Felony Theft	4.6	16.7	48.9	47.2	.001
Minor Theft	10.1	16.7	37.7	51.4	.000
Vandalism	8.7	16.7	37.6	47.4	.004
Illegal Services	4.4	28.6	29.8	38.4	.004
Weapons	8.0	33.3	41.3	43.6	.002
Extortion	12.5	33.3	38.6	47.5	.004
Drug Sales	16.0	16.7	26.7	37.1	.056
Alcohol	29.6	14.3	58.9	60.0	.000
Marijuana	26.0	14.3	54.9	50.0	.026
PCP, Psychedelics	12.0	16.7	29.0	52.7	.000
Speed, Barbiturates	4.1	0	30.8	42.8	.000
Cocaine	4.1	0	22.7	44.7	.000
Heroin, Other Opiates	4.4	0	12.8	31.4	.000

NOTE: "Regular" use means respondents reported using "a few times" or more often in the prior year.

or frequent involvement in those acts. For all gang types and nondrug crimes, fewer than half of the respondents reported more than three acts in the prior year. Gang members also do not appear to specialize. For the more serious gang types, the percentage of members reporting regular violence was only slightly lower than the percentage reporting regular property crimes. The similarities suggest a diverse pattern of behaviors among gang members within each type. Only for alcohol and marijuana use do a majority of respondents within the two most serious gang types report regular use. This further illustrates that drug use is intrinsic to gang life among more violent gangs. Finally, these trends did not vary among gang leaders. There were no significant differences between self-reported leaders and others in their self-reported regular involvement in drug use or delinquency.

The participation of members of "social gangs" in a range of delinquent acts also illustrates diversity within gangs. Fewer than 1 in 10 respondents in the "social gangs" reported regular individual involvement in most types of crime. These reports were consistent with their reports of collective gang

DRUG USE AND DRUG DEALING AMONG GANGS 655

involvement. It is uncertain, however, whether their delinquency occurred as part of a gang act or independently.

SOCIAL ORGANIZATION

In several studies (Dolan and Finney, 1984; Feldman et al., 1985; Hagedorn, 1988; Moore, 1978; Vigil, 1988), drug use and dealing were found to be endemic to gangs. Those studies also reveal covariation between the extent or severity of gang crime and drug involvement, however. Economic opportunity, normative adolescent experimentation and developmental progressions, presumed causal linkages with criminality, and specific gang and ethnic traditions are competing explanations for drug involvement by gangs. Little effort has been made to explain variation among gangs on drug use, and virtually no studies link gang social processes or structure to drug involvement or joint drug-crime behaviors. Accordingly, the analysis turns to the relationship between the social organization and processes of gangs and the severity of gang violence, other delinquency, and drug use.

A range of structural and process dimensions were compared by gang type. Formal structure included the presence of established leaders, rules or codes, formal roles, age stratification for roles, and roles for girls. The "serious delinquents" and "organizations" had the highest degree of formal structure (Table 6).[13] A higher percentage of "social" and "party" gangs reported frequent meetings. Since "meetings" possibly was interpreted as meaning both hanging out and more organized discussion of activities, these differences have mixed meaning with respect to social processes among gang members. Members of "social gangs" more often reported that initiation occurred before 13 years of age. There were no significant differences for gang identifiers (i.e., symbols, etc.).

Reports of specific roles for girls in the gang may indicate a formal structure among more active delinquent gangs. Prior studies (Campbell, 1984; Dolan and Finney, 1984; Thrasher, 1927) have identified roles for girls in gangs that confer status and offer excitement, such as provocation of fights, infiltration and spying on rival gangs, carrying messages, and carrying weapons. The latter occurs both for strategic and protective reasons, such as to avoid arrest of male gang members. Campbell (1984) reports that girls often are involved actively in drug use and sales by the gang. Girls are a distinct minority within gangs, however, and research has not been conclusive on the formality of female gang structures or whether their participation in gang processes and behaviors is auxiliary or integral to the gang's primary activities. The reports of specific roles for girls in the "serious delinquents" and

---

13. Comparisons of the mean age of gang members in each type established the age independence of the types and rejected the hypothesis that the types simply were similar gangs at different stages of organizational development.

656   FAGAN

Table 6.   Social Organization and Conventional Values, by
           Gang Types

	Gang Type				
	1	2	3	4	Significance, p (Chi-square)
Social Organization					
You can join before you are 13	65.9%	20.0%	38.9%	41.1%	.02
There are initiation rites	54.8	30.0	65.5	59.0	.20
The gang has established leaders	23.7	10.0	47.9	52.8	.01
The gang has regular meetings	64.9	75.0	40.8	51.3	.03
The gang has specific rules or codes	31.6	20.0	63.8	61.5	.000
Gang members have specific roles	33.3	20.0	52.9	65.0	.001
There are roles for each age group	27.8	20.0	52.8	40.5	.057
The gang has symbols and colors	66.7	100	88.9	79.2	.42
There are specific roles for girls	25.7	11.1	62.3	54.1	.001
Conventional Values*					
School is important to me	46.5	22.2	67.3	38.1	.051
School is important to the gang	58.1	44.4	81.8	63.4	.061
Work is important to me	52.5	14.3	72.0	57.1	.13
Work is important to the gang	20.5	0	34.0	15.2	.15
I have worked in the past 6 months	40.5	0	42.9	41.0	.18
I want to work	87.9	55.6	88.9	88.2	.059
Parents influence gang members	24.3	0	7.5	12.8	.10
Parents supervise me	53.5	40.0	25.0	28.6	.05
Parents are involved with gang	13.5	0	9.8	13.5	.72

* Percentage reporting "somewhat" or "very much."

"organizations" suggest that female roles may be more formal and integrated among more active and violent gangs and auxiliary among less cohesive and noncriminal gangs.

Reports of gang organization and social processes occurred more often among members of "serious delinquents" and "organizations." There were few differences between "serious delinquents" and "organizations" in reports of leadership, rules or codes of behavior, and specific roles within gangs, despite their different involvement in drug sales. Thus, there is little support for the hypothesis that drug selling by gangs as a collective act implies a formal organizational structure. Few members of "party gangs," a group with significant involvement in drug sales, reported that there was an organizational structure or social processes within their gangs. Formal organization exists for both "serious delinquents" and "organizations," despite their distinct patterns of drug use and differences in their involvement in drug selling. These patterns are typical of gang variation even within homogeneous social areas. What we simply may be seeing in these data are two distinct patterns

DRUG USE AND DRUG DEALING AMONG GANGS 657

of violence and drug involvement among cohesive gangs: the "fighting" gang, for whom drug use is an accompaniment to gang life, and the gang whose violence may be systemically related to their drug selling and use.

Conventional values also exist alongside deviant ones within gangs, regardless of their orientation toward crime and drug involvement. Most (over 87%) members of "serious delinquents," "organizations," and "social gangs" expressed interest in work, though many (over 40%) were unemployed for the prior six months. Most (over 58%) respondents from these three gang types value school. Although most individuals in all groups value work, few (no more than 34%) think that the gang values work. The gang apparently values education, however. The disparity between individual and collective gang norms on work may reflect either marginal participation of working members in their gang or simply the gang's realistic view of the limited work opportunities in their neighborhoods. The desire of members to work may reflect either a social bond or an economic imperative. Ironically, the "party gang," the strongest drug subculture but the least delinquent gang type, seems to be the most socially isolated in terms of conventional social values and beliefs.

For all gang types, parents are a negligible influence in their lives as gang members or as adolescents. Others have found similar weaknesses in parental influence over inner-city youths (Fagan et al., 1986). This may reflect the later developmental stages of respondents, when parental influence naturally is limited, but it also may reflect the general limitations on families in inner cities (Edelman, 1987; Wilson, 1987). Finally, these results are unequivocal about the absence of intergenerational parental influence on gangs.

SOCIAL PROCESSES

The results in Table 6 suggest an association between gang organization and their involvement in violence and drugs. The social processes within gangs that maintain the influence of these structures and cohesion among its members are examined in Table 7. Like many other facets of gang life, the maintenance of cohesion involves complex social processes. Spergel (1989) suggests that gang leaders use delinquent activities to mobilize the gang and sustain group cohesion. Klein (1971) views gang cohesion and delinquency as interactive, though cohesion often preceded delinquent activities and may be associated with collective and individual gang delinquency. Others argue that delinquency is related to status conflicts within gangs, and that gang delinquency may serve to restore cohesion that is threatened by conflict (Short and Strodtbeck, 1965). Unfortunately, there has been little critical review of gang research on cohesion and process to clarify these views. Table 7 examines differences between gang types for four social processes that reflect gang cohesion.

658   FAGAN

Table 7.   Social Processes and Codes within Gangs, by Type
           of Gang

	Gang Type			
	1	2	3	4
Process of Getting Involved				
I had friends in the gang	30.8%	70.0%	56.4%	53.8%
I was recruited by leaders	2.6	10.0	9.1	10.3
I partied with gang members	12.8	30.0	21.8	30.8
I hung out with gang members	51.3	20.0	45.5	38.5
I had business with gang members	17.9	20.0	20.0	12.8
Reason for Joining Gang				
It gave me status and identity	20.5	10.0	26.9	32.5
I was protected from other gangs	28.2	20.0	21.2	35.0
It gave me some good friends	15.4	20.0	17.3	27.5
It gave me a family feeling	33.3	10.0	17.3	30.0
To protect the neighborhood	28.2	50.0	17.3	27.5
I could meet girls	7.7	30.0	15.4	30.0
Violations That Provoke Sanctions				
Take someone's woman	19.5	11.1	21.4	42.5
Insult a neighbor or homeboy	12.2	0	14.3	27.5
Rip off a gang member	48.8	77.8	50.0	65.0
Use another gang's name, etc.	39.0	44.4	53.6	55.0
Snitch on a gang member	56.1	33.3	80.4	60.0
Chicken out in a fight	34.1	33.3	64.3	57.5
Fight with a neighbor or homeboy	4.9	0	16.1	20.0
Sanctions for Breaking Rules				
Nothing happens	61.1	55.6	24.5	35.0
The leader decides sanction	13.9	11.1	28.3	40.0
You have to defend the gang's name	11.1	11.1	24.5	27.5
You have to steal for the gang	8.3	22.2	7.5	20.0
You have to fight someone	11.1	22.2	28.3	47.5
You get beat up by the gang	16.7	0	32.1	40.0

NOTE: Percentages exceed 100% due to multiple responses within items.

Four processes were examined: process and reason for getting involved in
the gang, the types of rules violations that provoke sanctions, and the types of
sanctions for breaking rules. Responses for specific items within each of these
processes were analyzed using a multiple response procedure (SPSS, 1988).
This routine maps responses for items that have more than one value for each
case. Table 7 shows the percentage of gang members reporting whether each
of several specific features of each social process existed in their gang. This
method provides comparisons of the existence of each social process, but it
does not provide tests of statistical significance.

The processes for getting involved in gangs showed little consistent pattern.

DRUG USE AND DRUG DEALING AMONG GANGS 659

They reflect the generally informal social processes of gang affiliation, regardless of the extent of gang involvement in substance use or nondrug crimes. Initiation has various meanings, ranging from formal rites of initiation (e.g., fighting other gangs, running a gauntlet, participating in a shooting) to simply hanging around and being accepted by key members of the gang. Specific questions about processes of initiation revealed no significant differences across gang types. There were few reports of drafting or formal recruitment for any types.

As for reasons for getting involved, members of "organizations" more often reported that there were specific reasons for joining the gang. The attractions of gang life for the most seriously criminal youths in a neighborhood reflect the weakness (or absence) of conventional social institutions in those social areas and, conversely, the strength of gangs as institutions of social control and opportunity. The social immersion of its members within the gang is much greater. The gangs seem to fulfill the basic social needs that more formal social institutions and processes fulfill elsewhere.

In general, the processes for joining gangs and reasons for getting involved describe a multifaceted process that reflects natural opportunities for adolescent social interaction more than any formal recruitment process. There were several motivating influences for joining the gang. Joining may be a calculated act by some youths for protection, status, or economic opportunity. It also may reflect normative processes of adolescent development in specific neighborhoods with strong gang activity. For others, gangs may offer social supports and roles missing from their daily routines outside gang life. Researchers have long cited reports from gang members of the strong social and personal pleasure they derive from the "family feeling" of gang solidarity (e.g., Keiser, 1969). Whether gangs fulfill the role of family for their members, or provide an added dimension of familism beyond their natural families, is unclear from this study.

The use of force as punishment for violating gang codes was more often reported among the two more violent gang types. Of the possible violations listed, over 50% of the gang members reported that most of these acts would provoke a sanction within each of these two gang types. For the two other gang types, fewer than half the acts would provoke a response by more than a minority of their members. Similar trends were found for the specific sanctions. Members of the two more violent gangs more often reported that violent sanctions were used in their gangs, though by less than half of the members. Sanctions in general, violent or not, were rarely reported among "social" and "party" gangs.

Overall, the attractions of gang life and processes for enforcing gang norms and rules were most salient within the two more violent gangs. Comparison of the four social processes across gang types suggests that the gang types differed primarily in the existence of formal rules or norms that might provoke a sanction, and the existence of sanctions for breaking rules. Norms were in strongest evidence among "organizations" and "serious delinquents." Thus, the gangs with the most extensive involvement in substance use, drug sales, and violent crimes may be the most formally organized groups among a cohort of loosely affiliated gangs.

CONCLUSIONS

The complexity of the drug-crime relationship among gang members is typical of its equally complex relationship among inner-city youths. The patterns of drug use and crime among gangs suggest a skewed and spurious relationship. There is a positive association between drug involvement and serious collective gang acts, again similar to nongang urban youths. Also, members of gangs with greater involvement in substance use and drug selling more often reported that social processes were evident in their gangs to maintain and enforce gang rules and behavioral codes. The data support the contention that substance use and delinquency among gangs occur in gangs with well-developed organizational structures and social norms.

Drug use is widespread and normative among gangs, regardless of city, the extent or nature of collective violence, or their organization or social processes. Serious and violent behaviors occur among a majority of the gangs. Drug use occurs, however, both independently of other crimes and also as part of a general pattern of deviant behavior. Gang delinquency did not occur in the absence of drugs. The factors that shape and influence gang membership may result in joint patterns of drug use and violence, but also in drug use that is not accompanied by collective gang violence.

Patterns of drug selling also reveal a complex relationship with other gang behaviors. Serious crime and violence occur regardless of the prevalence of drug dealing within the gang. All gangs were involved to some extent in drug dealing, but it was most prevalent among gangs that were involved more heavily in PCP, heroin, and cocaine, regardless of their involvement in violence. Thus, involvement in use and sales of the most serious substances does not necessarily increase the frequency or severity of violent behavior. And there remains a small group of gangs who are heavily involved in drug use and dealing but avoid collective violence.

The complex and ambiguous patterns of delinquency and drug use or selling among gangs differ from patterns observed among adult offenders. The high risk among adult men of systemic violence from involvement in drug trafficking (Chaiken and Chaiken, 1989; Goldstein, 1985) does not appear to apply equally to all gang types or members. Some incidents no doubt are precipitated by disputes over drug sales or selling territories, but the majority

DRUG USE AND DRUG DEALING AMONG GANGS 661

of violent incidents do not appear to involve drug sales. Rather, they continue to be part of the status, territorial, and other gang conflicts that historically have fueled gang violence.

The discovery of similar gang types in three cities suggests some generalized social processes supportive of gang behaviors in urban areas. Thus, the important comparison of gang delinquency with nongang delinquency reaffirms the disproportionate involvement of gang members in delinquency. The patterns of delinquent and drug use behaviors among gang members are consistent with patterns observed among institutionalized delinquents and among the most serious and chronic offenders in general population studies. But the comparison also suggests that gangs are a marginal population in their neighborhoods, just as the institutionalized and multiple offenders in other studies were a small proportion of the adolescents in other social areas. This is not surprising—most urban youths do not join gangs (Baker, 1988),[14] and among those who describe themselves as gang members, their involvement ranges from fringe to core. It is likely that only a small percentage of gang members are "core" members (Klein and Maxson, 1989; Spergel, 1989). Thus, core gang members, who have the highest rates and severity of violence, are a marginal group within an already marginal population.

Social organization and other processes of gang cohesion offer only partial explanations of why gangs differ in violence or drug involvement. The transience of membership and leadership cliques and continuation suggest further that gang cohesion may have limited influence on behaviors. Curry and Spergel (1988) suggest that ecological factors, including residential transience, also are important influences on gang activity for Chicago gangs. Baker's (1988) interviews with African-American gang members in Los Angeles offer important clues to how urban form shapes gang cohesion and conflicts. The proliferation of gangs in urban areas with haphazard turf lines, routine activities that place gang members in frequent contact with other gangs and also on others' territory, access to weapons and income from crimes, all contribute to increases in different types of conflicts and opportunities for violence. The frequent contacts between gangs create frequent occasions for both prolonged organized assaults by one group of gang members, "gangbangs," and less organized attacks by individual gang members settling individual conflicts. Conflicts over drug territory are only one of many circumstances that may lead to collective gang violence.

In addition to urban topography, the social ecology of urban areas influences gang participation and patterns of violence. The marginality of the social areas with the highest rates of gang conflict suggests that these also are

---

14. Baker (1988) cites Los Angeles Police Department intelligence that estimates the gang population among African-American males at 25,000, or 25% of the city's estimated population of 100,000 African-American males between the ages of 15 and 24.

662   FAGAN

areas with the weakest social institutions. Thrasher (1927) noted nearly half a century ago that gangs could arise under conditions of social disorganization that in turn created social instability. Curry and Spergel (1988) linked these processes to residential mobility, poverty, and other socioeconomic variables. Several recent studies (Laub, 1983; Sampson, 1987, 1986; Shannon, 1984; Weis and Sederstrom, 1981) have linked social ecological factors with weakened formal and informal social controls and higher rates of adolescent violence. Thrasher (1927) noted the isolation from the surrounding society of "interstitial areas," where weak social institutions failed to provide effective social controls. Thus, variation in gang violence may reflect the extent of their social embedment in ecological areas that are cut off from normative social and economic influences.

Social isolation of gangs from both legitimate economic opportunity and routine interactions with mainstream society, and the limited influence of viable social controls, may lead to the development and ossification of gangs in a closed social system. In this context, the socialization of adolescents becomes skewed toward processes that sustain gangs as the dominant sources of social status and values, economic opportunities, affiliation, protection, and social control. Gang members in such areas may become inured to violence and also lose sight of other social norms or cultures. Lacking formal or informal social controls or opportunities, gangs may become the primary social influence. The undue reliance of inner-city youths on gang structures for basic social roles and opportunities may neutralize other conventional influences. Thus, one plausible explanation for variation in gang violence may lie in the relative social and economic isolation of their milieu and in the specific influence of social and legal controls and economic and criminal opportunities within those areas. Violence within gangs may reflect both the marginalization of gang members and the marginalization of the neighborhood itself.

REFERENCES

Aldenderfer, Mark S. and Roger K. Blashfield
    1984   Cluster Analysis. Beverly Hills, Calif.: Sage.

Anderson, Nancy and Orlando Rodriguez
    1984   Conceptual issues in the study of Hispanic delinquency. Research Bulletin:
              7:2–5. Hispanic Research Center. New York: Fordham University.

Baker, Robert
    1988   Homeboys: Players in a deadly drama. Los Angeles Times, June 26.

Biernacki, Patrick and Dan Waldorf
    1981   Snowball sampling: Problems and techniques of chain referral sampling.
              Sociological Methods and Research 10(2):141–163.

Black, Donald
    1983   Crime as social control. American Sociological Review 48:34–45.

DRUG USE AND DRUG DEALING AMONG GANGS 663

Bookin-Weiner, Hedy and Ruth Horowitz
1983   The end of the youth gang: Fad or fact? Criminology 21(4):585–602.

Campbell, Anne
1984   The Girls in the Gang. New Brunswick, N.J.: Rutgers University Press.

Cernkovich, Stephen A., Peggy C. Giordano, and Meredith D. Pugh
1986   Chronic offenders: The missing cases in self-report delinquency research. Journal of Criminal Law and Criminology 76:684–704.

Chaiken, Jan and Marcia Chaiken
1989   Drug use and predatory crime. In James Q. Wilson and Michael Tonry (eds.), Drugs and Crime—Crime and Justice: An Annual Review of Research. Vol. 13. Chicago: University of Chicago Press.

Chin, Ko-Lin
1986   Chinese triad societies, tongs, organized crime, and street gangs in Asia and the United States. Ph.D. dissertation, University of Pennsylvania.

Cooper, Barry M.
1987   Motor city breakdown. Village Voice, December 1:23–35.

Curry, G. David and Irving A. Spergel
1988   Gang homicide, delinquency, and community. Criminology 26:381–406.

Dolan, Edward F. and Shan Finney
1984   Youth Gangs. New York: Simon & Schuster.

Dundford, Franklyn W. and Delbert S. Elliott
1984   Identifying career offenders using self-reported data. Journal of Research in Crime and Delinquency 21:57–86.

Edelman, Marian W.
1987   Families in Peril. Cambridge, Mass.: Harvard University Press.

Elliott, Delbert S., and David Huizinga
1983   Social class and delinquent behavior in a national youth panel. Criminology 21:149–177.
1984   The Relationship Between Delinquent Behavior and ADM Problems. National Youth Survey Report No. 28. Institute for Behavioral Studies. Boulder: University of Colorado.

Elliott, Delbert S., David Huizinga, and Suzanne Ageton
1985   Explaining Delinquency and Drug Abuse. Beverly Hills, Calif.: Sage.

Erlanger, Howard S.
1979   Estrangement, machismo and gang violence. Social Science Quarterly 60(3):235–248.

Fagan, Jeffrey A., Elizabeth S. Piper, and Yu-Teh Cheng
1987   Contributions of victimization to delinquency in inner cities. Journal of Criminal Law and Criminology 78(3):586–613.

Fagan, Jeffrey A., Elizabeth S. Piper, and Melinda Moore
1986   Violent delinquents and urban youth. Criminology 23:439–466.

Fagan, Jeffrey A., Joseph G. Weis, and Yu-Teh Cheng
In press Drug use and delinquency among inner city students. Journal of Drug Issues 19(4).

664   FAGAN

Feldman, Harvey W., Michael Agar, and George Beschner (eds.)
    1979   Angel Dust: An Ethnographic Study of PCP Users. Lexington, Mass.:
              Lexington Books.

Feldman, Harvey W., Jerry Mandel, and Allen Fields
    1985   In the Neighborhood: A strategy for delivering early intervention services to
              young drug users in their natural environments. In Alfred S. Friedman and
              George Beschner (eds.), Treatment Services for Adolescent Substance Users.
              Rockville, Md.: National Institute of Drug Abuse.

Fields, Allen
    1985   Weedslingers: Young black marijuana dealers. In George Beschner and
              Alfred S. Friedman (eds.), Teen Drug Use. Lexington, Mass.: Lexington
              Books.

Gandossy, Robert P., Jay Williams, J. Cohen, and Henrick Hardwood
    1980   Drugs and Crime: A Survey and Analysis of the Literature. Washington,
              D.C.: National Institute of Justice.

Goldstein, Paul J.
    1985   The drugs-violence nexus: A tri-partite conceptual framework. Journal of
              Drug Issues 15:493–506.

Hagedorn, John
    1988   People and Folk: Gangs, Crime and the Underclass in a Rustbelt City.
              Chicago: Lakeview Press.

Hindelang, Michael, Travis Hirschi, and Joseph G. Weis
    1981   Measuring Delinquency. Beverly Hills, Calif.: Sage.

Horowitz, Ruth
    1983   Honor and the American Dream: Culture and Identity in a Chicano
              Community. New Brunswick, N.J.: Rutgers University Press.
    1987   Community tolerance of gang violence. Social Problems 34(5):437–450.

Johnson, Bruce D., Paul J. Goldstein, Edward Preble, James Schmeidler, Douglas
Lipton, Barry Spunt, and Thomas Miller
    1985   Taking Care of Business: The Economics of Crime by Heroin Abusers.
              Lexington, Mass.: Lexington Books.

Johnston, Lloyd D., Patrick M. O'Malley, and Jerrold G. Bachman
    1985   Use of Licit and Illicit Drugs by America's High School Students:
              1975–1984. Rockville, Md.: National Institute on Drug Abuse.

Keiser, R. Lincoln
    1969   The Vice Lords: Warriors of the Street. New York: Holt, Rinehart &
              Winston.

Klein, Malcolm W.
    1969   Gang cohesiveness, delinquency, and a street-work program. Journal of
              Research in Crime and Delinquency 6:135–166.
    1971   Street Gangs and Street Workers. Englewood Cliffs, N.J.: Prentice-Hall.
    1985   Gang involvement in cocaine rock trafficking. Grant application to the
              National Institute of Justice. University of Southern California, Social
              Science Research Institute, Los Angeles.

Klein, Malcolm W. and Lois Y. Crawford
    1967   Groups, gangs, and cohesiveness. Journal of Research in Crime and
              Delinquency 4:63–75.

DRUG USE AND DRUG DEALING AMONG GANGS 665

Klein, Malcolm W. and Cheryl L. Maxson
    1989   Street gang violence. In Marvin E. Wolfgang and Neil A. Weiner (eds.), Violent Crime, Violent Criminals. Newbury Park, Calif.: Sage.

Klein, Malcolm W., Cheryl L. Maxson, and Lea Cunningham
    1988   Gang Involvement in Cocaine Rock Trafficking. Final Report to the National Institute of Justice. Social Science Research Institute. Los Angeles: University of Southern California.

Laub, John
    1983   Urbanism, race and crime. Journal of Research in Crime and Delinquency 20:183–198.

Laub, John and Michael J. Hindelang
    1981   Juvenile Criminal Behavior in Urban, Suburban, and Rural Areas. Washington, D.C.: Office of Juvenile Justice and Delinquency Prevention.

Maxson, Cheryl L., and Malcolm W. Klein
    1983   Gangs: Why we couldn't stay away. In James Kleugel (ed.), Evaluating Juvenile Justice. Beverly Hills, Calif.: Sage.

Maxon, Cheryl L., Margaret A. Gordon, and Malcolm W. Klein
    1985   Differences between gang and non-gang homicides. Criminology 23:209–222.

Mieczkowski, Thomas
    1986   Geeking up and throwing down: Heroin street life in Detroit. Criminology 24:645–666.

Miller, Walter B.
    1975   Violence by Youth Gangs and Young Groups as a Crime Problem in Major American Cities. Report to the National Institute for Juvenile Justice and Delinquency Prevention. Washington, D.C.: U.S. Department of Justice.

Moore, Joan W.
    1978   Home Boys. New Brunswick, N.J.: Rutgers University Press.

Morash, Merry
    1983   Gangs, groups and delinquency. British Journal of Criminology 23:309–331.

Pennell, Susan and Christine Curtis
    1982   Juvenile Violence and Gang-Related Crime. San Diego: San Diego Association of Governments.

Piper, Elizabeth S.
    1985   Violent crime by juveniles: The lone wolf or the wolfpack? Paper presented at the annual meeting of the American Society of Criminology, San Diego.

Recktenwald, William and Nathaniel Sheppard, Jr.
    1984   Series on youth gangs in Chicago. Chicago Tribune, July 29 and 30, 1984.

Reiss, Albert J., Jr.
    1986   Co-offending influences on criminal careers. In Alfred Blumstein, Jacqueline Cohen, Jeffrey A. Roth, and Christy A. Visher, (eds.), Career Criminals and Criminal Careers. Vol. 2. Washington, D.C.: National Academy Press.

Sampson, Robert J.
    1986   Crime in cities: The effects of formal and informal social control. In Albert J. Reiss, Jr., and Michael Tonry (eds.), Crime and Justice: An Annual Review of Research. Vol. 8, Communities and Crime. Chicago: University of Chicago Press.

666   FAGAN

1987   Urban black violence: The effect of male joblessness and family disruption.
         American Journal of sociology 93(2):348–382.

Schwendinger, Herman and Julia Schwendinger
1985   Adolescent Subcultures and Delinquency. New York: Praeger.

Shannon, Lyle W.
1984   The Development of Serious Criminal Careers and the Delinquent Neighbor-
         hood. Office of Juvenile Justice and Delinquency Prevention. Washington,
         D.C.: U.S. Department of Justice.

Shaw, Clifford R. and Henry D. McKay
1943   Juvenile Delinquency in Urban Areas. Chicago: University of Chicago
         Press.

Short, James F. and Fred L. Strodtbeck
1965   Group Process and Gang Delinquency. Chicago: University of Chicago
         Press.

Spergel, Irving A.
1966   Street Gang Work: Theory and Practice. Reading, Mass.: Addison-Wesley.
1984   Violent gangs in Chicago: In search of social policy. Social Service Review
         June: 199–226.
1989   Youth gangs: Continuity and change. In Norval Morris and Michael Tonry
         (eds.), Crime and Justice: An Annual Review of Research. Vol. 12.
         Chicago: University of Chicago Press.

SPSS, Inc.
1988   SPSS-X Users Guide, 3rd. ed. Chicago: SPSS, Inc.

Stumphauzer, Jerome S., Esteban V. Veloz, and Thomas W. Aiken
1981   Violence by street gangs: East side story? In Robert B. Stuart (ed.), Violent
         Behavior: Social Learning Approaches to Prediction, Management, and
         Treatment. New York: Brunner-Mazel.

Suttles, Gerald D.
1968   The Social Order of the Slum. Chicago: University of Chicago Press.

Thio, Alex
1983   Deviant Behavior. 2nd ed. Boston: Houghton Mifflin.

Thrasher, Frederick M.
1927   The Gang: A Study of One Thousand Three Hundred Thirteen Gangs in
         Chicago. Chicago: University of Chicago Press.

Tracy, Paul E.
1979   Subcultural Delinquency: A Comparison of the Incidence and Seriousness of
         Gang and Nongang Member Offensivity. Center for Studies in Criminology
         and Criminal Law. Philadelphia: University of Pennsylvania.

Tracy, Paul E. and Elizabeth S. Piper
1984   Gang membership and violent offending: Preliminary results from the 1958
         cohort study. Paper presented at the annual meeting of the American
         Society of Criminology, Cincinnati.

Vigil, James Diego
1988   Barrio Gangs. Austin: University of Texas Press.

DRUG USE AND DRUG DEALING AMONG GANGS 667

Weis, Joseph G. and John Sederstrom
   1981   The Prevention of Serious Delinquency: What to Do? Washington, D.C.:
            Government Printing Office.

White, Helene R., Robert J. Pandina, and Randy L. LaGrange.
   1987   Longitudinal predictors of serious substance abuse and delinquency. Crimi-
            nology 25(3):715–740.

Whyte, William F.
   1943   Street Corner Society. Chicago: University of Chicago Press.

Wilson, William J.
   1987   The Truly Disadvantaged. Chicago: University of Chicago Press.

Wish, Eric D. and Bruce D. Johnson
   1986   The impact of substance abuse on criminal careers. In Alfred Blumstein,
            Jacqueline Cohen, Jeffrey A. Roth, and Christy A. Visher (eds.), Criminal
            Careers and Career Criminals. Vol. 2. Washington, D.C.: National
            Academy Press.

Wolfgang, Marvin E., Robert M. Figlio, and Thorsten Sellin
   1972   Delinquency in a Birth Cohort. Chicago: University of Chicago Press.

Yablonsky, Lewis
   1963   The Violent Gang. New York: Macmillan.

Jeffrey Fagan is Associate Professor in the School of Criminal Justice, Rutgers University. His current research includes studies of the impact of crack cocaine on criminal behavior, drug use and delinquency among inner-city adolescents, the comparative impacts of juvenile and criminal court sanctions on adolescent felony offenders, and the cessation of family violence.

668 FAGAN

APPENDIX.
SELF-REPORTED OFFENSE-SPECIFIC SCALES

Felony Assault
  Beat someone up so badly they probably needed a doctor
  Forced someone to have sexual relations with them
  Shot someone
Minor Assault
  Hit an adult or other youth in the neighborhood
Robbery
  Grabbed a purse and ran with it
  Used physical force to get money, drugs, or something else from someone
  Used a weapon to get something from someone
Felony Theft
  Bought stolen goods
  Taken things from a store worth more than $50
  Broken into a car to get something
  Broken into a building and taken something
  Taken a stranger's car without permission
Minor Theft
  Taken something from somebody's wallet or purse
  Stolen money from parents or other family members
  Stolen something at school
Vandalism
  Purposely damaged or destroyed property belonging to your school
  Purposely damaged or destroyed property not belonging to you or your
    family
Illegal Services
  Sold marijuana
  Sold angel dust, downers, speed, coke, or heroin
  Sold something you had stolen
Weapons
  Carried a weapon with the intention of using it in a fight
  Threatened an adult with a weapon
Extortion
  Threatened to hurt someone unless given something
  Threatened an adult
Drug Sales
  Sold weed (marijuana) or PCP cigarettes
  Sold angel dust, downers, speed, coke, or heroin
Alcohol Use
  Drank beer or wine
  Drank gin, vodka, or other liquor

DRUG USE AND DRUG DEALING AMONG GANGS 669

Marijuana
  Smoked marijuana
PCP or Psychedelics
  Smoked sherms or used dust
  Used acid
 Speed or Barbiturates
  Used downers, barbs, reds, speed, uppers, or other pills
Cocaine
  Snorted or shot cocaine, smoked crack
Heroin or other opiates
  Snorted or smoked heroin, smoked or ate opium, shot heroin

[19]

"CRACK," STREET GANGS, AND VIOLENCE*

MALCOLM W. KLEIN
CHERYL L. MAXSON
LEA C. CUNNINGHAM
University of Southern California

This investigation considers the connections among street gangs, "crack" cocaine, and violence associated with crack distribution during the initial years of crack proliferation. Data were extracted from the narcotics investigation files and homicide files of five Los Angeles Police Department and Sheriff's Department areas where both crack and gangs were prominent. The aims were to compare for 1983–1985, when crack first emerged as a significant problem, hypotheses about (1) gang involvement in crack distribution and (2) concomitants of gang involvement, particularly violence. The analyses confirm a dramatic growth in crack sales, an accompanying increase in gang members involved, but a declining rate of involvement, and inconsistent evidence on the impact of gang involvement on sales events. We infer that crack distribution, while including many individual gang members, was not primarily a street gang phenomenon.

Crack, or "rock" cocaine as it was first known in Southern California, exploded in south central Los Angeles before expanding to other places. Although Inciardi (1988) claims a longer history for crack, the early 1980s can be taken as its point of major initiation. The first major media report appeared in November 1984—"South Central Cocaine Sales Explode into $25 'Rocks'" (Los Angeles Times, November 25, 1984). The first article on crack cocaine in the professional literature (Klein and Maxson) appeared in 1985.

Although the history of Hispanic gangs in Los Angeles goes back to the first quarter of this century and that of black gangs to the early 1950s (Klein, 1971; Vigil, 1988), their drug involvement was principally an issue of use, not control of distribution. Significantly, the police and press reports of the Los Angeles crack explosion were that it was intimately tied to gangs and to gang involvement in distribution. The now infamous Crips and Bloods, black

* This project was supported by grant 85-IJ-CX-0057 from the National Institute of Justice, U.S. Department of Justice. Points of view or opinions in this report are those of the authors and do not necessarily represent the official position or policies of the U.S. Department of Justice. Gratitude is expressed to many officials of the Los Angeles Police Department and the Los Angeles County Sheriff's Department. To name a few would be unfair to all the others, but LAPD Chief Daryl Gates and Sheriff Sherman Block made it possible to work with all the rest. Thanks are also due to Daniel Glaser and several anonymous reviewers for their many fine comments on earlier drafts of this paper.

624   KLEIN, MAXSON & CUNNINGHAM

gangs prominent in the south central area, were soon singled out, and reports began to emerge of their exporting crack to other cities. Members of a national panel of experts reported, among other things, "growing proof that drugs are contributing to the alarming increase in gang violence" and that the Drug Enforcement Administration "has confirmed the presence of Los Angeles street gang members in 49 cities" (McKinney, 1988). Statewide data for California were notably similar in the increasing prevalence curves for gang-related and drug-related homicides over the past 10 years (Bureau of Criminal Statistics, 1988).

These are but a few of the indications of a growing belief about a close relationship among crack, gangs, and violence. It is that relationship that is the subject of this paper, and fittingly, it is from the investigative files of the police and sheriff's departments in Los Angeles that the data are taken. These data permit research on the confluence of gang activity and crack distribution, which, according to many enforcement and media reports, has led to unprecedented levels of violence. With other research beginning to yield data on crack elsewhere in the country (Belenko and Fagan, 1987, Inciardi, 1988; Mieczkowski, 1988; Skolnick, 1988), the Los Angeles data provide an early context for understanding some of the empirical and conceptual issues involved.

Further, our research procedures contrast considerably with those reported above, which provides some potential for useful debate. Other crack researchers, to date, have relied principally on ethnographic procedures, but we have employed statistical analyses of data taken from detailed police arrest and investigation files. Both types of data have limitations for establishing prevalence rates of drug sales, but they do complement each other. For example, our conclusions will be seen to be similar to those of Fagan (1989). In this paper, however, it is not prevalence that is at issue, but the specific question of gang involvement and its consequences. It is the gang versus nongang comparison in crack sales that relates to our hypotheses.

The adequacy of our established procedures to address these issues has been documented elsewhere (Klein et al., 1986). The gang/nongang designation, as determined from the extensive gang enforcement units in Los Angeles, has shown major differences in the character of gang and nongang violence (Maxson et al., 1985). Discriminant analyses suggested little impact on these differences attributable to biases in the police reporting, recording, and investigative processes from which gang/nongang designations are derived.

The use of official data to represent the behavior of law violators is always problematic, but extensive work on self-report versus official indicators of crime in the United States and abroad consistently shows concordance (Elliott et al., 1985; Hindelang et al., 1981; Klein, 1989). This has also been demonstrated for drug data (Bonito et al., 1976). There is no evidence in the

"CRACK," STREET GANGS, AND VIOLENCE 625

published literature that this concordance is differentially related to the distinction between gang and nongang youths (Tracy, 1979). Finally, in a study of crack arrests in New York City, Belenko and Fagan (1987) cite several indications of the reliability of their arrest statistics: (a) all officers are *required* to flag any case involving crack, thus at least increasing the reliability of arrest records; (b) 95.9% of the arrests were subsequently identifiable in the pre-arraignment files developed for the New York City Criminal Justice Agency; and (c) the reliability is sufficiently high to reveal a series of significant differences between powder cocaine and crack arrestees, the latter being more often male, black, and young and having few verified community ties and less extensive prior records (p.1, fn.1; pp.10–11, fn.2).

CONTRASTING HYPOTHESES

Because our research was designed in a period of ferment, ambiguity, and excitement, it addressed a mixture of immediate practical concerns, longer term policy issues, and conceptual questions raised by our past research on street gangs. Specifically, enforcement and media reports, echoed by political officials, proffered two propositions.

First, due to the advantages of crack over the traditional form of powdered cocaine,[1] neighborhood- and street-level distribution was given to and accepted by local street gangs. The presumed organizational and territorial characteristics of street gangs made them ideal for rapid, organized, and controlled distribution.

Second, widespread gang involvement in distribution would yield substantive differences in various aspects of crack sales incidents, especially an increase in violence associated with them. Gang members, it was asserted, have a high violence potential in any case, and mid-level distributors would employ gang members specifically to enforce their rules and to control territorial "rights."

These organizational and violence propositions, however, contrast significantly with hypotheses that can be derived from the sociological literature on street gangs and from the criminological literature on the relationship between drugs and violence. For instance, several decades of gang research have documented that street gang organization tends to be loose, cohesiveness low, and leadership unstable (e.g., see Hagedorn, 1988; Huff, 1989; Klein, 1971; Short and Strodtbeck, 1965; Vigil, 1988; Yablonsky, 1963). Traditional gangs combine poorly connected fringe members with high turnover and a

---

1. Advantages, in addition to relatively easy distribution and disposability, included lower sales price and easier addiction. The Los Angeles price varied between $10 and $25 per quarter-gram "rock." This low price, the flood on the market, the ease of rock manufacture, transportation, carrying, hiding, and the rapidity and intensity of the high all conspired to make the rock form of cocaine preferable to the powdered form.

626   KLEIN, MAXSON & CUNNINGHAM

smaller number of close-knit cliques of heterogeneous criminality (Klein, 1971). Only a few of the cliques might provide a basis for concentrated drug involvement (Short and Strodtbeck, 1965; Spergel, 1964).

Thus, although some potential exists for limited exploitation of gang cliques for purposes of crack distribution, a reasonable hypothesis, contrasting with police and press reports, is that street gangs would not become the principal mechanism for crack distribution in their neighborhoods. Some involvement would be predictable, but levels of street gang cohesiveness and organization, and ephemeral gang leadership, would work against a gang's development of effective sales networks.

The second common proposition, that gang involvement is a precursor of greater violence in crack distribution, is less obviously opposed by the literature. It is clear that gang law violators are more criminal and proportionately violent than are nongang offenders (Maxson et al., 1985; Tracy, 1979), but a fair summary of the extensive literature on the drug/violence connection is that this relationship involving drug *use* is weak and inconsistent (e.g., see Blum, 1972; Gandossy et al., 1980), although that involving drug *distribution* is perhaps stronger (Gropper, 1984). This latter conclusion, however, is based on a far more sparse ethnographic and anecdotal literature (see, e.g., McBride, 1981). At the time we undertook our research on crack and gangs, there was no literature on which to base directional hypotheses about the crack/violence connection and, therefore, no empirical base for accepting local enforcement claims about that connection. To the contrary, our hypothesis of limited gang involvement leads as well to a secondary hypothesis of minimal increases in distribution violence attributable specifically to gangs in the crack trade.

In sum, then, public reports of serious gang involvement and consequent increased violence associated with crack distribution accompanied a widely reported increase in crack availability in high gang areas of south central Los Angeles. Those reports are contrasted here with hypotheses derived from the sociological literature on gangs and the drug/violence connection. These hypotheses, of limited gang involvement and gang-derived violence, given the crack explosion, yield two general data predictions in the context of increased crack cocaine sales arrests:

1.   Street sales incidents would not show control of crack distribution by street gangs.

2.   Evidence would not demonstrate major changes in sales-related violence or in other variables attributable to street gang involvement in sales, either over time or as compared with nongang crack sales.

To state the conclusions early, cocaine sales arrests did increase dramatically. However, accelerations in gang involvement, while evident, were not at the levels we had been led to expect by enforcement and press reports; neither

"CRACK," STREET GANGS, AND VIOLENCE   627

were the differences in sales-related violence. The data are more consistent with predictions derived from the sociological literature. But we must caution the reader about two restrictions. First, the data refer only to arrests. Undetected drug transactions may follow different patterns (but see Fagan, 1989), and they can best be approached by ethnographic and biographical procedures. Second, the data refer to a period ending on December 31, 1985. Since that time, police and press reports have rather consistently reported a continued increase in Los Angeles of crack sales, gang involvement, and violence. Notably, however, some police officials are now acknowledging that gang involvement is mostly limited to special cliques or "drug gangs." Press reports have generally been slow to acknowledge these developments.

We begin our presentation of the study findings by reporting on the extent of cocaine sales incidents and the levels of gang involvement in those incidents. We then turn to the issue of whether gang involvement seems to make a difference. We document which case characteristics—incident, participant, and drug—distinguish gang-involved incidents from others and address whether those characteristics changed while levels of gang involvement in cocaine sales were increasing. Finally, we investigate the concern of violence associated with gangs and crack sales by utilizing two data sources. We report on indicators of violence from the cocaine sales incidents, but we rely chiefly on homicide data to assess gang/drug/violence connections. We report on drug aspects of gang and nongang homicides and look for evidence of increased drug involvement in violent incidents over this time period.

LEVELS OF GANG INVOLVEMENT IN COCAINE SALES

Underlying the aim of assessing the level and increase in gang involvement was the assumption that, as reported in the press, there had indeed been a major increase in cocaine sales since 1982. We begin our analysis by documenting that increase and then describe levels of gang involvement in sales incidents.

Five stations—three from the Los Angeles Police Department (LAPD) and two from the Los Angeles County Sheriff's Department (LASD)—with the highest combinations of cocaine sales arrests and reported gang activity in south central Los Angeles were selected for data collection. The purpose was not to be representative of any geographic area, but rather to capture the phenomena of interest at their points of highest concentration. Arrest logs in the five stations were reviewed for cases having at least one arrest for sale of cocaine (Health and Safety Code, section 11352) or possession for sale (section 11351). Simple possession for use was not included. The average cocaine seizure in our cases was about 13 grams, and cash seizures averaged

628   KLEIN, MAXSON & CUNNINGHAM

several hundreds of dollars. Thus, logging *sales* charges was seldom a function of charging high on simple drug *use* arrests. Details of the data extraction procedures are contained in the project's technical report (Klein et al., 1988).

Dramatic increases in the number of cocaine sales arrest cases were evident. In 1983, 233 such cases appeared across all five stations. In 1984, the number rose to 542, an increase of 133%. In 1985, the number increased to 1,114, an increase of an additional 106% or 375% above the 1983 numbers.[2] Note that these figures refer to *cocaine* sales arrest cases and not specifically to sales of cocaine in its *crack* form. Although our research design was framed in the context of the growth of the crack phenomenon and our expectations cite crack sales only, our analyses preceded an investigation of the presence of crack versus the powder form of cocaine in these incidents.[3]

Did gang involvement increase disproportionately? The answer, determined by using the extensive LAPD and LASD gang rosters,[4] is affirmative, but not nearly to the extent expected by our law enforcement informants. Defining gang involvement as the attribution of gang status to at least one arrestee in a case, gang-involved cases constituted 8.6% of all cocaine sales cases in the five stations in 1983, 20.8% in 1984, and 24.9% in 1985. The percentage increases are 142 and 20%, or 213% overall from 1983. Figure 1 illustrates how these data represent a major increase in gang involvement, yet a decelerating rate of change, and a 1985 level—25%—far lower than the informal estimates suggested to us by many of our police collaborators. During this three-year period, the explosion in cocaine sales was engaging a number of street gang members, but it was in no way dominated by gang involvement. Our literature-based hypothesis of limited gang involvement is supported.

Two less obvious but possibly alternative measures of increased gang

---

2. The cocaine sales arrest *incident* is the primary unit of analysis in this study. However, comparable increases can be seen in the number of *arrests* for these charges in the five stations. In 1983, the logs showed 380 arrests on cocaine sales charges. In 1984, arrests numbered 820, an increase of 116%. In 1985, the number rose to 2,123, a 159% increase over 1984 and a 459% increase over the 1983 arrest totals.

3. When the case file coding was completed, we found in fact that 87% of the incident case files reported the crack form of cocaine, with an average seizure of about 7.5 grams. These data are based on very thorough investigative techniques by the narcotics units, including laboratory determination of amounts seized and confirmation of the material as cocaine. Successful prosecution depends on such data, and the narcotics units were very concerned about having good cases for filing with the district attorney. Our observations within the stations confirmed the assiduousness with which these drug determinations were made.

4. Full details on this and other aspects of the data collection and coding are omitted due to space limitations. They are included in the full report available on request from the authors. Also, see Maxson et al. (1985) and Klein et al. (1986).

"CRACK," STREET GANGS, AND VIOLENCE   629

Figure 1.   Proportion of Cocaine Sales Arrest Incidents with
Gang Members in S. Central Los Angeles During
First Years of "Crack" Explosion (1983-1985)

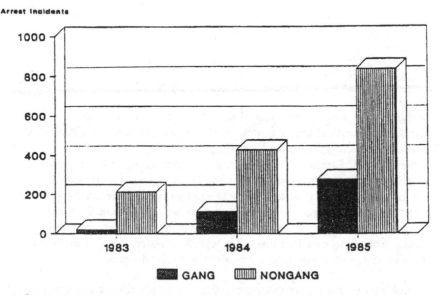

$\chi^2 = 31.25$; d.f. = 2; p < .001

involvement were considered: the proportion of gang members per case and
the proportion of members of the *same* gang in a case (indicating recruitment
and use of clique structures). For both measures, the enforcement expectation would be an increase over time. To apply these indicators with the reliability afforded by sufficiently large numbers, the time dimension was divided
into the four half years starting with the first half of 1984; 1983 case numbers
(20 gang cases) were too low for this analysis. For instance, the proportion of
roster-identified gang members among all arrested suspects (including those
charged with offenses other than cocaine sales) for each case was calculated
for all gang cases with more than one suspect. About 65% of the 384 gang
cases had multiple suspects. Table 1 presents the data.[5]

We also analyzed data for members of the same gang. The numbers are far
smaller (only 18% of all gang cases) because only cases with more than one
identified gang member and all gang names known are appropriate to the

---

5. This measure of gang involvement was also examined by month. Despite the low
number of cases in many of these time periods, the results are consistent with the analysis
by six-month time periods reported in Table 1, that is, no evidence for an increasing level of
gang involvement.

Table 1.   Mean Proportion of All Arrestees Who Were
Identified Gang Members for Four Half-Years
(Gang Cases with Multiple Suspects Only)

Period	Mean Proportion	Standard Deviation	N
First half 1984	.603	.288	24
Second half 1984	.593	.270	48
First half 1985	.551	.245	79
Second half 1985	.575	.246	89

analysis. The same-gang proportions dropped steadily from .78 to .53, a direction opposite to that required by the police/press reports but supportive of our contrasting, literature-based hypothesis.

Neither set of data offers support for an increasing level of gang involvement per case over the two-year period being measured. Indeed, if there is any trend at all, it is toward a *lower* level of gang member involvement on an event basis. Although the cocaine business was increasing dramatically and gang members were becoming more involved, they were not becoming a larger proportion of all who were involved. Rather, there is evidence of an increasing *nongang* presence even in gang-involved cases.

CORRELATES OF INCREASED GANG INVOLVEMENT

In order to assess the correlates, and presumably the effects, of increased gang involvement in cocaine distribution, detailed information was collected from the case files for each incident. As noted, the year 1983 was omitted because it had too few gang cases (20) to provide reliable estimates of gang/nongang differences. For 1984 and 1985, all cases from the five stations that had at least one roster-identified gang member arrestee were collected. An equal number of cases without gang arrestees was selected randomly in proportion to each station's contribution to the nongang total for each year.

Case records were located in station files, centralized storage facilities, and on microfilm. A pilot comparison of the availability of relevant information from different record sources yielded no substantial differences. Occasionally, case records could not be located and others were dropped when case materials indicated no arrests for cocaine sales. Those cases were not replaced because the nonsampled cases were exclusively nongang.

We turn next to the data comparing the characteristics of 384 gang incidents and 357 nongang cases to assess the possible effects of gang member involvement. We begin by looking at characteristics that distinguished gang and nongang homicides in prior research in order to determine whether those features also differentiate the two groups of cocaine sales incidents. We then

"CRACK," STREET GANGS, AND VIOLENCE   631

turn to unique aspects of drug sales events and examine what gang/nongang differences emerge. Finally, to assess gang impact we investigate changes in case characteristics occurring in this period of increased gang involvement.

GENERAL CHARACTERISTICS OF GANG AND NONGANG INCIDENTS

In previous research (Maxson et al., 1985) comparing gang-involved and nongang *homicides*, several variables were identified that significantly differentiated between them. Gang homicides were more likely to take place on the street, involve firearms, and include more suspects with different demographic profiles than nongang homicides. In the cocaine sales incidents, we found no evidence of gang/nongang differences in location and presence of firearms. About two-thirds of the incidents had street locations and about one-quarter had mentions of firearms, but neither varied significantly by gang involvement. However, statistically significant differences in *participant* characteristics paralleled those found previously for homicide cases. Cocaine sales incidents with gang involvement had slightly more suspects (2.16 vs. 1.81), and the suspects were more likely to be male, black rather than Hispanic, and younger (22.7 vs. 26.9 years) than cases without gang members involved.

DIFFERENCES IN DRUG CHARACTERISTICS IN GANG AND NONGANG COCAINE SALES

Keeping these confirmatory findings in mind, we can ask now whether gang and nongang cases differed overall with respect to special features of cocaine sales or possession-for-sale incidents, leaving aside for the moment the question of changes over time.

"CRACK HOUSE" INVOLVED

About one-third of all sales incidents took place in dwellings of some type, but crack houses—fortified residences redesigned for the purpose of retail sales of rock or crack cocaine and, therefore, known in Los Angeles as rock houses—were mentioned specifically in less than 6% of all cases, 5% in gang and 6% in nongang incidents. Police and press reports on gang involvement stressed these crack houses as symbolic of the intrusion of gang control into crack distribution. There, gang members could be assigned specific roles, such as lookout or enforcer, and could make use of their weaponry. Our doubts, based on previous findings of low cohesiveness and organizational potential among street gangs, led to a prediction of far lower gang domination of crack house operations than suggested by our police and media informants.

Clearly, reports of widespread use of gang-manned crack house cocaine distribution centers are contradicted by the data reported here. Street or car

632   KLEIN, MAXSON & CUNNINGHAM

sales locations were twice as prevalent as house or apartment locations, and type of location did *not* vary with gang involvement. If dwellings were perceived by law enforcement personnel as crack houses, they rarely labeled them as such in official reports.

FORTIFICATIONS

The surprisingly low level of crack house mentions could be an artifact of police recording practices. The recording of special fortifications—barred windows or doors, reinforced entrances, and so on—has more relevance to officers attempting a forced entry into a known sales location. Such fortifications were mentioned in 16% of gang and 17% of nongang incidents, or about half of the cases with home or apartment locations. With so many homes in the area having burglar bars, the 16 to 17% level of mention of fortifications is surprisingly low. Coupled with the lack of gang/nongang differences in frequency, we conclude that well-fortified crack houses, and their associated threats to officer safety and evidence retrieval, were the exception rather than the rule during this two-year period. The absence of gang-nongang differences again supports the hypotheses derived from the sociological gang literature.

SOURCE OF INFORMATION

This category refers to the means by which the police were alerted to the potential arrest situation. "Traditional" narcotics unit operations, such as receipt of information from paid or "turned" informants, citizen complaints, or anonymous tips, might be expected to be less common in gang-related cases because the openness of street gang activity might lead to more police-observed sales incidents and lead-up events (accidental discoveries in responding to calls on nondrug offenses). But the data reveal no such differences. About two-thirds of the arrest incidents were responses to prior information regarding drug activity. There were no gang/nongang differences relative to either existence of prior information or the source of prior information.

COCAINE INVOLVEMENT

Two measures were assessed here: cocaine taken in evidence and the mean amount of cocaine seized by the police. With cocaine mentioned very high in both sets of cases (96 and 97%), no differentiation is possible. But in these cases, the mean amount of coke seized also does not differ significantly. It is over twice as high in nongang cases (19.04 vs. 8.50 grams), which clearly does not support the expectation that gang involvement would yield more serious sales levels, but the variance is so high that the difference is not statistically significant. Even removal of "the outliers," the few cases involving very large

"CRACK," STREET GANGS, AND VIOLENCE   633

drug seizures, failed to yield a significant difference between gang and non-gang cases.

CRACK

Because the arrest logs that provided the sampling frame did not differentiate between forms of cocaine, it is only in the individual case files that one can find data about the presence of crack specifically (called "rock" in Los Angeles police files). As expected, however, crack was the predominant form involved. Gang cases more commonly included mention of crack, 92% compared with 81%, and the difference is statistically significant. However, the mean amount is actually, although not statistically, lower in gang cases (6.62 grams) than in nongang cases (8.49 grams). Thus, the 11% difference in prevalence is accompanied by a lower, but chance, difference in amount of crack involved. We are not dealing here with a major difference between gang and nongang cases.

OTHER DRUGS

All incidents were also coded for involvement of other drugs in order to assess whether gang sales events yielded higher levels of polydrug presence. Here again, no differences emerged. The marijuana percentages were 18 and 20%, and the next most common drugs, heroin and PCP, together were mentioned in only 4% of each set of cases.

CASH TAKEN

The files included the seizure of money as well as drugs. The percentage of cases with cash taken was significantly higher in gang cases (63 vs. 53%), but the actual amounts were not (means of $1,136 in gang cases and $764 in nongang cases). Thus, gang cases are somewhat more likely to involve crack and cash seizure, but the amounts obtained do not vary significantly with gang involvement. Further, the mean amounts of drugs and cash taken indicate the generally low levels of the distribution hierarchy involved in these incidents. Gangs had little effect at this level of the drug business.

MULTIPLE HANDLERS

Two enforcement-predicted characteristics of gang involvement that were expected to be measurable in case files were violence and organization. Our police collaborators were quite certain that gang cases were more violent, and we will report data on that later. They also thought that what gangs brought advantageously to crack distribution was their intrinsic organization. Indeed, two Los Angeles area courts have officially labeled street gangs as "unincorporated organizations," thereby making them more vulnerable to civil and criminal charges for court-order violations and conspiracy charges.

The case files were carefully coded for what we termed "multiple handlers." The term was used because of the relative absence of the role-specific argot reported in New York research reports (Goldstein, 1981)—"enforcers," "lookouts," "holders," and so on. Nevertheless, Los Angeles files did describe suspect activities that could be reasonably interpreted as division of labor in street sales. Some suspects warned of police surveillance or approach; some sold crack; some held money nearby; and some kept drugs or money in a nearby home, apartment, or car. Thus, one could describe distribution roles or "multiple handlers" in those incidents involving more than one suspect.

Multiple handlers should appear more commonly in gang-involved cases if gang organization is a factor in crack distribution. Given the fact that there were fewer than two suspects per case, however, a difference might be hard to find. And indeed, multiple handlers were coded in only 18% of all cases. They were more common in gang than nongang cases—21 vs. 15%, significant at the .05 level. However, this effect is likely the result of the more common appearance of multiple participants in gang cases. When we look at mentions of multiple handlers only among cases with more than one suspect, the gang/nongang difference is no longer statistically significant. Multiple handlers appear in 30% of gang cases with multiple suspects and in 24% of comparable nongang cases.

What do these comparisons mean? First, the vast majority of these cocaine arrest cases involved crack, but they yielded low numbers of suspects and low levels of drugs and cash. The crack phenomenon, as revealed in formal arrest activity, is increasingly widespread but undramatic. Second, there were few recorded differences between gang and nongang cases, and fewer still of any importance, as summarized in Table 2. Thus, there is little support for hypotheses derived from police and press reports of gang involvement; contrary expectations from the sociological literature hold up better. One could suggest that the *drug* parameters overwhelm the *gang* parameters. There is little evidence, certainly, that gang membership brings anything special to the crack trade.

DIFFERENCES OVER TIME

Did the increase in gang involvement yield concomitant growth in characteristics of cocaine sales incidents? As reported by the police and the media, the answer is in the affirmative. If it is actually in the negative, however, the sociologically derived hypotheses would be supported.

The issue was approached in two ways. First, a series of bivariate analyses was undertaken, comparing gang and nongang cases in the four half years covered, in which the numbers of gang and nongang cases were, respectively, 36 and 38, 70 and 71, 131 and 117, and 147 and 131. The second approach

Table 2. Summary, Gang/Nongang Differences in Sales Arrest Incident Characteristics

Variable	Police/Press Prediction	Sociology of Gangs Prediction	Result*
Crack House Involved	gang > nongang	no difference	no difference
Fortifications	gang > nongang	no difference	no difference
Source of Information	gang > nongang in traditional sources	no difference	no difference
Mean Amount of Cocaine	gang > nongang	no difference	no difference
Presence of Crack	gang > nongang	gang > nongang	gang > nongang
Mean Amount of Crack	gang > nongang	no difference	no difference
Presence of Other Drugs	gang > nongang	no difference	no difference
Cash Seized	gang > nongang	no difference	gang > nongang
Mean Amount of Cash	gang > nongang	no difference	no difference
Multiple Handlers	gang > nongang	no difference	gang > nongang
Multiple Handlers in Cases with 1 + Suspects	gang > nongang	no difference	no difference

* Based on chi-square statistics for categoric variables, *t*-test statistics for interval-level variables.

applied analyses of covariance to the case characteristics as dependent variables, to ask whether the impact of gang involvement "worsened" over time as the level of gang involvement increased. It is the contribution of the gang-time *interaction* to the overall variance that is important in this analysis.

Looking at the bivariate analyses first, did case characteristics change over time and did gang/nongang differences in each change over time? As seen in Table 3, the division of cases into the four time periods produces far lower cell sizes to be used for tests of statistical significance, especially in the earlier time periods. We report these tests cautiously, therefore, and look for broad and consistent patterns of change over time.

LOCATION

Over the four time periods, sales arrest incidents moved more into the streets. The street proportion moved from 55.5% to 60% to 59% to 68%. This trend could be explained equally well by changing law enforcement operational strategies as by changes in cocaine sales activity. The gang/non-gang differences were not significant in any of the four periods.

Table 3.   Characteristics in Gang and Nongang Cocaine Sales Events Over Four Time Periods

Incident Characteristics	First Half 1984 Nongang N=38	First Half 1984 Gang N=36	P	Second Half 1984 Nongang N=71	Second Half 1984 Gang N=70	P	First Half 1985 Nongang N=117	First Half 1985 Gang N=131	P	Second Half 1985 Nongang N=131	Second Half 1985 Gang N=147	P
Location Type												
Street	21 (55%)	20 (56%)	ns	47 (66%)	36 (51%)	ns	67 (57%)	79 (60%)	ns	83 (63%)	107 (73%)	ns
Dwelling	14 (37%)	16 (44%)		21 (30%)	30 (43%)		43 (37%)	43 (33%)		43 (33%)	33 (22%)	
All Other	3 (8%)	0		3 (4%)	4 (6%)		7 (6%)	9 (7%)		5 (4%)	7 (5%)	
Guns Present	11 (29%)	14 (39%)	ns	15 (21%)	23 (33%)	ns	30 (26%)	29 (22%)	ns	32 (24%)	25 (17%)	ns
Mean Number Guns per Incident with Guns	(N = 11) 1.54	(N = 14) 2.57	ns	(N = 15) 1.73	(N = 23) 2.22	ns	(N = 30) 1.7	(N = 29) 2.2	ns	(N = 32) 1.69	(N = 25) 1.76	ns
Prior Investigative Information	19 (51%)	16 (53%)	ns	45 (65%)	42 (62%)	ns	71 (63%)	86 (70%)	ns	90 (71%)	98 (70%)	ns
Cash Seized	16 (40%)	24 (67%)	*	36 (52%)	43 (61%)	ns	63 (54%)	80 (61%)	ns	74 (56%)	96 (65%)	ns
Mean Cash Amount	$837	$2,637	ns	$457	$1,050	ns	$1,120	$750	ns	$585	$1,120	ns
Crack/Rock Present	23 (60%)	31 (86%)	*	56 (79%)	60 (86%)	ns	102 (87%)	124 (95%)	*	107 (82%)	139 (95%)	**
Mean Number Participants Charged for Sales	1.58	1.75	ns	1.79	2.14	ns	1.73	2.1	ns	1.53	1.75	*

Participant Characteristics	First Half 1984 Nongang N=60	First Half 1984 Gang N=63	P	Second Half 1984 Nongang N=127	Second Half 1984 Gang N=150	P	First Half 1985 Nongang N=203	First Half 1985 Gang N=275	P	Second Half 1985 Nongang N=200	Second Half 1985 Gang N=258	P
Gender Male	49 (82%)	61 (97%)	**	115 (91%)	136 (91%)	ns	172 (85%) (N=202)	252 (92%) (N=274)	*	168 (84%)	246 (95%)	**
Race												
Black	31 (52%)	38 (60%)	*	88 (69%)	104 (70%)	ns	125 (62%)	199 (73%)	*	122 (61%)	180 (70%)	**
Hispanic	23 (38%)	25 (40%)		36 (28%)	45 (30%)		75 (37%)	75 (27%)		72 (36%)	78 (30%)	
Other	6 (10%)	0		3 (3%)	0		2 (1%)	0		6 (3%)	0	
Mean Age	27.7	22.6	**	25.9	21.5	**	26.9	21.8	**	27.2	21.6	**
Prior Arrest Record	38 (63%)	57 (90%)	**	95 (75%)	121 (81%)	ns	136 (67%)	227 (83%)	**	137 (69%)	225 (87%)	**
Mean Violence Priors	.53	.67	ns	.52	.78	ns	.43	.67	*	.42	.69	*
Mean Drug Sales Priors	.63	.63	ns	.74	.48	ns	.87	.75	ns	.82	.66	ns
Mean Drug Possession Priors	1.1	.65	ns	.62	.63	ns	.76	.65	ns	.76	.67	ns

NOTE: Chi-square statistics for categoric variables, t-test statistics for interval-level variables.

* p < .05   ** p < .01

"CRACK," STREET GANGS, AND VIOLENCE   637

PRESENCE OF FIREARMS

Guns reclaimed in arrest incidents are carefully recorded by the police. When present, they were coded for our analysis except for about 15 cases in which their location was so remote as to be inaccessible to the participants. Over the four half years, the proportion of cases with guns present decreased, somewhat surprisingly, from 34% to 27% to 24% to 21%. However, this change could be largely an artifact of the increase in street location noted above. The presence of firearms was recorded in the files of 8.8% of arrests at street locations and at 55.6% of residence locations. Gang/nongang differences were not significant in any of the four time periods. However, the decreasing presence of guns is more pronounced in gang (39 to 17%) than in nongang (29 to 24%) cases.

MEAN NUMBER OF FIREARMS

Within those cases in which guns were present, the mean number also decreased consistently, if slightly; the numbers were 2.12, 2.03, 19.95, and 1.72 guns per incident. This decrease, too, could well be due to the increase in street location. Gang/nongang differences were not significant in any of the four periods, although in each period the gang mean surpassed the nongang mean slightly. Even more than the trend for firearm presence, the decrease in number of guns was all in gang (2.57 to 1.76) rather than nongang (1.54 to 1.69) cases.

NUMBER OF PARTICIPANTS

Despite the increase in gang involvement over time, and the relationship between gangs and the number of incident participants, there was no appreciable increase in the average number of participants arrested for cocaine sales in our incidents over the four time periods. In each time period, there were slightly more participants in gang cases, but significantly so only in the last half of 1985.

GENDER

The proportion of male arrestees is always high in these incidents. It hovers around 85% for nongang and 93% for gang cases. These percentages did not vary substantially over time. Gang/nongang differences were statistically significant in all but the second time period (second half of 1984), but there is no pattern of increased differences over time.

ETHNICITY

The presence of "Anglos" in these cocaine incidents was virtually nonexistent; participants were principally black. However, the arrestees in gang cases were proportionately more often black than were nongang arrestees.

638   KLEIN, MAXSON & CUNNINGHAM

Nevertheless, the percentage of blacks never exceeded 73%, despite the expectation that crack sales in our five-station area was almost exclusively a black phenomenon. Although the ethnic differences attained statistical significance in all but the second period, the proportion of blacks never differed by more than 11% between gang and nongang cases.

AGE

Cocaine sales arrestees were modally in their twenties. Means were about 27 years for nongang participants and 22 years for gang participants.[6] There was no appreciable change over time. As expected, gang members were significantly younger in all four time periods.

PRIOR OFFENSES

The arrest histories were gathered from central data files maintained by the county, supplemented as necessary from state-derived rap sheets. From 63 to 75% of the nongang members arrested in the four time periods were found to have prior records. For gang members, the percentages ranged from 81 to 90%, confirming the expectation that gang members brought a more extensive criminal arrest background to the drug sales situation, despite their younger ages. Changes over time showed no particular pattern, such as enlisting more or less serious offenders. The gang/nongang differences were significant in all but the second time period.

PRIOR VIOLENCE

Gang members, as just noted, are somewhat more likely to have arrest histories, and they have more violent histories, as suggested by our police collaborators and prior research (Tracy, 1979). The proportion of gang members with arrests for violent charges was higher in all four time periods, significantly so in the last two periods. With the exception of the first period, the gang/nongang difference in violence records exceeded the difference in the proportion with prior records of all kinds; that is, the greater propensity toward violence was not merely a function of more extensive criminal behavior generally. Gang participants were more likely to have prior records and more likely even beyond that to have been arrested for assaults, weapons violations, and the like. The same holds true for robbery. Thus, we can reasonably expect to find more evidence of violence in the gang-involved sales incidents in our sample.

---

6. The mean gang age of 22 years speaks to two issues of interest. First, it yields no support for the claim by some that drug distributors have been employing juveniles in order to avoid adult prosecutions of dealers. Second, it reinforces the recognition that gangs in the 1980s are "street gangs," not juvenile gangs. The average age of gang homicide suspects, in Chicago and Los Angeles, is 19.

"CRACK," STREET GANGS, AND VIOLENCE   639

PRIOR DRUG ARRESTS

The final bivariate comparison has to do with prior arrests for sales and for possession of drugs. Here, we found no particular trend over time, and no significant gang/nongang differences during the four time periods for either sales or possession. However, in the eight comparisons (four periods × sales and possession), the nongang proportion with prior arrests equals or exceeds the gang proportion in seven and fails by only one percentage point in the eighth. This is in marked contrast to both the overall and the violence priors. This finding suggests that cocaine sales incidents throughout the two years were more in the hands of offenders experienced in drug matters, even when involving gang members. It is a point raised earlier, and to be raised again.

The 10 bivariate analyses yield some tentative conclusions. First, although there was an increase in street locations and a decrease in firearms presence (the latter, probably redundant, a function of the increasingly open locations), there were no other noteworthy changes over time despite the demonstrated increase in gang involvement. This does not indicate any major impact of gang involvement on the qualitative nature of the cocaine sales incidents under study.

We can add confidence to this conclusion by noting that results of bivariate comparisons of drug-specific characteristics are quite similar—few gang/nongang differences and minimal change over time. The same pattern appears with crack involvement. A higher likelihood of crack and cash taken in gang cases was evident in several time periods, but there is no indication that these gang patterns increased over time in comparison with nongang cases.

Second, *incident* characteristics do not differ between gang and nongang cases (location, weapons, number of participants), but *participant* characteristics do (gender, ethnicity, age, prior records except for drugs). Despite an occasional anomaly during the second time period, this seems to suggest that what gang members bring with them does not have much impact on the nature of the sales incidents themselves. We have already shown that the *level* of gang involvement in 1984 and 1985 was generally overstated. Now we can add that the concomitants of gang involvement may also have been overstated by police and press.

INTERACTION EFFECTS

Following the bivariate analyses, we undertook a series of analyses of covariance to see if we could tease out time or gang/time interaction effects on aspects of cocaine sales incidents. As noted earlier, the enforcement expectations were for substantial gang main effects; these hypotheses suggested that time main effects would be confounded by the increase in gang involvement in cocaine sales. Therefore, gang/time interaction was of particular interest to this study.

640   KLEIN, MAXSON & CUNNINGHAM

We selected a set of dependent variables that were most likely to show the gang/time interaction: street location, amount of cocaine and cash taken into evidence, mean age of suspects, and several aspects of the suspects' prior arrest records. The results were consistent with those of the bivariate analyses. Gang, time, and the gang/time interaction term explained very little variance in the dependent variables. Only on street location were the effects for time ($F = 7.64$) and the gang/time interaction ($F = 4.12$) statistically significant. For most of the dependent variables, R^2s ranged only from .01 to .06. The only exceptions were attributable to the strong main effects on suspect age. The R^2 for mean age of suspects charged with cocaine sales offenses was .15, but neither time nor the gang/time interaction term contributed significantly to the explained variance. Another exception is mean age of onset of criminal record, which is lower for gang members. Although the R^2 for this variable was .64, only mean age of suspects contributed to the explained variance. In this case, there were no significant main effects for either gang or time, nor was the gang/time interaction effect significant.

Consistent with the bivariate analyses, there were significant gang effects on some aspects of cocaine sales incidents (i.e., amount of cash, mean age of suspects, and prior arrest histories). The low amount of explained variance in the dependent variables indicates that factors other than gang and time should be examined, but the available data did not contain indices of such other variables. To test the notion of other, more explanatory variables, we turned to the example of jurisdictional differences in law enforcement field activity, investigation procedures, and case recording as well as possible jurisdictional differences in the nature of cocaine sales activity. Although such information was not collected specifically from the case files, our experience in the stations and interviews with officers suggested there would be such differences between our two cooperating departments.

To explore this possibility, we used a dummy variable for jurisdiction (LAPD v. LASD) as a proxy measure for unspecified jurisdictional differences. We selected street location, total number of suspects, and the amount of cocaine taken into evidence as dependent variables that would be most likely to show a jurisdictional effect. The amount of variance explained with jurisdiction included was quite similar to the initial results with only gang and time included. Time/jurisdiction interactions did not contribute significantly to the explained variance.

Thus, whatever may be the major factors that contribute to the variance in our data, they have not been tapped in this research. Gang involvement, time, jurisdictions, and their interactions yield relatively little. One might better turn to such issues as neighborhood or areal characteristics and the complex of variables that describe the drug distribution system. But that would constitute a very different project, geared toward very different questions.

VIOLENCE AND COCAINE SALES

When crack became a media event in Los Angeles, it was partly because of events that seemed to tie crack, gangs, and violence together. Most prominent was an incident in which a raiding group killed five young men in a brief burst of gunfire. This was variously described in the press as a gang retaliation, a drug territory retaliation, and both. The advent of gang participation in the fast burgeoning crack distribution system was an open invitation to speculations about gang-induced violence, based on assumptions about the nature of gang activity and about crack distribution (Hagedorn, 1988; Klein and Maxson, 1989; Reuter, 1988). Gang members might bring a greater familiarity with, or "propensity" for, violent approaches to conflict resolution. They may have more ready access to illicit firearms and automatic weapons. Such characteristics could be seen by drug distributors as prime qualifications for the "enforcer" or protective functions required by the large amounts of cash and drugs reputedly linked to crack house operations. The gang member armed with a shotgun pointed at the buyer purchasing crack through a small slot in an interior door was the picture often presented in our early law enforcement interviews.

Further, it was reported that gang members were recruited into drug operations specifically for their preexisting territorial claims over neighborhoods targeted for drug distribution. According to this view, coopting gang members into drug sales networks would reduce the potential for violence stemming from gang vs. drug territorial struggles. Others claimed that bringing gang members into drug distribution would merely carry ongoing gang rivalries into the drug scene; drug operations of one gang would be targets for rival gang retaliations.

There were two ways we could use available data to respond to these speculations. The first was to seek indices of violence in the sales arrest incidents already described. The second was to investigate aspects of drug involvement in homicides.

VIOLENCE IN COCAINE SALES INCIDENTS

The indices of violence available in cocaine sales incidents were few, for at least two reasons. First, most incidents involved sales of small volume. Front-line distributors are unlikely targets for violence-generating buyer rip-offs, and single sales transactions or arrests of front-line distributors are unlikely to involve turf disputes and retaliations. Indeed, a significant proportion of the incidents were "buy-bust" operations with narcotics officers as the buyers. Moreover, if a drug transaction precipitated violence and injury, the case typically would be investigated as a homicide or assault. Such charges would likely supersede drug sale charges and, therefore, not appear in narcotics arrest logs, the source of our population of incidents.

Second, most arrests were by narcotics or patrol officers whose primary purpose is to gather evidence useful in the prosecution of narcotics offenses. They are less concerned about intergang rivalries, rumors of impending or ongoing territorial conflicts, and gang-related motives. Gang unit officers typically have more concern for such matters, and they often pay less attention to drug paraphernalia and sales evidence. Therefore, we found that these arrest incidents presented few opportunities to investigate violence associated with cocaine sales. Indeed, occurrences of violence during these incidents were rare—7% in gang and 3% in nongang cases—and usually involved resisting arrest, rather than the type of drug-associated violence implied by our contrasting hypotheses.

Nevertheless, we can extract indices of violence *potential* from the cocaine sales arrest incidents. Once again, it is the comparison of gang with nongang cases and changes in the differences over time that address the issue of the gang/crack/violence connection. Relevant data were presented earlier, but we review them briefly here to provide the context for the supplemental data gathered to address gang/crack/violence relationships.

The presence of firearms, it will be recalled, did not distinguish gang from nongang cases, although the average number of guns in incidents with firearms did. Further, as crack sales flourished over time, the proportion of incidents with firearms decreased from 34% in the first half of 1984 to 21% in the second half of 1985. The levels are not high, and decline. The numbers of weapons also decreased steadily per incident with weapons, from 2.12 to 1.75. Decreasing trends in both presence and number were more evident among gang cases. Finally, proportion of gang members with prior arrests for violence remained relatively stable over time, which argues against the position that gang members were increasingly recruited by cocaine distributors to serve as their "muscle."

An additional point about the presence of firearms can be made. In the early stages of the project period, when there was much excitement about crack houses (the authors went on a 10-house raid with a sheriff's task force in a single evening), it was said that over a thousand crack houses were active on any given day. Further, we were told consistently that *every* crack house contained guns or that "almost every" busted crack house yielded guns of various kinds.

In our combined samples of 741 cases, crack houses were mentioned in only 39 cases (5%). Fortifications, a defining characteristic of crack houses, were mentioned in 121 (16%) cases. Clearly, this sets something of a ceiling on the "always a weapon" issue and therefore on weapons as harbingers of potential violence. Firearms were seized in 58% of the cases with crack house identifications and also in 58% of the cases in which fortifications were mentioned. Thus, again, the presence of weapons was greatly exaggerated by

"CRACK," STREET GANGS, AND VIOLENCE 643

our police collaborators. After all, it is commonly estimated that over 50% of American homes contain guns of some type.

None of these findings is conclusive about violence levels in cocaine sales, but they represent what is available. At best, they offer little support for the widely reported phenomenon of gang involvement in cocaine sales and violence during the 1984–1985 period.

DRUG INVOLVEMENT IN HOMICIDE

Because we anticipated that narcotics investigation files would be unlikely to yield much evidence of violence, we determined in the planning of the research to turn elsewhere. Sampling assault, weapons, and robbery incidents unfortunately would have taken far more resources than available funds would permit. We chose instead to use the most dramatic violent incidents—homicides—to address the question from the reverse direction: Is there evidence over our two-year period of more drug, cocaine, or crack involvement in gang than nongang homicides investigated in the five-station area?

Prior research had made us very familiar with homicide files. We had already developed data extraction and coding procedures for them. Further, if the drug/violence connection was increasingly obvious as dealers and distribution networks grew and came more into direct competition and conflict, it was most likely to be manifested in homicide.

A total of 123 1984–1985 gang homicides in the five-station area were available for data collection. For more than a decade, LAPD and LASD gang units have designated homicides as "gang" based on incident characteristics, knowledge of gang-related motives, and gang membership of either victims or suspects. In general, designation practices have been consistent over time in both jurisdictions (Klein et al., 1986). We matched the 123 gang homicides with 136 nongang homicides sampled randomly in proportion to each station's contribution to the five-station nongang homicide total for each year. Our first analysis, reported in Table 4, addressed the validation of gang/nongang differences found in our earlier homicide research (Maxson et al., 1985), assuring us that we were still dealing with consistent gang definitions. Five parameters were chosen for this purpose: location, presence of firearms, number of participants on the suspect's side, proportion of male suspects, and mean age of suspects. In all five comparisons, the gang/nongang differences were statistically significant, in the expected direction, and of the magnitude seen previously. Thus, we have the basis for valid comparisons with respect to the drug issues, of which we present four.

First, the most gross comparison is simply that of any drug involvement. In gang homicides, 84 of 123, or 68% of the cases showed evidence of drug involvement—paraphernalia, drug use or sales by victim or suspect, evidence of drugs at the scene, etc. The number of nongang homicides was 76 out of

644   KLEIN, MAXSON & CUNNINGHAM

Table 4.   Characteristics in Gang and Nongang Homicides
            (1984-1985)

Incident Characteristics	Nongang $N=136$	Gang $N=123$	P
Location Type			
Street	39 (29%)	82 (67%)	
Dwelling	65 (48%)	17 (14%)	**
All Other	32 (23%)	24 (19%)	
Guns Present	87 (64%)	112 (91%)	**
Mean Number Participants on Suspect Side	1.50	3.71	**
(Missing)	(7)	(1)	

Suspect Characteristics	Nongang $N=464$	Gang $N=615$	P
Male	438 (94%)	600 (98%)	**
Mean Age	27.7	20.0	**
(Missing)	(64)	(108)	

NOTE: Chi-square statistics for categoric variables, t-test statistics for interval-level variables.
** $p < .01$.

136, or 56%. Thus, gang homicides are somewhat more likely to reveal drug involvement than nongang homicides.

Second, when we compared gang homicide cases with and without drug involvement (see Table 5), we found few statistically significant differences with respect to the gang parameters—location, firearms present, and participant characteristics. Yet, when we compared nongang homicide cases with drug and without drug involvement, we found notable differences with regard to location, firearms present, number of suspect participants, and mean age. Of interest is that the differences were consistently in the direction of characteristics seen more often in gang than nongang homicides: more commonly street locations, firearms present, involving more participants and of younger ages. We interpret these second-order differences to mean that drug involvement has little impact on the *nature* of gang homicides—perhaps the import of "gang-relatedness" overwhelms the relevance of drug involvement. On the other hand, drug involvement is less common among nongang homicides, but when it is present, characteristics of the incident are quite distinct from those of other nongang cases. These results do not support the notion that gangs have unique and strong drug/violence connections.

Third, gang and nongang homicide files were coded for drug parameters,

"CRACK," STREET GANGS, AND VIOLENCE   645

Table 5.   Characteristics in Gang and Nongang Homicides (1984-1985) with and without Drug Involvement

Incident Characteristics	Nongang N=136			Gang N=123		
	Nondrug N=60	Drug N=76	P	Nondrug N=39	Drug N=84	P
Location Type						
Street	8 (13%)	31 (41%)		25 (64%)	57 (68%)	
Dwelling	37 (62%)	28 (37%)	**	4 (10%)	13 (15%)	ns
All Other	15 (25%)	17 (22%)		10 (26%)	14 (17%)	
Guns Present	29 (48%)	58 (76%)	**	33 (85%)	79 (94%)	ns
Mean Number Participants on Suspect Side	1.31	1.66	*	3.26	3.93	ns
(Missing)	(2)	(5)		(0)	(1)	

Suspect Characteristics	Nongang N=464			Gang N=615		
	Nondrug N=136	Drug N=328	P	Nondrug N=167	Drug N=448	P
Male	125 (92%)	313 (95%)	ns	162 (97%)	438 (98%)	ns
Mean Age	30.3	26.6	**	20.1	19.9	ns
(Missing)	(21)	(43)		(34)	(74)	

NOTE: Chi-square statistics for categoric variables, t-test statistics for interval-level variables.
* $p < .05$
** $p < .01$.

such as type of drug involved, mention of participant drug use or involvement in drug sales, and specification of explicit drug-related motives for the homicide (e.g., dealer rip-off, drug territory dispute). A gang-induced violence connection, as suggested by police and the press, should yield drug differences favoring the gang homicides. Cocaine was involved in 60% of the 160 homicides with any indication of drug involvement. Just over half of those 95 cases included specific mention of the rock form of cocaine—crack. There were no differences in type of drug among gang and nongang incidents.

About two-thirds of the drug homicides included an aspect of drug sales rather than merely drug use. Gang homicides were no more likely to involve drug sales than nongang homicides. Finally, a drug-related motive was indicated in just 27% of gang homicides with drug involvement, but in 47% of the nongang drug incidents, a statistically significant difference.

These results support the contention that despite the relative frequency of drug involvement in gang homicides, its *relevance* is more limited than public reports would suggest. The drug dimension of these homicides is perhaps a

646   KLEIN, MAXSON & CUNNINGHAM

function of gang member involvement in drug sales, but it is not often a *motive* for homicide. The more frequent mention of drug-related motives in nongang homicides could explain the differences in incident characteristics noted among nongang homicides when drugs are involved.

Finally, there is the time dimension. With the increasing gang involvement in cocaine distribution and all the expectations for a concomitant rise in violence, gang homicides in the area should have shown a proportional increase in drug involvement, at least as compared with nongang homicides. Table 6 reports the data.

Table 6. Drug Involvement in Gang and Nongang
          Homicides over Four Time Periods

	1984		1985	
	First Half	Second Half	First Half	Second Half
Gang[a]	71%	74%	67%	65%
Nongang[b]	43%	36%	72%	64%

[a] $\chi^2 = .63$; d.f. $= 3$; $p =$ ns.
[b] $\chi^2 = 12.62$; d.f. $= 3$; $p < .01$.

In some ways, these data are the most interesting in this section. Gang homicides manifest essentially no change in drug involvement, contrary to police expectations, but the *nongang* homicides show a dramatic change. The clear suggestion is that the portion of the gang world that got involved in severe violence was already tinged with drug connections, but that nongang homicide came to be drug tinged as the cocaine problem exploded. The gang/drug connection was already there; the cocaine explosion brought more violence to the *nongang* portion of the growing drug arena.

These are, of course, strong conclusions to be based on such indirect indications as drug mentions in homicide cases. The reader may wish to consider them with caution. We state them with some clarity in order to highlight the possibilities, and because they are directly contrary to police and press suggestions. The drug/homicide connection, to judge from all four of the above comparisons, is not basically a gang phenomenon. Gang homicides were not affected over time by the drug scene, but nongang homicides were. More broadly, Fagan (1989) has noted similar patterns in a three-city comparison. He reported relative independence among levels of gang membership, drug dealing, and violence and concluded, "One must look to factors other than drug involvement to explain violence among gang members" (p.19).

The fit between these suggestions and the data reported earlier is quite good. For the period of 1984 and 1985, the initial and major growth period for crack sales in Los Angeles, the purported gang connection seems in most

"CRACK," STREET GANGS, AND VIOLENCE   647

respects to have been considerably overstated. The implications for violence similarly seem to have been overstated. The more parsimonious hypotheses suggested by the professional literature are the ones supported by our data.

CONCLUSION

Arrests logged by narcotics officers in five districts of two large jurisdictions indicate that the growth in crack sales from 1983 to 1985 was very dramatic. Although the growth was accompanied by a major increase in street gang member involvement, the increase was primarily at the low volume, street level of sales. This parallels findings from New York (Fagan and Chin, 1989a), although the New York selling groups were not described in street-gang terms. Gang members seemed neither to have played a predominant role nor to have brought much extra violence or organizational character to crack distribution. We conclude, in line with the hypotheses derived from the literature, that the world of crack in Los Angeles belonged principally to the regular drug dealers, not to street gangs.

We should note also that more research is needed on this topic because of the unique situation of gangs in cities like Los Angeles, and because the crack and gang phenomena have spread rapidly throughout the country. Our data fit well with some of those of Belenko and Fagan (1987) in New York and of Mieczkowski (1988) in Detroit. In particular, Fagan and Chin (1989b) reported data on violence, gangs, and drug distribution that complement our data on the absence of a violence connection due to gangs.

But Skolnick (1988), using interviews with officials and a purposive sample of 39 inmates and wards in the California correctional system, claims a far greater involvement of gangs—especially in Northern California—in crack distribution, and at a higher organizational level. Skolnick's conclusions captured the approval of enforcement officials such as then California Attorney General Van de Kamp (Los Angeles Times, November 15, 1988). Our data were originally downplayed by Los Angeles officials because they do not go beyond 1985 and because of continuing reports of close gang/crack/violence connections (McKinney, 1988). But with new information and analysis of their own data by Los Angeles enforcement officials, the atmosphere in which our questions about the intensity of the gang/crack connection were not well received is now changing. The direct relevance of Skolnick's purposive correctional cohort to the issue of gang domination of street sales is unclear, and more careful analyses by the local police have revealed specialized "drug gangs" with peripheral relevance to traditional street gangs. In Los Angeles, as in many other cities, drug and gang problems may well intersect, but they do not thereby become a single, comprehensive social problem. Research on their confluence requires analysis of the gang and drug parameters separately, as well as in combination. In particular, assessments of gang involvement

648   KLEIN, MAXSON & CUNNINGHAM

must go beyond simplistic, undifferentiated depictions of street gangs to use the considerable knowledge base on street gangs available from the criminological literature of the past three decades.

REFERENCES

Belenko, Steven and Jeffrey Fagan
    1987   Crack and the Criminal Justice System. New York: New York City
              Criminal Justice Agency.

Blum, Richard H.
    1972   The Dream Sellers. San Francisco: Jossey–Bass.

Bonito, Arthur J., David N. Nurco, and John W. Shaffer
    1976   The veridicality of addicts' self-reports in social research. The International
              Journal of the Addictions 11:719–724.

Bureau of Criminal Statistics
    1988   Homicide in California, 1988. Sacramento: Office of the Attorney General.

Elliott, Delbert S., David Huizinga, and Susan S. Ageton
    1985   Explaining Delinquency and Drug Use. Beverly Hills, Calif.: Sage.

Fagan, Jeffrey
    1989   The social organization of drug use and drug dealing among urban gangs.
              Criminology 27:633–669.

Fagan, Jeffrey and Ko–lin Chin
    1989a   Initiation into crack and cocaine: A tale of two epidemics. Contemporary
              Drug Problems 16:579–618.
    1989b   Violence as regulation and social control in the distribution of crack.
              Presented at National Institute of Justice Technical Review Meeting on
              Drugs and Violence, Rockville, Md.

Gandossy, Robert P., Jay R. Williams, Jo Cohen, and Henrick J. Harwood
    1980   Drugs and Crime: A Survey and Analysis of the Literature. Washington,
              D.C.: U.S. Department of Justice.

Goldstein, Paul J.
    1981   Getting over: Economic alternatives to predatory crime among street users.
              In James A. Inciardi (ed.), The Drug–Crime Connection. Beverly Hills,
              Calif.: Sage.

Gropper, Bernard A.
    1984   Probing the links between drugs and crime. NIJ Reports/SNI 188
              (November).

Hagedorn, John
    1988   People and Folks: Gangs, Crime and the Underclass in a Rustbelt City.
              Chicago: Lakeview Press.

Hindelang, Michael J., Travis Hirschi, and Joseph G. Weis
    1981   Measuring Delinquency. Beverly Hills, Calif.: Sage.

Huff, Ronald C.
    1989   Youth gangs and public policy. Crime and Delinquency 35:524–537.

Inciardi, James A.
    1988   Crack Cocaine in Miami. Newark: University of Delaware.

"CRACK," STREET GANGS, AND VIOLENCE 649

Klein, Malcolm W.
  1971   Street Gangs and Street Workers. Englewood Cliffs, N.J.: Prentice–Hall.

Klein, Malcolm W. (ed.)
  1989   Cross-National Research in Self-Reported Crime and Delinquency. Dordrecht: Kluwer.

Klein, Malcolm W. and Cheryl L. Maxson
  1985   Rock sales in South Los Angeles. Sociology and Social Research 69:561–565.
  1989   Street gang violence. In Neil A. Weiner and Marvin E. Wolfgang (eds.), Violent Crime, Violent Criminals. Beverly Hills, Calif.: Sage.

Klein, Malcolm W., Margaret A. Gordon, and Cheryl L. Maxson
  1986   The impact of police investigations on police-reported rates of gang and nongang homicides. Criminology 24:489–512.

Klein, Malcolm W., Cheryl L. Maxson, and Lea Cunningham
  1988   Gang involvement in cocaine "rock" trafficking. Social Science Research Institute. Los Angeles: University of Southern California.

Maxson, Cheryl L., Margaret A. Gordon, and Malcolm W. Klein
  1985   Differences between gang and nongang homicides. Criminology 23:209–222.

McBride, Duane C.
  1981   Drugs and violence. In James A. Inciardi (ed.), The Drugs–Crime Connection. Beverly Hills, Calif.: Sage.

McKinney, Kay C.
  1988   Juvenile gangs: Crime and drug trafficking. Juvenile Justice Bulletin (September). U.S. Department of Justice, Office of Juvenile Justice and Delinquency Prevention.

Mieczkowski, Tom
  1988   Crack distribution in Detroit. Paper delivered at the annual meeting of the American Society of Criminology, Chicago.

Reuter, Peter
  1988   Youth gangs and drug distribution: A preliminary enquiry. Washington, D.C.: Rand.

Short, James F., Jr. and Fred L. Strodtbeck
  1965   Group Process and Gang Delinquency. Chicago: University of Chicago Press.

Skolnick, Jerome H.
  1988   The social structure of street drug dealing. BCS Forum. Bureau of Criminal Statistics. Sacramento: Office of the Attorney General.

Spergel, Irving
  1964   Racketville, Slumtown, Haulburg: An Exploratory Study of Delinquent Subcultures. Chicago: University of Chicago Press.

Tracy, Paul E.
  1979   Subcultural Delinquency: A Comparison of the Incidence and Seriousness of Gang and Nongang Member Offensivity. Philadelphia: University of Pennsylvania Center for Studies in Criminology and Criminal Law.

Vigil, James D.
  1988   Barrio Gangs. Austin: University of Texas Press.

650   KLEIN, MAXSON & CUNNINGHAM

Yablonsky, Lewis
    1963   The Violent Gang. New York: Macmillan.

Malcolm Klein is Professor of Sociology at the University of Southern California and Senior Research Associate in the Social Science Research Institute. From 1962 to 1968, he directed evaluation and basic research projects dealing with juvenile gangs. Since 1969, his research has centered on comprehensive criminal justice planning, evaluation of deinstitutionalization programs, and assessment of legislative impacts. His current research involves police handling of juvenile offenders and police investigation of gang-related homicides.

Cheryl Maxson is Research Assistant Professor of Sociology and Research Associate at the Social Science Research Institute, University of Southern California. Her current research and publication activity is concerned with the deinstitutionalization of status offenders, the nature of gang violence, and police identification and response to gang-related crime. Previous research topics have included predicting legislative change and evaluation of legislative implementation and impact.

Lea Cunningham is a Project Coordinator on the staff of the Social Science Research Institute, University of Southern California. She is currently involved with a project assessing the handling of status offending youths. The majority of her past research activities has been focused on the areas of gang involvement in violent crimes and drug distribution.

[20]

NEIGHBORHOODS, MARKETS, AND GANG DRUG ORGANIZATION

JOHN M. HAGEDORN

Researchers have debated whether gangs are selling drugs "freelance" or whether gang drug selling is more organized. Some have speculated that gangs are evolving into organized crime. This article uses contingency theory from the literature on organizations to examine the sources of variation in drug-selling organization of gangs from Milwaukee. In the turbulent environment surrounding drug selling, inflexible vertically organized drug businesses are unlikely to be successful. The failure of this kind of entrepreneurial drug gang in Milwaukee is described. Most gang drug sales in Milwaukee were by neighborhood-based, loosely organized operations. Neighborhood-based drug-selling organization varied according to the lucrativeness and stability of the drug market. Complexity of gang drug organization generally varied inversely to the degree that drug sales were centered on the neighborhood as a market. Ethnicity may also exercise an independent effect on organization. Research needs to pay more attention to organizational theory and the neighborhood context of gang activities and organization.

In the past decade, gangs across the United States have been selling cocaine (Fagan 1992). Researchers have disagreed on the degree to which gang drug selling is organized or "freelance" (e.g., Taylor 1990; Skolnick 1990; Jankowski 1991; Waldorf and Lauderback 1993). However, there are few empirical studies that have investigated variation in organization of gang drug selling.

To help explain gang drug dealing within poor neighborhoods, many gang researchers have used Wilson's (1987) concept of an "underclass" (Moore 1978, 1991; Sullivan 1989; Fagan 1992; Taylor 1990; Padilla 1992). They have argued that the expansion of drug dealing is fundamentally the result of

An earlier version of this article was presented at the 1993 annual meetings of the Society for the Study of Social Problems. Helpful comments on earlier drafts were made by Lupe Abendroth, David Curry, Mary Devitt, Clint Holloway, Rita Lewis, Joan Moore, Jorge Silva, Edward Smith, Stan Stojkovic, Angelo Vega, and Jerome Wonders. Jeff Fagan and the anonymous reviewers for the *Journal of Research in Crime and Delinquency* also made substantial contributions to the final form of the article. Send correspondence to John M. Hagedorn, UWM Urban Research Center, P.O. Box 413, Milwaukee, WI 53201.

decreased legitimate opportunities in the postindustrial era (cf. Scharff 1987; Harrell and Peterson 1992). Some underclass research follows Cloward and Ohlin (1960) in examining the influence of different kinds of neighborhoods on gangs (Bursik and Grasmik 1993) and on differences in gang drug dealing (Sullivan 1989; Fagan 1992).

Given the variation in gangs that has been noted from Thrasher ([1927] 1963) to Spergel (1989), it may be that many types of gang drug-dealing organizations exist. What factors influence organizational variation? Is organizational structure simply a matter of rational choice by gang "entrepreneurs"? Are neighborhood gangs evolving into organized crime? Or could organizational structure be influenced by the environment where drug sales take place? Might the relatively inflexible vertical organization of drug gangs be a poor fit with the turbulent conditions surrounding drug dealing? Could less structured gang drug organization vary by neighborhood as suggested by some underclass researchers? This article applies contingency theory from the literature on organizations to explore the relationship between gangs and drug selling in Milwaukee.

STUDIES OF GANG DRUG SELLING

Some studies of gang drug dealing have hotly debated whether gangs are more or less organized. Skolnick (1990) found ethnic variation: African American gangs were more "instrumental" and vertically organized than "cultural" Latino gangs. He made the distinction between instrumental gangs dedicated to the organized sale of drugs and cultural gangs, which resemble classic notions of neighborhood corner groups.

Waldorf and Lauderback (1993) sharply disagreed, finding both Latino and African American San Francisco gangs to be loosely organized with individual gang members engaged in freelance, not organized drug sales. Joe (1992) concurred in regard to Bay Area Asian gangs. Both Waldorf and Joe cited Joan Moore's (1978) research in East Los Angeles as supporting the freelance model against Skolnick. Fagan (1989) found variation in the social organization of gang drug selling in three cities. Esbensen and Huizinga (1993) did not find evidence of organized gang drug sales in survey research in Denver. Decker (1993) found freelance drug sales in gangs he studied in St. Louis. Williams's (1989) vivid description of a very loosely organized New York cocaine selling ring is consistent with these gang researchers' findings.

Skolnick (1990), however, argued that modern gangs are becoming more instrumental. Even Southern California cultural gangs, he said, are becoming more entrepreneurial and evolving toward more organized involvement in drug sales. Johnson, Williams, Dei, and Sanabria (1989) had earlier found that New York City crack selling operations were changing from the traditional freelance or Preble model (Preble and Casey 1969), where heroin users sold drugs only to buy more drugs for their own use. The lucrative profits of the crack trade, they said, led to the founding of drug-selling businesses of between 4 and 50 people. "In short, crack selling groups are moving towards the organizational structure very similar to legal businesses" (p. 35).

Taylor (1990, p. 4), summarizing Detroit's experience with the violent heroin and cocaine dealing Young Boys Incorporated (YBI), maintained that traditional "scavenger" youth gangs were "growth phases" in the evolution of "corporate" drug-dealing gangs. Consistent with Skolnick, Taylor (1993) said that as Detroit gangs began dealing crack, some appeared to have adopted a rational model of organization, were being emulated by others, and were branching out into other parts of the country. Since the break-up of YBI, Taylor found, corporate gangs have commenced "covert operations" (p. 21).

Mieczkowski (1986) had also initially found that Detroit's YBI had never practiced a freelance model. The YBI operated within a bureaucracy with defined roles and prohibition on the use of drugs by sellers. However, after the arrest of the YBI, Mieczkowski (1990a) argued that, overall in Detroit, "crack appears to be distributed largely by multiple units of small entrepreneurs rather than by any mega organization that controls the crack trade" (pp. 21-4). His study found that users still dominated street-level distribution in keeping with the traditional freelance view of drug selling.

Mieczkowski (1990b) also criticized notions of organized crime controlling the drug trade, pointing out that historically there has been little or no research into the nature of organized crime. He found law enforcement "structuralist" models "unworkable because they are excessively rigid." Rather, Mieczkowski argued for a "very loose, coalitional, and situational vision" of criminal drug syndicates (p. 103).

Most other gang/drug investigations are case studies of one gang and one neighborhood and therefore can tell us little about possible variation. For example, Padilla's (1992) "Diamonds" made a conscious decision to form a "business gang" in one Chicago middle-class neighborhood. We do not know, however, in what ways the Diamonds might differ from business gangs in other neighborhoods.

Jankowski and Organizational Theory

Jankowski's (1991) study is comparative: he looked at 37 gangs in three cities over 10 years. All gangs were business gangs that were driven by an entrepreneurial spirit, which is the fundamental "world view and behavior of gang members" (p. 101). His three types of gang organization—vertical, horizontal, and influential—were rationally chosen by gang members with little environmental influence (p. 68). Jankowski's gangs were cohesive structured organizations, which all had a "relationship" with organized crime (pp. 131-2). He sharply criticized researchers who have found that gangs are "loose associations," concluding that "groups that have loose organizations will not be able to operate efficiently for any long period of time" (p. 99).

Jankowski's study is unique in that he studied gangs as organizations, addressing a void in the literature. His work is limited, however, because of his adoption of the rational choice model: Both the gangs he studied and their individual members made rational decisions based on self-interest. Organizational theorists have found rationality of decision making in even formal organizations to be "rare in nature" (Weick 1976; also cf. Zey 1992; March and Olsen 1976). There is a deep literature describing organizations as "myths" (Meyer and Rowan 1981), as being "loosely coupled" (Weick 1976), or even comparing them to "garbage cans" of solutions waiting for the proper problem to solve (Cohen et al. 1972). Any of these theories might fruitfully be applied to the study of gangs, but Jankowski chose not to examine perspectives other than rational choice. One serious deficiency is his neglect of those theories that look at the relationship of the environment to organizational type.

For example, Jankowski's (1991) claim that gangs with loose organization fade away and only those with "tight structures" endure is inconsistent with contingency theory, one of the main strands of organizational thought. Lawrence and Lorsch (1969) point out that vertically structured organizations are better suited to stable environments, whereas more decentralized or loosely organized structures are more appropriate for dynamic environments. The main thesis of their classic work, *Organizations and Environments*, is that organizations do not perform well if their organizational structures do not fit the environment they face. [1]

Overall, the environment where drug dealing takes place is as "dynamic" as anything in the organizational literature. The fear of police raids, customers who are erratically acting addicts, potentially violent competition from other dealers or gangs, surveillance by hostile neighbors, and uncertainty in maintaining supplies are everyday occurrences. The task of drug dealing is also far from routine. The fear of violence or arrest makes every sale risky and demands varying methods of getting supplies, bagging or cooking the cocaine, and safely delivering the goods to the house or corner salesmen. Even the location where the product is sold might suddenly have to change.

Contingency theory would predict successful organizations formed under these conditions would be nonvertical, decentralized, flexible, and loosely or even barely structured operations. Gang drug selling, it could be predicted, would more likely be similar to Waldorf's freelance drug sales than to Jankowski's cohesive organizations or structuralist notions of organized crime. Gang drug sales, it could be hypothesized, may be relatively more organized and successful in environments (i.e., neighborhoods) where competition is curtailed, surveillance low, and where there is access to a stable, more affluent customer base. "Tightly organized" gang forms of the Jankowski mode would be "rare in nature" and likely to fail.

Variation in Drug Dealing and Neighborhoods

Organizational theory thus leads us back to examining different types of environments, or neighborhood conditions. Long ago Cloward and Ohlin (1960) argued that "delinquent responses vary from one neighborhood to another" (p. 161) based on characteristics of social organization within neighborhoods. According to Cloward and Ohlin, criminal subcultures and organizations developed only where close ties existed between conventional and criminal adults. In areas with few illegitimate opportunities, conflict or retreatist subcultures developed (cf. Spergel 1964).

More recently, Wilson (1987) has argued that some areas lack social organization due to the out-migration of the middle class and resulting spatial concentration of the very poor. Although Cloward and Ohlin saw the presence of criminal opportunities as pulling delinquents into crime, Wilson saw the absence of institutional controls as allowing crime to flourish. The lack of middle-class residents in underclass neighborhoods also inhibits the modeling of conventional behavior and allows for the diffusion of deviance. For Wilson, class differentiation ought to produce less deviance.

Although sociologists have not found empirical verification of Cloward and Ohlin's (1960) delinquent subcultures (e.g., Short and Strodtbeck 1965), the significance of "neighborhood effects" on gangs and drug dealing has reappeared in some current underclass research. Sullivan (1989) found the seriousness of criminal activity varied relative to local networks that provided access to legitimate work. Drug dealing was a full-time job and potential adult career for youth in Latino "La Barriada" and African American "Projectville," where legitimate opportunities were limited. But in White Hamilton Park, where access to legitimate jobs was available for most youth, drug dealing was often part-time work and merely a supplement to wages.

Curtis (1992) found that drug markets varied in Brooklyn and Williamsburg based on physical ecology, housing type, extent of political organization, and cultural differences. Centralized crack organizations developed in one neighborhood where five or six Mafia heads had historically dominated heroin trade, political organization was absent, Latinos were moving in, and crack sales took place in proximity to lower Manhattan's larger drug customer base.

Fagan (1992) found that neighborhood differences led to variation in gang or drug-selling organization. In the immigrant-populated and less economically distressed Washington Heights, drug-selling operations were reported as more formally organized, more profitable, and more violent than in homogeneously poor Central Harlem. In Central Harlem, drugs were sold only to local residents, whereas Washington Heights had a more diversified clientele of drug consumers, which led to more tightly defined territories where drug sellers could capture more lucrative markets.

This Milwaukee study examines how different kinds of poor neighborhoods have produced different kinds of gang drug-selling organizations. It critically applies contingency theory to the study of gangs in an era of vast expansion of illegal opportunity structures.

RESEARCH METHODS AND SOURCES OF DATA

The interpretations presented here draw on observation and extensive field work over a number of years, specifically on data from studies in 1987 and in 1992.[2] During the early 1980s, the author directed the first gang diversion program in the city and became acquainted with many leaders and other founders of Milwaukee's gangs. He has maintained a privileged relationship with many of them during subsequent years. The confidential interviews in this most recent study were conducted in late 1992 and early 1993. As in the original study, the research follows a collaborative model (cf. Moore 1978), in which gang members cooperate with academic staff to focus the research design, construct interview schedules, conduct interviews with their homeboys, and interpret the findings.

As part of our current study, we conducted 3-hour interviews with 101 founding members of 18 gangs: 90 were male and 11 female; 60% were African American, 37% Latino, and 3% White. Their median age was 26 years, with three quarters between 23 and 30 years old. Twenty-three of the respondents had been interviewed in the earlier 1987 study and were reinterviewed, whereas 78 others were interviewed for the first time in the second study. Members from 2 gangs interviewed in the earlier study could not be located.

To better understand the influence of neighborhood on gangs and drug dealing, we focused on three different neighborhoods and interviewed nearly all of the members of three gangs and 65 of the 152 original founding members from eight male gangs in those three neighborhoods. We also interviewed both leaders and rank-and-file members of a citywide drug gang. All quotes in the text are from gang members from the three neighborhoods or the citywide drug gang. All interviews were taped and transcribed. Respondents were paid $50.

The interview picks up the lives of the founding members since 1987, when our original study was done, and has them reflect on their personal lives, recounting their careers in the drug business and their pursuit of conventional employment. The interview extensively questions the gang members about the nature of their drug-selling operations, the relationship of the gang to drug dealing, and the neighborhood response to the gang. Data from the interviews were coded and recoded collaboratively by staff and typologies developed by constant comparative methods (Strauss 1987). The organizational types reported on here were presented back to many of our respondents for a validating "member check" (Lincoln and Guba 1985).

We also improvised means to ascertain the extent of drug dealing in our study neighborhoods. In the fall of 1993, study staff and gang members from each neighborhood who were intimately familiar with the drug trade went block by block in smaller sections of each neighborhood to count the number of drug houses and places where drugs are sold and to determine whether each was gang affiliated. Data gathered from this "dope house survey" may underestimate the actual extent of drug dealing due to limits of our informants' knowledge.

Other sources of data were also used. In our earlier study we compiled rosters of all those who had founded the major gangs in Milwaukee. In this follow-up research, our respondents were asked to update information including educational and employment status, extent of gang participation, drug use and involvement in drug sale of the founding members of their gang. We tracked this and other information on all 236 founding members of 14 male gangs and all 60 founding members from 4 female gangs.

Demographic characteristics of each neighborhood were taken from a neighborhood survey of the area, not drawn from larger census tracts. Fifty households in each neighborhood were randomly sampled and adult respondents were asked a series of questions by community interviewers in the summer of 1993. The interview questionnaire included questions on respondents' demographic characteristics, their participation in civic and community groups, kinship ties, and opinions on drug dealing and gangs (Moore and Hagedorn 1994).

BACKGROUND: GANGS AND
DECREASED LEGITIMATE OPPORTUNITIES

Before we look at variation between neighborhoods, we need to briefly sketch the background for the growth in Milwaukee gang drug sales in the mid- to late 1980s. Economic conditions deteriorated in Milwaukee during that time. Manufacturing jobs declined precipitously in the 1979-83 recession and did not ever completely recover. During the 1980s, Milwaukee lost 19% of its manufacturing job base (McMahon, Moots, and White 1992). Of the large firms that paid high wages and where many minorities had been hired (Trotter 1985), 37% were shut down. The Milwaukee area lost 42,000 manufacturing jobs while gaining 100,000 service jobs. The majority of all metropolitan jobs are now located in the suburbs, accelerating spatial mismatch of Milwaukee's "hyper-segregated" minority population with new jobs (Kasarda 1985).

These trends hit Milwaukee central city neighborhoods especially hard, with 1990 African American male unemployment rates exceeding 45% (Rose, Edari, Quinn, and Pawasarat 1992) compared to less than 3.7% of all area workers. As African American and other youths who founded Milwaukee's gangs in the early 1980s reached adulthood, they found few good-paying jobs (Hagedorn 1988). Most of the founders of Milwaukee gangs bobbed in and out of conventional employment and periodically sold cocaine as a means of survival (Hagedorn 1994). But there were major differences between neighborhoods in the organizational form of gang cocaine sales as well as the rise and fall of a notorious citywide drug gang. We will begin our examination of variation in gang drug organization by examining Milwaukee's infamous "Citywide Drug Gang."[3]

FINDINGS

Citywide Drug Gang

Many cities have had highly publicized prosecutions of well-organized drug gangs. Detroit's YBI is an example of the hubris of young men who lived high off the drug game only to fall to indictments and prison or into the grave. Are these instrumental gangs the wave of the future? Contingency theory would predict that such "rational" operations are unlikely to succeed in such a turbulent environment. What happened in Milwaukee?

Unlike any of the neighborhood gangs, the Citywide Drug Gang started out in the late 1980s as a drug gang, not based in any one neighborhood.

Although the leaders had moved to Milwaukee from the Chicago area, their operations were completely local. They claimed to follow the "laws and prayers" of a Chicago gang nation, but their gang was no more than a front for selling dope. They built their business with some common sense and lots of terror.

Q: Can you talk a little bit about what happened when the Citywide Drug Gang started out?

#225: Well, when they first started it, for one thing they had the guns, the dope, and the money, so they had the foundation. . . . They recruited so many people and put them up on this thing. As far as the business aspect they already said well hey we already got the work, we got the know-how, all we need is you to help us get it done . . . they wasn't scared, wasn't scared of nobody.

Q: Yeah, but here in Milwaukee it wasn't a neighborhood that you went to.

#225: No, no. Any neighborhood was ours. . . . Just move in that neighborhood and let everybody know we here.

Q: Don't the people that were there that were selling, or it was their neighborhood, didn't they get a little upset about that?

#225: What could they do? We was fully equipped. Any situation, we could handle it. We would outnumber them, so what could they do . . . like we went into one neighborhood and there was some peoples, . . . We just told them fuck 'em, they want a war, we took 'em to war, we smoked 'em out of it. Where ever they staying we shoot their house down. They ain't gonna stick around if they ain't got no house to sit in. 'Cause you know we all have different ways of going about it. You scare the shit out of them, there ain't gonna do nothing but just hit it.

Q: How did you get their share of the market? How did you get their customers?

#225: Easy. You give them a better product. You know, give 'em quality. I mean, first of all, when you set up in any type of business like that, you try to do something that the other person don't do, you know, and then we draw their confidence that way and then we got 'em. . . . Or even maybe, they might want one until tomorrow. That's something the person across the street wouldn't do, and that's what we'd do. Their confidence to go to you. Simple as that.

Q: So it's just basic business tactics is what you're doing, backed up with some muscle, right?

#225: Right. That's the whole key thing, backed up with muscle.

The half dozen core leaders of the Citywide Drug Gang personally ran drug houses scattered throughout Milwaukee. There were no franchises or partnerships that might reduce profitability for those on top. One of our respondents credibly reported he ran seven drug houses bringing in a quarter of a million dollars per week. The Citywide Drug Gang created what appeared to outsiders to be a tightly run centralized organization to run their multisite operations.

However, although a handful of leaders ran numerous drug houses all over Milwaukee, their style of organization was what Weber (1946) would term "pre-rational," lacking rules, and "executing the most important measures through personal trustees, table-companions, or court-servants" (p. 196). The Citywide Drug Gang leaders lived high off the hog, but they did not even pay their workers a salary. Here is the perspective from one of the "court-servants":[4]

> Q: Do you get paid in money, dope, or some of both?
>
> #225: Really to me at the time it was like living with a mom or a dad. They just take care of you, you know. They wouldn't really just dish you out some of the money. They would ask if you hungry, then a certain person would just stop and buy everybody something to eat. Or if we went shopping and then you could pick out what you want and one certain person pay for everything. It was like that. We had people that delivered us clothes, or we had people that steal clothes and bring it and everybody just picked their size and whatever you could wear grab. So it wasn't really pay. If you paid somebody you made it on your own, on the side.
>
> Q: The cars were the organization's cars, right?
>
> #225: Right, it was no personal car. No one had a car that was in you know, their personal name. But it was, and that's another reason I wanted to get out it was if you got a girlfriend, it's like . . . everybody had to know about it. I mean, you didn't have quality time. Really you had no personal life.
>
> Q: They took over everything.
>
> #225: Right. And I had, once I got hip to that I was like, fuck this, cause I, I'm a male, and sex, you know, I couldn't get the time for it. We couldn't even do that. You know, we went to a night club and we got a young lady, you know, talk to her or whatever. They might all jump up and say it's time to go, we got to go. You know, I can't say well I'll catch up with you, you know, you *gotta* go.

Like the YBI and other flamboyant gangs of drug dealers, Citywide Drug Gang members were indicted and taken off the streets within a few years. Their greed and centralized organization made their leaders easy targets for law enforcement and resentment from their workers. Here is a view from the top:

> Q: Some people have said that the Citywide Drug Gang fell because it went to your heads?
>
> #125: Yeah, we got too flamboyant, period. But the bottom line is once you got two or three hundred thousand dollars and I got fifty, sixty thousand dollars to put up, all the clothes I can wear, in a year's time all the jewelry I can wear, and anytime, two, three cars, you know, I feel like I'm unstoppable now, you can't do nothing to me. I'm rollin' in the street in a twenty-five thousand dollar car fully decked, they pull me over, yeah so what, I go to jail, what's my bail, two thousand? My homies just come get me, you know what I'm saying.

Here's a view from the bottom:

> Q: Talk a little bit about the demise of the Citywide Drug Gang.
> #225: It was crumbling anyway. . . . It was like everybody was living a lie. And we started getting hip to it. The money was only going into one hand. Only one person was profiting. We was just getting treated like kids.

Other gangs hated the Citywide Drug Gang's tactics of moving into their turf. Many gangs reacted to their tactics violently.

> Q: Did you ever get into it with the Citywide Drug Gang?
> #205: Right here, man, we in the heart of the ghetto. We is right there . . . you don't see nobody come in the turf but them orangutans. The Citywide Drug Gang tried to come in here and take over, but they couldn't, man. 'Cause we wouldn't let them. Hey man, we went 'round there one day, man, and . . . we had all guns in a car, . . . shouting . . . and then we go on up. Hey, . . . once they start to shoot. 'Cause they shooting at you. But we lit in on them. See the house there . . . buried, ain't no house there anymore. Still be the Citywide Drug Gang's but they don't come our way and lie like they did.

The Citywide Drug Gang members were indicted and sent to jail because they carelessly set up all their drug deals on a tapped phone. Several top members were murdered and dope dealers and gang members from all across the city snitched on them and helped them fall. Transcripts of the trial painted a ridiculous picture of the ineptness of the gang (Romenesko 1990).[5] Still, the fearsome image of the Citywide Drug Gang and the potential profits from invading others' turf and robbing other dope dealers have enticed a few other Milwaukee gangs to emulate this "new jack" style. Such tactics, however, have also brought resentment from other gangs and drug dealers, pressure from the police, and internal problems.

It seems likely that the turbulent world of drug dealing would tend to undermine such overambitious efforts to create non-neighborhood-based vertical drug-selling organizations. Cocaine sales may be more efficiently run in less flamboyant, more flexible, neighborhood-based selling groups. In Milwaukee, most gang drug sales take place by just such groups. How were these drug-selling gangs organized?

Gang Drug Selling in Hustletown,
Posse Park, and La Parcela

The turbulent conditions facing drug dealing led Milwaukee gangs to form loosely structured neighborhood-based drug-selling operations. Between different neighborhoods, however, type of gang drug organization varied based on the lucrativeness and stability of the market for drug sales. Generally, complexity of gang drug organization was related to the level of drug sales to neighborhood customers. Where poor neighborhood residents were the main customers for drug sales, gang organization remained at a low level and drug selling was freelance. However, when opportunities to sell to middle-class outsiders or Whites increased, the gang held together to form small businesses with a rudimentary division of labor, or created more flexible and efficient organizational forms.

Ecological factors also influenced how much money the gangs could make and how they were organized. Neighborhoods that were adjacent to White or middle-class areas had a greater opportunity to sell to outsiders than central-city areas isolated from affluent customers. They therefore produced more successful and efficient forms of drug selling. The degree to which drug markets were "closed" (only gang members were allowed to sell drugs in the neighborhood) also helped stabilize the drug-selling environment, increasing drug profits. Thus the type of neighborhood gang drug organization was basically contingent on the stability and lucrativeness of the illegal drug market.

Ethnicity, however, appears to have an independent effect on organization. Kinship ties in forming drug organizations, involvement with the gang as adults, and length of time selling cocaine all varied by ethnicity. To help sort out these matters theoretically, let us turn to an empirical examination of different kinds of loosely structured drug-selling groups within three different kinds of neighborhoods.

HUSTLETOWN

Hustletown is a 49-block,[6] homogeneously poor African American neighborhood. Poverty levels have increased to well over the 40% usually given as indicating underclass status. Over the past 10 years, residents have lost good jobs at area industries. By late afternoon each day, unemployed males stand on street corners and next to bars throughout the area. According to our survey of the area, 36% of our respondents were supported by AFDC (aid to families with dependent children) and 65% of all adult household members were unemployed, including 50% of all adult males. There are few community agencies in the area to help to control youth. On the other hand, our survey found that nearly one third of all residents owned their own homes and 56% reported that they had lived at the same address for 5 or more years.

TABLE 1: Neighborhood and Market Characteristics

Neighborhood	Ethnicity of Neighborhood	Population Turnover	Location of Neighborhood	Ethnicity of Customer	Percentage of Customers From Neighborhood	Nature of Market	Self-Report Gang Organization
Hustletown	98% African American	Relatively stable	Inner city	100% African American	100	Open to other gangs	Not at all organized
Posse Park	98% African American; Latino and White nearby	Unstable, gentrifying	Next to downtown	80% African American 20% White	30 to 80	Open to other gangs	Fairly organized
La Parcela	70% Latino; White, Asian, and African American	Considerable immigration	Next to downtown	Latinos, for some sellers up to 90% White	10 to 90	Closed to other gangs	Very organized
Citywide Drug Gang	NA, sold citywide	NA, sold citywide	Inner city	African American, 10% White	50	Take over local markets from others	Very organized

276

TABLE 2: Gang Organizational Characteristics

Organizational Type (example of gang)	Ethnicity	Division of Labor	Centralization	Relation of Drug Organization to Gang	Junior Groups	Same or More Gang Involvement as Adults 1987-1992
Freelance (Hustletown)	African American	NA, gang has dissolved	NA, gang has dissolved	Gang in name only; freelance drug selling	Junior groups independent of drug sellers	13% same or more gang involvement
Small business; network (Posse Park)	African American	Dopeman is leader; other roles for local drug selling	Single posse or loose network	Gang is foundation for drug posse or network	No junior groups	27% same or more gang involvement
Overlapping gang and drug organization (La Parcela)	Latino (mainly Puerto Rican)	Specialized roles in both gang and drug selling; gang leader is often dopeman	Decentralized sections in "turf" throughout neighborhood	Gang and drug organization overlap; drug selling may be kinship based	Junior groups part of gang and take roles in drug selling	57% same or more gang involvement
Drug gang (Citywide Drug Gang)	African American	Dopeman is leader; other roles in citywide drug distribution	Centralized with many citywide locations	Gang a front for dope game	Junior groups unrelated to drug business	NA, gang did not form until late 1980s

TABLE 3:   Dope House Survey

Neighborhood	Blocks Surveyed	Drug Houses	All Places Where Cocaine Was Sold	Percentage Gang
Hustletown	30	16	23	61
Posse Park	36	15	19	74
La Parcela	50	30	43	49

Hustletown corresponded in many respects to Cloward and Ohlin's (1960) "stable slum," where limited opportunities for criminal activities produced a conflict subculture. The selling of cocaine provided market opportunities for gang members to sell to neighbors, friends, and people from adjacent communities, even in the absence of prior criminal organization. Most (21) of the original 37 founding gang members of the Hustletown gang had been active in the neighborhood's wide-open cocaine trade.

The neighborhood was saturated with cocaine. Our dope house survey found that on 30 blocks in the center of Hustletown there were 16 dope houses, four bars where drugs were regularly sold, and three "strips" of several residential blocks where drugs were sold on corners to passersby. Most sales within the neighborhood were gang related, either by the Hustletown gang or a nearby rival. Of all drug-selling places, 61% (14) were run by gang members and 39% (7) were run by nongang independents.

Our interviews disclose how the original Hustletown gang, like gangs in other closely knit Milwaukee neighborhoods, fell apart as its members entered adulthood. Of the Hustletown founders, 60% were reported as "no longer involved" with the gang as adults. Independently minded junior gangs formed every few years, but the original gang members sold cocaine in Waldorf's freelance style. Following are three Hustletown gang members' description of what happened to the gang since our last study.

Q: Our last study was done in 1986 and we described how the gangs formed and what was happening to the founders of the gangs as they became adults. What has happened to the gang the last 5 years, since 1986? What's changed the most?

#205: We are not together any more. Everybody doing his own thing.

#105: They just broke up . . . the guys being in a gang are more of an individual thing now.

#208: Yeah . . . everybody just went their own way, that's the truth. Some of the other fellows who might hear me saying this right now might get upset. And say it ain't like that. But from my point of view man, there ain't no more gang.

Other gangs in similar neighborhoods also broke up.[7] The reasons why are the subject of speculation by gang members:

Q: How organized would you consider the gang?
#221: Right now? It's not organized at all right now.
Q: Why do you say that?
#221: Because it seems like a lot of them don't trust each other no more.

Hustletown's location played a role in potential profitability of the drug trade. Hustletown is tucked away in the middle of the inner city, surrounded by other poor neighborhoods. Opportunities to sell to more affluent outsiders are thus ecologically limited. Most drug sales by Hustletown gang members were to residents and friends, or addicts from the neighborhood or nearby areas, and mainly to women.

Q: How many different people do you sell to in the course of a week?
#223: Hundreds. About a hundred.
Q: What percentage of your customers come from the neighborhood? Just give
   a rough guess.
#223: Hundred (percent).

Q: How do you make sure you're not getting set up?
#208: For one thing I don't deal with no White folks. And when you see your
   customer, you know who your customer is. And you're certain. You ain't at all
   certain about White folks.
Q: When during the month are sales best?
#222: The first of the month. When women get their checks.

But even though Hustletown was a neighborhood where gang members had close ties to residents, the gang did not even enjoy a monopoly on dealing drugs. Six of the 16 dopehouses where cocaine was sold were run by nongang dealers.

Q: Are other people not in your gang allowed to sell in your neighborhood?
#222: They can. 'Cause everybody can make money.

But Hustletown founding members were acutely aware that not all gangs fell apart as theirs had. This respondent vividly describes the anarchy of the Hustletown drug market.

Q: Are other gangs in Milwaukee more organized than yours?
#208: Yes. There's some others you know, fellas out there organized . . . Like (in
   a nearby neighborhood) they all worked together. That's the way I see they

more organized. But the folks in our 'hood, they is like I want my own shit. You got six, seven, eight motherfuckers on one motherfucking corner or one block trying to sell dope. Everybody got a different kind of dope. It makes it kinda hectic to sell your products out there . . . It's like in our 'hood, hey, you get your motherfucking spot. Cool. You make your money. Cool. If you don't, you ain't hustling hard enough.

In Hustletown, drug customers were mainly poor neighborhood residents. The chaotic cocaine trade meant only scant profits for gang drug sellers. Other drug dealers and even other gangs were able to sell in Hustletown, further limiting profits. The original gang broke up and individuals sold drugs freelance. In Posse Park, however, gang drug selling took on a more organized form.

POSSE PARK

Posse Park is a 63-block neighborhood, which is undergoing gentrification and considerable movement of the population. Only about a third of the residents had lived at the same address for 5 or more years and only 14% owned their own homes. Our survey found only 46% of adult household residents were employed and 42% were on AFDC. Although Posse Park is 98% African American, middle-class Whites are invading to the south and poor Puerto Ricans press in on the east. The area is adjacent to downtown and a prize for gentrifying developers. Homes are being leveled and extensive housing rehabilitation is also going on. As we began our study, we were appalled by the sight of old, well-built homes from the poorer African American section of Posse Park being uprooted, placed on platforms, and transported to the gentrifying section, for repair and sale to middle-class Whites.

As in Hustletown, drug selling could be openly observed throughout the area. In a 36-block area in the middle of Posse Park, our staff counted 15 dope houses, two bars where cocaine was sold, and two corners in front of the bars where curbside sales were regularly made. Most (74%) of the places where drugs were sold were affiliated with one of three active area gangs.

Unlike Hustletown, which had a single gang representing the neighborhood, Posse Park was home to two of Milwaukee's most prominent gangs, which I will call Posse A and Posse B. Also unlike the Hustletown gang, the two major Posse Park gangs did not form junior groups, probably due to the more transitory nature of the population. Instead, a new gang, Posse C, formed in the neighborhood from the constantly shifting population and had begun to dominate the cocaine market.

Rather than fall apart as the Hustletown gang had, the adult members of each of the two Posse Park gangs banded together in different ways to more efficiently sell cocaine in a more unstable and competitive environment. Whereas 60% of the Hustletown founding members were reported as no longer involved in any way with the gang, only 10% of the two Posse Park gangs had lost all connection to the gang.

Posse A formed a small drug-selling business, which kept the tightly knit group of life-long friends together. Like the Hustletown gang, Posse A at first had started to break up into individual drug sellers. But one of the guys pulled everyone together.

> #129: When Joe was . . . selling his dope he didn't trust nobody . . . he didn't trust his own brother . . . And then, when Carl started it was like, I trust you. I'm gonna run my own shit. Joe wanted all the money for himself. He didn't want the whole gang involved. Carl was like, fellows, let's go for it.

What Posse A set up was a small business—a "drug store"—and they tried to make a go of it in various locations in and around the neighborhood. Here is a story of their start-up problems that should be familiar to many small businessmen.

> Q: You said before that you sort of tried it, failed, and that the business sort of stopped and started through the years. What do you mean by that?
>
> #109: It like, you know, when we first started we didn't know nothing about how to sell it. We just seen everybody else doing it and we just tried to do it, you know. We were seeing everybody else, and it just wasn't working.
>
> Q: Like what do you mean? Explain that to me.
>
> #109: For one, we was giving away too much dope for the price, for the money that we was taking in. And then, for the second part, we was sitting back smoking too much dope. And I think like the worst part of it all was we were going to buy dope and everything, and it'd be so mixed up [not pure cocaine], don't be worth selling. We bought it, we got stuck with it, and it don't be nothing but a loss, and at the time it'd be all our money tied up into it.
>
> Q: So it took a while before you figured out the mechanics of this, how to do it right?
>
> #109: Um-hum. It takes time, I say for a person just to jump off into it, if you don't know nothing about it like we did. You gonna end up wondering why in the hell did everybody else make money off it and we can't. And you sit there . . . you see the dope, you buy the dope, and then you're selling the dope. But then you see you ain't making nothing but what you paid for it, and then after awhile, you know, like we started asking questions, figuring out what are you going wrong at . . . you learn how to go about it without getting beat.

Posse B did not break up when they became adults either, but they did not form anything as elaborate as a small business. To use a yuppie word, they *networked* to sell cocaine.

> Q: How did the gang start selling dope?
> #201: We let everybody do things on their own but we still try to help one another, it's like a family thing. . . . You do your own personal business. If you need some help, then Posse B are there to help you.

Using the trust they had built up within the gang, Posse B members regularly pooled their money to buy heavier "weight," or larger quantities of cocaine, which they could purchase cheaper.

> Q: Do the guys ever pool their money to get enough to buy heavier weight?
> #201: Hmm, yes, yes. . . . About once a month.

Neither Posse A nor Posse B was a tightly organized drug-selling operation. Posse A saw degree of organization as related solely to efficiency in selling drugs and unrelated to the old gang.

> Q: How organized would you consider the gang?
> #213: It was fairly organized.
> Q: Why do you say that?
> #213: Everything else was covered by like answering the doors or stuff like that. But as far as people wanting to go outside and look for new customers, people didn't . . . want to do that. So that's what made it a lot of arguing, and just minor stuff.
> Q: Does the gang have officers or leaders?
> #213: No.

Although there was no longer a gang leader, that role was taken over by one of the members, Carl, who was the dopeman. Carl set the drug operation up and paid salaries to his fellow gang members who worked in one of his dope houses. He explains,

> Q: Does the gang have officers or leaders?
> 211: Oh, well it's like this right here. I'm the man, and like when pay time comes, you would deal with Joe for that. You wouldn't have to come see me for to get your money.

Posse A became a small business selling cocaine from two "stop 'n go" houses where cocaine could be purchased and smoked elsewhere and one "smoke house" where cocaine was both purchased and used. Members of Posse B sold both at various corners and at drug houses. Because Posse Park was gentrifying and adjacent to middle-class White areas, the opportunity existed to sell to outsiders, although the fear of getting busted limited those riskier transactions. Most respondents estimated about a quarter of their cocaine sales were to customers who lived outside the neighborhood and 10% of sales were to Whites. Although welfare recipients made up the greater part of their customers, workers were also a significant proportion of those "served." Here are two representative estimates:

> Q: How many different people do you sell to in the course of a week?
> #109: About 80, 90 different people.
> Q: What percentage of your customers come from the neighborhood?
> #109: About, I'd say about 30%.
> Q: What percentage of your customers are White?
> #109: It was like 10 of them. One was working out at the airport, driving around in the airport cabs, and another one working at night and then some was working in the nightclub. We had a couple come from there. And then a couple of them we just knew.

> Q: How many different people do you sell to in the course of a week?
> #211: Oh, man, that's hard there John, maybe a hundred or more.
> Q: What percentage of your customers come from the neighborhood and what percent White? Just give a rough guess.
> #211: 80% (from the neighborhood) and 10% White.
> Q: When during the month are sales best?
> #211: First of the month, the end of the month, anywhere from the 31st to the, say about the 6th. You get aid checks, social security checks, general assistance checks . . . Of course you also got working customers . . . (For them) weekends better.

Prostitutes, who worked the streets near downtown, helped the dope business by spending their money at the dopehouse and sometimes steering customers there.

> #217: Hookers . . . go out and get all these White rich people, not probably rich, but they have jobs, decent jobs, they might get them and . . . rob them . . . They come in and see a White man, might take him in the alley and suck his dick or whatever they do. They'll take all his money and . . . all that money will come to you. And then sometimes they might bring you another extra customer (who would) spend more than she do.

One factor limiting the profitability and organization of drug-selling operations was that, like Hustletown, Posse Park was an open market. Both gang rivals, People (Posse A) and Folks (Posse B), coexisted and at times even cooperated in drug sales. The frequent movement of people in and out of the area, and competition from independent dealers and other gangs made it difficult to sustain a monopoly on drug sales and expand an organization.

> Q: Are other people not in your posse allowed to sell in your neighborhood?
> #212: Yeah. It ain't like people fight over turfs no more.

> #202: Well I'm quite sure it's enough money out there for everybody you know . . . I mean I'll let him get his motherfucking money as well as I'm going to get mine. But I mean he can't be throwing salt on me to get his.

Other factors need to be considered in understanding why the gangs' drug businesses did not become even more structured. For example, more Posse Park gang members (46%) were working legitimate jobs while they sold dope than Hustletown gang members (19%), perhaps due to a closer proximity to legal job opportunities. This might tend to limit full-time involvement in drug sales and keep organization less structured. Half of Posse Park gang members had already moved out of the old neighborhood and looked elsewhere to make a new life, compared to only a third of Hustletown gang members.

Still, high potential profits, turnover of area customers, and heavy competition with Posse C led Posses A and B to stress consumer satisfaction and look for more efficient ways of making a profit. Although none of our Hustletown respondents was making "crazy money" or at least $10,000 per month, two of our Posse Park respondents became big-time dealers.[8]

Drug selling was less chaotic than in Hustletown, but still unstable. Running a drug store was certainly a more efficient way to sell cocaine than Hustletown's freelance sales. But like most small businesses, Posse A's drug store failed in less than a year when Carl went to prison. Attempts to start it back up continued on and off. We might speculate that drug businesses may be more lucrative than freelance sales, but may also be riskier and not persist as long.

Whereas drug sales were more profitable in Posse Park than in Hustletown, they were even more profitable in our third neighborhood.

LA PARCELA

La Parcela is by far the most heterogeneous of the three neighborhoods, made up of 95 blocks of Puerto Ricans, Mexicans, Whites, and, more recently, a scattering of African Americans. It is a historically Polish and German area, which in the past few decades has become a zone of first settlement for Latinos, with Asian immigrants settling nearby. Although there is constant population turnover, with 38% of those we surveyed saying they had lived at their present address for a year or less, still a third said they had lived at their present address for 5 or more years. A third also owned their own homes. Economic opportunities were marginally better than in the two African American neighborhoods. Of residents surveyed, 42% received AFDC and 50% of all adults reported they were employed. Latino gang members earned more money in legal employment than African Americans, averaging a legitimate income of $797 per month, compared to African Americans' $604 ($p = .08$).

Drug selling is even more prevalent in this area than in either Hustletown or Posse Park. In 50 blocks of this area surveyed by our staff, there were 30 drug houses, four bars where cocaine was regularly sold, six corners where drugs could be bought by passersby, and three other business establishments where cocaine was sold. Half of the places where drugs were sold were gang affiliated and half nongang. Although most gang members were Puerto Rican, most nongang drug sellers were Mexican who relied on independent networks to get their supplies. These dealers generally sold only within the Mexican community or distributed weight or large quantities to other dealers.

Like the neighborhood, gangs in La Parcela had fragmented. The two major Latino gangs that formed in this community in the late 1970s both suffered splits. One gang, La Parcela A, split in two when a gang member from one family killed a fellow gang member from another family. The area's largest gang, La Parcela B, had several new gangs split off from it. Then, rather than build itself as a monolithic vertical organization, La Parcela B decentralized into loosely coupled geographic sections, largely based on family ties.

Q: Do you consider La Parcela B to be a big group or small group?
#267: They're a big group but they're just all scattered around. They got their little smaller groups but they're all united as one.

Q: What has happened to the gang since our last study?
#243: They expanded. Yeah they got huge, more people. Yeah by expanded I mean different sections.

All of the La Parcela gangs considered themselves more organized than gangs in Hustletown or Posse Park, with formal junior gangs being groomed to eventually take their place. The junior gangs were not independent, like in Hustletown, but an integral part of the gangs' drug operations.

Q: Are the younger guys part of your operation or do they have their own?
#249: They part of my operation, man. They do what they are told to or else they can't be a member of the gang.

Almost to a man, gang members from all La Parcela gangs said that their gang was very organized, sometimes with a touch of humor.

Q: How organized would you consider the gang is?

#271: Very organized. They know the rules and regulations. They know where they stand in every position. Yeah they know when they're right and wrong. There's no point in them arguing with nothing cause they're already trained themselves.

Q: Does the gang have officers or leaders?

#271: Yes.

Q: How organized would you consider the gang?

#248: Very organized. Organized.

Q: Why do you say that?

#248: We served [sold cocaine] for so many years and we never got busted. Until we all got busted at the same time. It was very organized, yeah. We all got busted at one time.

What nearly all respondents meant by "very organized" was the existence of a gang structure, with leaders, rules and regulations, sections and other signs of gang organization. These gang activities were independent but overlapped with the dope business. Cocaine sales were not explicitly run by the gang, but rather were gang sanctioned. The gangs carried on their meetings and rivalries with other gangs as well as selling cocaine and other drugs.

La Parcela gangs' dope businesses were extremely flexible. Although the gang leader was often the main dopeman, the method of how gang members sold cocaine varied. Most La Parcela gang drug sales were franchise operations, where the gang leader/dopeman provided cocaine to individual gang members. These members sold on their own at corners or set up their own dopehouse, depending on local conditions and their own skills as entrepreneurs.

Q: Is the group selling and then it comes back to one person, or is everybody selling on his own?

#131: That's only in the movies . . . Everybody is selling on their own. Probably one guy will get a few ounces [of cocaine] and he'll say here's one for you and here's one for you. Just pay my money and the rest is yours. Just pay me the money for the stuff so that I can pay the guys back that I got it from.

Q: Is that the way it works with other La Parcela gangs?

#131: Yeah. Everybody is on their own.

Sometimes drug sales were organized around a few people, like the network in Posse Park. These groups were often relatives where trust was solid because everyone was "family." The drug business was a kind of "ethnic enterprise" (Butler and Herring 1981; Padilla 1992).

> Q: Is there a posse within the gang who sells or does the whole gang sell?
>
> #265: It wasn't the whole gang, just guys that we trusted, that were responsible enough. Just a few guys that were selling, that we trusted.
>
> #131: With us it includes me, Sharky, Ralph, Toots, and my cousin Durango. That's the main five and we're taking care of business itself. We're working together, I'm not working for myself, he's not working for himself, we're working together here and we made four thousand dollars and that's five of us at a thousand dollars each. If I made four thousand dollars on a deal, and there's four of us, each would get a thousand by now.
>
> Q: But you've got thirty members—you don't want to cut that four thousand thirty ways.
>
> #131: Yeah, especially if there's only five of them that you dealt with all the time.

Latinos we interviewed from La Parcela made one third more money selling drugs than African Americans. Latinos were also more likely to be big-time dealers, making more than $10,000 per month (Hagedorn 1994). La Parcela franchise drug selling proved to be more efficient than drug stores or freelance sales.

Like in Posse Park, the reason for higher profits can be found in understanding who were the gangs' customers. La Parcela gangs sold more to working and middle-class White customers from outside the neighborhood than gangs in Hustletown or Posse Park. Although some La Parcela drug-selling gangs sold mainly to friends and neighbors only within their "turf," others did a booming business with Whites from adjacent neighborhoods and nearby downtown. Also, rather than sell mainly to a welfare clientele, as in the other two neighborhoods, La Parcela customers were mainly working or middle class.

> Q: What percentage of your customers come from the neighborhood? Just give a rough guess.
>
> #273: About 10%.
>
> Q: What percentage of your customers are White?
>
> #273: All of them are. About 90%.
>
> Q: What percentage of your customers are working straight jobs?
>
> #273: Mostly all of them, about 70%.
>
> Q: What percentage of your customers are White?
>
> #245: We had a lot of them. Out of a hundred probably 40% could have been White, maybe 50%. Those are the ones that have the money.

#232: Yeah, we got the downtown people coming in. We even got people that live around the airport. And these are people they got their own businesses. They're users. You know. They're users and they come in and buy. And they like it. They'll come in three or four times a day not every other day. . . . I'd say about 50% (are from the neighborhood).

Why did more Whites buy cocaine in La Parcela than Posse Park, even though both were adjacent to downtown? Racism probably entered into the equation. The Whites who bought cocaine in La Parcela apparently found it more comfortable to buy from Latinos than from African Americans in nearby Posse Park. Whites also stand out more in African American neighborhoods and therefore may be shunned as a security risk. Gentrification in La Parcela also had led to opening many upscale taverns that catered to Whites. This increased the number of potential White customers.

Profits also increased because all La Parcela drug markets were closed to rival gangs. Each gang or family strictly regulated who could sell on their turf in a manner sharply different than in Hustletown or Posse Park. The chorus from all the gangs on this question was unanimous.

Q: Are other gangs allowed to sell in your neighborhood?

#273: Hell no, no other motherfuckers allowed into this neighborhood, bro. No motherfuckers—we fuck and kick ass, bro. I find some other motherfucker selling in our neighborhood . . . We fucked up the motherfucking neighborhood but hey, we keep ours clean [no other drug dealers], man.

#271: No that's breaking the rules.

#265: No, no. Even before, you couldn't do that and I don't think you could do it now, I doubt it. Get shot up.

Higher profits in La Parcela resulted from more Whites and outsiders buying cocaine from gang members, as well as drug markets that were closed to rival gang members. La Parcela gang structure was the most complex, with overlapping gang and drug organizations. Drug sales in La Parcela differed from Hustletown freelance sales or Posse Park drug stores mainly in the domination by the gang of all aspects of the drug transaction. In Posse Park and Hustletown, gang members did not care where the dope came from as long as the price was right. But in La Parcela, connections for weight were kept within the same gang.

Q: I don't want to know who they are, but are your connects from Milwaukee, from out of town, or both?

#267: Both. From the same gang, same organization.

The gang was overall more salient for Latinos than for African Americans. Gang involvement for many Latinos actually increased over the past 5 years, with 57% of La Parcela founding members reported as the same or more involved with the gang today than 5 years ago. Only 27% of Posse Park gang founders and only 13% of Hustletown founders were involved the same or more. Selling drugs was an activity related to gang involvement for Latinos, whereas it largely replaced gang involvement for African Americans.

This increased salience may reflect the stronger family traditions of Latino gang members or longer family involvement with gangs. The drug-selling business was also often more of a family affair than a strict business operation. Increased profits may also reflect more experience with the cocaine trade. Latino gangs in La Parcela had been selling cocaine for 5 or more years before cocaine became popular in Posse Park or Hustletown.

DISCUSSION

The economic transformation of our cities has prompted a vast expansion of the informal economy (Scharff 1987). Cocaine's easy availability, mega-profits, and short-term "high" have fueled the growth in illegal opportunity structures within poor neighborhoods (Hamid 1990). Several researchers have argued that these increased opportunities to sell cocaine have led to an evolutionary development of rationally organized drug gangs. Applying contingency theory to our data suggest that the situation is a bit more complex.

The turbulent environment of drug dealing is probably not a good fit for rational drug-selling organizations. The demise of Milwaukee's Citywide Drug Gang may be due to the foolishness and sloppiness of its leaders. Drug gangs elsewhere may have been more careful, covert, or "rational," and have survived in new forms. Overseas drug cartels may also be tightly organized, although Mieczkowski (1990b) urges caution even here. Evidence from Milwaukee and Detroit, however, suggest drug gangs are probably most successful when they avoid inflexible, vertical forms.

Our data indicate that rather than being at the end of an evolutionary development in drug sales, vertically organized drug gangs may more properly belong to an earlier period of the cocaine era (cf. Hamid 1992). Case studies suggest such vertical organizations' cocaine-powdered star may be setting, not rising. Drug distributors may tend to be organized vertically to the degree that their market can be stabilized. But for street-level dealing, vertical organization is probably not the strongest organizational structure, directly contrary to Jankowski's (1991, p. 100) claims. Waldorf's (Waldorf and Lauderback 1993) freelance and other loosely structured neighborhood-based operations are likely to be a better fit with a turbulent drug-selling environment than Skolnick's (1990) entrepreneurial gangs.

Our study points out that gang drug organization is probably not simply a matter of rational choice by career criminals. Rather, environmental conditions may exercise considerable influence on complexity of drug organization. Contingency theory may help explain variation within neighborhoods, although all the facts do not quite fit the theory. Milwaukee gang drug organization varied mainly based on the profitability of drug sales and the stability of the market. Where sales went only to low-income neighbors, there was little or no drug organization. But as sales to affluent Whites and outsiders increased, more efficient drug-selling structures were created.

However, more work is needed to flesh out this analysis. Ethnicity and other variables appear to be independently important, with stronger Latino kinship ties helping sustain gang involvement into adulthood. Latinos maintained membership in the gang while often using kinship groups to develop parallel drug-selling operations. African American adult gang members largely dispensed with the gang while selling drugs freelance or in small businesses. Most White adult gang members sold cocaine freelance while holding down a full-time job, reflecting relatively superior labor market opportunities (Hagedorn 1994). Cocaine markets may have grown less stable and profitable as crack sales replaced powder cocaine, and restabilized as crack declined in popularity. Changes in styles of use and drugs of choice may impact both profitability and gang structure. More social scientists need to apply contingency theory and other organizational analyses to gangs and drug-dealing ventures.

Some questions should be addressed in looking at gangs as organizations. In what ways do gang drug-selling organizations change over time? What conditions might produce lucrative and persisting gang drug organizations with a rational vertical structure? Is there a difference between gang drug selling in cities with long-term gang problems versus those cities where gangs have only emerged in the past two decades? Are there consistent ethnic "styles" as Waldorf (1993) found? Does gang involvement of drug sellers vary by ethnicity, or are our findings primarily local? Does drug organization vary by gang size or region? What different ways are female gang members organized to sell drugs and what are the sources of variation? Why is it that gangs in some cities do not even sell drugs (Klein and Maxson 1993)?

Gang studies also need to pay more attention to neighborhood conditions. Given the expansion in today's informal economy, a version of Cloward and Ohlin's (1960) opportunity theory may lay the basis for developing an underclass theory of gangs. Central to Cloward and Ohlin's approach was the notion that differences in neighborhood licit and illicit opportunities produced different kinds of gangs. Along with contingency theory, this article has tried to apply these general tenets to analyze neighborhood variation in drug dealing.

Gang drug dealing today can be best understood as a semiorganized response of young people to decreased opportunities in the postindustrial era. The debate whether drug gangs are freelance or highly organized does not account for the variety of gangs or gang drug-selling organizations. Most Milwaukee drug gangs are poorly organized operations whose goal is the economic survival of individual members, not the gang becoming a new Mafia. Is it not reasonable to conclude that such loosely organized gangs would wither away if good jobs became as plentiful as the opportunity to sell drugs?

NOTES

1. Emery and Trist (1965) proposed a continuum of four types of environments, which demand different organizational formats from Type I "placid, randomized" environments where classical markets grow, to Type IV "turbulent fields" where uncertainty arises from interorganizational competition and changing consumer characteristics and needs. Contingency theory also argues that organizational structure can be predicted by the nature of a business's task. When tasks are predictable, routine, and repetitive, or centralization is needed to coordinate simple identical units, a bureaucratic structure is appropriate. When tasks have to confront a changing, reactive environment, with much uncertainty, nonbureaucratic decentralized forms inevitably are most productive (Perrow 1979).

2. The follow-up study was funded by NIDA grant #RO1 DA 07218. The funding agency bears no responsibility for data or interpretations presented here.

3. The names of all gangs and neighborhoods have been changed. Many of the drug operations described in this article were continuing as this article was being written.

4. Both respondents quoted below were interviewed by Hagedorn. He had known them for the past 10 years and the interviews were emotional and self-reflective.

5. With huge profits, the Citywide Gangsters had tried to go into legitimate business, but with laughable results.

Q: Did you consider spending or investing the money you made in the community or neighborhood stores ?

#125: I wanted to buy me a store, but I couldn't find any good attorney who was at the same time he was good, he was still crooked that I could take that money to and form a good corporation. . . . Couldn't find anyone. So, nine out of ten you stuck with stacks of cash, . . . sometimes it'd just be sitting there.

Q: You couldn't figure out how to spend it?

#125: I mean, for real. Lot of times you see on the news when they catch drug dealers with all that money, they don't know what to do with it they got so much of it.

6. The three neighborhood boundaries were drawn up by gang members and do not correspond to census tracts or boundaries set by officials or neighborhood organizations. Hustletown and La Parcela residents were also surveyed in 1989 and the present survey was based on the first questionnaire (cf. Hagedorn 1991).

7. Another African American gang that broke up was from a housing project where drug selling by adult gang members was all freelance. A White gang also broke up. Gang drug sales in the White neighborhood closely resembled Sullivan's (1989) Hamilton Park where dealers usually held full-time jobs.

8. Mean monthly income from drug sales among all male Milwaukee gang members interviewed was $2,400 per month, a third of those who sold drugs averaged less than $1,000 per month, and only 3% brought in $10,000 per month (cf. Hagedorn 1994). Only one former Hustletown gang member could be classified as a big-time dealer, and he made his money almost solely outside of the neighborhood.

REFERENCES

Bursik Jr., R. J. and H. G. Grasmik. 1993. *Neighborhoods and Crime: The Dimensions of Effective Community Control*. New York: Lexington Books.

Butler, J. S. and C. Herring. 1981. "Ethnicity and Entrepreneurship in America: Toward an Explanation of Racial and Ethnic Group Variations in Self-Employment." *Sociological Perspectives* 34:79-94.

Cloward, R. and L. Ohlin. 1960. *Delinquency and Opportunity: A Theory of Delinquent Gangs*. Glencoe, IL: Free Press.

Cohen, M. D. et al. 1972. "A Garbage Can Model of Organizational Choice." *Administrative Science Quarterly* 17:1-25.

Curtis, R. 1992. "Highly Structured Crack Markets in the Southside of Williamsburg, Brooklyn." Paper prepared for publication for the Social Science Research Council, New York.

Decker, Scott. 1993. "Slinging Dope: The Role of Gangs and Gang Members in Drug Sales." Paper presented at Midwest Criminal Justice Association, Chicago.

Emery, F. E. and E. L. Trist. 1965. "The Causal Texture of Organizational Environments." *Human Relations* 18:21-31.

Esbensen, F. and D. Huizinga. 1993. "Gangs, Drugs, and Delinquency in a Survey of Urban Youth." *Criminology* 31(4):565-87.

Fagan, J. 1989. "The Social Organization of Drug Use and Drug Selling Among Urban Gangs." *Criminology* 27:633-67.

———. 1992. "Drug Selling and Licit Income in Distressed Neighborhoods: The Economic Lives of Street-Level Drug Users and Dealers." Pp. 99-146 in *Drugs, Crime, and Social Isolation*, edited by A. V. Harrell and G. E. Peterson. Washington, DC: The Urban Institute Press.

Hagedorn, J. M. 1988. *People and Folks: Gangs, Crime, and the Underclass in a Rustbelt City*. Chicago: Lakeview Press.

———. 1990. "Back in the Field Again: Gang Research in the Nineties." Pp. 240-59 in *Gangs in America*, edited by C. R. Huff. Beverly Hills, CA: Sage.

———. 1991. "Gangs, Neighborhoods, and Public Policy." *Social Problems* 38:529-42.

———. 1994. "Homeboys, Dope Fiends, Legits, and New Jacks." *Criminology* 32(2):197-219.

Hamid, A. 1990. "The Political Economy of Crack-Related Violence." *Contemporary Drug Problems* 17:31-78.

———. 1992 "The Developmental Cycle of a Drug Epidemic: The Cocaine Smoking Epidemic of 1981-1991." *Journal of Psychoactive Drugs* 24:337-48.

Harrell, A. V. and G. E. Peterson. 1992. *Drugs, Crime, and Social Isolation*. Washington, DC: The Urban Institute Press.

Jankowski, M. S. 1991. *Islands in the Street: Gangs and American Urban Society.* Berkeley: University of California Press.

Joe, K. 1992. "The Social Organization of Asian Gangs, the Chinese Mafia, and Organized Crime on the West Coast." Paper presented at the Annual Meetings of the American Society of Criminology, New Orleans, November.

Johnson, B., T. Williams, K. Dei, and H. Sanabria. 1989. "Drug Abuse in the Inner City." In *Drugs and the Criminal Justice System,* edited by M. Tonry and J. Q. Wilson. Chicago: University of Chicago Press.

Kasarda, J. D. 1985. "Urban Change and Minority Opportunities." Pp. 33-67 in *The New Urban Reality,* edited by P. E. Peterson. Washington, DC: The Brookings Institution.

Klein, M. W. and C. L. Maxson. 1993. "Gangs and Cocaine Trafficking." In *Drugs and the Criminal Justice System,* edited by C. Uchida and D. Mackenzie. Newbury Park, CA: Sage.

Lawrence, P. R. and J. W. Lorsch. 1969. *Organization and Environment: Managing Differentiation and Integration.* Homewood, IL: Irwin.

Lincoln, Y. S. and E. G. Guba. 1985. *Naturalistic Inquiry.* Beverly Hills, CA: Sage.

March, J. G. and J. P. Olsen. 1976. *Ambiguity and Choice in Orgnizations.* Bergen, Norway: Universitetsforlaget.

McMahon, W. J., G. F. Moots, and S. B. White. 1992. *Restructuring the Milwaukee Economy: 1979-1989.* Milwaukee: University of Wisconsin–Milwaukee Urban Research Center.

Meyer, J. M. and B. Rowan. 1981. "Institutionalized Organizations: Formal Structure as Myth and Ceremony." Pp. 303-22 in *Complex Organizations: Critical Perspectives,* edited by Mary Zey-Ferrell and Michael Aiken. Glenview, IL: Scott, Foresman.

Mieczkowski, T. 1986. "Geeking Up and Throwing Down: Heroin Street Life in Detroit." *Criminology* 24(4):645-66.

———. 1990a. "Crack Distribution in Detroit." *Contemporary Drug Problems* 17:9-30.

———. 1990b. "Drugs, Crime, and the Failure of American Organized Crime Models." *International Journal of Comparative and Applied Criminal Justice* 14:97-106.

Moore, J. W. 1978. *Homeboys: Gangs, Drugs, and Prison in the Barrios of Los Angeles.* Philadelphia: Temple University Press.

———. 1991 *Going Down to the Barrio: Homeboys and Homegirls in Change.* Philadelphia: Temple University Press.

Moore, J. W. and J. M. Hagedorn. 1994. "Gangs in the Community: Neighborhood Militia or Urban Terrorists?" Paper presented at the annual meetings of the Academy of Criminal Justice Sciences, Chicago, March.

Padilla, Felix. 1992. *The Gang as an American Enterprise.* New Brunswick, NJ: Rutgers University Press.

Perrow, C. 1979. *Complex Organizations: A Critical Essay.* New York: Random House.

Preble, Edward and John H. Casey. 1969. "Taking Care of Business: The Heroin User's Life on the Street." *International Journal of the Addictions* 4:1-24.

Romenesko, J. 1990. "The Last Days of the Struggle." *Milwaukee Magazine* 11(15):88-96.

Rose, Harold M., Ronald S. Edari, Lois M. Quinn, and John Pawasarat. 1992. *The Labor Market Experience of Young African American Men From Low-Income Families in Wisconsin.* Milwaukee: University of Wisconsin–Milwaukee Employment and Training Institute.

Scharff, J. W. 1987. "The Underground Economy of a Poor Neighborhood." Pp. 19-50 in *Cities of the United States,* edited by L. Mullings. New York: Columbia University Press.

Short, J. F. and F. L. Strodtbeck. 1965. *Group Process and Gang Delinquency.* Chicago: University of Chicago Press.

Skolnick, J. H. 1990. "The Social Structure of Street Drug Dealing." *American Journal of Police* 9:1-41.

294   JOURNAL OF RESEARCH IN CRIME AND DELINQUENCY

Spergel, I.A. 1964. *Racketville Slumtown Haulberg*. Chicago: University of Chicago Press.

————. 1989. *Youth Gangs: Problem and Response. A Review of the Literature*. Chicago: University of Chicago School of Social Science Administration, National Youth Gang Suppression and Intervention Project.

Strauss, A. L. 1987. *Qualitative Analysis for Social Scientists*. Cambridge: Cambridge University Press.

Sullivan, Mercer L. 1989. *Getting Paid: Youth Crime and Work in the Inner City*. Ithaca, NY: Cornell University Press.

Taylor, C. 1990. *Dangerous Society*. East Lansing: Michigan State University Press.

————. 1993, *Girls, Gangs, Women, and Drugs*. East Lansing: Michigan State University Press.

Thrasher, F. [1927] 1963. *The Gang*. Chicago: University of Chicago.

Trotter, J. W. 1985. *Black Milwaukee: The Making of an Industrial Proletariat 1915-1945*. Chicago: University of Illinois Press.

Waldorf, D. and D. Lauderback. 1993. "Gang Drug Sales in San Francisco: Organized or Freelance?" Institute for Scientific Analysis. Alameda, CA. Unpublished paper.

Weber, M. 1946. *From Max Weber*, edited by H. Gerth and C. W. Mills. Oxford: Oxford University Press.

Weick, K. E. 1976. "Educational Organizations as Loosely Coupled Systems." *Administrative Science Quarterly* 21:1-19.

Williams, Terry. 1989. *The Cocaine Kids*. Reading, MA: Addison-Wesley.

Wilson, W. J. 1987. *The Truly Disadvantaged*. Chicago: University of Chicago Press.

Zey, Mary. 1992. "Criticisms of Rational Choice Models." In *Decision Making: Alternatives to Rational Choice Models*, edited by Mary Zey. Newbury Park, CA: Sage.

Part V
Girls and Gangs

[21]

GIRLS' TALK
The Social Representation
of Aggression by
Female Gang Members

ANNE CAMPBELL

Rutgers University

The present study analyzes taperecorded accounts of fights given by female members of New York street gangs to fellow members. While such data may not be veridical, they can reveal much about the way aggression is socially represented to peers which in turn is likely to be constrained by gang norms about the propriety of aggressive behavior. Frequency data indicate that fights are not restricted to specifically female or gang member opponents, that the majority are one-on-one encounters and are a result of domestic and romantic disputes and matters of individual integrity rather than gang-related issues. A principal components analysis reveals three interpretable factors; group—personal, weapon—no weapon and victim—nonvictim. The five major reasons for the physical aggression are most clearly differentiated by a joint consideration of Factors I and III. The importance of these factors is discussed with reference to the social acceptability of limiting the extent and seriousness of the encounter.

Our knowledge of aggressive behavior is general and among females in particular is fragmentary and inadequate. Aggression, by virture of its low base rate of occurrence in public situations, has rarely been the object of observational methods except by dedicated anthropologists. Psychologists have in general confined their efforts to laboratory situations where the dependent measures, because of ethical restraints, have been artificial and noninjurious, such as attacks with styrafoam weapons, administrations of brief electric shock, or verbal attacks. Criminological work has frequently relied upon official

Author's Note: *I would like to express my appreciation to the girls in the gangs who tolerated my presence so cheerfully. Daniel Bibel assisted in statistical analysis. The work was funded by the Commonwealth Fund and the Daniel and Florence Guggenheim Foundation.*

criminal statistics with their inherent biases as a foundation for extensive theory building. One alternative to these approaches, and one certainly not devoid of methodological problems of its own, lies in the analysis of accounts of aggression given by participants to one another. This article will employ data of this kind.

There has been considerable popular concern in recent years over the increased rate of female criminal aggression as reflected in the Uniform Crime Reports of the United States and of other Western industrialized countries such as Great Britain. Between 1970 and 1979, the Uniform Crime Reports indicated that the percentage increase for juvenile females' involvement in aggravated assault was 75%; in weapon possession was, 107 % and for nonindex assault, 50.9 %. The rate of increase was substantially larger than that of boys, yet if we consider all those charged with the above offenses, the percentages of females are a modest 15%, 6% and 21%, respectively. Thus, it would be incorrect to suggest that female criminal aggression has reached alarming proportions. Nevertheless, if such a trend is more than artifactual and if it continues, we may anticipate a more egalitarian distribution of aggression in our society.

Figures such as these reveal little of the circumstances of the actors or the incidents that led to the final arrest and conviction. Much evidence suggests that delinquent acts are committed predominately by groups of youth (Erickson, 1971; Hindelang, 1976). This seems as true for girls as for boys (Campbell, 1981; Giordano, 1978). Furthermore, urban youth groups or gangs have been held responsible for a sizable proportion of juvenile assaultive arrests. Miller (1975) in a nationwide survey suggests that in New York, gang members account for 31.4% of such arrests. Comparable figures for Los Angeles are 44.5%, and for Chicago, 25.7%. Thus gangs would seem to be a fruitful area in which to investigate more fully the nature of female involvement in aggressive acts. However, according to police information, females constitute a minority of the gang population. Miller (1975) estimates membership at no more than 10% of the total gang membership in major urban areas. The New York City Police Department estimates concur with that figure. Tracy and Piper (1982) report a cohort study of youth born in Philadelphia in 1958 and subsequently arrested as juveniles. They found no white female gang members although 9.2% of all white female offenders were violent. Among black females, only 1% of violent offenders were gang members, while 16.4% of all offenders were violent. Giordano (1978) however in a comparative study of institutionalized female delinquents and a control group used a self-report method to estimate involvement in gangs and violence. Her results indicate that 55.6% of delinquent girls (compared to 18.1% of controls) had taken part in a gang fight; 79.6% versus 26.4% had carried a weapon such as a knife or gun and 59.6% versus 7.2% had used such a weapon in a fight. The data seem to indicate that official figures for female involvement in both violence and gangs are lower than self-report measures but that involvement in gangs and violence may be restricted to a small number of hard-core female offenders. As with males, gang membership and violent offenses seem to be correlated with a background of poverty and, consequently, minority status.

In a qualitative sense we know little of female gang members' involvement in aggressive behavior. Miller's work (Miller, in press) conducted in the 1960s suggests that the two female gangs he studied differed drastically in the amount of aggression displayed. The Molls (a white early-teens group) evidenced only one assault over a 30-month period, while the Queens (an older black group) had 18 incidents, higher even than some of his male gangs. Rice (1963) and Hanson (1964) writing at about the same period report on two New York girl gangs suggesting that they were subordinate to the male gangs and that their individual fighting was primarily the result of sexual jealousies, while group fights were at the behest of the male gang members who allowed the females to accompany them to intergang "rumbles." Rice paraphrasing the views of both writers notes,

If a girl fights as well as a boy—and Youth Board workers know girls who do—boys don't like her, and in no walk of life is a girl whom boys don't like an object of admiration or envy to other girls. (Rice, 1963, p. 153)

More recent work, however, suggests that among females today there is considerably more support for criminal acts, including aggression, than twenty years ago (Giordano, 1978). Bowker et al. (1979) in data derived exclusively from male gang members note that while females are often excluded from criminal acts, they are least likely to be excluded from aggression. Quicker (1974) reports a study of female Chicano gang members in Los Angeles noting that girls who are unable or unwilling to fight are not admitted to a gang. The loyalty that the gang demands may require physical combat and failure to join in is subject to sanction. Brown (1977) reporting on black gangs in Philadelphia suggests that girls, unlike boys, are not required to fight a "fair one" as an initiation rite but that progression from a "young girl" to an "old head" is dependent upon their actions in gang wars, at school (where one or more members of a gang may "sound" members of another), and on the street, if females trespass onto the gang's "turf." Within the gang, fights may result from sexual jealousy and from attempts to move up the status hierarchy by "coping the rep" of a higher female. Occasionally, girl members take on male members who have incurred their anger.

Accounts such as these indicate a number of ways in which female gang members may choose or be pressured to engage in aggressive acts. However, the sociological "gloss" necessarily provided by the authors removes the reader some distance from the circumstances of any given fight or social actor. Ideally, one would like to see data derived from detailed observations of actual fights as they occur. Unfortunately, firsthand accounts such as these tend to be few because of the low base rate of such behavior. The present data are composed of girl gang members' accounts of fights in which they were involved collected over a two-year period of full-time involvement with three New York City gangs. Under a dozen fights were actually witnessed during this time. Nevertheless, talking about fighting occupied quite a substantial portion of the social interaction among members. This point has also been noted by Miller (1966):

> Violence as a concern occupied a fairly important place in the daily lives of gang members but was distinguished among all forms of behavior in the degree to which concern took the form of talk rather than action. (Miller, 1966, p. 111)

Before taking social talk as our unit of analysis, some conceptual problems should be directly addressed. Whether or not self-reported accounts of behavior (particularly "deviant" behavior) should be assumed to be veridical is a matter of some debate. Among those who have used self-reported delinquency as an alternative to official police records, there has been much concern as to their validity. Studies that have mapped self-reported acts onto official police contacts, peer report and lie detector performance suggest that substantial positive correlations do appear (Farrington, 1973). No study to my knowledge has succeeded in obtaining a perfect fit. This may reflect inaccuracies either in the external validity measure or in the subject's self-report due to concealment, exaggeration, poor recall, or response sets. Many social psychologists (for example, Harré & Secord, 1972; Marsh 1982) suggest that the social representation of acts or beliefs constitutes a legitimate focus of research interest in its own right. Social understanding (and presumably prediction though such writers do not address this issue) may best be achieved by comprehending both the meaning and the personal and social significance accorded to a given act by the actor and his peers rather than by a microscopic behavioral analysis of a sequence of motoric actions. Selected pieces of behavior attain significance not merely by their form or frequency but by the way in which they are represented to others and the attributions that are then made by the audience to the actor. This seems to be particularly true of aggressive behavior. For many young people—traditionally lower-class males—the manner in which aggressive incidents are related to peers reveals a great deal about the parameters of acceptability of the act and its relationship to status acquisition.

The fact that fighting occupies such a prominent position in the lives of such youth has been frequently noted. The reasons for this have been explained thus:

(1) Concern with demonstrating "toughness" is a central concern of lower-class male adolescents.
(2) In a life of monotony and restricted opportunities, aggressive behavior is exciting and compensates for the tedium of repetitive labor or unemployment.
(3) Fighting in defense of the group reinforces individual loyalty and promotes a strong sense of "belonging."
(4) Individual reputation and status may be gained by outstanding feats of aggression.

With such benefits at stake, it is reasonable to suppose that social talk about aggression may not always be veridical. On the other hand, it would be unwarranted to assume that acts of aggression are nonspecifically exaggerated. It is hard to image a peer group who would endorse as evidence of status a member's announcement that he had shot an innocent child with a telescopic rifle (not that such events do not happen, but they are unlikely to be taken as evidence of bravery by peers. Such an act would be seen as "crazy" or "sick" by most gang members.) The way an incident of aggression is related indicates something about the acceptable or desirable limits of aggression employed by the audience. Indeed, Marsh (1982) argues persuasively that the peer group imposes strict limits on the degree of exaggeration that it will tolerate before calling the actor's bluff. The present study represents an analysis of girl gang members' *talk* about fights. The results may reveal much about the social representation of fighting in the peer group and further work would be required before we could conclude that such representations are accurate reflections of the behavioral sequences to which they refer.

METHOD

The data were collected as part of a two-year empirical investigation of three New York City gangs. The position of girls in the three gangs was identical; in all cases, girl members took a feminized version of their male gang's name and had their own leadership structure, initiation rites, and meetings. However, the major part of their time was spent with the male gang members "hanging out" at the clubhouse or on the street and visiting in one another's house. In many cases, female members were romantically involved and/or living with one of the male members. All the gangs were known to the Gang Information Units (then in operation) of the New York City Police Department. The girls ranged in age from 15 to 30. Gang one met, at that time, in the Upper West Side of Manhattan. Membership was both black and Hispanic and the female membership ranged between 10 and 13 members. Groups two and three were from the East New York and Sunset Park sections of Brooklyn, respectively. Membership was principally Hispanic with 2 or 3 white and black members. Their ages ranged between 15 and 24 and female membership numbered approximately 15 in both cases.

During the course of the two years, I heard scores of fight accounts but the following analysis is based upon 64 cases that were tape-recorded and so available for reliable coding and analysis. All the accounts were given in the presence of other gang members and were spontaneous. In some cases, I put specific questions to the girl to clarify or disambiguate certain statements.

RESULTS AND DISCUSSION

Each account was coded with reference to nineteen variables. In some cases, information was absent with respect to one or more variables and these were entered as missing data. The total number of cases did not drop below 58 for any variable. Most of the coding categories are self-explanatory: one, however, requires clarification. "Reason for fight" was classified as relating to one of the concerns as follows:

Criminal act: Physical aggression resulting from attempt to perpetrate or resist becoming the victim of a criminal act. (Includes attempts at robbery and resistance to rape.)

Intragang: Physical aggression resulting from a dispute over leadership or role within the gang.

Intergang: Physical aggression resulting from an ongoing feud with a member or members of another recognized street gang.

Domestic: Physical aggression resulting from a romantic or domestic relationship in which aggression is directed toward the partner. (Disputes about infidelity between partners would be included in this category but not fights concerned with seeking vengeance on a female rival, which would be coded in the following category.)

Integrity or loyalty: Physical aggression resulting from a perceived slight against the public reputation of an individual such as accusations of cuckoldry, promiscuity, cowardice or stupidity. Loyalty refers to fights undertaken on behalf of another person whose reputation has been so impugned.

Table 1 presents the frequencies associated with the 19 variables expressed as percentages with absolute members in parentheses. The targets of aggression were rather evenly spread across all categories indicating that aggression was not confined only to other gang members, nor especially to other females. Miller (1966) reported that approximately 66% of aggression was directed within the gang, and in a later report (Miller 1975) suggested that nongang targets appeared to be on the increase. This seems to be reflected in the current data. Rather, a small portion of fights were immediately related to gang membership (only a quarter were intra- or intergang fights). However, if we include criminal acts as resulting directly from gang membership, the figure increases to 40%. Surprisingly, the single largest category of reported fights related to domestic violence romantic partners. The severity of such fights ranged the full

TABLE 1
Frequence Distribution of Nineteen Fight Variables

Variable		Percent	Absolute Number N=64
1. Identity of opponent:	Female gang member	29.7	(19)
	Female non-gang	17.2	(11)
	Male gang member	23.4	(15)
	Male non-gang	29.7	(19)
2. Reason for fight:	Criminal act	16.1	(10)
	Intra-gang	12.9	(8)
	Inter-gang	11.3	(7)
	Domestic	35.5	(22)
	Integrity or loyalty	24.2	(15)
3. Location of fight:	Public place	59.7	(37)
	Private place	40.3	(25)
4. Observers present:		70.7	(41)
5. Number of protagonists:	= 1	70.3	(45)
	>1	29.7	(19)
6. Number of opponents:	= 1	74.6	(47)
	> 1	25.4	(16)
7. Started by:	Protagonist	65.0	(39)
	Opponent	35.0	(21)
8. Weapon carried by either party:	Lethal (e.g. gun, knife)	42.2	(27)
	Non-lethal	9.4	(6)
	None	48.4	(31)
9. Fight involved punching:		33.3	(21)
10. Fight involved biting:		9.5	(6)
11. Fight involved kicking:		23.8	(15)
12. Fight involved scratching:		6.3	(4)
13. Fight involved slapping:		19.0	(12)
14. Fight involved other assaultive acts:		14.3	(5)
15. Weapon used:	Yes	39.7	(25)
	No	49.2	(31)
	Threatened only	11.1	(7)
16. Fight ended:	Spontaneously by participants	67.7	(42)

(continued)

TABLE 1 (Continued)

Variable		Percent	Absolute Number N=64
	By observers or police	16.1	(10)
	Due to injury or death	16.1	(10)
17. Fight abandoned by:	Protagonist	22.2	(14)
	Opponent	58.7	(37)
	Neither party	6.3	(4)
	Both parties	12.7	(8)
18. Police involved:		14.1	(9)
19. Winner:	Protagonist	58.7	(37)
	Opponent	20.6	(13)
	Neither	20.6	(13)

spectrum from pushing and slapping through to hospitalization for internal injuries sustained by one girl in a violent sexual assault by her partner. As many fights were concerned with integrity and loyalty as with specifically gang-related issues.

Fights tended to happen in public places (such as streets, parks, beaches) more than in private establishments such as the clubhouse, a private apartment, or local bar. Related to this was the fact that observers were present on 70% of occasions. The majority of fights were one-on-one. Surprisingly, the girl herself often admitted to starting the physical aggression in spite of a more general philosophy of "We don't look for trouble, it looks for us." Although in half of the fights no weapon was carried by either party, where a weapon *was* present, it was most often a lethal one such as a gun or knife. Where some form of weapon was carried, it was generally used (25 out of 33 occasions). Other assaultive acts were scored such that any given case might be multiple coded. Punching and kicking, characteristically male tactics, were most often used. Slapping, a somewhat less acceptable tactic for males, also occurred frequently. Actions commonly associated with female fighting (biting, scratching) were least often admitted. In spite of the apparent ferocity of the fight, only 16% ended as a result of serious injury. In most cases, the fight was ended by the participants themselves. As one might expect, it was the opponent who was usually cited as being the first to abandon the fight, and the protagonist was consequently seen as having won. The fight came to the attention of the police on only 14% of occasions.

Frequency data alone cannot address the more important issue of the relationship between the fight variables. A most economical way of doing so is by principal component analysis. Consequently, the variable levels were treated as distinct variables and the data converted into scores on each of these new variables. The resulting data matrix was subjected to principal components analysis using orthogonal rotation. A Scree test revealed the first three factors to be critical, with eigenvalues and amount of variance accounted for dropping rapidly thereafter. Eigenvalues for the first five factors were 5.17, 4.80, 4.27, 2.72, 2.46. Variance accounted for was as follows: 17.1%, 15.9%, 14.1%, 9.0%, 8.1%. Consequently, a three-factor solution was examined. The significance of a loading was determined according to the Burt-Banks formula (Child, 1970). To achieve significance, a given variable had to show a loading of > .262 on the first factor, > .263 on the second, and > .264 on the third factor. Variables showing a significant loading on at least one factor are included in Table 2.

In evaluating the results, Factor II was the most clearly interpretable and may be labeled a *weapon-no weapon factor*. The positive pole was defined by do not use weapon (+ .79) and no weapon carried (+ .78). The negative pole was defined by use weapon (− .74) and lethal weapon carried (− .73). Ranged along the dimension were intermediate forms of assaultive behavior. The dimension, however clear, did not significantly differentiate the reasons for the fight (with the exception of personal integrity or loyalty that loaded in a positive direction).

However, Factors I and III when considered jointly did differentiate the reasons for the fight. Figure 1 plots all significant variables with respect to Factors I and III. The first factor may be tentatively labeled as a *group-personal* dimension. Intergang

TABLE 2
Variables Loading Significantly* on the First Three Components
Subsequent to Orthogonal Rotation

	I	II	III
Number of protagonist > 1	-.18	-.01	.61
Opponent female gang member	.50	.46	-.03
Opponent female non-gang	-.42	-.11	.17
Opponent male gang member	.45	.11	-.13
Opponent male non-gang	.27	-.15	-.73
Number of opponents = 1	-.26	-.17	.74
Number of opponents > 1	.37	.02	.53
Location public place	-.32	-.03	-.49
Location private place	.03	.44	-.30
Reason-criminal act	-.36	-.11	.56
Reason - inter-gang	.41	-.02	-.20
Reason - intra-gang	.06	.05	-.46
Reason - domestic	.01	.11	.61
Reason - integrity or loyalty	-.39	.32	-.15
Observers present	.63	-.07	-.04
No observers	-.07	-.22	.29
Ended spontaneously by participants	-.45	.10	-.36
Ended by observers or police	.34	.03	.33
Fight abandoned by opponent	.50	-.19	-.14
Fight abandoned by protagonist	-.84	-.20	.02
Fight abandoned by both parties	.84	.20	-.02
Fight abandoned by neither party	.02	-.52	-.09
Weapon carried - none	-.35	.78	.03
Weapon carried - lethal	.39	-.73	-.01
Weapon carried - non-lethal	.06	.49	.02
Punching	.02	-.47	-.08

TABLE 2 (Continued)

	I	II	III
Biting	.02	.48	-.31
Weapon used - no	-.01	.79	.12
Weapon used - yes	.04	-.74	-.10
Weapon used - threatened only	.01	.39	.07
Kicking	.01	.30	.11
Slapping	.48	.01	.48
Amount of variance explained	17.1	15.9	14.7

*Loadings that are significant are underlined. Nonsignificant loadings are included for the sake of completeness.

fights loaded in a positive direction, while personal integrity and crime fights loaded negatively. Intergang fights were characterized as involving specifically gang-member opponents of both sexes, lethal weapons, the presence of observers, and a tendency for the fight to be abandoned by the opponent or by both parties. By contrast, integrity or loyalty fights were characteristically against other nongang females, fought without weapons and abandoned by the protagonist or ended spontaneously by those involved. Crime fights loaded in the same direction. The significance of the fight being abandoned by the protagonist here was obviously different. Integrity fights may be seen as affairs of honor where the willingness to fight is more important than the inflicting of injury (in contrast to intergang fights where admission of withdrawal by the protagonist would be nothing less than cowardly). Fights resulting from attempts to perpetrate crimes on nongang females may also be ended by the protagonist not as an act of honorable restraint but as an expedient desire to leave the scene and avoid detention. Interestingly, crime fights were not especially likely to involve weapon use, according to female gang members. This dimension of group-personal fighting suggested a correlated interpretation: that of the locus of control of the seriousness of

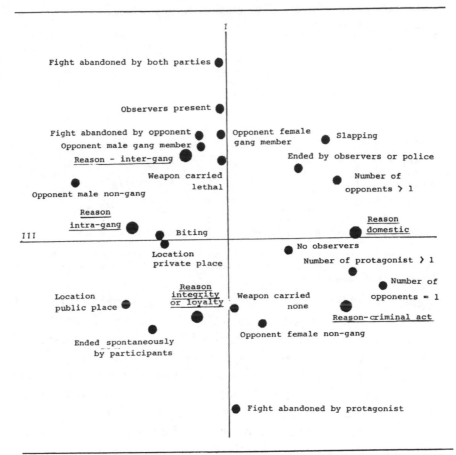

Figure 1: Fight Variables Plotted with Respect to Factors I (Group-Personal) and III (Victim-Nonvictim)

the fight. Intergang fights, as matters of public honor or "rep," occurred before observers. According to the girl's accounts, such fights, once begun, could not be honorably abandoned. Since weapons were likely to be involved, such fights were the most likely to result in injury. As such, they are nearer to popular conceptions of war than of street brawling. By contrast, personal integrity was more likely to be subject to the restraining or limiting codes of conduct evident in historical accounts of duelling and in contemporary analysis of aggression in British youth (Marth et al. 1978). The fight was likely to be ended by the fighters themselves with no dishonor being attributed if the girl herself admitted that she abandoned the fight. The absence of weapons similarly suggested that it was the willingness to become physically involved—to demand that honor be satisfied—that was more crucial than inflicting injury.

Factor II may be labeled as a *victim-nonvictim* dimension. Both domestic and crime fights loaded positively, together with the absence of observers, a single victim and a larger number of protagonists. Both types of fight were situations in which someone was picked on without the benefit of observers who might have intervened. The fact that domestic fights were not one-on-one affairs must be understood in the context of the living arrangements of the subjects themselves. In a domestic dispute, the girl might be attacked not only by her partner but by other members of the gang who joined in. Similarly, in the home, an attack by the girl on her partner might be joined by mothers, siblings, or children. The opposite end of the dimension was characterized by intragang fighting (and non-significantly by personal integrity and intergang fights). These fights did not seem to involve a victim, as such, since both parties willingly entered the confrontation. Intragang fights were closely associated with private locations (in this case usually the clubhouse) whereas domestic fights were not. This appeared paradoxical but many of the domestic fights occurred in parks, on the street, or in the subway. The high loading on this factor of male nongang opponent was enigmatic. It may have appeared in contrast to the domestic fighting that most often involved gang and family members.

CONCLUSIONS

It seems appropriate to stress once again that we are dealing not necessarily with matters of fact but those of social presentation. Bearing this in mind may be useful in interpreting the results. Studies of male gang members (such as Miller, 1966; Short & Strodtbeck, 1965; Yablonsky, 1962) accord no significance to domestic fighting. Two explanations spring to mind. Given Miller's (1975) suggestion that the mean age of gang members has increased over the last twenty years, it may be that age is the critical variable. We would not expect 14-year-old males to be involved in these kinds of disputes. On the other hand, sex may be a critical factor in terms of social presentation. Males are unlikely to gain kudos from public proclamations of having beaten up their partners. Females, however, are willing to report and discuss such events. For them, fights of this kind are intimately involved with their romantic and economic life—topics of some importance in their lives.

Similarly, fights over personal integrity are quite common among girls, yet in the male literature the overriding impression is of violence being a direct result of gang membership, as if there could be no challenge to an individual that was not an implicit challenge to the gang. The girls in this study often responded as individuals to attacks on their reputation or that of their lovers or children. Within the culture from which they come, failure to respond in this way would constitute deviance from an implicit prescriptive rule—"No one says that and gets away with it." It is my belief that such fights are equally common among male gang members and that individual fights can occur in the absence of other gang members. Females, however, may be particularly susceptible to this kind of attack since gang membership carries connotations of cheapness and inadequate maternal care of children as well as criminality.

Surprising, too, was the high proportion of male opponents and the relative frequency of weapon carrying and use. There is little doubt that fighting a male (and especially winning) carries a particular status among the girls (one that is unlikely to apply reciprocally to males fighting females). Similarly, use of weapons connotes toughness. The desire to portray oneself as a person who can take care of herself may inflate the reporting of both these factors.

The clarity of the weapon-no weapon factor in the principal components analysis was striking but perhaps less so than its inability to distinguish between fight reasons. Whether or not weapons are used seems to depend on variables unrelated to the type of fight. The present data suggest some tendency for intergang and crime fights to be more associated with weapon use. Clearly, further work on the determinants of weapon use is needed. Factor I (the group-personal dimension) suggested also a distinction in terms of the individual's ability to terminate the fight with honor. However, in spite of the significant loading of lethal weapon carrying, fight termination due to injury or death did not correlate with this type of encounter. If there are implicit limiting rules that serve to minimize the extent of injury (even when lethal weapons are carried), the present data did not tap them.

Both crime and domestic fights are characterized in terms of a victim set upon by more than one assailant in private. As perpetrators and victims in both cases, the girls indicate an implicit bracketing of these two forms. It is tempting to speculate when, as victims, both are seen as "unfair" but, equally, both may be seen as "necessary" when they are the perpetrators.

The visibility of all these fights to the police is low. Given that gang members are likely to be under closer police scrutiny than are other members of the community, this suggests that a very substantial portion of physical aggression occurs without recognition by the criminal justice system. Analysis of accounts offered by participants takes us some way toward an understanding of the social significance of aggression to members of lower-class youth subcultures.

REFERENCES

BOWKER, L., GROOD, H., & KLEIN, M. (1979). *Female delinquent gang activities.* Paper delivered to the American Society of Criminology, San Francisco, November.

BROWN, W. K. (1977). Black female gangs in Philadelphia. *International Journal of Offender Therapy and Comparative Criminology, 21*, 221-228.

CAMPBELL, A. (1981). *Girl delinquents.* New York: St. Martin's.

CHILD, D. (1970). *The essentials of factor analysis.* New York: Holt, Rinehart & Winston.

ERICKSON, M. L. (1971). The group context of delinquent behavior. *Social Problems, 19,* 114-129.

FARRINGTON, D. P. (1973). Self reports of deviant behavior: Predictive and stable? *Journal of Criminal Law and Criminology, 64,* 99-110.

GIORDANO, P. (1978). Girls, guys and gangs: The changing context of female delinquency. *Journal of Criminal Law and Criminology, 69,* 126-132.

HANSON, K. (1964). *Rebels in the streets: The story of New York's girl gangs.* Englewood Cliffs, NJ: Prentice-Hall.

HARRÉ, R. & SECORD, P. (1972). *The explanation of social behavior.* Oxford: Blackwell.

HINDELANG, M. J. (1976). With a little help from their friends: Group participation in reported delinquent behavior. *British Journal of Criminology, 16,* 109-125.

MARSH, P. (1982). Rhetorics of violence. In P. Marsh & A. Campbell (Eds.), *Aggression and Violence.* Oxford: Blackwell.

MARTH, P., ROSSER, E., & HARRÉ, R. (1978). *The rules of disorder.* London: Routledge & Kegan Paul.

MILLER, W. B. (1966). Violent crimes in city gangs. *Annals of the American Academy of Political and Social Science, 364,* 96-112.

MILLER, W. B. (1975). *Violence by youth gangs and youth groups as a crime problem in major American cities.* Washington, DC: U.S. Government Printing Office.

MILLER, W. B. (in press) *City gangs.* New York: John Wiley.

MOSKOVICI, S. (1963). Attitudes and opinions. *Annual Review of Psychology.* 231-260.

QUICKER, J. C. (1974). *The Chicano gang: A preliminary description.* Paper presented to the Pacific Sociological Association, San Jose, California.

RICE, R. (1963). A reporter at large: The Persian Queens. *New Yorker, 39,* 153-87.

SHORT, J. F. & STRODTBECK, F. L. (1965). *Group process and gang delinquency.* Chicago: University of Chicago Press.

TRACY, P. & PIPER, E. (1982). *Gang membership and violent offending: Preliminary results from the 1958 cohort study.* University of Pennsylvania. (mimeo)

YABLONSKY, L. (1962). *The violent gang.* New York: Macmillan.

Anne Campbell is an Assistant Professor at the School of Criminal Justice, Rutgers University. Her present research interest is in the social management of aggressive interactions with special reference to sex and social class differences.

[22]

Girls, Gangs and Violence:
Anatomy of a Backlash*

Meda Chesney-Lind
University of Hawaii at Manoa

REFLEXIVE STATEMENT

I have been working to break the silence about girls and their problems for over twenty years now, so it probably seems odd that I would consider writing a paper that basically attacks journalists for showing an interest in girls. Sadly, that is what I am compelled to do after a siege of media calls to me about the "problem" of girls in gangs. Perhaps the strangest was from a national television series that wanted me to produce a girl robber for their weekend program, but there have been many others. The reporters who call me are almost all young women themselves, but they quickly become aggravated with me when I won't confirm "what everybody knows"—that girls are more violent today.

As their lack of interest in the real problems of girls becomes clear, I find myself becoming increasingly frustrated and angry. I try to appeal to them as women, to establish that they were once girls, and that they, too, have likely suffered as a result of being born female. The damage done by the stories they have culled from the police files about girls a different color than they, living in a part of their city they don't understand, finding themselves in situations they cannot imagine, is hard to undo.

These days there is much talk about the differences between women and the need for many feminisms; that need has been made clear to me

---

*This paper is based on a presentation at the Annual Meeting of the American Society of Criminology, New Orleans, Louisiana, November, 1992. I am grateful for the helpful comments of Ruth Seydlitz, Marty Schwartz, Mike Lynch in the revision of this manuscript. Thanks also to Kathleen Daly, Laura Fishman, and Dragan Milovanovic for encouraging the author to pull this effort together.

in these conversations. The feminism these young women reporters feel close to has addressed issues very different from those of the girls who find gangs a partial answer to the many problems in their lives. Still, I feel compelled to try to define a sisterhood that can stretch that far and to try to pull together an understanding of girl gang members that makes their lives more accessible to others; this paper is part of that effort. It is also an attempt to make clear that the divides between women have been used by the media to demonize young women of color, thereby making them responsible for their own marginalization, while simultaneously warning their more privileged white sisters of the "dark" side of their efforts to seek a better life for women.

INTRODUCTION

Generally, the girls who find their way into the juvenile justice system have been invisible. The stereotype of the delinquent is so indisputably male that the general public, as well as those in criminology who study delinquency, rarely, if ever, consider girls and their problems.

Occasionally girls and women do occupy center stage, but only when their acts are defined as either very bad or profoundly evil. Such visibility was granted women's crime in the mid-nineteen seventies when the liberated "female crook" (Adler 1975a, p. 42) was discovered, and today a similar pattern is being seen with the media's intense interest in "girls in gangs." In both instances, these media crime waves were lodged within the larger silence about girls, their problems, and their delinquency. For this reason, there is often little with which to refute sensationalistic claims about girls' crime. More importantly, the relative lack of interest in this topic makes it difficult to craft an accurate understanding of girls and their relationship to their gangs.

RESEARCH ON GANGS

Existing theories of crime and delinquency, because they were constructed almost entirely with boys and men in mind, would appear to be fundamentally inadequate to the task of explaining young women's crime. Some contend, though, that despite their flaws, many of these theories can be adapted to explain female as well as male behavior (Canter 1982, Figueria-McDonough and Barton 1985; Giordano 1978; Simons, Miller and Aigner 1980; Smith and Paternoster 1987; Sommers and Baskin 1993).

Even these researchers, however, would likely concur that the degree of the androcentric bias found in theories of juvenile gangs is extreme. From the current gang frenzy that has gripped the United States comes a rather clear example of the problem. Martin Sanchez Jankowski's widely cited *Islands in the Streets* has the following entries in his index under "Women"

- "and codes of conduct"
- individual violence over
- as "property"
- and urban gangs

One might be tempted to believe that the last entry might refer to girl gangs and the emerging literature on girls in gangs (see Campbell 1984, 1990, Quicker 1983; Harris 1988), but the "and" in the sentence is not a mistake. Girls are simply treated as the sexual chattel of male gang members or as an "incentive" for boys to join the gang (since "women look up to gang members") (Jankowski 1991, p. 53).

Jankowski's work, as well as other current discussions of gang delinquency (see Hagedorn 1988) actually represent a sad revisiting of the sexism that characterized the initial efforts to understand visible lower class, male delinquency in Chicago over half a century earlier. Field work on gangs in Chicago clearly set the stage for decades of delinquency research. Then, too, researchers were only interested in talking to and following the boys. Thrasher studied over a thousand juvenile gangs in Chicago. He spends approximately one page out of 600 on the five or six female gangs he encountered in his field observation of juvenile gangs.[1]

During roughly the same period Shaw and McKay utilized an ecological approach to the study of juvenile delinquency. Their impressive works (1930, 1933, 1942) set the stage for much of the subcultural research on delinquency. In their ecological work, however, Shaw and McKay analyzed only the official arrest data on male delinquents in Chicago and repeatedly referred to these rates as "delinquency rates" (though they occasionally make parenthetical reference to data on female delinquency) (see Shaw and McKay 1942, p. 356). Similarly, their biographical work traced only male experiences with the law.[2]

Another major theoretical approach to gangs and delinquency focused on the subculture of lower class communities as a generating milieu for delinquent behavior. Here again, noted delinquency researchers concentrated either exclusively or nearly exclusively on male lower class culture. For example, Cohen's work on the subculture of delinquent gangs, which was written nearly twenty years after Thrasher's, deliberately considers only boys' delinquency. His justification for the exclusion of the girls is quite illuminating:

> My skin has nothing of the quality of down or silk, there is nothing limpid or flute-like about my voice, I am a total loss with needle and thread, my posture and carriage are wholly lacking in grace. These imperfections cause me no distress—if anything, they are gratifying—because I conceive myself to be a man and want people to recognize me as a full-fledged, unequivocal representative of my sex...I am reliably informed that many women...often affect ignorance, frailty and emotional instability because to do otherwise would be out of keeping with a reputation for indubitable femininity. In short, people do not simply want to excel; they want to excel as a man or as a woman (Cohen 1955, p. 138).

From this Cohen concludes that the delinquent response "however it may be condemned by others on moral grounds, has at least one virtue: it incontestably confirms, in the eyes of all concerned, his essential masculinity" (Cohen 1955, p. 140).

Feminist criminologists have faulted these and other theoretical schools of delinquency for assuming that boys' delinquency, even in its most violent forms, was somehow an understandable if not "normal" response to their situations. Girls who shared the same social and cultural milieu as delinquent boys but who were not delinquents were somehow abnormal or "over-controlled"(Cain 1989). Essentially, law abiding behavior on the part of at least some boys and men is taken as a sign of character, but when women avoid crime and violence, it is an expression of weakness (Naffine 1987).

For those with this conventional criminological perspective on gender, girls engaged in what are defined as "male" activities such as violent crime or gang delinquency are seen as seeking "equality" with their male counterparts (see Daly and Chesney-Lind 1988). Is that what is going on? A complete answer to that question requires a more careful and complex inquiry into the lives of these girls and the role of the gang in their world. But understanding has not been a major earmark of the current media interest in girls in gangs. Instead, the media has focused on the non-traditional, non-feminine, and sensationalistic aspects of these girls' behavior. A review of the media construction of the problem of girls in gangs will illustrate this quite clearly. This will be followed up by a summary of ethnographic and quantitative assessments of the girl gangs. Finally, this paper will offer a possible explanation for the intense media interest in this topic at this time.

MEDIA PORTRAITS OF GIRLS IN GANGS:

On August 6, 1992, a short-subject appeared on a CBS program entitled "Street Stories." "Girls in the Hood," which was a re-broadcast of a story that appeared first in January, 1992, opened with this voice over:

> Some of the politicians like to call this the Year of the Woman. The women you are about to meet probably aren't what they had in mind. These women are active, they're independent, and they're exercising power in a field dominated by men. In January Harold Dowe first took us to the streets of Los Angeles to meet two uncommon women who are members of street gangs (CBS 1992).

This story was one of many media accounts to have appeared since the second wave of the "liberation" hypothesis was launched by journalists. Where did this come from? Perhaps the start was an article entitled, "You've Come a Long Way, Moll" which appeared in the *Wall Street Journal,* January 25, 1990. This article noted that "between 1978-1988 the number of women arrested for violent crimes went up 41.5%, vs. 23.1% for men. The trend is even starker for teenagers" (Crittenden 1990, p. A14). But the trend was accelerated by the identification of a new, specific version of this more general revisiting of the liberation hypothesis. "For Gold Earrings and Protection, More Girls Take the Road to Violence" announced the front page of the *New York Times* in an article that opens as follows:

> For Aleysha J., the road to crime has been paved with huge gold earrings and name brand clothes. At Aleysha's high school in the Bronx, popularity comes from looking the part. Aleysha's mother has no money to buy her nice things so the diminutive 15 year old steals them, an act that she feels makes her equal parts bad girl and liberated woman (Lee 1991, p. A1).

This is followed by the assertion that "[t]here are more and more girls like Aleysha in troubled neighborhoods in the New York metropolitan areas, people who work with children say. There are more girls in gangs, more girls in the drug trade, more girls carrying guns and knives, more girls in trouble." Whatever the original source, at this point a phenomenon known as "pack journalism" took over. The *Philadelphia Inquirer*, for example, ran a story subtitled, "Troubled Girls, Troubling Violence" on February 23, 1992, that asserted:

> Girls are committing more violent crimes than ever before. Girls used to get in trouble like this mostly as accomplices of boys, but that's no longer true. They don't need the boys. And their attitudes toward their crimes are often as hard as the weapons they wield—as shown in this account based on documents and interviews with participants, parents, police and school officials. While boys still account for the vast majority of juvenile crime, girls are starting to catch up (Santiago 1992, p. A1).

This particular story featured a single incident in which an African-American girl attacked another girl (described as "middle class" and appearing white in the picture that accompanies the story) in a subway. *The Washington Post* ran a similar story entitled, "Delinquent Girls Achieving a Violent Equality in D.C." on December 23, 1992 (Lewis 1992).

In virtually all stories on this topic, the issue is framed in a similar fashion. Generally, a specific and egregious example of female violence is described. This is followed by quick review of the Federal Bureau of Investigation's arrest statistics showing what appear to be large increases in the number of girls arrested for violent offenses, and finally there are quotes from "experts," usually police officers, teachers, or other social service workers, but occasionally criminologists, interpreting the events.

Following these print media stories, the number of articles and television shows focused specifically on girls in gangs jumped. Popular talk shows such as "Oprah" (November, 1992), "Geraldo" (January 1993), and "Larry King Live" (March, 1993) did programs on the subject, and most recently NBC news had a story broadcast on its nightly news which opened with the same link between women's "equality" and girls' participation in gangs:

Gone are the days when girls were strictly sidekicks for male gang members, around merely to provide sex and money and run guns and drugs. Now girls also do shooting...the new members, often as young as twelve, are the most violent...Ironic as it is, just as women are becoming more powerful in business and government, the same thing is happening in gangs (NBC 1993).

For many feminist criminologists, this pattern is more than a little familiar. For example, a 1971 *New York Times'* article entitled, "Crime Rate of Women Up Sharply Over Men's" noted that "Women are gaining rapidly in at least one traditional are of male supremacy—crime" (Roberts 1971, p. 1).

A more expanded version of what would come to be known as the "liberation hypothesis" appeared in Adler's *Sisters in Crime* in a chapter entitled "Minor Girls and Major Crimes:"

Girls are involved in more drinking, stealing, gang activity, and fighting—behavior in keeping with their adoption of male roles. We also find increases in the total number of female deviances. The departure from the safety of traditional female roles and the testing of uncertain alternative roles coincide with the turmoil of adolescence creating criminogenic risk factors which are bound to create this increase. These considerations help explain the fact that between 1969 and 1972 national arrests for major crimes show a jump for boys of 82 percent—for girls, 306 percent (Adler 1975b, p. 95).

Of course, the female crime wave described by Adler (1975) and, to a lesser extent by Simon (1975) was definitively refuted by subsequent research (see Steffensmeier and Steffensmeier 1980; Gora 1982), but the popularity of this perspective, at least in the public mind, is apparently undiminished. It remains to be seen whether in the nineteen nineties something different might be going on, particularly with reference to girls and gangs. It is to that question, that this paper now turns.

TRENDS IN GIRLS ARRESTS

A review of girls' arrests for violent crime for the last decade (1982-1991) initially seems to provide support for the notion that girls are engaged in more violent crime. Arrests of girls for murder were up 12%, robbery arrests were up 48.7 and aggravated assault was up 70.3%. Indeed, arrests of girls for all Part One Offenses³ were up 62.1% (Federal Bureau of Investigation 1992, p. 218).

These increases may sound substantial despite the fact that they are actually considerably less dramatic than those that generated the first media version of a female crime wave. Between 1968-1977, for example, the total number of young women's arrests was up 61%, arrests of girls for robbery were up 112%, aggravated assault arrests of girls soared by 158.7%, and girls' arrests for Part One violent offenses were up 138.8% (Federal Bureau of Investigation 1978, p. 175).

To put these increases in perspective, though, only 2% of girls' arrests (4,889 arrests) in 1977 were for serious crimes of violence. By 1991 this figure had climbed to 2.9% (10,194 arrests out of a total of 343,506 arrests). Moreover, girls' share of serious crimes of violence (i.e. the sex ratio for these offenses) has changed very little during the two time periods. In 1977, for example, arrests of girls accounted for 10.6% of all arrests of youth for serious crimes of violence; in 1991, the comparable figure was 11.7% (Federal Bureau of Investigation 1978, p. 179; Federal Bureau of Investigation 1992, p. 222) . While many questions can be raised about the actual significance of such increases (e.g. the numbers involved are small and quite volatile), such an exploration is probably not salient. Changes in these sorts of official crime statistics failed to signal the rise of youth gangs (of either gender). As a consequence, it might be more useful to examine other sources of information on girls in gangs. Fortunately, there have been some excellent ethnographic studies of individual girls in gangs, and they seem a good starting point for a any discussion of major changes in the character of this form of female delinquency.

GIRLS IN GANGS⁴

Girls' involvement in delinquent gangs has never been of the same magnitude as boys. Traditional discussions of gang delinquency, reviewed earlier, stress the image of girls as playing auxiliary roles to boys gangs, if they are involved in gang activity at all. More recent criminological research seemed to confirm this impression. Miller's nationwide study of gangs, for example, in the mid-1970s, found the existence of fully independent girl gangs to be quite rare, constituting less than 10% of all gangs. He also noted that about half of the male gangs in the New York area had female auxiliary groups and of all the gangs known to exist in the Bronx and Queens areas of New York City, there were only six independent female gangs. Further, he reported that the crimes committed by the girl gangs were far less serious than males, and were no more violent than in the past (Miller 1975).

Miller (1980) also conducted an in-depth analysis on a Boston gang known as The Molls. This gang consisted of a core membership of 11 girls whose age ranged from 13 to 16. They were white and Catholic (mostly Irish). These girls seemed to fit the stereotype of inner-city working class girls, as they spent most of their time "hanging out" around street corners—looking and talking tough. They were known in the neighborhood as "bad girls." Their illegal activities included truancy, theft, drinking, property damage, sex offenses, and assault, in order of frequency. Truancy was by far their most common offense, occurring about three times as often as the next most common offense, which was theft (predominantly shoplifting).

These girls were closely associated with a male gang in the area known as the Hoods. The girls aspired "to become recognized as their girls," which they did by approving, supporting and abetting the criminal activities of the Hoods (Miller 1980, pp. 243-244). In fact, in order to be accepted by the Hoods the girls had no choice but to go along with their criminal activities. Contrary to popular belief, "the Molls did not flaunt their sexual exploits in order to win esteem" and they believed that to get the boys to like them was to imitate their behavior as much as possible, rather than be sexually accessible to them (Miller 1980, p. 244).

Rice reported similar findings in his study of a New York Gang, the Persian Queens. He noted that the gang was completely controlled by males and was oriented toward male activities. There is very little they could do to achieve power or prestige in the gang world. He also reported that if these girls fight, then the males will not like them; on the other hand, if they play a more feminine role, they are disregarded by the males, except for sexual gratification.

Similar findings have been reported in Philadelphia (Brown 1977) and in New York City (Campbell 1984). In general, while there have been some changes and some indications that girls are becoming more independent and aggressive, the majority of girls who are part of gangs are either the girlfriends of the male members or a "little sisters" subgroup of the male gang (see Bowker 1978, p. 184 and Hanson 1964).

There is abundant evidence that girls often join gangs for the same kinds of reasons as males, such as a sense of belonging, whereby the gang becomes a sort of "family." Brown (1977) found that friendships with fellow girl gang members is of utmost importance for girl gang members. Giordano's study (1978) arrived at the same conclusions. Gangs may also provide opportunities for relationships with boys (Flowers 1987, p. 137). Girls in gangs observed by Campbell very often engage in the same behavior as the boys, such as smoking pot, drinking, fighting, committing theft and "partying." Also, most of the fights the girls get into arise mostly from domestic or romantic disputes (Campbell 1984, p33). Summarizing these and other studies, Mann concluded that the stereotypical gang role for girls is "to conceal and carry weapons for the boys, to provide sexual favors, and sometimes to fight against girls who were connected with enemy boys' gangs" (Mann 1984, p. 45).

Other first hand accounts of girl gangs, while not completely challenging this image, have focused more directly on the race and class issues confronting girls who find themselves in gangs. Quicker's study of female Chicano gang members in East Los Angeles found evidence that these girls, although still somewhat dependent upon their male counterparts, were becoming more independent. These girls identified themselves as "homegirls" and their male counterparts as "homeboys," a common reference to relationships in the "barrio." In an obvious reference to "strain theory," Quicker notes that there are few economic opportunities within the barrio to meet the needs of the family unit. As a result, families are disintegrating and do not have the capability of providing access to culturally emphasized success goals for young people about to enter adulthood. Not surprisingly, almost all their activities occur within the context of gang life, where they learn how to get along in the world and are insulated from the harsh environment of the barrio (Quicker 1983).

Harris' study of the Cholas, a Latino gang in the San Fernando Valley echoes this theme. She notes that while the Cholas in many respects resembles male gangs, the gang did challenge the girls' traditional destiny within the barrio in two direct ways. First, the girls rejected the traditional image of the Latino woman as "wife and mother" (Harris 1988) supporting, instead a more "macho" homegirl role. Second, the gang supported the girls in their estrangement from organized religion, substituting instead a form of familialism that "provides a strong substitute for weak family and conventional school ties" (Harris 1988, p. 172).

One of the most interesting pieces of research on girl gangs comes from a study by Fishman (1988) of a black gang known as the Vice Queens. This gang was a female auxiliary gang to a boys' gang, the Vice Kings, that existed in Chicago during the early 1960s. Living in a mostly black community characterized by poverty, unemployment, deterioration and a high crime rate, the gang of about thirty teenage girls was loosely knit (unlike the male gang), and provided the girls with companionship and friends. Failing in school and unable to find work, the bulk of their time was spent "hanging out" on the streets with the Vice Kings, which usually included the consumption of alcohol and sexual activities, and occasional delinquency, most of which was "traditionally female" like prostitution, shoplifting and running away, but some of which was more serious (e.g. auto theft). They also engaged in fights with other groups of girls, largely to protect their gang's reputation for toughness.

Growing up in rough neighborhoods provided the Vice Queens "with opportunities to learn such traditional male skills as fighting and taking care of themselves on the streets." It was generally expected that the girls had to learn to defend themselves against "abusive men" and "attacks on their integrity" (Fishman 1988, p. 15). Their relationship to the Vice Kings was primarily sexual, having sexual relations and bearing their children, but with no hope of marriage.

Fishman notes that the Vice Queens were "socialized to be independent, assertive and to take risks with the expectations that these are characteristics that they will need to function effectively within the black low income community...As a consequence, black girls demonstrate, out of necessity, a greater flexibility in roles" (Fishman 1988, pp. 26-27). She also notes that there has been little improvement in the economic situation of the African-American community since the nineteen sixties; indeed, she believes that, if anything they face an even bleaker future than the Vice Queens she interviewed. In this context, she speculates that "black female gangs today have become more entrenced, more violent, and more oriented to 'male' crime (Fishman 1988, p. 28). These changes, she goes on to say, are unrelated to the women's movement, but are instead the "forced 'emancipation' which stems from the economic crisis within the black community (Fishman 1988, pp. 28-29)."

Fishman's bleak speculation about of the situation of girl gangs in contemporary poverty stricken neighborhoods has been largely confirmed by more contemporary research by Lauderback, Hansen and Waldorf on an African-American female gang in San Francisco. Disputing the "traditional notions of female gang members in which they are portrayed as maladjusted tomboys and sex objects completely dependent upon the favor of male gang members" (Lauderback, Hansen and Waldorf 1989), these interviewers found an independent girl gang who engaged in crack sales and organized "boosting" to support themselves and their young children. Looking past the gang's economic role in their lives, Lauderback and his associates noted that the gang "fills a void in the lives of its members" since their own family ties were "weak at best" prior to their involvement in the group (Lauderback, Hansen and Waldorf 1992: p. 25). All under twenty-five, abandoned by the fathers of their children, abused and controlled by other men, these young women wish they could be "doing something other than selling drugs and to leave the neighborhood," but "many felt that the circumstances which led them to sell drugs were not going to change" (Lauderback, Hansen and Waldorf 1992, p. 23).

Campbell's work on Hispanic gangs in the New York area (Campbell 1984, 1990) finds much the same pattern. Campbell noted that the girls in her study joined gangs for reasons that are largely explained by their situation in a society that has little to offer young women of color (Campbell 1990, pp. 172-173). First, the possibility of a decent career, outside of "domestic servant," is practically non-existent. Many have come from female-headed families subsisting on welfare, most have dropped out of the school and have no marketable skills. Their aspirations for the future were both sex typed and unrealistic with the girls expressing desires to be rock stars or professional models. Second, they find themselves in a highly gendered community were the men in their lives, while not traditional breadwinners, still make many decisions that circumscribe the possibilities open to young women. Third, the responsibility that young Hispanic women will have as mothers further restrict the options available to her. Campbell cites recent data revealing a very bleak future indeed, as 94% will have children and 84% will have to raise their children without a husband. Most will be dependent upon some from of welfare (1990, p. 182). Fourth, these young women face a future of isolation as a housewife in the projects. Finally, they share with their male counterparts a future of powerlessness as members of the urban underclass. Their lives, in effect, reflect all the burdens of their triple handicaps of race, class and gender.

For these girls, Campbell observes, the gang represents "an idealized collective solution to the bleak future that awaits" them. The girls have a tendency to portray to themselves and the outside world the gang in a very idealized and romantic manner (1990, p. 173). They develop an exaggerated sense of belonging to the gang. Many were loners prior to joining the gang, having been only loosely connected to schoolmates and neighborhood peer groups. Even the gangs closeness, as well as the "excitement of gang life", is more of a fiction than a reality. Their daily "street talk" is filled with exaggerated stories of parties, drugs, alcohol, and other varieties of "fun." However, as Campbell notes (1990, p. 176):

> These events stand as a bulwark against the loneliness and drudgery of their future lives. They also belie the day to day reality of gang life. The lack of recreational opportunities, the long days unfilled by work or school and the absence of money mean that the hours and days are whiled away on street corners. "Doing nothing" means hang out on the stoop; the hours of "bullshit" punctuated by trips to the store to buy one can of beer at a time. When an expected windfall arrives, marijuana and rum are purchased in bulk and the partying begins. The next day, life returns to normal.

Current research on girl gangs, then, have moved beyond stereotypical notions about these as simply the female auxiliaries of male gangs to more careful assessments of the role played by these groups in girls' lives. Of particular significance are those elements of female gangs that provide the girls with the skills to survive in their harsh communities while also allowing them to escape, at least for a while, from the bleak future that awaits them.

None of these accounts, even the most recent, confirms the stereotype of the hyper-violent, amoral girls found in media accounts of girls in gangs. Certainly, they confirm the fact that girls do commit a wider range of delinquent behavior than is stereotypically recognized, but these offenses appear to be part of a complex fabric of "hanging out," "partying," and the occasional fight defending one's friends or territory.

Historically, though, those activities that did not fit the official stereotype of "girls delinquency" have been ignored by those in authority. A clear documentation of this pattern is found in Shacklady-Smith's research on girl gang members conducted in Bristol between 1969-1972. She noted that delinquent girls and gang girls, the vast majority of whom were officially charged with the British equivalent of non-criminal, status offenses (like running away from home, being incorrigible, being a truant, etc.), had committed a wide range of delinquent behaviors, including fighting. Her figures indicated that nearly three quarters (73.3%) of her gang sample as well as 63% of her probation sample said they had "taken part in a fight." Said one girl:

> I reckon we fight as seriously as the boys. You know, if anybody comes up to us we'll smack a bottle in their faces. You know we say, "you try it", and they don't think we will use it on them. But we will if they try anything (Shacklady-Smith 1983, p. 86).

In the main, though, this behavior was ignored by official authorities according to her interviews:

> It's funny because once when I was down at the cop shop for fighting, this woman saw the swastika on my arm and forgot all about what she was looking for. They never did nothing-just told me to stop fighting. But the woman cop, she kept on about the swastika and Hell's Angels. What a bad lot they were for a girl to go around with, and how I had better stop going round with the Angels or else I'd get a really bad name for myself. Then she kept asking me if I'd had sex with any of 'em or taken drugs (Shacklady-Smith 1978, p. 83)

Shacklady-Smith's work, as well as the work of others who studied girls in gangs in earlier decades (Fishman 1988; Quicker 1983), suggests that girls have long been involved in violent behavior as a part of gang life. During earlier periods, however, this occasional violence was ignored by law enforcement officers far more concerned with their sexual behavior or morality. Shacklady-Smith's findings on the relative similarity of delinquent girls' and gang girls' activities also suggests the need to explore the degree to which girls in gangs are actually engaged in significantly different and more violent offending than their non-gang, but delinquent counterparts. A quantitative study of youth gangs in the state of Hawaii permits just such an exploration.

GIRLS IN GANGS IN HAWAII

Research on youth gangs in Hawaii has been conducted as part of an on-going study of the state's youth gang response system (see Chesney-Lind et al. 1992). Data gathered from files maintained by the Honolulu Police Department (HPD), which serves the City and County of Honolulu (on the island of Oahu where over three quarters of the state's population is located) permit a more quantitative assessment of girls' involvement in gang activity.[5]

Like other major cities, Honolulu has experienced a rapid growth in police estimates of gang activity and gang membership. In 1988, the HPD estimated that there were 22 gangs with 450 members; in 1991, the number of gangs has climbed to 45 with an estimated membership of 1,020, and by 1993 the number of gangs stood at 171 with 1,267 members (Office of Youth Services 1993).

Research on the characteristics of youth labeled by HPD as gang members commenced during August, 1991, and a demographic profile on a sample (N=361) of these youth was constructed. The sample was drawn randomly from a complete list of identification numbers for each gang youth contained in the HPD GREAT computer system.[6] Subsequent to this, additional information, particularly on prior offenses, was gathered from the HPD juvenile offender and adult offender records. Ultimately the profile was able to provide the ethnicity, gender, age, neighborhood, school (or previous school), zip code (at time of arrest), and offense history of youth identified as gang members as of August, 1991.

The general results of this research have been reported elsewhere (Chesney-Lind, et al. 1992), but these data also permit an examination of gender and gang membership. Only 7% of the suspected gang members on Oahu were female. About 70% of girls and 78% of boys were legally adults. While the bulk of both the men and women in the population of youth gang members were young (between 18-21 years of age), this was less true for women and for men. About half of the men (48.4%), but only slightly over a third of the women (37.5%) were in this age group. A third of the women were over twenty-six compared to only 13.4% of the men. There was, in fact, one woman in the data base who was 52 years old. Thus, the median age for women was 24.5 and 21.4 for men. Taken together, these findings make the use of the term "youth gang" somewhat questionable particularly for women labeled by police as gang members.

Virtually all the youth identified as gang members were drawn from low-income ethnic groups in the islands, but ethnic differences were also found between male and female gang members. The men were more likely than the women to have been drawn almost exclusively from immigrant groups (Samoan and Filipino); the women, by contrast, were more likely to be Native Hawaiian and Filipino.

Most importantly, women and girls labeled as gang members committed fewer of most offenses than men [see Table One] and they also committed less serious offenses [see Table Two]

Table One clearly indicates that both the males and female in this sample of suspected gang members were chronic but not serious offenders; the rank ordering of the most serious arrests in Table Two demonstrates that this pattern is particularly clear in the case of women suspected of gang membrship. Indeed, this rank ordering reveals, for the girls, a pattern that bears a very close relationship to typical female delinquency. For example, the most common arrest category for girls in 1991 in the U.S was larceny theft (F.B.I. 1992:p. 218), and the most common arrest category for these girls was larceny theft, followed by status offenses. For boys, the pattern is somewhat more sobering, with "other assaults" (which likely means fighting with other boys) as the most serious arrest for the bulk of these young men. In total, serious violent offenses (murder, sexual assault, robbery, and aggravated

Table One: Offense Patterns
Males and Females Labeled as Gang Members

Mean Number of:	Men:	Women:
Property Offenses	3.6	2.0
Violent Offenses	1.4	0.227
Drug Offenses	0.4	2.9
Status Offenses	1.6	2.0
Arrests	11.6	9.1
Incidents	7.6	5.6
	N = 337	N = 24

assault) accounted for 23% of the most serious offenses of males suspected of gang membership but none of the girls most serious offenses.

Finally, it is important to note that once police identified a youth as a gang member, they apparently remained in the data base regardless of patterns of desistence; for example, 22% of the sample had not been arrested in three years and there was no gender difference in this pattern.

Table Two: Rank Order
Most Serious Arrests of Suspected Gang Members by Gender

Females

Offense:	Percent:
1. Larceny Theft	38.1
2. Status Offenses	19.0
3. Drugs	9.5
4. Criminal Property Damage	4.76
5. Motor Vehicle	4.76
6. Other Assaults	4.76
	N = 21

Males

Offense:	Percent:
1. Other Assaults	27.0
2. Larceny Theft	14.0
3. Robbery	12.0
4. Burglary	7.9
5. Motor Vehicle	6.1
	N = 328

These patterns prompted a further exploration of the degree to which young women labeled by police as "suspected gang members" differed from young women who had been arrested for delinquency. To do this, a comparison group was created for those in the Oahu sample that were legally juveniles. Youth suspected of gang membership were matched on ethnicity, age, and gender with youth who were in the juvenile arrest data base, but who had not been labeled as gang members. A look at offense patterns of this smaller group indicates no major differences between girls suspected of gang membership and their non-gang counterparts. Indeed, the modal most serious offense for gang girls was status offenses, and for non-gang girls it was other assaults.

While the numbers were very small in this subsample (N=5), girls who were arrested for juvenile delinquency but not identified by the police as youth gang members were generally more seriously delinquent than girls suspected of gang activity. Girls suspected of gang membership had a mean of 5 arrests compared to 6.2 in the delinquent group. This pattern was consistent across all the arrest categories. Girls in the suspected gang group had .2 violent arrests compared to .8 in the delinquent group; they also had more arrests for property offenses (4.6 arrests compared to 3.7), and more arrests for status offenses (4.5, arrests compared to 4.4).

This finding is not totally unexpected. Bowker and Klein (1983), in an examination of data on girls in gangs in Los Angeles in the nineteen sixties, compared both the etiology of delinquent behavior of gang girls and their non-gang counterparts and concluded:

> We conclude that the overwhelming impact of racism, sexism, poverty and limited opportunity structures is likely to be so important in determining the gang membership and juvenile delinquency of women and girls in urban ghettos that personality variables, relations with parents and problems associated with heterosexual behavior play a relatively minor role in determining gang membership and juvenile delinquency (Bowker and Klein 1983, pp. 750-751).

In addition, similar studies, using comparison groups in Arizona (Zatz 1985) with Hispanic gangs and in Las Vegas (Shelden, Snodgrass and Snodgrass 1993) with African-American and Hispanic gangs, while not focusing on gender, found little to differentiate gang members from other "delinquent" or criminal youth.

Finally, research on official "careers" of non-white (71% of the non-white girls were African-American) and white girls, while not dealing specifically with gang girls, found far less serious and violent delinquency in the non-white girls than would be expected if they were "converging" with their black, male counterparts. In examining a cohort of youth first referred to Clark County in 1980, no difference was found in the types of offenses for which non-white and white girls were referred. Over a quarter of all the offenses resulting in referral to court were status offenses. Examining "personal" or violent offenses, these were found to comprise 6.5% of white girl's referrals and 4.7% of non-white girl's referrals. For boys, a sharper and more violent pattern obtained with 8% of the referrals of white males and 18% of non-white males. But about 60% of both groups were referred only once. In short, race plays a major difference in the length and seriousness of delinquent careers, but only for males (Shelden and Chesney Lind 1993).

Taken together, assessments of gang delinquency in girls, whether quantitative or qualitative, suggest that there is little evidence to support the notion of a new, violent female offender. Instead, what emerges is a more complex picture where some girls solve their problems of gender, race and class through gang membership. Clearly, girl's experiences with gangs cannot be simply framed as "breaking into" a male world. They have long been in gangs and their participation in these gangs, even their violence, is heavily influenced by their gender.

CONCLUSION

This review of the literature on girls in gangs suggests that girls have long been members of gangs, that their roles in these gangs have been considerably more varied than early stereotypes would have it, and that girls' occasionally violent behavior has, during other decades, been largely ignored. Since, there is little evidence of a radical change in girl's behavior in gangs over the past few decades, one must ask why these facts are being used now to construct a female crime wave?

A quick comparison of the articles that comprise each surge of media interest in crimes committed by girls and women suggests some answers to this question. While there are many similarities between the two media crime waves, there are some crucial differences. Those who tout both crime waves utilize a crude form of equity feminism to explain the trends observed and, in the process, contribute to the "backlash" against the women's movement (Faludi 1992). The age and ethnicity of the women in each of the crime waves does differ. In the stories that announced the first crime wave during the nineteen seventies, the liberated "female crook" was a white political activist, a "terrorist," a drug using hippie. For example, one story syndicated by the N. Y. Times service had pictures of both Patty Hearst and Friederike Krabbe (Klemesrud 1978). Today's demonized woman is African-American or Hispanic, and she is a violent teenager.

In both instances, there was some, small amount of truth in the image found in the articles. As this paper has shown, girls and women have always engaged in more violent behavior than the stereotype of women supports; girls have also been in gangs for decades. The periodic media discovery of these facts, then, must be serving other political purposes.

Yesterday, the goal may have been to discredit the young white women and their invisible, but central African-American counterparts (Barnett 1993) who were challenging the racism, sexism, and militarism of that day. Today, as the research on girls and gangs has indicated, young minority youth of both genders face a bleak present and a grim future. Today, it is clear that "gang" has become a code word for race.[7] A review of the media portrayal of girls in gangs suggests that beyond this, media stories on the youth gang problem can create a political climate where the victims of racism and sexism can be blamed for their own problems.

In short, this most recent female crime wave appears to be an attempt to reframe the problems of racism and sexism in society. As young women are demonized by the media, their genuine problems can be marginalized and then ignored. Indeed, they have become the problem. The challenge to those concerned about girls is, then, twofold. First, responsible work on girls in gangs must make the dynamics of this victim blaming clear. Second, it must continue to build an understanding of girls' gangs that is sensitive to the contexts within which they arise. Good ethnographic work is beginning to fill this void and explaining the utility and logic of the behavior of girls—including gang participation—as a response to being the economic and political margins. In an era that is increasingly concerned about the intersection of class, race and gender, such work seems long overdue.

NOTES

1. Thrasher did mention, in passing, two factors he felt accounted for the lower number of girl gangs: "first, the social patterns for the behavior of girls, powerfully backed by the great weight of tradition and custom, are contrary to the gang and its activities; and secondly, girls, even in urban disorganized areas, are much more closely supervised and guarded than boys and are usually well incorporated into the family groups or some other social structure" (Thrasher, 1927: 228).

2. In *Brothers in Crime*, for example, the delinquent and criminal careers of five brothers are followed for fifteen years.

3. Defined by the F.B.I. as murder, forcible rape, robbery, burglary, aggravated assault, larceny theft, auto theft, and arson (added in 1979).

4. A portion of this section is drawn from *Girls Delinquency and Juvenile Justice*.

5. For purposes of this discussion, it is sufficient to say that if the police in Honolulu are guilty of anything it is overdefinition of what constitutes a gang member. Two other counties, which tended to take a more conservative position about gang membership reported either no girls who met this definition (Kauai County) or so few the data would not be useful (Maui with 3 girls out of 71 suspected gang members).

6. GREAT is an acronym for Gang Reporting Evaluation and Tracking System.

7. Nearly half, (47%) of all young black men in Los Angeles between the ages of 21 and 24 made appearances in the Los Angeles Sheriff's Department's gang database (Muwakkil, 1993).

REFERENCES

Adler, Freda. 1975a. "The Rise of the Female Crook." *Psychology Today* 9:42-46, 112-114.

Adler, Freda. 1975b. *Sisters in Crime*. New York: McGraw Hill.

Barnett, Bernice M. "Invisible Southern Black Women Leaders in the Civil Rights Movement: The Triple Constraints of Gender, Race, and Class" *Gender and Society* 7:162-182.

Bowker, L. 1978. *Women, Crime and the Criminal Justice System.* Lexington, Mass,: Lexington Books.

Bowker, Lee. and Malcolm Klein. 1983. "The Etiology of Female Juvenile Delinquency and Gang Membership: A test of Psychological and Social Structural Explanations. *Adolescence.* 13: 739-751.

Brown, W. K. 1977. "Black Female Gangs in Philadelphia." *International Journal of Offender Therapy and Comparative Criminology* 21:221-228.

CBS. 1992. "Girls in the Hood." *Street Stories.* August 6.

Cain, M., ed. 1989. *Growing Up Good: Policing the Behavior of Girls in Europe.* London: Sage.

Campbell, A. 1984. *The Girls in the Gang.* Oxford: Basil Blackwell.

Campbell, A. 1990. "Female Participation in Gangs." In *Gangs in America,* edited by G. Ronald Huff. Newbury Park, Calif.: Sage.

Canter, R.J. 1982. "Sex Differences in Self-Report Delinquency." *Criminology* 20:373-393.

Meda Chesney-Lind, Nancy Marker, Howard Reyes, Yolanda Reyes, Anna Rockhill. 1992. "Gangs and Delinquency in Hawaii. Paper presented at the Annual Meeting of the American Society of Criminology Meetings, New Orleans, Louisiana, November.

Cohen, A. 1955. *Delinquent Boys: The Culture of the Gang.* New York: Free Press.

Crittenden, Danielle. 1990 "You've Come a Long Way, Moll." *Wall Street Journal* Thursday, January 25: A14.

Daly, K., and Chesney-Lind, M. 1988. "Feminism and Criminology." *Justice Quarterly* 5:497-538.

Faludi, Susan. 1991. *Backlash: The Undeclared War Against Women.* New York: Crown Publishers.

Federal Bureau of Investigation. 1978. *Crime in the United States—1977.* Washington, D.C.: U.S. Department of Justice.

Federal Bureau of Investigation. 1992. *Crime in the United States—1991.* Washington, D.C.: U.S. Department of Justice.

Figueria-McDonough, Josephina and William H. Barton. 1985. "Attachments, Gender and Delinquency." *Deviant Behavior* 6:119-144.

Fishman, L. T. 1988. *"The Vice Queens: An Ethnographic Study of Black Female Gang Behavior."* Paper presented at the annual meeting of the American Society of Criminology.

Flowers, R. B. 1987. *Women and Criminality*. New York: Greenwood Press.

Giordano, P., Cernkovich, S., and Pugh, M. 1978. "Girls, Guys and Gangs: The Changing Social Context of Female Delinquency." *Journal of Criminal Law and Criminology* 69:126-132.

Gora, JoAnn. 1982. *The New Female Criminal: Empirical Reality or Social Myth*. New York: Praeger Publishers.

Hanson, K. 1964. *Rebels in the Streets: The Story of New York's Girl Gangs*. Englewood Cliffs, N.J.: Prentice-Hall.

Harris, M. G. 1988. *Cholas: Latino Girls and Gangs*. New York: AMS Press.

Hagadorn, John M. 1988. *People and Folks*. Chicago: Lake View Press.

Jankowski, Martin Sanchez. 1991. *Islands in the Street: Gangs and American Urban Society*. Berkeley: University of California Press.

Klemesrud, Judy. 1978. "Women Terrorists, Sisters in Crime." N.T. News Service. *Honolulu Star Bulletin* January 16. C1.

Lauderback, David, Joy Hansen and Dan Waldorf. 1992. "Sisters are Doin' It for Themselves." Unpublished manuscript.

Lee, Felicia R. 1991. "For Gold Earrings and Protection, More Girls Take the Road to Violence." *New York Times* November 25.

Lewis, Nancy. 1992. "Delinquent Girls Achieving a Violent Equality in D.C." *Washington Post* December 23: A1, A14.

Mann, C. 1984. *Female Crime and Delinquency*. University: University of Alabama Press.

Miller, W. B. 1975. *Violence by Youth Gangs and Youth Groups as a Crime Problem in Major American Cities*. Washington, D.C.: U.S. Government Printing Office.

Miller, W. B. 1980. "The Molls." In *Women, Crime, and Justice*. Edited by S. K. Datesman and F. R. Scarpitti. New York: Oxford University Press.

Muwakkil, Salim. 1993. "Ganging Together." *In These Times*. April 5.

Naffine, N. 1987. *Female Crime: The Construction of Women in Criminology*. Sydney, Australia: Allen and Unwin.

NBC. 1993. "Diana Koricke in East Los Angeles." *World News Tonight*. March 29.

Office of Youth Services. 1993. *An Interim Report to the Legislature on the Gang Response System*. Honolulu: Office of Youth Services, State of Hawaii.

Quicker, J. C. 1983. *Homegirls: Characterizing Chicano Gangs.* San Pedro, California: International University Press.

Rice, R. 1963. "A Reporter at Large: The Persian Queens." *New Yorker,* October 19.

Roberts, S. 1972. "Crime Rate of Women up Sharply Over Men's." *New York Times,* June 13, p. 1, 72.

Santiago, Denis-Marie. 1992. "Random victims of Vengence Show Teen Crime." *The Philadelphia Inquirer* (February 23): A1.

Shaw, C. 1930. *The Jack Roller.* Chicago: University of Chicago Press.

Shaw, C. 1938. *Brothers in Crime.* Chicago: University of Chicago Press.

Shaw, C., and McKay, H. 1942. *Juvenile Delinquency in Urban Areas.* Chicago: University of Chicago Press.

Shacklady-Smith, Lesley. 1978. "Sexist Assumptions and Female Delinquency." *Women and Social Control.* Carol Smart and Barry Smart, editors. London: Routledge and Kegan Paul.

Shelden, Randall and Meda Chesney-Lind. 1993. "Gender and Race Differences in Delinquent Careers." *Juvenile and Family Court Journal.* Forthcoming.

Shelden, Randall G. Ted Snodgrass, and Pam Snodgrass. 1993. "Comparing Gang and Non-Gang Offenders: Some Tentative Findings." *The Gang Journal* 1:73-85

Simon, Rita. 1975. *Women and Crime.* Lexington: Lexington Books.

Simons, R. L., Miller, M. G., and Aigner, S. M. 1980. "Contemporary Theories of Deviance and Female Delinquency: An Empirical Test." *Journal of Research on Crime and Delinquency* 20:42-57.

Smith, Douglas and Raymond Paternoster. 1987. "The Gender Gap in Theories of Deviance: Issues and Evidence." *Journal of Research in Crime and Delinquency* 24:140-172,

Sommers, Ira and Deborah Baskin. 1993. "The Situational Context of Violent Female Offending." *Crime and Delinquency* 30:136-162.

Steffensmeier, D. J., and Steffensmeier, R. H. 1980. "Trends in Female Delinquency: An Examination of Arrest, Juvenile Court, Self-Report, and Field Data." *Criminology* 18:62-85.

Thrasher, F. 1927. *The Gang.* Chicago: University of Chicago Press.

Zatz, Marjorie. 1985. "Los Cholos: Legal Processing of Chicano Gang Members." *Social Problems* 33:13-30.

[23]

ACCOMPLISHING FEMININITY
AMONG THE GIRLS IN THE GANG

Karen Joe Laidler and Geoffrey Hunt*

Sociologists and criminologists in America have had a longstanding interest in youth gangs dating back to the pioneering work of Frederick Thrasher through to the subcultural theories of the 1960s–1970s to the present. Until recently, the primary focus was on the role of male gang members. In contrast, discussions about young women's involvement in gangs, with a few notable exceptions, have been typically shallow and sexist. In this paper we examine the meanings, expressions and paradoxes of femininity as they are understood and experienced by Latina, African American and Asian-Pacific American female gang members. The analysis, based on in-depth interviews with 141 gang members, is part of a long-term study (1990–present) of youth gangs in the San Francisco Bay Area.

Approximately 2 million American adolescents are involved in serious criminal offences (Inciardi et al. 1993). Because of this high prevalence rate for serious delinquency, criminal justice officials and researchers have shifted their attention from the 'typical' delinquent or what Inciardi et al. (1993) have called the 'garden variety' delinquent to that of the serious delinquent (Horowitz 1990). As a result of this shift in attention, interest in youth gangs has also occurred. This came about partly because of the belief that serious delinquents are more likely to be found in youth gangs and partly because of the perceived relationship between gangs, drugs and violence. The development of the drug trade in the 1980s signalled a transformation from the idea of gangs as 'transitory adolescent social networks to nascent criminal organizations' (Fagan 1990: 183).

Official estimates of the number of youth involved in gangs have increased dramatically over the past decade. Currently, over 90 per cent of the nation's largest cities report youth gang problems, an increase of about half since 1983, and police estimates now put the number of gangs at 4,881 and the number of gang members at approximately 249,324 (Curry et al. 1992). As a result, although the study of gangs is not new (the first major work was done by Thrasher in 1927) public concern about the involvement of young people in gang activity, and the perceived violence associated with this lifestyle, has soared.

Part of this concern about the increase in gangs has focused on the participation of women in gangs. While some researchers argue that girl gang membership is increasing, others have been more cautious, believing that participation has remained relatively stable over time. Estimates of girl gang membership today range from 10 to 30 per cent of all gang members (Campbell 1984; Chesney-Lind 1993; Curry et al. 1994; Esbensen and Huizinga 1993; Fagan 1990; Klein 1995; Moore 1991). These estimates, based on

* Respectively, Associate Professor, Sociology, University of Hong Kong; and Senior Scientist Institute for Scientific Analysis, Alameda, CA. Collection of data for this article was made possible by funding from the National Institute on Alcohol Abuse and Alcoholism (R01-AA10819), administered by Susan Martin, PhD.

ACCOMPLISHING FEMININITY

self-reports and community recognition (e.g. police, schools, youth agencies), include young women involved in all girl gangs and mixed (male and female) gangs.

There is little doubt that in recent years female gang participation has generated much public concern and media attention in the US, in large part because they are presumed to be rebelling against traditional notions of femininity. They are typically characterized as becoming more like their male counterparts: wild, hedonistic, irrational, amoral and violent (see Chesney-Lind 1993). Women's magazines like *Harper's Bazaar* try to illustrate vividly that these 'bad girls' have crossed the gender divide with photographs of girl gang members aiming guns with one hand, and throwing hand signs with the other hand (O'Malley 1993). Book length journalistic accounts provide similar impressions (Sikes 1997).

Yet are these young women defiantly challenging traditional gender roles? Although research on female gangs is relatively limited (compared to males), a number of perspectives have emerged. Traditional accounts (Cloward and Ohlin 1960; Cohen 1955; Miller 1958; Thrasher 1927) of female gang involvement have downplayed and minimized the role and motivations of girl gang members. They are portrayed in stereotypical ways from personal property to sexual chattel to maladjusted tomboys (see extended review in Joe and Chesney-Lind 1995). A more recent study continues to advance this male-centred view (Sanchez-Jankowski 1991). In essence, these accounts view the involvement of girls in gangs in relation to their sexuality. Their sexuality then serves as the basis for their identity as 'bad girls'. Other recent views offer a contrasting view, very similar to those in the media, of girl gang members seizing the streets, gaining independence from, and almost competing with, their male counterparts (Fleisher 1998; Taylor 1993). These contrasting accounts share, and at the same time suffer, from a one-sided, male-focused perspective, and fail to locate the situational context of being young, female, of colour, and poor.

How then do female gang members understand and accomplish femininity? How do they interpret their involvement in delinquency and violence? We explore these questions by first examining recent discussions about masculinity and 'bad girl' femininity on the streets. We then begin our analysis by looking at the different ways in which femininity is constructed within the family among a group of girl gang members. We then turn to examine how girls renegotiate and manage the paradoxes of femininity on the streets and at home.

Bad Girls and Femininity

Masculinities and crime has become the subject of much criminological interests and research in the last several years (Bourgois 1996; Collison 1996; Connell 1987; Jefferson 1996; Katz 1988; Messerschmidt 1986, 1993, 1997; Newburn and Stanko 1994). This new direction in the study of crime stems from wider discussions in the social sciences and arts on masculinities, and calls from within the discipline to 'take men seriously', particularly as the 'crisis of masculinity' heightens in post-modern society (Jefferson 1996). At a general level, this new orientation is trying to reconcile longstanding epistemological debates about the relationship (and dialectics) of social structure and interaction. In doing so, it locates acts of manliness within the broader economic and social class context, and at the same time, leaves room for human agency and interaction. Essentially

JOE LAIDLER AND HUNT

masculinities and crime studies examine 'varieties of real men' in relation to their differential access to power and resources, and how these different groups of men construct and negotiate with similarly situated others, the meaning of manliness (Messerschmidt 1997; Newburn and Stanko 1994). Messerschmidt (1993, 1997), in particular, suggests that the social structure situates young men in relation to similar others so that collectively they experience the world from a specific position and differentially construct cultural ideas of hegemonic masculinity, namely, dominance, control and independence (Joe and Chesney-Lind 1995).

Young males in gangs provide the example, par excellence, as they embody all of the problems of power in contemporary society: violence, guns, drugs, poverty, unemployment, decay of community life, and educational malaise. Young minority male gang members living in marginalized communities, have little access to masculine status in the economy and in education like their white middle and working class counterparts (Bourgois 1996; Joe and Chesney-Lind 1995; Messerschmidt 1997). This collectively experienced denial of access to 'legitimate' masculine status creates an arena for exaggerated public and private forms of aggressive masculinity. 'Street elite posturing' (Katz 1988) among male gang members with dramatized displays of toughness accounts for one cultural form of public aggressiveness. Male gang members' constant and aggressive pursuit of 'respect' represents another way to construct and affirm manliness in an alienated environment. Gang intimidation and violence are more than simply an expression of the competitive struggle in communities with little to offer, but rather, a vehicle for a meaningful identity and status. Gang banging then is a gender resource for young minority gang members to express their masculinity (Joe and Chesney-Lind 1995; Messerschmidt 1997). At the immediate level of interaction, then, the street is a battleground and theatre for young marginalized minority males to define, shape and do gender (Connell 1987).

This same level of theoretical interest has yet to be extended to women and crime, and raises a fundamental question for 'doing gender' and 'doing difference': if crime is a resource for expressing masculinity, how then are we to understand the experiences of women and their involvement in delinquency and crime? As Daly asks, 'would the claim that crime is a "resource for doing femininity"—for women and girls to "create differences from men and boys or to separate from all that is masculine"—have any cultural resonance?' (1997: 37).

Messerschmidt (1997) argued critically that the general tendency in criminological investigations has been to focus exclusively on differences in men's and women's crime, and as a result, women are conceptualized in masculine terms when they engage in 'typically' masculine crimes like violence. Therefore, we must look at both the similarities and differences between their involvement in crime to determine when crime is not a resource for doing masculinity.[1] From this vantage point, girls' participation in gangs offers an avenue for challenging and testing normative gender roles or what Connell (1987) calls, 'emphasized femininity'.

---

[1] Joe and Chesney-Lind's (1995) and Moore's (1991) analyses of gangs in Hawaii and East Los Angeles respectively, juxtapose female and male experiences in gang activity and highlight how gender is accomplished in gangs.

Partaking in the specific social situation of the gang, girls use the resources available to construct not masculinity but a specific type of femininity and notwithstanding, challenge notions of gender as merely difference (Messerschmidt 1997: 69).

Drawing from the limited but rich ethnographic studies on female gangs, Messerschmidt contends that female gang violence and displays of toughness are 'resources' for establishing a particular notion of femininity, that of the 'bad girl'. This street reputation and status translate as power for girls who operate within the patriarchal power structure of the gangs, the streets, and society. At the same time, girl gang members embrace and engage in some forms of 'culturally appropriate' femininity (1997: 83). Most ethnographic studies on female gangs, for example, find that gang girls concentrate on 'feminine activities' such as appearance and endless sessions of talking. Many also find themselves in typically gendered lower and working class jobs like janitorial services, babysitting and clerical work, and hold unrealistic feminine aspirations like rock singers and professional modelling (Campbell 1990; Joe and Chesney-Lind 1995).

These ethnographic studies further suggest that these two specific cultural forms of femininity frequently conflict with each other. Studies on Latina homegirls illustrate this point. Quicker (1983), Harris (1988) and Moore (1991) find some Chicana gang members adopt a 'macho' homegirl image, but in rejecting the Latino cultural norms of being a woman (i.e. wife and mother), male gang members and community residents view the girls as 'tramps' and not the type to marry. A significant focus for inquiry then is how girl gang members constantly negotiate a distinctive sense of femininity in different interactional settings within both their ethnic culture and delinquent subculture.

Research on African American girls also underscores the importance of focusing on cultural and ethnic differences across girl gang groups. Fishman (1988) and Lauderback et al. (1992) indicate that the adoption of a bad girl identity with exaggerated displays of toughness have less to do with rejecting or testing cultural gender norms and more to do with adopting 'greater flexibility in their roles' as they are expected to defend themselves against male violence (Fishman 1988: 15). At the same time, these female gang members are preoccupied with their responsibilities as young mothers including income generating strategies (e.g. drug dealing) and community activism (improving quality of life in their neighbourhoods; making the streets safe for their children) (Venkatesh 1998). Joe Laidler and Hunt (1997) show that African American female gang members are more likely to perceive the group as a source of autonomy, independence and empowerment from men than Latina gang girls, who are organized in relation to their male counterparts.

This article builds on these ethnographic studies and recent discussions on 'bad girl' femininity. It is specifically concerned with uncovering the meaning, expression and paradoxes of femininity as it is understood and experienced by Latina, African American and Asian-Pacific American female gang members. The analytical framework is based on several assumptions. The normative expectations of young women to be feminine and to be a teenager are often at odds. Generally, adolescence is a time for challenging authority, rebelling, seeking recognition among peers, independence; attributes that are associated with masculinity. Femininity, by contrast, starts early on in a girl's life, and is associated with passiveness, obedience, dependency, innocence, chastity and maturity. As Hudson (1984) has noted, 'adolescence is subversive of femininity; young girls' attempts to be accepted as "young women" are always liable to be undermined (subverted) by perceptions of them as childish, immature or any other of the other terms by which we define the status "adolescent"' (p. 32). McRobbie (1981) shows that English working class teenage girls respond to their contradictory position of being perceived as 'children' and expectations and fears of entering womanhood by forming tight knit groups. These peer groups are not oppositional, but rather a cultural form of resistance which offers an exclusive and private space for girls to define for themselves, 'what is feminine'. Membership in female gangs then operates in a similar fashion. Moreover, these conflicting normative standards constantly confront girl gang members in their interactions with family, their male counterparts and their homegirls and become the basis for evaluating themselves and other girls' femininity.

At the same time, it is important to underscore that notions of femininity are not fixed, but ever changing, depending on the situational context (Messerschmidt 1997). 'Being feminine' does not automatically change but is negotiated in the specific social contexts with interactions with other people. These notions may be contradictory in some settings, but are nevertheless seen as an accommodation to the setting. These interactions and negotiated definitions of femininity occur within the race, class and patriarchal constraints of a larger social structure. Young women's location within the social structure simultaneously affects their interactions and their notions of being feminine. This analysis heeds other recent critiques of Messerschmidt's recent work as being more structure than action oriented in his supporting evidence (see Jefferson 1996 for a fuller discussion), and examines not only how girl gang members reproduce normative gender expectations, but also how they resist and devise alternative forms of femininity. These alternative forms include but are not restricted to the 'bad girl'. The following discussion then, begins to tease out the construction and negotiation of femininity, particularly in relation to respectability among girl gang members in their interactions with family, homeboys and boyfriends, and homegirls and other young women.

Research Methods

The data for this analysis are drawn from a long-term, comparative qualitative study of ethnic gangs in the San Francisco Bay Area that began in 1991 and continues to the present. From 1991 to 1993, we conducted face to face interviews with over 600 self-identified male and female gang members (see Joe 1993; Waldorf 1993). The 65 female gang members interviewed were from seven different groups, and were located using the snowball sampling approach (Biernacki and Waldorf 1981). This sampling strategy relied on respondents referring members of their group or other groups to be interviewed. The same technique was used in our second study that extended our comparative research to Southeast Asian gangs in the same locale. In this effort, we interviewed 91 male and 19 female Southeast Asian gang members during 1993 through 1994. At present, we are engaged in a third study that revisits and explores other contemporary gang issues among males and females in the San Francisco Bay Area. We have included 57 of the female interviews from the current study for this analysis. From the three studies then, we will be drawing on a total sample size of 141 interviews with female gang members.

The in-depth interview involved a two-step process in which the interviewee first answered a series of questions from a quantitative schedule. The second step entailed a tape-recorded session, and members reflected on questions from a semi-structured guide about their gang experiences. This combined approach of a qualitative and close-ended questionnaire provided an opportunity to focus on the group's histories, organization and activities, personal demographics, alcohol and drug use, individual history and involvement with the group, and prior contact with the criminal justice system. We also asked the young women about power relations and gender expectations within the group, with the various males in their lives and with their families.

From the three studies, we recruited and trained five female and four male fieldworkers to conduct the female interviews. All of the fieldworkers were familiar with the gang scene in their communities, having either been directly involved in the street scene or as community workers (e.g. youth workers, public housing liaison). Given their role within the community, they had no difficulties in establishing rapport and trust with the girls. The interviews were conducted in a variety of settings ranging from the respondent's or peer's residence, parks, youth centres and coffee shops. The interview with the African American and Samoan girls were conducted in English. The Latinas and Vietnamese women were interviewed in English or their native language (or a combination), depending on their preference. The fieldworkers assisted in translating the Spanish and Vietnamese interviews. Interviews lasted from 90 minutes to three hours. We gave a 50-dollar honorarium in recognition of their participation and time.

Profile

The 141 young women in this study are current members of one of 44 different gangs.

Table 1 offers an overview of their personal characteristics. The 17 African American women belong to one of six groups. Unlike any of the other ethnic groups, four of the African American female gangs are organized as 'independent', without any affiliation or ties to any male group. The other two gangs are part of a larger 'mixed' group which includes females, but comparatively more male members. The African American women in the sample were older than the females of other ethnic gangs with a median age of 23 years (age range of 14 to 27). The members of the 'independent' groups had known each other since childhood, having grown up in the same neighbourhood. All of the African American women lived in or nearby public housing estates, and described their neighbourhoods as dangerous areas for themselves and their children. These are areas where 'people are outside smoking, getting high, drunk, loud and violent' [HG009], and more generally 'people look nasty. The streets are black, they stink. There's so much garbage. People look all dried up, they walking dead' [HG016]. Drug sales and prostitution are plainly visible on the streets in the afternoons, with activity heightening in the evening.

All of the African American women came from extremely marginalized backgrounds. Although slightly over 50 per cent of them reported that they lived principally with their mother and father until their mid-teen years, one of the parents, usually the father, often left home for months at a time due to alcohol and drugs. The majority of the girls stated that their fathers were either unskilled labourers or unemployed (data not shown). Over one-third of them lived only with their mother, and had had very limited or no contact at all with their fathers. Their mothers tended to be either working in the service sector or unemployed. Several of the girls reported that they had either cut off or limited their

TABLE 1   *Personal characteristics of girls in the gang*

	African American (N = 17)		Latina (N = 98)		Asian American (N = 26)		Total (N = 141)	
Age (median)	23 years		18 years		18 years		18 years	
Place of birth								
California	16	95.0%	57	59.0%	7	26.9%	80	56.7%
Other US	1	5.0%	3	3.1%	0	0.0%	4	2.8%
Mexico/Latina America	0	0.0%	38	38.8%	0	0.0%	38	27.0%
Vietnam	0	0.0%	0	0.0%	19	73.1%	19	13.5%
Domestic unit prior to 16 years of age								
Mother and father	9	52.9%	28	28.6%	16	61.5%	53	37.6%
Mother and stepfather	0	0.0%	5	5.1%	0	0.0%	5	3.5%
Mother only	6	35.3%	47	47.9%	3	11.5%	56	39.7%
Father only	0	0.0%	4	4.1%	3	11.5%	7	5.0%
Other relative	2	11.8%	9	9.2%	2	7.7%	13	9.2%
Other	0	0.0%	5	5.1%	0	0.0%	5	3.5%
Unknown	0	0.0%	0	0.0%	2	7.7%	2	1.4%
Education completed								
9th grade or less	4	23.5%	41	41.8%	6	23.1%	51	36.2%
10th grade	4	23.5%	16	16.3%	6	23.1%	26	18.4%
11th grade	6	35.3%	21	21.4%	9	34.6%	36	25.5%
12th grade	3	17.6%	16	16.3%	3	11.5%	22	15.6%
Junior College	0	0.0%	4	4.1%	0	0.0%	4	2.8%
Unknown	0	0.0%	0	0.0%	2	7.7%	2	1.4%
Employed full or part time	0	0.0%	29	29.6%	4	15.4%	33	23.4%
If employed, type of work								
Skilled	0	0.0%	6	20.7%	2	50.0%	8	24.2%
Service industry	0	0.0%	16	55.2%	1	25.0%	17	51.5%
Child care	0	0.0%	5	17.2%	0	0.0%	5	15.2%
Unskilled	0	0.0%	2	6.9%	1	25.0%	3	9.1%
Primary source of income								
Job	0	0.0%	24	24.5%	4	15.4%	28	19.8%
Family/friends	1	5.9%	39	39.8%	19	73.1%	59	41.8%
Public assistance	6	35.3%	16	16.3%	0	0.0%	22	15.6%
Hustles	7	41.2%	4	4.1%	3	11.5%	14	9.9%
Combination	3	17.6%	15	15.3%	0	0.0%	18	12.8%
Marital status								
Single	12	70.6%	76	77.6%	24	92.3%	112	79.4%
Living with partner	3	17.6%	14	14.3%	1	3.8%	18	12.8%
Married	1	5.9%	7	7.1%	1	3.8%	9	6.4%
Separated	1	5.9%	1	1.0%	0	0.0%	2	1.4%
Number of children								
None	3	17.6%	56	57.1%	24	92.3%	83	58.9%
One	7	41.2%	20	20.4%	1	3.8%	28	19.8%
Two	3	17.6%	13	13.3%	0	0.0%	16	11.3%
Three or more	4	23.5%	2	2.0%	0	0.0%	6	4.3%
Pregnant	0	0.0%	7	7.1%	1	3.8%	8	5.7%
Number of children residing with you								
None	1	5.9%	4	4.1%	0	0.0%	5	3.6%
One	7	41.2%	19	19.4%	1	3.8%	27	19.1%
Two	3	17.6%	10	10.2%	0	0.0%	13	9.2%
Three or more	3	17.6%	2	2.9%	0	0.0%	5	3.5%
Not applicable	3	17.6%	63	64.3%	25	96.2%	91	64.5%

contact with their mothers who were addicted to crack or heroin. Only 18 per cent of the girls had completed high school, and none of them reported any legitimate employment. The girls relied principally on hustling (drug sales and shoplifting) and public assistance to support themselves and their children.

Among the other ethnic groups, the majority of the young women belong to an 'auxiliary' group to a male gang. All of the Latina and 17 of the Asian-Pacific American girls belong to one of these groups that consider themselves 'separate but equal' to their male counterparts. The median age of the Latinas is 18 years of age with a range of 14 to 32. The Latinas come from more diverse communities and backgrounds than the African American girls. Among Latinas, half of them live in a highly congested and dense area in the city where the shops and residents are predominantly of Hispanic origins. Residential units vary with two major housing projects on either end of the community, transient motels used principally for short-term housing, prostitution and drugs, small apartment complexes, flats and single family homes. Most of the girls came to know each other from having a relative in the group or living on the same street or same public housing project. Gang alliances and rivalries were partly based on territory and ethnicity within the Latina community in San Francisco. The other half of the respondents live in a neighbouring city to San Francisco, which is experiencing an urban sprawl. Therefore, unlike their city counterparts, they did not live in a highly congested area, but instead lived in apartments and houses scattered throughout the city. Nearly 40 per cent of the Latinas were born in Mexico or Latin America, and immigrated with at least one parent. Almost 30 per cent of the girls lived with their mother and father. Nearly half of the girls indicated that they lived principally with their mothers, and several indicated that their fathers had either left the family or returned to their native land. When fathers were present, they were skilled, semi-skilled or unskilled labourers. Most mothers worked in the service sector or in unskilled positions. Among the 98 Latinas, approximately one-third reported that at least one of their parents had problems with alcohol or drugs.

Despite the median age of the Latinas, over 78 per cent had not completed high school. Forty per cent of them relied principally on their family and friends for money, and another 25 per cent supported themselves from employment, usually in the service industry. Over three-fourths of the girls were single. Forty-two per cent either had children or were about to give birth. Most of the girls reported that their children lived with them.

The median age of the Asian American females was similar to the Latinas at 18 years of age with a range of 15 to 21. The majority of Asian American girls were Chinese, Chinese Vietnamese and Vietnamese, and had immigrated from Vietnam. The girls came from different neighbourhoods, primarily working class houses and flats. Members came to know each other primarily through school or friends. Over 60 per cent of them live with both parents. The respondents' fathers work in small businesses and semi-skilled jobs, and their mothers work in the small business or in semi-skilled or service industry jobs. Most of the girls were still attending school, and relied principally on their family and friends for money. Only one was living with her partner and was pregnant.

Four Samoan girls were from one group with approximately 15 to 20 members. Members came to know each other through living in the same housing project or through a relative. The respondents' families were lower working class with fathers working in semi-skilled and unskilled labouring jobs and mothers in unskilled and service industry jobs. All the Samoan girls were still enrolled and attending high school.

JOE LAIDLER AND HUNT

Most relied on their families for money, but the eldest girl was married with one child, employed in the service sector, and dealt crack with her husband to supplement their income.

The female gang members in this study are similar to the girls reported in other research (Campbell 1984; Chesney-Lind and Hagedorn 1999; Fishman 1988; Harris 1988; Joe and Chesney-Lind 1995; Moore and Hagedorn 1996). They are young women of colour, from families that are either completely marginalized or barely surviving, and living in typically dense and congested neighbourhoods. They live in communities with limited employment prospects and few incentives to stay in school.

The Structure of Accomplishing Femininity

Much of recent gang research, and more generally, street life ethnographies have underscored the importance of 'respect' among inner city young minority men. In this masculine context, 'respect' demands deference to, and at the same time, commands status, power and authority in an environment with few legitimate avenues (e.g. employment, education) to attain a sense of esteem and importance for oneself and among one's peers. The 'pursuit of respect' (Bourgois 1996) and consequently affirmation of masculinity for young minority males is expressed through exaggerated demonstrations of bravado, fearlessness and aggressiveness with others on the street.

According to Messerschmidt, female gang members, like their male counterparts, constantly seek 'respect' from similarly situated others as a way of demonstrating and affirming power and status in a highly marginalized and patriarchal environment. While we recognize that female gang members operate in a male dominated environment, and may sometimes engage in what may be perceived as 'aggressive' masculine behaviours, it may have less to do with adopting the 'style' of their homeboys, and more to do with other contextual factors. Importantly, our respondents' interactions, evaluations of others and self definitions suggest that respect is highly gendered, and holds a very different meaning for females compared to males. For females, the notion of 'respect' should not be solely understood in masculine street terms of power and control. Among the young women in our study, respect is associated with the pursuit of respectability, one important dimension of 'being feminine'.

Respect has a lot to do with the way she presents herself. The way she acts around guys and girls at all times. She isn't a ho [whore], she's not all desperate with the drugs. She acts like a woman. Some girls kick back and don't have respect for the guys. Some homegirls [gang girls] see each other, and they start cussing [at each other and at the guys], 'fucking bitch this, fucking that, fucking asshole'. It starts getting ugly, and he'll hit her. Better calm down. They [those homegirls] got no respect for themselves. [F24]

Nearly all of the girls described respect(ability) in these highly gendered and normative terms regardless of their ethnic and cultural background. As the girls remind us, respectability involves both appearance and conduct. Her clothing, hairstyle, make-up, and stride signify her status as a reputable young woman. Yet her subtleness, restraint, and regard for others are also critical to distinguishing her from others. Skeggs (1997) notes the importance of appearance, conduct and distancing in her recent ethnography of the lives of Northwest working class women. She argues that respectability is a class signifier for differentiating those who are legitimate from those who are not. It is a distancing mechanism to identify the 'other'. And perhaps most importantly, 'respectability is usually the concern of those who are not seen to have it . . . It would not be of concern here, if the working classes had not consistently been classified as dangerous, polluting, threatening . . . pathological and without respect. It would not be something to desire, to prove and to achieve, if it had not been seen to be a property of "others", those who were valued and legitimated' (1997: 1). Still respectability in its normative form is not 'blindly accepted', women may express ambivalence, dis-identify or resist and devise alternatives (Skeggs 1997).

As the girls in this study suggest, the meaning of 'respectability' goes beyond the middle class notions of the term in other ways. Given their embeddedness in street life culture, and for some, at a very early age, respectability also means being aware and being able to stand up for oneself.

R: A homegirl has to have a mean head on her shoulders. She has to be responsible or respectable.

I: How do you do that?

R: Keep your head up and watch over the moves of others. You can't let nobody get you or you will be got.

The young women in this study, as we will see below, are well aware that to be entirely feminine and to be respectable in their highly marginalized communities is unrealistic and dangerous. Respect(ability) requires a sense of strength and independence. As Skeggs succinctly points out, 'to be completely feminine for most women would be almost impossible: it would be to be without agency, to be a sign of powerlessness' (1997: 102). And as she notes, the women in her study devise different forms of femininity, some of which are an expression of cultural resistance. Similarly then, among the young women in this study, respectability is negotiated and continually challenged in a number of interactional settings.

Interactions with family

There are a range of experiences and expectations among the girls in their family relationships. Regardless of the strength of their parental ties, all the girls believed that it is the family, particularly mothers, who should set the expectations and boundaries for them as girls and young women. In this normative context, it is the mother who they define as the primary caregiver and nurturer in their family. It is the mother who they look to for shelter, care, affection, support, discipline, guidance and structure. As Gina states, 'I got respect for mothers when they *care* for their children' [F38]. Because many respondents' fathers were absent (periodically or permanently), their mothers worked long hours. In these cases, the girls indicated that they or their elder sisters assumed the parental role, babysitting and caring for the younger ones in the family, preparing meals, and cleaning house. This assumption of the motherly role from early adolescence is consistent with other studies on female gang members (Fishman 1988; Joe and Chesney-Lind 1995).

In light of the girls' highly gendered expectations within their own family, some girls describe themselves as coming from a 'traditional' background whereby the mother and father 'expect me to be perfect. To do well in school. To avoid trouble' [F12]. Notably, several Latina and Asian immigrant girls consider themselves very 'traditional' in their appearance, conduct and aspirations, and take great pride in distinguishing themselves from their American born counterparts. By the same token, they rationalize some of their 'unconventional' activities as part of accomplishing femininity.

Rachel, a 22-year-old Mexican homegirl reports that she came to America when she was 12 years of age. Her father brought the family to California after labouring for three years here and believing he could provide them with a better life. She considers herself 'more like a Mexican girl' than the girls here. She holds traditional ideas about life events like the quincinera and weddings when a girl wears 'white' and has a large party for the family and friends. 'Girls from here just run away or don't bother' [F22]. She holds a great deal of respect for her parents who she states are always loving and giving her guidance. Although she has moved out on her own, she still retains a close relationship to them, and tries to live up to their expectations as a young woman and as a daughter. 'When I go to my mom's, I always help her clean house, take care of my niece. Help her to cook, do stuff around the house and take her to the store' [F22]. Her parents don't like the idea that she 'hangs around with trouble'. She has only had two boyfriends whom she has slept with because 'she is not that *kind* of girl'. She rationalizes her use of crystal methamphetamines as a way of losing weight and becoming attractive. 'I started using it because I had this boyfriend. He always used to tell me, You're too fat, you're ugly, nobody's gonna like you. So I started using it, knowing that you get skinny, I only use it now, you know, to lose weight' [F22].

Likewise, other Latina, Vietnamese, Samoan and Filipino girls find their families extremely traditional and conservative in their expectations of them as girls. The Vietnamese girls complain of the double standards and excessive controls they face as girls. Janet describes the differences in treatment between her brother and herself:

My family still holds Vietnamese traditions. Like they want me to come home after school, cook dinner, clean up the house, Can't go out, just got study. And that is it. No going out. Once in awhile but that is it. Your curfew is 9:00. No boys, they don't want you talking, you are too young for boys. They don't want you to get in love with boys, they might influence you and then you might drop out of school . . . My brother could go out all the time. After he got arrested, my parents try to watch out for us more, but the more they tell us what to do, we disobey them more. We lie to them . . . I mean I know better not to. [617]

Cindy, a 16-year old, echoes this view:

Like see parents, they don't understand that what it's like for guys, they think guys can't get pregnant so they get to go out all the time and they don't care. But when a girl goes out they think we're gonna come home pregnant. That is a big discrimination. Like we are all the same. We can't go out because they think girls are suppose to stay home, cook, clean and guys can just go out and have fun. That isn't right. [610]

All of the Vietnamese girls note that their parents were particularly strict with them throughout their early childhood and teen years. The girls contend that the imposition of curfews and restrictions are not solely to keep them out of trouble, but more importantly, to preserve them and therefore, their 'reputation'. The young women expressed a similar view to this 18-year old, 'Like the Vietnamese, they always think like, they care most about their reputation. Americans don't. In Vietnamese custom, they don't let girls in their teens date or go with boyfriends or even go out' [605]. In this case, her reputation refers to the preservation of her chastity and sexual innocence. But other Vietnamese respondents add that it is also the preservation of her innocence more generally; she should stay out of trouble at school and with the law. In terms of her

ACCOMPLISHING FEMININITY

parents, her reputation as a 'good girl' is an indicator of their reputation as 'good parents'. Some girls devise ways to 'please' their parents by maintaining the image of the 'good girl', and still engage in more 'liberating' experiences. For example, Susan reports that she brings home friends who are 'good girls' (e.g. dress conservatively, get straight As, and don't go out with boys) to make a good impression on her parents, but goes out to meet her homegirls in the gang to party and 'look for trouble' [614].

Paradoxically, despite our Vietnamese and a few of the Latina respondents' complaints of traditionalism and cultural gaps, many evaluate themselves in the gendered terms of their parents. They describe their transition from a 'good girl' to a 'bad girl', and believe that they are a disappointment to themselves and their families. This transition typically began in school as this 18-year-old Vietnamese woman notes:

Before I was always like a hard working student because my parents expected me to get good grades and also their friends would think that they had good kids who went to school everyday. They wanted their children to give them a good reputation. And I did get good grades and they were proud. But as I got into the peer pressure and the influence of my friends, I started cutting school. I was a very good student and a very good kid but from these influences, I am getting badder every day . . . I get into fights a lot. I don't stay home a lot no more. I know my parents always worry. [605]

While these young women complain about parental control, other gang girls describe almost a complete absence of parental expectations or controls. Approximately three-fourths of the African American young women and over one-half of the Latinas are critical of one or both parents. Most often, they vocalize their lack of respect for their fathers who rarely or sporadically surface, have drug or alcohol problems and/or are violent toward their mothers or them. Several young women judge their own mothers in relation to conventional standards of respectability and more generally, femininity.

I got along with my mom until I was a teenager. Till I could think my own thing and be my own person. She turned into an alcoholic. That's why I don't drink. I don't want to be like her. She used to beat me a lot. I can't stand her. She's a whore. She just don't get paid for her services. I tell her Ma ya know . . . make some extra money on the side. "Don't talk to me that way I'm your mother." I say so . . . your degrading yourself why can't I degrade you? She's had some awful dudes. I remember one guy came home drunk and beat her up and I went in there and bit his leg. Then when he threw me it was a big old oak dresser and she went nuts. He and she used to do coke. They'd try to play it off . . . oh no holier than though righteous bitch. I don't understand your coke addiction. Yeah mom you're stupid, you ain't never done nothing . . . But my dad he's old fashion. I can't live with him either. He believes a woman should be in the house cooking. Cleaning and having dinner ready by the time he gets home from work. Man I couldn't do that. No friends, no life nothing. [F9]

A few gang girls are not only angered by their mothers' drug use and associated problems (e.g. violence, money), but also, their mothers' inability to fulfil their roles and duties as parents. These girls have little respect for their mothers who they point out abandoned them early on for a life on the streets. To these girls, their mothers are everything they do not want to be.

Gang girls respond in different ways to what they perceived as their mothers' defiance toward and violation of conventional expectations of femininity and motherhood. African American respondents tend to completely sever ties to their mothers if they have problems with drugs. Their drug using mothers are perceived as adding another layer of risk to their current life at home and on the street. Latinas rarely cut off all ties, but instead either restricted their contact with their 'problematic' mothers or stand by their mothers, becoming the caregiver.

Although our respondents have quite diverse interactions within their families, they tend to develop conventional notions about gender roles, and in particular, what it means to be a woman and to be a mother. She is someone who is 'respectable'. She does not sleep around and she does not get heavily involved in drugs and alcohol. She looks after her family, providing care and affection. Importantly, they evaluate their own mothers, and sometimes themselves, in relation to this traditional good girl versus bad girl dichotomy. Some of our respondents acquire these expectations from an early age as they assume a parental role when their mothers are busy working or coping with family violence or drug problems. Many respondents who are from immigrant families develop strategies for fulfilling familial expectations of them as 'good girls'. Outside the family arena, however, the girls, in their interactions with other females and males, try to negotiate a balance between 'being respectable', 'being an adolescent' and 'being on the street'.

Interactions with homegirls and other women

There are two distinct arenas of interaction with other women in which girl gang members find themselves negotiating femininity. One arena involves the interaction they have among themselves. The second arena of interaction entails homegirls' encounters with other women outside of their group. In both arenas, the girls have very distinct notions and expectations of other female members' appearance and conduct that are clearly tied to their sexual reputation.

Don't be a flirt or anything, cause then you have no respect, you're supposed to stick by your old man. [F8]

Some girls are respected. Some girls are treated like hos. It depends on how you act . . . how many guys you slept with. [F012]

To get respect out on the street you should like not get all fucked up with all kinds of guys and do stupid things in front of guys . . . or going out with your friends and her getting into a fight and you causing it but running away and leaving her there. Make sure you can control your drugs and if you drink, just don't get too fucked up. Don't make a fool of yourself. [F23].

At times, they can be more judgmental regarding other girls' respectability than their male counterparts. Excessive drinking and drugging are defined as disreputable because like flirting and sleeping around, a young woman is likely to get out of control and become sexually promiscuous. This evaluative stance among homegirls is not surprising as others have noted that 'what is most significant about the stigma attached to sexual reputation is that young women police each other . . . Such policing has material effects in constricting young women's . . . expression of her sexuality and her freedom of action—her independence' (Lees 1997: 35). As in Lees' study of English girls (1997), we find gang girls spending a great deal of energy 'bitching' or casting doubt on others' reputations. This cross-cultural process operates not only as a mechanism of social control, but also of distancing and confirming one's own reputation.

Louisa, a 19-year-old Latina, vividly recalls why her group of girls broke off from their former set but continues to see the same problem with the younger members of her current gang. As she sees it, the 'problem' is the sexual promiscuity of other members, which reflects poorly on the respectable girls in the group (like her). *Their* conduct gives them a 'bad name', and gives rise to sexual harassment.

We use to belong to the Down Town Nortenas. They have guys and girls. Then we broke off from the girls, calling them the Down Town Max cause the girls were just real slutty, real hos, and it was like all the girls that respect themselves, that demand respect. We started our own group . . . These younger girls are out there being slutty with this guy and that guy, it makes everybody look bad, you know? Couple of the girls are real loose with their bodies and when we're kicking it with the guys, they start looking at us like . . . and we go NO HONEY . . . don't even think of me like that. Then they get all pissed off . . . and they say, well your homegirl . . . Just cause she does, doesn't mean that's me. [F009]

Hey (1997) also finds that bitching serves as a significant cultural practice for white working class English girls in their attempts at 'othering'. Othering or distancing carries enormous 'incentives', providing the means for claiming moral superiority, or more specifically, respectability over 'bad girls'. In this way, othering reinforces one's own identity and investments in femininity. In relation to the immediate group, othering strengthens the solidarity of members and at the same time, increases the conflict and competition with more peripheral members of the group and outsiders.

Despite the energy invested in 'the way a girl presents herself . . . the way she acts around other girls and guys' [F24], these young women are also confronted with the expectations and pressures of adolescence which often run counter to their efforts to be 'respectable'. This contradiction is clearest in the girls' desires to 'party', or more specifically, to drink and use drugs as noted above. Some of the Latinas and Asian-Pacific American females tend to avoid drinking and using drugs altogether, believing that these behaviours put themselves at risk of being branded by other homegirls and homeboys as being a 'druggie' or a drunk. Moreover, drinking and drugging are associated with promiscuity if a girl parties primarily with only homeboys. This 18-year-old Latina describes the setting:

I don't drink. There's a lot of girls who kick back, but they all get drunk and they be with all the guys in there so they wouldn't have no respect for them. I wouldn't let them disrespect me or tell me what to do. [F36]

Yet, with only a few exceptions, our respondents admitted that they had both experimented, and often regularly used alcohol and drugs (principally marijuana, but also *pingas* and crack cocaine). While a few of the homegirls reported drinking or using drugs in the presence of other homeboys and homegirls with little worry about others' perceptions, most of the respondents devised ways to drink or use drugs and maintain their respectability. The most common practice among Latinas and Asian-Pacific American homegirls involves 'safe partying' whereby the girls watch each others' back while drinking and drugging and at the same time, avoiding risky situations.

Like the drug use. It's all individual. I mean you ain't gonna go get high and drunk with some guy you just met you know. You gotta have your friends there to make sure you all take care of each other. We're not supposed to be using Pingas cause some girls ran into some problems, they got raped. [F39]

You gotta be open with them. If you think they're doing something stupid, don't be afraid to tell them. Tell them how it is. Make sure you're there for them all the time . . . Like you want to party. Somebody is gonna care for you so once they see you getting a bit too drunk and a guy comes around and tries to like try something with you. They won't let him. They'll be like, well you know she's wasted, you can't be talking to her right now. [F39]

Respondents rationalize the use of these strategies as a way to circumvent what they perceive to be the 'double standard' for young women. This suggests that the girls actively negotiate a distinctive sense of femininity, one that embraces normative notions of femininity, but also accommodates to the curiosities and pressures of a male oriented-adolescent culture.

Over half of the African American young women, and approximately one-fourth of the Latinas try to restrict heavy drinking or drugging as much as possible to private settings with only other homegirls. In this way, they do not risk negative evaluations from their male peers. Moreover, this partying with 'just the girls' provides freedom and privacy to explore issues of adolescence and femininity unhindered from male 'protection' and control. This private setting, usually at one of the girl's home or apartment, offers a venue for discovery, sharing and support.

One 17-year-old Latina recalls her first drinking session with her homegirls. They enjoyed themselves in this setting so much that it eventually became a regular custom for them to get together on their own to 'unload'.

The first time I drank, I drank with my homegirls at my house in the backyard and we were just drinking Millers. We got drunk. Fried. We had fun and then we started crying. So we went upstairs and went to bed. We were crying about whatever we was talking about. Now we pitch in, go to one of the girl's house, and kick back to drink. If you stay on the street, you'll get picked up. [F23]

Although girl gang members tend to provide each other with some degree of 'freedom' to party, they place distinct boundaries on what constitutes respectable behaviour. When a young woman (regardless of whether she is a member or an outsider living in the same neighbourhood) crosses the line from partying to chasing a high, female gang members define her in ways similar to male gang members. She is the antithesis of a respectable woman. Her drug use is not only out of control and 'unfeminine', but also ruins her sexual reputation because she is perceived to do 'anything' for a high. Many African American and Latina respondents refer to this 'type of girl' in sexualized terms like 'drug sluts', and 'hubba hoes', and rationalize their lack of empathy in this way: 'I can't respect a female that don't respect herself'. [G608]

Our earlier research also shows that female drug sellers hold similar moralistic views of women who have crossed over to become 'drug fiends' (Lauderback et al. 1992; Joe Laidler and Hunt 1997). Importantly, female drug sellers describe their own involvement in dealing as a vehicle for surviving (Joe Laidler and Hunt 1997; Venkatesh 1998). According to Dunlap and her colleagues' case study (1994), Rachel, a female crack dealer and user in New York was able to sustain an independent and successful business without resorting to violence and adopted ways to maintain her respectability to counter the image of her as a 'bad person'. Nevertheless, as Dunlap, Johnson and Manwar have pointed out (1994) women dealers as well as users are typically perceived as having crossed the boundaries of femininity and are stigmatized as 'whores' (1994: 7).

Given the girls' preoccupation with respectability, how then do we explain girl gang members' aggressive posturing and violence among girl gang members? How do we account for this paradox between their aspirations of 'being a young woman' and 'being bad'? At one level, female gang members' 'in your face' aggressive posturing is an

ACCOMPLISHING FEMININITY

attempt to 'look bad', (as opposed to 'being bad'), and is part of an overall protective strategy to the dangers of a highly masculinized street environment (Campbell 1984; Maher 1997). The girls' participation in violence is an expression of youth resistance as well as a power struggle among a group who are constrained by their race, class and gender (Messerschimdt 1997). As the young women in this study overwhelmingly agreed, fighting brings status and honour in a bleak and limiting environment. At another level, however, their participation in violence is also one of the few available resources for defending their reputation as a 'decent' girl and confirming to others that they are 'nobody's fool'. Respondents indicate that one of the major reasons for female on female violence is due to the 'slutty' behaviour of others.

Q: What is the most violent incident you've been involved in?

A: When I hit this girl over the head with a bat. She had screwed my dude. I walked in on them. After that, that bitch got up, went outside. That bitch slipped up one day, and I busted her on the head with the bat. [HG16]

These types of violent incidents usually occur after the girls have been drinking among themselves. Respondents indicate that drinking loosens them up, and provides courage for confronting other females who disrespect them by coming on to their boyfriends and partners. Janine, a 20-year-old Filipina, recalls the last serious incident arising when she and her homegirl were on their front steps drinking:

This was one of them days that I happened to be getting drunk and my homegirl was too. And we was sitting there, and I accidentally slipped, 'Oh, I seen that bitch with your man'. She was like, 'What? Well, why didn't you tell me this before?' I didn't know what to do. I'm drunk and just telling all. She had just got up and she just went out . . . She dropped her little cup with some E & J, and just stepped up to the girl. And that girl wasn't going out like no punk. She said, 'I'm fucking your man, so what?' And my homegirl she just dipped off into her ass. [HG011]

Leticia, a 20-year-old African American woman, describes her most recent fight was with a woman from her neighbourhood who sold her a gold ring that turned her finger green. She found the fight unsettling principally because it occurred when she was dressed up and situated in a party setting.

R: My cousin said they was rolling around. But you see I wasn't really trippin' because I was on the corner with my uncles and aunties getting drunk and high. I was chillin'. I wasn't in no kind of fightin' clothes. I was in some heels and a good dress and had my nails and hair done.

I: Where were you coming from?

R: It was one of them days. I thought I would be cute for the guys outside. They come up behind my back talking about, 'Where is my money or my ring at?' I says, 'Excuse me? You better get out of my face with that'. She was helluva taller than me . . . I am little short stubby. So I had to duck. And just had to catch and just knocked her down. And then two hos came up and started jumpin' me on my back. It was one on one at first until the two girls came and got on me. They almost stabbed me until my uncle came. (HG23)

As gang girls move out of the family arena and into the domain of their female peers, it becomes clear that they construct a distinctive sense of femininity. For them, femininity is, on the one hand, tied to conventional middle class notions of respectability whereby

JOE LAIDLER AND HUNT

young women do not openly draw attention to themselves in appearance and conduct. Sexual reputation is at the core of their definition of female respect(ability). Public displays of 'bad girl' behaviour are condemned through 'othering' or 'distancing'. On the other hand, gang girls would hardly accept total submission to normative notions of femininity. Being a young woman does not mean sacrificing exploration and independence. Hanging out and kicking back on the streets are an expression of this independence. However, gang girls also devise methods and rationales for engaging in behaviour more typically associated with their male counterparts on the streets like drinking and drugging. Importantly, however, the girls are always aware of the male gaze to the extent that they demarcate how far 'respectable' behaviour can be pushed, and vigilantly police themselves.

Interactions with homeboys and lovers

It is in the girls' interactions with homeboys and lovers that they become fully aware of the power of the male view. Accordingly, the girls quickly learn that the males in their lives have a number of general assumptions about and categories of women, all of which can be understood in sexualized terms. Tomboys dress, act and are treated like one of the guys. They are counted on when there are fights. Bitches hang around, but are not taken seriously, as they are loud, overly aggressive and bring unwanted attention. Sluts are only around to be passed around. They 'ask for it', by getting loaded, drinking too much and flirting. 'Good girls' are the antithesis of the slut. They know how to have fun but is always in check and in control.

In light of the girls' awareness of these definitions, and their own sense of femininity, how do gang girls understand their own relationships with homeboys and lovers? Our respondents uniformly agree that the men in their lives have certain conventional expectations of them. Natalie, a 24-year-old African American girl in an independent group succinctly summarizes this common view: 'He just want me to *act like a woman*' (her emphasis) [604]. The girls are very clear on what the men define as 'acting like a woman'. One of her defining features is domestic. Many of the girls in the auxiliary groups complain that they are constantly cleaning and cooking when they hang out with the homeboys at somebody's house, when they are partying, and when they have barbecues and picnics at the park. The girls' reaction to these expectations varies with some accepting this 'feminine duty', and others completely rejecting and confronting the males with the 'chores'.

In several of the African American and some of the Latina girls' relationships with their lovers, however, there are additional expectations. As Tanya, a 23-year-old African American girl, makes clear, she is in a very strained and contradictory position. Her 'nigger' (her words) boyfriend not only expects her to fulfil the traditional domestic duties of a housewife, but he also demands that she bring in her share of the household income. When she doesn't comply with both of these roles, he often resorts to violence.

He wants me to do everything for him. He wants me to cook his dinner, wash his clothes and shit, and he slaps me around when I don't do it . . . Because I didn't have his dinner ready when he came from outside selling his dope. And I didn't have his tennis shoes, wasn't white enough one time, so he beat me up . . . He is mean to me at times. He wants to control me. I go out to make money for my kids and he wants my money so he can invest it in his dope and get more dope. I am like what if somebody takes it off him, where is my money. It is gone. He wants me to be just down for him and do whatever he wants. He wants me to sell dope for him. But I don't. I sell it for myself to make money for my kids. [G607]

Tanya, and others in similar situations to her, indicate that they try to fulfil the domestic duties for their boyfriends or lovers, but are unwilling to be 'duped' into giving their income, usually from drug dealing or shoplifting, to them. She works for herself and her children. As indicated earlier, the gang girl's negotiated definition of femininity is based partly on normative notions of the 'good woman' but also, because of her marginalized position, is grounded in notions of autonomy and self-reliance.

According to the girls, homeboys and lovers hold other traditional expectations of them. In particular, they should act within the confines of 'appropriate respectable behaviour'. The list of 'don'ts' include not to flirt with men, not to sleep with men other than your boyfriend, not to take drugs or too much alcohol, and not to be loud and foul-mouthed especially in the presence of 'others'.

The guys say is isn't right for one of the homegirls to be looking like *that* in front of people. You know we have parties. It isn't right or we look like sluts out there. [F12]

In their interactions with homeboys, the girls realize that this is a double standard to which they are held accountable. They also recognize the power associated with their homeboys' expectations. The consequence of completely defying or resisting these expectations is to categorized as a 'bitch' or 'slut'. In the girls' interactions with her boyfriend, however, the consequences can be more severe, involving violence. Jenny, a 19-year-old African American woman, describes the fear she feels from her boyfriend's obsessive concern with her 'being a woman'.

I am afraid to look at other men because he is so jealous . . . He has a violent streak in him. He wants me to be passive all the time. He likes to speak for me, he likes to tell me what I should wear and how to act when I am out on the street with him. I don't like it, because I have my own personality. But if I try to say I don't like it, he wants to hit me. He thinks that it is his way of showing affection to me. We do fight, over me wanting to go out there and sell my dope. He wants me to give my dope to him. He gets jumped by the police and ends up in jail, and there goes the money for me and my son that I have to take care of. He pushes me around. Bitch you ain't shit, Bitch you can't go out. I am all kind of bitches but then I am supposed to be his woman. [G608]

Homegirls also recognize that homeboys and lovers constantly preach and regulate their behaviour in large part to protect their own image and status, that is, they don't want to be associated in any meaningful way with 'bad girls'. 'Bad girls' are simply for fun. But reputable girls don't make them out as fools. It is his image that is to be protected as 'master' rather than 'fool'.

Q: Are there any things that homeboys expect the women to do in the gang?

A: To watch out for themselves and not be just with any guy. Don't be with guy after guy after guy cause they don't like their homegirls to be talked about. And not to do any drugs. Doing drugs to make a fool out of yourself, they don't want cause they don't want people talking. [F23]

On partying, some girls, as noted above, try to avoid using or putting themselves at risk when partying with homeboys. Several respondents noted that not only did heavy partying put their reputation with the guys at risk, but it also presented dangers in terms of unwanted sexual advances and sometimes resulted in sexual assault. While some

JOE LAIDLER AND HUNT

homeboys try to take advantage of the homegirls when they are high, many girls report that the males took a protective and paternalistic attitude. Some girls interpret this paternalistic attitude as distinctively chauvinistic and took pride in resisting the homeboys' attempts to control them. Linda, a 24-year-old Chicana who reports moderately high levels of alcohol and marijuana use, reasons this way:

Yeah, the guys try to control us. They say, 'Hey girl, you know, slow it down'. But then, you know you don't like any guy telling a woman what to do, of course. So we just speed it up. Then that's when you start drinking faster and they're telling you this and that, and you don't like a guy to be telling you nothing while your drinking. And then you know conflicts start. Sometimes the guys even slap the girls to calm them down because everybody is all drunk and stupid. [F45]

Some of the Asian American homegirls also resist what they perceive to be homeboys' attempts at controlling them—in both their appearance and conduct. This 15-year-old Vietnamese girl notes the differences between her and some of the older girls. From her point of view, the older girls look more feminine, but are really to be admired for their ability to fight and defend themselves.

They [the guys] don't like it when we [the homegirls] dress like a guy with the baggy clothes. They will want us to wear dresses. They do! They go, 'You got to act more like girls'. We are all like a family. And then they tell us to act like a girl. Me and my best friend, we dress like a guy, talk like a guy, and they tell us talk and dress like a girl okay. We never dress like a girl. The older girls dress like 'girls'. You know how, like fancy and stuff that is how they dress. But they can fight too. [603]

It appears then that homegirls' definition of respectability involves both the adoption and rejection of some of the conventional roles of 'being a woman'. Yet it is important to point out that the girls' believe that autonomy and independence in their relationships with others, particularly males, are crucial to being respectable. According to several young women, independence means 'not being pushed around', 'having my opinions heard and counted', and 'standing up for what I believe in'. As Tanya and Jenny suggest, it also means 'taking care of business (to make money) so that we don't have to rely on anyone'. They have experienced too many disappointments with family and lovers.

Based on their interactions with homeboys, but particularly with lovers, the girls develop their own notions of men and masculinity as well. In their eyes, a man has to have respect for her as a woman and as an individual.

I don't like guys that don't have respect for girls. I wouldn't want to be with a guy that thinks of a woman that's less than a man is so he had to respect me. [F19]

We are looking for working men basically. Men that want to work and are going to be responsible. Like if they get us pregnant we want them to stay with us. We are looking for men that want to marry us hopefully one day. Whereas the men that we are left with are the street niggers that wear gold rings, wears gerry curls. You see, I am just with him because that is the environment that I am in, and I am trying to get out of this environment. I would like to have a man. Not no nigger that wants to beat me and makes me make money all the time and give it to him. I want somebody you know that cares about me and loves me, and loves my kids and helps me raise them, and give them a good family. [G07]

Despite these aspirations of finding a 'decent man' of someone who is 'nice', and has a job, many homegirls believe that this is only a dream as they do not have the resources to get out of their neighbourhoods to find a legitimate job nor meet a decent man.

Discussion/Conclusion

Good girls go to heaven but bad girls go everywhere. (Wurtzel 1998: 8)

The idea of the Madonna versus the whore has a long history, and has served the ranks of the middle class well as a method of 'distancing' the disreputable woman (that is, those from the working and lower classes). This patriarchal contrast of the 'good girl/bad girl' continues through the present, and permeates all social classes. As we have shown here, it serves as an 'othering' mechanism even among young marginalized women of colour.

The popular view of the gang girl today is someone who is essentially 'a bad ass'. She is similar to her male counterpart: aggressive, tough, crazy and violent. Yet as we have tried to show in this article, the young women in this study are situated in and must accommodate to the constraints of their structural position in society as well as on the streets. They are female, adolescents and young adults, of colour, poor, living under stressful family conditions and trying to negotiate a sense of identity, including what it means to be feminine. In other words, they *are affected by and affect* their structural position in society.

Our analysis has examined the girls' construction of femininity as they interact with family, other girls and young women, and with the males in their lives. A persistent theme throughout the analysis is the value the girls place on respect(ability). In all three interactional arenas we have looked at, their 'reputation' is one of the most salient markers of their identity as a young woman to the point that they would resort to violence to defend their status and honour. In their interactions with family, they expect their mothers and to some extent themselves to fulfil the normative roles of being female. Our respondents' experience a range with some parent(s) taking a traditional and controlling approach towards their daughters while other parent(s) have abandoned their daughters. Despite this variation, it is clear that the girls' evaluate their mothers' femininity and hold certain expectations about her respectability. In the girls' interactions with each other, they also construct distinct notions of femininity and respectability, and devise methods for resisting and exploring adolescence. As Hey (1997) rightly points out, female relationships are clearly structured in terms of patriarchal assumptions. Among the gang girls themselves, bitching, self-policing, and 'hidden' partying are clear indicators of the significance and ever-presence of the male gaze. The physical presence of males is not essential to the power and control they yield over females (Hey 1997). When homeboys and lovers are present, the girls are clearly aware of the importance of 'acting like a woman', but also define how far they are willing to do this, and refuse to give up their autonomy as individuals. For gang girls, respect(ability) in all three settings, means not only having a 'clean sexual reputation' but it also means being independent. The importance of independence must be underscored. In a recent historical analysis of court records, Davies (1999) found that despite the strong pressures of Victorian respectability in the middle and working classes, female 'scuttlers' in Manchester and Salford were relatively independent as they generated income from factory jobs and experienced some degree of freedom as they transitioned to adulthood and marriage. Given their presence on the streets and their sense of independence, these young working class women sometimes settled disputes and insults through physical fights in public.

What is the meaning then of gang girls' displays of 'toughness' or what Messerschmidt calls, 'bad girl femininity'? Their aggressive posturing is popularly perceived as an

JOE LAIDLER AND HUNT

attempt to 'become macho' like their male counterparts. As Miller's study (1998) shows, however, young women are clearly aware of the gendered nature of the streets, and their robbery strategies take this into account as they target other women who are less likely to fight back, manipulate men by appearing sexually available, or working with male partners. Their own perceptions of their involvement in the violent crime of robbery varies with some adopting a masculine identity and others contending that they are not criminal. Our respondents' experiences suggest that there are a number of reasons for 'acting bad' and for engaging in violence. To some extent, 'looking bad' (as opposed to 'being bad') is a protective strategy to the patriarchal environment at home and on the street. It is also a defence mechanism for coping with their 'emotional vulnerability and perpetual disappointment' (Hey 1997: 97). It is also a form of resistance to informal controls on their attempts to explore adolescence and femininity, and for demonstrating a sense of power in an environment that provides them with little status. In this connection, gang girl violence is also one of the very few resources for defending one's reputation as respectable. This is not to say that some gang girls may engage in violence for other reasons.

Middle class girls, by comparison, have a range of resources for exploring femininity and defending a reputation. When middle class girls come together, they are popularly known by adults and their peers as cliques and friendship groups (as compared to lower working class girls who are seen as gang girls). It is in the clique that middle class girls negotiate femininity and adolescence. 'Being nice' as opposed to 'being bossy' means demonstrating 'reliability, reciprocity, commitment, confidentiality, trust and sharing' (Hey 1997: 65). Middle class girls do draw on 'othering' or 'bitching' as a mechanism for demarcating others, but given their broader resources, they also invest a great deal of energy in exclusionary acts such as guilt and isolation, subtle but obvious displays of in versus out, and selective invitations to social activities and outings (Hey 1997).

This analysis has tried to demonstrate that the notion of the 'bad girl' is a complex one, riddled with questions of not only gender, but also class and ethnicity. Contrary to the idea that gang girls constantly engage in the construction of a 'bad ass' image, we suggest that the accomplishment of femininity occurs through interaction with others and is based in large part, but not exclusively, on acting and being respect(able).

REFERENCES

BIERNACKI, P. and WALDORF, D. (1981), 'Snowball Sampling: Problems and Techniques of Chain Referral Sampling', *Sociological Methods and Research*, 10: 141–63.

BOURGOIS, P. (1996), 'In Search of Masculinity', *British Journal of Criminology*, 36/3: 412–27.

CAMPBELL, A. (1984), *The Girls in the Gang*. Oxford: Basil Blackwell.

——(1990), 'Female Participation in Gangs', in C. R. Huff, ed., *Gangs in America*. 163–82. Newbury Park, CA: Sage.

——(1993), *Men, Women and Aggression*, New York: Basic Books.

CAMPBELL, A. and MUNCER, S. (1989), 'Them and Us: A Comparison of the Cultural Context of American Gangs and British Subcultures', *Deviant Behavior*, 10: 271–88.

CHESNEY-LIND, M. (1993), 'Girls, Gangs and Violence: Anatomy of a Backlash', *Humanity and Society*, 17: 321–44.

CHESNEY-LIND, M. and HAGEDORN, J., eds. (1999), *Female Gangs in America*. Chicago: Lake View Press.

CLOWARD, R. and OHLIN, L. (1960), *Delinquency and Opportunity: A Theory of Delinquent Gangs*. New York: Free Press.

COHEN, A. (1955), *Delinquent Boys: The Culture of the Gang*. Glencoe, IL: Free Press.

COLLISON, M. (1996), 'In Search of the High Life', *British Journal of Criminology*, 36/3: 428–44.

CONNELL, R. (1987), *Gender and Power*. Stanford, CA: Stanford University Press.

CURRY, G. D., BOX, R., BALL, R., and STONE, D. (1992), *National Assessment of Law Enforcement Anti-Gang Information Resources*, draft 1992, Final Report. West Virginia University: National Assessment Survey.

CURRY, G. D., BALL, R. and FOX, R. (1994), *Gang Crime and Law Enforcement Record Keeping*. Washington, DC: National Institute of Justice.

DALY, K. (1997), 'Different Ways of Conceptualizing Sex/Gender in Feminist Theory and Their Implications for Criminology', *Theoretical Criminology*, 1: 25–51.

DAVIES, A. (1999), 'These Viragoes are No Less Cruel than the Lads: Young Women, Gangs and Violence in Late Manchester and Salford', *British Journal of Criminology*, 39/1: 72–89.

DUNLAP, E., JOHNSON, B. and MANWAR, A. (1994), 'A Successful Female Crack Dealer: Case Study of a Deviant Career', *Deviant Behavior*, 15: 1–25.

ESBENSEN, F. and HUIZINGA, D. (1993), 'Gangs, Drugs and Delinquency in a Survey of Urban Youth', *Criminology*, 31: 565–89.

FAGAN, J. (1990), 'Social Processes of Delinquency and Drug Use Among Urban Gangs', in C. R. Huff, ed., *Gangs in America*, 183–222. Newbury Park, CA: Sage.

FISHMAN, L. (1988), *The Vice Queens: An Ethnographic Study of Black Female Gang Behavior*, paper presented at the Annual Meeting of the American Society of Criminology, Chicago (November).

FLEISHER, M. (1998), *Dead End Kids: Gang Girls and the Boys They Know*. Madison: University of Wisconsin.

HARRIS, M. (1988), *Cholas: Latino Girls and Gangs*. New York: AMS Press.

HEY, V. (1997), *The Company She Keeps*. Buckingham: Open University.

HOROWITZ, R. (1990), 'Sociological Perspectives on Gangs: Conflicting Definitions and Concepts', in C. R. Huff, ed., *Gangs in America*, 37–54. Newbury Park, CA: Sage.

HUDSON, B. (1984), 'Femininity and Adolescence', in A. McRobbie and M. Nava, eds., *Gender and Generation*, 31–53. London: MacMillan.

INCIARDI, J., HOROWITZ, R. and POTTIEGER, A. E. (1993), *Street Kids, Street Drugs, Street Crime: An Examination of Drug Use and Serious Delinquency in America*. Belmont: Wadsworth Publishing.

JEFFERSON, T. (1996), 'Introduction to Special Issue on Masculinities and Crime', *British Journal of Criminology*, 36/3: 337–47.

JOE, K. (1993), 'Getting in the Gang: Methodological Issues in Studying Ethnic Gangs', in M. De La Rosa and J. Adrados, eds., 234–57. *Drug Abuse Among Minority Youth: Methodological Issues and Recent Research Advances*, National Institute on Drug Abuse Research Monograph Series 130. Washington, DC: US Government Printing Office.

JOE, K. and CHESNEY-LIND, M. (1995), 'Just Every Mother's Angel: An Analysis of Gender and Ethnic Variations in Youth Gang Membership', *Gender and Society*, 9/4: 408–31.

JOE LAIDLER, K. and HUNT, G. (1997), 'Violence and Social Organization in Female Gangs', *Social Justice*, 24/4: 148–69.

KATZ, J. (1988), *Seductions of Crime*. NY: Basic Books.

KLEIN, M. (1995), *The American Street Gang: Its Nature, Prevalence and Control*. New York: Oxford University.

JOE LAIDLER AND HUNT

LAUDERBACK, D., HANSEN, J. and WALDORF, D. (1992), 'Sisters are Doin' It For Themselves: A Black Female Gang in San Francisco', *The Gang Journal*, 1: 57–72.

LEES, S. (1997), *Ruling Passions*. Buckingham: Open University.

MAHER, L. (1997), *Sexed Work: Gender, Race, and Resistance in a Brooklyn Drug Market*. New York: Oxford University Press.

McROBBIE, A. (1981), *Feminism and Youth Culture: From Jackie to Just Seventeen*. London: MacMillan.

MESSERSCHMIDT, J. (1987), *Capitalism, Patriarchy and Crime Toward a Socialist Feminist Criminology*. Totowa, NJ: Rowman and Littlefield.

——(1993), *Masculinities and Crime: Critique and Conceptualization of Theory*. Lanham, MD: Rowman and Littlefield.

——(1997), *Crime as Structured Action: Gender, Race, Class and Crime in the Making*. Thousand Oaks: Sage.

MILLER, J. (1998), 'Up It Up: Gender and the Accomplishment of Street Robbery', *Criminology*, 36/1: 37–66.

MILLER, W. (1958), 'Lower Class Culture as a Generating Milieu of Gang Delinquency', *Journal of Social Issues*, 3: 5–19.

MOORE, J. (1991), *Going Down to the Barrio: Homeboys and Homegirls in Change*. Philadelphia: Temple University.

MOORE, J. and HAGEDORN, J., eds., (1996), 'What Happens to Girls in the Gang?', in C. R. Huff, ed., *Gangs In America*, 2nd ed., 205–18. Thousand Oaks: Sage.

NEWBURN, T. and STANKO, E., eds. (1994), *Just Boys Doing Business*. London: Routledge.

O'MALLEY, S. (1993), 'Girlz N the Hood', *Harper's Bazaar*, October, 238–43, 272, 281, 284.

QUICKER, J. (1983), *Homegirls*. San Pedro, CA: International Universities Press.

SANCHEZ-JANKOWSKI, M. (1991), *Islands in the Street*. Berkeley: University of California.

SIKES, G. (1997), *8 Ball Chicks: A Year in the Violent World of Girl Gangsters*. New York: Anchor.

SKEGGS, B. (1997), *Formations of Class and Gender: Becoming Respectable*. London: Sage.

TAYLOR, C. (1993), *Girls, Gangs, Women and Drugs*. East Lansing, MI: Michigan State University Press.

THRASHER, F. (1927), *The Gang*. Chicago: University of Chicago.

VENKATESH, S. A., (1998), 'Gender and Outlaw Capitalism: A Historical Account of the Black Sisters of the United "Girl Gang"', *Signs*, 23/3: 681–709.

WALDORF, D. (1993), *Final Report of the Crack Sales, Gangs and Violence Study to the National Institute on Drug Abuse*. Alameda, CA: Institute for Scientific Analysis.

WURTZEL, B. (1998), *Bitches: In Praise of Difficult Women*. NY: Anchor.

Part VI
Policy and Practice

[24]

Gangs, Neighborhoods, and Public Policy*

JOHN M. HAGEDORN, *University of Wisconsin, Milwaukee*

This article uses research from three recent Milwaukee studies to show that deindustrialization has altered some characteristics of youth gangs. Gang members tend to stay involved with the gang as adults, and many have turned to the illegal drug economy for survival. Poor African-Americans in neighborhoods where gangs persist have both similarities and differences to Wilson's underclass concept. What characterizes these neighborhoods is not the absence of working people but the absence of effective social institutions. Public policy ought to stress jobs and investment in underclass neighborhoods, evaluation of programs, family preservation, and community control of social institutions.

Are today's youth gangs part of an "underclass"? What policies should communities adopt to control their gang problem? Based on recent gang research and experience in reforming Milwaukee's human service bureaucracy, we can address these questions and suggest practical local policies that go beyond the usual nostrums of "more cops" and "more jobs."

In the last few years a number of researchers have suggested that today's gangs have changed in some fundamental ways and may be part of an urban minority "underclass" (Moore 1985, Short 1990b, Taylor 1990, Vigil 1988). The nature of the "underclass," however, has been the subject of controversy (Aponte 1988, Gans 1990, Jencks 1989, Ricketts, Mincy, and Sawhill 1988, Wilson 1991). This paper uses data gathered from three different Milwaukee studies over the past five years to examine the changing nature of Milwaukee's gangs, the characteristics of Milwaukee's poorest African-American neighborhoods, and the relationship between gangs and neighborhoods.

For the first study, completed in 1986, 47 of the founding members of Milwaukee's 19 major gangs, including 11 of the 19 recognized leaders, were interviewed (Hagedorn 1988). That study described the origins of Milwaukee gangs, their structure and activities, and documented how gangs came to be seen as a social problem. It also tracked the education, employment, drug use, incarceration experience, and the level of gang participation of the 260 young people who founded the 19 gangs, including the 175 founders of 12 African-American male gangs.

A brief follow-up study in spring of 1990 looked at the patterns of drug abuse and the structure of gang drug dealing in three African-American gangs. This pilot study tracked the employment, incarceration, and drug use status of the 37 founding members of the three gangs since the original study. It began a process of exploring the relationship between Milwaukee gangs and drug dealing businesses or "drug posses."

Finally, as part of a human services reform plan, Milwaukee County commissioned a needs assessment in two neighborhoods where several of Milwaukee's gangs persist (Moore and Edari 1990b). Residents were hired to survey heads of households drawn from a probability sample of 300 households in ten census tracts in two neighborhoods. These neighborhoods had a high percentage of residents living in poverty and a clustering of social problems associated with the "underclass."

---

* This article is based on several previous papers. The first was presented April 24, 1990, to the U.S. Conference of Mayors in Washington, D.C. Two others were presented at the 85th Annual ASA meetings also in Washington, D.C., August 1990. Joan Moore, Carl Taylor, Howard Fuller, and Clinton Holloway made helpful comments on various earlier drafts. Social Problem's anonymous reviewers also added valuable insights. Correspondence to Hagedorn, University of Wisconsin-Milwaukee, Urban Research Center, P.O. Box 413, Milwaukee, WI 53201.

This article first looks at how Milwaukee gangs have changed due to deindustrialization. Second, the paper explores some volatile social dynamics occurring within poor but still heterogeneous African-American neighborhoods. Finally, based on the analysis of gangs and their neighborhoods, other underclass research, and on the author's own experience in reforming the delivery of social services, the article suggests several local policies to strengthen and assist community institutions with gang troubles.

Macro-Economic Trends and Gangs in Milwaukee

The underclass has been conceptualized as a product of economic restructuring that has mismatched African-American and other minority workers with radically changed employment climates (Bluestone and Harrison 1982, Kasarda 1985, Sullivan 1989). Milwaukee epitomizes this mismatch: between 1979 and 1986 over 50,000 jobs were lost or 23 percent of Milwaukee's manufacturing employment (White et al. 1988:2-6). African-American workers were hit especially hard. In 1980, prior to the downturn, 40 percent of all African-American workers were concentrated in manufacturing (compared to 31 percent of all city workers). By 1989, research in five all-black Milwaukee census tracts found that only about one quarter of all black workers were still employed in manufacturing (Moore and Edari 1990b). African-American unemployment rates in Milwaukee have reached as high as 27 percent over the past few years.

Another way to view economic changes in the African-American community is to look at social welfare over the last thirty years. Like European immigrants before them, African-Americans came to Milwaukee with the hopes of landing good factory jobs (Trotter 1985), and large numbers succeeded. But as industrial employment declined and good jobs were less available, reliance on welfare increased (Piven and Cloward 1987:83). In 1963, when black migration to Milwaukee was still rising, fewer than one in six of Milwaukee's African-Americans were supported by AFDC. However by 1987, nearly half of all Milwaukee African-Americans and two thirds of their children received AFDC benefits. Seven out of every ten Milwaukee African-Americans in 1987 were supported by transfer payments of some kind accounting for half of all 1987 black income in Milwaukee County (Hagedorn 1989a).

Coinciding with reduced economic prospects for African-Americans, Hispanics, and other working people, gangs reemerged in Milwaukee and other small and medium-sized cities across the Midwest. While the popular notion at the time was that these gangs had diffused from Chicago, gangs in Milwaukee and the Midwest developed from corner groups and breakdancing groups in processes nearly identical to those described by Thrasher fifty years before (Hagedorn 1988, Huff 1989). The economy may have been changing, but the way gangs formed had not.

In 1986 we interviewed 47 of the 260 Milwaukee gang founders or members of the initial groups of young people who started the 19 major gangs in the early 1980s. At the time of our interviews, the founders were in their early twenties and at an age when young people typically "mature out" of gang life. We asked the 47 founders to report on the current status of all the members who were part of the gang when it started. To our surprise, more than 80 percent of all male gang founders were reported as still involved with the gang as twenty to twenty-five year old adults.

We concluded at the time that the *economic basis* for "maturing out" of a gang—those good paying factory jobs that take little education, few skills, and only hard work—was just not there anymore. As Short wrote in a review recent of gang literature, "There is no reason to believe that boys hang together in friendship groups for reasons that are very different now than in the past. . . . What has changed are the structural economic conditions . . ." (Short 1990a).

Table 1 • *Employment and Adult Gang Involvement*

	% Black Male	% Hisp. Male	% Wh. Male	% Female
Full Time	9.7	10	10	8.6
Part Time	14.0	0	40	11.4
Unemployed	70.3	82.5	40	63.0
Involved with the Gang as an Adult	81.1	70	100	8.6
TOTALS N=260	N=175	N=40	N=10	N=35

Moore (1991) has also documented economic effects of deindustrialization on the "maturing out" process of Chicano gangs. She finds that members of recent gang cliques in East Los Angeles are less likely to have found good jobs than members of older gang cliques. She concludes, "It is not that the men from recent cliques were more likely to have dropped out of the labor market, nor were they more likely to be imprisoned. It may be that they could not get full-time, stable jobs."

The difficulty in finding a good job today is offset by the abundance of part-time jobs in the illegal drug economy. In preparation for a proposal to the National Institute on Drug Abuse to examine the impact of drug abuse and drug dealing on Milwaukee's gangs, we updated our rosters on the current status of the 37 founding members of three African-American gangs. By 1990, less than one in five (19 percent) of the founders, now in their mid to late twenties, were engaged in full-time work. However, three times as many of the founders (59 percent) graduated from the gang into drug "posses" or high-risk small businesses selling drugs. "High risk" is perhaps an understatement. Almost all of the 37 (86 percent) had spent significant time in prison since 1986, most for drug offenses. Three quarters (76 percent) had used cocaine regularly within the last three years, and three had been murdered. While five of the 37 were said to be working as entrepreneurs (called "hittin' 'em hard"), the others involved with drug distribution worked part time ("makin' it") or sporadically ("day one"), and continued to live on the margins.

Table 2 • *1990 Status of 37 Founding Members of Three African-American Gangs*

Involved in Regular Sales of Cocaine	Used Cocaine Routinely Since 1987	Spent Time in Prison	Presently Working Full Time	Murdered
59%	76%	86%	19%	8%
N=22	N=28	N=32	N=7	N=3

As Don, a leader of the 1-9 Deacons told us in 1985: "I can make it for two or three more years. But then what's gonna happen?" The answer to Don's question is now clear. The lack of access to good jobs has had a direct effect of making illegal drug sales, no matter how risky, more attractive to Milwaukee's gang founders as an occupation for their young adult years.

Frederick Thrasher pointed out sixty years ago: "As gang boys grow up, a selective process takes place; many of them become reincorporated into family and community life, but there remains a certain criminal residue upon whom gang training has, for one reason or another, taken hold" (Thrasher 1963:287). The loss of entry level manufacturing jobs appears to have turned Thrasher's "selective process" on its head. Today most of the young adult gang founders rely on the illegal economy for guarantees of survival. It is only the "residue" who, at this time in Milwaukee, are being "reincorporated into family and community life."

There are also some indirect effects of economic changes. In Milwaukee, most of the founders still identify somewhat with their old gang and often hang out in the same neighborhoods where they grew up, coexisting with a new generation of gang youth. This mixing of older members of drug "posses" with younger siblings and other young gang members has produced disturbing intergenerational effects. Older gang members with a street reputation employed in the fast life of drug dealing are modeling dangerous career paths for neighborhood youth. These intergenerational effects also appear in Anderson's latest work (1990). He finds that "old heads," older residents who upheld and disseminated traditional values, are being replaced by *new* "old heads" who "may be the product of a street gang" and who promote values of "hustling," drugs, and sexual promiscuity (103). This "street socialization" may contribute to reproducing an underclass rather than socializing young people into conventional lifestyles (Short 1990b, Vigil 1988).[1]

In summary, contemporary gangs have changed from the "delinquent boys" of fifties literature: There is a growing relationship between the youth gang, illegal drug-based distribution, and survival of young adult gang members in a post-industrial, segmented economy. Clearly, powerful *economic* forces are affecting contemporary gangs as Wilson and other underclass theorists would predict. But when we take a closer look at the impact of economic, demographic, and institutional changes on processes within Milwaukee's poorest African-American neighborhoods, the situation becomes more complicated.

Gangs and Neighborhood Segmentation

Gangs have always been associated with neighborhoods, and African-American gangs have been no exception. Thrasher found "Negroes" had "more than their share" of gangs (Thrasher 1963:132) as far back as the 1920s. In the neighborhood that Suttles studied, gangs were functional "markers" or signs by which neighborhood youth could know who may be harmful and who is not and thus were an important part of a neighborhood's search for order. Suttles' black gangs were not in any significant way distinct from white ethnic gangs (Suttles 1968:157). Similarly, the black Chicago gang members that Short and Strodtbeck (1965:108) studied were quite similar to non-gang black youth, though they were more lower class than white gang members. Until the 1960s, the sociological literature largely viewed black gangs as functional parts of black neighborhoods.

But things have been changing. Perkins, summarizing the history of black Chicago gangs, wrote that gangs first became disruptive to their communities in the 1960s due to the influence of drugs, corrupting prison experiences, and the failure of community-based programs (Perkins 1987:40-42). Cloward and Ohlin theorized that housing projects and other big city "slums" tended to be disorganized and "produce powerful pressures for violent behavior among the young in these areas" (Cloward and Ohlin 1960:172). They correctly predicted that "delinquency will become increasingly violent in the future as a result of the disintegration of slum organization" (203).

Increasing violence in central cities has prompted angry responses from residents. Cooperation by broad elements of the black community with police sweeps of gang members in Los Angeles and elsewhere and the founding of "mothers against gangs" and similar organizations throughout the country are examples of community hostility toward gangs. Gangs today are seen by both law enforcement and many community residents as basically *dysfunctional*. Today's gangs are a far cry from the "Negro" street gangs of Suttle's Addams area

---

1. Moore (1991) also finds a mixing of gang cliques in Los Angeles gangs. Short's (1990) 1960 Nobles were mainly employed in the early 1970s when they were restudied, in contrast to Vicelords, virtually all of whom had more prison experience, many of whom still identified with the Vicelords and were involved in illegal operations more than a decade after they were first studied.

which contained the "best-known and most popular boys in the neighborhood" (Suttles 1968:172).

Based on our Milwaukee interviews, we concluded that gang members reciprocated the hostility of "respectables." While the gang founders were hostile toward police and schools as expected, they also severely criticized African-American community agencies which they felt were mainly "phoney." The black founders agreed their gangs were dysfunctional for their neighborhoods: two thirds of those we interviewed insisted that their gang was "not at all" about trying to help the black community. Some were shocked at even the suggestion that their gang would be concerned about anything but *"green* power" (i.e., money). The role model of choice for many of the founders we interviewed was not Dr. Martin Luther King, Jesse Jackson, or any African-American leader, but Al Capone.

One explanation for this intra-community alienation in Milwaukee is the peculiar way black gangs formed. Gang formation in Milwaukee coincided with desegregation of the schools: a one-way desegregation plan that mandatorially bused only black children. While gangs originally formed from neighborhood groups of youth in conflict with youth from other neighborhoods, busing complicated the situation. School buses picking up African-American students often stopped in many different neighborhoods, mixing youth from rival gangs and transforming the buses into battlegrounds. Gang recruitment took place on the buses and in the schools as well as from the neighborhood. The black founders told us in 1985-86 that a majority of the members of their gangs no longer came from the original neighborhood where the gang formed.

Consequently, when the gang hung out on neighborhood corners, they were not seen by residents as just the "neighbors' kids" messing up. "I'll tell your Mama" did not work when no one knew who "mama" was or where she lived. Informal social controls were ineffective, so calling the police became the basic method to handle rowdiness and misbehavior as well as more serious delinquency. Hostility between the gangs and the neighborhood increased with each squad car arriving on the block.

A second explanation for intra-community hostility is provided by 1989 research in five of Milwaukee's poorest and all-black census tracts (Moore and Edari 1990b) where several of the gangs I had studied were founded. These neighborhoods exhibit many of the criteria of an "underclass" area, but they also differ in many respects from very poor ghetto neighborhoods described by Wilson and others.

Household income of the tracts was very low—1980 census data (*before* the eighties downturn) show more than 30 percent of the families in the five tracts living below poverty. The five tracts experienced a 42 percent population loss between 1960 and 1985. In 1989, when the interviews were completed, most (53.8 percent) respondents received AFDC and nearly twenty percent (19 percent) did not have a phone. A majority of residents in the five tracts presently live below the poverty line. The tracts certainly qualify as "underclass" areas by standard definitions (Ricketts and Mincy 1988).

But these neighborhoods are not uniformly poor. One quarter of the residents (28.6 percent) owned their own home—fifteen percent less than the city-wide average, but still a stable base within a very poor neighborhood. Half of the household heads lived at their current residence for five or more years. While stable employment had drastically declined in these tracts since 1980, still nearly one third of working respondents had held their current job for 10 or more years. Unlike the "densely settled ghetto areas" Sampson describes (1987:357) where residents have "difficulty recognizing their neighbors," 80 percent of the Milwaukee respondents said the best thing about their neighborhood *was* their "neighbors." Nearly three in five (59.2 percent) visited with neighbors at least once a week.

More striking were strong kinship ties, supporting earlier work by Stack (1974) and others. Nearly half of all respondents visited their parents every day and over ninety percent visited parents monthly. An even higher percentage visited siblings at least once a month.

Finally, more than three quarters belonged to families that held family reunions—and 77 percent of those respondents regularly attended those reunions. Even child protective clients, who are among the most transient residents, had extensive kinship networks (Moore and Edari 1990a).[2]

But the neighborhoods are not regarded positively by most residents. Less than one fifth (19.7 percent) said the neighborhood was a "good place to live," and 52 percent said they would move if they could. While respondents liked their neighbors as the best thing about their community, the top three worst things were said to be drugs (64 percent), violence (52 percent), and gangs (20 percent). About half said things had gotten worse the past two years, ·and a majority (54.5 percent) believed things will continue to get worse. And the problems were not "around the corner" or in an adjacent neighborhood, but right on the blocks where the interviews took place. The interviewers were often told by respondents to not go to a certain house or to avoid a certain side of the street because of dangerous drug or gang problems.

The area also has few basic social institutions. Zip code 53206 is a 20 by 20 square block area with 40,000 residents in the heart of Milwaukee, containing the census tracts where the interviews took place. This area has no large chain grocery stores. There are no banks or check-cashing stores in the entire zip code area. Bars and drug houses are in plentiful supply and the area has the highest number of Milwaukee drug arrests. Still, in 1989, this zip code area did not have a single alcohol/drug treatment facility. Even community agencies are located overwhelmingly on the periphery of 53206, circling the neighborhoods they serve, but not a part of them.[3] Community programs, churches, and social workers were seldom mentioned by survey respondents as a resource to call in times of neighborhood trouble.[4]

In summary, while these poor African-American neighborhoods have characteristics of Wilson's notion of the underclass, they also exhibit important differences. On the one hand, central city Milwaukee neighborhoods have been getting poorer due to deindustrialization and have experienced substantial population loss. They are home to the poorest and most troubled of all Milwaukee's residents. The area's lack of basic institutions is reminiscent of descriptions by Thrasher (1927) and Shaw and McKay (1969) and supports aspects of Wilson's underclass thesis.

On the other hand, large numbers of working class African-American families still reside in these neighborhoods. Some want to leave but cannot because of residential segregation (Massey and Eggers 1990) or lack of affordable housing. But many stay because they want to. Rather than neighborhoods populated overwhelmingly by a residue left behind by a fleeing middle and working class, as Wilson has described, Milwaukee's "underclass" neighborhoods are a checkerboard of struggling working class and poor families, coexisting, even on the same block, with drug houses, gangs, and routine violence.

This ecological coexistence explains much of the intra-community tension between poor and working families and underclass gangs. Clearly when drug deals gone bad turn into midnight shoot-outs, residents of a neighborhood will be scared and angry. Contrary to Wilson's claim, events in one part of the block or neighborhood are often of vital concern to those

2. Child protective clients, however, more than other residents, turned to police for help with problems than asking help from their relatives or neighbors.

3. In contrast, zip code 53204, a predominantly Hispanic area home to several Hispanic gangs, is dotted with community agencies, banks, merchants, and grocery stores. While this neighborhood is an area of first settlement for Mexican immigrants, it does not have the characteristics of social disorganization of the predominantly African-American 53206 neighborhoods. Those who use "percent Hispanic" as a proxy for social disorganization should take note of these findings (cf. Curry and Spergel 1988:387).

4. There are other institutions in the area with a high profile, particularly law enforcement. But the strong police presence plays to a mixed review. While most residents (38.3 percent) called the police for any serious problems in the neighborhood before they called relatives or friends, one in eight (12.1 percent) listed police as as one of the three top "bad things" about the neighborhood. Police are still viewed with suspicion and fear in African-American communities.

residing in other parts (Wilson 1987:38). With a lack of effective community institutions, residents can either ignore the gunshots in the night, arm themselves for self-protection, call "911"—or give in to the fear and despair by moving out.[5]

While Milwaukee neighborhoods are not the socially disorganized underclass areas reported by Wilson, neither are they the highly organized neighborhoods described by Whyte (1943) or Suttles (1968). Milwaukee's poor neighborhoods have segmented and an uneasy peace reigns between nervous factions. Suttles (1968) saw the 1960s Addams area as representing "ordered segmentation," where firm boundaries between ethnic neighborhoods helped make "a decent world within which people can live" (234). Instead, Milwaukee's neighborhood segments have become a prime source of instability.

This picture of neighborhood segmentation is consistent with Anderson's portrait of "Northton," a poor African-American community in a large eastern city (Anderson 1990). "Old heads" in Northton are not so much missing, as they have become demoralized and their advice shunned (78-80). Respectable residents are confronted by a growing street culture that increases community distrust of young people, victimizes neighborhood residents, and lures children into dangerous activities (92). Police simplistically divide the neighborhood between the "good people" and those linked to drug trafficking (202-3). Conflict between neighborhood segments inevitably increases, and "solidarity" is sacrificed to the imposed order of police patrols, vigilante justice, and prisons.

These heterogeneous but segmented neighborhoods in "Northton" and Milwaukee may be characteristic of many "underclass" communities across the United States (Jencks 1990). How to stabilize such neighborhoods is one of the major policy debates of the nineties.

Gangs, Neighborhoods, and Public Policy

In light of these findings, what do we make of this contradictory picture of gangs and their neighborhoods? What policies ought to be followed? The data suggest the drug economy flourishes in large part because of the absence of good jobs. It is hard to argue with the response from a 1986 interview:

> Q: OK, we're at the end here. The Governor comes in. He says, Darryl, I'm gonna give you a million dollars to work with gangs. Do what you want with it.
> A: Give 'em all jobs.

But while jobs are certainly needed, there is no reason to believe hundreds of thousands of good paying, entry-level jobs will appear anytime soon from either the private or public sector. In the absence of sufficient jobs, pressure will continue to mount for more police and more prisons as the policy option of choice to curtail violence. This militarization of our neighborhoods is inevitable unless community residents and public officials can be persuaded that alternative policies are plausible and can be effective. But what alternative policies should be advocated?

One popular option is to work with city hall and call for more federal resources to come to cities. While we clearly need more resources, a more critical issue is how money is spent. As Spergel says in summarizing his recommendations in the National Youth Gang Survey "the implications of our findings is that more resources alone for police or even human service programs would not contribute much to dealing effectively with the youth gang problem"

---

5. It must be remembered, however, that the illegal drug economy, while disruptive, is also sustained by local demand. Workers in drug houses assert that most Milwaukee cocaine sales are to people within the neighborhood, not to outsiders (in contrast to Kornblum and Williams [1985:11]). But when illegal activities bring trouble to the neighborhood, particularly violence, police are often welcomed in ousting drug dealers and combatting gang problems (Sullivan 1989:128).

(Spergel and Curry 1990:309). In the absence of institutional reform and guarantees that resources will get to those that need it, more resources alone will not necessarily contribute to solving gang problems.[6]

The development of effective policy will require a struggle within cities over where new and existing programs are physically located, who will be served, and how the massive public bureaucracies (which gobble most resources intended for the poor) should be structured. Rather than proposing specific new model gang programs or narrowly calling for a federal office of gang control (Miller 1990), our data suggest a focus on strengthening neighborhood social institutions. Our experience in reforming Milwaukee's human service system suggests that we should adopt four policies to strengthen neighborhood-level social control.

(1) Public spending and private investment must be concentrated in the most impoverished areas. This does not mean spend more human service dollars "for" the underclass by funding well intentioned programs run by middle-class white providers located on the periphery of the poorest neighborhoods. Rather, I suggest we should insist that money be spent mainly on programs physically located *in* underclass neighborhoods, run by people with ties to the neighborhoods they intend to serve. This policy has the effect of targeting programs for the underclass while also strengthening minority agencies or creating new agencies within very poor neighborhoods. These agencies provide not only services but also can provide jobs for neighborhood residents. As employment opportunities increase and better funded local agencies become centers for social action, pressures for working- and middle-class residents to flee should decrease.

For example, in Milwaukee, close examination of where human service dollars were spent by zip code exposed that less than 1 percent of $100 million of Department of Health and Human Service contract dollars in 1988 was spent on programs located in two of Milwaukee's poorest zip code areas (53206 and 53204). These two areas contain only eight percent of Milwaukee County's population but are home to 25 percent of Milwaukee's human service clients. These figures were used by our reform administration to direct several million dollars in purchase contracts to agencies physically located in the two zip code areas, helping build an institutional infrastructure. Boarded up buildings are being rehabilitated to house the new agencies, employing neighborhood youth in the rehabbing effort.

Redirecting existing money is not an easy task. When we sent more than "crumbs" to neighborhood organizations, the mainly white traditional agencies—which are located downtown or in integrated, more stable neighborhoods—howled "reverse discrimination" and lobbied against us. Funding new programs is a zero sum game: if agencies located in poor neighborhoods are to get funded, agencies located elsewhere stand to lose. Those providers will almost certainly have more political power and connections than poor neighborhood organizations.

But as our research shows, while very poor neighborhoods have been devastated by economic and demographic changes, they also have important strengths to build on. The residents who live in poor neighborhoods need stable, well-funded agencies and institutions in which to participate. This recommendation is a call for sustained local political struggle over *where* money is spent to better stabilize impoverished neighborhoods.

(2) Programs should be fully evaluated to see if they are having a positive impact on gangs or those most in need. It is not only important where the money is spent, but it is also critical whether anyone besides the agency or bureaucracy benefits. The inability of traditional agencies to serve the "hard to reach" has a long history: the Chicago Area Project (Schlossman, Zellman, and Schavelson 1984) was initiated to fill just such a gap. Geis cites the 1960s New York City

---

6. City hall may be as capable today of using academics against Washington for its own purposes as Washington in the sixties was adept in using academics to attack city hall (Gouldner 1968, Piven and Cloward 1971).

Youth Board as an example of the need for innovative programming to replace the traditional agencies which were unable "to respond readily to new ideas and approaches" (Geis 1965:43). And some programs do "work." Lizbeth Schorr lists numerous contemporary programs that have been effective and could be replicated (Schorr 1988).

Large public bureaucracies are seldom concerned with formal results of programs. Once programs are funded, their continuation is often all that is offered as proof of effectiveness. In Milwaukee, research on agencies which received more than $20 million dollars worth of contracts to work with delinquents discovered the Department of Social Services kept no records at all of client outcomes of these programs. Funding decisions were based almost solely on routine approval of the re-funding of those agencies funded the year before (Hagedorn 1989b).

Programs thus continue with no regard for their effectiveness for clients. Lindblom points out the apparent absurdity that "In an important sense, therefore, it is not irrational for an administrator to defend a policy as good without being able to specify what it is good for" (Lindblom 1959:84). James Q. Wilson, in a forum on "Can Government Agencies be Managed?" recommended the novel idea that managers be judged on program results, a prospect he doubted would happen because "It is in no one's interest in Washington, D.C.," to do it (Wilson 1990:33). Many organizational theorists have pointed out that program evaluation serves only ceremonial functions for public bureaucracies (Meyer and Rowan 1981, Weick 1976). If sociologists are not among those insisting that social programs be evaluated and show results for the clients they are intended to serve, who will?

(3) Fund family preservation programs. One of the most encouraging developments in the past decade in social work has been family preservation programs (Nelson, Landsman, and Duetelman 1990). These short-term, intensive, empowerment model programs, which focus not on an individual client, but rather the needs of the entire family, have been remarkably successful.[7] In dozens of states and cities, these programs, many of them modeled after the successful "homebuilders" projects funded by the Edna McConnell Clark Foundation, have reduced out of home placements and helped families learn how to stay together during a crisis.

Families where an older sibling is involved with gangs may be ideal candidates for these types of intensive, coordinated efforts. Our data show that many child protective clients have extensive family networks whose strengths could be utilized by intensive interventions. Milwaukee received a $1 million dollar grant from the Philip Morris Companies to fund a "homebuilders" model program. An agency located in one of the poorest areas of the city was awarded the contract to implement the program and collaborate with the public school system. As noted above, there was considerable resistance to the program from elements within the social welfare bureaucracy, where family-based, results-oriented programming was viewed as a threat to business as usual (Nelson 1988). Yet, strategies were developed to confront the opposition, and the program was implemented.

(4) Finally, large public bureaucracies should become more neighborhood based and more open to input from clients and the neighborhoods they serve. Reminiscent of the 1960s community control movement (Altshuler 1970), current research suggests that social control is least effective when imposed by outside forces. Community controls are strengthened most when informal community level networks are voluntarily tied to external bureaucracies and other resources

---

7. Recent control group evaluations have questioned these programs' effectiveness in reducing out of home placements. The main conclusion from the evaluations is the incapacity of social service bureaucracies to refer the appropriate clients to the programs. The evaluations found family preservation programs are so effective that social workers try to place families in the programs even though they do not fit project guidelines (cf. Feldman 1990, Schuerman et al. 1990, Yuan 1990). These evaluations also point out the important role social scientists can play in insisting programs be properly implemented.

(Figueira-McDonough 1991).[8] Public dollars for social programs today are largely used to support "street level bureaucrats" whose structure of work often makes it difficult to deliver services that improve the quality of life of their clients (Lipsky 1980). Diverse reform trends in policing, education, and social services all stress more community involvement in public bureaucracies (Chubb and Moe 1990, Comer 1972, Goldstein 1977, Kamerman and Kahn 1989). These reforms, insofar as they increase client and neighborhood control and break down existing bureaucratic barriers, merit support.

While Lipsky and others comment that it will be difficult to reform public bureaucracies in the absence of a social movement (Lipsky 1980:210, Wineman 1984:240), unfavorable conditions should not be an excuse for inaction. The Milwaukee experience of creating multidisciplinary teams of human service workers, moving them into the neighborhoods, and creating neighborhood councils to increase accountability is one example of such a reform.

Conclusion

Deindustrialization has altered the nature of gangs, creating a new association between the youth gang, illegal drug-based distribution, and survival of young adult gang members in a post-industrial, segmented economy. While it would be a mistake to see all gangs as drug-dealing organizations, the lack of opportunity for unskilled delinquents creates powerful strains on gang members to become involved in the illegal economy. Without a major jobs program, illegal trade in drugs and related violence seem likely to continue at unacceptable levels (Goldstein 1985, Johnson et al. 1989).

Although neighborhood changes are clearly relevant to gang activities, Wilson's characterization of the underclass as living in neighborhoods from which middle and working class African-Americans have fled and abandoned social institutions (Wilson 1987:56) does not fully apply in cities like Milwaukee. Instead, there are deteriorating neighborhoods with declining resources and fractured internal cohesion. In cities like Milwaukee, it is not the absence of working people that define underclass neighborhoods but more the absence of effective social institutions. Without community controlled institutions, conventional values will have diminished appeal, neighborhoods will segment, solidarity will weaken, and working residents will continue to flee. The research on Milwaukee is consistent with the basic tenet of social disorganization theory, that the lack of effective institutions is related to crime and delinquency. The data support Spergel and others who call for "community mobilization and more resources for and reform of the educational system and job market" (Spergel and Curry 1990:309) as the most effective approach to gang control.

This article does support Wilson and others who call for massive new federal jobs programs. While lobbying for new state and federal job programs, social scientists should also focus on ways to encourage private and public investment in poor neighborhoods and advocate for more community control of social institutions. This means a stepped up involvement by academics in the workings of the large public bureaucracies which control resources needed to rebuild these communities.[9]

In the words of C. Wright Mills, bureaucracies "often carry out series of apparently rational actions without any ideas of the ends they serve" (Mills 1959:168). All too often the

8. This was also Suttles' conclusion: as community ties to external forces increased, so did its internal social control—it became more "provincial" (1968:223-224). Social disorganization and social control, Sullivan also points out, is not linear, but varies widely between poor neighborhoods (Sullivan 1989:237).

9. This recommendation is not a call for revisiting the Chicago Area Project which relied on private financing and performed a "mediating role" with local institutions (Schlossman and Sedlak 1983, Sorrentino 1959), nor is it a call for a new war on poverty with built in antagonism between city hall and short lived federally funded agencies (Marris and Rein 1967, Moynihan 1969). Rather, it is a call for academics to directly engage in local struggles over how and where large public bureaucracies distribute existing resources.

ends public bureaucracies serve are not helpful for poor communities. This article can be read as a call for social scientists to step up the struggle to make public bureaucracies more rational for the truly disadvantaged.

References

Altshuler, Alan A.
   1970   Community Control, The Black Demand for Participation in Large American Cities. New York: Pegasus.
Anderson, Elijah
   1990   Streetwise: Race, Class, and Change in an Urban Community. Chicago: University of Chicago Press.
Aponte, Robert
   1988   "Conceptualizing the underclass: An alternative perspective." Paper presented at Annual Meetings of the American Sociological Association. August. Atlanta, Georgia.
Bluestone, Barry, and Bennett Harrison
   1982   The Deindustrialization of America: Plant Closings, Community Abandonment, and the Dismantling of Basic Industry. New York: Basic Books.
Chubb, John E., and Terry M. Moe
   1990   Politics, Markets, and America's Schools. Washington, D.C.: The Brookings Institute.
Cloward, Richard, and Lloyd Ohlin
   1960   Delinquency and Opportunity. Glencoe, Ill: Free Press.
Comer, James P.
   1972   Beyond Black and White. New York: Quadrangle Books.
Curry, G. David, and Irving A. Spergel
   1988   "Gang homicide, delinquency, and community." Criminology 26:381-405.
Feldman, Leonard
   1990   "Evaluating the impact of family preservation services in New Jersey." Trenton, N.J.: New Jersey Division of Youth and Family Services.
Figueira-McDonough, Josefina
   1991   "Community structure and delinquency: A typology." Social Service Review 65:68-91.
Gans, Herbert J.
   1990   "The dangers of the underclass: Its harmfulness as a planning concept." New York: Russell Sage Foundation, Working Paper # 4.
Geis, Gilbert
   1965   "Juvenile gangs." Washington, D.C.: President's Committee on Juvenile Delinquency and Youth Crime.
Goldstein, Herman
   1977   Policing a Free Society. Cambridge, Mass.: Ballinger Publishing.
Goldstein, Paul J.
   1985   "The drugs-violence nexus: A tripartite conceptual framework." Journal of Drug Issues 15:493-506.
Gouldner, Alvin
   1968   "The sociologist as partisan: Sociology and the welfare state." The American Sociologist May: 103-116.
Hagedorn, John M.
   1988   People and Folks: Gangs, Crime, and the Underclass in a Rustbelt City. Chicago: Lakeview.
   1989a   "Roots of Milwaukee's underclass." Milwaukee, Wis.: Milwaukee County Department of Health and Human Services.
   1989b   "Study of youth released from residential treatment, day treatment, and group homes in 1989." Milwaukee, Wis.: Milwaukee County Department of Health and Human Services.

540 HAGEDORN

Huff, C. Ronald
   1989   "Youth gangs and public policy." Crime and Delinquency 35:524-537.
Jencks, Christopher
   1989   "Who is the underclass—and is it growing." Focus 12:14-31.
Johnson, Bruce, Terry Williams, Kojo Dei, and Harry Sanabria
   1989   "Drug abuse in the inner city." In Drugs and the Criminal Justice System, ed. Michael
           Tonry and James Q. Wilson, Chicago: University of Chicago.
Kamerman, Sheila B., and Alfred J. Kahn
   1989   "Social services for children, youth, and families in the United States." Greenwich,
           Conn.: The Annie E. Casey Foundation.
Kasarda, John D.
   1985   "Urban change and minority opportunities." In The New Urban Reality, ed. Paul E.
           Peterson, 33-65, Washington, D.C.: The Brookings Institute.
Kornblum, William, and Terry Williams
   1985   Growing Up Poor. Lexington, Mass: Lexington Books.
Lindblom, Charles E.
   1959   "The Science of 'Muddling Through.' " Public Administrative Review 19:79-88.
Lipsky, Michael
   1980   Street-Level Bureaucracies: Dilemmas of the Individual in Public Services. New York:
           Russell Sage.
Marris, Peter, and Martin Rein
   1967   Dilemmas of Social Reform, Poverty and Community Action in the United States.
           Chicago: University of Chicago.
Massey, Douglas S., and Mitchell L. Eggers
   1990   "The ecology of inequality: Minorities and the concentration of poverty, 1970-1980."
           American Journal of Sociology 95:1153-1188.
Meyer, John M., and Brian Rowan
   1981   "Institutionalized organizations: Formal structure as myth and ceremony." In Complex
           Organizations: Critical Perspectives, ed. Mary Zey-Ferrell and Michael Aiken, 303-321.
           Glenview, Ill.: Scott, Foresman, and Company.
Miller, Walter
   1990   "Why the United States has failed to solve its youth gang problem." In Gangs In
           America, ed. C. Ronald Huff, 263-287. Beverly Hills, Calif.: Sage.
Mills, C. Wright
   1959   The Sociological Imagination. London: Oxford University Press.
Moore, Joan W.
   1985   "Isolation and stigmatization in the development of an underclass: The case of Chicano
           gangs in East Los Angeles." Social Problems 33:1-10.
   1991   Going Down to the Barrio. Philadelphia: Temple University Press.
Moore, Joan W., and Ronald Edari
   1990a "Survey of Chips clients: Final report." Milwaukee, Wis.: University of Wisconsin-
           Milwaukee Urban Research Center.
   1990b "Youth initiative needs assessment survey: Final report:." Milwaukee, Wis.: University of
           Wisconsin-Milwaukee.
Moynihan, Daniel P.
   1969   Maximum Feasible Misunderstanding: Community Action in the War on Poverty. New
           York: The Free Press.
Nelson, Douglas
   1988   "Recognizing and realizing the potential of 'family preservation.' " Washington, D.C.:
           Center for the Study of Social Policy.
Nelson, Kristine, Miriam J. Landsman, and Wendy Deutelman
   1990   "Three Models of Family-Centered Placement Prevention Services." Child Welfare 69:3-21.
Perkins, Useni Eugene
   1987   Explosion of Chicago's Black Street Gangs. Chicago: Third World Press.
Piven, Frances Fox, and Richard A. Cloward
   1971   Regulating the Poor: The Functions of Public Welfare. New York: Pantheon.

1987   "The contemporary relief debate." In The Mean Season: The Attack on the Welfare State,
          ed. Fred Block, Richard A. Cloward, Barbara Ehrenreich, and Frances Fox Piven, 45-108.
          New York: Pantheon.
Ricketts, Erol, and Ronald Mincy
    1988   "Growth of the underclass: 1970-1980." Washington, D.C.: Changing Domestic Priorities
              Project, The Urban Institute.
Ricketts, Erol, Ronald Mincy, and Isabel V. Sawhill
    1988   "Defining and measuring the underclass." Journal of Policy Analysis and Management
              7:316-325.
Sampson, Robert J.
    1987   "Urban black violence: The effect of male joblessness and family disruption." American
              Journal of Sociology 93:348-382.
Schlossman, Steven, and Michael Sedlak
    1983   "The Chicago Area Project revisited." Santa Monica, Calif.: Rand Corporation.
Schlossman, Steven L., Gail Zellman, and Richard Schavelson
    1984   Delinquency Prevention in South Chicago. Santa Monica, Calif.: Rand Corporation.
Schorr, Lisbeth
    1988   Within our Reach. New York: Doubleday.
Schuerman, John R., Tina L. Pzepnicki, Julia H. Littell, and Stephen Budde
    1990   "Some intruding realities." Chicago: University of Chicago, Chapin Hall Center for
              Children.
Shaw, Clifford R., and Henry D. McKay
    1969   Juvenile Delinquency and Urban Areas. Chicago: University of Chicago.
Short, James F.
    1990a   "Gangs, neighborhoods, and youth crime." Houston, Tex.: Sam Houston State University
              Criminal Justice Center.
    1990b   "New wine in old bottles? Change and continuity in American gangs." In Gangs in
              America, ed. C. Ronald Huff, 223-239, Beverly Hills, Calif.: Sage.
Short, James F., and Fred L. Strodtbeck
    1965   Group Process and Gang Delinquency. Chicago: University of Chicago.
Sorrentino, Anthony
    1959   "The Chicago Area Project after 25 years." Federal Probation 23:40-45.
Spergel, Irving A., and G. David Curry
    1990   "Strategies and perceived agency effectiveness in dealing with the youth gang problem."
              In Gangs in America, ed. C. Ronald Huff, 288-309, Beverly Hills, Calif.: Sage.
Stack, Carol B.
    1974   All Our Kin. New York: Harper Torchback.
Sullivan, Mercer L.
    1989   Getting Paid: Youth Crime and Work in the Inner City. Ithaca, N.Y.: Cornell University
              Press.
Suttles, Gerald D.
    1968   The Social Order of the Slum. Chicago: University of Chicago.
Taylor, Carl
    1990   Dangerous Society. East Lansing, Mich.: Michigan State University Press.
Thrasher, Frederick
    [1927]
    1963   The Gang. Chicago: University of Chicago.
Trotter, Joe William
    1985   Black Milwaukee: The Making of an Industrial Proletariat 1915-1945. Chicago:
              University of Illinois.
Vigil, Diego
    1988   Barrio Gangs. Austin, Tex.: University of Texas Press.
Weick, Karl E.
    1976   "Educational organizations as loosely coupled systems." Administrative Science Quarterly
              21:1-19.

542 HAGEDORN

White, Sammis, John F. Zipp, Peter Reynolds, and James R. Paetsch
    1988   "The Changing Milwaukee Industrial Structure." Milwaukee, Wis.: University of Wisconsin-Milwaukee, Urban Research Center.

Whyte, William Foote
    1943   Street Corner Society. Chicago: University of Chicago.

Wilson, James Q.
    1990   "Can government agencies be managed?" The Bureaucrat 9:29-33.

Wilson, William Julius
    1985   "Cycles of deprivation and the underclass debate." Social Service Review 59:541-559.
    1987   The Truly Disadvantaged. Chicago: University of Chicago.
    1991   "Studying inner-City social dislocations: The challenge of public agenda research." American Sociological Review 56:1-14.

Wineman, Steven
    1984   The Politics of Human Services. Boston: South End Press.

Yuan, Ying-Ying T.
    1990   "Evaluation of AB 1562 in-home care demonstration projects." Sacramento, Calif.: Walter R. McDonald and Associates.

[25]

The Little Village Project: A Community Approach to the Gang Problem

Irving A. Spergel and Susan F. Grossman

Based on substantial preliminary evidence, a four-year Gang Violence Reduction Project has demonstrated its effectiveness in terms of process and outcome. An innovative approach in the prevention and control of a serious gang violence problem was based on key interrelated strategies of community mobilization, social intervention, suppression, opportunities provision, organizational development, and targeting. A team of community youth workers, tactical police officers, adult probation officers, and representatives of a neighborhood organization operated under the aegis of the Chicago Police Department. Of special interest was the interrelated practice roles of police tactical officers and community youth workers, many of whom were former gang members.

Key words: *community; gangs; police; violence; youths*

Community organization and direct services are not easily combined in the modern lexicon of social work methods. The current rhetoric distinguishing community and personal empowerment from various treatment modalities, however defined, may be insufficient for planning and dealing with the complex problems of troubled and troublesome people in fragmented, impoverished, and segregated communities (Mondros & Wilson, 1994). An older tradition of service delivery, interagency coordination, and social reform may need to be reinvigorated in more interactive and creative ways (Brager, Specht, & Torczyner, 1987; Ross, 1967). The complex present-day problems of juvenile delinquency and street gang crime may be a means to develop and test new service delivery, interagency coordination, and institutional reform strategies.

Youth gang crime and delinquency are major social problems that are no longer confined to inner-city areas. Both are now present in small as well as medium-size cities, suburban areas, and rural areas (Curry, Ball, & Decker, 1995; Klein, 1995a; Miller, in press; Spergel, 1995). However, there is no "hard" evidence that any specific social services or a suppression strategy has by itself contributed to the prevention or reduction of gang crime—either gang violence or gang-related drug dealing. Claims by various social intervention projects (for example, Goldstein, Glick, Carthon, & Blancero, 1994) or police departments about effective reduction of the problems have not been supported by good evidence. Gang crime fluctuates, is often seasonal and cyclical, and is more serious at some times and less so in others (Illinois Criminal Justice Information Authority, 1996; Klein,

1995b). Nevertheless, the trend for gang crime, especially gang violence, has been upward in scope and severity at least since the mid-1980s.

Traditional outreach, youth work, and gang work have emphasized direct counseling, crisis intervention, mediation, or mentoring and most recently has targeted younger at-risk youths. Group work interest in the youth gang problem has a long history (Puffer, 1912; Spergel, 1995; Thrasher, 1927). Street gang work flourished in the late 1940s through the early 1960s but declined until the early 1990s. Currently, youth gang work is experiencing a rebirth within a broader, more collaborative interagency and community framework in a variety of contexts: schools, inner-city neighborhoods, American Indian reservations, residential centers, and prisons.

Evaluation of a series of single-dimensional social outreach programs in the 1960s and 1970s suggested little positive impact of these efforts alone. Miller (1962) in Boston and Gold and Mattick (1974) in Chicago reported no positive changes resulting from the programs they assessed; Klein (1968), in his evaluation of a Los Angeles County probation project, reported negative effects. Spergel, Castellano, Pleas, and Brown (1969) and Spergel (1995), in their evaluations of the Woodlawn Organization's Youth Manpower Project in Chicago, stated that the project assisted in the development of two major criminal gang structures—the Blackstone Rangers, later the Black P. Stone Nation and more recently the El Rukns, and the Devil's Disciples, later the Black Gangster Disciples, currently the largest gang in Illinois. Fragmentation of program and policy, lack of cooperation, and conflict among social and criminal justice agencies and local and national community organizations may have indirectly contributed to the failure of many gang control and prevention efforts.

Police interest in street gangs in their current serious criminal form evolved in the 1960s in Chicago and Los Angeles. Police responses, characterized by the creation of specialized gang units and a suppression or attack strategy, coincided with the weakening or demise of the social intervention approach. A suppression strategy by law enforcement came to be associated with increased arrests, improved prosecution, and longer sentences, but there was no consistent evidence of improved community control or a decline in the problem (Howell, 1996). Currently, suppression is the dominant approach in various social contexts: the local community, schools, public housing projects, or prison.

An effective approach to youth gang problems was developed in Philadelphia during the early 1970s. A Crisis Intervention Network (CIN) project involved a youth agency collaborating citywide with school personnel, police officers, adult probation officers, and a network of block clubs or small neighborhood resident groups. A sharp reduction of gang homicides followed and was associated with the project throughout the 1970s. However, an evaluation of this project was not conducted. Moreover, during this period a gang drug economy arose and may have mitigated the violence aspect of the gang problem. Further, some questions were raised about a change in police recording practices, which may have been related to changing homicide rates (Klein, Maxson, & Miller, 1995; Spergel, 1995).

The Little Village Gang Violence Reduction Project in Chicago represents an interorganizational and community approach to the youth gang problem in its most violent form. This approach is characterized by a team of community youth workers, probation officers, tactical police officers, and a community organization carrying out interrelated strategies involving social intervention, social opportunities provision, social control, and gang suppression within a framework of community activism. Applying the model in the community has reduced the problem of gang violence in Little Village in comparison to control areas in Little Village and elsewhere in Chicago over a four-year demonstration period (Spergel & Grossman, 1996). A principal factor in the reduction of gang violence has been the close collaboration of community youth workers, many who are themselves former gang members, and police officers, as well as probation officers and representatives of local organizations and residents through targeting hard-core gang youths (that is, those who possess guns, are repeat offenders, and are influentials in gang crime), particularly those who are in their middle to late teenage years or early 20s. The process of collaboration of workers from disparate agencies is of special interest in this discussion.

Little Village Project Model

The Little Village Gang Violence Reduction Project is a variation and further elaboration of the Philadelphia CIN Project. The Little Village Project also is based on a research and development process conducted between 1987 and 1991. The project is currently related to a follow-up national comprehensive, communitywide approach to gang prevention, intervention, and suppression being tested in 10 other cities. Funding for these initiatives has come mainly from the Bureau of Justice Assistance and the Office of Juvenile Justice and Delinquency Prevention (OJJDP) of the U.S. Department of Justice. The elements of the approach, as indicated above, consist of the following interrelated strategies (Spergel et al., 1994): community mobilization, opportunities provision, social intervention, suppression, organizational change and development, and targeting.

Community Mobilization

Community mobilization is the involvement of local citizens and organizations, including local residents and groups, youth agencies, police and probation officers, and former gang youths, in a common enterprise. Not only community and agency leaders but also street-level staff must be coordinated into a team. This integration is particularly important in communities with a chronic gang problem that are disorganized or seriously fragmented in their approach to that problem and where high levels of gang activity, especially violence, are present.

Opportunities Provision

This opportunities provision is based on the premise that relevant opportunities, such as more and better jobs, special education programs, and training programs, are critical to meeting the needs of low-income youths at particular points in their developmental cycles. For example, training and job opportunities should be accessible to older gang youths who, for a variety of reasons such as maturation and pressures to raise a family, may be ready to leave the gang. Remedial educational programs and alternative schools as well as work on family support structures may be required for younger youths at risk of becoming gang members.

Social Intervention

Social intervention refers to outreach to gang youths in the streets or in problematic social contexts and is based on the assumption that many youths are not able to use available opportunities to become adequately connected to legitimate social institutions. The primary purpose of the social intervener is to mainstream alienated youths. Social intervention must be ecological in nature, dealing appropriately with the individual, the gang structure, and the environmental resources in an interactive and interdependent way. The various modalities of social intervention—crisis counseling; individual and family counseling; and referral for services and resources such as drug treatment, jobs, training, educational programs, and some recreation—must be related not only to case management, advocacy, and coordination of agency programs, but also to resource development in particular social and physical contexts.

Suppression

Suppression for purposes of gang control requires the application of a variety of informal as well as formal controls on the behavior of individual youths and the structure and process of their gangs. Not only supervision and surveillance, arrest, probation, and imprisonment, but also positive communication with youths, information sharing with other agency service and control providers, and joint decision making among agency and community group representatives are essential elements of social control. Suppression also must be viewed as an integral component related to the other strategies described here.

Organizational Change and Development

Units of workers within and across key organizations must collaborate through a closely knit structure that develops a common set of objectives for reducing and preventing gang crime and mainstreaming gang youths or those at risk. The team must develop effective procedures to achieve these objectives. Mutual trust, interdependence, and high levels of morale need to evolve from a carefully supported and nurtured process of organizational change and development at the administrative level as well.

Targeting

A team of workers from different disciplines must be established to target specific youths, gangs, and social contexts who or which induce crime situations. Consensus must be achieved about who and what should be targeted in a particular community. Limited resources must be combined and focused on certain aspects of the problem. Essential to targeting is clarity and consistency of definition about who is a gang youth, what is a gang, and what is a gang incident. Only a relatively small number of youths in particular gangs are likely to be highly at risk or chronic gang offenders. The target youths often are from troubled or dysfunctional families and are located in certain neighborhoods, hangouts, schools, parks, streets, stores, or school buses (Spergel et al., 1994).

Little Village and the Gang Problem

The Little Village community was selected as a test of this strategic model. Criteria for selection were that the community had a serious problem of gang violence and preferably only a moderate drug problem, a more complex problem when interrelated with gang violence. There had to be sufficient institutional and community strengths to produce a significant and measurable program effect. The ages of the youths to be targeted, initially 17 to 24 years, were determined on the basis of the requirements of a Federal Urban Violence Reduction block grant, mandating that the age group responsible for most of the serious gang violence be targeted.

Until the 1970s Little Village, or La Villita, was a community of aging Central Europeans residing in small bungalows and apartment buildings. In 1992 Little Village had a population of 80,000, of which more than 90 percent were Mexican and Mexican American. It is a low-income area but does not have much public housing and is not one of the poorest communities in Chicago. Currently in the community is a wide array of small businesses and educational, medical, social, cultural, and religious institutions. A sizable number of factories are in the area, which provide jobs for the local population. The community, southwest of Chicago's central business district, consists of six beats of the 10th District of the Chicago Police Department. These beats became the boundaries for program implementation and evaluation purposes.

Gang violence in Little Village involved chronic, serious turf fighting mainly between two gangs: the Latin Kings and the Two Six. Many members of the two gangs had known each other for years, had attended the same elementary schools, and were occasionally from the same immediate or extended families. Each gang comprised about 10 to 15 sections identified by the names of particular neighboring streets or aggregations of such streets. The Latin Kings were the older, more established gang that lived in the eastern section in somewhat poorer three-story apartment housing. The Two Six comprised younger youths and lived in the western section in better bungalow-type housing with somewhat larger families.

The two gangs accounted for about 70 percent of the serious gang violence (gang homicides, batteries with firearms, and assaults with firearms) in Little Village. Furthermore, older gang youths, ages 17 to 24 and mainly male, accounted for about 75 percent of the serious gang violence in the target area. The Latin Kings were the more violent and criminal group; the Two Six engaged in more property crime. About 90 percent of the youths initially contacted ($n = 108$) by the project were already known to the Cook County Adult Criminal Court.

Gang Violence Reduction Project

The goal was the absolute or relative reduction of serious violence among gang youths served in the project, compared to similar nonserved or noncontacted gang youths in the area or across similar gang areas over time. About 200 hard-core youths in the two gangs were targeted over the four-year project period. The mechanism for achievement of the goal was a team of workers consisting of a unit of police officers, including two full-time tactical officers, a part-time neighborhood relations sergeant, and a part-time clerical officer; a unit of three full-time Cook County Criminal Court adult probation officers, including a supervisor (and more recently one juvenile court intensive probation supervisor liaison); and a unit of community youth workers, including a full-time supervisor and two full-time and two part-time workers located at the School of Social Service Administration (SSA), University of Chicago, under the general direction of the senior author, who also acted as a coordinator of the overall project. Also closely related to the project team was the director of the Neighbors Against Gang Violence (NAGV), an independent local organization formed with the aid of the project coordinator and his assistant. NAGV comprised representatives of three Catholic churches, a Protestant church, a jobs agency, two boys and girls clubs, a major local youth agency, the local alderman's office, a large Latino community organization, and several local residents.

Each project unit carried out its organizational mission and simultaneously targeted hard-core gang youths in a collaborative fashion. Initial contacts were generally made by community youth workers, who were based on the streets. The targeted gang youths also were known to other units of the project through arrest, probation, family work, recreation, and religious contacts. One marked distinction from the original design of the project was that NAGV workers, although expected to encourage the development of local services and provide an interagency coordination function, instead performed mainly family services and recreational functions, focusing on younger male siblings in the families of the targeted youths. Early in the development of NAGV, several communitywide neighborhood meetings were held, although there was limited follow-up of concerns expressed by neighborhood residents and insufficient involvement by nonproject local organizations in the work of the Gang Violence Reduction Project. The project did not attempt and was not able to address general problems of interagency fragmentation and community development.

Over time, a high degree of interrelatedness and consistency of objectives and field operations developed among project workers. The tactical officers were on the streets at least four nights a week from 4:30 PM to midnight and later. Occasionally they were in court in the mornings or on special assignment. The community youth workers worked similar late afternoon and night hours but on a staggered basis so that all nights and days of the week were covered. In addition to street contacts, much of the community youth workers' time was taken up with job placement, school referrals and transfers, and occasional court appearances.

The probation officers were on duty two or three nights per week. Their caseloads were more inclusive of different types of gang offenders, particularly drug dealers or those convicted of drug offenses, than those of the police and community youth workers and included gang youths who were not from the immediate Little Village area. The NAGV workers, particularly the director who was the organization's only full-time worker, seemed to be available almost all of the time. The team members, including NAGV, met at least once every two weeks for general reporting, project development, and special targeting of youths who were recently most actively involved in violent activities. The group also met periodically for case management purposes, that is, to exchange information and plan treatment and contacts for youths in the program. These case management sessions lasted up to two hours and were conducted over a two-month period two or three times per year. More than 200 youths were assessed as to progress and treatment planning over each series of case management meetings.

The project workers regularly met for formal meetings at the probation office in the Little Village community. Sometimes meetings were held at the 10th District police station, although such meetings were not always comfortable for community youth workers, several of whom as former gang members were well known to some nonproject police officers. Meetings were also held at the SSA. Occasionally the district police commander, liaison officers of the police department's Research and Development Division, and the deputy chief of probation as well as the associate director of the Illinois Criminal Justice Information Authority (the State Planning Agency) attended project meetings. Each component unit also had separate weekly meetings in its own agency setting. Each unit continued to report to its administration and abide by its overall departmental regulations. Nevertheless, mechanisms were devised to facilitate almost daily communication and interaction. All of the workers had beepers, and police officers and probation workers had agency radios. Several police officers and community youth workers had cellular telephones. All of the police officers, community youth workers, and probation officers had access to and generally used protective vests. They also used their own or agency vehicles and regularly observed, but did not necessarily interact with, each other openly in the community.

Project Worker Relationships

Community Youth Workers and Police Officers

The most unusual and innovative relationships that developed were those between the police tactical officers and the community youth workers. The two tactical officers were in their late 20s and early 30s, originally with limited experience in dealing with gangs. Only one was of part-Mexican ancestry. The two officers had some college credit. All of the community youth workers were in their 20s, Mexican American, and from the target neighborhood. They were either former gang influentials or had grown up in the company of gang members. The community youth work supervisor and one of the senior community youth workers were college graduates; one community youth worker had a year of junior college, and two others were completing general equivalency diploma (GED) or evening high school classes. One had spent eight years in prison for a gang homicide; two had police records but had not served time in prison. Whereas the two tactical officers had been with the project since its inception four years earlier, the community youth workers had been on board for shorter, varying periods. During the first two years of the project, a half dozen community youth workers had to be replaced, mainly for reasons related to

deficiencies in job performance. A few of the community youth workers were arrested for a variety of crimes off the job, such as stalking, traffic offenses, and probation violation.

Police and community youth workers shared a deep commitment to the project's goals and objectives. Police continued to be identified with their police peers in the tactical units but did not focus on making a certain number of arrests per day. The community youth workers functioned as youth workers but also were closely identified with the legitimate aspirations and interests of youths in the gangs from which they had originated. They were deeply concerned about gang violence and were prepared to reduce it by nearly any means possible.

Each of the workers, especially the police officers and community youth workers, sought information that would contribute to the project mission and shared such information with each other formally and informally. It was easier for probation officers and the neighborhood organizers to share information and collaborate with other staff; they were not at opposite ends of the ideology pole. The community youth workers and police officers were embedded in networks of relationships and situations that made teamwork problematic at first. The officers had to learn to communicate with gang youths in a manner that demonstrated genuine concern for the welfare of the youths and their families; they had to be as much concerned with prevention as with arrest. They learned to understand the youths. The officers referred the youths to community youth workers for jobs and school programs and collaborated with them but were careful not to be seen as too closely affiliated to avoid threatening the relationships of the workers with the gang members.

At first the project's police officers were regarded as "kiddy cops" by their peer officers. When the officers first began to talk to gang youths, they were regarded as gang members themselves by local residents, who sometimes reported their activities to the police. Project officers moved about in their unmarked cars, getting to know gang sections. They were soon able to identify the various gang structures, leaders, and hard-core youths to be targeted.

The officers were instrumental in solving a high percentage of aggravated batteries and homicides in and out of the area in which local gang youths were involved. The other district tactical officers eventually came to depend on the project officers for critical information and advice about gang problems. County police and agents of the Federal Bureau of Investigation also found their information and contacts valuable. The district's police tactical teams began to use a similar approach as that of the project police, learning to better communicate with gang youths and in the process to more effectively carry out their law enforcement functions.

The community youth workers were embedded in a network of gang relationships although they were no longer engaged in fighting or in criminal behavior. The workers not only had to develop new quasi-professional skills related to referrals of gang youths to agency services or job placement, but they also had to learn to collaborate with police and probation officers in such a way that gang conflict was prevented or at least controlled. To the extent possible, the workers assisted the police to avoid arrest of the wrong youths and helped gang youths avoid probation violations by getting them to report to their probation officers on time. The workers learned to trust the project police officers and provided them with many leads to solve gang crime incidents.

The community youth workers were able to maintain the respect of gang youths while continuing to influence them through advice, counseling, job placement and school referrals, and encouragement to become more closely aligned with legitimate institutions and practices. Gang members eventually came to understand and accept not only the community youth workers' helping role but also their relationship with police and probation officers. This understanding helped gang youths avoid harassment from the police and incarceration and made life more tolerable in the community. Gang youths were helped to better distinguish "good" and "bad" cops and were advised on how to handle the latter in a "better way." They respected the new role of the community youth workers in protecting the resident bystanders as well as themselves from gang shootings.

Other Project Personnel

All of the project workers were enmeshed in a variety of interdependent project relationships. Probation staff sought the assistance of community youth workers in getting probationers to show up for regular contacts, to obtain jobs, and to return to school. The NAGV workers assisted community youth workers with supplementary information about gang youths, contacts with family, and services for training and jobs. The NAGV workers were quick to alert project workers to new graffiti, shootings, and community situations that could lead to further intergang conflict. This information was shared with both police officers and community youth workers.

A much closer relationship between the police and probation officers was established. The police officers now shared information about a gang case with probation officers within a matter of minutes, rather than weeks and having to wait for information to filter through agency channels. Police officers, probation officers, and community youth workers together supervised gang youths at graffiti "paint outs"; youths who put up the graffiti now expunged it. Project workers together were involved in softball games with gang members from the warring groups without mishap, although the games were played outside the neighborhood. Police and probation officers and community youth workers participated together with various factions of gang youths in group counseling sessions at the SSA. These sessions, however, did not progress to the point that members of the opposing gangs were present in the same session. At the same time, members of the two gangs occasionally participated with each other in basketball games and more general training workshops on the border between, or outside, the two gang territories. They also participated together in local citizen group meetings sponsored by the various project units.

The close relationships of police officers, community youth workers, probation officers, and NAGV workers with each other in working with hard-core gang youths contributed to project staff cohesion and high morale. All of the workers were highly visible to each other in the community, contributing to a high level of accountability and quality job performance. For example, the community youth workers could not "goof off" or engage in nonconstructive behavior (for example, drinking beer) with the gang youths in the streets or not show up for scheduled interagency meetings. The police officers maintained a high level of professional activity and came to be well respected by the gang youths, the community youth workers, and neighborhood residents.

Integration of Research and Demonstration

A key aspect of the project was the integration of program operations and evaluation. The SSA research team was the sole evaluator; although the team worked closely with the community youth workers, it was separate from them. The evaluators regularly disseminated information about the content, nature, and scope of the gang problem and progress of the project. They obtained aggregate crime data from the Crime Analysis Section of the Chicago Police Department and the Early Warning System of the Illinois Criminal Justice Information Authority. The evaluation team identified certain gangs, streets, age groups, and shifts in crime patterns that were useful to the program team. For example, information that more juveniles ages 14 to 16 were becoming involved in serious gang crime was the basis for lowering the age of the youths to be targeted. Information that most gang crimes were occurring between 6:00 PM and midnight and that female gang members were not substantially involved in serious gang violence aided the project's focus.

The evaluators performed a variety of tasks essential to measuring project impact and outcome. Community surveys of residents ($N = 200$) and local community organizations or agency representatives ($N = 100$) at two time periods on their perceptions about the nature and scope of the gang problem in Little Village and the comparison community—Pilsen—were useful in assessing changing levels of gang crime and the effects of policing with respect to these levels. Data from interviews of three cohorts of youths ($n = 194$) entering the program, as well as police data, court data, and detention data, were critical in determining the effectiveness of the project. Police data on the nontargeted

youths arrested along with members of the target gangs at program entry were useful in the construction of control groups. Also critical were tracking data. Each project worker was surveyed as to what services and activities were provided and what progress was made by program youths. The extent of coordination among project workers was also determined. The aggregate results of each periodic evaluation were given to program personnel at intervals varying from three months to one year. These analyses provided preliminary but important estimates about the differential effects and effectiveness of the project.

Community youth workers were essential to the evaluators in locating and relocating targeted youths for yearly research interviews. The youth workers assisted in obtaining consent from the youths and their parents for interviews. They corrected information about youths' names and addresses (gang youths had street names and often used aliases). The meaning of the grouped data also was more clearly established with the aid of interpretations from community youth workers, police officers, and other project workers. However, names or identifying information about gang youths was not shared by researchers with program personnel or anyone else. Confidentiality and protection of data were strictly observed.

Results

Process

Although only preliminary data are available on the effectiveness of the Gang Violence Reduction Project, the results appear to be consistently positive. Analysis of data for the 125 targeted youths, mainly cohort I and cohort II over three years, on whom there is program information thus far, indicates that almost all (98.4 percent) had contact with community youth workers, and a large proportion (36.8 percent) were contacted and sometimes arrested by project by police. Smaller percentages were contacted or served by probation officers (10.4 percent) and NAGV (14.4 percent). Almost half (45.6 percent) of the targeted youths received contacts or services from more than one group of project workers, primarily police officers and community youth workers. The majority received some kind of informal counseling or support from project personnel (95.2 percent). Family contacts were made for almost two-thirds (64.0 percent) of the targeted individuals served. Similarly, about two-thirds (65.6 percent) of the gang youths were involved in some type of athletic activity (basketball nights, baseball games) with project staff. Assistance or job-related referrals were made for nearly two-thirds (64.0 percent), and slightly more than half (53.6 percent) received assistance or referral related to a school problem. Finally, police and probation personnel reported that they had engaged in suppression activities for 31.2 percent of the 125 youths.

The impact of the project (as well as youth maturation) on school and job attainment appears to be striking. The proportion of individuals in cohorts I and II who graduated from high school or received GED certificates rose from 25.3 percent at the first baseline interview to 51.6 percent at the third annual interview. Similarly, the proportion of individuals in cohorts I and II who were currently employed increased from 30.8 percent at the first interview to 76.0 percent at the third interview. The increase was smaller for the Latin Kings, but employment for members of this gang was more steady over the three years of project service (Spergel & Grossman, 1996).

Outcome

Arrests for a three-year preprogram interval for targeted youths were compared to a three-year program period for control youths (Grossman et al., 1996). The program youths experienced a relative reduction in gang crime, especially gang violence, compared to the two groups of control youths (that is, nontargeted gang youths receiving some services but not receiving coordinated intensive service or contacts and nontargeted or nonserved contacted youths from the same gangs who were arrested for the same incidents in the first program year). Crime patterns of program youths were compared not only with those of other similar groups but with themselves in the preprogram period, controlling for age in a modified cohort analysis (Grossman, Spergel, & Jacob, 1997).

Table 1 presents the results of a multivariate analysis using, as an outcome measure, police data on arrests for violent crime—which included homicide, aggravated battery, battery, aggravated assault, assault, armed robbery, and robbery—in the three-year project period for program and comparison group youths. The two comparison groups were generated from police arrest data about individuals arrested along with the project youths from cohort I. The first of these groups included individuals who were not known to project staff ($n = 85$). The second group consisted of individuals who had had limited contacts or services from the project team even though they were never directly targeted for service or contacts ($n = 42$). Variables controlling for the influence of age, gang affiliation, prior criminal history, targeted versus comparison group status, and "contact" nontargeted comparison group status were

Table 1

Model Predicting Arrests for Violent Crime in the Three-Year Project Period

Variable	ß	t	$p > t$
Intercept	1.173179	2.891	0.0043*
Individual is younger than 19	−0.103985	−0.569	0.5700
Individual is a Two Six member vs. a Latin Kings member	0.080611	0.596	0.5516
Arrests for violent crime in the three years before the project	0.201759	3.190	0.0016*
Individual is a project youth vs. a control group youth	0.158240	0.838	0.4027
Individual is control group youth who received services or was known to project staff vs. not receiving services or being a project youth	−0.341323	−1.876	0.0620
Individual is age 19 or older and a project youth vs. all others	−0.599957	−2.241	0.0261*

NOTES: Arrests for homicide, aggravated battery, battery, aggravated assault, assault, armed robbery, and robbery based on Chicago Policy Department classification. Overall adjusted R^2 for the model = .0790, $N = 216$, $df = 6$.
*The coefficient is statistically significant in the model.

included in the model, as was an interaction term controlling for both age and project service. Together these variables accounted for about 8 percent of the variance in arrests for violent crime in the three-year project period. The strongest predictor of outcomes was prior history; those who had been arrested for more violent crimes in the three-year preproject phase were more likely to be arrested for such offenses in the project period. Still, taking prior history into account, the project had a significant effect in reducing violent criminal activity, particularly for youths who were older when the project began. Those who were 19 or older did better over time and had fewer arrests when they received project services and contacts compared to project cases who were younger or to individuals from both comparison groups regardless of age. Similar analysis using the same variables for the combined first and second cohorts of project youths and control group cases revealed the same results for the interaction of age and service or contact variables (beta = 0.556392, $t = 2.418$, $p = .0163$, $N = 270$). None of the other variables, with the exception of prior arrests for violent crime, attained statistical significance in the equation.

However, looking at police arrest data in the third program year only, the younger age group did better during the program years than the older group. They did not do as well in the comparison of the three-year program versus three-year preprogram periods. Age or maturation and program effects interacted to produce different position results for these older youths.

Table 2 discusses self-reported crime data for youths from cohort I receiving coordinated services versus those who had contact with only community youth workers. The coordinated service group included youths who were served by community youth workers and police officers; police officers and NAGV; community youth workers and probation officers; community youth workers, police officers, and probation officers; community youth workers, police officers, and NAGV; or all four types of project team members. Three individuals were served by community youth workers and NAGV; however, they were not included in the coordinated service group because they were receiving the

same type of services (that is, variations of social intervention). Therefore, these three youths were excluded from the analysis, as were seven others who were interviewed but apparently received no services.

The coordinated services group had a significantly higher average number of reported total crime at the baseline interview compared to the noncoordinated group. Significant differences also existed at baseline in relation specifically to violent crimes; the coordinated services contact youths reported slightly more than twice the number of violent crimes on average compared to those receiving services from community youth workers only. This is consistent with the key objective of the project to target the most violent and criminal youths in the gangs; however, at the time of the third interview, a different picture emerged. The coordinated services contact group had averages similar to those in the noncoordinated group for all crimes as well as for violent and property crimes. The coordinated group had a slightly lower average number of reported days selling drugs and greater decreases over time in the number of reported crimes. Their average decrease between the first and third interviews for days selling drugs was slightly more than five times greater than those in the noncoordinated group; their declines were up to twice as great in the other categories of crime.

The results of the analysis of official police arrest data are similar to the outcomes for self-reported crimes (Table 3). In the first project year (October 1992 to September 1993), the coordinated services group had higher average numbers of arrests in all categories examined, with the exception of arrests for drug-related crimes (Table 4), which were identical for both groups. However, in the third project year (October 1994 to September 1995), differences between the groups were much smaller. In addition, in all categories in which declines occurred over time, the declines were greater for the coordinated services group. Further, the coordinated group had declines in both the Gang Violence Reduction Project (GVRP) and "Hotspots" violence indexes (see Table 3 for list of crimes), whereas the community youth workers only group experienced increases in

Table 2

Self-Reported Crimes for Individuals Receiving Coordinated Services versus Those Having Contact with Only Community Youth Workers, Comparing First Program Year and Third Program Year (First Cohort)

	Self-Reported Total Crimes						Violent Crimes[a]					
	At Baseline		At Third Interview		Difference		At Baseline		At Third Interview		Difference	
Group	M	N	M	N	M	N	M	N	M	N	M	N
Coordinated services	76.6*	28	11.1	28	−65.5 †††	28	46.6 *	27	8.3	27	−38.3 ††	27
Community youth workers only	37.5	25	6.1	25	−31.4 ††	25	20.5	26	3.5	26	−17.0 †	26
Total	58.2	53	8.7	53	−49.5 †††	53	33.8	53	5.9	53	−27.9 †††	53

	Average Property Crimes[b]						Average Days Selling Drugs					
	At Baseline		At Third Interview		Difference		At Baseline		At Third Interview		Difference	
Group	M	N	M	N	M	N	M	N	M	N	M	N
Coordinated services	29.8	28	2.6	28	−27.2 ††	28	154.7	27	69.3	27	−85.4	27
Community youth workers only	15.7	26	2.4	26	−13.3 ††	26	91.7	28	75.4	28	−16.3	28
Total	23.0	54	2.5	54	−20.5 †††	54	122.6	55	72.4	55	−50.2	55

Notes: For differences within groups between time periods: † $p \leq .05$, †† $p \leq .01$, ††† $p \leq .001$. For differences between groups within time periods: * $p \leq .05$.

[a] Includes robbery with and without a weapon, threats with and without a weapon, gang intimidation, battery with and without a weapon, homicide, and drive-by shootings.

[b] Includes writing gang and nongang graffiti, destroying property worth $300 or less, entering or breaking into a building to commit a theft, stealing a car for joy riding, and breaking into a car and stealing parts.

Table 3

Police Arrest Data for Individuals Receiving Coordinated Services versus Those Having Contact with Community Youth Workers Only: First Project Year versus Third Project Year

Group	Average No. All Arrests			Average No. of Arrests for GVRP Index Offenses[a]		
	First Project Year	Third Project Year	Difference	First Project Year	Third Project Year	Difference
Coordinated services (n = 31)	1.39**	0.65	−0.74 ††	0.26	0.19	−0.07
Community youth workers only (n = 31)	0.61	0.48	−0.13	0.10	0.16	+0.06
Total (n = 62)	1.00	0.56	−0.44 †	0.18	0.18	0.00

Group	Average No. of Arrests for Hotspots Violence Offenses[b]			Average No. of Arrests for Property-Related Offenses[c]		
	First Project Year	Third Project Year	Difference	First Project Year	Third Project Year	Difference
Coordinated services (n = 31)	0.16*	0.13	−0.03	0.61*	0.06	−0.55 ** ††
Community youth workers only (n = 31)	0.00	0.10	+0.10	0.16	0.16	0.00
Total (n = 62)	0.08	0.11	+0.03	0.39	0.11	−0.28 †

NOTES: For differences between groups within time periods: *p ≤ .05, **p ≤ .01. For differences within groups between time periods: †p ≤ .05, ††p ≤ .01. GVRP = Gang Violence Reduction Project.
[a] Includes robbery with and without a weapon, assault, aggravated assault, battery, aggravated battery, and murder.
[b] Includes aggravated battery, aggravated assault, and murder.
[c] Includes all arrests related to burglaries, thefts, motor vehicle damage and criminal trespass of motor vehicles, damage to property including graffiti, and trespass-related charges.

Table 4

Adult Police Arrest Data for Individuals Receiving Coordinated Services versus Those Having Contact with Community Youth Workers Only: First Project Year versus Third Project Year

Group	Average No. of Drug-Related Arrests[a]		
	First Year	Third Year	Difference
Coordinated services ($n = 31$)	0.06	0.16	+0.10
Community youth workers only ($n = 31$)	0.06	0.10	+0.04
Total ($n = 62$)	0.06	0.13	+0.07

[a]Includes possession of marijuana, possession of a controlled substance, and distribution or delivery of a controlled substance.

both these categories. The coordinated services group also underwent statistically significant declines in arrests for property-related crimes, whereas the noncoordinated group experienced no change.

The one category in which outcomes differed relative to self-reported crime was with respect to drug-related arrests for possession as well as for manufacture and delivery (Table 4). However, the number of arrests in this category was small. There was no evidence of increase in the most serious drug-related crimes of manufacture and delivery; most of the arrests related more to drug use or possession.

An additional analysis of first- versus third-year program periods, especially for the first cohort, controlling for respondent's age indicated similar patterns; the coordinated services–contact group generally experienced either greater declines or had lower averages of reported criminal activity in the third year, using self-report data, regardless of age. When official police data were used, differences between the youth workers only and coordinated groups were still present. However, differences between the two types of services–contact groups were greater among those who were younger. Again, the coordinated group had larger declines in arrests on average for younger and older program youths over time. Further analysis will focus on clarifying the aspects of the program and other characteristics of individuals—who seemed to have experienced greater decreases in criminal activity over time—under different conditions.

Aggregate crime data about the most serious gang-motivated violent incidents also indicated positive change. Little Village had the lowest increase in gang violence compared to six similar mainly Hispanic areas in Chicago with similar attributes and high levels of gang violence when a four-year program period was compared to an equivalent four-year preprogram interval (Grossman et al., 1996). The level of serious gang violence for the members of the Latin Kings and Two Six gangs generally (including those targeted and not targeted) was also lower or in some cases declined compared to other nontargeted or nonserved Latino or black gangs in the same police district for the same four-year program period compared to the four-year preprogram period.

Comparing Little Village and Pilsen at the beginning of the project and two years later indicated a greater statistically significant reduction in the perceived level of gang violence and gang property crime among residents ($N = 200$) and groups and organizations ($N = 100$) in Little Village. Further, Little Village residents viewed the police as more effective than Pilsen residents viewed them in addressing the gang problem in their community (Spergel & Grossman, 1996).

Conclusion

The Gang Violence Reduction Project was expected to target a significant number of hardcore and some peripheral gang members. Not only individual, but areawide rates of gang violence were to be lowered, relatively and absolutely, after a reasonable period. Furthermore, the perceptions of Little Village residents about rates of gang crime were expected to be lower compared to those of residents of Pilsen, an almost identical community nearby without the program.

The Gang Violence Reduction Project is a pioneering, cross-disciplinary, community-based effort to control and prevent serious gang crime, especially gang violence. Evidence of success was achieved based on realistic strategies generated within a theoretical framework consistent with social work values as well as theories from other disciplines, particularly social disorganization, opportunity, and anomie. The project idea is now being accepted as a possible extension of community policing. Integration of tactical police and adult probation efforts is planned. It is not clear, however, whether and how the community youth work component will be adapted.

Project ideas continue to be the basis for the development of two major programs from the OJJDP to prevent and control the gang problem in other large and medium-size cities of the United States: the OJJDP Comprehensive Communitywide Approach to Gang Prevention, Intervention, and Suppression Program and the Safe Futures Program. Of special interest to the office is further testing of the effectiveness of the combination of the community youth workers' and police officers' roles as part of a community-based approach in the reduction of the gang problem.

The Gang Violence Reduction Project may contribute to social work theory through its invigoration or further elaboration of the values of coordination as a key framework for the development of community organization practice. Community organization practice is not simplistically an issue of gaining power for those population groups who are disenfranchised. Practice should be based on realistic assumptions that social organization, community, and political systems often are complex, fragmented, and disassociated and can affect youths differently at different stages of development. Social workers can better address social problems through improved integration across organizational and community relationships. Methods of community organization, interagency coordination, and institutional change can be integrated through interrelated but complementary organizational and service delivery practices.

Furthermore, much of community organization practice must consider an individual outcome as well as organizational change. Analysis of and prescriptions for social problems must not be based on ideology or notions in the abstract but related to specific facts and concerns by clients themselves, including gang youths and residents in particular communities.

The response to social problems such as gang violence is often stereotypic or opportunistic for organizational development or political purposes. Nevertheless, the problem of inadequate agency or community response can be overcome through a local and broader community interactive and collaborative process with appropriate incentives and constraints as well as good leadership (Spergel, 1995). No single agency, community group, discipline, or approach alone is sufficient to successfully address a complex problem such as gang crime. ∎

References

Brager, G., Specht, H., & Torczyner, J. L. (1987). *Community organizing* (2nd ed.). New York: Columbia University Press.

Curry, G. D., Ball, R. A., & Decker, S. H. (1995). *Developing national estimates of gang-related crime.* (Report to the National Institute of Justice). St. Louis: University of Missouri, Department of Criminology and Criminal Justice.

Gold, M., & Mattick, H. W. (1974). *Experiment in the streets: The Chicago youth development project.* Ann Arbor: University of Michigan, Institute for Social Research.

Goldstein, A. P., Glick, B., Carthon, W., & Blancero, D. (1994). *The prosocial gang.* Thousand Oaks, CA: Sage Publications.

Grossman, S. F., Lyndes, K., Barrios, E., Littleton, A., Jacob, A., & Spergel, I. (1996). *The Little Village Gang Violence Reduction Project evaluation progress report.* Chicago: University of Chicago, School of Social Service Administration.

Grossman, S. F., Spergel, I. A., & Jacob, A. (1997). *Use of the Modified Cohort Design Analysis.* Chicago: University of Chicago, School of Social Service Administration.

Howell, J. C. (1996). *Review of youth programs.* Washington, DC: U.S. Department of Justice, Office of Juvenile Justice and Delinquency Prevention, National Youth Gang Center.

Illinois Criminal Justice Information Authority. (1996, August). *Street gangs and crime* [Research Bulletin]. Chicago: Author.

Klein, M. W. (1968). *From association to guilt: The group guidance project in juvenile gang intervention.* Los Angeles: University of Southern California, Youth Studies Center, & Los Angeles County Probation Department.

Klein, M. W. (1995a). *The American street gang.* New York: Oxford University Press.

Klein, M. W. (1995b). *Street gang cycles.* In J. Q. Wilson & J. Petersilia (Eds.), *Crime* (pp. 217–236). San Francisco: Institute for Contemporary Studies.

Klein, M. W., Maxson, C. L., & Miller, J. (1995). *The modern gang reader.* Los Angeles: Roxbury Press.

Miller, W. B. (1962). The impact of a "total community" delinquency control project. *Social Problems, 19,* 168–191.

Miller, W. B. (in press). *The growth of youth gang problems in the United States: 1970–1995.* Washington, DC: U.S. Department of Justice, Office of Juvenile Justice and Delinquency Prevention, National Youth Gang Center.

Mondros, J. B., & Wilson, S. (1994). *Organizing for power and environment.* New York: Columbia University Press.

Puffer, J. A. (1912). *The boy and his gang.* Boston: Houghton Mifflin.

Ross, M. G. (1967). *Community organization, theory and principles* (2nd ed.). New York: Harper & Row.

Spergel, I. A. (1995). *The youth gang problem: A community approach.* New York: Oxford University Press.

Spergel, I. A., Castellano, T., Pleas, J., & Brown, P. (1969, February). *Evaluation of the youth manpower demonstration of the Woodlawn Organization* (Submitted to the Office of Economic Opportunity). Chicago: University of Chicago, School of Social Service Administration.

Spergel, I. A., Chance, R., Ehrensaft, K., Regulus, T., Kane, C., Laseter, K., Alexander, A., & Oh, S. (1994, October). *Gang suppression and intervention: Community models* [Research summary]. Washington, DC: U.S. Department of Justice, Office of Juvenile Justice and Delinquency Prevention.

Spergel, I. A., & Grossman, S. F. (1996). *Evaluation of a gang violence reduction project: A comprehensive and integrated approach.* Chicago: University of Chicago, School of Social Service Administration.

Thrasher, F. M. (1927). *The gang.* Chicago: University of Chicago Press.

_____

Irving A. Spergel, PhD, is George Herbert Jones Professor, School of Social Service Administration, University of Chicago, 969 East 60th Street, Chicago, IL 60637; e-mail: iasperg@midway. uchicago.edu. Susan F. Grossman, PhD, is assistant professor, Loyola University School of Social Work, Chicago, and former research director, Gang Violence Reduction Project, School of Social Services, University of Chicago.
The Chicago Police Department (Agency Award No. D50401) and the Illinois Criminal Justice Information Authority (Agency Award No. 11866-01-02) funded the program and the research. All views and conclusions expressed in the article are those of the authors and do not necessarily represent those of the above agencies. Laura Anderson, Louis Arata, Javier Avila, Elisa Barrios, Lisa DeVivo, Ayad Jacob, Joshua Levy, Annot Littleton, Kathryn Lyndes, Rolando Sosa, and Kwai Ming Wa assisted with community gang problem assessment, project planning, data collection, access to youths, and data analysis.

Original manuscript received September 23, 1996
Accepted December 21, 1996

[26]

Gang Suppression Through Saturation Patrol, Aggressive Curfew, and Truancy Enforcement: A Quasi-Experimental Test of the Dallas Anti-Gang Initiative

Eric J. Fritsch
Tory J. Caeti
Robert W. Taylor

In 1996, the Dallas Police Department began an anti-gang initiative that was designed to reduce gang violence. Five defined target areas that were home to seven of the city's most violent gangs received overtime-funded officers to implement several different enforcement strategies. The strategies included saturation patrol and aggressive curfew and truancy enforcement. Control areas were selected, and preintervention and postintervention measures of gang violence and offenses that were reported to the police were analyzed. The findings indicated that aggressive curfew and truancy enforcement led to significant reductions in gang violence, whereas simple saturation patrol did not. In addition, there were no significant reductions in offenses reported to the police. The significance of these findings and policy implications is discussed.

For years, police agencies have pursued tactics designed to deal with the proliferation of gangs and gang violence. According to the National Youth Gang Survey, the primary strategy in many jurisdictions is suppression (Spergel and Curry 1990). Suppression tactics include tactical patrols by law enforcement, vertical prosecution by district attorneys, and intensive supervision by probation departments. Generally, suppression involves the arrest, prosecution, and incarceration of gang members. Although suppression is the primary strategy in many jurisdictions, it is also frequently viewed as the least effective (Spergel and Curry 1990).

In 1996, the Dallas Police Department received an anti-gang initiative grant from the Office of Community Oriented Policing Services to combat violent gang activity. The grant period lasted from June 1, 1996, through

ERIC J. FRITSCH: Assistant Professor, Department of Criminal Justice, University of North Texas. TORY J. CAETI: Assistant Professor, Department of Criminal Justice, University of North Texas. ROBERT W. TAYLOR: Professor and Chair, Department of Criminal Justice, University of North Texas.

May 31, 1997. In 1996, the city of Dallas had 79 gangs with 6,145 documented gang members. In addition, there were 1,332 gang-related incidents recorded in 1996. The Dallas Police Department targeted five areas, made up of a varying number of patrol beats, which were home to seven of the most violent gangs in Dallas. In the year preceding the grant, the targeted gangs accounted for 18 percent of the known gang members in Dallas and were responsible for approximately 35 percent of the gang-related violent crimes.

The primary objective of the grant was to fund overtime enforcement in the five targeted areas in hopes of significantly decreasing violent gang activity through suppression. Gang Unit officers teamed with Interactive Community Policing (ICP) officers to develop innovative enforcement strategies for each of the targeted areas. Subsequently, teams of six to eight officers were assembled and received overtime pay to implement the developed strategy. These officers were freed from calls for service and instead spent their time implementing and carrying out the particular enforcement strategy. Although tactics such as "buy-bust" operations and warrant service were employed during the grant period, the vast majority of overtime funds were spent on three suppression tactics: aggressive curfew enforcement—juvenile curfew ordinances were strictly enforced whenever suspected gang members were encountered;[1] aggressive truancy enforcement—officers worked closely with local school districts in enforcing truancy laws;[2] and saturation patrol—officers conducted high-visibility patrols in target areas, stopping and frisking suspected gang members or other suspicious persons that they observed and making arrests when appropriate. The research reported in this article assessed the effectiveness of these strategies in reducing gang-related violence and gang-related offenses reported to the police.

LITERATURE REVIEW

The Police Role in Dealing With Gangs

Several authors, while noting that gangs per se probably cannot be eradicated, believe that the police can manage and, in effect, suppress the more negative aspects of gang activity (Huff and McBride 1993; Owens and Wells 1993; Rush 1996). The various strategies adopted by law enforcement to deal with gangs have been well documented (Dart 1992; Huff and McBride 1993; Jackson and McBride 1996; Johnson, Webster, Connors, and Saenz 1995; Klein 1993, 1995; Knox 1994; Spergel 1995; Weston 1993). Some have advocated the use of specialized patrols, especially foot patrol (Wilson and Kelling 1989); others have embraced a philosophy best represented by the

GREAT program, which integrates schools and law enforcement and teaches resistance (Howell 1996); and still others have advocated traditional and non-traditional law enforcement suppression techniques (Houston 1996; Johnson et al. 1995; Needle and Stapleton 1983; Rush 1996). However, empirical evaluations of the prescribed strategies have been few in number.

Gang suppression by law enforcement has also often included a broad range of tactics that frequently have taken the form of crackdowns. Crackdowns typically have involved "a sharp increase in law enforcement resources applied to the previously under-enforced laws, with a clear goal of enhancing general deterrence of the misconduct" (Sherman 1990b, p. 2). Most often, crackdowns have been effective initially, have had a short residual deterrent effect, and have been followed by an eventual return to preintervention levels of crime (Sherman 1990b). Generally, greater successes have been found in strategies focusing on specific offenses, offenders, and places than by simply increasing presence (Sherman 1990b). Although Sherman (1990b) has provided an extensive review of police crackdowns, including those emphasizing suppression of drug sales, drunk driving, prostitution, subway crime, and various other serious and nonserious crimes, no gang-specific crackdowns were examined or discussed in his review.

Gang crackdowns have not been evaluated systematically (Klein 1995). Some authors have dismissed the use of the crackdown entirely. "In the case of youth gang interdiction, this tactic is analogous to an attempt to put out a forest fire with a water bucket" (Shelden, Tracy, and Brown 1997, p. 212). However, a crackdown can be, and often is, a coordinated effort by a law enforcement agency to stop a certain type of crime or an offender using more than simple police presence. Indeed, the role of crime analysis in directing and supporting police crackdowns is growing; however, to date, very little empirical research examining well-coordinated crackdowns directed by crime analysis has been conducted. The studies that have been done have shown dramatic results, as was the case in the Minneapolis "hot-spots" research (Sherman 1990b) and the Kansas City Gun Experiment (Sherman, Shaw, and Rogan 1995).

Gang problems and behaviors vary widely from city to city as well as within cities (Weisel and Painter 1997). In accordance, it is doubtful that one strategy will be effective across and within all jurisdictions. Some law enforcement agencies have adopted a philosophy of total suppression, in which any gang member or wanna-be has been targeted, such as in the Los Angeles Police Department's (LAPD) Community Resources Against Street Hoodlums (CRASH) (Freed 1986; Klein 1993). Others, such as the Los Angeles Sheriff's Operation Safe Streets (OSS), have adopted a philosophy of target suppression, in which the police have only targeted hard-core gang members (Freed 1986; Klein 1993). Still others, such as the Oxnard, California, Police Department's Gang-Oriented Comprehensive Action Program (GOCAP) and the Westminster, California, Tri-Agency Resource Gang Enforcement Team (TARGET), have focused on information sharing and intelligence gathering to identify, arrest, and successfully prosecute gang members (Kent and Smith 1994; Owens and Wells 1993).

Most of the current prescriptive literature has focused on community-oriented tactics. Some have recommended that the police stop trying to eradicate gangs and that they communicate with gang youths in such a way as to demonstrate respect, acceptance, and concern for gang youths (Spergel 1995). The literature has also concluded that law enforcement alone cannot solve the gang problem—in fact, the typical police organization is ill-equipped and poorly structured to deal with gangs (Rush 1996). Dealing with gangs requires a comprehensive approach that involves all members of the criminal justice community, schools, community leaders, and the like (Owens and Wells 1993; Rush 1996). A fundamental problem with all of the aforementioned strategies, but especially the latter, has been the lack of reliable, well-documented, well-designed, empirical evaluations of the strategies and tactics employed (Klein 1993, 1995; Knox 1994; Spergel 1995).[3] In fact, some of the evaluations of the tactics have been gleaned from newspapers (Freed 1986).

A recent review of several gang efforts has questioned the efficacy of police responses in dealing with the problem (Weisel and Painter 1997). In describing the gang enforcement tactics in five major cities in the United States, Weisel and Painter (1997) noted that "none of the agencies engaged in any identifiable long-term planning process or conducted research to monitor the changing nature of the problem. None . . . engaged in meaningful evaluations of effectiveness of specialized or other departmental efforts related exclusively to gang enforcement" (p. 83). In fact, some evaluative statements have been based on hunches because of the lack of empirical data. For example, Klein (1993) has said, "my informed hunch is that suppression programs, left to their own devices, may deter a few members but also increase the internal cohesiveness of the group" (p. 312). Indeed, much of the current literature has concluded that traditional law enforcement tactics alone will have little effect on reducing, managing, or suppressing gangs (Huff and McBride 1993; Rush 1996; Shelden et al. 1997; Spergel 1995).

Empirical Evaluations of the Effect of Police on Gang Activity

Spergel (1995) has concluded that the strategy of targeting gangs and gang members only for suppression purposes is flawed. However, in evaluating the effectiveness of suppression, Spergel also noted that "We have no systematic or reliable assessments of the effectiveness of a gang suppression strategy by criminal justice agencies, particularly law enforcement" (p. 198). Indeed, his analysis of the literature assessing the effectiveness of gang suppression by law enforcement consisted of a series of anecdotal comments from newspaper articles—hardly a scientific source. Klein (1995) reviewed several sweep programs that were undertaken in California. Operation Hammer, which was conducted by the LAPD, was a preannounced, media-covered gang sweep of Los Angeles that resulted in 1,453 juveniles being arrested; however, 1,350 were released without formal charges being filed. In the end, the operation was characterized by Klein and some LAPD officials as "all show" that was only for public relations. However, Klein also reported that when he rode along with Los Angeles County Sheriff's officials on a gang sweep that was not announced, not covered, and that was coordinated among several different targeted areas, the results were much different. Whereas Operation Hammer provided serious gang members with good laughing material, the Sheriff's sweep produced no humor among the arrestees that night.

Evaluations of community-based gang prevention programs are increasing. However, many of these have been qualitative and did not measure the impact of the program on crime in general or even on gang-related crime. For example, Thurman, Giacomazzi, Reisig, and Mueller (1996) evaluated a community-based gang prevention program implemented in Mountlake Terrace, Washington. Their evaluation included direct observation, focus group interviews, and official crime statistics. The program purported to provide an alternative outlet in which youths at risk or already involved in a gang could spend their time (Thurman et al. 1996). The official crime statistics used in the study were general calls for service to the police, with no breakdown given between gang-related calls for service and regular calls for service. Although Thurman et al. concluded that the intervention "appears to be a cost-effective gang prevention and intervention program" (p. 292), no data on crime; effect on the number of gang members, gang-related crimes, or gang-related calls for service; or other statistical evidence were offered to support this conclusion. Furthermore, the extent and scope of the gang problem in the area, the demographic characteristics of the community, and the crime statistics for the community were not discussed. The authors concluded that the program "offers an effective alternative to traditional law enforcement approaches which typically rely on police crackdowns and curfews to regulate gang activity" (Thurman et al. 1996, p. 279), yet no evidence was offered to show that these latter techniques were ineffective or have not been effective in the past—either nationally or in Mountlake Terrace.

Palumbo, Eskay, and Hallett (1992) evaluated three gang prevention programs, including Arizona New Turf, GREAT, and Community Reliance Resource Effort (CARE). They found that although all of the programs were well implemented, there was no effect on the gang problem, even though police officers, students, and members of the community felt positively about the programs. Indeed, the majority of the community-based programs may fall victim to a common criticism—they sound good, feel good, look good, but do not work good. Many of the evaluations of these community programs have relied on qualitative data that typically show that everyone surveyed or interviewed thought the program was effective and useful, but no quantitative empirical support has been offered to indicate the impact on the gang problem, gang-related crime, or the gang members served by the program.

Much of the current literature has been dismissive, perhaps prematurely, of the ability of the police to suppress gang activity in that there are virtually no empirical studies that support such a claim. As Klein (1993) noted,

> The message is not so much that suppression does or does not "work": evidence one way of the other is sorely lacking. *There are logical, as well as experiential, reasons to believe that suppression programs can have deterrent effects and thus, by our reasoning, can contribute substantially to gang and drug activity prevention.* (P. 308; emphasis in original)

Curfew and Truancy Enforcement

The literature assessing curfew and truancy enforcement is still in its infancy; most existing studies have focused on tactics, descriptions of programs, and legal issues (Friend 1994; Garrett and Brewster 1994; "Juvenile Curfews" 1994; Ruefle and Reynolds 1995; Watzman 1994). Curfews have received attention recently because of their perceived effectiveness in reducing juvenile crime and juvenile victimization. Much anecdotal reference about their effectiveness has appeared in the popular media (LeBoeuf 1996; Ruefle and Reynolds 1995), but the existing academic literature on curfew and truancy enforcement has been limited to a few articles on the number of arrests and the various types of ordinances that have been enacted.

Hunt and Weiner (1977) studied a Detroit curfew that was specifically designed to reduce criminal gang activity by youths. They used before and after comparisons of crime rates and criminal temporal activity and concluded that the curfew enforcement seemed to effectively reduce or suppress the relative level of crime during curfew hours, although they also found evidence of temporal displacement (i.e., gang-related crime increased during noncurfew hours). Ruefle and Reynolds (1995) surveyed metropolitan police departments serving populations of more than 200,000 and found that curfews in one form or another existed in 59 (77 percent) of the 77 largest American cities. The Dallas Police Department's internal analysis revealed that following adoption of its aggressive curfew enforcement program, juvenile victimization during curfew hours dropped 17.7 percent and juvenile arrests dropped 14.6 percent from the previous year (Click 1994). Statistics from Phoenix, Arizona, revealed that 21 percent of all curfew violators were gang members. Furthermore, a 10 percent decrease in juvenile arrests for violent crimes occurred following implementation of an aggressive curfew program (LeBoeuf 1996). Decreases in various other juvenile crimes occurred in several other metropolitan areas (Chicago, Denver, Jacksonville, New Orleans, North Little Rock) that employed curfew programs (LeBoeuf 1996).

Truancy has been linked to a variety of negative consequences for youths (e.g., drug use, delinquency, unemployment) and for society (i.e., daytime crime, auto theft, vandalism) (Garry 1996; J. R. Martin, Schulze, and Valdez 1988; Rohrman 1993). However, the impact of aggressive truancy enforcement on crime rates remains essentially unevaluated. One evaluated program used a small squad of officers to enforce truancy laws; although numerous arrests were made, the impact on felonies and misdemeanors in the area was nominal (J. R. Martin et al. 1988). However, the study did not control for whether the crimes under study were committed by adults or by juveniles.

METHODOLOGY

A quasi-experimental design was used for the evaluation reported in this article. The main objective of the initiative was to decrease gang-related violence in the five targeted areas. The five areas were composed of patrol beats and were selected on the basis of two criteria.[4] First, the areas had experienced a large amount of gang violence in the preceding year. Second, they overlapped some of the defined Enterprise Zones and Renaissance Areas in Dallas. Enterprise Zones are designated by the city to encourage economic development in an area, and businesses receive tax breaks for locating in the Zones. A Renaissance Zone is an area in which neighborhood organizations use federal funds to design and implement programs to reduce crime and disorder.

To estimate the impact of the enforcement strategies on crime, it was important to select control areas for comparison purposes. Four control areas were selected based on a two-stage selection process. First, the number of violent gang-related offenses from June 1, 1995, through May 31, 1996, for each patrol beat in the same patrol division as the corresponding target area was determined from data provided by the Dallas Police Department Gang

Unit. Second, the beats with the largest number of violent gang-related offenses during the time period were matched with a corresponding target area and served as control areas.[5] The target and control areas were sufficiently similar to allow comparison and estimation of the efficacy of the gang suppression effort.

Two data sets were used to measure the anti-gang initiative's impact on crime. First, offenses reported to the police from June 1, 1995, through May 31, 1997, were obtained from the Crime Analysis Unit of the police department. Murder, rape, robbery, aggravated assault, burglary, auto theft, theft, arson, other assault, criminal mischief, drug offenses, and weapon offenses were analyzed. The last two offenses were measured by number of arrests rather than reported offenses. Second, data from the Gang Unit on all of the gang-related offenses reported to the police from June 1, 1995, through May 31, 1997, were collected. Several offenses were aggregated into the category of violent gang-related offenses.[6]

Because of the small sample size, gang-related property crimes were not analyzed. Final determination of whether an offense was gang related was made by Gang Unit detectives after a follow-up investigation based on police department criteria for gang-related crime.[7] Report formats clearly indicated that the offense was gang related by both a checked box and a narrative. Annual precomparisons and postcomparisons of crime in general and gang-related violence in particular were analyzed for each target and control area to determine the anti-gang initiative's impact on crime. For each comparison, a paired samples *t* test was computed to determine statistically significant differences between the mean values over two time periods. In instances in which statistically significant differences existed, efforts were made to determine the particular strategy employed during the time period (curfew enforcement, truancy enforcement, or saturation patrol).

Limitations

Determining the generalizability of any evaluation of a gang suppression strategy is at best difficult; at worst, it is impossible. One specific problem with gang intervention strategy evaluation is the fact that police, prosecutor, and legislative definitions of gangs, gang-related crime, and gang members differ widely (Caeti, Fritsch, and Hemmens 1995; Curry, Ball, and Decker 1996). A second problem occurs when there is wholesale adoption of any gang intervention strategy without looking carefully at evaluations of the strategy and its assumptions, especially suppression strategies. This practice is ill-advised and could in fact be destructive (Klein 1995). Therefore, results must be interpreted with caution and replicated across and within several

TABLE 1:   Mean Number of Violent Gang-Related Offenses per Month by Area

	Target Area			Control Area		
Area	Time 1	Time 2	t Test	Time 1	Time 2	t Test
Area 1	6.8	1.8	3.69*	2.9	2.6	0.46
Area 2	5.1	3.8	1.03	10.2	5.7	2.31*
Area 3	2.0	1.0	1.65	7.6	3.8	3.06*
Area 4	3.5	1.0	4.33*	1.9	2.3	−0.53
Area 5	3.5	1.3	3.04*	1.9	2.3	−0.53
All areas combined	20.9	8.9	7.21*	22.6	14.3	3.76*

NOTE: Time 1 = Year 1 (June 1995 through May 1996); Time 2 = Year 2 (June 1996 through May 1997).
*$p < .05$.

jurisdictions before broad and definitive conclusions can be drawn about the overall usefulness of a particular strategy. The fact that definitions of gang-related crime vary makes this caution all the more salient.

FINDINGS

Gang Violence

Table 1 compares the mean number of violent gang-related offenses in the five target areas per month with those in the four control areas. Overall, there was a statistically significant decrease (57 percent) in gang-related violence in the target areas during the grant period. Statistically significant decreases in gang violence were observed during the anti-gang initiative in the control areas as well, but the overall decrease was less substantial than in the target areas—37 percent in the control areas in comparison to 57 percent in the target areas.

Compared with the year prior to the anti-gang initiative (June 1, 1995, through May 31, 1996), there were statistically significant reductions in violent gang-related offenses in Target Areas 1, 4, and 5 during the grant period (June 1, 1996, through May 31, 1997). There was approximately a 73 percent reduction in violent gang-related activity in Target Areas 1 and 4 and a 64 percent reduction in Target Area 5. Little change in gang violence occurred in the control areas for these beats; indeed, Control Areas 4 and 5 experienced a 22 percent increase in gang violence during the grant year.

This increase in Control Areas 4 and 5 could be due to displacement of gang activity by the initiative. That is, increased police activity in a targeted area may have forced gang members into areas of the city with a lesser law enforcement presence. Gang violence may have moved to another area instead of being eradicated. To investigate the possibility of displacement, the number of violent gang-related offenses for the 33 nontarget beats, contiguous to target beats, was determined and comparisons were examined. The sample size for each beat was small, which precluded the use of a paired samples *t* test; therefore, the raw frequencies were analyzed. Of the 33 beats contiguous to target beats, 15 experienced a decrease in gang violence during the grant period, whereas 10 experienced an increase and 8 experienced no change. Although the anti-gang initiative may have displaced some gang violence to other beats, the extent of displacement appears to have been minimal.

Further analysis was conducted to identify the strategies employed in Target Areas 1, 4, and 5 to determine which of them might be responsible for the significant decrease in gang violence. The strategies were obtained from weekly and monthly reports written by the sergeants responsible for a target area; they documented the overtime-funded enforcement strategies that were employed in the area during the study period. Of the strategies used in each area, the vast majority of overtime hours were spent on curfew enforcement in Target Area 1 (80 percent of overtime hours) and truancy enforcement in Target Areas 4 and 5 (89 percent of overtime hours). Therefore, concentrated efforts to enforce truancy and curfew laws had a positive impact on reducing gang violence.

In addition, there was also a 46 percent reduction in gang violence in Target Area 3 during the grant period and a 25 percent reduction in Target Area 2, but these reductions were not statistically significant. Differently, there were statistically significant decreases in gang violence in Control Areas 2 and 3, even though these areas did not receive overtime-funded enforcement strategies. There was a 44 percent reduction in violence in Control Area 2 and a 50 percent reduction in Control Area 3. However, these control areas may have received extra attention from the Gang Unit during on-duty hours. Because enforcement strategies in the five target areas were overtime funded, more on-duty time may have been spent in the control areas that did not have any overtime funds. Unfortunately, quantitative data to support this statement were unavailable.

It is important to recognize that the main strategies employed in Target Areas 2 and 3 differed from those in the other areas. Of the documented strategies in each area, the vast majority of overtime hours was spent on undirected saturation patrol. Officers in Target Areas 2 and 3 also employed other suppression strategies, such as truancy and curfew enforcement, but to a much lesser degree than did officers in Target Areas 1, 4, and 5. Therefore, saturation patrol to increase police presence alone was not effective in decreasing the level of gang violence in these areas.

Offenses Reported to the Police

Data were collected on index violent and property crimes reported to the police. In addition, data were obtained on other assaults, criminal mischief, drug offenses, and weapon offenses. The following two hypotheses were tested:

> *Hypothesis 1*: Increased officer presence led to decreases in reported offenses, especially for suppressible crimes such as robbery, auto theft, burglary, and criminal mischief.
> *Hypothesis 2*: Freedom from responding to calls for service led to greater officer-initiated activity, which resulted in more arrests for drug and weapon offenses.

Table 2 compares the mean number of offenses reported to the Dallas Police Department per month during the grant year with the number of offenses reported per month during the prior year. As shown in Table 2, there were statistically significant increases in reported robberies (23.8 percent increase) and auto thefts (15.4 percent increase) in the target areas during the grant period. In addition, there were statistically significant decreases in reports of criminal mischief (15 percent decrease) and arrests for weapons violations (30 percent decrease) in the target areas. The statistically significant decrease in criminal mischief was also observed in the control areas during the grant period, despite the lack of overtime-funded enforcement strategies; thus, the decrease cannot be attributed to activities generated by the overtime funding in the target areas.

Neither of the two hypotheses were supported by the data. In fact, the direct opposite effect was noted in a few instances. For example, statistically significant increases in robbery and auto theft were observed in the target areas, perhaps because increased police presence encouraged the reporting of offenses due to the increased availability and presence of officers, but no data relevant to this explanation were available. Also, there was a statistically significant decrease, rather than the hypothesized increase, in arrests for weapons violations, which may be due to the deterrent effect of the increased presence of officers in these areas. Indeed, it is plausible that the strategies deterred gang members from visible criminal mischief and from carrying weapons once the word got out that the police were being more active. However, data were not available to support or refute this explanation.

TABLE 2:   Mean Number of Offenses Reported to Dallas Police Department per
            Month

Offense	Target Area			Control Area		
	Time 1	Time 2	t Test	Time 1	Time 2	t Test
Index violent						
Aggravated assault	92.3	90.4	0.30	65.6	74.9	−0.99
Murder	3.7	2.6	1.26	2.8	1.3	2.16
Rape	5.5	5.3	0.16	6.3	7.0	−0.60
Robbery	61.0	75.5	−2.42*	47.1	44.5	1.15
Index property						
Arson	2.3	2.3	0.00	3.4	3.6	−0.24
Auto theft	142.6	164.6	−2.66*	160.4	174.3	−1.34
Burglary	129.3	141.5	−1.76	154.1	168.5	−1.40
Theft	349.8	366.9	−1.69	348.6	388.2	−2.73*
Part II offenses						
Assault	181.6	239.3	−1.55	148.3	211.1	−1.81
Criminal mischief	181.9	154.7	2.56*	208.3	181.7	3.19*
Drug offense[a]	86.4	107.1	−1.84	53.1	57.5	−0.62
Weapon offense[a]	19.5	13.8	3.25*	10.7	10.3	0.21

NOTE: Time 1 = Year 1 (June 1995 through May 1996); Time 2 = Year 2 (June 1996
through May 1997).
a. Based on the number of arrests.
*$p < .05$.

DISCUSSION AND CONCLUSION

This study found that, consistent with previous research, undirected saturation patrol has little affect on reducing crime (Sherman 1990b). In short,
simply adding more police officers without direction was not effective.
Unfortunately, this conclusion has been overgeneralized to mean that policing and patrol does not work. Fortunately, other research has shown that
directed patrol (whether directed toward offenders, places, victims, or
offenses) was effective in varying degrees (Abrahamse, Ebener, Greenwood,
Fitzgerald, and Kosin 1991; S. E. Martin 1986; S. E. Martin and Sherman
1986; Sherman, 1990a, 1990b, 1992; Sherman et al. 1995). The research
reported in this article provides support for the latter statement because the
aggressive enforcement of truancy and curfew laws was effective in reducing
gang-related violence in target areas. This finding needs replication, particularly in a true experimental design.

Enforcement of curfew and truancy is frequently a low-priority task of officers, but it can have an impact on gang violence and may potentially have an even greater impact on juvenile victimization. For example, the number of homicides in Dallas (citywide) that involved a juvenile victim (excluding child abuse deaths) dropped from 18 during the year prior to the anti-gang initiative to 7 during the initiative. Furthermore, the number of gang-related juvenile homicide victims dropped from 6 during the first time period to 2 during the second (Caeti 1997).

We also found little effect on the number of offenses reported to the police. Increased officer presence did not lead to a decrease in offenses reported to the police. Sherman (1990b, 1992) reported that both increases and decreases in calls for service have been noted as the result of a crackdown. Thus, the validity of using calls for service as a measure of effectiveness must be questioned. In addition, freeing officers from responding to calls for service did not lead to greater officer-initiated activity, such as drug and weapons arrests. The question "What do officers do with their time?" needs greater empirical attention. Furthermore, suppressible crime was not affected greatly by the initiative overall. Perhaps this was because the enforcement activities that relied on curfew and truancy enforcement only had appreciable effects on the crimes that juvenile offenders commit. Indeed, criminal mischief and weapons offenses decreased dramatically in the targeted areas. Individuals who commit robberies and other serious felonies may be unaffected by curfew or truancy enforcement because they may be adults and/or not in the school system.

Many police scholars have concluded that traditional police activities and goals (preventive patrol, rapid response, investigations, etc.) have failed to achieve crime reduction and have increased problems of police-citizen alienation (Kelling 1978). However, more recently, Kelling (1996), in discussing how to define the bottom line in policing, noted the following:

> A basic purpose of police is crime prevention. The idea that police cannot do anything about crime and that they stand helpless in the face of demographics, drugs, gangs, or whatever is unacceptable—often . . . a "cop-out" that covers lack of strategic commitment and absence of planning and implementation. (P. 31)

Police gang suppression activity may not affect gang membership or the conditions that create gangs. However, it is possible that those activities affect the nefarious effects of gangs—crime and violence.

Would we really care if kids joined gangs if gangs did not engage in criminal activity? Probably not; in fact, some positive gang values (group cohesiveness, loyalty, respect, discipline, etc.) are encouraged to a large extent in legitimate activities, such as youth sports, clubs, and various other groups. In any case, the gang suppression activities of law enforcement probably cannot and perhaps should not be concerned with the "whys" of gangs. As Spergel (1995) noted,

> The police cannot be held responsible for basic failures of youth socialization; lack of social and economic achievement by families, deficiencies of schools, decreased employment opportunities for African-American youth, the extensive street presence and accessibility of sophisticated weaponry, and the extensive racism and social isolation that appear to be highly correlated with the gang problem in some low-income minority communities. (P. 191)

The police should, however, concern themselves with a more narrow mission of developing effective strategies to address the crime problems that gangs create. The idea that the police can change the underlying socioeconomic conditions that give rise to gangs or to the infinite reasons why kids join gangs is naive and unrealistic. This is not to say that other community agencies should not focus on such endeavors. The simple fact of the matter is that the police are designed, organized, staffed, and trained to deal with crime, not social services.

Although strategies that use offender-, place-, and crime-specific techniques are in their infancy and require greater empirical attention, much of the recent literature that has evaluated such strategies is promising (Sherman 1990b, 1992). For example, when overtime-funded officers were freed from calls for service in Houston, substantial reductions in suppressible crimes soon followed (Hoover and Caeti 1994). The philosophy is that

> police agencies can impact the level of crime and disorder in a community. The police *do* make a difference. Saying that crime and disorder are a product of social and economic forces the police cannot and should not affect is rejected. (Hoover and Caeti 1994, p. 1)

The police should coordinate with other public agencies in their efforts to deal with gangs, and these efforts should be focused on the criminal problems that gangs create. Interagency cooperation and information-sharing models provide promise as well, especially the ability to successfully prosecute serious and habitual offenders (Owens and Wells 1993). Recent technological advances in the areas of computer mapping, object-oriented databases, management information systems, and offender identification and tracking all bode well for the ability of the police to increase their effectiveness in managing crime, particularly gang crime. More empirical evaluation research is needed concerning which law enforcement strategies can lead to reductions in gang violence and victimization through gang violence.

NOTES

1. Dallas has a nocturnal curfew ordinance that requires individuals (not accompanied by their parent or guardian) younger than age 17 to be in their residence between the hours of 11 p.m. and 6 a.m. on weeknights (Sunday through Thursday) and between the hours of 12 a.m. and 6 a.m. on weekends (Friday and Saturday).

2. The State of Texas truancy law requires juveniles between the ages of 7 and 16 to be enrolled in and attending school. Enforcement activity was conducted between the hours of 10 a.m. and 3 p.m. weekdays, concentrating on the gang-ridden target areas.

3. The Office of Juvenile Justice and Delinquency Prevention (OJJDP) has developed a comprehensive gang suppression and intervention strategy based on community models (Spergel, Curry, Chance, Kane, Ross, Alexander, Simmons, and Oh 1994). The Bureau of Justice Assistance (BJA) (1997) has also published a monograph on *Urban Street Gang Enforcement*, which is a comprehensive overview of the various tactics employed by all agencies who come into contact with gangs. These works are very extensive, yet they are completely prescriptive—there is little mention or review of any empirical studies that evaluate the police role in dealing with gangs.

4. The target areas were composed of the following patrol beats: Target Area 1—Beats 513, 514, and 515; Target Area 2—Beats 412, 413, 414, 415, 416, 417, and 419; Target Area 3—Beats 311, 312, 314, and 316; Target Area 4—Beats 112, 113, 115, 154, and 156; and Target Area 5—Beats 141, 143, 144, 145, 146, and 152.

5. The following beats comprise the control areas, which did not receive the overtime-funded enforcement strategies under the anti-gang initiative: Control Area 1—Beats 552, 553, and 555; Control Area 2—Beats 423, 425, 426, 427, 445, 448, and 456; Control Area 3—Beats 325, 326, 327, and 328; Control Areas 4 and 5—Beats 114, 116, 131, 134, and 135. Because Target Areas 4 and 5 were in the same patrol division, the same control area was used for both.

6. Capital murder ($n = 2$); murder ($n = 19$); attempted murder ($n = 5$); aggravated assault ($n = 415$); misdemeanor assault ($n = 167$); sexual assault ($n = 1$); deadly conduct ($n = 64$); aggravated robbery ($n = 56$); robbery ($n = 46$); injury to a child ($n = 5$); terrorist threats ($n = 16$); retaliation ($n = 4$); and cruelty to animals ($n = 1$).

7. According to Dallas Police Department policy, an incident should be considered gang-related activity when participants, acting individually or collectively, are known to be gang members or gang associates and the criminal activity engaged in is aggravated assault, assault, robbery, homicide, possession for sale of narcotics, shooting at house and/or car, arson, retaliation/witness tampering, auto theft, criminal mischief (graffiti), sexual assault, kidnapping, or burglary. Officers may also consider an incident as street gang activity when (1) the participants are identified as gang members or associates who are acting individually or collectively to further any criminal purpose of the gang; (2) a reliable informant identifies an incident as gang activity or a participant as a gang member; (3) an informant of previously untested reliability identifies an incident as a gang activity and it is corroborated by other existing circumstances or independent information; (4) there are strong indications that an incident is gang related, such as the nature of the offense (i.e., drive-by shooting) or the fact that the participants were wearing/using common identifying signs, symbols, or colors; or (5) gang members or associates are identified through existing police gang intelligence files.

REFERENCES

Abrahamse, Allan F., Patricia A. Ebener, Peter W. Greenwood, Nora Fitzgerald, and Thomas E. Kosin. 1991. "An Experimental Evaluation of the Phoenix Repeat Offender Program." *Justice Quarterly* 8:141-72.

Bureau of Justice Assistance. 1997. *Urban Street Gang Enforcement*. Washington, DC: National Institute of Justice.

Caeti, Tory J. 1997. "Who's Killing Our Kids? An Analysis of Juvenile Homicide Victims in Dallas 1993-1997." Research Initiation Grant Project, University of North Texas, Denton.

Caeti, Tory J., Eric J. Fritsch, and Craig Hemmens. 1995. "Bangin' in the Legislature: A Comparison of State Statutory Responses to Gangs." Presented at the annual meeting of the American Society of Criminology, Boston.

Click, Benjamin R. 1994. "Statistics in Dallas Encouraging." *Police Chief* 61 (12):33-6.

Curry, G. David, Richard A. Ball, and Scott H. Decker. 1996. "Estimating the National Scope of Gang Crime From Law Enforcement Data." *National Institute of Justice: Research in Brief.*

Dart, Robert W. 1992. "Chicago's 'Flying Squad' Tackles Street Gangs." *Police Chief* 59:96-8.

Freed, David. 1986. "Policing Gangs: Case of Contrasting Styles." Pp. 288-91 in *The Modern Gang Reader*, edited by M. W. Klein, C. L. Maxson, and J. Miller. Los Angeles: Roxbury.

Friend, Charles E. 1994. "Juvenile Curfew." *Policy Review* 6:1-4.

Garrett, Dennis A. and David Brewster. 1994. "Curfew: A New Look at an Old Tool." *Police Chief* (December):29-61.

Garry, Eileen M. 1996. "Truancy: First Step to a Lifetime of Problems." *Juvenile Justice Bulletin* (October).

Hoover, Larry T. and Tory J. Caeti. 1994. "Crime-Specific Policing in Houston." *Texas Law Enforcement Management and Administrative Statistics Program Bulletin* 1 (9).

Houston, James. 1996. "What Works: The Search for Excellence in Gang Intervention Programs." *Journal of Gang Research* 3:1-16.

Howell, James C. 1996. *Youth Gang Violence Prevention and Intervention: What Works*. Washington, DC: National Institute of Justice.

Huff, C. Ronald and Wesley D. McBride. 1993. "Gangs and the Police." Pp. 401-16 in *The Gang Intervention Handbook*, edited by A. P. Goldstein and C. R. Huff. Champaign, IL: Research Press.

Hunt, A. Lee and Ken Weiner. 1977. "The Impact of a Juvenile Curfew: Suppression and Displacement in Patterns of Juvenile Offenses." *Journal of Police Science and Administration* 5:407-12.

Jackson, Robert K. and Wesley D. McBride. 1996. *Understanding Street Gangs*. Incline Village, NV: Copperhouse.

Johnson, Claire M., Barbara A. Webster, Edward F. Connors, and Diana J. Saenz. 1995. "Gang Enforcement Problems and Strategies: National Survey Findings." *Journal of Gang Research* 3:1-18.

"Juvenile Curfews and Gang Violence: Exiled on Main Street." 1994. *Harvard Law Review* 107 (7):1693-710.

Kelling, George L. 1978. "Police Field Services and Crime: The Presumed Effects of a Capacity." *Crime & Delinquency* 24:173-84.

———. 1996. "Defining the Bottom Line in Policing: Organizational Philosophy and Accountability." Pp. 23-36 in *Quantifying Quality in Policing*, edited by L. T. Hoover. Washington, DC: Police Executive Research Forum.

Kent, Douglas R. and Peggy Smith. 1994. "The Tri-Agency Resource Gang Enforcement Team: A Selective Approach to Reduce Gang Crime." Pp. 292-96 in *The Modern Gang Reader*, edited by M. W. Klein, C. L. Maxson, and J. Miller. Los Angeles: Roxbury.

Klein, Malcolm W. 1993. "Attempting Gang Control by Suppression: The Misuse of Deterrence Principles." Pp. 304-13 in *The Modern Gang Reader*, edited by M. W. Klein, C. L. Maxson, and J. Miller. Los Angeles: Roxbury.

———. 1995. *The American Street Gang: Its Nature, Prevalence, and Control.* New York: Oxford University Press.

Knox, George W. 1994. *An Introduction to Gangs.* Bristol, IN: Wyndham Hall.

LeBoeuf, Donni. 1996. *Curfew: An Answer to Juvenile Delinquency and Victimization?* Washington, DC: Office of Juvenile Justice and Delinquency Prevention.

Martin, Joe R., Arnie D. Schulze, and Mike Valdez. 1988. "Taking Aim at Truancy." *FBI Law Enforcement Bulletin* 57:8-12.

Martin, Susan E. 1986. "Policing Career Criminals: An Examination of an Innovative Crime Control Program." *Journal of Criminal Law and Criminology* 77:1159-82.

Martin, Susan E. and Lawrence W. Sherman. 1986. "Catching Career Criminals: Proactive Policing and Selective Apprehension." *Justice Quarterly* 3:171-92.

Needle, Jerome A. and W. V. Stapleton. 1983. *Police Handling of Youth Gangs.* Washington, DC: American Justice Institute, National Juvenile Justice System Assessment Center.

Owens, Robert P. and Donna K. Wells. 1993. "One City's Response to Gangs." *Police Chief* 58:25-7.

Palumbo, Dennis J., R. Eskay, and Michael A. Hallett. 1992. *Do Gang Prevention Strategies Actually Reduce Crime?* Washington, DC: National Institute of Justice.

Rohrman, Doug. 1993. *Combating Truancy in Our Schools: A Community Effort.* Washington, DC: National Institute of Justice.

Ruefle, William and Kenneth Mike Reynolds. 1995. "Curfews and Delinquency in Major American Cities." *Crime & Delinquency* 41:347-63.

Rush, Jeffrey P. 1996. "The Police Role in Dealing With Gangs." Pp. 85-92 in *Gangs: A Criminal Justice Approach*, edited by J. M. Miller and J. P. Rush. Cincinnati, OH: Anderson.

Shelden, Randall G., Sharon K. Tracy, and William B. Brown. 1997. *Youth Gangs in American Society.* Belmont, CA: Wadsworth.

———. 1990a. "Police Crackdowns." *National Institute of Justice Reports* (March/April).

Sherman, Lawrence W. 1990b. "Police Crackdowns: Initial and Residual Deterrence." *Crime and Justice: A Review of Research* 12:1-48.

———. 1992. "Attacking Crime: Police and Crime Control." Pp. 159-230 in *Crime and Justice: A Review of Research*, vol. 14, edited by M. Tonry and N. Morris. Chicago: University of Chicago Press.

Sherman, Lawrence W., James W. Shaw, and Dennis P. Rogan. 1995. "The Kansas City Gun Experiment." *National Institute of Justice: Research in Brief.*

Spergel, Irving A. 1995. *The Youth Gang Problem.* New York: Oxford University Press.

Spergel, Irving A. and G. David Curry. 1990. "Strategies and Perceived Agency Effectiveness in Dealing With the Youth Gang Problem." Pp. 288-309 in *Gangs in America*, edited by C. R. Huff. Newbury Park, CA: Sage.

Spergel, Irving A., David Curry, Ron Chance, Candice Kane, Ruth Ross, Alba Alexander, Edwina Simmons, and Sandra Oh. 1994. *Gang Suppression and Intervention: Problem and Response.* Washington, DC: Office of Juvenile Justice and Delinquency Prevention.

Thurman, Quint C., Andrew L. Giacomazzi, Michael D. Reisig, and David G. Mueller. 1996. "Community-Based Gang Prevention and Intervention: An Evaluation of the Neutral Zone." *Crime & Delinquency* 42:279-95.

Watzman, Nancy. 1994. "Curfew Revival Gains Momentum." *Governing* 7:20-1.

Weisel, Deborah L. and Ellen Painter. 1997. *The Police Response to Gangs: Case Studies of Five Cities*. Washington, DC: Police Executive Research Forum.

Weston, Jim. 1993. "Community Policing: An Approach to Youth Gangs in a Medium-Sized City." *Police Chief* 60 (August):80-4.

Wilson, James Q. and George L. Kelling. 1989. "Making Neighborhoods Safe." *Atlantic Monthly* (February):46-52.

[27]

CHILDHOOD RISK FACTORS FOR ADOLESCENT GANG MEMBERSHIP: RESULTS FROM THE SEATTLE SOCIAL DEVELOPMENT PROJECT

KARL G. HILL
JAMES C. HOWELL
J. DAVID HAWKINS
SARA R. BATTIN-PEARSON

Adolescents who join gangs are more frequently involved in serious delinquency compared with those who do not, yet few studies have conducted a prospective examination of risk factors for gang membership. The present study uses longitudinal data to predict gang membership in adolescence from factors measured in childhood. Data were from the Seattle Social Development Project, an ethnically diverse, gender-balanced sample (n = 808) followed prospectively from age 10 to 18. Logistic regression was used to identify risk factors at ages 10 through 12 predictive of joining a gang between the ages of 13 and 18. Neighborhood, family, school, peer, and individual factors significantly predicted joining a gang in adolescence. Youth exposed to multiple factors were much more likely to join a gang. Implications for the development of gang prevention interventions are discussed.

Youth violence, property crime, and substance abuse result in enormous monetary, social, and personal costs. These and other criminal acts have been consistently linked to gang membership (Howell 1997). Thus, it is important

This research was supported by a research grant (No. 2158) from the Office of Juvenile Justice and Delinquency Prevention (OJJDP), a grant from the National Institute on Drug Abuse (No. 1R01DA09679), and a grant from the Robert Wood Johnson Foundation. The authors would like to thank Robert Abbott and Cynthia Shaw for lending their statistical and editorial expertise, respectively. Correspondence should be addressed to Karl G. Hill, Social Development Research Group, University of Washington, 9725 3rd Avenue, NE, Suite 401, Seattle, WA 98115; phone: (206) 685-3859; e-mail: khill@u.washington.edu.

JOURNAL OF RESEARCH IN CRIME AND DELINQUENCY, Vol. 36 No. 3, August 1999 300-322
© 1999 Sage Publications, Inc.

to learn why youth join gangs and how to interrupt this process. The present study uses longitudinal data to predict gang membership in adolescence, from neighborhood, family, school, peer, and individual factors measured in childhood.

Gang members are more likely than nonmembers to commit violent offenses and property crime and to use drugs (Spergel 1995; Thornberry 1998). Bjerregaard and Lizotte (1995) found that, when compared with nongang members, gang members were more than twice as likely to carry a gun and to engage in serious delinquency and more than three times as likely to engage in drug sales. Similarly, Esbensen and Huizinga (1993) found measures of drug sales and use, as well as serious and minor delinquency, to be substantially higher for gang members than nongang members. Battin et al. (1998) found that gang membership contributed to criminal behavior over and above the contribution of having delinquent peers. The relationship between gang membership and crime is robust and has been reported in virtually all studies of gang behavior in the United States regardless of historical period, methodology and design, or sample (Howell 1997).

It is imperative to learn why youth join gangs to better understand how to prevent them from joining gangs, but this question has not been well studied. The first gang theorists viewed gang delinquency as a result of social disorganization, endemic to slum areas (Shaw and McKay 1931, 1942; Thrasher [1927] 1963). One outgrowth of this line of reasoning was control theory, suggesting that entry into deviant peer groups is a function of a lack of social control experienced by youth (Hirschi 1969). Deviant groups such as gangs also have been viewed as the context for differential association through which criminal behaviors are learned (Sutherland and Cressey 1978). Other theorists described delinquent subcultures within the lower- and working-class communities (Cohen 1955; Cohen and Short 1958) that the earlier Chicago theorists believed to be the origin of gang formation. Miller (1958) suggested that youth who engage in gang delinquency are behaving in a manner consistent with lower-class culture. Finally, strain theorists suggested that delinquency and gang involvement arise as an adaptation to structural pressures: blocked conventional opportunities lead to frustration, which leads to antisocial acts and the pursuit of gain through illegitimate opportunities (Cloward and Ohlin 1960). Recent contributors to gang theory have revived the social disorganization tradition (Bursik and Grasmick 1993; Spergel and Curry 1993), often embedding it in the underclass concept of social disadvantage and economic inequality (Fagan 1996; Short 1996; Wilson 1987, 1996).

RISK FACTORS FOR GANG MEMBERSHIP

Reviews of the last 30 years of longitudinal research have identified a number of predictors of delinquency and violence (Hawkins et al. 1998; Lipsey and Derzon 1998; Loeber et al. 1991) and substance abuse (Hawkins, Arthur, and Catalano 1995; Hawkins, Catalano, and Miller 1992; Simcha-Fagan, Gersten, and Langner 1986). Although delinquency, violence, and substance abuse are not synonymous with gang membership, predictors of these behaviors provide a starting point for examining the predictors of gang membership. These predictors of delinquency, violence, and substance abuse are summarized in Table 1.

Several of the factors in Table 1 have been found to distinguish gang from nongang members in cross-sectional studies (see Howell 1997). These include neighborhood factors such as availability of drugs (Curry and Spergel 1992, Hagedorn 1988, 1994a, 1994b), family factors such as poor family management and low bonding to family (Adler, Ovando, and Hocevar 1984; Bowker and Klein 1983; Friedman, Mann, and Friedman 1975; Maxson, Whitlock, and Klein 1998), school factors such as low commitment to school (Bowker and Klein 1983; Maxson et al. 1998), peer factors such as association with delinquent peers (Fagan 1990; Maxson et al. 1998; Vigil and Yun 1990), and individual factors such as fewer conventional beliefs (Fagan 1990) and positive attitudes about gang membership (Friedman et al. 1975).

Moore (1978, 1991) retrospectively examined family histories of gang members, although without the benefit of a comparison group. Gang members reported frequent conflict and abuse among their parents, child abuse, family member alcoholism and drug addiction, and family trouble with the police.

To date, only two longitudinal studies have reported prospective data on gang participation: the Rochester Youth Development Study (Bjerregaard and Smith 1993; Lizotte et al. 1994; Thornberry et al. 1993) and the Denver Youth Survey (Esbensen and Huizinga 1993; Esbensen, Huizinga, and Weiher 1993). In the Rochester Study, Bjerregaard and Smith (1993) examined factors associated with gang membership using waves two and three of their study (covering ages 13 to 15) and found substantial similarity among males and females in the risk factors associated with gang participation. They found that, in Rochester, neither social disorganization nor poverty was significantly related to gang membership. However, they acknowledged that because the study oversampled high-risk youth, the range of the social disorganization variables was limited. Having low expectations for completing school significantly predicted gang membership among females but not among males. Having delinquent peers was significant for both groups.

TABLE 1: Summary of Risk Factors for Delinquency, Violence, and/or Substance Abuse
from Prior Cross-Sectional and Longitudinal Studies

Community risk factors
    Extreme poverty[SDVC]
    Disorganized neighborhoods[SDVC]
    Low levels of attachment to the neighborhood[SDV]
    High rates of mobility[SD]
    Availability of firearms[VL]
    Availability of drugs[SVC]
    Community norms favorable toward antisocial behavior[SDVC]
School risk factors
    Academic failure[SDVC]
    Low degree of commitment to school[SDVLC]
Family risk factors
    Family history of problem behavior[SDVLC]
    Poor family management practices[SDV]
    High levels of family conflict[SDVC]
    Favorable parental and sibling attitudes toward antisocial behavior[SDVL]
    Family poverty[SDVLC]
Individual and peer risk factors
    Constitutionally based risk factors (low autonomic arousal,
       sensation-seeking)[SDV]
    Early and persistent antisocial behavior[SDVLC]
    Favorable attitudes toward antisocial behavior[SDC]
    Association with peers who engage in problem behavior[SDVLC]

NOTE: S = Predictive of substance abuse in prior longitudinal studies, D = Predictive of
delinquency in prior longitudinal studies, V = Predictive of violence in prior longitudinal
studies, L = Predictive of gang membership in prior longitudinal studies, C = Distinguish
gang members from nongang members in prior cross-sectional studies.

Neither attachment to parents nor family supervision was a significant predictor of later gang membership. Low self-esteem also was unrelated to gang
membership. Early sexual activity was significantly related to gang membership for both sexes, and the association was significantly stronger for females
than for males. These analyses may be somewhat confounded, however, by
the fact that the predictors were drawn from wave two of their study, whereas
gang membership was a measure that combined waves two and three. Thus,
clear statements as to whether these factors were predictors or consequences
of gang membership are difficult to make from these analyses.

In the Denver sample, Esbensen et al. (1993) examined differences at
wave three of their study (males and females, ages 11 to 17) for those youth
who were either gang members, nongang street offenders (committed rape,
robbery, or aggravated assault), or neither at wave four (ages 12 to 18). Compared with nonoffenders, both gang members and nongang street offenders

reported (1) higher levels of commitment to delinquent peers; (2) lower commitment to positive peers; (3) higher levels of normlessness in the family, peer group, and school context; (4) more negative labeling by teachers; and (5) higher tolerance for criminal activity on the part of their peers. However, no differences were observed among the three groups with respect to social isolation, perceived limited opportunities, and self-concept measures. The only factor that distinguished gang members from street offenders was that gang members reported significantly more negative labeling by their teachers. Esbensen and his colleagues found no differences among the three groups in their involvement in a range of activities (including school-year job, summer job, attending school, school athletics, school activities, community athletics, community activities, and religious activities). They suggested that this finding calls into question the assumption that getting youth involved in such activities will prevent or reduce gang involvement.

These studies provide an important base for examining the predictors of gang membership. However, a limited number of possible predictors of gang membership have been studied, and these have been limited to factors either just prior to or during the typical period for initiation of gang membership. The extent to which childhood experiences during the elementary grades predict adolescent gang membership has not been examined longitudinally. The present study examines prospectively a range of childhood predictors of adolescent gang membership.

METHOD

Sample

Seattle has been characterized as an "emerging gang city" (Spergel and Curry, 1993); however, little empirical research has documented the nature or extent of gang membership in Seattle. Self-reported studies conducted in the 1970s and 1980s found that the proportion of gang members in Seattle youth populations studied ranged from 10 percent (Hindelang, Hirschi, and Weis 1981) to 13 percent (Sampson 1986).

The present study examines predictors from ages 10 to 12 of joining a gang between ages 13 and 18, using longitudinal data from the Seattle Social Development Project (SSDP). Data are from a multiethnic sample of males and females followed prospectively from 1985, when participants were in the first semester of the fifth grade (age 10), to 1993, when participants were 18 years of age. Data on gang membership were collected annually starting with the age 13 survey. The sample consists of 808 fifth-grade students attending 18 elementary schools serving high crime neighborhoods of Seattle in the fall of 1985. To select the schools, we met with members of the Seattle Police Department to review neighborhood crime statistics and then approached the feeder-elementary schools for those neighborhoods with higher crime rates. The 18 elementary schools represented approximately 25 percent of the total number of elementary schools in Seattle at that time. The 808 who consented to participate in the longitudinal study represent 77 percent of the population of fifth graders in these schools serving high-crime neighborhoods. Of the 808 students, 396 (49 percent) were female, 372 (46 percent) were European American, 195 (24 percent) were African American, 170 (21 percent) were Asian American, 45 (2 percent) were Native American, and the remaining 26 students were of other ethnic backgrounds (primarily Hispanic). A substantial portion of subjects were from low-income households. Median annual family income in 1985 was approximately $25,000. Forty-six percent of parents reported a maximum family income of less than $20,000 per year, and more than half of the student sample (52 percent) had participated in the National School Lunch/School Breakfast Program at some point in the fifth, sixth, or seventh grade, indicating that they came from families living in poverty.

Assessments

Data were obtained from multiple sources, including the youth, their parents or adult caretakers, teachers, school records, and King County court records. Data were collected in 1985 when most participants were 10 years old ($M = 10.3$, $SD = .52$) and then in the spring of each year through 1991. Data for the present study were collected again in the spring of 1993 when most subjects were 18 years old and those progressing normally in school were graduating from high school. In Grades 5 and 6, surveys in project schools were group-administered questionnaires completed in class. Youth who left project schools were individually interviewed. Starting in 1988, all students were individually interviewed in person. The interviews asked for the youth's confidential responses to a wide range of questions regarding family, community, school, and peers, as well as their attitudes and experiences with gangs, alcohol, drugs, drug selling, violence, weapon use, delinquency, and victimization. The interviews took about one hour. Early in the study youth received a small incentive (e.g., an audiocassette tape) for their participation; later they received monetary compensation. Participation rates were high; 94 percent of the sample (757 participants) completed the age 18 assessment in 1993. School, police, and court records were obtained from 1985 through 1993. In addition, adult caretakers (83 percent of whom were the subject's mother) were interviewed at recruitment in the fall of fifth grade (age 10) and annually each spring from 1986 through 1991.

Constructs

Gang membership was the primary outcome variable for these analyses. It was measured from age 13 to 18 by the question, "Do you belong to a gang?" followed by "What is the name of the gang?" to distinguish gangs from informal peer groups. Gang questions were not asked of the youth prior to age 13. Youth who reported that they were a member of a gang and could provide a name were coded as belonging to a gang during that wave. The most commonly named gangs were the Bloods, the Crips, and the Black Gangster Disciples. The use of self-report to determine gang membership has been used and advocated in similar gang studies and by gang researchers (Bjerregaard and Smith 1993; Esbensen and Huizinga 1993; Hindelang et al. 1981; Klein 1995; Sampson 1986; Savitz, Rosen, and Lalli 1980; Thornberry et al. 1993).

Risk factors for gang membership. Predictors were measured at ages 10 through 12. For continuous measures, the mean of the age 10 through age 12 values was used. For the categorical predictors of family structure and learning disabled, the fall 1985 values were used. Family structure was obtained from in-depth living calendars completed by the parents. Five categories were constructed: two parents (biological or adoptive) in home, one biological parent and one stepparent, one parent alone, one parent living with other adults, and no parents in the home. To investigate the possibility that possible strains associated with blended families might lead to higher probability of child problems, families with a stepparent were tested separately from other two-parent families. Furthermore, to represent the concept of risk exposure, all predictor variables were dichotomized, where one represented being in the highest quartile of risk on that predictor and zero represented the remainder, following Farrington (1989, 1998). A list of these predictors and the indicators that operationalized them is provided in the appendix.

For the present analyses, we sought to operationalize the constructs summarized in Table 1 using data available on the sample at ages 10 through 12. Some predictors of interest were not measured at these ages (e.g., community norms favorable to antisocial behavior, low autonomic arousal, sibling involvement in gangs), although they were measured in later waves of the study. Because the present study examines the childhood predictors of adolescent gang membership, predictors added in the adolescent interviews were not included in this analysis.

Several potential predictors were included in the analysis that have not been confirmed as risk factors for substance use, delinquency, or violence. Their addition was guided by the social development model, the theory that guides the Seattle Social Development Project (Catalano and Hawkins 1996). The number of youth in trouble in the neighborhood was added to examine the impact of neighborhood opportunities for antisocial involvement. Bonding to family was added to examine its impact, family structure was included to examine its contribution, and religious service attendance was included to examine the contribution of this form of involvement in prosocial activities.

Analysis

Logistic r and odds ratios. All regressions were prospective in design, predicting joining a gang between the ages of 13 and 18 from constructs assessed at ages 10 through 12. Given the dichotomous nature of the dependent variable, gang membership during adolescence, logistic regression was used.

Farrington (Loeber, Farrington, Stouthamer-Locker, and Van Kammen 1998) has shown that correlational measures such as the product-moment correlation, or the logistic r, give a misleading impression of predictive efficiency because they are greatly affected by the base rates of the predictors and outcomes such that the maximum correlation is often much less than 1.0. After reviewing a variety of alternatives, Farrington concluded that the odds ratio is a preferred way of presenting predictive efficiency because it is not affected by sample size, changes in base rates, or other factors. Thus, two strategies were used in the bivariate logistic regressions: First, each regression was run using the continuous measure of the predictor and the logistic r and significance were recorded. Next, each regression was run using a dichotomized high-risk quartile measure of the same predictor and the logistic r, significance, and odds ratio for gang initiation in the high-risk group were recorded. To identify childhood predictors of adolescent gang membership, separate bivariate logistic regressions were run for each potential predictor.

Effect of exposure to multiple risk factors. To obtain an assessment of the effects of exposure to multiple risk factors in childhood on later gang membership, an index was created that counted the number of significant risk factors to which each youth was exposed. Respondents were then divided into four approximate quartiles on their level of risk exposure and a logistic regression was run on this categorical measure of number of risk factors and adolescent gang membership, with each successive level of risk compared to the quartile of lowest risk.

RESULTS

Gang prevalence. Cumulatively, 15.3 percent of the sample self-reported ever belonging to a gang between the ages of 13 and 18. Membership peaked at age 15 (6 percent), with about equal percentages (almost 5 percent) reporting gang membership at ages 14, 16, and 18. The prevalence of gang membership was much higher among males (21.8 percent) than among females (8.6 percent). Twenty-six percent of African American adolescents in the sample, 12 percent of Asian American youth, 10 percent of European American youth, and nearly 20 percent of other groups, primarily Native Americans, reported having belonged to a gang. These data are summarized in Table 2. Although African American youth were more likely than other ethnic groups to join gangs, they constituted a minority of the sample who became gang members.

Gang membership by risk. The last column of Table 3 presents the odds ratio for gang membership at ages 13 to 18 associated with being in the worst quartile on each of the predictors at ages 10 to 12. In addition, columns 3 and 4 in Table 3 show the prevalence of gang membership for those in the worst quartile on each predictor and for the remainder of the sample, respectively. For example, 29.7 percent of those reporting the greatest availability of marijuana at ages 10 to 12 became gang members compared with 10.6 percent of those who reported that marijuana was less available in their environments at ages 10 to 12.

Table 3 also presents the logistic *r* for the dichotomized predictors. Logistic regressions also were conducted using the full continuous predictors where available. These analyses provided similar logistic *r*s and significances to their dichotomized counterparts, although occasionally the continuous predictor logistic *r* was stronger. These results are not tabled. Twenty-one of the 25 constructs measured at ages 10 to 12 predicted joining a gang at ages 13 to 18. Predictors of gang membership were found in all domains measured.[1]

Neighborhood-level predictors. Youth from neighborhoods in the top quartile of availability of marijuana had more than three times greater odds of joining a gang than those from other neighborhoods (odds ratio [OR] = 3.6).

TABLE 2:   Gang Involvement by Gender and Ethnicity (total *N* = 808)

	Gender		Ethnicity				
	Number (and column percentage of category)						
	Who Have Ever Belonged to a Gang by Age 18						
	Female	*Male*	*European American*	*African American*	*Asian American*	*Other*	*Total*
Yes	34 (8.6)	90 (21.8)	38 (10.2)	51 (26.2)	21 (12.4)	14 (19.7)	124 (15.3)
No	362 (91.4)	322 (78.2)	334 (89.8)	144 (73.8)	149 (87.6)	57 (80.3)	684 (84.7)
							808 (100)

NOTE: Other consists primarily of Native Americans.

Similarly, youth from neighborhoods in which many young people were in trouble had three times greater odds of joining a gang than youth from other neighborhoods (OR = 3.0). Level of attachment to the neighborhood was less strongly related to gang membership (OR = 1.5).

Family-level predictors. Family structure predicted gang membership. When compared with youth living with two parents (either biological or adoptive), youth living with one parent (OR = 2.4), youth from homes with one parent and other adults (OR = 3.0), and youth with no parents in the home (OR = 2.9) had greater odds of joining a gang. Youth from families with one biological and one stepparent were not significantly more likely than youth living with two parents (biological or adoptive) to become gang members.

Parental attitudes favorable to violence when youth were between the ages of 10 and 12 also predicted later gang membership (OR = 2.3), as did sibling antisocial behavior (OR = 1.9) and poor family management practices (OR = 1.7). Gang membership in adolescence was not significantly predicted by parental drinking or attachment to parents at ages 10 to 12. Logistic regressions were run separately for attachment to mother and attachment to father, and results were not significant (not shown in Table 3).

School-level predictors. School-related variables at ages 10 to 12 also predicted later gang membership. These included being identified as learning disabled (OR = 3.5), poor academic achievement as assessed by standardized test scores (OR = 3.1), low attachment to school (OR = 2.0), low commitment to school (OR = 1.8), and low educational aspirations (OR = 1.6).

Peer-level predictors. Friends engaged in problem behaviors, as assessed by how many of the youth's three best friends at ages 10 to 12 did things that got them in trouble with the teacher or had tried alcohol without their parents'

TABLE 3: Risk Factors at Ages 10 to 12 for Adolescent Gang Membership and Observed Gang Prevalence and Odds Ratios for Those at Risk in Childhood

_1_	_2_	_3_	_4_	_5_
		Observed Adolescent Gang Prevalence for Those at Low Risk on Each Factor (percentage)[b]	_Observed Adolescent Gang Prevalence for Those at High Risk on Each Factor (percentage)_[b]	_Odds Ratio for Those at High Risk_
Potential Childhood Risk Factor	_Logistic r_[a]			
Neighborhood				
Availability of marijuana	.23***	10.6	29.7	3.6
Neighborhood youth in trouble	.21***	10.4	26.4	3.0
Low neighborhood attachment	.05*	13.8	19.5	1.5
Family				
Poverty: low household income	.12***	12.7	23.3	2.1
Family structure				
Two parents (biological or adoptive) at home (n = 279)[c]				
One biological parent; one stepparent (n = 71)	.00(ns)	10.0	12.7	1.3
One parent only (n = 143)	.12**	10.0	21.0	2.4
One parent and other adults (n = 44)	.11**	10.0	25.0	3.0
No parents in home (n = 33)	.08*	10.0	24.2	2.9
Parent drinking	.00(ns)	15.3	15.2	1.0
Sibling antisocial behavior	.10**	12.8	21.7	1.9
Poor family management	.07*	13.5	20.6	1.7
Parent proviolent attitudes	.13***	13.2	25.7	2.3
Low attachment to parent(s)	.04(ns)	13.3	20.1	1.5

School				
Low academic aspirations	.06*	13.8	19.9	1.6
Low school commitment	.09**	13.3	21.4	1.8
Low school attachment	.12**	12.8	23.0	2.0
Low academic achievement in elementary school	.20***	11.1	27.6	3.1
Identified as learning disabled (*n* = 62)	.16***	13.6	35.9	3.6
Peer.				
Association with friends who engage in problem behaviors	.09**	13.2	25.8	2.0
Individual				
Religious service attendance	.00(*ns*)	15.3	15.3	1.0
Antisocial beliefs	.11***	13.1	22.7	2.0
Respondent drinking	.05*	13.8	20.1	1.6
Respondent marijuana initiation (*n* = 60)	.16***	13.6	36.7	3.7
Violence	.20**	11.4	28.4	3.1
Personality/individual difference				
Externalizing	.17***	12.0	26.4	2.6
Internalizing	.03(*ns*)	14.1	18.8	1.4
Hyperactive	.09**	13.4	21.3	1.7
Poor refusal skills	.08*	14.2	22.7	1.8

NOTE: *ns* = nonsignificant.
a. Median *n* for bivariate logistic regressions = 786.
b. At risk is defined as being in the worst quartile on the risk factor. For the categorical predictors of family structure, learning disabled, and marijuana initiation, the *n* for the category is provided.
c. Logistic regressions for family structure compare each subsequent family structure category against the first category (two parents, biological or adoptive, in household).
*p < .05. **p < .01. ***p < .001.

knowledge, was significantly associated with later gang membership (OR = 2.0).

Individual-level predictors. At ages 10 to 12, having tried marijuana (OR = 3.7) and self-reported violence as assessed by fighting, throwing objects, and hitting a teacher (OR = 3.1) were predictive of gang membership at ages 13 to 18. Youth high in externalizing behavior as rated by fifth- and sixth-grade teachers had more than two times greater odds of joining a gang as compared with other youth (OR = 2.6). Other significant individual-level predictors included rejection of conventional beliefs (OR = 2.0), poor refusal skills (OR = 1.8), hyperactivity as rated by fifth- and sixth-grade teachers (OR = 1.7), and early initiation of drinking (OR = 1.6). Religious service attendance at ages 10 to 12 did not significantly predict gang membership in adolescence.

Interactions of risk factors with gender. The differential impact of each risk factor on males and females was examined by conducting logistic regressions on the full sample entering each risk factor along with gender and the Factor × Gender interaction term (results not tabled). Results indicated substantial similarity among males and females in the risk factors associated with gang participation: Only the Family Structure × Gender interaction term was significant, such that the effect of single-parent households on subsequent gang membership was stronger for girls than it was for boys.

The impact of multiple risk factors. To assess the impact of exposure to multiple risk factors in childhood on later adolescent gang membership, an index was created that counted the number of significant risk factors to which each youth was exposed. Because 21 significant predictors of gang membership were found, scores could range from 0 to 21. Actual scores ranged from 0 to 19, divisible into approximate quartiles of youth exposed to 0 to 1 risk, 2 to 3 risks, 4 to 6 risks, and 7+ risks. A logistic regression was run on this categorical measure of risk factor exposure and adolescent gang membership, with each level of risk compared to the base 0 to 1 risk. These results are presented in Table 4. Note that for each successive quartile of risk the odds of joining a gang approximately doubled, such that those youth with exposure to 7 or more risks in elementary school had more than 13 times greater odds of joining a gang than those exposed to 0 to 1 risk. The fact that exposure to more risks increased the odds of gang membership suggests that, in spite of possible covariation among these factors, each of these significant factors contributed to overall risk for gang membership.

TABLE 4: Odds Ratios for Adolescent Gang Membership for Numbers of Risk Factors Experienced at Ages 10 to 12

Level of Risk at Ages 10 to 12		n	Observed Adolescent Gang Prevalence (percentage)	Odds Ratio[a]
No risk	0 to 1 risk factors	148	3.4	
Low risk	2 to 3 risk factors	219	9.6	3.0***
Medium risk	4 to 6 risk factors	235	14.0	4.7***
High risk	7+ risk factors	206	31.6	13.2***
Total		808		

NOTE: Odds ratios for each category are in comparison to the first category (no risk); $N = 808$.
a. Odds ratio for joining a gang compared to no-risk category (0 to 1 risk).
***$p < .001$.

DISCUSSION

Logistic regression was used to identify risk factors at ages 10 through 12 predictive of joining a gang between the ages of 13 and 18. Factors from every domain of children's experience—the neighborhood, family, school, peer, and individual—significantly predicted joining a gang in adolescence. The strongest predictors at ages 10 to 12 were the availability of marijuana in the neighborhood, many neighborhood youth in trouble, living with one parent and another nonparent adult in the home, having initiated marijuana use, having engaged in violence, low academic achievement, and being identified as learning disabled in school; all of the predictors had odds ratios between 3 and 4 for those youth with these characteristics. Note that the present analyses assess the independent childhood predictors of later gang membership. Multivariate models testing specific theoretical hypotheses using time-varying predictors would be a reasonable next step.

Some of these results replicate predictors identified in previous longitudinal studies of gang membership (family structure and poverty, low academic aspirations, delinquent peers, prior delinquency, and alcohol and drug use). The present results indicate that these factors predict later gang membership from as early as ages 10 to 12. In addition, this study identified factors previously unstudied in longitudinal analyses that predicted gang membership, including living in a neighborhood in which many youth are in trouble and drugs are available, sibling antisocial behavior, poor family management practices, parent proviolent attitudes, low attachment and commitment to school, being identified as learning disabled, being rated by teachers as high on externalizing behavior and hyperactivity, and having poor refusal skills.

Analyses of the effect of exposure to multiple risk factors indicated that exposure to a greater number of risk factors in childhood greatly increased the risk of joining a gang in adolescence. These findings support intervention strategies that target youth in neighborhoods, families, or schools exposed to multiple risk factors.

At the community level, the strongest measured predictors of gang membership were the availability of marijuana and the number of neighborhood youth in trouble, supporting cross-sectional results reported by Spergel and Curry (1993). These findings suggest that prevention efforts that reduce opportunities for antisocial involvement in the neighborhood may help in reducing later gang membership.

Family composition (one parent in the home versus two) and poor family management significantly predicted gang membership, whereas attachment to mother or father did not. These results support findings from Decker and VanWinkle's (1996) ethnographic interviews of gang members who, although they were more likely to come from single parent homes, would choose their family over the gang if forced to choose. It does not appear from these data that gangs provide new families for children who have failed to bond to their own families. Helping parents to develop skills to better manage their children may reduce risks for gang membership, particularly for girls.

Sibling antisocial behavior and parents' proviolent attitudes also predicted later gang membership. Intervention efforts may be directed productively at these family influences toward gang membership. If preventing gang membership is a goal, preventive intervention efforts to reach the younger siblings of delinquent adolescents are clearly supported by the present data, as are parent-focused interventions that encourage parents to adopt and express nonviolent solutions to problems and conflict situations.

These data show the importance of elementary school experiences in predicting later gang membership. Poor school achievement, attachment, commitment, and aspirations at ages 10 to 12 all predicted later gang membership, as did being identified as learning learning disabled in elementary school. These results suggest that elementary schools that increase academic success for all students can reduce the risk that their students will later join gangs.

Note that involvement in the form of religious service attendance at ages 10 to 12 was not a significant predictor of later gang membership. This finding is interesting given the mixed findings on participation in religious activities in preventing delinquency in adolescence (Bainbridge 1989; Benda

1995; Cochran, Wood, and Arneklev 1994; Evans et al. 1996; Fernquist 1995; Free 1994; Hirschi and Stark 1969; Maxson et al. 1998).

Research by Moffitt (1993) and Bartusch et al. (1997) highlights the importance of childhood delinquency in initiating a pattern of life course persistent antisocial behavior. Furthermore, recent analyses by Hawkins et al. (1997) found that an early age of initiation of alcohol mediated almost all other early risk factors for alcohol abuse at age 18. These studies, coupled with the present finding that early initiation of problem behaviors such as violence and marijuana use predicted later gang membership, highlight the importance of preventing or delaying initiation of such behaviors well before most youth join gangs.

Overall, gang membership appears to result from antisocial influences in neighborhoods, families, and peer groups; failure to become successfully engaged in school; and early initiation of problem behaviors. These findings provide guidance for gang prevention. We should not wait until adolescence to begin gang prevention efforts: The present results suggest that preventive interventions in the elementary grades could have a significant impact on adolescent gang membership. Moreover, these findings highlight the importance of multiple-component prevention strategies addressing risks across several domains.

APPENDIX
Item List for Measures of Predictors of Gang Membership

DEMOGRAPHICS

Gender (youth interview)

* Female, Male

Ethnicity (youth interview)

* Asian American, African American, European American, Other (primarily Native American)

NEIGHBORHOOD

Availability of marijuana (youth interview)

* Do you know anyone who has tried marijuana?
* Have you ever had a chance to try marijuana?

- If you had the money, and wanted to get marijuana, do you think you could get some?

Neighborhood youth in trouble (youth interview)

- Lots of kids in my neighborhood are in trouble.

Low neighborhood attachment (youth interview)

- I know many people in my neighborhood.
- I like my neighborhood.
- I feel safe in my neighborhood.

FAMILY

Poverty (parent interview)

- Approximately what is your family's total yearly income before taxes?

Family structure (parent interview)

The variety of family structures in the sample were combined into the following five categories:

- both parents (biological or adoptive) at home,
- one biological parent and one stepparent,
- one parent alone,
- one parent with other adults living in home, and
- other adults only (no parents).

The last four family structures were each compared with the case in which the child had both parents (biological or adoptive) at home.

Parent drinking (parent interview)

- How often do you drink beer, wine, or liquor?
- If you are living with a spouse or partner, how often does your spouse or partner drink beer, wine, or liquor?

Sibling antisocial behavior (youth interview)

- If you have brothers and sisters, do any of them smoke cigarettes?
- Do any of your brothers or sisters smoke marijuana?
- Have any of your brothers and sisters ever been suspended from school?
- Have any of your brothers or sisters ever been picked up or arrested by the police?

Poor family management (youth interview)

- When you are away from home, do your parents know where you are and who you are with?
- The rules in my family are clear.

Parent proviolent attitudes (youth interview)

- How do you think your parents feel (or would feel) about you hitting or threatening to hit someone?

Low attachment to parents (youth interview)

- Would you like to be the kind of person your mother is?
- Do you share your thoughts and feelings with your mother?
- Would you like to be the kind of person your father is?
- Do you share your thoughts and feelings with your father?

SCHOOL

Low educational aspirations (youth interview)

- If you could go as far as you wanted in school, how far would you like to go?

Low school commitment (youth interview)

- I do extra work on my own in class. (reversed)
- When I have an assignment to do, I keep on working on it until it is finished. (reversed)

Low school attachment (youth interview)

- I like school. (reversed)
- Most mornings I look forward to going to school. (reversed)
- I like my teacher this year. (reversed)
- I like my class this year. (reversed)

Low academic achievement in elementary school (school records)

- Score for the California Achievement Test (from school records). This is a combined score of three subtests (reading, math, and language).

Identified as learning disabled (school records)

- Special Education designation as learning disabled (from school records).

PEER

Association with friends who engage in problem behavior (youth interview)

This scale reflects the mean amount of time a student spends with each of three best friends, providing the friend gets in trouble with the teacher, or drinks.

- Does your best friend do things that get her or him in trouble with the teacher?
- Has your best friend tried beer, wine, or liquor when his or her parents did not know about it?
- How often do you see your best friend?

- Does your second best friend do things that get her or him in trouble with the teacher?
- Has your second best friend tried beer, wine, or liquor when his or her parents did not know about it?
- How often do you see your second best friend?
- Does your third best friend do things that get her or him in trouble with the teacher?
- Has your third best friend tried beer, wine, or liquor when his or her parents did not know about it?
- How often do you see your third best friend?

INDIVIDUAL

Religious service attendance (youth interview)

- How often do you attend religious services?

Antisocial beliefs (youth interview)

- Is it okay to take something without asking if you can get away with it?
- To get ahead you have to do some things that are not right.
- You have to be willing to break some rules if you want to be popular with your friends.
- If a friend asked to copy your exam, would you let your friend copy it?
- At school, sometimes it is okay to cheat.
- It is fun to do things you are not supposed to.

Respondent drinking (youth interview)

- Have you ever drunk beer, wine, whiskey, gin, or other liquor?
- How many times in the past month have you drunk beer, wine, whiskey, gin, or other liquor?

Respondent marijuana initiation (youth interview)

- Have you ever smoked marijuana?

Violence (youth interview)

- How many times in the past year have you picked a fight with someone?
- How many times in the past year have you thrown objects such as rocks or bottles at cars or people?
- How many times have you hit a teacher in the past year?

Externalizing (teacher interviews)

- Achenbach's (1991) broad-band externalizing scale consisting of 66 teacher-rated items reflecting the subdimensions "inattentive," "nervous-overreactive," and "aggressive."

Internalizing (teacher interviews)

- Achenbach's (1991) broad-band internalizing scale consisting of 25 teacher-rated items reflecting the subdimensions "anxious" and "social withdrawal."

Hyperactive (teacher interviews)

- Achenbach's (1991) scale consisting of teacher-rated hyperactive behavior (e.g., items such as "fidgety," "restless," and "distracted").

Poor refusal skills (youth interview)

Items included in this scale assessed the appropriateness of responses to the following scenarios involving peer pressure for antisocial behavior:

- If you were at a party and one of your friends offered you a beer, what would you do?
- If one of your friends asked you to skip school, what would you do?

NOTE

1. To examine the effect of risk factors due to early gang experience, individuals who indicated gang membership at the earliest age this question was available (age 13) were deleted in an exploratory analysis. Results from this analysis were consistent with those presented in the article and are available from the first author.

REFERENCES

Achenbach, T. M. 1991. *Integrative Guide for the 1991 CBCL/4-18, YSR, and TRF Profiles.* Burlington: University of Vermont, Department of Psychiatry.

Adler, Peter, Carlos Ovando, and Dennis Hocevar. 1984. "Familiar Correlates of Gang Membership: An Exploratory Study of Mexican-American Youth." *Hispanic Journal of Behavioral Sciences* 6:65-76.

Bainbridge, William S. 1989. "The Religious Ecology of Deviance." *American Sociological Review* 54(2):288-95.

Bartusch, Dawn J., Donald R. Lynam, Terrie E. Moffitt, and Phil A. Silva. 1997. "Is Age Important? Testing a General Versus a Developmental Theory of Antisocial Behavior." *Criminology* 35(1):13-48.

Battin, Sara R., Karl G. Hill, Robert D. Abbott, Richard F. Catalano, and J. David Hawkins. 1998. "The Contribution of Gang Membership to Delinquency Beyond Delinquent Friends." *Criminology* 36(1):93-115.

Benda, Brent B. 1995. "The Effect of Religion on Adolescent Delinquency Revisited." *Journal of Research in Crime and Delinquency* 32(4):446-66.

Bjerregaard, Beth and Alan J. Lizotte. 1995. "Gun Ownership and Gang Membership." *Journal of Criminal Law and Criminology* 86:37-58.

Bjerregaard, Beth and Carolyn Smith. 1993. "Gender Differences in Gang Participation, Delinquency, and Substance Use." *Journal of Quantitative Criminology* 9:329-55.

Bowker, Lee H. and Malcolm W. Klein. 1983. "The Etiology of Female Juvenile Delinquency and Gang Membership: A Test of Psychological and Social Structural Explanations." *Adolescence* 18:739-51.

Bursik, Robert J., Jr., and Harold G. Grasmick. 1993. *Neighborhoods and Crime: The Dimension of Effective Community Control.* New York: Lexington Books.

Catalano, Richard F. and J. David Hawkins. 1996. "The Social Development Model: A Theory of Antisocial Behavior." Pp. 149-97 in *Delinquency and Crime: Current Theories*, edited by J. David Hawkins. New York: Cambridge University Press.

Cloward, Richard A. and Lloyd E. Ohlin. 1960. *Delinquency and Opportunity: A Theory of Delinquent Gangs.* New York: Free Press.

Cochran, John K., Peter B. Wood, and Bruce J. Arneklev. 1994. "Is the Religiosity-Delinquency Relationship Spurious? Social Control Theories." *Journal of Research in Crime and Delinquency* 31(1):92-123.

Cohen, Albert K. 1955. *Delinquent Boys: The Culture of the Gang.* Glencoe, IL: Free Press.

Cohen, Albert K. and James F. Short. 1958. "Research in Delinquent Subcultures." *Journal of Social Issues* 14:20-37.

Curry, G. David. and Irving A. Spergel. 1992. "Gang Involvement and Delinquency among Hispanic and African-American Adolescent Males." *Journal of Research in Crime and Delinquency* 29:273-91.

Decker, Scott H. and Barrik Van Winkle. 1996. *Life in the Gang: Family, Friends, and Violence.* New York: Cambridge University Press.

Esbensen, Finne-Aage and David Huizinga. 1993. "Gangs, Drugs, and Delinquency in a Survey of Urban Youth." *Criminology* 31:565-89.

Esbensen, Finne-Aage, David Huizinga, and Anne W. Weiher. 1993. "Gang and Non-Gang Youth: Differences in Explanatory Variables." *Journal of Contemporary Criminal Justice* 9:94-116.

Evans, T. David, Francis T. Cullen, Velmer S. Burton, Gregory R. Dunaway, G. L. Payne, and Sesha R. Kethineni. 1996. "Religion, Social Bonds, and Delinquency." *Deviant Behavior* 17(1):43-70.

Fagan, Jeffrey. 1990. "Social Process of Delinquency and Drug Use Among Urban Gangs." Pp. 183-219 in *Gangs in America*, edited by C. R. Huff. Newbury Park, CA: Sage.

———. 1996. "Gangs, Drugs, and Neighborhood Change." Pp. 39-74 in *Gangs in America*, 2d ed., edited by C. R. Huff. Thousand Oaks, CA: Sage.

Farrington, David P. 1989. "Early Predictors of Adolescent Aggression and Adult Violence." *Violence and Victims* 4(2):79-100.

———. 1998. "Predictors, Causes, and Correlates of Male Youth Violence." Pp. 421-75 in *Crime and Justice*, Vol. 24, edited by M. Tonry and M. H. Moore. Chicago: University of Chicago Press.

Fernquist, Robert M. 1995. "A Research Note on the Association Between Religiosity and Delinquency." *Deviant Behavior* 16(2):169-75.

Free, Marvin D. 1994. "Religiosity, Religious Conservatism, Bonds to School, and Juvenile Delinquency Among Three Categories of Drug Users." *Deviant Behavior* 15(2):151-70.

Friedman, C. Jack, Fredrica Mann, and Alfred S. Friedman. 1975. "A Profile of Juvenile Street Gang Members." *Adolescence* 10:563-607.

Hagedorn, John M. 1988. *People and Folks: Gangs, Crime and the Underclass in a Rustbelt City.* Chicago: Lakeview Press.

———. 1994a. "Homeboys, Dope Fiends, Legits, and New Jacks." *Criminology* 32:197-217.

————. 1994b. "Neighborhoods, Markets, and Gang Drug Organization." *Journal of Research in Crime and Delinquency* 31:264-94.

Hawkins, J. David, Michael W. Arthur, and Richard F. Catalano. 1995. "Preventing Substance Abuse." Pp. 343-427 in *Crime and Justice: A Review of Research: Vol. 19. Building a Safer Society: Strategic Approaches to Crime Prevention*, edited by M. Tonry and D. Farrington. Chicago: University of Chicago Press.

Hawkins, J. David, Richard F. Catalano, and Janet Y. Miller. 1992. "Risk and Protective Factors for Alcohol and Other Drug Problems in Adolescence and Early Adulthood: Implications for Substance Abuse Prevention." *Psychological Bulletin* 112:64-105. [SDRG #86]

Hawkins, J. David, John W. Graham, Eugene Maguin, Robert D. Abbott, and Richard F. Catalano. 1997. "Exploring the Effects of Age of Alcohol Use Initiation and Psychosocial Risk Factors on Subsequent Alcohol Misuse." *Journal of Studies on Alcohol* 58:280-90.

Hawkins, J. David, Todd Herrenkohl, David P. Farrington, Devon D. Brewer, Richard F. Catalano, and Tracy W. Harachi. 1998. "A Review of Predictors of Youth Violence." Pp. 106-46 in *Serious and Violent Juvenile Offenders: Risk Factors and Successful Interventions*, edited by R. Loeber and D. P. Farrington. Thousand Oaks, CA: Sage.

Hindelang, Michael J., Travis Hirschi, and Joseph G. Weis. 1981. *Measuring Delinquency.* Beverly Hills, CA: Sage.

Hirschi, Travis. 1969. *Causes of Delinquency.* Berkeley: University of California Press.

Hirschi, Travis and Rodney Stark. 1969. "Hellfire and Delinquency." *Social Problems* 17(2):202-13.

Howell, James C. 1997. "Youth Gang Violence Prevention and Intervention: What Works." Report to the U.S. Department of Justice, Office of Juvenile Justice and Delinquency Prevention.

Klein, Malcolm. 1995. *The American Street Gang.* New York: Oxford University Press.

Lipsey, Mark W. and James H. Derzon. 1998. "Predictors of Violent or Serious Delinquency in Adolescence and Early Adulthood: A Synthesis of Longitudinal Research." Pp. 86-105 in *Serious and Violent Juvenile Offenders: Risk Factors and Successful Interventions*, edited by R. Loeber and D. P. Farrington. Thousand Oaks, CA: Sage.

Lizotte, Alan J., James M. Tesoriero, Terence P. Thornberry, and Marvin D. Krohn. 1994. "Patterns of Adolescent Firearms Ownership and Use." *Justice Quarterly* 11:51-73.

Loeber, Rolf, Farrington, David P., Stouthamer-Loeber, Magda, and Van Kammen, Welmoet B. 1998: *Antisocial behavior and mental health problems: Explanatory factors in childhood and adolescence.* Mahwah, NJ: Lawrence Erlbaum Associates, Inc.

Loeber, Rolf, Magda S. Stouthamer-Loeber, Welmoet Van Kammen, and David P. Farrington. 1991. "Initiation, Escalation, and Desistance in Juvenile Offending and Their Correlates." *Journal of Criminal Law and Criminology* 82:36-82.

Maxson, Cheryl L., Monica L. Whitlock, and Malcolm W. Klein. 1998. "Vulnerability to Street Gang Membership: Implications for Practice." *Social Service Review* 72:70-91.

Miller, Walter B. 1958. "Lower Class Culture as a Generating Milieu of Gang Delinquency." *Journal of Social Issues* 14:5-19.

Moffitt, Terrie E. 1993. "Adolescent-Limited and Life-Course-Persistent Antisocial Behavior: A Developmental Taxonomy." *Psychological Review* 100:674-701.

Moore, Joan W. 1978. *Homeboys: Gangs, Drugs and Prison in the Barrios of Los Angeles.* Philadelphia: Temple University Press.

————. 1991. *Going Down to the Barrio: Homeboys and Homegirls in Charge.* Philadelphia: Temple University Press.

Sampson, Robert J. 1986. "Effects of Socioeconomic Context on Official Reaction to Juvenile Delinquency." *American Sociological Review* 5:876-85.

Savitz, Leonard D., Lawrence Rosen, and Michael Lalli. 1980. "Delinquency and Gang Membership as Related to Victimization." *Victimology* 5:152-60.

Shaw, Clifford R. and Henry D. McKay. 1931. *Social Factors in Juvenile Delinquency. Report on the Causes of Crime, Vol II. National Commission on Law Observance and Enforcement.* Washington, DC: U.S. Government Printing Office.

———. 1942. *Juvenile Delinquency and Urban Areas.* Chicago: University of Chicago Press.

Short, James F., Jr. 1996. *Gangs and Adolescent Violence.* Boulder, CO: Center for the Study and Prevention of Violence.

Simcha-Fagan, Ora, Joanne C. Gersten, and Thomas S. Langner. 1986. "Early Precursors and Concurrent Correlates of Patterns of Illicit Drug Use in Adolescence." *Journal of Drug Issues* 16:7-28.

Spergel, Irving. 1995. *The Youth Gang Problem.* New York: Oxford University Press.

Spergel, Irving A. and G. David Curry. 1993. "The National Youth Gang Survey: A Research and Development Process." Pp. 359-400 in *The Gang Intervention Handbook*, edited by A. Goldstein and C. R. Huff. Champaign, IL: Research Press.

Sutherland, Edwin and Donald Cressey. 1978. *Principles of Criminology.* 10th ed. New York: Lippincott.

Thornberry, Terence P. 1998. "Membership in Youth Gangs and Involvement in Serious and Violent Offending." Pp. 147-66 in *Serious and Violent Juvenile Offenders: Risk Factors and Successful Interventions*, edited by R. Loeber and D. P. Farrington. Thousand Oaks, CA: Sage.

Thornberry, Terence P., Marvin D. Krohn, Alan J. Lizotte, and Deborah Chard-Wierschem. 1993. "The Role of Juvenile Gangs in Facilitating Delinquent Behavior." *Journal of Research in Crime and Delinquency* 30:55-87.

Thrasher, Frederic M. [1927] 1963. "The Gang: A Study of 1,313 Gangs in Chicago." Abridged with a new introduction by J. F. Short, Jr. Chicago: University of Chicago Press.

Vigil, James D. and Steve C. Yun. 1990. "Vietnamese Youth Gangs in Southern California." Pp. 146-62 in *Gangs in America*, edited by C. R. Huff. Newbury Park, CA: Sage.

Wilson, William J. 1987. *The Truly Disadvantaged: The Inner City, the Underclass, and Public Policy.* Chicago: University of Chicago.

———. 1996. *When Work Disappears.* New York: Knopf.

[28]

PROBLEM-ORIENTED POLICING, DETERRENCE, AND YOUTH VIOLENCE: AN EVALUATION OF BOSTON'S OPERATION CEASEFIRE

ANTHONY A. BRAGA
DAVID M. KENNEDY
ELIN J. WARING
ANNE MORRISON PIEHL

Operation Ceasefire is a problem-oriented policing intervention aimed at reducing youth homicide and youth firearms violence in Boston. It represented an innovative partnership between researchers and practitioners to assess the city's youth homicide problem and implement an intervention designed to have a substantial near-term impact on the problem. Operation Ceasefire was based on the "pulling levers" deterrence strategy that focused criminal justice attention on a small number of chronically offending gang-involved youth responsible for much of Boston's youth homicide problem. Our impact evaluation suggests that the Ceasefire intervention was associated with significant reductions in youth homicide victimization, shots-fired calls for service, and gun assault incidents in Boston. A comparative analysis of youth homicide trends in Boston relative to youth homicide trends in other major U.S. and New England cities also supports a unique program effect associated with the Ceasefire intervention.

Although overall homicide rates in the United States declined between the 1980s and 1990s, youth homicide rates, particularly incidents involving firearms, increased dramatically. Between 1984 and 1994, juvenile (younger than 18) homicide victimizations committed with handguns increased by 418 percent, and juvenile homicide victimizations committed with other guns in-

This research was supported under award 94-IJ-CX-0056 from the National Institute of Justice, Office of Justice Programs, U.S. Department of Justice. Points of view in this article are those of the authors and do not necessarily represent the official position of the U.S. Department of Justice. The authors would like to thank Paul Evans, James Jordan, Gary French, and the members of the Boston Gun Project working group for their support in this research enterprise; Glenn Pierce and Baron Briggs for the acquisition of some of the data; and Stephen Brimley, Christiana Briggs, and Lisa Sanbonmatsu for their excellent research assistance. We would also like to thank Lois Mock for her sound advice and patience in the completion of this research.

creased 125 percent (Fox 1996). During this time period, adolescents (ages 14 to 17) as a group had the largest proportional increase in homicide commission and victimization, but young adults (ages 18 to 24) had the largest absolute increase in numbers, and there was a good deal crossfire between the two age groups (Cook and Laub 1998). All of the increase in youth homicide was in gun homicides (Cook and Laub 1998). For many cities, the bulk of this dramatic increase in youth homicide occurred in the late 1980s and early 1990s. In Boston, youth homicide (ages 24 and younger) increased more than threefold—from 22 victims in 1987 to 73 victims in 1990 (see Figure 1). Youth homicide remained high even after the peak of the epidemic; Boston averaged about 44 youth homicides per year between 1991 and 1995.

At the same time that the United States was experiencing this sudden increase in youth violence, the capacity of police departments to design and implement creative new operational strategies also increased through the advent of "community" and "problem-oriented" policing (Goldstein 1990; Sparrow, Moore, and Kennedy 1990). In Boston, an interagency problem-solving intervention, based in part on a tight link between research, the design of interventions, and operations, has shown much promise in reducing youth homicide (Kennedy, Braga, and Piehl 1997; Kennedy, Piehl, and Braga 1996). Nationally, without the support of a formal evaluation, the Boston program has been hailed as an unprecedented success (see, e.g., Butterfield 1996; Witkin 1997). This article describes the results of a National Institute of Justice-funded evaluation of Boston's youth homicide reduction initiative. Our analyses of Boston's youth homicide prevention program suggests that it was a very effective intervention; not only was the intervention associated with a significant reduction in youth homicide victimization, it also was associated with significant reductions in shots-fired calls for service and gun assault incidents.

THE BOSTON GUN PROJECT AND
THE OPERATION CEASEFIRE INTERVENTION

Problem-oriented policing holds great promise for creating a strong local response to youth homicide problems. Problem-oriented policing works to identify why things are going wrong and to frame responses using a wide variety of often untraditional approaches (Goldstein 1979). Using a basic iterative approach of problem identification, analysis, response, evaluation, and adjustment of the response, problem-oriented policing has been effective against a wide variety of crime, fear, and order concerns (Braga, Weisburd et al. 1999; Eck and Spelman 1987; Goldstein 1990). This adaptable and

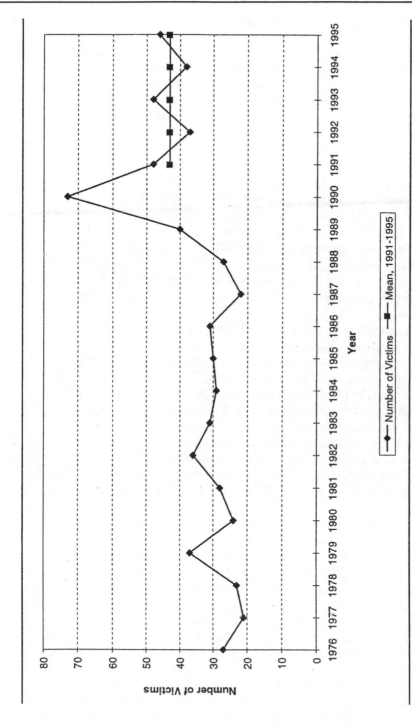

Figure 1: Boston Homicide Victims Ages 24 and Younger

197

198 JOURNAL OF RESEARCH IN CRIME AND DELINQUENCY

dynamic analytic approach provides an appropriate framework to uncover the complex mechanisms at play in youth homicide and develop tailor-made interventions to reduce youth homicide victimization.

The Boston Gun Project is a problem-oriented policing initiative aimed at reducing homicide victimization among young people in Boston. *Youth* was initially defined as "age 21 and under" and, as the project developed, "age 24 and under."[1] Sponsored by the National Institute of Justice, the project was designed to proceed by (1) assembling an interagency working group of largely line-level criminal justice and other practitioners; (2) applying quantitative and qualitative research techniques to create an assessment of the nature of, and dynamics driving, youth violence in Boston; (3) developing an intervention designed to have a substantial, near-term impact on youth homicide; (4) implementing and adapting the intervention; and (5) evaluating the intervention's impact. The project began in early 1995 and implemented what is now known as the Operation Ceasefire intervention beginning in the late spring of 1996.

Core participating agencies, as defined by regular participation in the Boston Gun Project Working Group over the duration of the project, included the Boston Police Department; the Massachusetts departments of probation and parole; the office of the Suffolk County District Attorney; the office of the U.S. Attorney; the Bureau of Alcohol, Tobacco, and Firearms; the Massachusetts Department of Youth Services (juvenile corrections); Boston School Police; and gang outreach and prevention "streetworkers" attached to the Boston Community Centers program. Other important participants, either as regular partners later in the process or episodically, have included the Ten Point Coalition of activist Black clergy, the Drug Enforcement Administration, the Massachusetts State Police, and the office of the Massachusetts Attorney General.

Project research showed that firearms associated with youth, especially with gang youth, tended to be semiautomatic pistols, often ones that were quite new and apparently recently diverted from retail (Kennedy et al. 1996; Kennedy et al. 1997). Many of these guns were first sold at retail in Massachusetts, and others were smuggled in from out of state. Project research also showed that the problem of youth homicide was concentrated among a small number of chronically offending gang-involved youth.[2] Only about 1,300 gang members—less that 1 percent of their age group citywide—in about 61 gangs were responsible for at least 60 percent of all youth homicides in the city. These gangs were well known to the authorities and streetworkers; gang members were also often well known and tended to have extensive criminal records (Kennedy et al. 1996). Chronic disputes, or "beefs," among gangs appeared to be the most significant driver of gang violence (Braga, Piehl, and Kennedy 1999).

The research findings were discussed and analyzed within the working-group problem-solving process and were instrumental in the development of an operational strategy. The research findings and the working-group process thus led to the Operation Ceasefire intervention (for a complete discussion of the program development and implementation process, see Kennedy, Braga, and Piehl 1999). Operation Ceasefire included two main elements: (1) a direct law-enforcement attack on illicit firearms traffickers supplying youth with guns and (2) an attempt to generate a strong deterrent to gang violence. The working group framed a set of activities intended to systematically address the patterns of firearms trafficking identified by the research. These included the following:

- Expanding the focus of local, state, and federal authorities to include *intrastate* trafficking in Massachusetts-sourced guns, in addition to interstate trafficking.
- Focusing enforcement attention on traffickers of those makes and calibers of guns most used by gang members.
- Focusing enforcement attention on traffickers of those guns showing short time to crime and thus most likely to have been trafficked. The Boston Field Division of ATF set up an in-house tracking system that flagged guns whose traces showed an 18-month or shorter time to crime.
- Focusing enforcement attention on traffickers of guns used by the city's most violent gangs.
- Attempting restoration of obliterated serial numbers and subsequent trafficking investigations based on those restorations.
- Supporting these enforcement priorities through analysis of crime gun traces generated by the Boston Police Department's comprehensive tracing of crime guns and by developing leads through systematic debriefing of, especially, arrestees involved with gangs and/or involved in violent crime.

The "pulling levers" strategy, as the second element came to be known by working-group members, involved deterring violent behavior by chronic gang offenders by reaching out directly to gangs, saying explicitly that violence would no longer be tolerated, and backing that message by "pulling every lever" legally available when violence occurred (Kennedy 1997, 1998). Simultaneously, streetworkers, probation and parole officers, and later churches and other community groups offered gang members services and other kinds of help. The Ceasefire working group delivered this message in formal meetings with gang members, through individual police and probation contacts with gang members, through meetings with inmates of secure juvenile facilities in the city, and through gang outreach workers. The deterrence message was not a deal with gang members to stop violence. Rather, it was a promise to gang members that violent behavior would evoke an immediate and intense response. If gangs committed other crimes but refrained from violence, the normal workings of police, prosecutors, and the rest of the criminal justice system dealt with these matters. But if gang members hurt people, the working group focused its enforcement actions on them.

When gang violence occurred, the Ceasefire agencies addressed the violent group or groups involved, drawing from a menu of all possible legal levers. The chronic involvement of gang members in a wide variety of offenses made them, and the gangs they formed, vulnerable to a coordinated criminal justice response. The authorities could disrupt street drug activity, focus police attention on low-level street crimes such as trespassing and public drinking, serve outstanding warrants, cultivate confidential informants for medium- and long-term investigations of gang activities, deliver strict probation and parole enforcement, seize drug proceeds and other assets, ensure stiffer plea bargains and sterner prosecutorial attention, request stronger bail terms (and enforce them), and focus potentially severe federal investigative and prosecutorial attention on, for example, gang-related drug activity. The multitude of agencies involved in the working group assessed each gang that behaved violently and subjected them to such crackdowns. These operations were customized to the particular individuals and characteristics of the gang in question and could range from probation curfew checks to DEA investigations.[3]

The Ceasefire crackdowns were not designed to eliminate gangs or stop every aspect of gang activity but to control and deter serious violence. To do this, the working group explained its actions against targeted gangs to other gangs, as in "this gang did violence, we responded with the following actions, and here is how to prevent anything similar from happening to you." The ongoing working-group process regularly watched the city for outbreaks of gang violence and framed any necessary responses in accord with the Ceasefire strategy. As the strategy unfolded, the working group continued communication with gangs and gang members to convey its determination to stop violence, explain its actions to the target population, and maximize both voluntary compliance and the strategy's deterrent power.

A central hypothesis within the working group was the idea that a meaningful period of substantially reduced youth violence might serve as a "firebreak" and result in a relatively long-lasting reduction in future youth violence (Kennedy et al. 1996). The idea was that youth violence in Boston had become a self-sustaining cycle among a relatively small number of youth, with objectively high levels of risk leading to nominally self-protective behavior such as gun acquisition and use, gang formation, tough street behavior, and the like: behavior that then became an additional input into the cycle of violence (Kennedy et al. 1996). If this cycle could be interrupted, a new equilibrium at a lower level of risk and violence might be established, perhaps without the need for continued high levels of either deterrent or facilitative intervention.

DETERRENCE AND CRIME PREVENTION

The Operation Ceasefire intervention is, in its broadest sense, a deterrence strategy. Deterrence theory posits that crimes can be prevented when the costs of committing the crime are perceived by the offender to outweigh the benefits of committing the crime (Gibbs 1975; Zimring and Hawkins 1973). Most discussions of the deterrence mechanism distinguish between "general" and "special" deterrence (Cook 1980). General deterrence is the idea that the general population is dissuaded from committing crime when it sees that punishment necessarily follows the commission of a crime. Special deterrence involves punishment administered to criminals with the intent to discourage them from committing crimes in the future. Much of the literature evaluating deterrence focuses on the effect of changing certainty, swiftness, and severity of punishment associated with certain acts on the prevalence of those crimes (Blumstein, Cohen, and Nagin 1978; Cameron 1988; Cook 1977, 1980; Paternoster 1987; Sherman 1990; Sherman and Berk 1984; Weisburd, Waring, and Chayet 1995). In addition to any increases in certainty, severity, and swiftness of sanctions associated with youth violence, the Operation Ceasefire strategy sought to gain deterrence through the advertising of the law enforcement strategy and the personalized nature of its application. It was crucial that gang youth understood the new regime that the city was imposing.

The pulling-levers approach attempted to prevent gang violence by making gang members believe that consequences would follow on violence and gun use and choose to change their behavior. A key element of the strategy was the delivery of a direct and explicit "retail deterrence" message to a relatively small target audience regarding what kind of behavior would provoke a special response and what that response would be. Law enforcement agencies in Boston increased the cost of gang-related violence. The deterrence principles applied in the Operation Ceasefire intervention could be regarded as a "meso-deterrence" strategy. Beyond the particular gangs subjected to the intervention, the deterrence message was applied to a relatively small audience (all gang-involved youth in Boston) rather than a general audience (all youth in Boston) and operated by making explicit cause-and-effect connections between the behavior of the target population and the behavior of the authorities. Knowledge of what happened to others in the target population was intended to prevent further acts of violence by gangs in Boston.

The effective operation of general deterrence is dependent on the communication of punishment threats to the public. As Zimring and Hawkins (1973) observe, "the deterrence threat may best be viewed as a form of advertising" (p. 142). One noteworthy example of this principle is an evaluation of Massachusetts' 1975 Bartley-Fox amendment, which introduced a mandatory minimum one-year prison sentence for the illegal carrying of firearms. The high degree of publicity attendant on the amendment's passage, some of which was inaccurate, was found to increase citizen compliance with existing legal stipulations surrounding firearm acquisition and possession, some of which were not in fact addressed by the amendment (see Beha 1977). Zimring and Hawkins further observe that "if the first task of the threatening agency is the communication of information, its second task is persuasion" (p. 149). In his article on the misapplication of deterrence principles in gang suppression programs, Malcolm Klein (1993) suggests that law enforcement agencies do not generally have the capacity to "eliminate" all gangs in a gang-troubled jurisdiction, nor do they have the capacity to respond in a powerful way to all gang-offending in such jurisdictions. Pledges to do so, though common, are simply not credible. The Operation Ceasefire working group recognized that, for the strategy to be successful, it was crucial to deliver a credible deterrence message to Boston gangs. Therefore, the Ceasefire intervention targeted those gangs that were engaged in violent behavior rather than expending resources on those who were not.

IMPACT EVALUATION

Like most evaluations of crime prevention programs (Ekblom and Pease 1995), our evaluation design departs from the desirable randomized controlled experimental approach. The Operation Ceasefire strategy was aimed at all areas of the city with a serious youth violence problem. There were no control areas (or control gangs) set aside within the city because of the following: (1) The aim was to do something about serious youth violence wherever it presented itself in the city, (2) the target of the intervention was defined as the self-sustaining cycle of violence in which all gangs were caught up and to which all gangs contributed, and (3) the communications strategy was explicitly intended to affect the behavior of gangs and individuals not directly subjected to enforcement attention (Kennedy et al., 1996). Therefore, it was not possible to compare areas and groups affected by the strategy to similar areas and groups not affected. Our analysis of impacts within Boston associated with the Ceasefire intervention follows a basic one-group time-series design (Campbell and Stanley 1966; Cook and Campbell 1979); we also use a nonrandomized quasi-experiment to compare youth homicide trends in Boston to youth homicide trends in other large U.S. cities (Cook and Campbell 1979; Rossi and Freeman 1993).

Within-Boston Outcome Measures: Homicide and Gun Violence

The key outcome variable in our assessment of the impact of the Ceasefire intervention was the monthly number of homicide victims ages 24 and younger. The Ceasefire intervention mostly targets violence arising from gang dynamics; our earlier research suggests that most gang members in Boston are ages 24 and younger (Kennedy et al. 1996; Kennedy et al. 1997). Therefore, our impact evaluation focuses on the number of youthful homicide victims in this age group. The homicide data used in these analyses were provided by the Boston Police Department's Office of Research and Analysis. The youth homicide impact evaluation examined the monthly counts of youth homicides in Boston between January 1, 1991, and May 31, 1998; the preintervention period included the relatively stable but still historically high postepidemic years of 1991 to 1995 (see Figure 1).

Beyond preventing youth homicides, the Ceasefire intervention was also designed to reduce other forms of nonfatal serious violence. As such, our evaluation also examines monthly counts of citywide shots-fired citizen calls for service data and citywide official gun assault incident report data. These data are available for a slightly shorter time period than our homicide data set due to lags in the Boston Police Department's data collection and preparation procedures. These data are examined for the January 1, 1991, through December 31, 1997, time period. The computerized Boston Police Department incident data have what is, for our purposes, an important shortcoming—the records do not capture the age of the victim (this is, of course, also true for shots-fired calls for service). To assess the effects of the intervention on gun assaults in specific age groups, we collected information on the age of the victim from hard copies of gun assault incident reports for the study time period. Because the collection and coding of this information was a time-consuming task, we chose to collect these data for one high-activity police district. District B-2 covers most of Boston's Roxbury neighborhood and has a very dense concentration of gangs; 29 of 61 identified gangs (47.5 percent) had turf in B-2 (Kennedy et al. 1997). Furthermore, there were 217 homicide victims ages 24 and younger in Boston between 1991 and 1995; a third of these victims were killed in B-2 (71 of 217, 32.7 percent).

Gangs

Simple Pre/Post Comparisons

In these analyses, we selected May 15, 1996, the date of the first direct communications with Boston gangs, as the date Ceasefire was implemented because all elements of the strategy—the focus on gun trafficking, a special interagency response to gang violence, and the communications campaign with gangs—were in place as of that date. No other rival programs were implemented in Boston even roughly close to this time period (Piehl, Kennedy, and Braga 2000). The well-known large reduction in yearly Boston youth homicide numbers certainly suggests that something noteworthy happened after Operation Ceasefire was implemented in mid-1996. As discussed earlier, Boston averaged 44 youth homicides per year between 1991 and 1995. In 1996, the number of Boston youth homicides decreased to 26 and then further decreased to 15 youth homicides in 1997. It is noteworthy that the yearly total of youth homicides in 1997—the first full calendar year of data after the implementation of Operation Ceasefire—represents the smallest number of youth homicides in Boston since 1976. This suggests that it was unlikely that the youth homicide reduction was due to a regression to the mean number of yearly youth homicides of the pre-youth homicide epidemic years. Figure 2 presents the monthly counts of youth homicides in Boston during the study time period. The time series shows a 63 percent reduction in the mean monthly number of youth homicide victims from a pretest mean of 3.5 youth homicides per month to a posttest mean of 1.3 youth homicides per month. This simple analysis suggests that Operation Ceasefire was associated with a large reduction in youth homicides in Boston (see also Piehl et al. 2000).

Generalized Linear Models

Generalized linear models were used in our deeper analysis of impacts associated with the Ceasefire intervention to analyze the time-series data (Dobson 1990; McCullagh and Nelder 1989). Generalized linear models are an extension of traditional linear models that allow "the mean of a population to depend on a *linear predictor* through a nonlinear *link function* and allows the response probability distribution to be any member of an exponential family of distributions" (SAS Institute 1993:4). This allows the technique to be applied to a wider range of problems. Generalized linear models are constructed by selecting the appropriate link function and response probability distribution. Because the underlying data were counts, a Poisson regression in a log-linear model was selected to model the monthly counts. The SAS Institute's GENMOD procedure was used to calculate the maximum likelihood estimate of the Ceasefire intervention effect parameters on the outcome

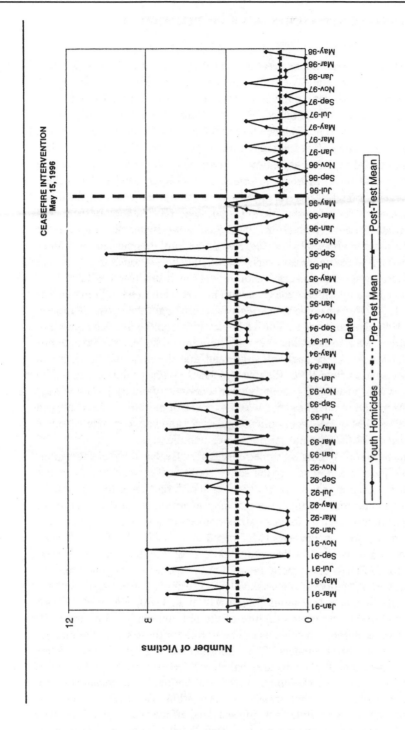

Figure 2: Monthly Counts of Youth Homicides in Boston

measures and to compute the associated probability values. The parameters for the intervention effects were also expressed as incidence rate ratios (i.e., exponentiated coefficients). Incidence rate ratios are interpreted as the rate at which things occur; for example, an incident rate ratio of .40 would indicate that, controlling for other independent variables, the Ceasefire intervention was associated with a 60 percent reduction in the number of youth homicides. Following social science convention, the two-tailed .05 level of significance was selected as the benchmark to reject the null hypothesis of "no difference." Likelihood ratio tests were used to determine whether adding the intervention variable provided statistically significant improvement of the model fit to the data (Aldrich and Nelson 1984). Finally, we present the results of the deviance statistic divided by the degrees of freedom; this measure examines the dispersion of the dependent variable and indicates whether these data are appropriate for the Poisson regression model (SAS Institute 1997:285).

As noted, we considered the Ceasefire intervention to be fully in place as of May 15, 1996. For convenience, we therefore begin the "post" period on June 1, 1996. Beyond our qualitative observations on the implementation of the program, we also examined the youth homicide time series for exogenous structural breaks; these analyses suggested that the maximal break in the series occurred in June 1996 (Piehl et al. 1999:13). The preintervention time series was composed of the monthly counts between January 1991 and May 1996; the intervention time series was composed of monthly counts between June 1996 and May 1998 for homicide measures and between June 1996 and December 1997 for nonfatal serious violence indicators.

In any time series, there are three sources of noise that could obscure intervention effects: *trend*, meaning the series could drift upward or downward; *seasonality*, meaning the series could spike at different times (e.g., homicide increases in summer months); and *random error*, meaning that even if the series was detrended and deseasonalized, observations would fluctuate randomly around some mean level (McDowall et al. 1980:14). If a time-series model does not account for these sources of error, the intervention analysis will be confounded. The general class of auto regressive integrated moving average (ARIMA) models can be used to good effect in detecting these three sources of noise in a time series (McDowall et al. 1980). We used ARIMA models to unravel the error structure of the preintervention time series for each outcome measure to guide us in accounting for these sources of noise in our generalized linear models.[4] The important findings of this exercise are discussed here, and the details are available on request from the *Journal of Research in Crime and Delinquency*. None of the outcome measures exhibited statistically significant serial autocorrelation. However, all outcome measure time series exhibited varying seasonal effects; that is, all time series had either seasonal moving averages (a shock that is felt once each season and then disappears), seasonal autocorrelation (e.g., August 1991 figures correlated with August 1992, August 1993, and so on), or both. To account for these seasonal effects in our models, we included dummy variables for each month. None of the time series data showed significant nonseasonal autocorrelation (i.e., monthly counts serially correlated); therefore, we did not estimate a nonseasonal autoregressive component in our models.

The preintervention time series varied in whether a trend was present. Youth homicides and youth gun assault incidents in B-2 were relatively stable during the preintervention time series, whereas citywide shots-fired calls and citywide gun assault incidents in B-2 exhibited simple linear downward trends. To account for trends in the series, we included a simple linear trend variable in the model.[5] Finally, months do not have an equal number of days. Therefore, the probability that a violent event could occur in a given month increases or decreases. For example, January has 3 more days (31 days) than February (28 days) to experience a youth homicide. To account for these differences in monthly interval lengths, we allowed the interval length in the GENMOD to vary according to the number of days per month.[6] Inserting youth homicides as the dependent variable, the basic model was as follows:

Monthly Youth Homicide Count = Intercept + Intervention
+ Trend + Month Dummy Variables + Error.

Table 1 presents the results of the Poisson regressions controlling for trend and seasonal effects. The Ceasefire intervention was associated with a statistically significant decrease in the monthly number of youth homicides; according to the incidence rate ratio, the Ceasefire intervention was associated with a 63 percent decrease in the monthly number of youth homicides. The Ceasefire intervention was also associated with statistically significant decreases in the monthly numbers of citywide gun assault incidents, citywide shots-fired calls for service, and youth gun assault incidents in district B-2. According to the incidence rate ratios, the Ceasefire intervention was also associated with a 25 percent decrease in the monthly number of citywide gun assault incidents, a 32 percent decrease in the monthly number of citywide shots-fired calls for service, and a 44 percent decrease in the monthly number of youth gun assaults in district B-2. The likelihood ratio test result was also significant, confirming that the intervention variables significantly improved the fit of the models to the data. The deviance divided by degrees of freedom results were only slightly higher than 1.0; this suggests that the Poisson distribution was appropriate for the youth homicide, city gun assault incidents, and B-2 youth gun assault incidents models (see SAS Institute 1997:285). The results for the shots-fired calls for service model, however, suggested that these data were overdispersed. The significant reduction in shots-fired calls

TABLE 1: Results of the Poisson Regressions Controlling for Trend and Seasonal Effects

	Youth Homicides	Gun Assaults	Shots Fired	B-2 Youth Gun Assaults
Incidence rate ratio	0.37	0.75	0.68	0.56
Parameter estimate	−0.9948	−0.2886	−0.3854	−0.5814
Standard error	0.2501	0.0514	0.0271	0.1339
Chi-square	15.8217	31.5819	202.6158	18.8439
Probability > chi-square	0.0001*	0.0001*	0.0001*	0.0001*
Likelihood ratio test chi-square	16.6259	31.9418	206.8892	19.6072
Probability > likelihood ratio test chi-square	0.0001*	0.0001*	0.0001*	0.0001*
Trend	−0.0014	−0.0093*	−0.0119*	−0.0093*
January	−0.0213	−0.0108	−0.0008	−0.0442
February	2.8335*	2.8736*	2.8356*	3.1343*
March	−0.0185	0.0508	−0.0111	0.0382
April	0.3767	1.0479*	1.0473*	0.9969*
May	0.1890	0.1048	0.3272*	0.1842
June	1.1827*	1.1471*	1.5021*	1.1553*
July	0.3444	0.2728*	0.4407*	0.4252*
August	0.1410	0.3388*	0.4416*	0.1975
September	1.3472*	1.1825*	1.2423*	1.2634*
October	0.3486	0.1141	0.2507*	0.1807
November	0.6932*	0.9248*	1.0636*	0.7601*
Log likelihood	47.5647	19680.27	111620.60	1535.6891
Deviance/df	1.12	1.65	9.18	1.47

NOTE: December was the reference category for the month dummy variables.
$*p < .05$.

for service associated with the Ceasefire intervention remained after the model was run with a correction for overdispersion.[7]

The youth homicide and gun violence reductions associated with the Ceasefire intervention could have been caused or meaningfully influenced by other causal factors (see Piehl et al. 2000). We therefore controlled for changes in Boston's employment rate as measured by the Massachusetts Department of Employment and Training, changes in Boston's youth population ages 5 to 24 as measured by the U.S. Bureau of the Census, changes in citywide trends in violence as measured by the robbery data reported in the Federal Bureau of Investigation Uniform Crime Reports, changes in homicide victimization among older victims (ages 25 and older), and changes in youth involvement in street-level drug market activity as measured by Boston Police Department arrest data. Admittedly, these controls are far from ideal. For example, measuring changes in Boston's citywide youth population does not directly measure population changes among our target audience—gang-involved youth offenders. However, these variables represent the best available information on these alternate endogenous explanations for Boston's decrease in youth homicide. When these control variables were added to our models, our findings did not substantively change. The significant reductions in youth homicide, shots-fired calls for service, gun assault incidents, and youth gun assault incidents in B-2 associated with Operation Ceasefire remained when the control variables were added to our Poisson regression models (see Table 2).

Youth Homicide Trends in Boston
Relative to Youth Homicide Trends in Other Cities

Although the within-Boston analyses support that a large reduction in youth homicide and gun violence was associated with the Ceasefire intervention, it is necessary to distinguish youth homicide trends in Boston from national trends in youth homicide. Many major cities in the United States have enjoyed noteworthy reductions in homicide and nonfatal serious violence (see, e.g., Blumstein and Rosenfeld 1998); the reductions in other cities could be associated with a number of complex and tightly interwoven endogenous or exogenous factors such as positive changes in the national economy, shifts in the age distribution of offending populations, or the stabilization of urban drug markets. Moreover, many cities, most notably New York (Kelling and Bratton 1998), have implemented crime prevention interventions that have been credited with substantial reductions in violence. The following analyses provide insight on whether Boston's reduction in youth homicide was part of national youth homicide trends and whether the program impact associated with the Ceasefire intervention was distinct in magnitude from other youth homicide reductions occurring at the same time as the Ceasefire intervention. Furthermore, because other cities were also taking intervention action to reduce youth homicide, these analyses will suggest whether any program impact in Boston was larger than, or distinct from, any other deliberate interventions implemented during the same time period. A priori, we predicted that Boston would experience a significant reduction in monthly youth homicide counts associated with the timing of the Ceasefire intervention.

To compare youth homicide trends in Boston to national youth homicide trends, we analyzed youth homicide data for the largest cities in the United States. By rank ordering U.S. Census population data in 1990 and 1996, we selected 41 of the most populous cities in the US.[8] Boston was ranked 20th in population size among these cities in both 1990 and 1996 with an average population of about 565,000. We then obtained monthly counts of the number of homicide victims ages 24 and younger for the 41 comparison cities from Supplementary Homicide Report (SHR) data for the time period of

TABLE 2: Results of the Poisson Regressions Controlling for Rival Causal Factors, Trend, and Seasonal Effects

	Youth Homicides	Gun Assaults	Shots Fired	B-2 Youth Gun Assaults
Incidence rate ratio	0.28	0.81	0.72	0.58
Parameter estimate	−1.2578	−0.2081	−0.3234	−0.5378
Standard error	0.3500	0.0684	0.0353	0.0018
Chi-square	12.92	9.25	84.00	9.75
Probability > chi-square	0.0003*	0.0024*	0.0001*	0.0018*
Likelihood ratio test chi-square	14.11	9.33	84.99	10.04
Probability > likelihood ratio test chi-square	0.0002*	0.0023*	0.0001*	0.0015*
Population age 5 to 17	0.0001	−0.0001	0.0001*	0.0001
Population age 18 to 24	−0.0001	−0.0001	−0.0001*	−0.0001*
Employment rate	14.1371	1.0363	9.1317*	9.6738
Robbery index crimes	−0.0002	−0.0001	−0.0001	−0.0002
Youth drug arrests	−0.0048*	0.0001	0.0005*	0.0015
Adult homicide	0.0163	0.0078	0.0027	0.0290
Trend	−0.0306	−0.0287*	−0.0543*	−0.0746*
January	0.1706	−0.1961	−0.3295*	−0.6819*
February	2.8743*	2.7125*	2.5749*	2.6565*
March	0.1093	−0.1007	−0.2715*	−0.4667
April	0.5568	0.9265*	0.8413*	0.6060*
May	0.3411	0.0050	0.1526*	−0.1287
June	1.1215*	1.0326*	1.2701*	0.7736*
July	0.2483	0.1820*	0.2035*	0.0954
August	0.1776	0.2666*	0.2418*	−0.0966
September	2.0265*	1.1420*	1.2052*	1.0413*
October	0.6295	0.0789	0.1756*	−0.0030
November	0.8130*	0.9127*	1.0206*	0.6868*
Log likelihood	52.7188	19684.46	111677.47	1542.29
Deviance/*df*	1.07	1.67	8.27	1.40

NOTE: December was the reference category for the month dummy variables.
*$p < .05$.

January 1991 through December 1997. After a close examination of these data, 2 cities (Washington, D.C. and New Orleans) were excluded due to extensive missing data. This left us with 39 major U.S. cities in the comparison group.

Recognizing that youth homicide trends can vary greatly across 39 major U.S. cities, we built a model that would maximize our ability to control for the various sources of error in the time series of each city. After a number of analyses,[9] we decided on the following model:

Monthly Count of Youth Homicide = Intercept + Trend + Trend Squared + Month
   Dummy Variables + Intervention + Autoregressive (1) Component + Error,

where trend controls for simple linear trends within each time series, trend
squared controls for nonlinear trends within each time series, month dummy
variables control for monthly seasonal effects within each time series, intervention estimates the effect of the intervention within each time series, and
autoregressive (1) component estimates an overall AR(1) serial lag-one correlation components for each time series.

The SAS GENMOD procedure does not allow the estimation of an
autoregressive component in generalized linear models. However, the SAS
GLIMMIX macro allows autoregressive components to be estimated in generalized linear mixed models (see Littell et al. 1996). Mixed models are generally used by statisticians to estimate random effects in statistical models.
However, they can also be used to estimate a variance component that is different from that assumed by generalized linear models. In our fixed-effects
model, the GLIMMIX macro simply allows us to estimate a variance component that includes an AR(1) coefficient in a generalized linear Poisson regression model. GLIMMIX also automatically corrects for overdispersion in the
distribution of the dependent variable by estimating an overdispersion coefficient (see Littell et al. 1996). Finally, we also accounted for the varying number of days per month.

Table 3 presents the results of the Poisson regressions for the 39 comparison cities plus Boston.[10] Four cities—Boston, Jacksonville, Dallas, and Virginia Beach—had differences in youth homicides at the time of the intervention that were statistically significant at the .05 level; Boston had the largest
estimated effect. Because our cross-city analysis involved 40 statistical tests,
the expected number of effects significant at the .05 level is two. Thus, we
need to be especially sensitive to the possibility of Type II error in our results.
We would expect that 14 percent of the time we would find four or more statistically significant effects by chance alone. However, these cities would be a
randomly selected set; we made an a priori prediction that Boston would have
a significant reduction. The probability of finding four or more successes one
of which is Boston (or any specific city) by chance alone is .0155. The
inter city results, therefore, fit what would be expected if Boston had a
change that was not due to chance alone. However, the statistical analysis
cannot provide a basis for determining whether this was the case. Nonetheless, on the basis of these results, we can conclude that there was no national
trend that explains the change in youth homicide that occurred in Boston at
the time of the Operation Ceasefire intervention.

Examination of the trends in youth homicides in the other cities with significant intervention coefficients also supports the distinctiveness of the

212   JOURNAL OF RESEARCH IN CRIME AND DELINQUENCY

TABLE 3:   Results of the Poisson Regressions for 39 Comparison Cities Plus Boston

City	Estimate	Standard Error	df	t	Prob (t)	AR(1)
Albuquerque, New Mexico	−0.1195	0.5783	24.18	−0.21	0.8380	0.1751
Atlanta, Georgia	−0.0336	0.3635	22.42	−0.09	0.9273	0.1973
Austin, Texas	−0.5207	0.4801	28.89	−1.08	0.2870	−0.0780
Baltimore, Maryland	0.2505	0.1974	26.03	1.27	0.2155	0.0134
Boston, Massachusetts	−1.1351	0.3771	25.98	−3.01	0.0057*	−0.0009
Charlotte, North Carolina	0.2948	0.4321	27.30	0.68	0.5009	0.0197
Chicago, Illinois	0.1764	0.1421	24.03	1.24	0.2264	0.2671
Cleveland, Ohio	0.2811	0.3947	21.94	0.71	0.4839	0.0877
Columbus, Ohio	0.3246	0.3478	21.83	0.93	0.3610	0.0470
Dallas, Texas	−0.5254	0.1786	28.79	−2.94	0.0064*	−0.1270
Denver, Colorado	−0.6698	0.4514	24.55	−1.48	0.1505	0.0576
Detroit, Michigan	0.2675	0.1873	21.57	1.43	0.1677	0.2207
El Paso, Texas	−0.1672	0.6274	28.03	−0.27	0.7918	−0.0866
Fort Worth, Texas	0.1385	0.4273	24.45	0.32	0.7485	0.1756
Fresno, California	0.0347	0.4260	25.14	0.08	0.9357	0.1952
Honolulu, Hawaii	−0.0443	0.6515	27.94	−0.07	0.9463	−0.0447
Houston, Texas	−0.3069	0.1972	24.97	−1.56	0.1322	−0.0108
Indianapolis, Indiana	−0.0577	0.3267	27.65	−0.18	0.8611	−0.0313
Jacksonville, Florida	−0.5670	0.2693	29.28	−2.11	0.0439*	−0.1637
Kansas City, Missouri	−0.5239	0.3483	24.75	−1.50	0.1452	0.0106
Los Angeles, California	−0.2324	0.1421	26.09	−1.64	0.1140	−0.0156
Long Beach, California	−0.3046	0.4892	24.59	−0.62	0.5393	0.1625
Memphis, Tennessee	−0.0328	0.3147	23.78	−0.10	0.9178	0.1029
Milwaukee, Wisconsin	−0.3408	0.2659	28.52	−1.28	0.2102	−0.1194
Nashville, Tennessee	0.1387	0.2936	31.11	0.47	0.6400	−0.1854
New York, New York	0.1583	0.1442	23.63	1.10	0.2833	0.1144
Oakland, California	−0.1766	0.3877	23.11	−0.46	0.6530	0.1336
Oklahoma City, Oklahoma	0.2657	0.6092	28.94	0.44	0.6659	−0.0299
Philadelphia, Pennsylvania	0.3227	0.1659	25.19	1.95	0.0629	0.0177
Phoenix, Arizona	−0.4195	0.2500	26.31	−1.68	0.1053	0.0207
Portland, Oregon	−0.3787	0.5133	30.06	−0.74	0.4663	0.0107
San Antonio, Texas	−0.2199	0.2907	30.09	−0.76	0.4553	−0.1754
San Diego, California	0.2118	0.5302	22.54	0.40	0.6933	0.1404
San Francisco, California	0.1256	0.4518	27.36	0.28	0.7831	0.0357
San Jose, California	−0.2445	0.6483	24.19	−0.38	0.7094	0.2625
Seattle, Washington	0.4182	0.6829	22.71	0.61	0.5463	0.1630
St. Louis, Missouri	−0.5068	0.2925	24.22	−1.73	0.0959	0.0772
Tucson, Arizona	−0.1741	0.4770	25.63	−0.37	0.7180	0.0143
Tulsa, Oklahoma	0.0213	0.6573	28.78	0.03	0.9744	0.1115
Virginia Beach, Virginia	1.2287	0.5968	29.43	2.06	0.0485*	−0.1935

NOTE: Deviance = 3613.23; dispersion parameter = 0.8616.
*$p < .05$.

Boston case (Figure 3). Virginia Beach, for example, shows a significant increase in youth homicides occurring in June 1996, although the yearly counts of youth homicides were stable between 1995 and 1997.[11] The declines in Dallas and Jacksonville both began months earlier than that in Boston. We are unaware of any known connection between youth homicides in these four cities. Although based on exploratory analysis, the presence of these differences undermines the argument that the changes in Boston reflect trends in other major U.S. cities.

Of course, other cities may have experienced a sudden significant decrease in youth homicide either before or after Boston experienced its significant decrease in youth homicide, and these might be missed by the single-time-period analysis presented in Table 3. Therefore, we conducted an exploratory analysis to identify abrupt significant youth homicide reductions in the comparison cities occurring in other months during the time series. We performed our main analysis of youth homicides in 39 major U.S. cities with a varying intervention point from month 12 to month 72 in the time series.[12] Five out of 39 cities experienced a sudden significant youth homicide reduction at some point in the time series.[13] These cities were Philadelphia; Tucson, Arizona; Dallas, Texas; Los Angeles; and New York City. A sharp and sustained break will lead to significant before and after differences for several time periods around the intervention. This is because the analyses are, in essence, comparisons of two means adjusted for other factors (Piehl et al. 1999). For this reason, significant break points in Boston are found in months 65 through 67 rather than just in month 66 (the June 1996 start date). Results in the 5 cities with significant breaks indicate that each had a series of successive significant breaks.

Although five cities experienced large reductions in youth homicide at some point within the time series, it is difficult to make a direct link between youth homicide trends in the five cities and Boston, as the yearly trends across cities look different. Philadelphia experienced significant reductions in monthly counts of youth homicides in months 36 (December 1993) through 38 (February 1994), 30 months before the implementation of Operation Ceasefire (Figure 4). This was followed by a steady increase in youth homicide between 1994 and 1997 (Figure 4). Tucson experienced significant decreases in monthly youth homicide counts between month 59 (November 1995) and month 60 (December 1995). This sudden decrease was followed by an increase in Tucson youth homicides in 1997 (Figure 4). Dallas experienced a significant decrease in the monthly count of youth homicides between month 63 (March 1996) and month 65 (May 1996). Although this significant reduction coincides with the implementation of Operation

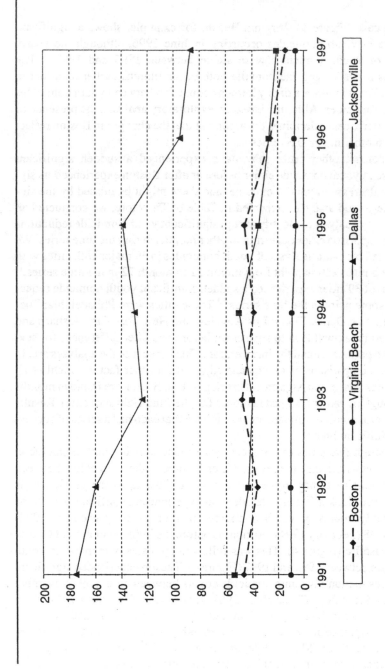

Figure 3:   Youth Homicide in Boston, Dallas, Jacksonville, and Virginia Beach, 1991 to 1997 (annual)

Ceasefire, youth homicide in Dallas declined almost linearly between 1991 and 1997 (Figure 4).

Los Angeles experienced a significant reduction in monthly counts of youth homicides during months 30 and 31 (June and July 1993). New York City experienced sudden significant reductions in monthly counts of youth homicides during months 39 and 40 (March and April 1994) and also during months 44 and 45 (August and September 1994). As in Dallas, youth homicide trends in Los Angeles and New York show steep declines during the mid 1990s (see Figure 5). Superficially, the steady declines in New York, Los Angeles, and Dallas seem different from the trajectory of youth homicide in Boston. Overall, the results from this analysis do not support the idea that changes in Boston either followed or trailed national changes or changes in other major cities.

We also used this technique to examine whether Boston's youth homicide reduction could have been influenced by decreases in regional youth homicide trends. We obtained monthly counts of the number of homicide victims ages 24 and younger for 29 large New England cities[14] from SHR data for the time period of January 1991 through December 1997. The majority of the New England cities experienced very small numbers of youth homicides and did not exhibit any discernable trends. The youth homicide time series of 11 (37.9 percent of 29) New England cities were analyzed statistically.[15] When the main analyses were run with the varying intervention point, none experienced a significant reduction in the monthly count of youth homicides.

Careful within-city studies are necessary to unravel youth homicide trends in these cities. Without the benefit of a detailed analysis, it is difficult to know whether there is some broad link between the youth homicide trajectories in such diverse cities. Although some cities may have experienced a similar decrease, these analyses suggest that Boston's significant youth homicide reduction associated with Operation Ceasefire was distinct when compared to youth homicide trends in most major U.S. and New England cities.

The Role of Preventing
Illegal Firearms Trafficking

Finally, there is the question of what degree, if any, of violence reduction in Boston should be attributed to the prevention of illegal firearms trafficking. Trafficking was, of course, one of the principal original foci of the Gun Project and attention to trafficking one of Operation Ceasefire's two fundamental planks. Evaluating the particular contribution of supply-side interventions in Boston is, we believe, essentially impossible. Antitrafficking efforts were

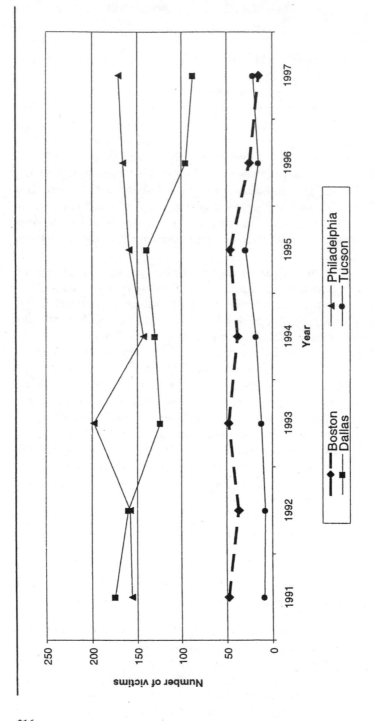

Figure 4: Youth Homicide in Boston, Dallas, Tucson, and Philadelphia, 1991 to 1997 (annual)

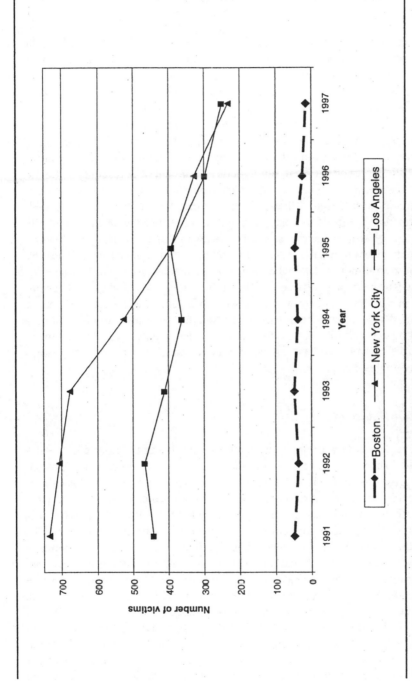

Figure 5: Youth Homicide in Boston, Los Angeles, and New York City, 1991 to 1997 (annual)

implemented at the same time as violence deterrence efforts, and both might be expected to influence, for example, gun carrying, gun use, and the mix of illegal guns found on the street. A stand-alone trafficking prevention intervention would not face these difficulties and could lead to definitive answers on the impact of supply-side interventions. Operation Ceasefire, however, was not a stand-alone trafficking prevention intervention.

Here, as well, the distinctive characteristics of the decline in homicide and shootings in Boston offer the best insight into what might have happened. Two things are certain. First, supply-side efforts cannot be responsible for the abrupt reductions in gun-related violence over the summer of 1996. Boston trafficking cases follow that reduction rather than anticipate it. Second, antitrafficking efforts in Boston did nothing to reduce the existing stockpile of illegally acquired and possessed firearms in Boston. Those guns held by gang members in Boston in May of 1996 were, for the most part, still held by them several months later when the violence reached its new, lower equilibrium. The change that had occurred was not in the extent of gun *ownership* but in gun *use*. The principal impact therefore was nearly certainly a demand-side, deterrence-based effect rather than a supply-side effect. It may well be that antitrafficking efforts strengthened and prolonged that impact. Whether any such effects were large or small cannot be independently established in this case.

CONCLUSION

The Boston Gun Project was an attempt to bring problem-oriented policing to bear on one important problem, youth violence, in one city, Boston. The project assembled a working group with members from a wide variety of agencies and representing a wide variety of law enforcement, social service, and other operational capacities (Kennedy et al. 1996). It went through a variety of shifts typical of problem-solving operations: shifts in the problem definition, in the shape of the intervention, and in the management and membership of the core operational partnership. Its core operational intervention, Operation Ceasefire, was designed to operate anywhere in the city where youth violence was a serious problem and was intended to interrupt the self-sustaining cycle the Gun Project hypothesized to be driving youth violence in the city (Kennedy et al. 1996). The pulling-levers deterrence strategy at the heart of Operation Ceasefire was designed to influence the behavior, and the environment, of the core population of chronic-offender gang-involved youth Gun Project research found to be at the heart of the city's youth violence problem (Kennedy 1997).

As we have noted, these interests and diagnoses—the desire to operate wherever youth violence presented itself and the belief that there was essentially one dynamic, which had to be addressed, driving violent behavior by various groups in various places within the city—made a classic experimental evaluation design impossible. It was appropriate neither from the viewpoint of participating agencies nor from the perspective of the forces believed to be driving youth violence to set aside particular areas, groups, or individuals as controls. There are thus irreducible limits to attributing any violence reduction in Boston to any particular operational intervention.

This article makes a weaker but still meaningful case: that there was an innovative intervention implemented, there were subsequent substantial reductions in youth violence in Boston, the timing of those reductions is consistent with the intervention having impact, those reductions were robust relative to proxy measures of rival causal factors in the city, the reductions in Boston were significantly larger than those in most other American cities at the time, and the large and abrupt changes that characterized the reduction in Boston differed from those of other American cities. There seems, then, to be reason to believe that something distinct happened in Boston and that its impact was both larger and of a different character than either secular trends or deliberate interventions then operating in other cities.

The results of the impact evaluation support the growing body of research that asserts that problem-oriented policing can be used to good effect in controlling crime and disorder problems (Braga, Piehl, et al. 1999; Clarke 1992; Eck and Spelman 1987; Goldstein 1990). In particular, the Ceasefire intervention suggests a new approach to controlling violent offenders from a more focused application of deterrence principles. In contrast to broad-based "zero tolerance" policing initiatives that attempt to prevent serious offending by indiscriminately cracking down on minor crimes committed by all offenders, the pulling-levers deterrence strategy controlled violence by focusing on particular groups that were behaving violently, subjecting them to a range of discretionary criminal justice system action, and directly communicating cause and effect to a very specific audience. Unfortunately, we were not able to collect the necessary pretest and posttest data to shed light on any shifts in street-level dynamics that could be associated with the pulling-levers deterrence strategy. Our research efforts during the pretest phase were focused on problem analysis and program development. A priori, we did not know what form the intervention would take and who our target audience would be. In this regard, our assessment is very much a "black box" evaluation. Additional research on the deterrence mechanisms of the pulling-levers approach to controlling offenders is necessary.

We believe that the research presented here shows that the Boston Gun Project was a meaningful problem-oriented policing effort, bringing practitioners and researchers together in new ways, leading to a fresh assessment of the youth violence problem in Boston, and leading to operational activities that were a substantial departure from previous practice. The principal intervention, Operation Ceasefire, was likely responsible for a substantial reduction in youth homicide and youth gun violence in the city. At first blush, the effectiveness of the Operation Ceasefire intervention in preventing violence may seem unique to Boston. Operation Ceasefire was constructed largely from the assets and capacities available in Boston at the time and deliberately tailored to the city's particular violence problem. Operational capacities of criminal justice agencies in other cities will be different, and youth violence problems in other cities will have important distinguishing characteristics. However, we believe that the working-group problem-solving process and the pulling-levers approach to deterring chronic offenders are transferable to other jurisdictions. A number of cities have begun to experiment with these frameworks and have experienced some encouraging preliminary results (see, e.g., Coleman et al. 1999; Kennedy and Braga 1998). These cities include Minneapolis, Minnesota; Baltimore; Indianapolis, Indiana; Stockton, California; Lowell, Massachusetts; Los Angeles; Bronx, New York; High Point, North Carolina; Winston-Salem, North Carolina; Memphis, Tennessee; New Haven, Connecticut; and Portland, Oregon.

The Boston Gun Project applied the basic principles of problem-oriented policing to a substantial public safety problem. Addressing this problem required the involvement of multiple agencies and the community as well as substantial investments in analysis, coordination, and implementation. The experience of the Gun Project suggests that deploying criminal justice capacities to prevent crime can yield substantial benefits. The problem-solving orientation of the project means that the problem definition, the core participants, and the particulars of the intervention evolved over the course of the collaboration. Operation Ceasefire itself was highly customized to the goals of the collaboration, the particular nature of the youth violence problem in Boston, and the particular capacities available in Boston for incorporation into a strategic intervention. Therefore, Operation Ceasefire as such is unlikely to be a highly specifiable, transportable "technology." However, certain process elements of the Boston Gun Project, such as the central role of the line-level working group and the use of both qualitative and quantitative research to "unpack" chosen problems, should be generally applicable to other problem-solving efforts. Using the working-group problem-solving approach, criminal justice practitioners in other jurisdictions will develop a set of intervention strategies that fits both the nuances of their youth violence problem and their operational capacities. Although the resulting package of interventions may not closely resemble the tactics used in Operation Ceasefire, the frameworks will be similar.

NOTES

1. We expanded our study to include youth ages 24 and younger when Boston Gun Project research revealed that street gangs were an important driver in youth gun violence. Most Boston gang members were between the ages of 14 and 24 (see Kennedy, Braga, and Piehl 1997).

2. During the problem analysis phase of the project, the authors did not provide or press a definition of *gang* on the members of the working group. Defining gang is a core problem in analyzing and understanding gang- and group-related youth crime and violence (Ball and Curry 1995). The character of criminal and disorderly juvenile gangs and groups varies widely both within and across cities (Curry, Ball, and Fox 1994). The members of the working group used a definition that could be reduced to self-identified group of kids who act corporately (at least sometimes) and violently (at least sometimes) (see Kennedy et al. 1997).

3. There were, in fact, only two major Ceasefire crackdowns. In May 1996, the Vamp Hill Kings were subjected to a multiagency operation that included street drug enforcement and drug market suppression, warrant service, stepped-up street enforcement by the Boston Police Department (10 arrests), Operation Night Light probation visits to suspected gang members (38 home visits, 10 probation surrenders), parole visits, 4 Department of Youth Services surrenders, seizure of pit bull dogs by animal control, special bail conditions established for cases presented to Massachusetts district courts, and 4 cases accepted for prosecution by the U.S. Attorney (3 pled guilty, 1 was deported). In August 1996, the Intervale Street Posse was subjected to a similar multiagency operation that included 15 federal arrests on drugs and homicide conspiracy charges (those federally charged were held out of state on pretrial detention) and 8 state drug arrests prosecuted by Suffolk County District Attorney.

4. We pursued these analyses to ensure that we were accounting for possible sources of error in our generalized linear models and did not use auto regressive integrated moving average (ARIMA) models to measure intervention effects. Identifying appropriate ARIMA models for evaluation purposes can be a very subjective exercise. As Gary Kleck (1995) suggests,

> Experts in ARIMA modeling also commonly point out difficulties that even experienced practitioners have in specifying time series models. Specification is very much an art rather than a science, so that different researchers, using the same body of data, can make substantially different, even arbitrary, and, as a result, obtain sharply different results. (P. 354)

5. The trend variable was simply the month number from the start to the end of the time series (i.e., for the January 1991 through December 1997 series, the trend variable ranged from 1 to 84). We also ran the model (Dependent Variable = Intercept + Month Dummies + Trend + Error) on the preintervention series with trend squared. Trend squared did not improve the fit of the model to any of the preintervention time series. The trend variable improved the fit of the model to all of the preintervention time series with the exception of youth homicides. This was not surprising because the youth homicides were very stable during the preintervention times series.

6. The OFFSET option sets the interval length in the GENMOD procedure. We created a series of if-then statements that assigned the appropriate interval lengths per month in the offset specification.

7. We ran separate models with the PSCALE and DSCALE options in the SAS GENMOD procedure. The PSCALE option uses the Pearson's chi-square divided by the degrees of freedom as the dispersion parameter, and the DSCALE option uses the deviance statistic divided by the degrees of freedom as the dispersion parameter. Neither option altered the significant reductions in shots-fired calls for service associated with the Ceasefire intervention.

222   JOURNAL OF RESEARCH IN CRIME AND DELINQUENCY

8. We ranked the top 40 cities according to U.S. Census population estimates in 1990 and 1996. In this procedure, we observed that Fresno, California, and Tulsa, Oklahoma, were not in the top 40 in 1990 but were in the top 40 in 1996. St. Louis, Missouri, and Oakland, California, were in the top 40 in 1990 but not in the top 40 in 1996. Rather than exclude either pair of cities, we decided to keep both pairs in the sample. After Boston was removed from this group of populous cities, we were left with 41 cities.

9. Relative to other models, this model fit the data best, and, by allowing trend, trend squared, month, and autocorrelation effects to vary within each city, we believed that it best allowed the model to reflect the reality of heterogeneous error structures across the city time series. We compared the goodness of fit of the various models by examining the deviance statistics; a smaller deviance indicates a better fit of the model to the data. The deviance of the reported model was 3,613.23. Other models included a model predicting monthly counts of youth homicides as a function of month effects within each city, intervention effects within each city, and an autoregressive component within each city (deviance = 4,130.26); a model predicting monthly counts of youth homicides as a function of simple linear and nonlinear trends within each city, intervention effects within each city, and an autoregressive component within each city (deviance = 6,403.99); a model predicting monthly counts of youth homicides as a function of simple linear and nonlinear trends within each city, month effects within each city, and an autoregressive component within each city (3,680.77); and a model predicting youth homicides as a function of simple linear and nonlinear trends within each city, month effects within each city, intervention effects within each city, and a simple variance component within each city (3,611.80). Note that including an autoregressive component within each city time series does not supply a significantly better fit when compared to a model with a simple variance component within each city time series. Although there is almost no autocorrelation in the Boston time series, there are a number of cities that have strong autocorrelations in their respective time series (see Albuquerque, Atlanta, Chicago, Detroit, Fort Worth, Fresno, San Antonio, San Jose, and Virginia Beach in Table 3). Therefore, we felt that it was important to include an autoregressive component in our model. Finally, also note that the addition of the intervention variable does not significantly improve the fit of the overall model to the data. A priori, this is what we expected. A significant improvement in fit would indicate a strong nationwide effect coinciding with the implementation of Operation Ceasefire. This would suggest that there was nothing unique about Operation Ceasefire's effect on youth homicides in Boston.

10. Earlier drafts of this article contained somewhat different results than reported here. Specifically, in the intercity analysis in this article, several additional cities are found to have statistically significant results. Prior analyses were based on the SAS GLIMMIX macro available for version 6.12 of SAS. That macro calls the SAS procedure Proc Mixed. Due to an error in that version of Proc Mixed, the degrees of freedom are estimated incorrectly when the Satterthwaite method is used (SAS Institute 1998). This, in turn, led to the incorrect calculation of p values associated with the t tests performed on the parameter estimates. This article presents the correct p values. This error, which is limited to models with specific variance structures, including AR(1), has been resolved in later versions of SAS.

11. The Supplementary Homicide Report data reported the following yearly counts for youth homicides in Virginia Beach: six in 1995, seven in 1996, and six in 1997. The June 1996 significant break was due to a period of four months without youth homicides followed by a period of six months with one youth homicide each.

12. The intervention point could vary from month 12 to month 72 only rather than the full time period of month 1 to month 84. Twelve months were excluded at either end of the time series to ensure enough data to identify trends and autocorrelation in the time series.

13. For this analysis, we used the standard of a p value of .01 or less to define a significant break. We chose this level to decrease the risk of Type II error in an analysis that involved 50 tests

in each of 40 cities (expected to yield 100 breaks if a .05 level were used). However, we chose not to move to an even more stringent alpha level both because the temporal nature of the data made it likely that the within-city tests were not independent and because exploratory analyses should not be overly restrictive. Although using a .05 level would identify a number of additional significant breaks, these are in the form of one- or two-month spikes rather than sustained change.

14. We selected all New England cities with populations of more than 60,000. These 29 cities were Bridgeport, Danbury, Hartford, New Britain, New Haven, Norwalk, Stamford, and Waterbury in Connecticut; Brockton, Cambridge, Fall River, Framingham, Lawrence, Lowell, Lynn, New Bedford, Newton, Quincy, Somerville, Springfield, and Worcester in Massachusetts; Portland, Maine; Nashua and Manchester in New Hampshire; and Cranston, Pawtucket, Warwick, and Providence in Rhode Island. Although it has only 50,000 residents, we included Burlington in this pool because it was the only major "city" in Vermont.

15. These cities included Bridgeport, Hartford, New Haven, Stamford, and Waterbury in Connecticut; Providence, Rhode Island; and Lynn, Lowell, Springfield, and Worcester in Massachusetts.

REFERENCES

Aldrich, John and Forrest Nelson. 1984. *Linear Probability, Logit, and Probit Models*. Paper Series on Quantitative Applications in the Social Sciences. Beverly Hills, CA: Sage.

Ball, Richard and G. David Curry. 1995. "The Logic of Definition in Criminology: Purposes and Methods for Defining 'Gangs.' " *Criminology* 33:225-46.

Beha, James A. 1977. " 'And Nobody Can Get You Out': The Impact of a Mandatory Prison Sentence for the Illegal Carrying of a Firearm on the Use of Firearms and on the Administration of Criminal Justice in Boston-Part I." *Boston University Law Review* 57:96-146.

Blumstein, Alfred, Jacqueline Cohen, and Daniel Nagin, eds. 1978. *Deterrence and Incapacitation: Estimating the Effects of Criminal Sanctions on Crime Rates*. Washington, DC: National Academy of Sciences.

Blumstein, Alfred and Richard Rosenfeld. 1998. "Explaining Recent Trends in U.S. Homicide Rates." *Journal of Criminal Law and Criminology* 88:1175-216.

Braga, Anthony A., Anne M. Piehl, and David M. Kennedy. 1999. "Youth Homicide in Boston: An Assessment of Supplementary Homicide Report Data." *Homicide Studies* 3:277-99.

Braga, Anthony A., David L. Weisburd, Elin J. Waring, Lorraine Green Mazerolle, William Spelman, and Francis Gajewski. 1999. "Problem-Oriented Policing in Violent Crime Places: A Randomized Controlled Experiment." *Criminology* 37:541-80.

Butterfield, Fox. 1996. "In Boston, Nothing Is Something." *New York Times*, November 21, p. A20.

Cameron, Samuel. 1988. "The Economics of Crime Deterrence: A Survey of Theory and Evidence." *Kyklos* 41:301-23.

Campbell, Donald T. and Julian Stanley. 1966. *Experimental and Quasi-Experimental Designs for Research*. Chicago: Rand McNally.

Clarke, Ronald V., ed. 1992. *Situational Crime Prevention: Successful Case Studies*. New York: Harrow and Heston.

Coleman, Veronica, Walter C. Holton, Kristine Olson, Stephen Robinson, and Judith Stewart. 1999. "Using Knowledge and Teamwork to Reduce Crime." *National Institute of Justice Journal*, October:16-23.

Cook, Philip J. 1977. "Punishment and Crime: A Critique of Current Findings Concerning the Preventive Effects of Punishment." *Law and Contemporary Problems* 41:164-204.

224 JOURNAL OF RESEARCH IN CRIME AND DELINQUENCY

————. 1980. "Research in Criminal Deterrence: Laying the Groundwork for the Second Decade." Pp. 211-68 in *Crime and Justice: An Annual Review of Research*, Vol. 2, edited by Norval Morris and Michael Tonry. Chicago: University of Chicago Press.

Cook, Philip J. and John H. Laub. 1998. "The Unprecedented Epidemic in Youth Violence." Pp. 27-64 in *Youth Violence*, edited by Michael Tonry and Mark H. Moore. Chicago: University of Chicago Press.

Cook, Thomas and Donald Campbell. 1979. *Quasi-Experimentation: Design and Analysis Issues for Field Settings*. Boston: Houghton Mifflin.

Curry, G. David, Richard Ball, and Richard Fox. 1994. *Gang Crime and Law Enforcement Record Keeping* (NCJ 148345). Washington, DC: National Institute of Justice.

Dobson, Annette. 1990. *An Introduction to Generalized Linear Models*. New York: Chapman and Hall.

Eck, John E. and William Spelman. 1987. *Problem-Solving: Problem-Oriented Policing in Newport News*. Washington, DC: National Institute of Justice.

Ekblom, Paul and Ken Pease. 1995, "Evaluating Crime Prevention." Pp. 585-662 in *Building a Safer Society: Crime and Justice*, Vol. 19, edited by Michael Tonry and David Farrington. Chicago: University of Chicago Press.

Fox, James Alan. 1996. *Trends in Juvenile Violence*. Washington, DC: U.S. Department of Justice, Bureau of Justice Statistics.

Gibbs, Jack P. 1975. *Crime, Punishment, and Deterrence*. New York: Elsevier.

Goldstein, Herman. 1979. "Improving Policing: A Problem-Oriented Approach." *Crime & Delinquency* 25:236-58.

————. 1990. *Problem-Oriented Policing*. Philadelphia: Temple University Press.

Kelling, George L. and William J. Bratton. 1998. "Declining Crime Rates: Insiders' Views of the New York City Story." *Journal of Criminal Law and Criminology* 88:1217-32.

Kennedy, David M. 1997. "Pulling Levers: Chronic Offenders, High-Crime Settings, and a Theory of Prevention." *Valparaiso University Law Review* 31:449-84.

————. 1998. "Pulling Levers: Getting Deterrence Right." *National Institute of Justice Journal*, July:2-8.

Kennedy, David M. and Anthony A. Braga. 1998. "Homicide in Minneapolis: Research for Problem Solving." *Homicide Studies* 2 (3): 263-90.

Kennedy, David M., Anthony A. Braga, and Anne M. Piehl. 1997. "The (Un)Known Universe: Mapping Gangs and Gang Violence in Boston." Pp. 219-62 in *Crime Mapping and Crime Prevention*, edited by David Weisburd and J. Thomas McEwen. New York: Criminal Justice Press.

————. 1999. "Operation Ceasefire: Problem Solving and Youth Violence in Boston." Unpublished report submitted to the National Institute of Justice. Available on request from authors.

Kennedy, David M., Anne M. Piehl, and Anthony A. Braga. 1996. "Youth Violence in Boston: Gun Markets, Serious Youth Offenders, and a Use-Reduction Strategy." *Law and Contemporary Problems* 59:147-96.

Kleck, Gary. 1995. *Targeting Guns: Firearms and Their Control*. New York: Aldine de Gruyter.

Klein, Malcolm. 1993. "Attempting Gang Control by Suppression: The Misuse of Deterrence Principles." *Studies on Crime and Crime Prevention* 2:88-111.

Littell, Ramon C., George A. Milliken, Walter W. Stroup, and Russell D. Wolfinger. 1996. *SAS System for Mixed Models*. Cary, NC: SAS Institute, Inc.

McCullagh, Peter and John Nelder. 1989. *Generalized Linear Models*. 2nd ed. New York: Chapman and Hall.

McDowall, David, Richard McCleary, Errol Meidinger, and Richard Hay. 1980. *Interrupted Time Series Analysis*. Sage University Series on Quantitative Applications in the Social Sciences. Newbury Park, CA: Sage.

Paternoster, Raymond. 1987. "The Deterrent Effect of the Perceived Certainty and Severity of Punishment: A Review of the Evidence and Issues." *Justice Quarterly* 4:173-217.

Piehl, Anne M., Suzanne J. Cooper, Anthony A. Braga, and David M. Kennedy. 1999. "Testing for Structural Breaks in the Evaluation of Programs." NBER working paper no. 7226, National Bureau of Economic Research, Cambridge, MA.

Piehl, Anne M., David M. Kennedy, and Anthony A. Braga. 2000. "Problem Solving and Youth Violence: An Evaluation of the Boston Gun Project." *American Law and Economics Review* 2:58-106.

Rossi, Peter H. and Howard E. Freeman. 1993. *Evaluation: A Systematic Approach*. 5th ed. Newbury Park, CA: Sage.

SAS Institute. 1993. *SAS/STAT Software: The GENMOD Procedure*. Release 6.09, technical report P-243. Cary, NC: SAS Institute, Inc.

———. 1997. *SAS/STAT Software: Changes and Enhancements through Release 6.12*. Cary, NC: SAS Institute, Inc.

———. 1998. "V6 SAS Note: PROC MIXED Can Return Incorrect DF with DDFM=SATTERTH and REPEATED." February 18 (http://www.sas.com/service/techsup/unotes/V6/E/E660.html).

Sherman, Lawrence. 1990. "Police Crackdowns: Initial and Residual Deterrence." Pp. 1-48 in *Crime and Justice: A Review of Research*, Vol. 12, edited by Michael Tonry and Norval Morris. Chicago: University of Chicago Press.

Sherman, Lawrence and Richard Berk. 1984. "The Specific Deterrent Effects of Arrest for Domestic Assault." *American Sociological Review* 49:261-72.

Sparrow, Malcolm, Mark H. Moore, and David M. Kennedy. 1990. *Beyond 911: A New Era for Policing*. New York: Basic Books.

Weisburd, David, Elin J. Waring, and Ellen F. Chayet. 1995. "Specific Deterrence in a Sample of Offenders Convicted of White Collar Crimes." *Criminology* 33:587-607.

Witkin, Gordon. 1997. "Sixteen Silver Bullets: Smart Ideas to Fix the World." *U.S. News and World Report*, December 29, p. 67.

Zimring, Franklin and Gordon Hawkins. 1973. *Deterrence: The Legal Threat in Crime Control*. Chicago: University of Chicago Press.

[29]

SHOOTINGS, GANGS AND VIOLENT INCIDENTS IN MANCHESTER: DEVELOPING A CRIME REDUCTION STRATEGY

Crime Reduction Research Series Paper 13

Karen Bullock and Nick Tilley

May 2002

The views expressed in this briefing note are those of the authors, not necessarily those of the Home Office (nor do they reflect Government policy).

Introduction

The Targeted Policing Initiative (TPI) forms part of the Government's Crime Reduction Programme. The TPI comprised a range of evaluated action projects. This briefing note summarises a report that describes the preliminary research on one of them, based in Manchester. The project to which this report relates is unusual in that it involved a problem-oriented approach requiring a relatively long, six-month research phase prior to putting measures in place. It is also unusual in attempting to address a major crime problem, serious gang-related violence rather than volume crime. In both of these respects, it draws inspiration from an apparently very successful initiative in Boston, Massachusetts, Operation Ceasefire, which was associated with a rapid decline in numbers of fatalities caused by use of guns or knives (Kennedy et al, 1996; Braga et al, 1999).

The Boston project, like the one being developed in Manchester, also used a problem-oriented approach. The idea in both cases was to gather as systematically as possible reliable information about the nature of the problem and to formulate practical proposals to deal with it in the light of that information. The Boston strategy was to produce a rapid and sustainable reduction in injuries and deaths caused by firearms. Given its purpose, the analysis in Boston was not framed around those underlying social conditions that might foster gangs. Rather, it aimed to identify more immediate ('proximate') and modifiable conditions for violent events to occur. This approach has been followed in Manchester.

Methods of research

Using mainly police sources, two data sets were constructed and analysed. These related to shooting incidents and to individuals involved in shootings and/or gangs. In addition a small sample of young men believed by the police to be involved in gangs and gang violence were interviewed about shootings and stabbings and about the circumstances leading up to their involvement in gangs. A semi-structured practitioner focus group was run to canvass informed opinion. Finally, social services files relating to a small subset of gang-members were consulted. None of the data sources used is without problems. Data on shooting incidents and individuals relate only to those known to and recorded by the authorities. Those interviewed do not comprise a random sample, but were again those known to the authorities who could be readily contacted. Files consulted relate to those suspected by project workers to have had difficulties, again not a random sample.

Main findings

Shootings

1. Violence in general, gun violence in particular and fatal shootings most specifically are concentrated in some specific small areas of South Manchester.

2. Victims of gun violence in Manchester are mainly young, black or mixed race males, who have criminal records.

3. Suspected perpetrators of serious gun violence in Manchester tend to have similar attributes to victims.

4. Those who have been victims of shootings are at increased risk of repeat incidents.

5. The total annual cost of firearms related violence in South Manchester is estimated as £5 million.

6. Young black (and mixed race) male victims of shootings in South Manchester were generally known to have been involved in gangs.

7. About 60 per cent of shootings are thought to be gang related.

Gangs

8. There are differences in the make-up, origins, activities, and organisation of the four main South Manchester gangs, though members of all are involved in a wide range of criminal behaviour.

9. Gang-membership comprised a mix of same-age local friendship groups, blood relatives and recruits.

10. Gang-related criminal behaviour includes drug-related offences, but only as one element of a patchwork of violent and non-violent crime.

11. Rates of arrest for gang-members tend to fall as they age.

12. Gangs in South Manchester are loosely area-based.

13. Alliances are sometimes formed between some South Manchester gangs, but conflict is endemic and easily triggered.

14. Firearms carrying by gang-members is at least partly protective and police intelligence records suggest that it may also be part symbolic and part instrumental for the commission of violent crime.

15. There are strong norms of non-co-operation in police enquiries into gang-related shootings, in particular in giving evidence, which undermine successful prosecution of offenders.

Ways forward: The proposed crime reduction strategy

The primary concern is to save lives and to reduce serious injury. So what are the most promising interventions to try? On the basis of the preliminary analysis, a strategy, involving police and partners is sketched out. Three elements can be adapted from the Boston project. These are:

1. Applying co-ordinated leverage to gangs through highly publicised multi-agency targeted crackdowns, aimed at gangs using firearms, possessing firearms or taking part in serious assaults

2. Enhancing strong community relations, to obtain neighbourhood support for the targeted crackdowns and to stimulate community efficacy in informal social control and reduction in incivilities

3. Engagement with gang-members to elicit information, to transmit consistent messages about targeted crackdowns, and to provide diversionary services.

Three additional elements are proposed to address the differing conditions for an initiative in Manchester. These are:

4. Development of inter-gang mediation services, to head off and diffuse tensions that risk leading to serious incidents of violence, including shootings

5. Protection for victims and repeat victims

6. Sensitisation of agencies to the implications of their actions for gangs and the risks to their members, especially in the light of the provisions of Section 17 of the Crime and Disorder Act (1998).

References

Braga, A., Kennedy, D. and Piehl, A. (1999) *Problem-Oriented Policing and Youth Violence: An Evaluation of the Boston Gun Project,* Unpublished Report to the National Institute of Justice, Washington DC.

Kennedy, D., Piehl, A. and Braga, A. (1996) 'Youth violence in Boston: Gun markets, serious youth violence, and a use-reduction strategy', *Law and Contemporary Problems,* Vol 59, No. 1, pp. 147-196.

Acknowledgements

The authors would like to thank Ralph Corrigan and Steve Shropshire of Greater Manchester Police for their assistance in this project.

Karen Bullock is a member of the Policing and Reducing Crime Unit, Home Office.
Nick Tilley is a professor of sociology at Nottingham Trent University currently on secondment to
the Policing and Reducing Crime Unit, Home Office.

Name Index